JUBAL

THE LIFE AND TIMES OF

General Jubal A. Early, CSA,

Defender of the Lost Cause

CHARLES C. OSBORNE

*Algonquin Books of
Chapel Hill*
« 1992 »

Published by
ALGONQUIN BOOKS OF CHAPEL HILL
Post Office Box 2225
Chapel Hill, North Carolina 27515-2225

a division of
WORKMAN PUBLISHING COMPANY, INC.
708 Broadway
New York, New York 10003

LIBRARY OF CONGRESS CATALOGING-IN-
PUBLICATION DATA
Osborne, Charles C., 1930–
   Jubal: The Life and Times of
   General Jubal A. Early, CSA, Defender of
   the Lost Cause / Charles C. Osborne.
      p.   cm.
   Includes bibliographical references
   and index.
   ISBN 0-945575-35-1
      1. Early, Jubal Anderson, 1816–1894.
   2. Generals—United States—Biography.
   3. Generals—Southern States—Biography.
   4. Confederate States of America. Army—
   Biography.   I. Title.
   E467.1.E13083   1992
   973.7'45—dc20   92-11982
                                                CIP

10   9   8   7   6   5   4   3   2   1
First Edition

For Philla, Tom, and Caroline

« CONTENTS »

Illustrations   ix
Maps   xi
Preface   xiii

PART ONE

One: Foothills Idyll   3
Two: Soldier Apprentice   8
Three: Military Governor, Country Lawyer   22
Four: A Shedding of Tears   34

PART TWO

Five: "The Fun Has Just Commenced"   55
Six: The Spur of Ambition   72
Seven: "Very Able and Very Brave"   84
Eight: Pinnacle of Pride   101
Nine: "Here Comes Old Jubal!"   117
Ten: Underwriting the Army   140
Eleven: Watch Charm Victory   164

PART THREE

Twelve: Essay in Retribution   177
Thirteen: Change of Heart   186
Fourteen: "A Great Mind to Curse"   203
Fifteen: The Trouble with the Cavalry   215
Sixteen: On a Darkling Plain   228
Seventeen: Lynchburg Rescued   245

< vii >

CONTENTS

Eighteen: "The Most Exciting Time"   261
Nineteen: "More Formidable Than Ever"   277

PART FOUR

Twenty: "The Altar of Revenge"   297
Twenty-one: A Worthy Opponent   312
Twenty-two: Fateful Lapse   328
Twenty-three: "The Stars Had Fallen"   349
Twenty-four: Last Stand   378

PART FIVE

Twenty-five: Reconstruction and Railroad Politics   401
Twenty-six: A Matter of Money   420
Twenty-seven: Seeking the Lost Cause   429
Twenty-eight: "Tom-Tom Warfare"   454
Twenty-nine: A Farewell Kiss   469

Abbreviations   479
Notes   481
Bibliography   521
Index   531

< viii >

« ILLUSTRATIONS »

Following page 174

General Jubal A. Early

Joab Early

Ruth H. Early

John D. Imboden

J. E. B. Stuart

James Longstreet

D. H. Hill

Harry T. Hays

P. G. T. Beauregard

William Barksdale

Richard S. Ewell

Thomas J. Jackson

"Extra Billy" Smith

Confederate Troops in
Frederick, Maryland

John Sedgwick

Cadmus Marcellus
Wilcox

"Fighting Joe" Hooker

John Brown Gordon

Robert E. Rodes

Robert H. Milroy

William W. Averell

John McCausland

Thomas L. Rosser

"Black Dave" Hunter

Thomas H. Carter

Stephen Dodson Ramseur

George Crook

Lew Wallace

Horatio G. Wright

Jubal's Men on the
Potomac

Francis Blair's Home

Philip H. Sheridan

Kershaw's Men on Their
Way to the Valley

Fitzhugh Lee

John Pegram

James L. Kemper

William Mahone

Robert E. Lee on
Traveller

Jubal Early in Old Age

« MAPS »

page 67   *First Manassas*   July 21, 1861

79   *Williamsburg*   May 5, 1862

93   *Cedar Mountain*   August 9, 1862

123   *Antietam*   September 17, 1862

136   *Fredericksburg*   December 13, 1862

153   *Chancellorsville*   May 3, 1863

161   *Chancellorsville*   6:00 P.M., May 4, 1863

171   *Winchester*   June 14, 1863

190   *Gettysburg*   6:00 P.M., July 1, 1863

206   *Rappahannock Station*   November 7, 1863

218   *Averell's Raid*   December 1863

234   *Wilderness*   May 6, 1864

253   *Early's Route*   June 12–July 17, 1864

256   *Lynchburg*   June 17–18, 1864

266   *Movement of Valley Army*   July 4–18, 1864

272   *The Monocacy*   July 9, 1864

322   *Theater of Operations*   August 7–September 18, 1864

334   *Winchester*   September 19, 1864

343   *Fisher's Hill*   September 22, 1864

363   *Cedar Creek*   5:40 A.M.–C. 7:30 A.M., October 19, 1864

365   *Cedar Creek*   7:30 A.M.–9:30 A.M., October 19, 1864

376   *Cedar Creek*   Union counterblow, starting at 4:00 P.M., October 19, 1864

388   *Waynesboro*   March 2, 1865

« PREFACE »

CONSIDERING his stature as a military leader during the Civil War and as a battler for the Confederate cause afterward, it is curious that—until now—Jubal Early has had only one biographer, Millard K. Bushong, a fellow Virginian. I, a native of Massachusetts, may seem an odd person to be writing about a Virginian and uncompromising Confederate like Early. Yet his life was such a clear definition of that term that it caught the attention of a Yankee like me with an interest in the Civil War and the South, stimulated when I was a magazine correspondent there in the late 1950s and early '60s.

This interest has been greatly reinforced by a totally fortuitous family connection. Like many of the Northerners who participated in the war, I am related, in my case by marriage, to numerous Virginians. My wife's mother grew up in Richmond and Clarke County; as I found out when I was well into this biographical endeavor, my mother-in-law's grandfather, Col. Thomas H. Carter, was General Early's chief of artillery during the critical phases of the 1864 Valley campaign. It has been gratifying to discover—and report—that Colonel Carter was in every way an exemplary soldier, as he seems to have been a virtually irreproachable man, recognized as such by General Early.

The general was not irreproachable—certainly not in the terms established in his day—and this, to me, is one of the most interesting aspects of his life. Irreligious and profane in a pious age, unbuttoned and misanthropic in a society whose manners were rooted in formality

and *politesse,* independent in thought to the point of eccentricity, Early
was an anomaly.

« A GREAT MANY people helped me in this endeavor, among whom
I will try to mention the most generous and effective—begging the
indulgence of those whom I shall inevitably but inadvertently leave
out. I am enormously indebted to the skilled archivists and librarians
at the Library of Congress, the Connecticut State Library, the New
York Public Library, and the New-York Historical Society; comparable
was help provided by the staffs of the Southern Historical Collection
at the University of North Carolina, the Manuscript Department at
Duke University, the Alderman Library at the University of Virginia,
the Virginia Historical Society, the Museum of the Confederacy, and
the Virginia State Library. David Ward, at the Edsel Ford Library of the
Hotchkiss School in Lakeville, Connecticut (near my home), made the
school's set of Official Records available to me on a circulating basis.
Also most helpful with research were Marie Capps of the United States
Military Academy at West Point; Mary Ann Johnson, the late Gertrude
Mann, Virginia Williams, and Dr. Francis Amos of Rocky Mount, Virginia; Eda and Susan Williams of Richmond; Alexander and Charlene
Sedgwick of Charlottesville; Gary Cardwell of Danville, A. V. Tuck
of Monroe, Cornelia Noble O'Dowd of Waco, Texas, Ted and Elva
Osborne and Doris Jackson of Washington, D.C., and John Hennessy
of Niskayuna, New York.

I must thank such descendants of Jubal Early as Jim Early and Jean
Early Dugan for genealogical information and for letting me see family
records and correspondence. Aleice Pinkerton, another descendant,
supplied family pictures. Louis Plummer also helped with pictures, as
did Philip Kunhardt and Michael Gannett. Nick Fasciano wrought the
excellent maps so essential to discussion of campaigns and battles.

For comments and criticism of the war narrative I am beholden to
Civil War military experts Brian Pohanka and Harris Andrews, who
saved me from many a gaffe—but are not responsible for the mistakes that slipped through despite their vigilance. Without the support
and encouragement of friends like Jane Alexander I would never have
begun; nor could I have finished without the active participation of

Philla Osborne (Isabelle Carter Crocker), Colonel Carter's great-great-granddaughter. She not only read the manuscript for grammar and sense but put up with the crotchety self-regard of the author during all the interminable years it took him to produce this book.

Cornwall, Connecticut,
October 1991

PART ONE

CHAPTER ONE

Foothills Idyll

OHN WISE, a traveler to Franklin County, Virginia, in 1862, remarked in his memoirs on the ruggedness of the landscape and the
plain character of the people. Most of the country Wise and his companions traversed en route from the Blue Ridge to the county seat, Rocky
Mount, is rough foothill country, with wooded, craggy heights scored
by stony stream valleys. On the uplands, Wise noted, "all that is visible
is the winding road, with the blue sky above it, and the massed tree
tops below, and the curling smoke of some mountain distillery, with
nothing to break the stillness but the heavy hammering of the log cock
upon some dead limb, or the drumming of the ruffed grouse far away."

In a valley, Wise caught a glimpse of "a mountain cabin, whence a
woman smoking a pipe, and innumerable tow-headed children hanging
about her skirts, eyed us silently."

He was impressed by a logger "in shirt sleeves, with trousers stuck
into his cowhide boots, leaning against his load so intent on scrutiny
of us that he barely noticed our salutation." Others encountered along
the way included a "woman on horseback, with long sunbonnet, and
coarse, cotton riding-skirt, and bag slung at the saddle bow, and small
boy, with dangling bare feet riding behind her."

Everybody got around on horseback. On days when the stage was
due in Rocky Mount, bringing news of the war, the main street of the
town was lined with saddle-horses; women riders would slip off their
riding skirts and tie them to the saddles, "revealing their plain homespun dress," while they went about their business—selling chickens
and farm produce, and purchasing sundries. The men rode to Rocky

Mount separately; their principal occupation when in town, according to Wise, was horse-trading.

Rocky Mount is named, aptly enough, for the flinty and precipitous terrain on which it is built. It had taken a year of war to penetrate the immemorial seclusion of the place, perched upon its hill, still without a railroad or a telegraph. In more settled times, the months and years passed in a changeless pattern broken occasionally by court days with their drunken fights, political campaigning, and religious revivals.

The main street sloped steeply between houses and stores to the courthouse, clerk's office, and county jail. About halfway down the street stood the tavern, a venerable structure with a bar, a porch lined with benches and comfortable chairs, and a local war hero in residence. Brig. Gen. Jubal Anderson Early, a native of Franklin County, was at home recuperating from a serious wound suffered at the Battle of Williamsburg on May 5, 1862.[1]

At the ambitious age of 46, his career only temporarily set back by his wound, Early bore all the singular marks of his maturity. Most striking was his appearance: shoulders as stooped as those of a man far older; piercing dark eyes; thin, grizzled hair and beard. A handsome sculpted nose, pursed lips, and thickset jaws communicated determination and an appearance of profound self-confidence. The general habitually wore a large white slouch hat, adorned with a black plume. Complementing the flamboyance of the hat, in the field or in cool weather, was a long white overcoat that fell dramatically to his heels.

In tones incongruously high and piping (one acquaintance likened its timbre to the sound of a "Chinese fiddle"), Early's voice expressed his opinions in terms that were often blunt, sarcastic, and disrespectful, and always, in Wise's view, "interestingly lurid and picturesque." Not least, the general was scathingly profane, spitting out oaths with streams of tobacco juice from a plug that was seldom absent from his jaw.[2]

Waiting for the stage to arrive, the patrons of the tavern delighted in getting General Early to talk about the men and events of the war. He enjoyed the lion's role his listeners gave him. Mistrustful of anyone's popularity, including his own, scorning the multitude and its views, he nonetheless liked a convivial drink, and he loved to talk.

Wise described the tone of Early's discourse: "With his admiring throng about him on the tavern porch . . . General Early, in my opinion, said things about his superiors, civic and military, and their conduct of affairs, sufficient to have convicted him a hundred times over before any court-martial." But the general never spoke ill of Robert E. Lee, recently appointed to command of Confederate armies in the east, and Early accurately predicted Lee's future successes.[3]

Early may have considered his preeminence on the tavern porch a kind of compensation—for the pain of his wound, and for past disappointments and asperities. The general may, in fact, have been as contented in the summer of 1862 as he had been since childhood, or would be until old age.

<< HE WAS BORN Jubal, son of Joab, son of Jubal, son of Jeremiah, son of Jeremiah. The original Jeremiah, descended from John, a seventeenth-century immigrant from Ireland, gave all ten of his children biblical names beginning with *J*. The patriarch thus began a family custom that endured down to young Jubal's generation. Settling in what is now Madison County, Virginia, the first Jeremiah established himself as a planter, married the daughter of a prominent resident named Buford, and prospered. When he died, at age 90, he left an immense estate to his offspring.[4]

Jeremiah the younger, who lived in Bedford County (neighboring Franklin to the northeast) invested a portion of his inheritance, along with his brother-in-law James Callaway, in the Washington Iron Works in Rocky Mount. There they converted the existing bloomery, a relatively primitive smelting operation, to an up-to-date furnace and forge. The enterprise advertised as far away as South Carolina, where one display, dated July 21, 1779, offered "POTS, KETTLES, CAMP-KETTLES, OVENS, SKELLETS, FLATIRONS, SPICE MORTARS, FIRE DOGS, SMITHS ANVILS, FORGE ANVILS, FORGE HAMMERS, WAGGON BOXES, STOVES, or any other kind of castings that may be wanted."[5]

Jeremiah died soon after the advertisement appeared, and Jubal's grandfather and namesake inherited a share, along with two brothers.

Grandfather Jubal was married in 1790, but died within a couple of years, leaving two infant sons—Henry and Joab—who were placed under the guardianship of Samuel Hairston, a family friend.

The elder Jubal and his brother John were the first of the Early line to buy land and settle in Franklin County. The two bought their first parcel, 15 acres on Gill's Creek, from Anthony Pate in 1789 for 15 pounds. It was Jubal senior who probably built the house, in the Red Valley section about 18 miles north of Rocky Mount, where young Jubal was born on November 3, 1816. He was the second son and the third of ten children—five girls and five boys. (For Judith, Jubal, and Joab, their parents kept up the family custom of biblical names beginning with *J*.)[6]

<< RUTH, JUBAL'S mother (who married his father in 1812, having grown up with him), was the daughter of Samuel Hairston and Judith Saunders. Of Scottish background, the Hairstons were descended from an immigrant named Peter, who had departed Scotland in 1746 after fighting on the losing side in the Battle of Culloden, the disastrous climax of Bonnie Prince Charlie's rebellion of 1745 against Britain's King George II. In the years since Peter Hairston's arrival in North America, his descendants had established themselves, mainly in Henry County (next door to Franklin on the south), as one of the principal slave-owning planter families in the region, as were the Saunderses.[7]

Joab's social prominence led him naturally to the assumption of important local offices: member of the Virginia legislature from 1824 to 1826, colonel of the Franklin County militia.[8] At one time or another, Joab held upward of 1,000 acres in the central portion of the county, where he raised tobacco and such other crops as corn, hay, and produce.[9] Considerable land was planted in tobacco, the main cash crop of the region.[10]

<< LAPPED IN wealth and unassailable social position—albeit in a remote part of the world—the setting for Jubal's growing-up was as genteel and serene as any antebellum ambience that could be imagined. Perhaps as a consequence of his own orphaning, Joab, a generous father, showered his children with love and attention. All ten got an education, including the girls. Jubal's older brother Sam went to the

College of William and Mary. The two youngest daughters were sent
to Salem to attend boarding school. For Jubal, lessons at a local one-
room school were followed, in his mid-teens, by stints at school in
Lynchburg and at the Danville Male Academy.

At home during the summer, the girls were urged to invite friends
for long stays. Their father thoughtfully provided a flower garden for
his daughters, planted between the vegetable garden and the house. In
season, everybody went to the races, held at one of Franklin County's
two tracks, or "race paths," as they were called; Joab and his sons
entered the family's horses, some of which had literary names like
Tristram Shandy, to match their speed with other local coursers. In the
fall, the boys and their father might go hunting for partridge.[11]

The family's serenity was harshly broken in 1832 when Jubal's mother
died. "She was a most estimable lady," he wrote much later, "and her
death was not only the source of the deepest grief for her immediate
family, but caused universal regret."[12]

Late in the same year, the 16-year-old Jubal was beginning the process of applying to West Point. The application was made through
Nathaniel H. Claiborne, a resident of Rocky Mount and the district's
representative in Congress. Claiborne wrote the required recommendation to Lewis Cass, the secretary of war, attesting to Jubal's moral
character, and remarking that Franklin County had never before sent
a cadet to the Military Academy. Cordial recommendations were also
forthcoming from teachers. Joseph P. Godfrey, who had taught Jubal at
Lynchburg, emphasized the applicant's "peculiar" aptitude for science
and "extraordinary mathematical genius." Eugene Weld, signing his
letter as "Preceptor of Danville Male Academy," was more measured
in his pupil's praise, but he certified that young Early had covered all
the basic ground in Latin and Greek, and "moreover attended a little
to the study of the French language."

Early was accepted as a cadet candidate in April 1833, with an
entrance test to be passed in June, and his final status to be determined
by the results of examinations in January 1834. Directed to report to
the Military Academy between June 1 and June 20, Jubal Early allowed
such a prudent margin of time to make the long journey to West Point
that he arrived at the end of May.[13]

« CHAPTER TWO »

Soldier Apprentice

*I*N THE 1830S, the last leg of a Southerner's journey to the Military Academy was a steamboat voyage from New York City—the vessel breasting the broad Hudson, a sea flowing between spectacular banks, up to West Point. Seen from the deck of a boat, Break Neck Mountain, the Crow's Nest, and the other heights that surmount the river at that place might have been put there for no other purpose than to assert the brute dominance of physical nature—glowering in winter dusk or summer thunderstorm, hulking and benign in the glow of a May noonday.

Whatever visage the mountains showed on the day of Jubal Early's arrival, their shapes and dimensions, like those of the river itself, were a vivid contrast to the familiar proportions of Virginia's Franklin County and its environs. As the boat approached the West Point dock, the scene was almost calculatedly inspiring. But it might easily have induced affrighted second thoughts in some new cadets—thoughts opposed in varying degrees by youth, with its reserves of optimism and untested resolve. Another antidote to doubt was ambition. Early's choice of West Point is the first clear indication of a major ingredient in his character—a tightly coiled spring of motivation that would impart energy to his actions throughout his life.

Given Jubal's comfortable circumstances and educational attainments, he could probably have gotten into virtually any college he wished. His reasons for choosing the Military Academy certainly did not include social aspirations. Many boys attended West Point in order to achieve or maintain position in society—as well as to get a free education; though he came from a province of Virginia remote from the power and glitter of the Tidewater, Early did not need West Point to confirm his class status, nor was his family poor.[1]

Scope for initiative was both more subtle and more far-reaching. The Military Academy was a national institution. It offered graduates a set of credentials that could open up the world outside the boundaries of Franklin County, of Virginia, or of the South itself. Evidence of this breadth was the unique course of study. American higher education displayed no counterpart to the Military Academy curriculum, which was largely the handiwork of the renowned Sylvanus Thayer. As Jubal Early was entering West Point, Thayer was winding up his last year as Academy superintendent, a position he had held since 1817. In his time, Thayer firmly set the Military Academy on the path it has essentially followed ever since.[2]

Thayer had begun by dispensing with most of the standard nineteenth-century American college curriculum (the classics, supplemented by logic and ethics, or moral philosophy). He went on to establish the best engineering school in the country. The classics were replaced by mathematics and the physical sciences. Cadets had to take French so that they could read the untranslated texts by European mathematicians and military experts, imported by Thayer, that comprised the bulk of the volumes in the Academy library.[3]

When Jubal arrived at West Point, these academic challenges lay three months in the future. In June, he was confronting severe physical changes in his mode of life that must have given him pause as he compared it to the tenor of his days in Virginia. He learned that the price of his chance to step onto a wider stage than that offered by Franklin County was high: the loss of independence, mobility, even identity.

Alighting from the steamboat at West Point's Hudson River dock, Jubal followed his luggage, loaded in a horse-drawn cart, up the steep hill to the Academy. He immediately found himself immersed in the rigors of the institutional welcome extended to new cadets. First he was robbed—as he might have fumed about it later—of the money in his pocket. After signing in at the adjutant's office, the newcomer reported to the treasurer, who took all his cash and credited it to a West Point account set up in his name. From that moment until he left the Academy, Early would be permitted, officially, to carry no pocket money.[4]

Next in the sequence of humiliations was a harsh introduction to new living conditions. Cadets were housed in the North and South Barracks, stone structures of four and three stories, respectively, containing 90 rooms; most of the rooms were mere cells, 13 feet by 10. From the quartermaster, young Early drew necessary gear: a chair, two blankets, a supply of stationery, soap, a candlestick and candles, a broom, a basket, a slate and an arithmetic text, a tin dipper, and washbasin. The floor was the bed, to be shared with as many as four or five others.[5]

As an "animal," or "plebe," Jubal was at the very bottom of the Military Academy hierarchy. For the next few days, even before being fitted for a uniform, he learned the lesson of his lowliness and inadequacy over and over again from upper-class cadet instructors, who braced the newcomers, barking every word in an exaggerated manner, meting out swift punishment for ineptitude. They put their charges through four daily hours of classroom work in arithmetic, followed by introductory exercises in close order drill.[6]

Resistance to all of this was natural. For Jubal Early, the effort to contain explosive feelings of resentment and outraged pride was doubtless strenuous. Yet the rigors of the system soon began stamping impressions on a mind that was receptive and malleable enough, for all its prickliness. Jubal was already digesting the essential maxims of West Point: obedience, regularity, reverence for authority—though he would always interpret these principles in his own way. Strict order, public chastisement, and stiff-backed example would reinforce hierarchical teachings learned at home: honor, as interpreted by the traditions of an officer caste; proper behavior for an officer, who did no work with his hands, looked down on merchants and other moneygrubbers, and told the truth.

Part of the officer's status, as reflected in his training at the Academy, was orthodox religion. Since 1825, Sylvanus Thayer had required every cadet, regardless of faith, to attend High Church Episcopalian services each Sunday. Jubal Early was not an Episcopalian at home; no such church stood in Rocky Mount (nor would it until 1875, founded—the effort beginning in the '40s—with Early's help). From his days at West Point on, at the rather limited points where organized religion touched his life it would take an Episcopalian form.[7]

It must all have been bewildering and daunting as well as insulting. But Jubal did not make things easier for himself. Throughout life, his manner in the company of his fellows would often be preoccupied and self-absorbed—looking through acquaintances met in the street, giving offense. Jubal had a hard time making friends.[8]

Introduction to military life may have been lonely and hard. The entrance examination, at least, turned out to be easy. In a typical test, a cadet was asked to define a fraction, read a few lines from a history book, and write a dictated sentence or two on the blackboard. A physical examination was not much more rigorous than the educational test. Candidates were weighed and measured, and were inspected for deformities and rotten teeth. The eye test challenged the subject to tell whether a coin displayed at a distance of 14 feet was "heads" or "tails."[9]

Jubal passed these tests easily enough, and his first West Point success was published in an order dated June 15, 1833. For the next two months, a tent in the annual summer encampment on the Plain was to be the cadet's home. The schedule was demanding. Drill and instruction began at 5:30 A.M. and ended at 5:00 P.M. Infantry drill, musketry, fencing, riding, small unit tactics, artillery drill, and range firing were the subjects. Military chores—guard duty and fatigue details—rounded out the day, and there were constant inspections and parades. Somehow, there was also time for cadets with the strength and the inclination to swim in the Hudson, go for walks in the scenic hills near the Academy, read, and even take dancing lessons.[10]

As a plebe, Jubal was probably under too much pressure to enjoy any of these diversions. He did spend some of his free time writing letters home, which Joab answered promptly and warmly. On August 7, the father wrote of his fond anticipation of Jubal's return home on the regular second-class-year furlough, which was an eternity in the future— two summers off. In answer to a question, he reported poor sales of the current tobacco crop, but added that the corn crop was the best in years and signed off tenderly: "All join in love to you . . . my dear son."[11]

Summer ended abruptly near the end of August with a return to barracks. On September 1, Cadet Early rose at dawn, fell in for roll-call, cleaned his room and accoutrements, and breakfasted at 7:00. At 8:00, he reported to his first class—in mathematics, judged the most important element in the West Point curriculum, along with French, worth, by Sylvanus Thayer's reckoning, a third as much as mathematics. The class lasted three hours.[12]

Instruction in mathematics was directed by Albert E. Church, described by one cadet as "an old mathematical cinder, bereft of all feeling." Another pupil remarked that "there never was a colder eye or manner than Professor Church's." Under Church's eye, Jubal studied algebra, geometry—including a difficult application called mensuration—and trigonometry.[13]

Following the mathematics class—and an hour of study in his room—Jubal returned to the classroom at noon for instruction in French. Claudius Bérard was the schoolmaster, a native of France who had a curious background for a teacher at a military school. Threatened with conscription into Napoleon's armies, he had hired a substitute. The stand-in was killed in Spain; under the rules, his death canceled Bérard's exemption and subjected him to the draft all over again. His response was flight from France.[14]

Mess call sounded at 1:00 P.M., interrupting the French class for an hour. At 2:00, Jubal and his classmates resumed their instruction and recitations for two more hours. From 4:00 P.M. until sundown, the schedule called for drill, parades, and recreation. The cadets ate supper at sunset, after the flag was hauled down; the meal lasted half an hour. Fifteen minutes after rising from the table, all the men were to be in their rooms, where they studied until 9:30. When the bugle sounded taps at 10:00, everyone was to be in bed.[15]

Jubal Early was a probationer through the semiannual examinations in January 1834, a two-week ordeal whose results confirmed his membership in the Corps of Cadets. His standing was generally good. He was one of 84 men who received warrants—admission certificates—out of a class of 97; among the 97, Early's test results placed him tenth in mathematics and 31st in French. In June, at the year's end, he was ninth in mathematics but still 31st in French, among those admitted. Early's overall class rank, under general merit, was 11th.[16]

< 12 >

Not good at all was Jubal's conduct rating, which placed him 203d in the total cadet body of 242. The Early spirit was too impatient and unbending for success in comportment. But regardless of classroom proficiency, accumulation of 200 or more demerits spelled expulsion. Jubal got 142 in his plebe year. "I was not a very exemplary soldier . . . ," he later wrote. "I had very little taste for scrubbing brass and cared very little for the advancement to be obtained by the exercise of that most useful art." [17]

Despite the low conduct mark, Jubal was advanced to the status of third classman. His promotion gave his family—especially his father—much gratification. As brother Samuel, three years older and Joab's firstborn, had written as early as February 1834, "Pa seems to be almost intoxicated with your progress. . . . The old man is very much wrapped up with the notion of your success and it ought to be a very great stimulus to perseverance with you. . . . His whole heart seems fixed upon it and I believe much of his happiness will depend on it . . ." [18]

Stirrings of doubt disturbed this picture of achievement. The diligent student was unsure of future benefit from so much effort. Where was it all leading? One discouragement that Jubal confided to his family was the prospect of low pay for career officers—a lieutenant got $1,000 a year. Sam was reassuring. "I agree with you entirely . . . ," he wrote in March. The "want of pecuniary inducement and the little happiness to be enjoyed" were excellent reasons for leaving the army after obligations of service—one year of active duty in return for the free education—were satisfied. Considering alternative employments, Sam, a budding lawyer, declared his preference for law over medicine "because if not more lucrative it is at least more agreeable and a fair road to the success to which your ambition aspires." Also on the list of possible professions, Sam pointed out, was engineering. And what was West Point if not an engineering school? [19]

The major discouragement was the mortifying day-to-day grind of West Point itself. Ambition, worn down, gave way—at least for the moment—to irresolution. Might it be possible, Jubal wrote, to contemplate quitting? Back came a tactful Sam, in full agreement as before about the undesirability of an army career, but unwilling to see Jubal abandon West Point. Graduates of the Academy, Sam advised, can do other things besides soldiering. Finally, Sam pointed out that times were hard. Jubal would regret leaving his present situation "for any you could obtain in this country—money is scarce—people are hard run and prospects are gloomy in every respect, it seems to me."[20]

Encouraged or grudgingly acquiescent, Jubal pressed on. As a third classman, he took French, analytical geometry, and fluxions (a form of calculus), along with drawing ("elements of the human figure . . . ; topography with the pen, pencil, ink and colours"). The course, intended to equip future officers with the skills to make sketches and maps in the field, was taught by Robert W. Weir, who was appointed the year Early entered West Point and remained there 42 years. Weir was to establish himself as a well-known artist, commissioned to paint "The Landing of the Pilgrims" in the National Capitol.[21]

In June 1835, Early stood higher than at the same time a year before: 12th in mathematics, 22d in French, ninth in drawing—ranked in a class of 76, where he finished eighth in general merit. But the conduct score deteriorated: with 189 demerits, Jubal placed 223d in the total cadet body of 240.

Jubal's conduct rating may have suffered, at least partly, from an angry dispute with a cadet named Lewis A. Armistead. Early made some scathing remark to Armistead on the parade ground as the cadets marched to mess; the quarrel continued at the meal, and Armistead ended by breaking a plate over Early's head. For this, Armistead was dismissed from the Academy. (He was to die at Gettysburg during Pickett's charge.)[22]

Following the summer furlough, the second class year was devoted to drawing, chemistry, and natural philosophy, or physics. The physics professor was William H. C. Bartlett, one of the Academy's most brilliant graduates. As a West Point teacher, he became one of the most prominent astronomers in the United States, building his own observatory at the Academy, but he was far from a perfect preceptor. The second class year was particularly hard, cadets said, on account of Bartlett; part of the trouble was the difficulty of the material itself, and part was the fact that Bartlett, a nervous man afflicted with a poor digestion, was an uninspiring teacher.[23]

In the fall of Early's second class year, news of war reverberated from

< 14 >

the heights above West Point. The outbreak of fighting seemed heaven-sent to Jubal, who strove to reconcile yearnings for military fame with abhorrence for the routine of a soldier's life.

The war on everyone's tongue was the uprising of Texans under Samuel Houston, seeking independence from Mexico. The conflict, pitting American settlers in Texas against the Mexican government, appealed greatly to young Early's sense of right and wrong. He wanted very badly to go to Texas; his blood was fired, and he saw possibilities, in joining the Texans' cause, of a rapid advancement of his career that would obviate the need to finish up at West Point.

Writing passionately to Joab, Jubal marshaled his arguments to win permission for an expedition to Texas and money to cover the cost. The thinking in the letter is not original. But the writing reveals in detail, and for the first time in Jubal's own voice, much about his eloquent way with words—which occasionally sound a lawyerly note—his biases and ideals, his lofty goals and his pugnacity.

The letter pleads for the right of the Texans to secede from Mexico. Their right, Jubal believed, was based on the recognition, in the Mexican constitution of 1824, that the states were independent, "as our State Governments are." Early went on to argue for the Texans' right of self-preservation. Though Mexico had induced Americans to settle in Texas, Early continued, the Mexican regime of Antonio López de Santa Anna persecuted them and tried to kill them off.

Helping the Texans, wrote Jubal, was an obligation. Young Early compared the Texan cause favorably with "our own" in the American Revolution. Jubal reminded his father that liberty had been "driven from the old world and the only asylum for it is in the new. If it cannot find one there, where can it find one?"

The peroration was an appeal to Joab's concern for Jubal's future:

Oh! My dear Father, will you not let me go? . . . I do not believe I shall become a Buonaparte or a Bolivar. I have no such ridiculous idea, but I believe that I can gain some fame, at least I wish to make the attempt; and I believe I can gain the confidence of the Texans by taking part in their cause now, and reap the reward of my exertions after their independence is established. There will be no established characters to contend with; all will be new and the road to civil distinction will be open and easy. I will not have to wait until others have passed off the stage before I can come on it, as would be the case in this country. You seem to attach such importance to a start in the world. Therefore, I shall have all the *start* imaginable.

Jubal implored his father to borrow the money to send him off to Texas, the debt to be repaid following success there. "Do not laugh at this project," he begged. "I am in earnest and consider it plausible, however chimerical you may think it. I propose it from an unwillingness to cause you expense."

A postscript followed the signature: "I have written this letter and confined it to one subject because my whole soul is taken up with the subject. I am well." [24]

<< THOSE WHO have made—or heard—similar youthful appeals to parental authority will not be surprised that Jubal, persuaded that his goal was after all impractical, remained at the Military Academy. He duly finished his second class year, ranking 11th in general merit in a class of 58. He stood 13th in physics, 18th in drawing, 19th in chemistry. Again, a good scholastic record was offset by an abysmal conduct grade; with 196 demerits (hair-raisingly close to the finality of 200), he stood 17th from the bottom in a cadet corps of 216. [25]

A substantial number of demerits may well have flowed from a further display of pugnacity and ill temper. The incident seems to have pitted Early against his classmate Joseph Hooker, who would be known during the Civil War as "Fighting Joe." Early was in the audience at a debating society contest in which the topic was slavery. Hooker, a native of Hadley, Massachusetts, asserted that owners of slaves killed them when they were too old or sick to work. Early leaped to his feet and denounced the statement as an outrageous lie. Hooker objected to the interruption, and Early said nothing more. But after the debate, he waited for Hooker outside and kicked him. Hooker, whether scared of Early or prudent in avoiding trouble, did not fight back. [26]

Men in their final year were expected to set an example. Whether

< 16 >

or not Early tried to shine his brass any brighter as a first classman than before, he finished scarcely higher in conduct than in the previous year. He was given 189 demerits, which placed him, in a corps of 211, 195th. In his senior year, the disciplinary record shows the only arrests of his West Point career—though the infractions were trivial: six days' confinement to quarters for visiting other cadets after taps; three days' confinement for ignoring the orders of a guard.[27]

In suffering chastisement for unauthorized hobnobbing with his fellows, Jubal showed he had gotten better at making friends—though who they were and how close they were to him are unanswered questions. Jubal acknowledged his general unpopularity; but he did have friends. It was, he said, just a question of getting to know him.[28]

Disregarding the instructions of guards and others in authority was to become a lifelong predilection that would get Early into trouble again. Yet, notwithstanding his transgressions, the senior cadet was permitted to join a group of upperclassmen privileged to take their meals at the house of a Mrs. Thompson, "below the hill," along with his classmate John C. Pemberton and others. Mrs. Thompson's spinster daughters cooked and served such delicacies as hotcakes for breakfast, and the occasional roast of beef, "served left over—finally as a delicious hash— all week." It must have been a welcome respite from the salt meat, cabbage, and potatoes at the mess hall.[29]

First classmen trained with artillery, and studied engineering. The course was acclaimed as the pinnacle of the first class year and of all four years at the Point. Given West Point's preeminence as a school of engineering, it was widely acknowledged that a graduate who did not choose to be a career soldier or a mathematics teacher had a good chance of employment as a civil engineer.[30]

The professor was Dennis Hart Mahan, an Academy graduate (class of 1824) who had spent four years in France studying civil engineering and European military affairs. A small, irascible "skeleton of a man," as one student described him, he was the author of numerous texts on engineering that were used at West Point for 40 years. Most were translated into several foreign languages.

As time went on, Mahan began to flesh out his course with occasional sessions devoted to military strategy and tactics. But these interludes

JUBAL

had probably scarcely begun in Early's time. Indeed, many cadets complained of too little instruction on the art of war. Armed with their
Academy French, cadets could—some probably did, though Jubal apparently did not—plow through the European texts in the library. (He
did read a fair amount of ancient and modern history in English.) By
and large, Early and his classmates benefited little from examination of
the military theories, most of them products of Napoleon's recent campaigns, with which European professional soldiers were—theoretically,
at least—acquainted.[31]

Fifty cadets completed the first class program, led by a Connecticut
native named Henry W. Benham. The future Confederate commander
Braxton Bragg ranked fifth; John Sedgwick, who was to become one
of the abler of the Union generals, came in 24th, and Hooker was
29th. Early's messmate, John Pemberton, the Philadelphian who was
to surrender Vicksburg to Ulysses S. Grant, ranked 27th. Early finished
18th, ranking seventh in engineering, 21st in artillery, and 33d in moral
philosophy.[32]

The record was sufficiently creditable for graduation in good standing, and Early could choose the branch he would serve in: artillery. In
June 1837, freshly appointed a second lieutenant, he bade farewell forever to West Point. But the pressure on him did not ease. A war against
the Seminoles, sputtering inconclusively in Florida, demanded United
States troop reinforcements. Denied the usual postgraduation leave of
absence, Early and many of his classmates were ordered immediately
to Fortress Monroe, Virginia, to train recruits.[33]

« IN THE swelter of the Virginia summer, the duty—whipping some
800 recruits into shape—was arduous. Jubal Early, taking his first look
at the men available to the United States Army from (mostly Northern)
urban recruiting centers, may have seen little to choose among any of
them, and come to conclusions about the caliber of such soldiers that
would endure for life.[34]

Respite from this martial scut work would have been welcome indeed. Jubal got leave in late July or August, and went to White Sulphur
Springs, the resort in the Virginia hills. There, it seems, he met a girl
from Philadelphia named Lavinia, and fell in love. When it came time

to go to war, plans were made to meet again the next year; addresses were exchanged.

« "AFTER ALL, Florida is the poorest country that ever two people quarreled for," wrote a military surgeon named Jacob Rhett Motte in *Journey into Wilderness*, his account of the Seminole War. Motte characterized the peninsula as "a perfect paradise for Indians, alligators, serpents, frogs, and every other kind of loathsome reptile." He wondered why, "in the name of common sense," the Indians had not simply been allowed to enjoy life in the "land of their fathers," where "[e]very day served but to convince us of their determination to fight or die." [35]

The United States' war aim was twofold. The government wanted to continue opening up the Florida peninsula, acquired from Spain in 1819, for settlement; this goal encompassed removing the Indians wholesale from Florida and resettling them in the West. Also, in removing the Seminoles, Washington hoped to placate irate slave owners whose property had run away to Florida and taken refuge with the Indians. [36]

Lieutenant Early arrived at Tampa Bay in October. Reporting to Company E, Third Artillery, he discovered that the company commander, Capt. Elijah Lyon, was too ill to carry out his duties and the unit's two first lieutenants were on detached service; Early's introduction to active campaigning would include command of the company. [37]

On January 6, 1838, he marched his men out of Fort Taylor as part of a column led personally by Thomas S. Jesup, the major general commanding the Florida forces. The column was made up of 600 dragoons and 400 artillerymen—all regular troops—reinforced by 500 Tennessee and Alabama volunteers. The going was difficult. The column had to cut its own road for guns and wagons through dense stands of hardwood called hammocks, bypassing cypress swamps and traversing stretches of pine flats interspersed with nearly impenetrable growths of saw palmetto. The men, many barefooted, had their clothes torn and their flesh lacerated by the saw palmetto, and in places they marched up to their waists in water. [38]

On January 24, the company of dragoons riding at the point of the column drew fire from a party of several hundred Indians occupying a hammock girdled by a creek. The position was near a ford, called Locha-Hatchee, over the Jupiter River. Ten companies of artillerymen, including Early's, attacked the hammock from the left; dismounted dragoons rushed the position from the front; on the right, the volunteers either got lost or held back out of fear. In any case, they never engaged the Indians. Early, not a man to brag, later reported that he had "heard some bullets whistling among the trees," but "none came near me and I did not see an Indian." The skirmish was decided when a detachment of 15 dragoons led by two junior officers swam the creek in the rear of the Indian position and emerged on the dry land of the hammock exhausted and sodden, their ammunition ruined. Though the dragoons were all but incapacitated, their appearance seems to have unnerved the Seminoles, who ran away. The whites' casualties were seven killed and 30 wounded. The Indians' loss was at least one killed and left on the ground; any other dead, along with wounded men, were carried away.[39]

Early's company joined the pursuit of the Indians, many of whom were captured.[40] On his return to garrison, Lieutenant Early was reminded of the world beyond the hammocks and swamps of Florida. The young officer's mail included a letter from E. G. Tapton, a fellow West Pointer, which addressed a private matter of great importance to Jubal. Tapton's letter made a bantering reference to Lavinia, in connection with a projected get-together at White Sulphur Springs in August 1838 of "all the ladies of P.A. (Miss Lxxx)." Tapton predicted that "it will be hard indeed if we can't get a wife apiece out of all that number."

Unlike Early, Tapton, it appears, was in a position to see Lavinia from time to time, as he reported in a tone that might have been intended to get under his correspondent's sensitive skin: "By the way, I find you have taken up seriously my (*suppressed*) intention of becoming your rival for the beautiful [creature] hinted at above—don't be alarmed, comrade, I consider your ground too sacred to undermine you. But don't come at me with pugnacious intent . . . because I assert my admiration of her. Oh . . . I took her out in the moonlight and descanted most poetically on starry heavens, nightbirds' songs, balmy breezes, etc., etc., then wound up by portraying a certain *distant lover* sleeping on the cold soil of Florida, wrapped up in his cloak and his

< 20 >

glory, dreaming of sweet home and his sweeter Lavinia!! Need I say that I found an attentive [audience] . . ." Tapton ended this equivocal message with assurances that he was not trying to supplant Early in the lady's affections, but only endeavoring to promote Jubal's interest "by all the romance I could attach to your situation." Jubal may not have believed this, but there was little he could do.[41]

<< LIEUTENANT EARLY remained in Florida until spring brought hot weather. Since the Seminole War was deemed to be over—it actually sputtered on for three more years—and since, as Early recalled it later, it "had not been my purpose to remain permanently in the army . . . I determined to resign for the purpose of going into civil life."[42] While awaiting the clearance of his resignation papers, Jubal applied for leave—hoping, no doubt, to spend part of it at White Sulphur Springs with his friends and his Lavinia. When leave was approved, the young man started for home, via Nashville and Louisville. On arrival in Louisville, he read in a newspaper that the army had been enlarged and that he had been promoted to first lieutenant.

In his memoirs, Early remarks, rather offhandedly, that he might have stayed in the army if he had known of his promotion before submitting his resignation. At the time, his second thoughts were probably heartfelt; apart from the slight benefits of promotion, the army might now have seemed a veritable refuge. Visions of "civil life" may well have embraced marriage; but that dream now lay in ruins. About this time, Jubal Early learned—perhaps from a clipping mailed to him by Lavinia herself—that the young lady from Philadelphia had married another man.[43]

CHAPTER THREE

Military Governor, Country Lawyer

GOING TO West Point had been a means of answering the call of ambition. But after a taste of active army duty—mainly tedious days in garrison and intermittent immersions in the Florida swamp—Jubal was quite ready for civilian life, even if he had to live it as a frustrated bachelor on the relatively narrow stage of Franklin County, and even if he had only vague ideas about what his role there should be.

First, he must earn a living. In light of views exchanged with brother Samuel in correspondence to and from West Point, the law now seemed a logical profession. In the fall of 1838, Jubal Early commenced the study of law under Norborne F. Taliaferro, a prominent Rocky Mount attorney destined, before long, to become a judge. In due course, certified by the Franklin County Court and by an examining board, Early embarked, aged 23, on a career that was to engage him—with an interval for service in the Mexican War—for most of the next 20 years. The junior counsel, handling small cases involving such matters as wills and minor lawsuits (most of them disputes over small debts), began to acquire a reputation as a capable and honest practitioner. But the law—notwithstanding its relative advantages as a career—was no high road to wealth.

Jubal hardly seemed to care. Fees were anything but exorbitant (five dollars was a standard charge for defending a suit). But Early's interest in his profession, whatever its focus, was not the money. Jubal was said to be generous with his time, willing to help poor clients or those in distress, and not unduly concerned about payment. He was, for that matter, an indifferent businessman, careless about keeping track of who owed him how much, "and the consequence," he later admitted, "was that my practice was never very lucrative." [1]

Early's growing standing as a lawyer did not rest on a flamboyant courtroom manner or an ability to sway juries. He was more effective in arguments before a judge, especially on appeal. Early had no trouble framing or articulating his thoughts. But as he saw it, he was different from other lawyers—and other men. He had little talent, in his own estimation, "for popular speaking as generally practiced in the States." In Jubal's view, his lack of this faculty, which he clearly denigrated, could be explained by other aspects of his nature. In his *Autobiographical Sketch*, he wrote, "I was never blessed with popular or captivating manners, and the consequence was that I was often misjudged and thought to be haughty and disdainful in my temperament." [2]

In saying this about himself, Early revealed both a deep vulnerability and his defense against it. He knew he lacked conventional charm, and the knowledge must now and then have been painful. His response to the pain was a furious denial that his charmlessness was important, with the corollary that intelligence and moral energy, which he did possess in full measure, were superior to charm in any form. But stating the denial in so many words would have seemed childish. Instead of arguing the possible truth of his defense against pain, Early customarily took the offensive, attributing poor judgment to real or imaginary critics who mistook evidences of brains and moral force for hauteur and disdain.

<< AT THIS stage, a lack of ingratiating ways was no great obstacle. However he appeared to the world, Jubal seemed to be off to a good enough start in his career. But like many young lawyers, he sought to enhance his visibility by entering politics. Running as a Whig, he won one of Franklin County's two seats in the Virginia House of Delegates in 1841 and went to Richmond for the 1841–42 session as the youngest member of the legislature. [3]

Early's identification with the Whigs arose primarily from his background as a well-educated, professionally bent member of the planter class. Southern Whigs, more or less influenced by the Virginia-born statesman Henry Clay, were a diverse lot. By and large, they agreed in supporting tariff protection; government-subsidized roads, railroads, and canals; a national bank; and the economic goals of commerce and industry as well as those of agriculture. They were also broadly opposed to the deliberate expansion of the United States, whether or not at the expense of other nations such as Mexico. This political framework seemed to suit many Southerners who were businessmen, professionals, and planters of commercial crops; Southern iron, coal, and salt-mining interests supported the protectionist planks in the Whig platform.[4]

In Richmond, the freshman legislator joined a Whig majority at a session that ran from December through March. Petty matters—of great import, of course, to local interests—made up much of the agenda. In December, Jubal joined the many who were presenting petitions for private bills. He apparently sought to smooth out legal problems following a cousin's death; asking for authorization "to make sale of certain property belonging to the estate of Abner Early, deceased," the petition was framed as a bill, and passed.

Weightier issues were also addressed. The legislators wrestled with policy and appropriations for public education, and expended much effort on the financing and management of insane asylums. They also debated subsidies for canals and the growing network of railroads. Like a true Whig, Jubal voted in January 1842 with those who were in favor of a state loan to the Richmond, Fredericksburg & Potomac Railroad.

Early, the army veteran and West Point graduate, got two chances during the session to stay in touch with military affairs. A petition from constituents in Franklin County asking for authority to form a new militia company of cavalry became law in March. The other matter involved the financial struggles of the fledgling Virginia Military Institute, founded only three years before in Lexington as the nation's first state military school. A law authorizing a $1,500 appropriation for the institute, passed earlier, was threatened with repeal. Francis Smith, head of the institute, wrote to Early in February, complaining that the annual salaries of two valued professors were only $700 and $500, respectively. These stipends, asserted Smith, were inadequate to permit the professors to remain at VMI and support their families; their pay, he urged, must be increased. Smith also wrote that money was needed to build housing for 150 cadets. Jubal's reply, near the end of the session, was a vote with the majority rejecting repeal of the appropriation.[5]

As the session wound down, Jubal's constituents, including members of his family, were urging him to declare his candidacy for another term. He complied. But in the elections, held in April 1842, the Whigs were badly beaten in Franklin County and across the state. Early lost his seat to his old legal preceptor, Norborne Taliaferro, a prominent Democrat.

In the role of friend, Taliaferro was able to ease the pain of defeat for his young opponent. The older man held the posts of prosecuting attorney in Franklin and Floyd counties. Vacating these jobs on his election to the legislature, Taliaferro arranged for Early's appointment as his successor in both counties—positions that Early held until the reorganization of the state under a new constitution in 1851, and with time out to serve in Mexico.[6]

<< JUBAL'S IMPULSE to go to war in Mexico was not entirely logical. In the elections of 1844, his Whig convictions had led him to vote for Henry Clay, who lost the presidential race to James K. Polk. Among the campaign positions taken by Clay was opposition to the annexation of Texas, which took place in the waning months of the Tyler administration. But when, under Polk, annexation led to war with Mexico, Early—not long since a passionate supporter of the Texans' cause—felt an urgent need to participate.[7]

The urge to rejoin the colors, like most of Jubal's attitudes at this period, had complicated roots. The life of the law was busy enough and even moderately productive, but the routine was stultifying. The commonwealth attorney busied himself with prosecutions for fighting—the most serious common offense—or, at the other extreme, for disturbing a church service. Where, in all that, was the thrill of risk surmounted, of aspirations fulfilled?[8]

Mexico offered a badly needed stimulus. Only ten years had passed since Houston's Texas rebellion had stirred the West Point cadet to ardent espousal of the Lone Star—now vindicated by the backing of the United States. And though military life, as Early well knew, could be dreary and frustrating, wartime always offered the possibility of action, excitement—and advancement.

Military employment was close at hand. On December 30, Jubal was appointed major of volunteers, serving in the Virginia Regiment under Lt. Col. Thomas B. Randolph and Col. John F. Hamtramck, the commanding officer. Both were West Point graduates, and both veterans of the War of 1812.[9]

By the second week in January, the first troops were being sent to Fortress Monroe. They were the vanguard of a regiment that had been expanded from ten to 12 companies, assembling for the voyage to Mexico at the fort on Old Point Comfort, at the mouth of the James River.

For them, and for Major Early, who was soon to join them, the prospect of combat was remote. But dread of the dangers they might face in Mexico filled the thoughts of those close to them. On the eve of his departure for Fortress Monroe, Jubal received a letter from his younger sister Elizabeth, who wrote: "Let me beg of you my dear a lock of your hair when you write *you must not forget it* . . ."[10]

Mustering the men at Fortress Monroe, Major Early found himself in effective command; neither Hamtramck nor Randolph was on hand. On his own, Jubal struggled with a welter of problems ranging from inadequate quarters—in the depths of winter—to the hasty training of the raw recruits. The worst problem was inadequate clothing. Uniforms that had been ordered were slow in arriving, and many men, thinking they would be issued uniforms immediately on joining up, had reported with no more than the clothes they wore. The clothing shortage had resulted in one death from exposure.

For Major Early, another acute difficulty was Colonel Hamtramck, whose apparent disinclination to be with his troops was but one of his trying characteristics. Capt. James Lawson Kemper, the regimental quartermaster and a future governor of Virginia, found his commanding officer "affable and easy" in his manners—but not notably bright, and fussy about military niceties. The colonel insisted that officers wear spurs and sword and keep a servant.[11]

On January 15, Randolph arrived and took charge. A week later, Hamtramck himself was on hand to supervise embarkation of the first six companies. As of January 28, under Randolph's command, 485 officers and men, in two ships, were on their way to Point Isabel, near the mouth of the Rio Grande.[12]

Early seized on Hamtramck's presence as a chance to take a few days off for personal business. But the moment he returned to Old Point Comfort, the colonel departed once more, this time in order to make the trip to Mexico via Mississippi riverboat and New Orleans, a much more pleasant journey than the winter sea passage that Early and the men faced, sailing in the troop transports from the Virginia coast. Early was left in charge of embarking the last contingents of the regiment, with whom he would make the voyage. As they waited for the transports, Kemper made friends with Jubal; the two had fun with other officers one evening at an impromptu party, trading stories about college. Kemper also saw another side of the major, who quarreled bitterly with the assistant adjutant general of the post—the commandant's executive officer—and was evicted from his quarters. Kemper, who lived off the post, invited Early to become his roommate until the embarkation.

<< THE BARQUE *Exact* sailed with three companies on February 2, and Early departed on March 1 with the remaining troops in the *Sophia Walker*, bringing the total aboard both ships to approximately 400 officers and men. As the troops were embarking, Kemper witnessed a demonstration of the major's harsh singlemindedness (some might call it cruelty). Striving to embark the maximum number of troops to campaign in Mexico, Early forced a sick man to board one of the ships. Kemper and others grew angry at "such wantoning with life," especially since the man had been rousted from the post hospital where all knew there were several cases of smallpox.

Bad weather and sickness, including smallpox, burdened the voyage with misery. Two men on the *Sophia Walker* were buried at sea. Kemper asserted that during the first week on board, he was "the sickest of suffering mortals." On March 10, he noted the ship's position off the mouth of the Rio Grande: "I am hoping with an agony of intensity to reach land today."[13]

The ship did sight land that day, dropping anchor. Boats brought news of a victory by Gen. Zachary Taylor over the Mexicans at Buena

Vista on February 22–23. Though no one knew it, the American triumph marked the end of active campaigning in northern Mexico. By the time the entire Virginia Regiment was ashore in Mexico, the principal drama of the war was unfolding far to the south. Having landed 12,000 men at Veracruz, Gen. Winfield Scott was driving toward Mexico City, which American forces would capture on September 14.[14]

For the Virginians and their compatriots in northern Mexico, the war settled into the routine of an occupying army. Assembled for the first time on Mexican soil at Camargo, on the Rio Grande, the Virginia Regiment marched on April 4 to China, 55 miles west. Six companies, under Randolph, established a garrison at China; the rest of the regiment, commanded by Early—Hamtramck was down with sickness—marched to Monterrey, relieving an Ohio regiment as garrison.[15] Before moving into the town, Early and his men camped near Taylor's headquarters. Here Early met Jefferson Davis, colonel of the 1st Mississippi Rifles, who had been painfully wounded at Buena Vista. Shaking Davis's hand, Early was "struck with his soldierly bearing." Davis laid the groundwork for a lifelong friendship with Early by paying him compliments on "the order and regularity" of his camp.[16]

Perhaps inspired by such evidence of competence, a command from General Taylor made Major Early military governor of Monterrey, a post that he relished and filled with distinction. Intimations of glory in battle may have beckoned Early to Mexico, but the gritty reality of his garrison assignment now became an exemplary seminar in which Jubal refined his approach to the arts of training and leading soldiers.

No slackness was tolerated in camp. "Being a rather strict disciplinarian," he remembered, ". . . and naturally regarded by inexperienced troops as harsh in my treatment of them, I was by no means popular with the mass of the regiment [during most of the Mexican tour] . . . but I can safely say that, on the day they were mustered out . . . I was the most popular officer in the regiment, and I had the satisfaction of receiving from a great many of the men the assurance that they had misjudged me in the beginning and were now convinced that I had been their best friend all the time."

At Monterrey, morale was high, partly because the major took good care of his troops, paying close attention to their health and enforcing high standards of camp hygiene. Early's men, drilling daily, got credit for good conduct. Hamtramck, returning from sick leave in June, wrote warm words of praise, remarking that "our improvement astonishes even our own officers and soldiers here." Indeed, the results of Early's methods brought a high luster to his reputation with his peers. Fellow officers—and the Mexicans themselves—gave Early credit for keeping better order in the city of Monterrey than anyone ever had.[17]

One colleague who complimented Early directly on his governance of Monterrey was a fellow Virginian, an army paymaster named David Hunter. Early would remember him kindly—until the two men collided as bitter adversaries in the next war.[18]

<< HOWEVER HARD Major Early worked to keep his men healthy, a harsh climate and the primitive hygiene practiced in nineteenth-century armies led to much sickness. Between April and the end of the year, 60 men of the regiment died, and 98 were discharged, too broken down by disease for further service. In June, when Early was ordered to march his command south to Buena Vista, the number of sick in the regiment reached 134, its highest level.

Until well into the twentieth century, the dangers and miseries of sickness were just items on a long list of the costs of campaigning. As he had shown in the embarkation at Fortress Monroe, Early could be hard on a sick man. But one of the sick in Early's command was a young man from Rocky Mount named Moses Greer Noble, who had run away from home at 17 to join the Virginia Regiment. When he fell ill, Early kept an avuncular eye on him, and after the boy lapsed into feverish unconsciousness, the major installed the patient in his own cot, sleeping on the tent floor until the sickness passed. Noble gave Jubal credit for saving his life.[19]

With regard to health, the move from Monterrey was fortunate. Buena Vista was considered a salubrious post, boasting a relatively hospitable climate and sufficient supplies of fresh vegetables, fruits, and meat. Assembled once again, the regiment began, in general, to regain its health.[20]

But Jubal was an unhappy exception. A cold and fever contracted during the summer and fall of 1847 developed into a painful chronic arthritis that bent his powerful frame; it was to remain with him for the rest of his life.[21] In October, Early was sent home on sick leave, spending about three months with his father, brothers Sam and Robert, and other members of the family in the Kanawha Valley. There, Early family ventures in farming and in the salt manufacturing business were prospering.[22]

Traveling back to Mexico in the new year, the convalescent had a close call. At one o'clock in the morning of January 8, Jubal was abed in his stateroom aboard the steamboat *Blue Ridge*, which was navigating the Ohio River just below its confluence with the Kanawha. As often happened on river boats of the period, the vessel's boilers exploded, killing 14 people. Jubal was not injured. But his escape was narrow; the blast destroyed half the stateroom, and hot fragments of boiler sliced through the deck, burning and cutting Early's feet as he jumped out of his berth. In the dark and cold, the survivors, huddled on deck, suffered considerable exposure before they could get ashore and find shelter. Astonishingly, Jubal's arthritis actually got better—"a decided improvement . . . ," Early recalled, "though I would not advise blowing up in a western steamboat as an infallible remedy."[23]

<< Before Major Early had been back in Mexico more than a fortnight, the treaty concluding the war was ratified by the United States Senate. In due course, the Virginia Regiment marched to Brazos, the American supply base near the mouth of the Rio Grande, to await shipping back to Fortress Monroe. The volunteers arrived during the first week of July.[24]

Jubal was out of the army himself by the end of summer, having discharged his bronzed, bearded men in July. "They were anything but *parlor* looking boys," reported a Petersburg newspaper that covered the regiment's last muster, "and their appearance clearly showed that, though they had never been in battle, they had experienced pretty rough service." So they had.[25]

And so had Jubal. Back home as Rocky Mount's most prominent Mexican war veteran, he attracted attention. Already, at 32, the returned soldier, bent with arthritis like a man more than twice his age,

< 30 >

bore little resemblance to the tall, upright youth the citizens of Franklin County had last seen. Early was already grizzled.

Also changed was his view of life. Jubal's Mexican experience, for all its costs, and despite its dearth of action, had played out on a far wider stage than that afforded by life in Rocky Mount. Now, youthful indecision was replaced by a new determination. As if to force the pace of hometown existence, whatever the reaction of his fellow citizens, and to maintain as broad an arena as he could for the possibilities of drama in his own life, Jubal Early embarked on a course whose consequences resonate in the talk of Rocky Mount to this day.

<< ON HIS RETURN to town from the army, Jubal had taken a room at the tavern, where he spent a good many nights. Other nights, he would stroll a short distance up the hill from the tavern to a small house he owned on a side street just off North Main. Waiting for him there was a woman named Julia McNealey, who served him supper, and later accompanied him to bed. Julia, who was about 17 when Jubal took up with her, married Charles M. Pugh in 1871; throughout most of the years until her marriage, she was as close to being Jubal Early's wife as anybody ever came. Over nearly two decades, she bore him four children, whom Jubal seems to have supported and to have regarded as his own. Certainly he was not ashamed of them, bestowing his surname on them, and making one, Jubal L., his namesake.[26]

In the mid-nineteenth century as in any era, many men, even in small, rural communities, kept company with women who were not their wives, though most took pains to keep such connections out of sight. That Jubal chose to challenge the rules as unabashedly as he did offers a fascinating insight into a character by now largely formed.

Self-preoccupied, vulnerable, and standoffish, Jubal suffered perhaps more than the usual bachelor's loneliness. He needed female companionship, but the bitter experience of rejection by the faithless Lavinia seems to have soured him on taking his chances with conventional wooing and wedding. On the other hand, an unconventional connection with a woman of lower social standing (implicit in her acceptance of the arrangement) gave his egocentric soul plenty of scope.

< 31 >

It allowed him as much control as he would have had in marriage, and—perhaps most important—it did not force him to commit himself emotionally as would a relationship with someone of his own class.

Ultimately, the affair with Julia was an expression of Jubal's self-assertiveness, now in full, arrogant flower. What he had decided was right, he seemed to be declaring, and was therefore beyond criticism. The affair was nobody's business but his own. He wanted the world to see that he cared nothing for what most people thought of him; if there were busybodies and bluenoses in town who did not like what he was doing, so much the worse for them.

《 HOWEVER DIM the community's views of Jubal's sexual conduct, no stain seems to have attached thereby to his reputation as a lawyer. Presumably because voters trusted his honesty and ability, Early was elected to the post of prosecuting attorney in Franklin County after a new Virginia constitution, promulgated in 1851, made such offices elective rather than appointive.[27]

Meanwhile, Jubal kept up his private practice. The majority of cases were routine, many involving disputes over land. The work was often boring—a far cry from life as a military governor. The extraordinary case of Indiana Choice must have seemed a godsend. In 1851, Early was the plaintiff's attorney in a lawsuit so unconventional as to suggest that he took it on, at least partly, as yet another way of challenging Franklin County's notions of propriety. The issue arose in the emotionally charged arena of race.

Wife opposed husband in the case, which alone made it highly unusual. The lawsuit was brought by a white woman named Cassandra Choice against her husband, Gresham, a middling-prosperous Franklin County farmer who owned 14 slaves. Cassandra had been married once before; in her household had been a young free black woman named Indiana, who had stayed with Cassandra when she was widowed, and came along with her when she married Gresham Choice. Since Indiana's free status was vouched for only by her word and that of her friend Cassandra, and was unsupported by documentary evidence, Gresham claimed her and her three children as slaves. The suit, on behalf of Indiana, was Cassandra's bold answer to her own husband's claim. Jubal argued the case before a jury in a court presided over by his mentor and friend Judge Norborne Taliaferro, and won. Indiana Choice and her children, declared "free and not slaves," were awarded damages of one cent.[28]

Though Jubal's view of slavery and his attitude toward black people were at bottom profoundly racist, his assumption of Indiana Choice's cause reveals an imaginative ability to see beyond lawyerly considerations of property to the human issues in the case. And, as a local aristocrat with *noblesse oblige* to dispense, he could well have enjoyed his role as defender of two otherwise defenseless women. There they were, both courageous and high-spirited, both possibly attractive, pitted against a pettifogging domestic tyrant bent on exploiting legal technicalities to satisfy his greed and pride of possession. The case, and its outcome, must have given Jubal great satisfaction.

Not quite as rare in Franklin County as suits over freedom from slavery were cases of divorce. Jubal might take such jobs when they were offered, and when he was available. But in 1859, he turned a divorce case down, pleading a conflicting court appearance on the day fixed for taking depositions. Later, represented by another lawyer, the man whose wife was seeking the divorce was making his deposition at a crossroads store with two of his brothers as witnesses when armed men rode up and shot the three dead. The incident might have seemed a kind of portent of the far wider domestic violence to come—which Early did not attempt to avoid, though he tried hard to avert it.[29]

CHAPTER FOUR

A *Shedding of Tears*

TO REACH the meeting chamber on the second floor of Mechanics Hall in Richmond, a member of the Virginia Secession Convention of 1861 had to pass through a room near the entrance of the building. This lobby was thronged with women, young and old, pretty and plain, but all more or less affluent; their voices, in the modulated accents of the Tidewater, gently rose and fell, a counterpoint to the whisper of the rich materials of their hoopskirted dresses as they moved about. To the men wending their way through the room en route to the convention floor, these ladies, like damsels testing the knightly hero in a fable, addressed a question: "Are you a secessionist?"

The women required an affirmative answer. If they got it, chances were that they would laugh and tease the man a bit—making a mildly flirtatious fuss over him ("He'll do!"), and pretending to make way for him through the enchanted barrier of their crinolines. If the answer, however politely evasive, added up to a "no," their reaction, could they have brought it to pass, would have turned the man to stone.[1]

The ladies in the anteroom—and upstairs in the hall, where first-comers were allotted special seats in honorable segregation to the right of the president's chair—would not have been there if they had not felt certain of the rightness of their position. They were secure in the knowledge that they represented a powerful sentiment among the white people of Richmond, and of eastern Virginia. In that part of the state, slaves constituted up to 36 percent of the population, and the urge to separate Virginia from the Union ran strongest.[2]

As the drama of secession in the Old Dominion evolved, the ladies of Mechanics Hall would turn out to have the last word. But in early 1861, that outcome was far from clear. Though most Virginians were confused over the issue, secession was not the express sentiment of the people as a whole. As the Convention gathered in mid-February, the great majority of its delegates—Jubal Early among them—would encounter the cold wrath of Mechanics Hall's genteel Furies.

Early had run as a Unionist delegate from Franklin County; his hill country roots, hardly less than his views, would have condemned him in the eyes of upper-class Richmond secessionists. He and a fellow Unionist, Peter Saunders, had defeated secessionists Hugh Dillard and Abram Booth Hancock; Early's margin of victory, by his own account, was 1,060 out of approximately 1,800 votes cast.[3] The tally was a fair reflection of local voters' uncertainty. Most were still against immediate secession—and opposed to the "ultra-secession party," as Fleming Saunders called it in a letter to his brother Peter. Fleming reported that many of his rabid secessionist neighbors in Campbell County (near Franklin) were moving away—to the South.[4]

Across the state, 145,697 voters had elected 152 delegates of whom only about 30 were in favor of immediate secession. In the same election, the voters also approved a provision—opposed by the secessionists—requiring the Convention to refer any final decision on leaving the Union to the electorate.[5]

‹‹ IN ALL THIS, Virginians, like other Americans, were reacting as best they could to the explosion of events set off by the election of Abraham Lincoln as president in November 1860. His emergence as a leader largely elected by Northerners challenged Southerners to guard their own sectional interests—embodied primarily in the institution of slavery, which many saw the North as bent on abolishing. That perception, particularly in the deep South, led to a clamor for independence.

Action swiftly followed. South Carolina seceded on December 20, 1860, and other states left the Union in rapid succession: Mississippi, Alabama, Florida, Georgia, Louisiana, and Texas. Stunned by these defections, Virginians were profoundly ambivalent.

The dilemma was intricate. Virginia was a truly Southern state. It was tied to the region through its way of life, rooted in a society dominated by a patrician planter class that prospered in an agricultural economy based on slavery. But Virginia's geography and history made for strong ties to the North. Washington, seat of government of the United States, was in Virginia's front yard. Wealthiest of the Southern states, Virginia looked to the neighboring North as the principal market for its crops, an economic connection too valuable to be severed without much damage and pain.

Most important was a memory of Virginia's contribution to the nation's creation and growth. Thoughtful people facing the prospect of secession were very much alive to the devoted part played by Virginians in the origins of the Union. Men such as George Washington and Patrick Henry had helped shape the Revolution. By reason of Virginia's role—through men like Washington, James Madison, and Edmund Randolph—in the Constitutional Convention of 1787, the state had been a midwife in the birth of the United States. Washington, Madison, and other Virginians, as executives, legislators, and jurists, had had much to do with guiding the Union through its painful early years.

Against this background, the restrained reaction of most Virginians to news of the Union's crisis was understandable. Though many admitted the right of a state to secede under extreme provocation, relatively few regarded the election of Lincoln as sufficient, in itself, to justify secession forthwith. (That view was loudly proclaimed by Henry A. Wise, a former governor and a leader of the outspokenly secessionist minority.) On the other hand, there was general agreement among the citizens that the federal government had no legitimate power to coerce a state.[6]

Such was the theme of a resolution passed early in a special session of the Virginia General Assembly that gathered on January 7, 1861. But though an active—to some, a radical—majority favored taking measures to prepare for war, the legislature scarcely knew its own mind. The record of the session traced the changes of mood—now rising to hope of peace, now yielding to despair. On January 14, the General Assembly passed a bill establishing the Secession Convention, which was to meet on February 13.

On January 19, the day Georgia seceded, a joint resolution passed both Virginia houses calling for a peace conference. The body was to meet in Washington, where Virginia commissioners were to join

< 36 >

those from other states and try to work out a compromise, based on amendments to the Constitution, that would at least guarantee slavery's status quo.[7]

Another joint resolution, passed on the 21st, probably expressed the ultimate position of most Virginians. It stated that "if all efforts to reconcile . . . differences [should] prove to be abortive, then . . . every consideration of honor and interest demands that Virginia shall unite her destiny with the slave-holding states of the South." On the 29th, the day after Louisiana seceded and the day before Texas withdrew from the Union, the Virginia General Assembly voted one million dollars to arm the state.[8]

<< THE RICHMOND *Examiner*, a leading secessionist newspaper, dismissed the members of the newly elected Secession Convention as a collection of "old fogies who have not represented Virginia in the past thirty years." But Jubal Early was proud to be a part of it. "A deliberative body containing more general talent and worth," he later wrote, "had rarely, if ever, assembled in the state."[9]

Broadly speaking, the delegates belonged to three factions. The three-score secessionists agitated for their cause while they waited for the right moment to bring about the separation of the state from the Union. Moderates, about 70 strong, held a range of views. Many came to the Convention acknowledging the doctrine of secession, but only as a final resort; others made remaining in the Union conditional on the federal government's forbearance on the issue of coercion. Standing with the Unionists at first and holding the balance of power, the moderate faction increasingly lost strength in defections to secessionist ranks, and eventually dissolved. The Unionists, numbering about 50, recognized no right of secession, though many felt the pull of loyalty to state and region; in the minds of a good number, federal authorities had no right to enforce United States law in states that had already seceded. Still, most opposed Virginia's secession to the end.[10]

As the curtain rose on the Convention, the Unionists, aggressively exploiting their strength in combination with the moderates, struck the first blow. They swiftly elected John Janney, a Unionist, as president. But their dominance of the Convention persuaded the Unionist

< 37 >

leaders to adopt, at least initially, an overall strategy of delay: unlike the secession conventions of other states, Virginia's was in no hurry.

Part of the strategy of delay was the establishment of a Committee on Federal Relations, which the Unionists dominated; they had seven members, working in concert with ten moderates and against four secessionists. The committee's function was as a deliberative sponge, to absorb all resolutions offered from the floor on Virginia's posture toward the United States, and to keep any significant prosecession decisions from being made.

To fend off precipitate action on a key question—what Virginia would actually do in the face of an attempt by Washington to coerce it—the Committee on Federal Relations took a number of resolutions on the subject under advisement, promising to make a report and submit recommendations for action at some appropriate future date. In the meantime, the Convention marked time while it waited for a report from the Peace Convention, which had begun its work in Washington on February 4, and for Abraham Lincoln's inaugural address.[11]

During the lull, with many of their opponents absent, the secessionists struck back, winning their first significant victory. South Carolina, Georgia, and Mississippi had sent commissioners to the Virginia Secession Convention to urge its immediate adoption of a secession ordinance. The Virginia secessionists managed to slip through a resolution seating the commissioners on the Convention floor and offering them a chance to say anything they wanted.[12]

Word spread like brushfire. On February 18 and 19, the ladies were in the hall by eight in the morning, some with knitting to help pass the time until the session opened at noon. All the balconies were packed; windowsills, aisles, steps, every cranny of the chamber held nests of eager spectators. Hundreds were turned away. Acclaimed by the vociferous claque of Richmond firebrands in the audience, the emissaries from the new Confederacy—Jefferson Davis had been elected its president on February 9—trumpeted the glories of leadership and prosperity that would be Virginia's reward for joining their cause. In response to this, a few of the waverers among the moderates began changing sides. Other hearts were doubtless stirred out of indecision by blasts of war talk from the most fiery speakers.[13]

On February 20, as the oratorical roar faded, Jubal Early entered the fray for the first time—with logic, humor, and common sense. He was responding to a resolution calling on the Committee on Federal Relations to investigate reports that the United States authorities were sending arms and troops to reinforce forts in and near Virginia. The secessionists had written this resolution to convert wavering delegates by stirring up their suspicion and fear of the North. Calm down, advised Early. He pointed out that federal support of military outposts was only to be expected; the president had a constitutional right to defend public property. Fears that the Washington government was trying to cow the people of Virginia, he continued, were groundless; the only risk posed by the forts' guns were to those thoughtless enough to "run their heads into the mouth of one of them." The resolution was tabled for the time being.[14]

But the seeds of mistrust planted by the resolution germinated. On February 23, Early had to rise again to dissuade those who still fretted to investigate the reinforcement of the forts. A particular concern was Fortress Monroe, Jubal's home depot in two wars. At this fort, it was claimed in dire tones, water had been let into the moat; sentinels were going their rounds and calling the hours all night; no fewer than 13 of the fort's guns were aimed at the town of Hampton. These were ominous facts, the Convention was warned, and should be published to alert the people to hostile federal intent.

Nonsense, said Jubal. The pure light of day would show anyone with eyes that nothing had really changed. There had been water in the moat at Fortress Monroe for 30 years, and he had fished in it. As for the sentinels, they were customary in military establishments, and were there "principally to prevent some of the men who were a little inclined to spree, from getting out. If the sentinels were required to cry the hour of the night, it was because they might be inclined to sleep, and to prevent them from being frozen in extremely cold weather. It was also done to prevent them from leaving their posts."[15] For all he knew, Early added, there might indeed be 13 guns pointed at Hampton. If so, the number was less than would have been the case if the fort's armaments had ever been complete under federal defense plans, of long standing, that had nothing whatever to do with the present crisis. Anyway, though half the fort faced the land, 125 of its 175 guns were aimed at the sea.

For all its quirky wisdom, the speech was not persuasive. The efforts of Early and other Unionists (notably John S. Carlile and John S. Jackson) to turn the resolution aside were to no avail, and in passing it the secessionists posted yet another gain. Through the bitter debate, the push and pull of forces in the struggle between the secessionists and their opponents became clearly marked. In the end, many moderates may have been swayed by the dark warning of a secessionist named Peter B. Borst: "May not these fortifications prove to Virginia, by and by, what the wooden horse proved to Troy?" [16]

<< TWO DAYS after this clash, the Convention embarked on another battle that was to unleash an unprecedented outbreak of hot-eyed anger against the North. It was a storm that disrupted the Convention and exploded beyond Mechanics Hall. The clash fed voracious pro-South sentiments that had recently been building—especially in the capital city, but also in the countryside.

The fray began when a Unionist delegate named Samuel McDowell Moore launched a frontal attack on the seceded states, and urged that Virginia refrain completely from joining any confederacy not willing to abolish the international slave trade, prohibited under United States law. The seceded states, Moore asserted, wanted nothing more than to reopen the trade in order to reduce the price of slaves.

John Goode, a secessionist lawyer from Bedford County and acquaintance of Early's (from county court appearances), made his side's heated reply to Moore. Goode emphasized that the men meeting in Montgomery, Alabama, capital of the Confederate states, had expressly prohibited any reestablishment of the African trade. But, Goode went on, that was not the point. What mattered was the right to own slaves. And who, he inquired, had betrayed Virginia and the other states of the South? The backstabber was the North—which had spurned humble overtures for peace, rejecting conciliation until slave owners should bow down and renounce their property. Would Virginia submit to *that*?

Goode never finished his speech. Mechanics Hall exploded with ear-splitting volleys of clapping and cheering. Goode himself, shouting for

< 40 >

order, was drowned out. The president ordered the building cleared of spectators, and one man who resisted the sergeant-at-arms was arrested.

The frenzy in the hall sought release in the streets and alleys of Richmond, where a rabble roamed with torches. The mob—with a core of toughs paid, some said, by slave traders—harassed "submissionists," burned their effigies and hung minatory nooses in the windows of their hotels; demonstrators rallied noisily around the radical secessionists of the Convention, serenading them with brass bands and displaying Confederate flags.[17]

<< BUOYED BY these demonstrations of support, the secessionist cause drew yet more strength from the failure of the Peace Convention. Its proposals, submitted to Congress on February 27, were rebuffed, and more moderates undoubtedly defected as a consequence.[18]

Unionists also lost moderate adherents in the aftermath of Lincoln's inaugural address, delivered March 4. The president's speech asserted his intention "to hold, occupy and possess the property and places belonging to the government." But the speech, which Early and others characterized as "enigmatical," seemed conciliatory in some of its passages. "We are not enemies, but friends," the president declared. "Though passion may have strained, it must not break the bonds of affection. The mystic chords of memory, stretching from every battlefield and patriot grave, to every living hearth and hearthstone . . . will yet swell the chorus of the Union, when again touched, as surely they will be, by the better angels of our nature."

Lincoln disclaimed all intention—believing he had no right—to interfere with slavery where it was already in place. "The government," he declared, "will not assail you. You can have no conflict without being yourselves the aggressors." Lincoln made it clear that he still regarded the Union as intact, and that he would be diligent, as required by the Constitution, in seeing that "the laws of the Union be faithfully executed in all the states."[19]

In the Virginia Secession Convention, a common reaction to Lincoln's speech was fury, vented in stormy oratory. On March 6, the inaugural address was denounced as a threat and an augury of war: "I accept the vaticination of President Lincoln," said one delegate. "It is not the first time that the Almighty has placed the words of prophecy in the mouth of a wicked man." [20]

Directly bucking this powerful current of secessionist feeling against Lincoln, Jubal Early took the floor once again. His speech was a forthright defense of the president and an impassioned stand in favor of the Union, which he called the "fairest fabric of government that was ever erected." It was not, Early declared, that he approved of Lincoln's election, or that he endorsed the president's policy any more than any other delegate. But Early was willing, he said, to allow Lincoln to be faithful to his inaugural vow to carry out the law in all the states. Early blamed the Confederate states, seceded "from this Union," for the perception that the president was bent on crushing the South. If it had not been for the secessionists, Early argued, "the declaration of President Lincoln that he would execute the laws in all the states would . . . have been hailed as a guarantee that he would perform his duty, and that we should have peace and protection for our property," meaning slaves. Early finished with a recommendation that the Convention postpone all action until the Committee on Federal Relations, still under control of moderates and Unionists, submitted its report and recommendations. [21]

Early's speech achieved a level of calm, good sense, logic, and optimism about the future of the United States as high as any reached at the Convention. Unfortunately, when John Goode replied to his speech, Jubal's reaction showed how close to his well-ordered exterior lay a volcano of raw anger: Early the patriot and orator sought the way of conciliation; Jubal the man was perilously quick to take violent offense. In a yet more intemperate era, the clash provoked by Goode's remarks might well have led to a duel.

Goode derided Early, to the accompaniment of delegates' applause and laughter, for "his syren song 'wait.' " Early was determined, Goode said with heavy irony that drew a laugh, "not to be precipitated into any hasty action." Was the Convention, Goode asked, to submit to having its agenda thwarted by a Federal Relations Committee that had become "the slaughterhouse and the burial place of all the resolutions that have been sent to them for their consideration?"

"No," Goode answered himself. "The patience of the country is exhausted." Then, the speaker struck the spark that ignited Jubal's rage.

As an instance of popular frustration, Goode cited—of all places likely to infuriate its proud representative—Franklin County, and the discourse changed from debate to personal vendetta. "Yesterday," Goode went on, "letters came to me from the mountains of Franklin, stating that the patience of the people, [Early's] own constituents, was well nigh exhausted." Goode continued, at some length and with great heat, to urge "decisive, emphatic, earnest action. . . . I earnestly appeal to this Convention to speak today, and to let the voice of Virginia go back to Washington upon the electric wire, that she will resist any and all attempts at coercion at all hazards and to the last extremity." [22]

Impatience now fed Early's growing wrath. Having already spoken, he was obliged to wait, under the rules of the Convention, to be recognized again. When the chair did get around to him, he had to state that he was claiming a personal privilege in order to hold the floor. The *ad hominem* flavor of the quarrel was significantly sharpened.

Goode, Jubal said, "whose impatience has been so great and who has kept up the steam so high, not contented with the opportunities afforded to him for letting it off in this Convention, has on one or two occasions, let it off in the streets." This sally, a reference to the mobs of secessionist partisans promenading through the city, was designed to wound Goode by associating him with these plebeians.

Goode "undertakes," Jubal continued, "to stand between me and my constituents, and he tells this Convention and the country that he has communications from my home, showing that the patience of my constituents is exhausted." Early clearly did not believe it. He challenged Goode to disclose the basis of this information.

Early's reference to Goode's public discharge of steam found its mark. Insulted by the imputation of vulgar rabble-rousing, Goode stopped just short of denouncing Early as a liar: "When he says that I have sought occasions to harangue the people, I tell him that he makes the assertion without foundation in fact."

Feelings between the two men were now running very high, and adjournment for the day did not end the matter. But as if the antagonists were fearful that a face-to-face encounter might generate emotions too violent for control, the dispute proceeded through an exchange of letters. Initiated by Early, the correspondence was delivered back and forth between the principals' hotels and on the Convention floor by friends.

In this matter of delivery, as in others, the affair partook of the etiquette of dueling. But the friends undoubtedly tried to mediate, and the letters themselves showed that the antagonists were increasingly willing to patch things up. From the evening of March 6, and throughout the 7th and 8th—when Goode was ill and stayed away from the Convention—the letter writers hammered it out. Early wanted to know whether Goode had meant to call him a liar, or even imply that he had been guilty of deliberate misrepresentation.

Finally, Goode backed away. Having given the matter thought, and having read the account of the March 6th debate in the Richmond *Enquirer*, Goode realized, he wrote on the 7th, that he had simply misunderstood Early, adding "that I did not design to impute to you falsehood or willful misrepresentation, but simply to deny the truth of your statement as I understood it at the time." Fair enough, Early responded. And for his part, he had not meant any offense either. All he had had in mind was to show how hastily he believed Goode was acting on the issue of secession.[23]

In the end, the affair became the basis of a fast friendship. The matter ended amicably partly because, however volatile his temper, Early could be reasonable, and the men had enjoyed a cordial relationship in the past. But it was Goode who backed down—albeit from a shaky position.

<< AS THE BLUSTERY, mercurial weather of March symbolized the course of the Convention that month, Jubal's Pyrrhic victory over Goode stood for the position of his fellow Unionists at the beginning of the second week of March. Until then, the Unionists had held the honors. But they were increasingly under pressure from secessionists emboldened by the Peace Convention's collapse and the storm unleashed by Lincoln's inaugural. The pro-Confederates were taking the offensive, calling on the Federal Relations Committee to report a secession ordinance, and offering a resolution to arm the state against the intention of the United States to "plunge the country into civil war." On

March 7 and 8, the Unionist leadership had to resort to parliamentary maneuvers to forestall possibly awkward votes.[24]

On March 9, when the Committee on Federal Relations issued a preliminary report, the first phase of the Convention ended. At the same moment, the opposing factions exchanged strategies. The Unionists, once in favor of delay, and still in control of the Federal Relations Committee, now wanted the Convention to pass its majority report forthwith, submit it to the Lincoln administration, and adjourn until the fall—an interval they believed would provide a cooling-off period in which North and South could devise some sort of compromise.[25]

The report, supplemented on March 19, did not make any recommendations for or against the secession of Virginia, though the committee condemned the use of force by the Lincoln administration against any state. On the other hand, the panel showed how hard it had been working to keep Virginia in the Union by neutralizing the pressure to abolish slavery. The report included drafts of 14 possible constitutional amendments for submission to Congress and called for an immediate conference of the border states and a national convention, all designed to keep the Union intact on some basis that would recognize and preserve slavery.[26]

This effort reeked of desperate improvisation. But hope and confidence increasingly buoyed the secessionists, who wanted no part of compromise. They refused to sign the committee's majority report. Now it was they who were all for delay. Their new plan was to stall, prevent passage of the majority report, wait, and keep agitating until public opinion should swing their way. They were sure it would.[27]

« THROUGHOUT MARCH and well into April, as the pressures mounted —Lincoln hardening his determination to keep the Union intact—the Unionist-dominated Virginia Convention staved off the growing movement to secede. A principal hope of delegates opposed to secession was Lincoln's secretary of state, William H. Seward, who appeared to be trying to steer the president clear of confrontation with the Confederacy.

On that issue, the Unionists worried about their own secessionist brethren, whose urge to confront Lincoln was growing. On April 4, Unionists and their moderate allies had to muster 88 votes—against 45—to stifle a proposed secession ordinance. On the 8th, still trying to forestall the crisis, the Convention appointed a three-man committee to seek an interview with Lincoln. With a view toward compromise, its members were carefully selected: George W. Randolph, Thomas Jefferson's grandson and a secessionist; Alexander H. H. Stuart, Unionist; and William Ballard Preston, a moderate and a friend of Early's. Their assignment was to inform the president directly of Virginia's condemnation of armed coercion and find out what he intended to do about the seceded states. Delayed on the journey to Washington by bad weather, the commission arrived late on April 12.[28]

On the Convention floor that day, Jubal Early rose to present a powerful argument in favor of remaining in the Union: it was aimed at the self-interest of the planters and farmers among the Convention members, including many of the most outspoken of the pro-Confederates. In some passages, the speech was a bold bid, albeit made too late, to influence the farmer who owned no slaves by appealing to his pocketbook.

Jubal spoke at large for Virginia, the South's leading tobacco state, and in particular for his home county, where tobacco was not only grown but processed for the market. The tobacco, he pointed out, was raised by those possessing no slaves as well as slave owners. Early asserted that the rights of men with no slaves should be "regarded and protected" along with those of slave owners.

But the real issues, Early said, were markets and capital. Manufacturers of tobacco products were dependent on Northern capital—disbursements from commission merchants—for the money to buy the tobacco and treat it. This financial mechanism depended in turn on such centers of distribution as Baltimore and New York, the primary markets for Virginia's tobacco. As Jubal explained it, the target for Southern tobacco was the large population of Americans outside the South. "The consumption of the article of tobacco depends on the number of mouths to be supplied, and as they have more mouths at the North, there is more tobacco consumed there."[29]

« The hour was very advanced for such a sensible statement to matter much. Shots had already been fired in anger. On April 13, at 9:00 A.M., Randolph, Stuart, and Ballard were shown into the presence of Lincoln. The president may or may not have known that Charleston's harbor batteries had opened fire on Fort Sumter beginning at 4:30 A.M. on the previous day. He handed the committee members a memorandum setting out his intention to hold Sumter—answering force with force—and repossess any federal property seized before his inauguration. The presidential paper also referred to the part of his inaugural address renouncing any intent to invade or use force beyond the minimum needed to take back federal property. The president talked with the committee for a considerable while; as they recalled the conversation and the memorandum, Lincoln seemed to want them to go home and tell Virginia that there was to be no general war.[30]

As news of the Sumter bombardment detonated in Richmond, secessionists were joyful to see their ranks swell with Virginians inspired by the smell of gunpowder. Recognizing the stink of death and ruin, Jubal Early rebuked those who greeted the warlike news with such glee. He was appalled by the rising bellicosity of the Convention, and stood up to "confess that my heart is bowed down with sorrow . . . that Virginians are ready to rejoice at such an event." Early utterly rejected the idea that the bombardment had done anything to bolster the fortunes of the seceded states, and predicted that the people of Virginia would never embrace their cause.[31]

Events were moving very swiftly. On April 15, the Convention received word—unconfirmed by official proclamation—of Lincoln's call for 75,000 volunteers to "suppress the combination" of seceded states. Virginia was expected to furnish its share of the troops—three regiments, 2,340 officers and men.

Here, to the likes of Randolph and Ballard, was naked coercion. The president's appeal (quickly answered by many Northern states) was not only a drawing of swords but an act of betrayal. In the Virginians' conference with Lincoln, he had not even hinted at the deployment of 75,000 men against the South. Outraged, Ballard immediately proposed an ordinance of secession. Other moderates joined Ballard in his feeling that Virginia should secede before taking part in the hostilities they saw Lincoln organizing against their fellow Southerners.

Stuart remained steadfast in his effort to keep his state with the Union in spite of Lincoln's action. Wait, Stuart urged; there was no actual fighting going on (Sumter had surrendered without bloodshed); the "present seat of war" was far away—perhaps it could be kept that way, and general war averted. On the other hand, a seceded Virginia, next door to Washington, would court invasion and could become a killing ground.[32]

In support of Stuart, Jubal Early again stood fast. Hold on, he advised the Convention, for confirmation of the call for volunteers. It was hard, he said, for him to credit the notion that responsible men in Washington had taken such an extreme step. It was impossible to believe that Secretary of State Seward, "a statesman" of prudence and discretion, could have lent his support to such a proclamation.[33]

Stuart and Early changed few minds. The secessionist fuse was well alight. Henry Wise read a telegram from South Carolina's Governor Francis Pickens. "We can sink the fleet if they attempt the channel," said Pickens's wire. "If they land elsewhere we can whip them. I have here now near 7,000 of the best troops in the world and a reserve of 10,000 more on our railroads. . . . Please let me know what Virginia will do."

What the Old Dominion would do was already apparent to anyone with eyes and ears. By April 14, many Unionist delegates were afraid to talk publicly against secession; in the city streets, according to one observer, they could hear "the indignant mutterings of the impassioned storm which threatens every hour to sweep them from existence."[34]

On April 16, the Convention went into secret session. One reason given to the public was the confidential nature of the report to be expected from the committee sent to interview Lincoln. But the Union supporters saw it, rightly, as a sign of imminent crisis and resisted the closing of the Convention's doors. The effort was unsuccessful, along with others by pro-Union forces to prevent the outright rejection of every proposition looking toward compromise.

Though the secret proceedings were stenographically reported—and the transcripts later published—exactly what took place in the closed-door sessions remains mysterious. The mood in the Convention seems to have been frenzied. According to one participant, evidently a Union sympathizer, the secessionist leaders appear to have revealed that they had been conspiring to launch a revolution. They wanted to take Virginia out of the Union and launch armed action against the federal government without sanction by normal constitutional authority.

As a Unionist delegate from western Virginia named Waitman T. Willey remembered the proceedings, "The scenes witnessed within the walls of that room . . . have no parallel in the annals of ancient or modern times. On the morning of the 17th, Mr. Wise rose in his seat and drawing a large Virginia horse-pistol from his bosom laid it before him and proceeded to harangue the body in the most violent and denunciatory manner. He concluded by taking his watch from his pocket and, with glaring eyes and bated breath, declared that events were now transpiring which caused a hush to come over his soul."

Led by Wise, the radical secessionists told the Convention how they had organized a force to seize the arsenals at Harpers Ferry and Norfolk. They had asked Governor Letcher for permission to carry out these missions in the name of Virginia, but Letcher refused to authorize the raids on grounds that he had pledged not to open any hostilities without consulting the Convention.

John Imboden, later to serve as a cavalry officer under Jubal Early, was the man in charge of the insurrectionists' artillery. The gunners had been recruited in the Shenandoah Valley town of Staunton, in Imboden's home county of Augusta. In his account of the crisis, Imboden recalled that the revolutionary group decided to execute their plans regardless of the governor. At the moment of decision, as if on cue, a dispatch arrived from Norfolk: "The powder magazine here can be taken and the Yankee vessels captured and sunk so as to obstruct the harbor. Shall we do it?" The answer, given by Wise, was in the affirmative.

Denunciation of Wise's coup in the Convention hall was swift and impassioned. One delegate called it treason because it involved the people in a war that most of them opposed. Another delegate, John Baldwin of Augusta County, denouncing the act as contrary to the efforts of the

Convention to seek compromise, wanted to know who was in charge and where the activists came from. Wise replied that he assumed all the responsibility, and asked Baldwin to support the movement now that it was "on the march," and "aid the people who have waited on the convention too long in vain, in seizing arms for their own defense." Baldwin continued to protest. Wise told him that the "patriotic volunteer revolutionists" were Baldwin's own constituents, "his friends and neighbors of Staunton . . . marching under my orders to take their own arms for their own defense. . . . Shall they be doomed unsupported to bloody beds?"

According to Imboden, this sally silenced Baldwin, who "looked aghast." At that moment, the delegates were "thrown into bewildering excitement by Mr. Baylor, Baldwin's colleague, rushing by, almost over seats and down aisles, making his way to Wise. It might be to assail him; but no, it was to grasp his hand, with tears streaming down his cheeks and exclaiming, 'Let me grasp your hand; I don't agree with you; I don't approve your acts; but I love you; I love you.' " [35]

This, or something like it, was the atmosphere that compassed passage, on April 17, of the ordinance of secession. The act was entitled "An ordinance to repeal the ratification of the Constitution of the United States by the State of Virginia, and to resume all the rights and privileges granted under said Constitution." The vote was 88 in favor, 55 opposed, including Jubal Early. He cast his negative vote in the hope "even against hope" that war might still be prevented, and because he found it "exceedingly difficult to surrender the attachment of a lifetime to that Union which . . . I had been accustomed to look upon (in the language of Washington) as the palladium of the political safety and prosperity of the country." [36]

Early felt the vote to secede as the loss of a cherished ideal, which he mourned publicly. "The adoption of the ordinance wrung from me bitter tears of grief," Early later wrote, and he was not alone. But even now, Jubal did not completely give in to the new secessionist majority, which, in passing the ordinance, had given the Convention's endorsement to Wise's coup.

Galvanized by the vote, Wise's raiders descended on Harpers Ferry on April 18. Word had reached the Federal garrison, which had set fire to the buildings before abandoning the arsenal. Though the store of small arms was largely destroyed, much of the valuable machinery for making and repairing weapons was saved, and later moved to Richmond. On the 21st, Virginians occupied the Navy Yard at Norfolk, which Federal forces had set afire, then evacuated. The raiders found an enormous dump of military supplies untouched by the flames, including more than a thousand heavy cannon.

By plunging Virginia into hostilities at the moment of secession, Wise and his group doubtless hoped, in part, to nullify the significance of the popular vote legally required to ratify the ordinance.[37] But the secessionists wanted absolutely nothing left to chance. In the Convention, they passed a resolution providing for an address to the people that would set forth the reasons for ratification.[38]

<< VIRGINIA WAS bent on war. As a military man who held a general's commission in the state militia (as did a great many men less fit for high rank than he), Early now signaled his acquiescence—though his approach was very practical. On April 21, the delegates were debating an ordinance to appoint Robert E. Lee the commander of all the state's armed forces. Early offered an amendment that would enable the government to appoint none but qualified commanders to serve under Lee. "The necessities of the state," said Jubal, "require that all the Generals of Militia be decapitated. I offer my own head on the block as a willing victim for the good of the Commonwealth."[39]

In the end, "the good of the Commonwealth" was the standard on which Jubal Early aligned his conduct—along with many others, not least Lee. Fealty to the Union, however attractive to the soaring mind of an idealist, was still only a concept, while loyalty to Virginia had the primal resonance of blood. On the day of his resignation from the United States Army, Lee had written to his sister: "With all my devotion to the Union and the feeling of loyalty and duty as an American citizen, I have not been able to make up my mind to raise my hand against my relatives, my children, my home."[40]

There is no doubt that Early would have sympathized. Responding to Lee's formal installation as Virginia's military commander, Jubal declared his loyalty to the state whether or not it was right for the commonwealth to pull out of the Union. He had been opposed to secession all along, he said, and he had no regrets. Yet, he declared, "As we are now engaged in this contest, all my wishes, all my desires and all the energies of my hand and heart will be given to the cause of my state. Whether we have the right of secession or revolution, I want to see my state triumphant."[41]

The issue became unmistakably clear on May 23 when an overwhelming majority of the state's voters approved the ordinance of secession. Jubal now signed it. Having already offered his services to the governor, he accepted a colonel's commission in the Virginia militia and was assigned to the command and training of volunteers who had begun assembling in Lynchburg.[42]

« TAKING UP arms against the Union was a final act. Unlike many of his compatriots, Jubal Early would never look back again. But not many of his comrades-in-arms over the bloody four years to come would turn out to be the radical secessionists who had let loose the war in which the soldiers bled. With his taste for sour ironies, Jubal Early became fond of taunting the few identifiable secessionists in gray uniform who came his way, especially when the circumstances were less than amusing. One of his better-known targets was John C. Breckinridge. A former vice-president of the United States, Breckinridge was a presidential candidate of Southern extremists in 1860 (though not a true advocate of secession), and Early's second-in-command during part of 1864. That fall, in full retreat from defeat in the Third Battle of Winchester, Early was riding with Breckinridge; in the chaos and horror of his army's rout, Early took occasion to mock his celebrated subordinate: "Well, General," he crowed, "what do you think of the 'rights of the South' in the territories now?"[43]

PART TWO

<< CHAPTER FIVE >>

"The Fun Has Just Commenced"

*J*UBAL EARLY was eager to make war. But his ardor did not completely suppress his ambivalence about soldiering and military life. His attitude showed in his dress, which was determinedly civilian. In the first months of the war, some Southern officers and a great number of the men were still wearing a mixture of uniform and civilian clothes. But Early's mode of dress was not only downright unmilitary; it was not even the garb of a lawyer or other man of importance in civil life. To one observer, it looked like the attire of "a farmer in ordinary circumstances"; to another, Jubal's raiment made him look like a stage driver. A third observer, who thought Early's scruffiness a pose, was reminded of Plato's speech to Diogenes, "that he showed his vanity by his rags." [1]

Early, who was vain enough to think of himself as a careful and fastidious dresser—"most particular . . . about the cut and fit of my clothes"—disagreed. It was simply, he asserted, that during the war he was almost always in camp or in the field, without the time or resources to get new clothes.

Whatever the excuse for his appearance, Early's old aversion to spit-and-polish scarcely concealed a rigorous intellectual and emotional commitment to the wartime requirements of his soldier's profession. This aspect of his attitude toward the war created a reputation that was to last. Many would come to regard the military intellect of Jubal Early, combined with a cool bravery and imperturbability under extreme pressure, as second to none in the Confederate States Army. [2]

Certainly, in the tests put to him during the first months of the Civil War, Jubal Early acquitted himself well. He had two chances to shine in battle. In the first, he won praise and earned promotion for reaching the field "at an opportune, critical moment" and commanded his forces "with sagacity, decision and successful results." In the second, he acted with an impetuosity that some said was recklessness, while others called it courage and persistence. In the lengthy intervals when there was no fighting, he struggled, often furiously and usually effectively, to make an army out of men he considered almost irremediably spoiled for useful military employment by having lived as civilians most of their lives, which was basically true of him as well. (The apparent inconsistency, like that in his attitude toward dress, never occurred to him.)[3]

Unlike P. G. T. Beauregard, Thomas J. Jackson, Barnard Bee, James Longstreet, and many others in the corps of senior Confederate officers, Jubal could not show a record shimmering with the glaze imparted by the fires of Mexican War combat. But there was little he had not learned at Fortress Monroe and Monterrey about turning volunteers into some semblance of soldiers. He knew his recruits.

« AND THEY were to know him. For the Virginia volunteers mustering at Lynchburg in the spring of 1861, the first hint that war might be more than a Maytime lark with hometown friends might well have been their introduction to Colonel Early. Some of these boys, cocksure and boastful of marksmanship that could fillet a jackrabbit at 100 yards, were anxious to hone their skills on Yankee targets. Many had been persuaded to sign up by the promise—at any rate, the prospect—that each would be issued a rifle, the weapon of choice for the up-to-date man-at-arms. What very few realized was the scarcity of such modern ordnance, not only in Virginia but throughout the South; all the arsenals of the Confederacy, from the Rio Grande to the Potomac, contained but 15,000 rifles—along with 120,000 deficient percussion muskets and some antique flintlocks. Many of the fresh recruits were forced to begin their new lives as soldiers without the personal weapons the young Southerner was supposed to set so much store by. A number, feeling insulted, reacted with anger. Loud recriminations and rumors of mutiny reverberated through the camp.

But it all died down when Colonel Early confronted his restless

< 56 >

charges. The level gaze of his dark eyes was enough to make most men abandon any notion of crossing the colonel; his high, argumentative voice was persuasive, asserting with mingled ridicule and reason that the shortage of weapons was a universal problem, and that the men would be armed as soon as human effort and ingenuity could overcome the deficiency. Though the grumbling would never stop, most of the new privates refrained from mutiny or immediate desertion. Early reported the problem to Richmond, and the high command let him know they were well satisfied "with the manner in which you repressed the difficulty among the companies under your command with regard to their arms."[4]

It may have been about this time that the men in Early's charge gave him a nickname. Inspired by respect for his acerbic but fair approach to command and his air of premature age, as well as by amusement over his old-fashioned name, they took to calling him "old Jube" or "old Jubilee."[5]

<< Maj. Gen. Robert E. Lee, commanding Virginia's forces in the confused period following the Old Dominion's secession, was doubtless grateful that Jubal was available for service in Lynchburg, a transportation center that made it a logical manpower and supply depot. Early, only one of many officers designated to run "camps of instruction," or recruiting centers, had gotten his orders on May 6: take charge of Virginia troops being formed as units at the hurriedly improvised Lynchburg camp. There, the colonel was to organize five regiments of infantry and one of cavalry, using men from counties in the Lynchburg region; he was to get them ready for combat as soon as he could.[6]

The order was challenging. Early's temper, which was to be abraded by the frustration of dealing with the recruits, was also to be severely tested by horrendous problems of supply. On May 16, the day of his arrival in Lynchburg—he had spent some time at home in Franklin on personal business—Early was already writing to Lee's headquarters in Richmond about the state of affairs at Camp Davis, as the depot for Virginia troops had been christened.

In his report, Early acknowledged that some work had already been done. Lt. Col. Daniel Langhorne, from whom Early was taking over, had mustered in two companies of cavalry and nine companies of infantry. That was fine as far as it went, but the companies were largely unarmed. One cavalry company had about 50 sabers, but 20 men were entirely without arms; the troopers with sabers had no other weapons. In view of the shortages, cavalry troopers from companies formed earlier in the counties had been advised to bring their own double-barreled shotguns to Lynchburg; but few such weapons could be found, and the prices of guns offered for sale were prohibitive. As for the infantry companies, they had no arms of any kind.

It was clear that equipping five regiments of infantry and one of cavalry would mean starting from scratch. For the foot soldiers, Early estimated he would need 5,000 stands of muskets and rifles,[7] along with equivalent numbers of other kinds of gear such as knapsacks, canteens, and blankets. For the mounted troops, the requirement was 1,000 cavalry arms (including pistols and carbines), supplemented by suitable quantities of saddles, bridles, saddle bags, and other horse equipment.

Meanwhile, as the men awaited the means of waging war, they must live. Even the simplest necessities were lacking. Early found a serious shortage of mess pans and camp kettles. There were not nearly enough tents, and the supply was "of an inferior quality and make." Lynchburg was a city with the industrial means of remedying these wants, but in immemorial fashion, military bureaucracy had intervened to handcuff the local commander. The assistant quartermaster, a Captain Gilmor, told Early that he had orders from Richmond "to make no contract for the manufacture of any articles without orders from headquarters."

In his report to the high command, the colonel suggested that such orders be issued forthwith. In the meantime, what could not be made or found could be dispensed with or replaced by an expedient: if there were no tents, idle tobacco factories could supply shelter; horses could be stabled in empty warehouses.[8]

Within five days of Jubal's report, the critical deficiency of weapons began to be corrected. Under Lee's prodding, the fledgling Confederate Ordnance Department started shipping the first of one thousand muskets, along with 60,000 rounds of ammunition. It was enough to outfit 10 companies, which were formed as a regiment of infantry. As more muskets arrived in camp, they were issued to enough men to form another infantry regiment. Sufficient cavalry weapons were scraped up to outfit a mounted regiment. These units, the 24th and 28th Virginia Infantry and the 30th Battalion Virginia Volunteers (later the 2d Virginia Cavalry) were sent by rail—not without difficulty and delay, as Early saw it—to Culpeper Courthouse. There, Col. Philip St. George Cocke was organizing defenses against a gathering threat of Northern invasion. The 24th Virginia—with one company from Franklin County—came under Early's personal command; while he remained in charge at Lynchburg, the regiment was turned over to Lt. Col. Peter Hairston.[9]

Through the end of May and the first weeks of June, Colonel Early soldiered on at Camp Davis, cobbling together some of Virginia's first contributions to the Confederate war effort. The major preoccupation remained the hunt for weapons. Trying to equip volunteer cavalry companies that were riding in on good mounts but armed worse than many a local farmer, the colonel kept pestering Richmond, whose armories were nearly as bare as Lynchburg's; he also kept his ear to the ground. Hearing of sabers and pistols in nearby Henry County, he sent a party to lay hands on them.[10]

« AFTER FEDERAL troops occupied Alexandria in late May, Southern military thinking became increasingly focused on the area of Manassas Junction, a key rail point just south of Bull Run. On the last day of May, Brig. Gen. Beauregard assumed command of a Manassas force of about 15,000 men. On June 19, Early—ordered to the line at last!—reported to Beauregard, who placed Early in charge of his army's 6th Brigade, comprising the 24th and 7th Virginia and the 4th South Carolina Regiments. The brigade's assignment was to watch the crossings of Bull Run close to its confluence with the Occoquon River.[11]

Beauregard considered the mission important enough to attach a three-gun section of the Washington Artillery, a crack unit, to Early's brigade. Reporting for duty, Lt. Charles Squires, commanding the section, found the colonel riding along a road near the stream. In his war reminiscences, Squires described Early's saddle as "old-fashioned," and his saddle bags as "still older." The former artillery officer also tried to reproduce Jubal's voice orthographically: "He asked me, 'Are you M-i-s-t-e-r S-q-u-i-r-e-s?' I answered, 'Yes.' 'W-e-l-l, I am C-o-l. E-a-r-l-y. You will halt here and when the infantry comes up, follow behind.'" Squires saw a lot of the colonel during this period and began a lifelong friendship with him.[12]

« BY MID-JULY, it was evident that a Federal army was lumbering southwestward from Alexandria via Centreville toward Manassas. The Union force comprised about 37,000 men commanded by Maj. Gen. Irvin McDowell, whom Early had known at West Point. Early and his brigade were still on the right, or eastern, end of the Confederate line, posted behind Blackburn's Ford, one of the Bull Run crossings. The unit was in reserve, with orders to support either the 4th Brigade, defending Blackburn's Ford under the blunt, bearlike Brig. Gen. James Longstreet, or the 3d, guarding McLean's Ford (on the far Confederate right), under the steady, sagacious David R. Jones, also a brigadier general.

The stage was set for a sharp clash at Blackburn's Ford that was to be a prelude to the First Battle of Manassas. Not long after noon on July 18, Union fire opened on the Confederate positions opposite Blackburn's Ford, and a two-company reconnaissance force boldly approached Longstreet's men, who were soon firing back. Longstreet, worried that the assertiveness of the Federal advance signified substantial support, asked Early for reinforcements; and soon there came an order from Beauregard directing the 6th Brigade to back Longstreet up. Leading the men personally, Early brought along the 7th Louisiana Regiment, under Col. Harry T. Hays, the 7th Virginia—led by Col. James L. Kemper, Jubal's old comrade from the Mexican War—and the Washington Artillery section under Lieutenant Squires. Musket fire spattered the column as it double-quicked down the road toward the ford; Jubal's reaction was a bitter joke. Addressing a colonel riding at his knee, Early asked, "What do you think of secession now?" "Oh, the fun has just commenced." "Well," said Early, "you'll get enough of it before it's over."[13]

Though the Federal advance did not turn out to be strongly supported, Longstreet's concern was not misplaced. In a sharp exchange of fire, his men managed to repulse an attempt by the enemy to cross Bull

Run before Early's reinforcements arrived. When they did, Longstreet immediately put the 7th Louisiana into line to relieve his 17th Virginia and part of his 11th Virginia. Hoping to stop any subsequent Union assault before it began, he then ordered his line to cross Bull Run in an attack of its own, and requested that Colonel Early bring the rest of his command—the 7th and 24th Virginia Regiments—up to lend support.

At this point, effective cooperation between Early and Longstreet faltered. No 6th Brigade troops crossed Bull Run in support of Longstreet's attack. Early may have misunderstood his colleague's request, or he may have ignored it, believing there was not enough room in the narrow crossing to accommodate the hundreds of men Longstreet was already trying to cram into its few yards of width.

Undoubtedly contributing to the loss of coordination were the miasma of battle and the newness of the men to combat. But even veterans might have been rattled by the predicament in which Early's men found themselves. For all Longstreet's concern, the Confederate position at the ford was reasonably secure against a general assault over the crossing, but the individual fighting man was quite vulnerable. Federal troops stood on elevated ground overlooking the Confederates, who occupied open fields only partially screened by trees along Bull Run. Plunging fire from the Northern bank was bound to hurt and distract the Southerners. For raw troops hearing the malevolent buzz of the first bullets fired at them on purpose, and seeing what those balls could do to their comrades' heads, limbs, and bellies, the marvel is that they did not simply run away—though the thought of encountering their colonel on their way to the rear may have given some of them pause. Others, profiting from their training at his hands, had already learned to act the soldier.[14]

In any case, their impulse was to stand and fight. Unfortunately, other Southern troops were in the line of their fire. In the process of being formed in line—whether to relieve Longstreet's men or to support them in attack—the 7th Virginia reacted to enemy volleys by shooting, without orders, over the heads of the men on the line of the stream to their front. Longstreet tried to stop the 7th Regiment's fire by riding up and down in front of them, but it was no good; he had to dismount and lie down until all the muskets were empty. Still, no Confederate soldiers seem to have been hurt by the Virginians' undisciplined "friendly" fire.[15]

In the meantime, Squires's guns dampened the Federal musketry, and the 7th Virginia advanced. The men Longstreet had sent across the stream hit the Northerners in their flank, accelerating a withdrawal that was already in progress. The fight was over—a minor but very satisfying victory for the Confederates, paid for with scant loss. Longstreet's casualties were 15 killed, 53 wounded, and two missing—probably prisoners.[16]

Early's men bivouacked that night along Bull Run, relieving most of Longstreet's brigade, which Early acknowledged had "borne the brunt of the fight." All in all, the 6th Brigade had not had so bad a time of it; they were now blooded veterans, who had driven the Yankees back. Most had suffered little damage, save the bullet-holed jacket here and the dented canteen there, which merely bolstered their youthful sense of their own immortality. Less sure of the future, Early next day ordered the troops, using bayonets and any other improvised entrenching tools they could find, to dig in along the banks of the stream.[17]

<< AMONG THE proud new veterans, there were some who believed that the recent scuffle (which Beauregard grandiosely called the Battle of Bull Run) was the end of the campaign—that the enemy would depart and never return. But most realized that the fight was only a curtain raiser.

On the evening of the 19th, Beauregard summoned his brigade commanders to a conference at his headquarters at the McLean house, not far from Early's position. There, to the group of officers seated on the lawn in the summer twilight, the commanding general outlined his aggressive plans for the immediate future. Beauregard counted heavily on the cooperation of an army under Gen. Joseph E. Johnston that was confronting a Federal force in the Shenandoah Valley commanded by Brig. Gen. Robert Patterson. Because it would enable the Confederates, by concentrating, to oppose McDowell on something like even terms, this plan of cooperation had the blessing of the Confederate authorities; but its execution depended on Johnston's ability, before moving to join Beauregard, to defeat or slip away from Patterson.

Though he had no assurance that Johnston would be able to accomplish this elusive goal, Beauregard made his plans on that assumption. Also intrinsic to the plan's success was another assumption, for which Beauregard had no evidence: that Johnston, in moving from the Valley, would send part of his force on the cars of the Manassas Gap Railroad and join Beauregard south of Bull Run, while the rest would march via Ashby's Gap and attack McDowell's right flank. At that point, Beauregard's army, now reinforced, would hammer the Federal left.

During the meeting on July 19, Beauregard learned—on excellent authority—that Johnston intended to dispatch his entire army by rail. But Beauregard was unconvinced. Since he had planned it that way, he persuaded himself that Johnston was sure to send a part of his force so as to attack McDowell's right flank. On that basis the general ordered his army to attack across Bull Run as soon as the sound of gunfire announced the beginning of Johnston's assault, probably around dawn the next morning—the 20th. "Now, gentlemen," Beauregard exhorted, "let tomorrow be their Waterloo." [18]

But next day's events did not unfold as Beauregard had said they would; there was no noise of battle where Johnston was supposed to be attacking off to the left—which was to have been the signal for the forward movement of Early's men. Actually, no fighting took place on the 20th, and, though Early did not know it, almost nothing was happening the way Beauregard had planned. To begin with, Johnston in fact arrived by train at Manassas Junction on that day, and the bulk of his army was en route by the same means. Another problem was the confusion in Beauregard's mind about McDowell's intentions. The Louisianian seemed to be assuming that McDowell would either sit still and wait for the Confederates to attack him, or compliantly attack Beauregard at his strongest point—on the right, near Blackburn's and McLean's fords. [19]

On the steamy morning of July 21, Early and his men remained near the McLean house, where they were once more acting as a reserve backing up Jones or Longstreet. It was the latter who again called on one of Early's regiments for support as Federal batteries opened fire from the heights north of Blackburn's Ford. Early sent forward six companies of the 24th Virginia, along with two companies of Hays's 7th

Louisiana. Then came a request for another regiment; the remaining eight companies of the 7th Louisiana, with Early at their head, now came up.

The colonel discovered that Longstreet had moved all his men across Bull Run; they were under cover in the dead ground at the foot of the Union-occupied heights. Moving to join Longstreet's units were the companies of the 24th Virginia; the 7th Louisiana men had been ordered to form a supporting line among the trees on the south bank. Federal guns in front and over on the right pounded the neighborhood of the ford and made crossing risky.

Longstreet, who was waiting for an order from Beauregard to attack up the hill, braved the fire to ride across and reconnoiter the far side of the stream. On his return, he sent Early off to the right, with the 7th Virginia and the Louisiana regiment, under orders to cross Bull Run at McLean's Ford and silence the enemy guns firing from that flank.

While his force was moving toward McLean's Ford, Early rode ahead to see what he would be up against. On rising ground, he found a lookout posted in a tree, who was able to tell him that the route to the battery was in its field of fire most of the way. Early's men would have to advance, a bit like the Light Brigade at Balaclava, along an open valley, with a climb at the end up a bare slope to the gun position. The lookout also observed that the battery enjoyed substantial infantry support. (Early later learned that an entire infantry brigade lay in wait for attackers behind works protected by an abatis, or entanglement of felled trees.)[20]

« AT THIS MOMENT, around 11:00 A.M., a courier galloped up to relay an order from Beauregard: withdraw forthwith to the south side of Bull Run. Early told the courier about the Longstreet order he was carrying out. Informed that the order from Beauregard overrode Longstreet and applied to everyone, Early felt a strong sense of relief. Trying to take those guns, he was persuaded, would have meant "certain destruction," "the annihilation or utter rout of my two regiments."

Even with this reprieve, the danger was not past. The meanderings of Bull Run, the strong Federal presence on the north bank, and the similarity between Federal and Confederate uniforms at this stage of the war—a lethal source of confusion throughout the Bull Run battle—required cautious forethought in getting everybody safely back across the stream. Early handled it personally. Fearing that the Louisiana regiment, marching back to McLean's Ford from the north bank, might be fired on by Jones's men guarding the ford, Early rode over to see Jones and warn him to have his troops hold their fire.

Jones did as he was asked. Then he inquired whether Early had gotten an order from Beauregard directing him to bring his brigade to headquarters. On this day, Beauregard issued many orders that went astray, or disappeared, or could not possibly be carried out, or for many reasons had null effect. The directive to Early referred to by Jones was one of the disappearing variety. Fortunately, Jones had received it—in the form of a note appended to an order addressed to *him*. The note, in pencil, simply said: "Send Early to me." Early got the message as the heat of the day approached its peak, between noon and 1:00 P.M. The firing off to the left was growing heavier by the minute.[21]

Colonel Early had no way of knowing why he was being sent toward the mounting din of battle. But if he sensed that his command was needed to reinforce a Confederate position under dire threat, he was right. General McDowell had not attacked the Confederate right, where Beauregard was strongest, but instead had looped around in the opposite direction and attacked the Southern left flank, which was relatively weak. By the time the summons to Early reached him and sent him on his way, Beauregard, with Johnston close by, was in deep trouble; he was barely, frantically fending off an extremely threatening Federal assault on Henry Hill some five miles to the west of Blackburn's Ford. Here Thomas Jackson had already come by his sobriquet, "Stonewall"; here Barnard Bee, who had coined it, had suffered a mortal wound, and Francis Bartow, commander of an earlier reinforcing contingent sent from the right flank, had died, rallying his men with their battle flag in his hands.[22]

Despite the urgency of his situation, General Beauregard's directive to Early was vague to the point of opacity. Nevertheless, the colonel immediately set about gathering his brigade to make the march to Beauregard's field headquarters, which Early understood to be somewhere off to his left, possibly near Mitchell's Ford—about four miles to the west over the zigzagging country tracks. The colonel dispatched a staff officer, Lt. Fleming Gardner, to find out where Beauregard might be. Sending word to Hays to bring on his Louisianians as fast as possible, and ordering Kemper to get his Virginians ready, Early asked Longstreet to return the six companies of his own 24th Virginia detached earlier. The reply from Longstreet suggested that Early make a switch: the 13th Mississippi Regiment, under Col. William Barksdale, resting in the woods to Early's immediate left, was under orders to join Longstreet; let Early take that regiment, urged Longstreet, and he would keep the 24th Virginia companies. The arrangement would save time, and avoid exposure of both regiments to Federal artillery fire as they traveled back and forth in the neighborhood of Blackburn's Ford. Early promptly agreed. Barksdale was also in accord, and as soon as his men could be fallen in, they were marched off to join Early's column hurrying westward. It was about 1:00 P.M. [23]

The way led hour after hour uphill, through fields, sometimes following a farm track. Men fell out to fill their canteens with muddy water from puddles, and to pick berries and persimmons. Wasps nesting in one persimmon patch attacked the stragglers, who ran every which way in the terrible heat; when Colonel Barksdale, stout and fussy, rode up to see what the matter was, he blundered into the heart of wasp territory, much to the hilarity of his men. [24]

As the marchers slogged toward the prospect of death or maiming, their spirits were assailed by signs that the battle was going badly. One of Beauregard's staff officers, also looking for the general, galloped up to announce that word had just been received at Manassas Junction that 6,000 Union troops were on their way from the Valley. Stragglers moving to the rear told the 6th Brigade men that it was all up with them. These "recreants," as Early called them, told the officers that riding onto the field would be suicidal, since the enemy was shooting anyone on horseback. No one in his brigade, Early noted with pride, reacted to these woeful tidings by falling out of ranks. [25]

Up on Henry Hill, around 3:00 P.M., Beauregard realized that his battle was approaching a crisis. His battered brigades were holding off the Union offensive, but fresh Federal troops were pushing hard against his left flank and threatening to turn it. Although one of Johnston's

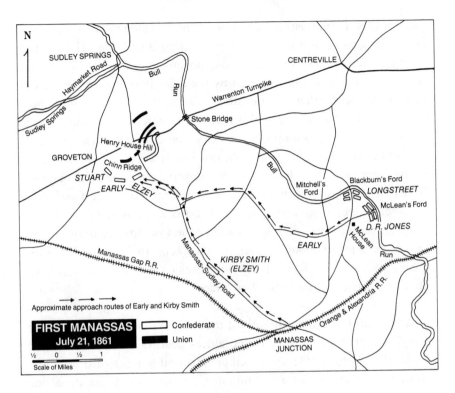

N

SUDLEY SPRINGS
CENTREVILLE
Haymarket Road
Bull
Sudley Springs
Warrenton Turnpike
Run
Stone Bridge
Henry House Hill
GROVETON
Chinn Ridge
STUART
Bull
EARLY ELZEY
Mitchell's Ford
Blackburn's Ford
LONGSTREET
McLean's Ford
D. R. JONES
McLean House
Manassas Gap R.R.
Manassas-Sudley Road
KIRBY SMITH (ELZEY)
EARLY
Run
Orange & Alexandria R.R.

Approximate approach routes of Early and Kirby Smith

FIRST MANASSAS ☐ Confederate
July 21, 1861 ■ Union

MANASSAS JUNCTION

½   0   ½   1
Scale of Miles

newly arrived brigades, under Col. Arnold Elzey, was sent to stifle this threat, Beauregard badly needed another brigade to nail the vulnerable flank down. As these thoughts fluttered through the general's mind, he got word that a sizable dust cloud had been spotted to the southwest, approaching his left. Before long, he could see the cloud, and then a marching column. Was it Confederate reinforcements, or Union troops from Patterson's Valley force? The distance was too great for the general to identify the flag at the head of the column. If it were the enemy, Beauregard would have to inform Johnston and give the order to retreat. But if the advancing column were Southern, the timing and the angle of its approach would bring it into action on the left in an almost perfect position to roll up the enemy line.[26]

« RIDING IN agitated search of instructions, one of Early's aides encountered a Beauregard staff man: orders were vague—just head for the front. Not much later, Early himself met an aide to General Johnston; the senior commander had left Beauregard on Henry Hill to run the fight there, and was managing the movement of other troops being funneled into the battle. Relayed by the aide, Johnston's order was a little more specific than Beauregard's: move to the left of the front line. The colonel forthwith turned his men in that direction, and in a short while ran into Johnston himself. Exactly where, he asked the general, should he position his brigade? Johnston hardly knew; he had not been on the spot long enough to scout the country. But he sensed that the best place for Early's command was on the far left of the Confederate line. There, along with other newly arrived troops, notably Elzey's brigade, the 6th Brigade might stabilize the Confederate position and maybe even inflict enough damage on the enemy to tip the odds toward a Southern victory. Keep marching, Johnston told the colonel, until there is no one on your left—then attack.[27]

<< BEAUREGARD, staring intently at the column of soldiers with its flag hanging inert from its staff in the airless heat, decided that it was a Federal relief force. He sent a senior officer off to tell Johnston—then hesitated. "Let us wait a few minutes," he shouted to the departing officer, "to confirm our suspicions . . ." Once again he fixed his eye on the distant flag. Then, a breath of wind floated the flag away from the staff just long enough for the general to recognize the colors of a Confederate regiment in the 6th Brigade. The general's fierce anxiety turned instantly to elation. Here, in the shape of Jubal Early, was victory, imminent and triumphant.[28]

<< IT WAS about 4:00 P.M. Despite the uphill march in the heat, Early had pushed and chivied his men six miles in three hours. No small accomplishment for a green command, it was one that Jubal and his men would repeat many times, though (perhaps unjustly) his troops would never enjoy the reputation of "foot cavalry" later accorded the soldiers commanded by Stonewall Jackson.

Now Early swung his brigade in on the left of Elzey's. As he was positioning the regiments for the attack, the men were punished by the accurate fire of Federal skirmishers on the slope of Chinn's Ridge, to

< 68 >

the Southerners' front. As he was to note with great satisfaction and pride, Early's green cohorts did not flinch despite their inability to return the skirmishers' long-range fire with their old smoothbores.

Then, in this tense moment of unfolding battle, the colonel got word from Col. J. E. B. Stuart, in charge of a party of cavalry and some guns operating out of sight even farther to the left than Early. Stuart's message to Early must have been a tonic: coordinate with me and my guns, hit the enemy now, and he will break. Noticing that Elzey's brigade, on his right, was advancing, Early ordered his men forward in line of battle toward a Federal line visible on top of Chinn's Ridge while Stuart's guns fired from the extreme left into the enemy's flank. Shaken by the artillery fire and by the advance of Early's and Elzey's seemingly fresh troops, the Union soldiers on the hill began moving to their rear. As Early's men reached the top of Chinn's Ridge, they halted in full view of thousands of Federal troops milling around at the bottom of the slope and beginning to flee the battlefield in large numbers.

The impetus of the Federals' retreat, soon to become a rout, was increased by a general advance of the entire Confederate force on the line of Henry Hill, from Early's position on the left to the units on the far right where the Southern line touched Bull Run. In the few minutes of action, 6th Brigade losses were 12 killed and 64 wounded, out of approximately 1,500 men.[29]

Early's brigade joined in the desultory pursuit of the Federals, but went only a short distance before forming a defensive line and making a hungry, exhausted camp, miles from their baggage and supplies. Amid the confusion of the evening, President Jefferson Davis appeared on the field, and in due course appeared at Early's camp, renewing the acquaintance begun 14 years before in Mexico. Lacking orders and uncertain as to what to do, Jubal asked his commander in chief for instructions. Davis was noncommittal: stay put, he said, and get some rest.

Colonel Early did the little he could—there were no rations, and no one had eaten since early morning—to see that his men were comfortable. As soon as they were settled, he rode with his staff in search of orders from Beauregard or Johnston. Finding neither general, and returning to camp toward midnight across the desolation of the main battlefield, the colonel bedded down on a pallet of wheat.[30]

<< THE FORTUITOUS arrival of Early's brigade and its action alongside Elzey's on the left end of the Confederate line set off the retreat that led to McDowell's debacle at the First Battle of Manassas. By almost any standard, Early's handling of his brigade, both on the march from the McLean house and in the relatively short burst of action on Chinn's Ridge, was highly effective. Thanks to Jubal Early, the star of P. G. T. Beauregard rose high and shone bright—albeit only briefly—and the Louisiana general's gratitude never diminished, as Early would discover years later when it was his turn to need some help. In the short run, Beauregard repaid Early by recommending him for a promotion to brigadier general that was approved in August and made effective as of the day of battle.[31]

Early himself evidently realized how lucky he had been to arrive in just the right place at precisely the right time. He never claimed to have tipped the balance of contending forces with his command, though he obviously thought he and the troops had done a good job, and praised his men for the "cool and deliberate manner" in which they had deployed for battle under fire. With his penchant for logic, he would have found it repugnant to hog credit for the victory when it seemed so clear that his effort was not unique. He put the case to readers of his memoirs: when a small force has been fighting for hours against difficult odds "until it has become exhausted and is beginning to give way, and then fresh troops come up and turn the tide of battle, the latter are said to have saved the day and often reap all the glory." People forget, Early urged, "that, but for the troops whose obstinate fighting enabled the fresh ones to come up in time, the day would have been irretrievably lost before the appearance of the latter. It is an old saying that 'it is the last feather that breaks the camel's back,' yet the last feather would do no harm but for the weight that precedes it. The *first* feather contributes as much as the last to the catastrophe."[32]

<< EARLY ALSO acknowledged that McDowell himself had something to do with the "catastrophe." But he showed a surprising generosity to McDowell. Possibly he retained warm feelings left over from the Academy, where McDowell had been a class behind him.[33] The

Union's Manassas defeat, said Jubal, was actually the fault of old Winfield Scott, general in chief of the Union army. Early suggested that Scott, unwilling to entrust the battle to McDowell, who had no experience commanding troops, controlled the entire action from his desk in Washington. Whoever may have been in charge, as Jubal pointed out, the Union lost its chance by delaying its assault; McDowell (or Scott) could have overwhelmed the Confederates on July 18 if the Federals had hammered the center of the Southern line at the same time they were attacking its right at Blackburn's Ford. Johnston's army would not yet have been on the field, and Union forces would have outnumbered the Confederates by more than two to one.

Early's charity to McDowell also included praise for the Union commander's distress and indignation over the conduct of Federal troops, who stole and killed livestock, pilfered other property, and burned buildings belonging to civilians during the campaign of First Manassas. Early quoted, in its entirety, an order McDowell issued on July 18, threatening jail—or worse—for any Federal soldier caught "committing the slightest depredation," and insisting that the soldiers' conduct should be the same as it would be at home. Union forces, the order concluded, were "here to fight the enemies of the country, not to judge and punish the unarmed and helpless, no matter how guilty they may be. When necessary, that will be done by the proper person." In Early's eyes, McDowell had honestly tried to fight the campaign "according to the principles of civilized warfare."

It was to be a point of enormous importance to Early, who held McDowell up as the last Union commander even to attempt preventing his troops from savaging noncombatants. This was untrue, but the distortion arose from the unforgiving violence of Early's feelings, which would be directed against commanders—notably John Pope, William T. Sherman, David Hunter, and Philip Sheridan—whom Jubal blamed for *deliberate* barbarity toward civilians. His response to the Union's policy of total war would be retribution in kind and lifelong hatred.[34]

« CHAPTER SIX »

The Spur of Ambition

I N THE AFTERMATH of the July 21 battle, manned balloons sent aloft by "Professor" Thaddeus S. C. Lowe kept a nervous watch on the advanced Confederate positions outside Washington and Alexandria. But the aeronautics did the Federals little good, in Jubal Early's view; he saw the balloons as just one sign of an excessive Yankee caution. In fact, the Confederates were also cautious as the two armies devoted the fall and winter of 1861–62 to refitting and reorganizing. It was an unsettling period of transition, unmarked by significant fighting, that created or confirmed many of Jubal Early's deepest biases, crotchets, and pet hates.[1]

Early's brigade, supported by a cavalry company and a battery of guns, now consisted of the 24th Virginia and the 5th and 13th (later the 23d) North Carolina Regiments. In October, the brigade was combined with that of Brig. Gen. Richard S. Ewell—a man of almost as many quirks and eccentricities as Early—in a division commanded by the dapper Mississippian Maj. Gen. Earl Van Dorn.

Until now, the Confederate forces along Bull Run had been loosely organized in brigades, whose commanders reported directly to the army commander, General Johnston. Subordination to supreme authority was the only form of military submission Early could unhesitatingly accept; the insertion of Van Dorn into the chain of command thus constricted Jubal's independence, and undoubtedly irked him.

Other sources of irritation were not lacking. Until it went into winter quarters, Early's command changed camps a number of times, and on each occasion Jubal fumed at the time it took—two or three days—

to make the move. The main problem was the immense amount of private baggage piled up by officers and men alike. Early tried to educate at least the officers in the wisdom of reducing personal impedimenta as much as possible, and tried to persuade them to send their excess luggage home. He admitted failure. "[I]t was very provoking," he grumped, "to see with what tenacity young lieutenants held on to baggage enough to answer all their purposes at a fashionable watering place in time of peace."

In March, when the army was ordered to abandon the line of Bull Run, the private trunks, boxes, and portmanteaus were added to the piles of military stores and supplies slated for shipment to the rear. As it turned out, there was not nearly enough transportation to move even the vital military supplies, which included large quantities of clothing, blankets, and salted meat. When everything that had to be left behind was put to the torch, Jubal soothed his keen distress at the military consequences of the burning—he believed it affected the course of the entire war—with the knowledge that the fires were also consuming the messy and unmilitary accumulation of baggage.[2]

Just as unmilitary, General Early felt—as he did throughout his wartime service—was the custom of officers bringing their wives along on campaign. This, the general thought, was unfair to the men, who could not bring their wives into camp. He also regarded it as unseemly—a kind of social degradation that placed an officer's spouse on the same level as that of a camp follower, that is, a whore. Most of all, he saw the wives as an endless source of distraction from the urgent business at hand—prosecuting a war. After failing to persuade the women to leave, Early issued "peremptory orders" that got rid of some, but not all, of the most irritating spouses.[3]

The officers' failings were compounded by the shortcomings of the rank and file. Men failed to reenlist or deserted or went absent without leave and misbehaved in other ways that drew the full measure of Early's disapproval. In this he showed his tendency to mistrust and derogate subordinates. It made him few friends, but the urgency of wartime helped him justify it. In a February 1862 letter to James Kemper, Early complained of those who looked after their convenience and comfort in the face of a formidable enemy, and declared that from now on it would be his "vocation . . . to *watch* those under me. . . . This is a painful state of things . . . in an army that is fighting for its homes and the very existence of its country." Conscription, he declared, was necessary to prevent the army from simply melting away.[4]

<< THESE QUESTIONS got the airing they did, of course, partly because there was time to air them. But though the military respite of 1861–62 allowed space to find solutions to the army's problems, the free time and leisure of life in camp and winter quarters was not an unmixed blessing. Crowding, dirt, and contagion killed many men; the officers, with or without wives, fretted—and some drank too much.

This number may have included Jubal Early; the first winter of the war gave rise to a story—among the first of many—containing such a suggestion. The anecdote shows Jubal in a very dim light, as a quarrelsome spoilsport at the sort of convivial, sentimental feast dear to the hearts of nineteenth-century warriors. The source of the ill feeling was a wholly inappropriate and mean-spirited Virginia chauvinism that reflected very badly on Early, though the episode was by no means the last time that he and other Virginians would be accused of such bias during the war and afterward.

One winter day, the senior officers of Johnston's and Beauregard's commands held a ceremony at Van Dorn's headquarters in honor of Maryland regiments of the army, for which girls from home had sewn flags out of the material of their gowns. The occasion was poignant; the Marylanders, whose state had remained with the North, had left their homes to fight with the South. Following the presentation of the flags by the young ladies, the officers enjoyed a substantial luncheon. All went well until someone proposed a toast to Barnard Bee, Francis Bartow, and C. F. Fisher, dead heroes of the July battle. To everyone's astonishment, Jubal Early objected to the toast on the grounds that it mentioned no Virginian (Bee was from South Carolina, Bartow was Georgian, and Fisher from North Carolina). Voices now rose along with tempers; Generals Beauregard, Johnston, and Van Dorn tried in vain to calm the excited officers. Then a doctor whom hardly anyone knew rose and subdued the contenders with a conciliatory speech. The toast was drunk in total silence as Early and members of his party started to

< 74 >

leave. In the doorway, Early paused and said, "Didn't I stand up for old Virginia?"

It was now after dark and snow was falling. Early did not return immediately to his camp, but was not missed for a while. When staff members did turn out to look for him, one of the officers found him in the woods, fast asleep with his back against a tree.

Research has provided no independent confirmation of this story, but it has the ring of truth; Early was certainly capable of striking the harsh, incongruous note. The question is whether a sober Early would have been so imprudent and reckless as to insult almost everyone in the room as he did. Samuel Ferguson, the source of this version of the story, seems to have been present at the luncheon. He never stated that Early was intoxicated; only the story's ending suggests overindulgence.[5]

<< IN APRIL 1862, Maj. Gen. George B. McClellan launched his grand maneuver to outflank the Confederacy: a march to Richmond up the peninsula between the York and James rivers. Partly in response— and mainly because the line of Bull Run was no longer tenable—Johnston withdrew his army to the neighborhood of Richmond. On April 9, Jubal Early reported to Maj. Gen. John Magruder, in charge of defenses on the lower Peninsula. These consisted at that time of a line between Yorktown and the Warwick River, which Magruder occupied with 10,000 men. Using "Quaker" guns made of wood and moving men back and forth to create an aura of activity and strength, Magruder skillfully managed to convince McClellan (commanding 105,000) that he was opposed by 100,000 Confederates.[6]

The Southern high command, more realistic in their appraisals, felt that even when reinforced by Johnston's army, their maximum force of around 56,000 was too small to defend the length of the Yorktown–Warwick River line. Orders to withdraw to a shorter line started a Confederate retreat toward Richmond that was plagued by bottomless mud and constant, chilly rain. By nightfall on May 3, the glum, sodden columns were filing past fortifications built months earlier by Magruder to guard Williamsburg, Virginia's first capital. The largest of these works, Fort Magruder, near the intersection of the Yorktown and Hampton roads, was surrounded by smaller redoubts and entrenchments.

< 75 >

The army kept on marching toward Williamsburg, about two miles west. Jubal Early's brigade now consisted of the 24th Virginia, the 5th and 23d North Carolina, and the 38th Virginia—all but the first unblooded. The 2d Florida Regiment and the 2d Mississippi Battalion were attached to the brigade for the time being. About 2,300 strong, the brigade formed the rear guard of the Confederate army as part of a division under the scrappy North Carolinian Maj. Gen. Daniel Harvey Hill. On the night of May 3, Early's men went into camp about two miles west of Williamsburg.[7]

Next day, the advancing Federals caught up with the Confederate cavalry screen and threatened to overtake the main body in the open near Williamsburg. General Johnston ordered Confederate troops to hold Fort Magruder and some of its outlying redoubts long enough to enable him to get his supply trains safely away. Following a Federal attack on Fort Magruder begun early on May 4, a division commanded by James Longstreet reinforced the defenses at noon, launched a counterattack, and threw the Union force back. The Southern actions seemed to stabilize the line and assure the success of the general retreat, which was to resume at nightfall.[8]

But that assurance was far from complete. While attention was focused on the action on the right, a Federal brigade under Brig. Gen. Winfield Scott Hancock had marched boldly around the Confederate left and seized two unmanned redoubts from which Union artillery began to pour flanking fire into Fort Magruder. The fire was destructive enough, and the Confederates could see that if the guns were supported by infantry, the Southerners' position could become very awkward. But though Longstreet had not known of Hancock's presence until his guns opened fire, the Confederate general had foreseen such a danger, and had asked D. H. Hill to send him a brigade that could be brought up quickly if it became necessary to stiffen the left end of the line. The brigade was Early's.[9]

<< As of 3:00 P.M., they were halted, wretched and hungry, in the rain on the campus of the College of William and Mary, when the order came to move to Longstreet's support. Off they trudged, taking up

a position to the left of Fort Magruder overlooking a wheat field with woods on the far side, directly to the south.[10]

On arrival, Jubal was immediately inspired with thoughts of a glorious offensive. From the other side of the woods below the wheatfield came the crash of artillery in rapid fire. Federal guns, Jubal was certain, were close by, firing across his front on Fort Magruder. An attack through the woods might hit the guns in the rear and result in their destruction or capture.[11]

As Jubal was savoring this prospect, Hill arrived on the ridge, riding ahead of the rest of his division. Hill explained that, on Longstreet's orders, these troops were being positioned to Early's rear to support him in case of enemy attack. But when Early expounded his thoughts about taking out the Union guns beyond the woods, Hill was most intrigued. He rode down through the wheat to make a quick reconnaissance of the woods, learning little except that the ground was swampy and choked with underbrush; there was no telling how far it was through the woods to the guns, or where, exactly, the artillery might be. All the same, Hill felt that a brigade assault on the guns along the lines Early was suggesting stood a good chance of success.

Permission was obtained from Johnston, who urged caution, and Longstreet told Hill to accompany the attack in person and make sure that it did not slow down the rearward movement of the army. Hill, all eagerness to gain some glory at the head of the North Carolina regiments, unhesitatingly agreed to Longstreet's stipulation.

Calculating—really just hoping—that he would be closest to the guns when he emerged from the woods, Early took his place, as proud leader of the Virginia regiments, posting his old command, the 24th, on the far left, and deploying the 38th to its right. Next in line were the 23d and 5th North Carolina Regiments, the latter on the extreme right.

Confusion ruled the action from the outset. Saying nothing to Early, Hill started his regiments toward the woods; Early, assuming that he was expected to conform, waved his men forward. The veterans of the 24th moved off with alacrity; but the green ranks of the 38th, commanded by Lt. Col. Powhatan B. Whittle, hesitated. When the 38th did get started, it was 50 yards behind its sister regiment to the left.[12]

Spurring and cursing his mount downhill through the boggy under-brush in the woods, Early led his men to the bottom of a ravine and up the slope beyond. Tasting the triumph just ahead as the sound of the guns grew louder, he ordered no pause at the bottom of the ravine to dress his own ranks or see whether the 38th Virginia to his right was aligned with the 24th; nor did he try to ascertain where the North Carolina regiments were.

Hill had managed to preserve his units' cohesion on the march down-hill through the woods, but on the upslope beyond the ravine they encountered such dense undergrowth that Hill paused to get his bear-ings. Having no real idea where the Virginia regiments were, Hill sent a staff officer through the woods to the left to find them and try to coordinate the attack with them.

The two wings of the assault were now like deaf, blind whales swim-ming at the bottom of the sea. In his eagerness, Early was the first to regain sight, as the 24th Virginia emerged from the swampy under-brush.

When Early looked out into the open field beyond the woods, he could see, about a hundred yards to the left, a group of guns sited among a cluster of farm buildings along a north-south fence line. Supported by infantry in a redoubt and in woods behind them, the guns were firing across Early's front from left to right; their targets were Fort Magruder, about half a mile to the west, and a couple of smaller Confederate-held redoubts within closer range. "Follow me!" Early bellowed, and jumped his horse over a fence out of the woods into an open field. Swinging the 24th Virginia in a line headed for the guns, Early led the regiment forward.[13]

Case shot and canister slashed the ranks of the Virginians as they struggled through the muck in the field toward the Federals, and many fell. The artillery fire spared Jubal, a conspicuous target in the saddle, but musket balls smashed into his left shoulder and neck, and others partially blinded his horse. Bleeding and in pain, his horse nearly dis-abled, Jubal stayed in action, riding away from the guns to find the other regiments and send them in support of the 24th.

His way led him toward the 5th North Carolina, which had emerged from the woods and was now advancing toward the guns and the infan-

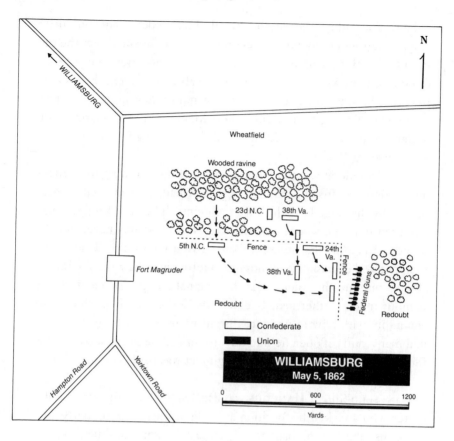

try in the redoubt. The North Carolinians, under Col. D. K. McRae, strove at the double-quick across the muddy field to catch up to the Virginians. From where they had left the woods, McRae's men had four or five times as much ground to traverse as the Virginians, under fire all the way. But they pushed to the fence line to join the 24th.

The Confederate onset had rattled the Union gunners momentarily, but they soon relaid their pieces and began to put fire on the advancing infantry, who were also victims of a withering volume of musketry from short range as they approached the Federal position. The artillerymen then commenced, in an orderly fashion, to limber up and withdraw to the shelter of the redoubt and the woods to their rear. There they resumed fire, pausing as the Federal infantry launched a counterattack to drive the Confederates back.

Faint and giddy from loss of blood, Jubal rode toward one of the Confederate-held redoubts, intending to dismount and direct the fight from there. But trying to get off his maimed horse was so painful and difficult that he knew he would never be able to remount; he also realized that he was no longer up to commanding troops. He rode slowly to the rear, finding Longstreet at Fort Magruder and bringing him up to date on the action he had just left, then making for the hospital in Williamsburg.[14]

The Confederate assault faltered just as it was throwing the Federals into serious confusion, mainly because it had gone in totally unsupported by the brigade's other two regiments. The 38th Virginia finally emerged from the woods, but the 23d North Carolina never did. Hill found both regiments, and sent them eastward toward the Union force, then ordered everyone to withdraw. In retreating, the 24th Virginia was able to run into the woods near the original gun position and escaped without much further loss, but the 5th North Carolina, which unaccountably withdrew to its more distant point of exit from the woods, had many yards of open field to traverse under fire of the intact Federal force before reaching cover. The regiment was badly cut up.[15]

« WINFIELD SCOTT HANCOCK was dazzled by the valor of the Confederates who attacked his position at Williamsburg. "Immortality ought to be inscribed in the banners of the 24th Virginia and the 5th North Carolina," he later wrote.[16] Their bravery was even noted in the normally scornful columns of the Northern press. But their courage was in vain, expended in a "futile, bungling action" (in Douglas Southall Freeman's words) that had no effect on the outcome of the larger battle. It was the action in the center and on the right that succeeded in holding the Federals off long enough to permit Johnston to pull back into the defenses of Richmond. The fight on the left made no strategic difference whatever.

Tactically, the blundering cost little. Hancock was not tempted to push his counterattack very far. But losses in Early's brigade on May 5 were appalling—at least 600 killed and wounded, around 24 percent of the brigade strength and 38 percent of the total Confederate loss. Considering the fact that only two regiments were fully engaged, the brigade's casualties were in a class with the worst of the war. The 24th Virginia had 30 men killed, 93 wounded, and 66 missing; in the 5th North Carolina, of 415 who had emerged from the woods to attack the guns, only 75 were left to answer roll call the next morning.[17]

Jubal's own wound was bad, though not likely to carry him off. The bullet that hit him in the neck did little damage, but the other minié ball struck his arm just in front of the shoulder joint and ran around his back to the opposite shoulder. Bone deflected the ball away from vital organs and thus saved his life, but the patient was very sore and weak from loss of blood. Early left the hospital and found succor for a few days with a friend living in New Kent County near Williamsburg. From there, by ambulance and James River steamboat, he proceeded to Richmond and a bed at the American Hotel. As soon as he was strong enough to travel by coach, he took himself home to Franklin County.[18]

There his thoughts about the past year must have provided satisfaction. From Lynchburg through Manassas, the record was unalloyed success, attested by his promotion to general officer's rank. As for Williamsburg, that could be seen at least as a mixed success—forgetting the wound, which carried its own ego-soothing cachet (it proved to the world and to himself that he was brave). Though the operation against Hancock was a complete tactical failure (as Jubal himself later admitted), the brigade's performance, from his point of view, did it— and him—great credit. In a draft of his report, Early highlighted a moment just after he was wounded: ". . . though I was suffering intensely, I could not but feel a thrill of enthusiasm as I saw the admirable order in which the men advanced in an open field under fire of artillery, directly upon the enemy. . . . I have never seen anything to eclipse the conduct of the 5th North Carolina and the 24th Virginia on this occasion." Early's official report called the "gallantry" of this attack "unsurpassed in the annals of warfare." The men were certainly brave; more to the point, all Early's attention to drill had been rewarded.[19]

But however great his own sense of gratification, it may have been just as well for Jubal that the Battle of Williamsburg and his particular part in it were soon to be overshadowed by the Seven Days' battles. Meanwhile, in the Williamsburg affair's aftermath, the mills of rumor and intrigue ground out their measures of blame and recrimination. Because of the losses, it was rumored, D. H. Hill was contemplating shifting any blame to Early, claiming he had never ordered the brigade to attack, and implying that Jubal had been impetuous and reckless. Hill would later assure Early that far from contemplating any such thing, he positively exonerated Jubal from charges of recklessness, and had twice recommended him for promotion after the battle. Longstreet's report, in its brief mention of Jubal's wounding, characterized the assault as "impetuous." [20]

That charge had some merit. The attack had been blind: the guns that were the objective were hidden from the attackers by the woods, which also concealed the number of artillery pieces and the strength of their infantry support. The woods themselves were virtual *terra incognita;* Hill had made a cursory inspection of the forest's edge that should have demanded a more careful scrutiny of its interior. Early himself made no reconnaissance, nor did he order any. If the Federals had posted pickets in the woods, the guns, forewarned, might have been trained directly on the Virginians when they emerged from cover, and they might have suffered even more severely. On the other hand, the price of reconnoitering might have been the very delay that Longstreet had forbidden.

Even as things worked out, Jubal was right in believing that the coordination of all four regiments in the assault force, especially if supported by one of the brigades in the division reserve, could have driven Hancock off the field or bagged a substantial fraction of his command (Hancock's line of retreat lay across a narrow mill dam). This outcome was frustrated by the terrain, by the inexperience of the troops and their regimental officers, by a divided, muddled command, and by Early's own overweening haste. Hancock, handling his troops with admirable coolness and skill, made a substantial contribution to the Confederate reverse.

Hill was the senior commander, detailed by Longstreet to supervise the attack, but Early was the man in immediate charge of the operation, who took the position closest to the objective. In his haste, Early failed to assure coordination, and his distance from Hill almost guaranteed faulty communications. [21]

A conservative commander armed with the results of a thorough reconnaissance might have canceled the attack, asked for more troops to support it (consent would have been unlikely), or tried to find a different route to the guns. In similar circumstances on July 21, Early had made an effort to scout the ground his brigade would have to negotiate to attack the battery behind McLean's Ford. In the future, his conduct would be inconsistent: now cautious, now aggressive; now he would take pains to reconnoiter, now he would not bother. At Williamsburg, the spur of ambition was sunk deep in his side, and he was all driven energy and unheeding force.[22]

CHAPTER SEVEN

"Very Able and Very Brave"

O N JUNE 26, 1862, doctors at a hospital in Lynchburg gave Jubal Early, still much debilitated from his wound, reluctant permission to return to duty. But their orders were firm: no riding—which, effectively, meant no fighting. In predictable defiance of medical advice, Early—who seems to have sent his horses ahead from Franklin County to Richmond—clambered onto his own charger as soon as he could after reaching the capital on June 28. He then cantered off in search of General Lee and a body of troops to command. Jubal, his injured left arm still in a sling, was scarcely able to mount, even with assistance. How much it hurt Jubal to ride is impossible to say; his arthritis must have been aggravated by the trauma of the gunshot wound. But as the injured often do when forced to work around their disabilities, he and his body probably found ways to compensate. Certainly Early, his left arm weakened, would not have minded riding with his right— or sword—hand holding the reins, however unmilitary that would have looked. (In any case, generals very rarely drew their swords.) That he could ride at all demonstrates consummate horsemanship.

Lee was in the neighborhood of Fraser's Farm, where one of the last of the Seven Days' battles was then raging. On the night of his arrival, Early found Lee too preoccupied to talk to him. Jubal slept on the ground, and next day, July 1, Lee appointed the general to command a brigade until lately led by Arnold Elzey, who had been wounded earlier in the Seven Days' campaign.

These battles—from Mechanicsville (June 26) to Malvern Hill (July 1)—transformed the atmosphere of the war in the East. Seizing the initiative, Lee blocked McClellan's plan to take Richmond from the Peninsula. The Confederates maintained this aggressive posture through the summer of 1862, defeating the Federals at Second Manassas in August and holding them off—albeit at great cost—on the Antietam in September.

But for Lee, the Seven Days' campaign was, notwithstanding its ultimate strategic benefits, a source of frustration. Lee wanted to outmaneuver and destroy McClellan, who believed himself outnumbered and was trying to disengage and get his army off the Peninsula. Lee's object had been frustrated—partly through his own shortcomings as a newly fledged army commander, partly through the failure of his key subordinates, among them Stonewall Jackson. Aided in part by Jackson's laggard and indecisive role at White Oak Swamp on June 30, McClellan's men were able to fend off a blow that Lee had hoped would be fatal. On July 1, Lee was exhausted and unwell, but still determined to catch up with McClellan and finish him off.

As he was about to part from Lee to take up his new command, Early expressed anxiety that McClellan might get away. With unusual asperity, Lee answered, "Yes, he will get away because I can not have my orders carried out."[1]

Early's new brigade was part of the command of Stonewall Jackson, whom Jubal encountered leading troops along the road to Malvern Hill, soon to be the scene of the Seven Days' final battle—and Early's first action after returning to duty.

It was just as well that he was not seriously tested in the Battle of Malvern Hill. In any event, he was to be substantially, and successfully, tried in a number of engagements later in the summer of 1862, including the battles of Cedar Mountain, Second Manassas, and Antietam. His performance in these battles was to help build the reputation he would enjoy—until after Stonewall's death at Chancellorsville—as a fighting general second only to Jackson himself.[2]

« MALVERN HILL was not a success for the Confederates. Poor communications, execrable staff work, unfavorable terrain, and Lee's mental and physical weariness, among several causes, led the Southerners into a tactical nightmare. McClellan's position, on the ridge of Malvern

Hill and the terrain just north of it, was virtually impregnable. Numerous batteries, including some heavy rifled siege guns and large-caliber howitzers, commanded not only the open fields leading to the Union-occupied high ground but the terrain farther north where Confederate troops were assembling. Supporting the Union guns, infantry, including sharpshooters, lay in cover, ready to repel any Confederates who survived the concentrated artillery fire. In the Federal rear, two gunboats provided additional support.[3]

Apart from his command problems, Lee confronted two physical challenges. The more obvious was the Union artillery. The other was the dense wooded terrain, slashed by ravines, choked with swamp and underbrush, that his men would have to negotiate just to gain the bottom of the slopes approaching the Federal position on Malvern Hill. The Confederate commanding general proposed to post his own artillery so as to lay a converging fire on the Federal guns; with the Union batteries neutralized—or at least distracted—Lee would then send his infantry up the hill.[4]

The Confederate guns were ineffective—too few in number and brought into action separately so that the Federal gunners could concentrate their fire and destroy the opposing batteries piece by piece. The infantry assault was delayed through the day during the lopsided artillery combat; when the foot soldiers were ordered on the attack against the center of the Union line, notwithstanding the failure of the Confederate guns, the result was a catastrophe. The troops lost cohesion in the woods on the way to the attack; emerging from cover, they were mown down by the Union fire from the heights.[5]

Early and his brigade, part of a division under Richard Ewell in Jackson's command, spent most of the day in reserve on the Confederate left. The brigade, about 1,000 officers and men, included remnants of seven regiments: the 13th Virginia, 25th Virginia, 31st Virginia, 44th Virginia, 52d Virginia, 58th Virginia, and 12th Georgia.

Toward sunset, Jackson ordered Ewell's division and another into action. Ewell accompanied Early as he moved his brigade forward through the woods toward the battle; they marched under what Early called "terrific" artillery fire, with shells bursting in the treetops. After moving some considerable way through the woods, the head of the column came to a "small blind road" giving onto a clearing, the former site of a mill drawing power from a creek that flowed between Early's brigade and the enemy. Ewell ordered everyone to halt while he and a guide who was supposed to know the country rode ahead to reconnoiter a way across the creek.

Ewell soon rode back and gave the order for Early to hurry forward with his brigade. Then something bizarre occurred. Instead of simply letting Early continue to take his brigade across the creek and into action, Ewell suddenly ordered the lieutenant colonel commanding the lead regiment to move the men forward at a double-quick pace through the clearing to the creek, cross it, and then turn left through the woods to a road on the other side. To Early, Ewell said, "We will have to go this way," and galloped off in an entirely different direction across the old mill dam, turning into yet another road leading to the scene of combat.

"I had no option but to follow him," Early later wrote. But Ewell's action must have seemed utterly cracked. Why turn responsibility for the brigade over to a regimental commander when Jubal was right there and very hearty if not entirely hale? Why drag the brigade commander away from his command? No ready answer to these questions comes to mind. But it is very difficult not to believe that Ewell wanted somehow to keep Early, a man he probably already admired and wanted to retain as a brave, capable subordinate, from getting his head blown off in a battle that was clearly going badly for the South. And it is possible that Jubal remembered how dangerous it was to emerge blind from woods into the concentrated fire of a disciplined, well-positioned enemy force. If Jubal thought otherwise, it is hard to see why he did not even remonstrate with Ewell for plucking him so abruptly away from his brigade.

However all that may have been, the indisputable effect of Ewell's maneuver, which followed a looping detour through the woods, was to separate Early from his command at a critical moment. When Ewell left him to look for Hill, Early attempted as best he could to find his brigade. But it was no easy matter. Failing light—evening was now well advanced—deepened the confusion into which the Union fire was throwing the Confederates, who were straggling back through the murky woods in large numbers; Early kept mistaking some of these fugitives for his own men. Moreover, the rough going in the woods had combined with orders misunderstood and wrong turns taken by the brigade's different regiments at different times to scatter Early's command all over the landscape. He eventually found three of his seven regiments—all shattered in previous battles—and joined their pitiful aggregate of 300 men to a defensive line being formed in growing darkness by Ewell and Hill. Orders were to stay in place. Union artillery fire continued unabated until 9:00 P.M., when Hill and Ewell retired, leaving orders for Early and his men to remain where they were until next day. They did, trying to get some sleep, aware that they were surrounded by dead and maimed men, the wounded moaning and crying, Early recalled, in "truly heartrending" fashion.

The morning light revealed the "appalling" sight of the battle's toll— the wounded and dead of both sides. Looking to the right, Early saw a group of a dozen or so unwounded Confederates. He approached the little band and recognized Brig. Gen. Lewis Armistead—dismissed from West Point for breaking a plate over Jubal's head—with a few men of his brigade. Where, Early asked, were the rest? "Here," replied Armistead, "are all I know anything about except those lying out there in front." Early and his brigade, reassembled after the battle, had been spared such terrible losses. The murderous Union artillery had killed and wounded 33 of his men (out of approximately 1,300). As for any effect on the enemy, the brigade, as Early acknowledged, "did not draw trigger at all." [6]

<< AFTER MALVERN HILL—despite Lee's disappointment with its outcome—McClellan was a beaten man. Richmond was safe. When the Union high command formed a new Army of Virginia under Maj. Gen. John Pope, Lee contemplated a bold move to defeat it in its turn.

Lee's aggressive inclination may have been spurred by the behavior of his antagonist. Pope had come swaggering out of the West, where, he said, "We have always seen the backs of our enemies." From his "headquarters in the saddle," Pope issued bombastic predictions of victory over the rebels, which cracked Jackson's face in a grim smile. Jackson's men laughed over the response Richard Ewell was supposed to have

< 88 >

made: "By God, he'll never see the backs of my men. Their pants are out at the rear and the sight would paralyze this western bully." [7]

In mid-July, Pope's force was occupying the region between Culpeper and Gordonsville. Lee's plan to defeat him was simple, if risky: he would divide his own army, sending part, under Jackson, to swing west and north of Pope to cut his communications with Washington. When Pope reacted, Jackson would keep him pinned until Lee, with Longstreet's corps, could come up and join in a battle of annihilation.

For the moment, Pope was not only threatening the Virginia Central Railroad at its key station in Gordonsville but waging a war of attrition in the region around Culpeper; bent on living off the land and scourging what he could not use, he had his men destroy standing crops needed not only by Confederate troops but by the local citizens. This conduct aroused the cold fury of the Southern soldiers, and stimulated the passion of their commanders to do Pope in. [8]

Jackson's force, consisting initially of his own and Ewell's divisions— about 12,000 men—was to have this assignment. "I want Pope to be suppressed," wrote Lee in a dispatch to Jackson that also informed him that reinforcements were on their way: the 10,000-man "Light Division" commanded by Maj. Gen. Ambrose Powell Hill, and the 2d Brigade of Louisiana Volunteers, about 2,000 strong. These reinforcements would bring Jackson's strength to about 24,000. [9]

On the five-day march to Gordonsville, Jubal fretted, as he often did in tedious circumstances. He was upset because almost a month had gone by since he had reported back to duty, and he was still holding the temporary command of Elzey's very small brigade. He was cross because his old brigade, of First Manassas fame, had been broken up and its regiments assigned to brigades commanded by men with less rank than he. Jubal worried that Elzey's return to duty upon recovery from his wound would displace Early and cast him into outer darkness under the provisions of recently passed legislation: the new law mandated removal of officers from brigade or division command when the constituent units of the command "left the service," as had been the case with the regiments of his old brigade. Jubal assumed that his failure to be assigned a new permanent command—his former permanent status having dissolved with the dissolution of his old brigade—subjected him to the irreversible operation of this pernicious law. If this were so, he stewed, did it mean that the Confederate authorities had lost confidence in him? In that case, he would offer his services to the state of Virginia. In the meantime, it sometimes seemed that his superiors considered him to have committed a crime in suffering his wound at Williamsburg; they were certainly punishing him for it.

All of these concerns found their outspoken way into a letter Early dispatched to General Lee on July 23 from camp near Gordonsville. Within two short weeks, Lee—amid worries about Pope and McClellan and the defense of Richmond—found time to send a soothing reply. Yes, Lee said, it is true that Elzey last commanded the brigade, and when he gets back it "may be considered proper to assign him to it. But surely you would be considered entitled to another command." Lee assured Jubal "that confidence in your zeal and ability has been increased instead of diminished by your service, and that the honourable wound you received at Williamsburg in the defense of your country is viewed as a badge of distinction and claim for high consideration instead of crime, as you suppose." [10]

‹‹ LEE'S LETTER was written August 5. Two days later, Jackson's army was on the march toward Culpeper in search of Pope. On August 9, Ewell's division led the army, with Early's brigade, now 1,500 strong, at its head; behind Early was a brigade commanded by Brig. Gen. Isaac Trimble, followed by the Louisiana brigade, under Col. Henry Forno. Next came three brigades of Jackson's old division, now led by Brig. Gen. Charles Winder: the Stonewall Brigade (Col. Charles Ronald), the 2d Brigade (Col. Thomas S. Garnett), and the 3d Brigade (Col. William B. Taliaferro). A. P. Hill's division brought up the army's rear. [11]

About midmorning, the men of Early's leading regiment came upon a body of Confederate cavalry sitting their horses in the road. The horsemen were contemplating a group of Federal cavalry visible in the open fields on a low ridge some 800 yards away to the northeast and to the right of the road. Ewell ordered Early to reconnoiter to the right with his brigade, in the direction of a ridge called Cedar (or Slaughter's) Mountain. In obeying the order, Jubal took a section of field guns with him. The guns advanced and opened fire on the Union cavalry, which trotted to the rear. But the fire was returned, ominously, by Federal artillery out of sight behind the ridge.

The presence of artillery meant a strong probability of infantry, at least in support, though none could be seen. Early was ordered back to the Culpeper Road and sent north along it about a mile, to an intersection with a road coming in from the left that led to Madison Court House. Arriving at the junction about 11:30, he could see that the Federal horsemen, in a challenging attitude, were back on their ridge. It looked as if Jackson had bumped into Pope—or at least part of Pope's force. The Federals were standing their ground.[12]

With Ewell, Jackson now worked out a plan of attack. Ewell was to take two brigades eastward over the shoulder of Cedar Mountain and attempt to turn the left flank of whatever Union force lay in front. Jubal Early was to take his brigade north along the Culpeper Road toward the enemy center. Winder would get orders to render support to Early. With Taliaferro's and Garnett's brigades Winder was also to extend his left—through woods that ran along the left side of the Culpeper Road—so as to envelop the Union right flank. The Stonewall Brigade would be in reserve—available to press the attack either on the left or in the center. Artillery on both Confederate flanks would pour converging fire into the Union lines and compensate for any weakness in Jackson's center, where only one brigade (Early's) was initially disposed.[13]

Jubal got his orders from Jackson about noon. But he was told to wait until Winder sent word that he was prepared to follow up in support. While he waited, Early made a thorough reconnaissance of the country in front of him. His reward was the discovery of a route by which he could advance unobserved most of the way toward the only visible enemy—the cavalry standing on its ridge to the northeast.

At approximately 2:00 P.M., a courier from Winder brought news that he was on his way. Early moved out, with the 13th Virginia under Col. James A. Walker serving as skirmishers and covering the left flank, and the 12th Georgia on the right. As the brigade emerged from its covered approach into the view of the Federal cavalry, the startled troopers turned and galloped off—under scattered long range fire from

Early's men that emptied a saddle or two. In later years, a soldier in the 12th Georgia used to say that Jubal borrowed a rifle and fired the first round at the Federal horsemen.[14]

The brigade now advanced across a narrow track leading from the Culpeper Road to Mrs. Crittenden's farm and marched up onto the ridge lately occupied by the enemy cavalry. As they reached the crest, Union batteries posted on another higher ridge to the northeast took the Confederate infantry under a fire that was accurate and punishing; a shell burst close beneath Jubal's horse and covered him with dust. As men fell, Early told the brigade to move back into the shelter of the reverse slope and lie down. There they formed a line stretching eastward a little less than a half mile from the Culpeper Road on the left, and awaited the order to attack.

But since Winder was still not on the field, Jubal dispatched his brother Samuel, now a lieutenant on his staff, to urge Winder to hurry up, simultaneously sending another aide, Maj. Andrew L. Pitzer, to request artillery from Winder, Ewell, or Jackson. Then Jubal cast his intelligent eye over his present military environment.[15]

From his position on the ridge recently occupied by the Union cavalry, he could see much of what was to be the battlefield. His left lay along the Culpeper Road, with thick woods on the other side. These woods, which extended as far as he could see, struck Jubal as a source of grave danger: if the enemy moved through the trees under cover, they could turn the Confederate left flank.

To the right of the road, in front, the open ground sloped down to a little watercourse, a branch of Cedar Run. Beyond the stream, on a gradual upslope, was a wheatfield stretching from the center to the right; next to the road, and cutting in to the north behind the wheat, was a cornfield. The top of the upslope where the grain grew was the ridge from which the precise Union gunfire was coming. It seemed to Early that the ridge concealed a gully where a large body of infantry might be hiding.[16]

To the right, open fields sloped down in the rear to another branch of Cedar Run. A mile beyond the stream directly to the right rose the shoulder of Cedar Mountain, where Ewell had taken two of his brigades. Early's eye quickly took in an alarming fact: a gap at least one

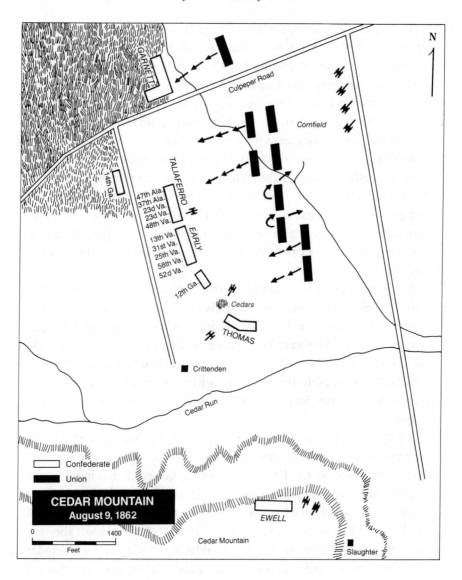

CEDAR MOUNTAIN
August 9, 1862

mile wide yawned between the right of his line and Ewell's brigades
on Cedar Mountain. To the right but closer to Early, a grove of cedars
occupied a knoll that dominated the grain fields. When the guns he had
asked for arrived, Early proposed to put them next to the cedar grove,
from which they could engage the Federal artillery behind the ridge

in front, and take on any enemy infantry that might attack through the grainfields. They could also cover the gap on the right.[17]

These guns were soon under Early's hand; Ewell's chief of artillery, Maj. A. R. Courtney, seems to have divined Jubal's need, and in timely fashion sent a section of three pieces galloping along the Culpeper Road and into the fields in Early's rear. Unlimbering under his direction at the cedar grove, these pieces were soon in action.

At this point—sometime between 2:30 and 3:00 P.M.—Ewell's guns on Cedar Mountain and Winder's pieces, now in position near the road, joined the artillery chorus, which was echoed by the Federal guns; a duel began that was to last nearly three hours. It was not long before the converging fire that Jackson had envisaged began to have an effect: one or two of the Union batteries were forced to change position.[18]

In the meantime, Early stationed the 12th Georgia Regiment to the right of the cedars, both to support his guns and to make some show, with the few troops at hand, of closing the dangerous gap between him and Ewell. The 12th Georgia was a scrappy fragment of a regiment commanded by a 65-year-old captain named William F. Brown, who had succeeded to the command when the regiment's colonel and its second-in-command had both disgraced themselves by acts of cowardice.[19]

To Winder, whose men were still making their way forward, Early sent two messages. In the first, impressed by the effect of the Confederate cannonade on the Union guns, he suggested that Winder might exploit the situation by using the cover of the woods on the left of the road to position infantry for a flank attack on the busy Federal batteries. In the second message, based on observation of—and guesses about—infantry movement on and behind the ridge in front, he warned Winder that the Federals might be preparing to penetrate the woods on the left and mount their own flank attack.

The latter message, carried through the smoky racket of the burgeoning artillery duel by Lt. Sam Early, was to be prophetic. Unfortunately, it reached Winder moments after he had been struck by a shell and mortally wounded. His second-in-command, Colonel Taliaferro, was not with Winder. But Lieutenant Early was able to give the message to Stonewall Jackson himself, who, close to 4:00 P.M., was just arriving at Winder's position.[20]

About this time General Early watched while a body of Union infantry topped the ridge in front and advanced through the cornfield toward his position. Well out of musket range, this contingent, with skirmishers in front, halted and lay down among the concealing cornstalks. But Jubal could see that the enemy formation extended past the right end of his line. Moreover, because the ground to the right of the cedars inclined away rather sharply, Early feared that the Federal infantry, covered by the slope, could all too easily reach the guns he had posted near the cedars. He immediately sent a courier to Jackson with a request for a brigade to stiffen that vulnerable quarter. The reinforcement was promised.

At this tense moment, Jubal would have been elated had he known that Forno's and Trimble's brigades, with Ewell, had found a place from which to launch an attack on the Federal left. But he would have scowled if he had been told that fire from his own guns and other Confederate batteries farther to the left near the road swept the field in such a way as to deny Ewell's men any safe route of attack.[21]

The battle seemed to be developing spontaneously, without much direction from Jackson. And now, like an onlooker at the scene of a terrible accident, Early watched the unfolding of a crisis arising from this lack of management. The emergency arose when A. P. Hill, whose division was bringing up the rear of Jackson's march toward Culpeper, heard the banging of artillery ahead; he ordered his division's heavy guns forward. Two batteries galloped heedlessly through Early's line and, totally unsupported by infantry, unlimbered in the open field on his left front. The guns were only 150 yards from the hidden Union troops in the corn, well within musket range. Aghast, Early observed the Union line, concealed from the Southern gunners by the tall corn, begin to advance on the exposed batteries.[22]

Spitting and cursing as he snapped his tobacco quid from jaw to jaw, Jubal gave a piercing shout of command that sent his brigade forward to the rescue. The men surged over the crest, yelling in excitement, and hurled themselves down toward the guns. This sudden apparition shook the blueclad foot soldiers, who hesitated long enough to give Jubal's sprinters time to win the race. Reaching the batteries, the Southerners fired a volley from among the startled gunners—who had scarcely awakened to their danger before being rescued, and who now loaded canister and blasted the Federals back into the cornfield. Then the cannoneers added shot and shell to the fire of other Confederate batteries exchanging salvos with their Union counterparts. Meanwhile, Jubal ordered the 12th Georgia, posted to the right of the cedars, to wheel to its left and pour a flanking musket fire into the retreating Union infantry. After 5:00 P.M., as the potential disaster on Early's front was receding, the artillery duel sputtered out.[23]

Almost immediately the main infantry battle opened in sudden ferocity. Heavy musket fire on the Confederate left announced a Federal attack through the woods, as Early had predicted. But the bluecoats were also advancing in front—on Early and on Taliaferro's brigade, posted to Jubal's left next to the road. Mindful of the gaping hole in the line between the right end of his brigade and Ewell's men on Cedar Mountain, Early galloped off toward the cedars in great anxiety.

At this vital moment, the promised reinforcements, a brigade from Hill's division under Brig. Gen. Edward L. Thomas, arrived and were posted to the right of the Georgians. Early remained on the right for a while to make sure Thomas would be able to withstand a Federal attempt to slice through the gap. He was reassured: even though the Union line overlapped the Southern position in that direction, Thomas's men were able to stop the Federal advance, their volleys seeding the rows of grain with dead and wounded men.[24]

From where he was riding near this action, Early could not see what was happening over on the left end of his brigade line; as soon as he felt Thomas had things under control, he spurred back to take a look. The sight was surely a shock. He could see that though the exposed guns had gotten away safely, most of his regiments had pulled back from the ridge they had been holding, opening an interval into which the enemy was rapidly pouring. Early heard men saying that the Federals had turned the Confederate left flank, news confirmed by loud Northern cheers and the emergence from the woods of grimy, exhausted Southerners. Many were wounded and unarmed, all were on their way to the rear. They said the Federals had sliced in behind the regiments in the woods on the far left and shattered the position there.

Now the Federals, rolling up the Southern line, were approaching the road and the flank of Taliaferro's brigade. Regiments began to break, including one in the vaunted Stonewall Brigade, the reserve now thrown into the fight. In fact, all the Confederates in this part of the field gave ground, though some stood for a while, and others such as the 13th Virginia preserved their organization. Samuel Buck, a sergeant commanding a company in the 13th Virginia, recalled that "all were badly broken and every effort was needed to form under such a terrible fire. One of my men ran by me and I could not hold him to the line. The next day he came to me and said, 'Sergeant, I heard you begging men to rally and heard you say to me, "For God's sake, rally," but indeed I could not stop.' This was a fact, he could not stop."

The Confederate units that fell back—even the 13th recoiled as much as 200 yards—exposed the left and rear of Early's line. As he inspected the scene, he could see scattered groups of his men standing firm; but it was all too clear that his flank was in the air, and that enemy troops were already behind him.

Stonewall Jackson now began to take personal charge of a battle that was slipping out of his grasp, rallying troops to the left of the road and along it and leading them forward himself until Taliaferro begged him to go to the rear. The general inspired his men with the sight of his slight figure, his sword aloft in his hand, and with the sound of his high voice shouting, "Rally, brave men, and press forward! Your general will lead you. Jackson will lead you. Follow me!" [25]

Early was probably unaware of this. As far as he could see, what was left of his force, the 12th Georgia and Thomas's brigade, anchored on the cedars, was all that was holding the center of the Confederate line together. If they gave way there, all would be lost, and Early knew it. [26]

Obeying this logic, he sent Maj. Samuel Hale to do what he could to rally the broken units on the left of his line and rode back to lend resolve to the troops holding the key to the position. These men were of stout heart. When Early ordered old Captain Brown of the 12th Georgia to hold on "at all hazards," the captain earned Early's respect with his reply: "General, my ammunition is nearly out, don't you think we had better charge them?"

Jubal, unwilling to lose such men, said no. Meanwhile, partly through Jackson's personal intervention, partly because the Federal attack was short-handed, unsupported, and disorganized by passage through the woods, and largely because of A. P. Hill's timely arrival on the field with his division, the momentum of the battle was reversed. Branch's brigade of Hill's division launched a massive counterattack through the woods on the left; Colonel Walker of the 13th Virginia rallied his men, and they, along with parts of other regiments, returned to the attack; remnants of Taliaferro's brigade also resumed the offensive. Early, still fearing an onslaught through the dreaded gap on the right against troops now seriously low on ammunition, kept the 12th Georgia and Thomas's men where they were, with orders to hold—if necessary with the bayonet—at all costs, until they could see the entire Confederate line begin to move forward.[27]

The final action of the day was a sad blunder by the Federals. A body of Union cavalry appeared, charging headlong down the Culpeper Road. This rash effort, which was a ghastly fiasco (only 71 of 164 troopers rode back unwounded), signaled a general Union admission of failure. The entire Federal force, a 9,000-man detachment of Pope's army under Maj. Gen. Nathaniel P. Banks, withdrew. Jackson's men, including Early's brigade, followed for a short distance, then halted. They remained in the vicinity of the battlefield for two days.[28]

<< JACKSON CAME close to losing the battle of Cedar Mountain. If he had, the story of his military career—and that of the Confederacy— might have been quite different. Banks, whom Jackson had so decisively beaten in the Valley in the spring, would have avenged himself, a victory made doubly sweet because his force was half the strength of Jackson's. The reasons for Jackson's near failure have been variously attributed: he is charged with, among other lapses, a failure to investigate the wooded ground to his left, clearly a source of danger; a lack of

control over the elements of his command, many of which (including Early's brigade) Jackson left on their own to fight without any particular direction; secretiveness about his plans and poor communications with his commanders; failure to utilize his entire strength.

These charges have a degree of substance. But Jackson, in possession of the field, claimed a victory. Banks had helped him by rashly attacking—against the spirit of his orders from Pope—when attacked, instead of holding his ground. Banks had enough strength for defense, but not for offense. The potentially lethal assault on the Confederate left was undermanned.

Even so, it came within an ace of unhinging the whole Southern position and nearly led to the rout or annihilation of Jackson's two leading divisions. That this did not happen is substantially attributable to Jubal Early. From the outset, he made careful reconnaissances of the ground where he was to operate. He observed what he could of the entire arena of battle, and drew from these analyses exactly the conclusions he needed for effective action.

Master of the crucial center, which he anchored on the excellent military position represented by the cedars, he held the disparate pieces of Jackson's battle together until damage elsewhere on the field could be repaired. Placing his guns in precisely the right place, positioning the 12th Georgia and Thomas's brigade just where they should have been, he managed to negate the dire effect of the Federal move around the Confederate left. If Early's position had given way completely, the Federals could conceivably have sliced through the gap on his right, bagging Ewell's entire division as well as destroying Winder's, and could have posed a deadly threat to Hill. At best, Jackson would have had to organize a night retreat with the Rapidan at his back and Pope presumably moving to reinforce Banks. As it was, Jackson could report the capture of 400 prisoners, one gun, three colors, and many small arms. Counting 229 dead and 1,047 wounded, Stonewall had lost but 6 percent of his force; Banks, with total casualties, including prisoners, of 2,381, had lost 30 percent.[29]

Though Jackson pursued Banks a short way toward Culpeper late on the 9th, Stonewall took serious note of intelligence furnished by Stuart that Pope was approaching with his whole force. Jackson elected to pull out. On the night of August 11, he executed a carefully organized, uneventful withdrawal behind the barrier of the Rapidan.[30]

« JACKSON WAS always stingy with praise, but he gave Jubal his due. Jackson stated in his report that "Early's right had held with great firmness." For Jubal's division commander, "Old Bald Head" Ewell, no praise was too lavish for inclusion in his report, and he made an official recommendation of promotion. Ewell lauded Early for "gallant and effective service," and for "repulsing repeated attacks of the enemy, contributing largely to driving him from the field." The division commander remarked on Jubal's courage, noting that Early was still "so enfeebled from the effects of a wound received at Williamsburg as to be unable to mount his horse without assistance."[31]

Writing to his friend Lizinka Brown in Nashville (whom he would later marry) Ewell made his admiration of Jubal explicit: "General Early is an excellent officer and ought to be a Major General." In the same letter, a comment Ewell had not included in his report touched on Jubal's chronic restlessness: "He is dissatisfied, as well he may be, and talks sometimes of going out to join Bragg [in Tennessee]. He is very able and very brave and would be an acquisition to your part of the world."[32]

But Jubal never really meant a word about going west. And Ewell was glad when Early stayed right where he was.

< 100 >

« CHAPTER EIGHT »

Pinnacle of Pride

*J*UBAL EARLY was hardly a superstitious man—nor were his superiors in the Confederate army. But all undoubtedly acknowledged
the role of chance in war. It is certain that luck—allied with skill,
sagacity, and courage—furnished a substantial measure of Early's success in the opening months of the Civil War. To shine in battle, a man
must be exposed to the glare of action: fortune placed Jubal on the field
of battle soon enough and often enough to shine, while shielding him
(except at Williamsburg) from the dangers of modern rifled firearms.

During the remainder of 1862, Jubal prospered and his stature grew.
At First Manassas and Cedar Mountain, chance had placed him in
situations where a good performance was essential—and where he had
delivered excellence. At Second Manassas, Antietam, and Fredericksburg, the hazards of war would help him to help himself in much the
same manner. But how might he fare when luck ran against him, or
when hope seemed forlorn?

He had gotten one answer at Williamsburg. Another came in an
unheralded but—certainly from Jubal's viewpoint—significant river
crossing on August 22, about a fortnight after the Cedar Mountain
battle. Since that encounter, Lee had decided to reinforce Jackson with
troops that had hitherto formed the Richmond defense force, assault
Pope in central Virginia, and destroy him before McClellan could pull
his army out of the Peninsula and join Pope. Jackson was to turn Pope's
right flank, cut the Federal army's communications with Washington,
and then bring Pope to battle against the concentrated forces of Long-

< 101 >

street and Jackson. After disposing of Pope, Lee would then defeat McClellan—finally.

On August 22, obedient to this plan, Jackson was marching along the right bank of the upper Rappahannock, looking for an unguarded crossing. In the steamy afternoon, Ewell's division—to which Early's brigade belonged—arrived opposite Warrenton Springs. There, though the bridge leading to the resort had been destroyed, the river was fordable.

Jackson could see no signs of the enemy. He decided to send Ewell's division across the river a brigade or two at a time, let them feel out the situation, and cross the rest of his command over if all seemed well. Accompanied by two batteries, a brigade under Brig. Gen. Alexander R. Lawton, which had recently been added to Ewell's division, started wading across through a thundershower near the wrecked bridge. Early's brigade teetered over on top of a dilapidated old dam a mile or so downstream, noting, as the rain continued, that the water was rising. Darkness fell as the last companies were filing across the dam, canceling the crossing of Col. Henry Forno's Louisiana Brigade. Ewell himself had come across, directing Jubal to position his troops in a scrubby pine thicket close to the dam; he also ordered Early to establish communications with Lawton, whose men had supposedly all made the crossing near the Springs. Then Ewell returned to the other bank. In the morning, presumably, the river would be lower, and Forno could cross in safety.[1]

Eager to link up with Lawton, Early sent his trusted aide, Maj. Andrew Pitzer, off into the rainy murk upstream to the left. In a surprisingly short time the major was back, accompanied by six privates and a sergeant of the enemy's cavalry, with all their arms and equipment. Pitzer had run into them in the dark on the road to the Springs. They had ordered him to surrender, but he had persuaded them—for all Pitzer knew, it was true—that they were surrounded by two entire brigades of trigger-happy Confederates, and that their only chance of survival was to follow him back to his headquarters as *his* prisoners.[2]

Major Pitzer's hardihood and presence of mind did him credit, but the discovery of the Union soldiers and their bold behavior in the vicinity of Early's position alarmed the general. How many other bluecoats were wandering around out there? Jubal, aware that Pope's entire army might lie nearby north of the Rappahannock, ordered no further attempt that night to reach Lawton. If a substantial Federal force were in the neighborhood, capture of a messenger and disclosure of the Southern presence might mean annihilation. For the balance of the wet, miserable night, the orders—to men who had eaten nothing since crossing the river—were to sit tight and stay quiet.

Morning brought the sun, cheering the men as they warmed up and dried off. But Jubal's mood was somber. The river at his back was still lapping its banks—far too deep and rapid to be crossed. At first light, he had sent a courier to find Lawton, who, it turned out, had never made it to the north bank. In fact, he had only crossed the two batteries and one regiment—the 13th Georgia—of his brigade over the water before the raging stream cut them off.

Early, of course, was also cut off, facing a Federal force of unknown strength that might also quickly separate him from the very tenuous support offered by the Georgians and Lawton's batteries. Luck was certainly not running Jubal's way, and had not been since the river crossing. But no matter. For all his anxiety and frustration, his actions were those of an imperturbable professional. Jubal ordered a courier to jump into the angry Rappahannock and swim to the other bank with a written message for Ewell or Jackson: capture or slaughter of Early's entire force was a real threat, the message said; Lawton's contingent was also in grave danger. The only solution might be to slip away upstream, pick up Lawton's men en route, and make for Waterloo Bridge, four miles to the north. Did Jackson agree?

Not exactly. Stonewall was evidently still hoping that he could push his whole force over the river at Warrenton Springs, or near it. In a reply to Early's message, Jackson's orders were to link up with Lawton's guns and the 13th Georgia and hold on. Jubal was told to get everyone into a defensive position Stonewall had spotted. The position Jackson had in mind was formed by the angle of a creek running into the Rappahannock a little below Jubal's location in the scrub. The tributary, swollen by the rains, was too full for the enemy to cross, Jackson felt; but if the Federals threatened to do so in significant force, Early was to head for Waterloo Bridge. Jackson would stay abreast of him on the opposite bank, covering his movement with artillery fire. In the meantime, repair work would begin on the wrecked Warrenton Springs bridge.[3]

Moving into the creek angle, the worried Jubal observed that the tributary's waters were falling with a rapidity that was equally apparent to the Union cavalrymen who now trotted into view on the far bank. At the same time, a quick glance at the Rappahannock to Jubal's rear revealed its continuing impassability; both retreat and reinforcement were still ruled out.

But an attack by Union troops across the creek was now a definite threat. Toward afternoon, Federal infantry appeared on the opposite bank, and the situation, in Early's view, became "critical." Jubal was cool in the measures he took to guard his men and himself. He pulled his infantry away from the creek bank into the concealment of the woods, along with Lawton's batteries, and settled down to wait. The Federals across the creek made no move—evidently as unsure of Confederate strength and intentions as Early was of theirs.[4]

As the afternoon wore along, the uneasy monotony was suddenly broken by the clatter of hoofs from the direction of the Springs. The horsemen were two regiments of Confederate cavalry under Brig. Gen. Beverly Robertson, along with two guns. Returning from a successful raid on Pope's headquarters, the troopers had more or less blundered into Early's disadvantageous situation, but they were all the more welcome as timely reinforcements. They even had ideas for stirring things up. On the way in, Robertson explained after greeting Early, he had spotted what appeared to be a Union ammunition train. How about seeing if his guns, firing from the vicinity of the Springs, could do the wagons some damage? Early agreed that this sounded like a good plan; he probably saw it at least as a way of diverting the enemy's attention from his position and taking his men's minds off their peril.

Robertson's guns were soon in action. The train, it turned out, was well guarded; a six-gun battery replied to Robertson's fire, opening a cannon duel that crashed and fulminated in the twilight with little effect on either side, though Jubal detached two of Lawton's eight 10-pounder Parrott rifles and sent them to Robertson to back up his less accurate smooth-bore horse artillery.[5]

As night approached, the river still surged at a level too high for crossing, though on the right, the water in the creek was now easily fordable. At the same time, the Union infantry seemed to be moving around to Early's left, as if seeking to certify his doom by first pinning him against the river and then squeezing him into it.

Darkness brought a dense fog, and the sounds of advancing enemy infantry. Suddenly a crash of Union musketry lit the woods and brought leaves and twigs fluttering down on Early's men where they lay on the ground. Their orders, which they obeyed with what Jubal called "great coolness," were not to reply to this volley; they could not afford to expend ammunition on an unseen target. Compelled to lie still and wait for the enemy to come yet closer and fire yet another volley, Jubal and his men abode in mounting apprehension. Time passed. But the Federals neither moved nor fired.

Then came sounds that must have frozen the Confederates in utter incredulity: suddenly, the Federals gave three cheers and a "tiger," the loud yell that often followed such huzzahs. It was as if the Union men had decided, with official encouragement, that they had accomplished their purpose, whatever it may have been, and that it was now time for self-congratulation. The Southerners could have had no idea what any of it meant. Early waited a few more minutes until he felt that the Federals would make no further move; then he ordered two of his guns, loaded with canister and manhandled out of the woods, to open rapid fire into the gloom in front. Shortly, he could hear the Federals moving off, their night's activity evidently at an end. In a short while, the only signs of the enemy were, as Jubal noted, the awful noises made by wounded men.[6]

Just as Early was beginning to feel that his command might be spared a night attack after all, his sense of relief was jarred by news that Jackson was about to dispatch the remainder of Lawton's brigade to join the 13th Georgia, resuming the movement across the Rappahannock interrupted the day before by the flooding river. "Instead," as Freeman would write, "of permitting the hungry troops on the left bank to return to safety, that strange man Jackson was exposing more troops. . . . To Early, it seemed incomprehensibly rash." It was certainly true that

Jubal believed the opposition was strong enough to crush Ewell's whole division—had it been present—if ever Pope or his subordinates could get themselves organized.

But Jackson was not quite so maddeningly stubborn as Jubal supposed. Stonewall had, in fact, become more and more concerned about the safety of Early and his men. Jackson sent an aide over the river to deliver detailed instructions on a possible route of escape to Waterloo Bridge. At one point during the 24th, Jackson swam his horse across the flooding Rappahannock to supervise the bridge repair work in person, riding in the water near the bridge abutments on the far side of the stream while the engineers toiled. Under his stern eye, they constructed a roadway capable of bearing the weight of artillery. It was ready by 4:00 P.M. [7]

Jackson also communicated his concern to Ewell. General Lawton, arriving at Early's camp ahead of his men, reported that he had seen Jackson's orders to Ewell directing the division commander to cross at daylight, investigate the situation, and if he saw fit, pull everybody back to the south bank. Early seized on this intelligence to fire a dispatch off to Ewell declaring that the enemy was unquestionably on the scene in very heavy force. Now, Jubal urged, was the hour for withdrawal: daylight would give the Federals too much of an opportunity to hamper a recrossing, especially with all the guns that the enemy could be heard moving toward the Springs—ordnance that could be sited to fire directly on the temporary bridge and the nearby ford. Ewell, responsive to the urgings of a trusted subordinate, promptly crossed to discuss the situation with Early; about 3:00 A.M. on the 25th, he ordered the guns and all of Early's and Lawton's men back over the stream.

Once more on the right bank, Early felt not only relieved but vindicated as he saw to the feeding of his ravenous men, of whom he was very proud. They and he had conjured with the ill fortune of the rain-swollen river and the Yankee host. His belief in the enemy's overwhelming strength was to be confirmed when Pope's report showed that he had ordered every infantryman of his army—except for one corps under McDowell—to concentrate at Warrenton Springs on August 23. In terms of forces actually present in Early's vicinity, numbers are hard to pin down. But members of Union army corps under Sigel, Banks, and Jesse Reno may have numbered about 25,000, accompanied by scores of cannon. Early faced this cohort, with no chance of retreat or success in a fight, leading about 1,500 muskets, Robertson's troopers, and a handful of guns. Jubal knew that this evil spell had been broken, in great part, by the ineptitude of the Union officers confronting him on the river, who seemed to have thought he outnumbered *them*.

But Jubal also knew the magic wrought by his own abilities. Jackson, in his hardheaded way, knew it too, after considering the crossing operation, and reflecting on Pope's orders, the rising of the river, and the ordeal of the men isolated on the wrong side of the Rappahannock. He noted that Early had lost not one man killed or wounded. From Stonewall, the performance wrung one of his rare utterances of outright praise: "In this critical situation," he remarked in his report, "the skill and presence of mind of General Early was favorably displayed." [8]

« On August 25, Jackson resumed his swing around Pope's right flank. Marching 25 miles that day, his command crossed the river above Waterloo Bridge, and spent the night near Salem. During the march on the 26th, it began to be clear that the few Federals Jackson's men encountered along the way knew nothing of his movement, and that no preparations had been made to defend against it.

By the evening of the 26th, Stonewall's three divisions were astride Pope's supply line at Bristoe Station, south of Manassas Junction on the Orange & Alexandria Railroad. By midnight two infantry regiments of Trimble's brigade and a contingent of cavalry were in joyous possession of mountains of stores heaped up for Pope's army at the Junction, the old Confederate base. Jackson's "foot cavalry" had completed one of the epic marches in military annals, some of his men having covered as many as 54 miles in two days. While their comrades feasted on the Union commissary stores and sutlers' supplies at Manassas Junction, the three brigades of Ewell's division drew duty as rear guard at Bristoe.

About the time the lucky Confederates at the Junction were beginning to sample such commodities as fancy meats, prepared mustard, canned lobster salad, cake, and Rhine wine, Pope's army was becoming aware of the enemy presence in its rear. The Federals soon began to

< 107 >

react. Jackson ordered Ewell to delay any Union move up the railroad toward Manassas Junction; but he was to fall back in that direction if the opposition became substantial, since Stonewall did not want a general engagement just yet.

Ewell followed orders. As approaching Union forces applied greater and greater pressure, he put Early in charge of covering a withdrawal of the division toward Manassas. Lawton and Forno pulled their men out under cover of Early's brigade, Jubal posting the 13th Virginia under Col. James A. Walker—the unit he relied on most since its magnificent recovery at Cedar Mountain—as rear guard for his other regiments. Under Early's eye, the whole withdrawal proceeded with silken smoothness. As a finishing touch, Ewell ordered that the harnesses, saddles, and other equipment of horses killed during the movement be removed and carried to the rear; this was to show the enemy that the withdrawal was being conducted with icy deliberation, as indeed it was.

The price paid by Jubal's men for their soldierly performance was high: by the time they reached Manassas Junction, the delicacies were gone. The hungry men had to be content stuffing their haversacks with hardtack and salt meat—"all of the plunder obtained at that place which they could get," in Early's sympathetically grumpy words. But there should have been consolation, for Jubal and his men, in the view Jackson expressed in his report—that the "withdrawal of infantry and artillery was conducted with perfect order." [9]

It was now Jackson's task to find suitable ground on which to await Lee's arrival with Longstreet and the rest of his army. Stonewall chose a low ridge near the hamlet of Groveton on the Warrenton Turnpike, not far from the battlefield of First Manassas. The ridge was creased along much of its length by the bed of a graded but unfinished railroad. Taking a position behind this road grade, Jackson placed his force with Taliaferro's division in the center. On the right he stationed Ewell, with Lawton's and Trimble's brigades; on the left, Early was put in charge of his own and Forno's brigades. [10]

Toward sunset, a Union division marched into view along the Warrenton Pike. Jackson determined to attack it, advancing with the troops to

Early's right. A fierce encounter now broke out. Just before sundown, Early received an order to advance to the front with his command; in the gathering darkness, baffled by the terrain, which was interrupted across his axis of advance by a deep cut in the railroad line, Early never directly engaged the enemy, though Union artillery fire ripped through his formations and inflicted some casualties. When it got too dark to tell friend from foe, Jubal halted in place.[11]

His part in what turned out to be an inconclusive clash was moot. Other results of what Early called "the affair at Groveton" were much clearer. Heavy losses among the units that had been directly engaged included the severe wounding of William Taliaferro and Richard Ewell, who took a bone-shattering bullet in the knee. Ewell, losing his leg below the knee to the surgeon's knife, would be out of action for many months. For now, by seniority, Lawton would succeed to the command of Ewell's division instead of Early.

The Federals pulled back during the night, leaving Jackson in possession of the field. But he was keenly aware that darkness would only afford an interval. The enemy, Jackson later wrote, "did not long permit us to remain inactive or in doubt as to his intention to renew the conflict."[12]

<< ON AUGUST 29, Stonewall expected an attack from the east, and he had correctly surmised that Pope's intention was to destroy him before Lee could arrive on the field. But he had no way of knowing where Pope might strike his line, now ranged along the unfinished railroad.

Enemy movement from Manassas toward the Confederate right suggested to Jackson that the Federals might try to turn his right flank. In an eloquent demonstration of his trust in Early, Stonewall ordered Lawton to detach Jubal, who was to take charge of his own brigade and Forno's and a battery. These units were to post themselves on the extreme right of the line and guard against the flanking maneuver Jackson feared. To Early's left in the Confederate line were Taliaferro's division, now commanded by Brig. Gen. William E. Starke; then came Lawton's division (less Early's and Forno's brigades); on the far left was A. P. Hill's division. Hill had deployed his men in two lines in order to strengthen the defense at a point where dense woods—blocking fields of artillery fire and masking the approach of enemy attackers—extended here and there into the Southern position and weakened it.

Over on the right, Early set up his guns on the ridge, and sent two regiments (under the trusty Colonel Walker of the 13th Virginia) out toward Manassas as a strong outpost. But the anticipated Federal envelopment never materialized. Instead, around 10:30 A.M., Early's contingent became a welcoming party for the advance elements of Lee's army, part of Longstreet's command under Brig. Gen. John Bell Hood. These reinforcements now marched up from the west and extended the Confederate line of battle to Jackson's right so that it curved southeastward across the Warrenton Pike in the direction of Manassas.[13]

Early, considering himself relieved from his flank guard assignment, waited for no orders to pick up his command and move back to the left to rejoin Lawton, whose men were under attack. But as Early started off, Pope was obviously shifting his heaviest assaults to Hill's position on the far left. Ordered to back up Hill, Early kept right on marching until his brigades were in a position to support Hill's Light Division.[14]

From around noon until 6:00 P.M., Pope threw successive waves of troops against Hill's lines behind the railroad grade. The Federal assaults were beaten back; but as the sun was beginning to set, some of the Confederate units were running out of ammunition, and Pope seemed to have inexhaustible reserves of fresh troops. A weakly held boundary between two of Hill's brigades—those of Maxcy Gregg and Edward L. Thomas—gave the Federals a golden chance. An attack by five Union brigades forced Gregg's men back 300 yards from the railroad line to the top of a rise. Powder and bullets almost gone, ranks sadly thinned, Gregg's exhausted soldiers prepared to fight with bayonets and rocks. In support, Forno's brigade kept the Federals from turning Lawton's flank and getting in behind Hill. Meanwhile, Early was summoned to rescue Gregg.[15]

At this moment in the crisis, one of Gregg's men later recalled, "a shout behind us paralyzed [us] with dread." Some turned their heads, half expecting a Union attack from the rear. But the yell came from the throats of Jubal's brigade and a regiment of Louisianians he had picked up en route back to the front after replenishing its ammunition.

Their combined counterattack slammed the Federals back across the railroad line and some hundreds of yards farther. Hill's orders had been not to go beyond the railroad, but the impetus of Early's men was too powerful to be restrained. Jubal yelled at his officers to stop the men, but they kept going. Finally, he shouted, "Well, damn you, if you will go, go on!" The charge cost Early's men few casualties, he noted, but Jackson reported that they drove the enemy off the railroad line "with great slaughter." [16]

Early's counterattack, which came (as Hill recounted) "at a most opportune moment," shut down the last Federal assault of the day. Jubal's men slept where they were, aware that the night was only a pause in the battle. Under cover of darkness, Hill's men went to the rear to refill their cartridge boxes, leaving Early's to hold their position.

<< ALL HANDS had reason for satisfaction. Despite long odds (Pope had outnumbered Stonewall roughly three to one) and serious casualties (Gregg's brigade lost more than 600 men), Jackson had succeeded in holding Pope until Lee could concentrate his whole force. Tomorrow should, according to the plan that was so far working so well, be a day of victory for the South.

Pope, whose own plan—to defeat Jackson and Lee separately—was plagued by poor judgment and faulty information, thought it was he who had won on August 29. When the 30th dawned, the Union commander, possibly misled by a shortening of Jackson's line, evidently believed that Jackson had quit the battlefield. Moreover, Pope seemed to have very little concern about where Longstreet was, and did not, in fact, believe he had arrived on the battlefield. At the end of a long morning of waiting on both sides, Pope pushed forward once more. [17]

To begin with, the Union assault aimed at Jackson's center and left, then shifted to the left. Early, sour because he was still occupying a portion of Hill's front line, grew more unhappy as he came to the realization that his brigade constituted the extreme left flank of the entire Confederate position. He had been given to understand that a number of Hill's brigades were stationed in the woods on his left. But no one had told him that they too had been ordered to the rear for more ammunition, and that no troops had taken their places. Early discovered his

< III >

flank was unprotected when Federal sharpshooters in the woods to his left began picking off members of his brigade, not least a lieutenant in the 13th Virginia, his pet regiment, whom Early described as "very valuable."

This casualty may have been Lt. J. T. Hillroy of Company A, who mounted a personal response to one particularly troublesome Union marksman firing from up in a tree some 1,000 yards off to the left. The lieutenant borrowed a rifle from one of his men and lay down behind a stump on the rim of the railroad cut about 20 yards above the company position. Taking careful aim, he fired. In Buck's account, the "Yankee at once returned the fire and the second shot took effect, putting a bullet in his eye and killing him instantly." The lieutenant "never spoke, but we heard that awful 'thud' and the next moment his lifeless body rolled down the embankment bleeding like a beef. I shall never forget the scene as long as I live."

Emboldened by the vacuum they were encountering, some of the Union skirmishers walked forward, firing at likely targets as they advanced. Early—no doubt wondering how long the riflemen would remain unsupported—sent word to Hill. In timely fashion, troops arrived at the point of danger and drove the marksmen back.[18]

As they had the day before—Pope believing that the Confederates would collapse under the next attack—the Federals kept on assaulting Jackson's line throughout the afternoon. But Jubal's men saw very little action, some of them ending up in a reserve line. Others, including the 49th Virginia, commanded by Col. William Smith—a former and future governor of Virginia—got caught up in another counterattack that swirled them perilously and gloriously forward beyond where they had been ordered to stop.[19]

But the furious action on Jackson's front, along with Pope's delusions, came to an end late in the afternoon when Longstreet launched his force upon the exposed Union left flank. As Pope's army reeled backward from this shock, Jackson's men moved forward in their turn. The stage seemed set for a reenactment of July 21, 1861. But a stiff rear-guard action by United States regulars on the Henry Hill, memorable to survivors of the first battle, allowed the Federals to avoid a disastrous rout.[20]

<< SINCE LEE still hoped to trap Pope and finish him off before he could reach the defenses of Washington, only half a day's rest was allowed Jackson's weary, depleted ranks before their resumption of the march. Under a downpour on the afternoon of August 31, they set off in a renewed search for Pope's flank. They slogged northward, turned east on reaching the Little River Turnpike, and spent the night at Pleasant Valley. Because their wagons, with food and other supplies, were far behind them, they were hungry as well as wet and tired, and thus reduced to cadging ears of corn from the farmers' fields as they passed by.[21]

Late the next afternoon, Jackson's men encountered a Federal force blocking the highway at Ox Hill, near the old mansion of Chantilly. Under lowering skies and the threat of yet more rain, Stonewall formed a line of battle on a wooded ridge south of the road, with Hill's division on the right, Lawton's in the center, and Starke's on the left.[22]

Early's brigade and another in Lawton's division were in reserve as the fighting commenced with a Union attack launched by the division of Maj. Gen. Isaac I. Stevens. As the Confederates were coping with this assault, the volleys of musketry were answered by the onset of a violent thunderstorm, its crashing bolts and vivid lightning an exaggerated echo of the roar and flash of battle. Floods of rain, driven by a high wind, lashed the Confederate soldiers' faces as they tried to beat back the assault.[23]

As a battle scene, it was more unnerving and confusing than many. Though the principal action was on the Confederate right, Starke, on the left, anticipated an attack on his position. Moreover, he perceived a gap between his extreme left and the turnpike. Fearing that the Federals might turn his flank, he asked Early to move his brigade from its reserve position and plug the gap. It was a logical request: Early's men were not engaged, and because Starke's line curved to the left, they were fairly close to the terrain Starke was worried about. Perhaps mistrusting Starke, who was new to division command and his junior in rank, Early was reluctant to consent to the request. Before agreeing, he rode over to the left and had as good a look at the terrain as the dense woods and the weather's distractions permitted.[24]

The position seemed tenable. Urged by Starke, who felt the situa-

< 113 >

tion was critical, Early moved his brigade off without waiting for orders from Lawton or Jackson, relying on the Louisiana brigade that was in the front line to cover the position he was leaving. On the way to his new position, marching by the left flank with his left regiments in the lead, Jubal heard a racket of musketry that seemed to be coming from the position he had just left. On arrival at the new position, he discovered that the 13th, 25th, and 31st Virginia Regiments, which had been deployed on his brigade's right and were now last in his column of march, were not with him. Quickly he sent Lt. Sam Early back to find out what was going on. The three regiments were, it turned out, briskly fighting off a contingent of Federals, who had broken through the Louisianians in the front line. The Tigers' brigade commander, Col. Henry B. Strong—succeeding Forno, who had been wounded at Manassas—was new at his job. Under attack from an unexpected quarter, he had tried to change his brigade's front, and made a mess of it. The Louisiana regiments, in disarray, ran back through the units of Early's brigade that were about to march off to the left. To their credit, the commanders of the three Virginia regiments kept these units where they were, forming a barrier behind which the Louisiana men could rally.[25]

This Federal success was to have no sequel, however local or temporary, on that day. In the nasty, jumbled firefight of Chantilly, the Union forces got the worst of it once more. They were repulsed everywhere along the line, and went into retreat as night fell. Two of their division commanders, Maj. Gen. Philip Kearny and Maj. Gen. Isaac Stevens, were killed, and Union losses, about 1,000 killed and wounded, were twice those of the Confederates.[26]

Even during the worst of the storm and the fighting, Early's men enjoyed a huge joke. Col. William Smith of the 49th Virginia, known as "Extra Billy," was just as unmilitary in his dress as Jubal; but unlike the general, he had little use for West Pointers. At Chantilly, his headgear was a lofty beaver hat. When the rain commenced, Colonel Smith raised a blue cotton umbrella and kept his hat, his coat, and his saddle dry. There is no evidence that Early had anything to say about this breach of military punctilio, but it made the soldiers laugh. "Come out of that umbrel," one soaked, ragged fellow shouted. "I see your legs; come out of that hat, want it to bile the beans in!" [27]

Notwithstanding Extra Billy's declaration of independence—which Jubal might even have grinned at himself—General Early was at his proudest, of himself and his men, following this action. In his report (filed *after* Antietam, where pride might also have been pardoned), he is referring to the Chantilly fight when he asks to "be excused for referring to the record shown by my own brigade, which has never been broken or compelled to fall back or left one of its dead to be buried by the enemy, but has invariably driven the enemy when opposed to him and slept upon the ground on which it has fought in every action, with the solitary exception of the affair at Bristoe Station, when it retired under orders, covering the withdrawal of other troops." [28]

True enough—though Jubal was talking about his post-Williamsburg brigade, the once-despised leavings of Arnold Elzey.[29] It was Jubal's brigade now. And now, Early had reached a peak of military success, as measured by his own men as well as his ablest peers and superiors. The men were veterans; they had seen their share of action. But they knew that their losses in combat under Early were much more bearable than those of other brigades. From the abortive Rappahannock crossing through the Chantilly fight, by Early's account, the brigade had lost 27 killed and 181 wounded. By contrast, Trimble's brigade had lost almost twice as many at Second Manassas alone. This may simply have been luck—not being where the fighting was heaviest, the fire hottest over a long period of time. But it is clear that Jubal cared about his men, and not only because without them he could not be effective. He shared their danger and hardships, and he tried to keep them alive and sound. The rank and file sensed this concern, and were grateful in their fashion.

Respectful at bottom though never adulatory, the men's attitude toward their general owed a good deal to the comic possibilities inherent in the oddity of his appearance and manners. The degree of risk they would take to enjoy these possibilities was demonstrated in an incident later in the war. One day in the summer of 1864, Early rode over to confer with his distinguished subordinate John Breckinridge.

As usual, Early was dressed in a nondescript gray suit, and was wearing a hat with a plume. Some of the men standing near the conference between the two generals noticed that a member of Breckinridge's mounted escort was wearing an outfit and a hat that bore a striking resemblance to Early's garb and headgear. Struck by the resemblance, one of them shouted, "Look at Jube's brother!"

"This opened the ball," as another witness recalled the scene. "Forgetful of danger, a hundred voices took up the cry, and 'Jube's brother!' 'Jube's brother!' was echoed on every side. Old Early heard the noise, and looking up, saw his double, who half sheepishly joined in the general laughter." Early, all business, paid no more attention, continuing his conversation with Breckinridge. Then, "some rascal, bolder than the rest, cried out: 'Jube, why don't you go and kiss your brother?' "

At this, Early lost his temper. He rode up to the group, members of the 12th Georgia Battalion, and gave them the side of his tongue, citing them for every known crime. He finished by telling them he would provoke a fight for their "special benefit, and put them in the forefront of it, where he hoped that every one of them would be killed and burn in hell through all eternity."

The fight materialized next day as the 12th Georgia Battalion, acting as skirmishers, stopped a Union cavalry attack with apparently little loss. Far from being demoralized by their punishment for concocting the outrageous "brother" joke, they had behaved just as Early would have wished—and perhaps as he intended.[30]

Early's fellow commanders and his superiors naturally viewed him in a different light. The respect he had earned from Stonewall Jackson provides the measure of his reputation. As he had shown at Second Manassas and Chantilly, Jubal was not only reliable and proficient in carrying out orders, but also capable of independent action—of using his own judgment to take appropriate steps without orders. Gaining greater responsibility and promotion along the way, he would enjoy the pinnacle of his military career for a good while to come.

< 116 >

CHAPTER NINE

"Here Comes Old Jubal!"

EPTEMBER 2, 1862, was a day of rest, badly needed. It was to be the last for some time as Lee's army prepared yet another aggressive move—an invasion of Maryland. For breakfast on the 2d, Jubal Early, like his men, had a couple of ears of green corn and boiled fresh beef, the remains of the booty from Manassas Junction. Irksome but not surprising was the lack of salt and bread.[1]

Along with General Lee, who had worried since leaving Richmond about the provisioning of his army, Early was much concerned; the Confederate commissary department was ineffective, and the food captured at Manassas was running out. Jubal acknowledged that "green Indian corn and boiled beef without salt are better than no food at all by a good deal." But sharing the common diet, he was sharply conscious of its debilitating effect on the troops, whom it afflicted with diarrhea.[2]

The rank and file had other woes not shared by Early, rumpled and casual though he was: some men were dressed in worn, tattered remnants of uniforms, patched and mended, with brimless hats and ropes holding up their trousers; many marched with naked feet.[3]

The march that began on September 3 would lead to the bloody standoff on Antietam Creek. There, displaying his penchant for being in the right place at the proper time, Jubal would play an important part in a Confederate counterattack that may have prevented a Union victory during the early phase of the battle. Before the day was far advanced, he succeeded to the command of Ewell's old division, though his new position was rendered nominal by the fact that all the division's brigades except his own were crippled by casualties. Later in the

year at Fredericksburg, his division commander's status now on a confirmed footing, Jubal would earn promotion by leading another counterstroke that had much to do with changing the course of the battle. As
a witness—albeit secondhand—of what he deemed Union misconduct
toward Fredericksburg civilians, Early nursed a growing hatred of the
Northern invader.

<< ON SEPTEMBER 6, flour and salt were issued at Frederick, Maryland,
where Early and his brigade arrived late in the day, bivouacking near
Monocacy Junction just east of the city. (It would not be Jubal's last
visit to the vicinity of the Junction.)[4]

For three or four days, while they rested in enemy country, officers and men of the Army of Northern Virginia had leisure to reflect
on what they were doing in Maryland. Among the numerous reasons
for the invasion, perhaps the most important was the defeat of an old
adversary who had escaped once before. In the aftermath of Second
Manassas, Lee had become aware that the hapless Pope, stripped of
high command after his failed campaign, had been replaced as Union
army leader by George McClellan. This was very good news; Lee knew
his opponent as a cautious general whom he felt he could defeat—and
with whom it was possible to take chances in order to do so. The chance
Lee took, in defiance of hoary military principles, was to divide his
force (as he had against Pope and as he would again). The Confederate commander proposed to send Jackson to capture Harpers Ferry—
removing the Federal base as a threat to his communications, denying
the services of its garrison to McClellan, and scooping up quantities of
supplies badly needed by the Army of Northern Virginia. Lee gambled
that Jackson could take Harpers Ferry in time to rejoin him before
McClellan challenged him in the field.[5]

On September 10, Jubal and his brigade, with Lawton's division,
broke camp near Monocacy Junction and accompanied Stonewall to
Harpers Ferry. The march route led westward through Frederick to
Williamsport, where Jackson's force would cross the Potomac back
to the Virginia side, then return eastward to Loudoun Heights. As the
troops of Jubal's brigade tramped through the mostly deserted Frederick streets—fewer Marylanders than expected seemed to support the

< 118 >

Southern cause—they saw two little girls, one about ten, the other six or so; the elder was waving a small United States flag (of the sort, Jubal noted later, known as a "candy flag") and reciting "Hurrah for the Stars and Stripes" over and over in "a dull, monotonous tone."

The soldiers thought this was pretty funny—except for one man who was irritated by the spectacle. Early came on the scene as the man was threatening to take the flag away from the child. Jubal told the fellow he was a fool, and ordered him to leave the girl alone; "she could do no harm with her 'candy flag.' " In Early's opinion, this episode—or a similar incident involving a United States flag witnessed by a member of another brigade—may have been the basis of the famous "Barbara Frietchie" affair celebrated in the poem of that name by John Greenleaf Whittier.[6]

<< JACKSON WAS outside Harpers Ferry with his command by September 14. Abetted by two divisions detached from Longstreet's force that occupied key heights to the north and east of the town, Jackson prepared to attack on the 15th. As the hour of the assault drew near, Early noted that the ground over which his brigade would have to approach the enemy was difficult: the men would have to enter a deep declivity from which all cover had been cleared, then mount a steep slope covered with "thick brush that had been felled so as to make a formidable abbatis [sic]." Jubal found this prospect "by no means comforting." [7]

Before the assault could be launched, the Federals raised a white flag. Against the outnumbered Union garrison, Lee's object had been gained without great loss at Harpers Ferry, though fighting at Crampton's Gap and South Mountain to protect the divided wings of Lee's army from McClellan's oncoming juggernaut would be more costly.

Leaving A. P. Hill's division at Harpers Ferry to take the surrender and organize the captured supplies, Jackson marched the rest of his command rapidly northward to Sharpsburg. There he joined Lee on September 16 near Antietam Creek, where the army commander had taken up a position following the clash with McClellan two days before at South Mountain. As it was eventually established, Lee's line ran southeastward from a point near the Potomac, then curved south

< 119 >

and ran roughly parallel to the Hagerstown Pike. The position covered Sharpsburg and blocked the principal approach to the town across Antietam Creek via the Rohrbach Bridge, later known as the "Burnside Bridge." [8]

When Jackson's force arrived toward the end of the day, it was eventually posted on the left end of Lee's main line. Early found himself detached with his command on the far left of Stonewall's contingent; with Early was the division's brigade of Louisianians, once more under Harry Hays, who had recovered from a wound suffered in June at Port Republic. The division's other two brigades, commanded by Col. James Walker and Col. Marcellus Douglass, bedded down near a small whitewashed brick chapel (the famous Dunkard Church) half a mile or so to the south. Only a brigade of cavalry under Stuart, with a few guns, was farther to the left than Early's detachment. [9]

To Early's right in Lee's line was the division commanded by Brig. Gen. J. R. Jones, who had taken over from the relatively junior William Starke. There was some skirmishing until nightfall between McClellan's men and Confederates of Hood's division in the woods north and east of the Dunkard Church. [10]

Trying to get some rest after the firing died down, senior officers like General Early had reason to brood about their side's chances in the battle that was certain to begin in earnest next day. The bad diet and sorefootedness that worried Jubal and many other commanders, notably Lee himself, had contributed to unprecedented straggling in an army never noted for its march discipline. Since September 1, straggling had cost the Army of Northern Virginia more than one-fifth of its strength. As one of Jackson's officers wrote in a letter to his family, "I am completely tired out with our constant marching. . . . It is too much as the state of our ranks show, and if Jackson keeps on at it, there will be no army for him to command."

Nor for Lee. But the men with the spirit and the endurance to stay in ranks were the cream of the army. As one officer put it, "None but heroes are left."

Still, even these paragons were outnumbered better than two to one, manning a line too long for their strength. They would be in serious trouble if McClellan attacked simultaneously all along their line. Alter-

natively, reinforcing a defense against a concerted assault on one sector
of the line could weaken others to the breaking point. With the Potomac River only three miles to the Confederates' rear, retreat might spell
not just defeat but disaster. Lee, defying conventional soldiers' wisdom
in this as in the matter of dividing his forces, was gambling again.

Lee might know exactly what he was doing. But if his worried subordinates had even surmised that the Federals also did—that they had
captured the Confederate general's plans for the Maryland campaign—
the Southerners' concern might have been closer to despondency. All
the same, the bizarre fact was that a staff officer had, thoughtless or
unaware, used a copy of Lee's orders to wrap some cigars, and then left
the package behind in his bivouac when the army moved. There, an
alert Federal soldier discovered the little parcel, and soon McClellan
knew as much as Lee about what Lee intended to do and what risks
he was taking. Though Lee had learned that McClellan possessed his
"lost orders," few others in the Confederate army knew it.[11]

<< As soon as there was light enough to see, the battle opened with
the concentrated fire of Federal artillery, soon answered by Confederate guns. Not long after, Jackson ordered Early to move his brigade off
to the left to support Stuart's guns, which were firing from Nicodemus
Hill. Jackson knew that if the Federals captured the hill—with or without the guns—his position would become untenable. But one brigade,
he felt, should do the job; Hays was told to take his brigade to join
Walker and Douglass. These units moved across the Hagerstown Pike
and now faced the enemy near the Miller farm. There, in the famous
cornfield, they were to take much of the brunt of the first full-scale
Federal onset.[12]

Jubal, moving to join Stuart, saw ominous signs of a Union attempt
to turn the Confederate left flank; Stuart was concerned enough to pull
some of his guns back from their position on Nicodemus Hill and move
them to Hauser's Ridge, farther to the rear and to the right. As this was
happening, Stuart—presumably in touch with Jackson via courier—
told Early that Lawton had been wounded; Jubal was to link up with
the division's other brigades and take over divisional command.[13]

Up to this point, uninformed by anything but the terrific din of ar-

< 121 >

tillery and musketry (one New Yorker called it "a savage continual thunder"),[14] Early appears to have had little notion of what was happening elsewhere on the field. But he seems to have appreciated the importance of his role on Jackson's left. Now, in carrying out his orders to concentrate the division, Early showed how his taste for independent action influenced his decisions. In his report, Early says that Jackson had ordered him to "carry my brigade back and take command of the division." In other words, he was to move his brigade to the right and join the division's other brigades where they were, in the general neighborhood of the Dunkard Church. Instead, he determined to place his brigade as he saw fit—in close contact with the enemy—and bring the division's other brigades up to join it. This course of action was never challenged. If it had been, Early's justification might well have been his fear that the Federals were trying to turn his left flank, and that removing his brigade would allow them to do so.[15]

Accordingly, he left the 13th Virginia, now a 100-man vestige, to support Stuart. With his other regiments, he marched back to the position he had occupied in the early morning. There he discovered two regiments. One was the 27th Virginia under Col. Andrew J. Grigsby, an able officer whose penchant for bad language reputedly rivaled Early's. The other was the 9th Louisiana under Col. Leroy A. Stafford. Together, they comprised a couple hundred men who were all that was left, for fighting purposes, of Jones's division. Jones had been wounded, and Starke, his replacement, had been killed. Thus was Early first made aware of the terrible toll of Antietam. He left his brigade in position with the remnant units he had found there and went off to bring the others to him.

Amid growing signs that large Union forces were pushing to envelop the Confederate left flank, Jubal entrusted his brigade to the command of the flamboyant Extra Billy Smith of the 49th Virginia and placed Grigsby in charge of the two regiments rallied from the wreckage of Jones's division. He then rode southward toward the Dunkard Church in search of Hays's, Walker's, and Douglass's men. There he discovered that they, like Jones's command, had been so badly hurt that they had been sent to the rear, no longer capable of fighting. Assailed by Union infantry and artillery of Joe Hooker's corps, they had been

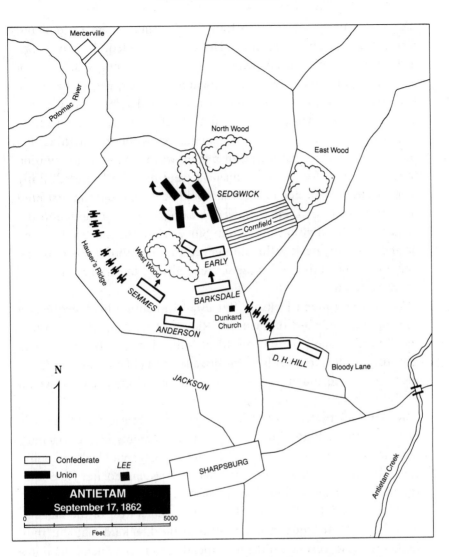

Confederate
Union

LEE

ANTIETAM
September 17, 1862

0   5000
Feet

blasted down in their tracks. Hooker himself summed it up: "In the time I am writing, every stalk of corn in the northern and greater part of the field was cut as closely as could have been done with a knife, and the soldiers lay in rows precisely as they had stood in their ranks a few minutes before. It was never my fortune to witness a more bloody, dismal battlefield."

In Walker's brigade, suffering 30 percent casualties overall, the veteran 12th Georgia (linchpin of Early's right flank at Cedar Mountain) lost at least 59 of its 100 men. Douglass was killed. In Hays's brigade, every regimental commander was a casualty, along with six out of every ten men. The survivors, their ammunition expended, had been relieved by Hood's division, which had launched a desperate counterattack that succeeded in pushing the Federals back across the pike.[16]

Neither Early nor anyone else had ever experienced anything like this. "After having discovered that there was nothing of the division left on the field for me to command except my own brigade," Early recalled, he sent an aide to see what could be done about the shattered units that had retired. He then went looking for Jackson, to report the condition of his division and inform Stonewall of the menace building on the Confederate left. Jubal believed that this threat was opposed only by his own brigade and the scratch units led by Grigsby, a total of about 1,400 men.[17]

When Early found Jackson, Stonewall was sitting his horse near a concentration of guns on Hauser's Ridge, behind the church. From there he could see something of the unfolding battle on his front. Jubal got orders to return quickly to his brigade and hold on until reinforcements could be found and sent to join him. Jackson said he would attend to this as soon as he could.[18]

Riding back to the point where he had left his brigade and Grigsby's ragtag adjuncts, Early found the enemy movements in their vicinity more menacing than ever. He sent his aide Maj. Samuel Hale galloping off to find Jackson and tell him that danger was immediate; Hale soon returned with word that reinforcements were about to be sent.

At this point, Jubal's troops were in the woods west of the Hagerstown Pike about a quarter mile north of the Dunkard Church; they formed an east-west line running perpendicular to the pike. The line's right flank ended in the woods opposite the middle of a field, about 200 yards wide, that lay between the woods and the road. This field sloped up to form a plateau in rear of Early's line; the rising ground and the cover of the woods concealed the line from anyone looking north along the Hagerstown Pike from the vicinity of the Dunkard Church.

Just as Hale finished delivering Jackson's news of reinforcements, there came a most disconcerting sound of field guns—from Early's right and rear. Jubal had been anxiously scanning the view in front and to his left, "not dreaming that there was any immediate danger to my right." He had seen Confederate troops in action fairly far across the pike to the southeast, so he assumed Lee's line covered the flank in that direction. On hearing the new sound of artillery, he began by taking "it for granted that this was one of our batteries that had opened on the enemy."

This comforting hypothesis was immediately challenged when a soldier who was standing close to the summit of the plateau—and was thus able to see over it—declared the guns belonged to a Federal battery. This was confirmed by Major Hale, who cantered up for a look. But Jubal was not convinced without seeing for himself. He looked. There they were—men in blue serving a group of guns on the pike that were firing down it in the direction of the Dunkard Church.

As Jubal watched the battery at work, he observed a substantial body of infantry near the guns. He could see all too clearly that there were no other Confederate troops between him and the church, and that the Union infantry was moving westward across his rear into the gap. A Federal advance in that direction represented a major crisis, Early believed; if the enemy should seize the woods they were now entering, they could easily capture Hauser's Ridge and other heights behind the church. Then they could take the entire Confederate line in reverse and destroy Lee's army.

Early realized that though cut off, he was now under extreme pressure to hold his position. He needed reinforcements more desperately than ever. Union troops were still moving up on the left and in front, squeezing him back into contact with those recently arrived in his rear. Fortunately the plateau intervening between Jubal's men and the Federal column near the battery meant that the enemy at Early's back probably had no idea he was there—yet. If they found out, Early was sure they could quickly annihilate his little contingent. But just in case, he coolly and quietly hooked the right end of his line back through the woods, refusing it and facing it southeast to do what it could to guard his rear.

Now the Union body to the rear started moving forthrightly into the woods toward the rising terrain behind the church. Early knew this was the decisive moment. He started marching his brigade off to the west, parallel to the Federal axis of advance and moving in the same direction. Meanwhile, he told Grigsby to maintain a line facing the Federal advance on the left and in front, and check the threat from that quarter while falling slowly back toward the church. As Early's column followed along with the Union attack units, the ridge flattened out. But the Confederates maintained concealment by judicious use of numerous outcrops and ledges of limestone that dotted the woods, which were otherwise fairly open and free of underbrush.

When Early's lead regiment, Smith's 49th Virginia, reached a gap in this system of ledges, the Confederates could see the enemy advancing with flankers deployed between the main body and Early's men. With this target in view, Jubal ordered Smith to open fire. The Union flankers, surprised by the sudden volley from their right, quickly ran back to join the main body.

Early now became aware of two brigades of Confederate reinforcements approaching him and the Federals from the western end of the woods behind the church. Early ordered rapid fire. Capt. John R. Phillips of Company K, 31st Virginia, captured the moment in his diary. Early, Phillips wrote, "hurled himself . . . into the thickest of the fight and shouted, boys, hold them, you have plenty of reinforcements coming, hold them . . ."[19]

The Federals answered the Confederate fire with a couple of volleys and then started withdrawing toward the pike. As they had more than once before, the men of Jubal's brigade got excited, defied orders, and pursued the retreating bluecoats, driving them well across the pike. This was dangerous, particularly since the enemy was still moving up from the left, though Grigsby had been able to slow their advance somewhat. At this point, these Federal formations, still marching forward in successive lines of battle, were substantially reinforced.

But now, also, the deadly Union thrust through the woods toward Hauser's Ridge had been repulsed. And now all the Confederate reinforcements were on hand—most of three brigades. These, with Early's, Grigsby's, and Stafford's forces, turned on the Union battle lines advancing west of the pike. As the Federals headed for what they thought was the Confederate left flank, their line of march drew

< 126 >

them perpendicularly across the front of the reinforced grayclad cohort, which opened fire. Slicing into the Union flank, the Confederate volleys were devastating. Added to the metal of the artillery on Hauser's Ridge, the weight of fire in the opening minutes of the counterstroke was so heavy, according to one witness on the Union side, that hundreds "were disabled in a moment." In the confusion, Federal units trying to change front panicked and opened fire on each other. The 15th Massachusetts lost 318 men in a few minutes, the worst casualties of any Union regiment on this day. The unwounded survivors turned and fled northward. Though the Confederate pursuit was checked, the Union offensive was at an end in this portion of the field by about 9:45.[20]

<< EARLY AND his men spent the balance of this long and horrible day quietly, in a position not far from where they had begun it, aware that they might have to repel another attack at any moment. Of events on other parts of the field during the remaining hours of September 17, Jubal knew little until much later, when the reports of both sides gave him a sense of the battle's main features. Around midday, an increase in the din of combat to Early's right, near the center of Lee's line, might have provided a hint of the ordeal of D. H. Hill against a desperate challenge by two Federal divisions.

But to officers and men of Early's rank and below on the far left of the Confederate line, its far right—about two miles to the south— might as well have been in Mexico. There was no way of knowing that McClellan had ordered an assault by Maj. Gen. Ambrose Burnside on the Confederate right around 10:00 A.M., or that by midday his troops had still not gained a foothold on the Confederate side of Antietam Creek—or that this delay had enabled Lee to send Jackson the reinforcements that had helped Early repulse the Federals on the left. Though the Rohrbach Bridge was in Federal hands by 1:00 P.M., Jubal and his men could have had no idea that their fate depended on the fact that it took Burnside another two hours to organize a follow-up assault. (Once launched, the attack seemed on the point of succeeding—Lee's flank about to be turned and Union soldiers skirmishing in the purlieus of Sharpsburg.)

Of A. P. Hill's arrival on the field from Harpers Ferry at the last pos-

< 127 >

sible moment, and of his surprise counterattack on Burnside's exposed left flank and the resulting frustration of the Federal assault on Lee's exhausted and attenuated force, Early could only have heard vague rumors over the next few hours.

<< LATE ON the 17th, as soon as he felt fairly sure the Federals would mount no more assaults on the Confederate left, Early rode off to find the missing brigades of his putative divisional command. This melancholy errand was hardly successful; Jubal discovered only 100 men of Douglass's brigade, assembled by Maj. J. H. Lowe, the senior officer surviving. Lowe got orders to bring these men up to Early's position and deploy them to the right of his brigade. Next day, Harry Hays appeared with 90 of his Louisianians, and a little later 200 men of Walker's brigade turned up under the command of a captain, Walker having been disabled, though not seriously hurt, by a shell fragment.

On September 18, the two armies faced each other in relative inaction. That night, Lee withdrew beyond the Potomac and ended his Maryland campaign. Early's command, marching as a rear guard, was the last Confederate infantry, he believed, to regain the Virginia shore.[21]

Jubal felt the honor of this post, and indeed it did him credit. That he had earned the distinction was reflected in the reports of his superiors. Lee's report of the battle mentioned that Early "attacked with great resolution the large force opposed to him." Once again, Jackson allowed himself to praise his aggressive subordinate, observing that "General Early attacked with great vigor and gallantry the column on his right and front."

Such opinions were the currency of advancement for Jubal and his peers. As the Army of Northern Virginia pulled itself together near Winchester following the back-to-back campaigns against Pope and McClellan, rumors of promotion charged the autumn air with the sharp scent of organizational politics. Men began lining up, and lining each other up. At the head of the parade were Longstreet and Jackson, who were awarded the rank of lieutenant general, to accompany their respective designations as commanders of the 1st and 2d Corps.

< 128 >

With his cultivated nose for the odors of advancement and his justified sense of achievement, Early had high hopes. His claim to divisional command rested partly on the severe wounding of senior officers,
and in that sense he was a mere replacement. But he knew that his
right to higher command was more substantial than that. He had performed very well since returning from medical leave. At Antietam, he
had handled his brigade and its attached units with skill and effect—
changing fronts twice (a risky maneuver) and breaking up a potentially
catastrophic Union attack. He had done so, moreover, at a cost that
was a fraction of that in the rest of the division, which had suffered 38
percent casualties overall. Early's losses in killed and wounded were
9 and 15 percent, respectively, of the division's. Overall Confederate
losses were 11,724, or 23 percent of those engaged.[22]

If Jubal based any expectations on reflections such as these, they
were to be dashed. Jackson recommended only Isaac Trimble among
his brigadier generals for promotion to major general, and used the
word "brilliant" in citing Trimble's attack on Manassas Junction with
two small regiments during the campaign against Pope.

Lee, sending his recommendations to Richmond on October 27, included both Early and Trimble on his list of officers to be promoted.
Each, Lee proposed, was to command a division—Early to continue
permanently in that role if Ewell could not return to duty, and if another
general senior to Jubal (Edward Johnson) was likewise not fit for service
in the field. Perhaps because Early had few if any friends in high places
besides Lee, the politics of preferment left him with the temporary responsibility of divisional command, but without the substantive rank.
One consolation might have been Trimble's failure to gain promotion,
in spite of Jackson's unusually eloquent recommendation (as well as
Lee's).[23]

‹‹ THE CONFEDERATE government made its decisions about these matters against the background of a battle well fought, even if it had been
very costly, and even if strategically unsuccessful in that it ended Lee's
Maryland campaign. Abraham Lincoln was forced to make decisions
against a vastly different background: horrendous casualties; a botched

battle against inferior numbers. McClellan had not only failed to destroy Lee, but had allowed him to escape. Although "Little Mac," who would not bow to pressure, was left in command for a few weeks after Antietam, Lincoln meant to keep him there no longer than it took to find a general who would do as his commander in chief wished.

The choice was Ambrose Burnside. Told to advance on Richmond, he moved his command to Fredericksburg, arriving November 19. By this time, the Army of the Potomac, which McClellan had—exercising his real skill—recruited, refitted, drilled, and polished, was a formidable adversary once more. Against it, the Army of Northern Virginia, resupplied by rail from Richmond and rested, its ranks stiffened with returned stragglers, conscripts, and convalescent wounded, cast a far longer shadow than the skeleton army on the Antietam scarcely three months earlier.[24]

Lee sent Longstreet to mark Burnside's progress down the Rappahannock and block the route to Richmond. Jackson soon followed, marching southward up the Valley, then crossing into Madison County. There was a story, surely a favorite among the troops, that related how General Early, leading his division one day on this march, gave Stonewall a piece of his mind. It seems that Early, riding with his command as it brought up the rear of Jackson's column, received a message from Stonewall. Reading it, Jubal learned that "the Lieutenant General commanding desires to know why he saw so many stragglers in rear of your division today."

Early's reply was in two parts. The first asserted that most of the stragglers Jackson had seen belonged to the other divisions marching ahead. That was fair comment—certainly unsurprising and no doubt largely true. But the reply's second part was astonishing. "[T]he reason the Lieutenant General commanding saw so many stragglers in rear of my division today," Early snappishly informed Jackson, "is probably because he rode in rear of my division."

If Jackson ever got this or a similar communication from Early, he apparently made no response. If Early sent such a communication to his corps commander, he got away with it. In that case, Jubal must have felt that his fighting reputation gave him a form of immunity; perhaps, in his arrogant way, he simply did not care. As a Confederate veteran was to observe, "nobody but Old Jube would have presumed to flip Stonewall that way." That much seems indisputable.[25]

A few days before Jackson's corps arrived in Fredericksburg, Early bivouacked near Orange Court House, Virginia, in the vicinity of Montpelier, the former home of the late president James Madison. Its incumbent owner, a Mr. Carson, invited the general and his staff to come over to the house. As George Greer, a young staff officer, remembered the occasion, Carson did not greet them when they arrived, and never appeared. But they were shown hospitably enough to the library, "a very agreeable room." The seven officers sat and chatted. Time passed— an hour; two hours. Growling stomachs spoke of the good meal they had been hoping for at Montpelier—a repast of a splendor suggested to Dr. Whitehead, the divisional surgeon, by the "rich furniture, &c." in the library. The doctor said he supposed that Carson "would have plenty of Burgundy, Champagne, &c."

Finally, supper was announced. The table was laid with great elegance. But when the meal was served, faces fell. Along with some biscuits, coffee, bread, and butter, there were five eggs "to soothe the ravening of seven hungry stomachs." No meat was provided. In place of wine, sparkling or still, there was buttermilk.

The officers maintained a polite silence until the servant had left the room. Then, recalled Greer, they burst out: "D——d such a supper!" "What horrid coffee!" "These biscuits have too much lard in them!" As a junior member, Greer got no egg.

The general presumably claimed an egg. But it can scarcely have improved his mood. Early "ate in silence for a few moments," Greer reported, "when giving a grunt he rose from the table using a very vulgar expression. 'I'll be damned if I ain't going home and get something to eat.' He soon had his overcoat on and we were soon on our way with no good idea of the proprietor of Montpelier."[26]

« FACING BURNSIDE at Fredericksburg, Lee's resources made him a wealthy man, militarily speaking, compared to his pauper's status against McClellan at Sharpsburg. Opposing 125,000 Federals with 78,000 men (some of whom, in December, lacked shoes), Lee was still outnumbered. But he had substantial reserves to hold his solid position south of the Rappahannock and an amplitude of guns—so many that he was unable to site them all. Even so, the Federals could throw a far greater weight of metal from their heavy artillery, sited on Stafford Heights just east of the Rappahannock; numerous large, rifled pieces outranged the Southern guns. The Federals also disposed of many field batteries. But these advantages were partly offset by the vulnerability of Union infantry in any attack on the Confederate defenses.

Recognizing that his opponent would have to attack in order to gain the decisive victory Lincoln hoped for, Lee had the strategic advantage. For once, he could afford to assume the defensive and wait for the enemy to come to him. And by December 11, it seemed clear that Burnside intended to cross the river at or near Fredericksburg and attack there—the evidence being the completion, under heavy fire, of five pontoon bridges, three opposite the town and two a mile or so downstream.

To cover his pontoniers—who were to suffer heavily anyway under Confederate rifle fire from the waterfront—Burnside ordered the town shelled. The shelling drove out civilian refugees too poor or too stubborn to have evacuated their homes under the mere threat of war. Lee found the bombardment repugnant. "These people," he said of the Federals, "delight to destroy the weak and those who can make no defense. It just suits them!"

Undoubtedly the general found it difficult to believe that civilized men would do such a thing. But he might have had an equally hard time believing his own good fortune. Burnside's choice of a place to assault could hardly have suited an opponent better as a place to defend. Lee's position was based on a ridge rising steeply above the Rappahannock behind the town of Fredericksburg on his left and continuing some three and a half miles to flat terrain below the town to his right. On that flank, which Lee entrusted to Jackson's corps, the ridge sloped up more gradually, but the numbers and dispositions of the defenders were concealed by woods from the ridge crest down to the line of the Richmond, Fredericksburg & Potomac Railroad. From the railroad to the river, the country was generally open; a high bank on their side concealed the river itself from the Confederates. On the left, where Longstreet commanded, the crest of the ridge, Marye's Heights, offered good artillery positions, and a stone wall and sunken road some distance below the crest furnished virtually impregnable cover for infantry.

Before Burnside had telegraphed his intentions by building his pontoon bridges, Lee had prudently sent two of Jackson's divisions, Early's and D. H. Hill's, down the river to block any Union crossings closer to Richmond. Now Jackson ordered them to return. Meanwhile, Stonewall placed the divisions of A. P. Hill and William Taliaferro (recovered from his wounds and once more at the head of his old command) along the ridge line—Hill in front and Taliaferro in reserve.

One topographical anomaly in Powell Hill's front seemed to offer danger, though apparently Hill had trouble seeing how it could be more than slight. Along most of the front, the woods ended at the rail line. The principal exception was a ravine that projected a triangle of boggy woods eastward across the railroad for several hundred yards, its 200-yard base on the rail line. Tangled undergrowth and icy dampness— the weather was brutally cold—made the ravine seem such an unlikely avenue for attack that Hill felt it need not be physically occupied by defenders.

Hill posted the brigade commanded by Brig. Gen. James H. Lane to the left of the triangular gap; on its right was Brig. Gen. J. J. Archer's brigade. Unfortunately—whether or not by design—Lane's right flank was 250 yards from the leftward boundary of the swampy aperture, while Archer's left rested about 150 yards to the right of the gap. These intervals, added to the 200-yard width of the triangle at its widest, created an opening in Hill's line that was almost a third of a mile wide. As a precaution, Hill stationed Maxcy Gregg's brigade behind the gap, some 500–600 yards to the rear of Lane's and Archer's line. If Jackson knew of this weakness in his line—it seems unlikely—he did nothing to change or augment Powell Hill's defensive alignments.[27]

During the cold, windy night of December 12–13, the divisions of Harvey Hill and Jubal Early marched back upstream to join Jackson, arriving in a dense fog. That night, though neither general—nor anyone else on the Confederate side—could have known much about it until later, some of the Federals who had entered Fredericksburg across the bridges discovered the abandoned houses of affluent citizens departed before the armies had assembled. These Union soldiers, perhaps partly out of anger at the stiff resistance they had encountered—put up by Mississippians under Barksdale—took to looting and wrecking after the defenders withdrew.[28]

« REPORTING ON the 13th to Stonewall, who had unaccountably dressed himself that dreary morning in a splendid new uniform coat presented to him by Jeb Stuart, Early got orders to align his division to the right of Taliaferro's. Both Early's and Taliaferro's units were deep in the woods, which hid the enemy from them as they were hidden from the Federals. When Harvey Hill's men arrived, they were sent to occupy open ground in a third line behind Early's division.[29]

Jubal believed the weakest part of the Confederate line was its extreme right, where the wooded ridge gave way to flat open terrain that was well within range of the big Union batteries on the heights across the river. Only Jeb Stuart, with two cavalry brigades and three batteries of horse artillery, was watching this vulnerable part of the field. For that matter, if Burnside had thrown the full weight of his force opposing Jackson—some 55,000 men in a "grand division" under Maj. Gen. William Franklin—against that part of the line, he might have turned the Confederate flank, severed Lee's communications with Richmond, and destroyed his army. But Jackson had concealed the size of his force so skillfully in the woods that Burnside apparently thought most of Stonewall's corps was still downstream guarding the lower crossings. When the Union commander did attack, he initially used only one division—about 4,500 men under Maj. Gen. George Gordon Meade.[30]

The fog was burning off and Jubal's men were filing into position when the Federal artillery opened fire. The batteries seemed well directed; despite the cover of the woods, the Union gunners, spotting the likely positions of the defenders, soon found their range.

About noon, the artillery fire was augmented by a roar of musketry off to the front. Early's curiosity and concern were quickly answered with the arrival of a courier from Archer, in search of A. P. Hill; Archer needed help, the courier said, against a heavy attack on his left. The courier had scarcely spoken when an officer of Jackson's staff drew rein and gave Early an order to move his division to the right and counter an enemy maneuver in that direction—reinforcing Jubal's concern about the right end of the line.

He had been about to send a brigade to support Archer. Jackson's order made him hesitate, but he decided to get a supporting brigade ready to move anyway. Early was instructing Col. Edmund N. Atkinson, commanding Lawton's brigade, to prepare for the advance when further news arrived with Lt. Ham Chamberlayne, adjutant of Powell Hill's artillery, who announced that heavy concentrations of the enemy had penetrated the gap (the lieutenant called it "an awful gulf") on Archer's left. This lunge was threatening to trap Archer's brigade and capture Hill's divisional batteries. Only an immediate counterattack, Chamberlayne said, would make any difference to this outcome.

With this news, Jubal decided to ignore Jackson's order for a move to the right. He told Atkinson to get moving in support of Archer. For reasons that are not clear (there had been plenty of time), Early had not reconnoitered the terrain immediately to the front; he asked Chamberlayne what direction the support brigade should take. The lieutenant informed Early that all Atkinson had to do was thrust straight ahead and he would collide with the enemy column that had breached the line. But Chamberlayne also said that one brigade would not be enough to seal the gap. Early responded by ordering another brigade (the one he had commanded, now under Col. James Walker) to move up and advance on Atkinson's left.

The situation was as bad as Early had feared. Meade's division, now supported on its right by the division of Maj. Gen. John Gibbon, had braved lethal artillery fire to get to the boggy ravine; pouring through, they had turned Archer's left. They had also hit Lane's brigade, to the left of the gap, and pushed it back. Union infantry driving straight ahead had surprised Gregg's brigade and shaken it up, mortally wounding Gregg; but the unit had pulled itself together and held on.

Now Atkinson's brigade encountered the Union force that had outflanked Archer. The collision propelled a large number of the Federals back down the hill and over the railroad. Early's battle-seasoned men, their blood up and pride in their crusty commander surging, began to crow a bit over the predicament of Hill's proud veterans' reeling—some

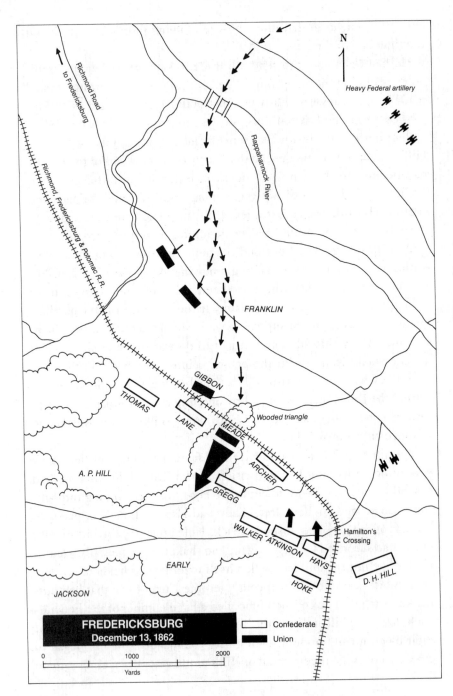

N

Heavy Federal artillery

to Fredericksburg

Richmond Road

Rappahannock River

Richmond, Fredericksburg & Potomac R.R.

FRANKLIN

GIBBON

THOMAS

LANE

MEADE

Wooded triangle

A. P. HILL

ARCHER

GREGG

WALKER

ATKINSON

HAYS

Hamilton's Crossing

EARLY

HOKE

D. H. HILL

JACKSON

FREDERICKSBURG
December 13, 1862

☐ Confederate
■ Union

0   1000   2000
Yards

of them running—from the shock of the Union attack. The reinforcers shouted, "Here comes old Jubal! Let old Jubal straighten that fence! Jubal's boys are always gettin' Hill out o' trouble!"

Hill acknowledged this timely assistance in his report: The brigades of "that gallant old warrior came crashing through the woods at the double-quick . . . ," Hill wrote, and "the enemy, completely broken, fled in confusion."[31]

The Confederate drive carried out into the open country beyond the rail line and even panicked some Union gunners enough to abandon their pieces. But it also exposed the counterattackers to lethal fire from the heavy Federal guns on Stafford Heights. Atkinson had already been badly wounded when it became obvious to Col. Clement A. Evans, his successor, that his brigade had to pull back.

Successful though it seemed, Atkinson's surge ended badly for him. Too gravely hurt to be moved back to his own lines, he had to be left behind to fall into Federal hands. Also, through no fault of his or anyone in his command, Atkinson's counterattack had failed to clear more than a sizable fraction of the Federals from behind Archer's position on Hill's front.

Walker's counterstroke, farther to the left, was perhaps more substantive. Early's old brigade repulsed one of the Federal units that had moved through the gap, but the effort ended, like Atkinson's, out in the open. Walker withdrew on spotting a fresh column of Union attackers moving into the woods to his left; he set up a line in the woods, then detached his old regiment, the 13th Virginia, to hit the advancing enemy column in its flank. This attack, coinciding with a counterthrust from the front by the brigade of Edward Thomas of A. P. Hill's division (Thomas had been a bulwark on Early's right at Cedar Mountain), inflicted heavy losses and reestablished Hill's line on the left of the gap.[32]

Meanwhile, to the right, Archer's brigade, still under heavy pressure from front and rear, was once more yielding ground. Learning this from a courier, Early ordered another brigade, under Col. Robert F. Hoke, to back Archer up. Just as Hoke was moving out, an order arrived from Jackson: take the whole division forward. The last brigade, Hays's, was sent in to support Hoke.

Some of the Federals who had gotten around behind Archer were in

Hoke's path when he reached the scene of action. His momentum and the surprise of his arrival threw the bluecoats back, to the great relief of Archer, who was barely holding onto his right as his ammunition began to run out; Hoke's impetus hurled the enemy back to his reserve line on the railroad. Then a second charge, joined by General Archer himself, cleared the line of the railroad, captured some prisoners and small arms abandoned on the field, and left the Federals occupying a fence line some distance to the east of the railroad.[33]

‹‹ "THE ENEMY was very severely punished for this attack," Early recalled; the Federals' reaction was to refrain from any further aggressive moves against the Confederate right. The battle's outcome unfolded on the left, above the town, where wave after wave of Union soldiers bravely tried to gain the heights, and failed in a welter of blood.[34]

Burnside would have had a better chance if he had concentrated from the first on attacking Jackson, particularly on the extreme right, where both Early and Jackson feared a Federal assault. It was substantially Early's accomplishment that Franklin's men did not succeed in attacking where they did, though the Confederates were fortunate that Burnside and Franklin failed to support the tough, brave brigades of Meade and Gibbon.

Through his ability to make rapid, audacious decisions—including a willingness to ignore an order from Stonewall—Jubal contributed significantly to the Federals' discouragement by driving them back after they had gone far toward achieving their objective in the assault through the swampy gap. The Federal repulse and the timeliness and flair of Early's conduct were of a praiseworthy piece with his performance in previous actions. But his role at Fredericksburg introduced some significant differences; command of a division entailed new problems of management. Though Jubal cannot really be faulted for it, he effectively lost control of Atkinson's and Walker's brigades, which went too far in pursuing the enemy.

In his thinking about the day's events, General Early must have conceived considerable respect for the Pennsylvanians of Meade's division who had come so close to breaking through Jackson's lines. But his view of the Federal high command, which had ordered the shelling of

Fredericksburg, and of the men who had ransacked the houses of its citizens, was full of bitter scorn. This battle marks an intensification of Jubal's hate for the Northern foe. According to a story that is difficult to doubt, Early, Lee, and the Confederate cavalry commander Wade Hampton were together watching the Federals withdraw two days after the battle. Jubal said he "wished they were all dead." Lee chided Early for the violence of this expression, and said he "did not wish they were all dead but that they would go home and mind their own business." Then Lee rode off. As soon as he was out of earshot, Early snarled to his companion, "I not only wish them all dead but I wish them all in Hell." [35]

<< CHAPTER TEN >>

Underwriting the Army

*T*HERE, staunchly defending their camp, stand the Georgians of Clement Evans's brigade. And there, proud in the assault, come the North Carolinians of Hoke's brigade. The air is white with flying snowballs, and blue with the oaths and joyful shouts of the boy soldiers. Heavy snow has fallen, as happened a number of times during the winter of 1862–63, on the camps of Early's division on the Rappahannock near Port Royal; "the fleecy element," as Jubal characterized it, helps relieve the tedium of winter quarters.

To Jubal, it is all great fun. His postwar description of the snowball fight is a facile parody of the style of official reports: he has Hoke's men making "a bold dash at the Georgians, pelting them most unmercifully with their well pressed balls, and giving the usual Confederate yell. . . . [T]here was no withstanding the shock of their onset."

The North Carolinians capture the Georgians' camp, but are repulsed in their turn, General Hoke himself falling into the hands of the pursuers. Evans's men prudently refrain from trying to seize their opponents' camp, "magnanimously" releasing the captured general after "his having been well wallowed in the snow." After the fight, there are jokes at divisional headquarters at the expense of a young officer "who was himself captured under suspicious circumstances on Hoke's retreat." He is charged with skulking, ". . . and there was some reason to suspect that he did not stand the storm of snow balls as he did that of shot and shell on many another occasion."

This comment, seasoning the light-hearted narrative of the mock battle, might seem mere nineteenth-century sentimentality. But Early

< 140 >

was essentially devoid of sentimentality. Here, notwithstanding his sport with the notion of brave men playing at combat, speaks a nature full of pessimism, of fears, felt but unexpressed at the time of the snowball fight, that much of the worst lay ahead.[1]

« STILL, JUBAL had immediate reasons for satisfaction: his promotion to major general, to date from January 17, and his permanent assignment to command of the division he had led at Fredericksburg. The unit was now officially known as Early's division.[2]

Pleasure in this well-deserved advancement may have been offset by the frustrations of camp life. A major problem stemmed from another antidote to the wintertime blues. A favorite pastime, for an active minority, was theft, particularly of civilian property. The Louisiana troops of Hays's brigade, known throughout the army for their lawless and unorthodox ways, were blamed for much of the stealing. Finally, on December 30, 1862, Hays was forced to issue an order threatening to shoot future perpetrators. The order may have been Early's idea, since most of the complaints from outraged citizens were directed to him. Whatever the reason for the order, Hays received a stream of messages from General Early accusing the Louisianians of thievery. Believing the charges exaggerated, Hays finally revolted. He informed his regimental commanders that he would request their signatures on a petition to be submitted to General Lee requesting transfer of the Louisiana Brigade from Early's command to some other. All but one colonel, a native Virginian (in command of the 7th Louisiana) named Davidson Penn, an old friend of Early's, signed the petition with Hays.

To reach Jackson and Lee, the document first had to be sent through channels to Early. Furious, he summoned the Tigers' senior officers. When they were assembled in his tent, Jubal glared at the group and growled, "Gentlemen, this is the most remarkable document that I have had the honor to receive from you; but I am glad to see that there is one man of sense among you—Penn didn't sign it."

Early then read a lengthy bill of particulars citing the repeated occasions on which the Tigers' crimes had brought disgrace upon the division. All of this evil he had so far patiently endured, Jubal declared; his reward was this insulting transfer petition. In his high-pitched voice, he shouted, "Who do you think would have such a damn pack of thieves but me? If you can find any Major General in this army such a damn fool as to take you fellows, you may go!"

This was too much for Col. Leroy Stafford of the 9th Louisiana, who burst out laughing. The whole tent exploded with mirth, and soon everybody was chortling at the silly scene while Jubal broke out a jug and poured drinks all around. Thanks to Early's firmness and his sense of the absurd, the Tigers would remain.[3]

<< FOR THEM and for almost everybody else in Lee's army, there was little of a warlike nature to do along the front of the Rappahannock through the winter and early spring of 1863. James Longstreet took two of his divisions off to southeast Virginia and North Carolina, leaving the divisions of Lafayette McLaws and Richard Anderson under the direct command of Lee. By late April, Brig. Gen. John B. Gordon, wounded badly at Sharpsburg leading the 6th Alabama, had arrived to take command, in Early's division, of the brigade led so ably through the snowball fight by Clement Evans (who returned to regimental command). The battle-scarred, charismatic Gordon was to be a major figure in the development of Jubal Early's career.[4]

Of far greater significance from all points of view was the change, as of January 26, in the Union high command. Joe Hooker, who succeeded Burnside in the wake of the Fredericksburg debacle, had apparently come far since his run-in with Jubal after the slavery debate at West Point. Hooker was an intelligent soldier who reorganized the infantry and cavalry of his army along efficient lines that were to endure through the war. He was a brave man who liked to ride conspicuous light gray horses in battle, and he talked a belligerent game that gave credence to his "Fighting Joe" sobriquet. No stranger to ambition, he had been heard referring to the need for a military dictator, presumably himself, to run the war and the country. He was known as a bitter critic of Burnside, especially for ordering Hooker's men into repeated, futile charges up the heights above Fredericksburg. Burnside's vain attempt in January 1863, in the notorious "mud march," to push his army through the winter gumbo of Virginia's roads led to Hooker's appointment as his successor. If Lee, no doubt aware that Early was a classmate of Hooker,

< 142 >

inquired about how far the Union general might actually have come since Academy days, Jubal unquestionably told him. If so, the information—that Hooker was not to be feared though his army (more than twice the size of Lee's) was potentially formidable—could have helped the Confederate commander develop the bold strategy he was to adopt in early May at the Battle of Chancellorsville.

<< IN WINTER quarters, the two armies stood about where they had been in December, facing each other across the Rappahannock in the vicinity of Fredericksburg. Among the likeliest Federal moves to be anticipated when campaigning should resume, Lee and his senior generals felt, was a crossing of the Rappahannock at or below Fredericksburg and an attempt to turn the Confederate right flank. Early, who had in March been assigned a position on the Confederate line not far from where he and his division had been in December, felt the vulnerability of his right flank even more than he had then. He saw an added reason for concern in the fact that most of the trees that had furnished concealment in December had been cut down over the winter for shelter and firewood.[5]

Among the trees that were left, limbs were smeared with green where buds and spring leaves emerged; in some places on the wooded hills, the white sepals of anemone set off the light blue blossoms of houstonia. Around some of the farms behind the Confederate line, peach and cherry trees in full bloom stated spring's cheerful case. Lee and his generals had no eyes for these seasonal attractions, their thoughts preoccupied with Hooker and what he might do.[6]

<< FOR JUBAL EARLY, the new campaign opened before dawn on April 29, when a brigade of Federal infantry, taking advantage of heavy fog, crossed the river in boats, and landed just downstream from the mouth of Deep Run, one of two creek-sized tributaries of the Rappahannock on Early's front, and seized a bridgehead. Before long, three pontoon bridges were in place, and a division of infantry, with guns, was brought across. Another landing a mile or so downstream led to the laying of additional bridges and the crossing of a second division, accompanied by artillery.[7]

As fog dissipated, Confederate commanders could see that the slopes rising from the river on the opposite bank were crowded with troops, coloring blue much of the visible terrain all the way from a point opposite Fredericksburg to the extreme right end of the Confederate line—a distance of about six miles. Was this host, as it seemed, getting ready to launch a major attack in the neighborhood of Fredericksburg? Or was it a feint, to draw attention from a movement elsewhere? [8]

Through the 29th, Lee still seemed to believe in the former; he concentrated most of his men along the old December front, once more occupying Fredericksburg with Barksdale's Mississippians. Meanwhile, the Federals made no aggressive moves on the Confederate side of the stream, though large groups of infantry moved in purposeful fashion down the opposite slopes as if heading toward the bridges. While fog no longer concealed the Union movements, the Confederates' view of the crossings was partially blocked by the curtain of a high bank rising on the Confederate side between the water and level ground. [9]

Daylight on April 30 revealed very little change, though the Union bridgeheads had been fortified, and the Federals seemed to be connecting them with a trench line. But as the day wore on, the relative immobility of the Union forces indicated that Hooker was employing a ruse; this was confirmed for Lee by Jeb Stuart's cavalry scouts. According to Stuart, Hooker had launched a massive turning movement around the Confederate left, dispatching the better part of three corps across the Rappahannock and the Rapidan above their confluence. From there, these units were marching southeast through the Wilderness toward Chancellorsville and Lee's rear at Fredericksburg. Determined to nail Hooker before the Union general could attack him, Lee played his risky but (so far) trusty hole card: he divided his army, leading its larger portion westward toward Hooker, and leaving the smaller to guard Fredericksburg and hold off any attack by the Union forces remaining there. [10]

Lee chose General Early for this mission. His most important assignment to date, it consisted in protecting the Confederate rear and preserving Lee's freedom of maneuver against Hooker. The mission came down to underwriting the very existence of the Army of Northern

Virginia. Early was principally entrusted with the task of keeping the Federal troops at Fredericksburg from capturing the heights above the city—or at least delaying such an outcome as long as possible. Seizure of the heights would enable the Federals to cut Lee's communications with Richmond and destroy his supply depots at Hamilton's Crossing, a few miles below Fredericksburg, along with Guiney's Station, on the Richmond, Fredericksburg & Potomac Railroad. Even more important, possession of the high ground would open the way into Lee's rear, where the Union force could crush him against the oncoming main body under Hooker.[11]

Early would not have been surprised if he had been told that this was just what Hooker had in mind. (The Union commander, in fact, envisaged nothing less than a classic double envelopment—Cannae on the Rappahannock.) What Jubal would have thought if he had known— as he probably did—that the force opposing him was the 6th Corps under the command of another classmate, Maj. Gen. John Sedgwick, can only be guessed; Sedgwick had a rising reputation as one of the North's most capable generals, as Jubal presumably knew.[12]

Early was ready enough to accept the honor of the trust placed in him. But he was aggrieved as well as appalled by his relative weakness, whoever his opponent might be. He was to execute his assignment with only the 9,000 muskets of his own division augmented by Barksdale's 1,500-man brigade (of McLaws's division) and some 56 artillery pieces, under the command of Lee's chief of artillery, Brig. Gen. William N. Pendleton, and Lt. Col. Snowden Andrews.[13]

Against this force, as the 30th dawned, Sedgwick commanded the Union 1st and 3d Corps in addition to his own 6th, with nearly 60,000 men and more than 100 guns, many of them heavy siege pieces. (During the day, the 3d Corps was ordered to join Hooker, reducing Sedgwick's force to about 40,000 men.)[14]

Lee's final orders, issued to Early on April 30, were three in number: first, he was to observe the Federals and pin them down if possible, keeping his weakness a profound secret; second, if the enemy's numbers overpowered him, he was to retire toward Guiney's Station and protect the supplies and the railroad; finally, if he ascertained that the Federals near Fredericksburg were pulling out or significantly reducing their force there, he was to march to join Lee at Chancellorsville, posting a guard strong enough to hold whatever troops the enemy might leave behind at the town.[15]

« THE FREDERICKSBURG front lay quiet all day on May 1. On the 2d, the scene remained much the same, though Early noted a slight strengthening of the infantry occupying the opposite slopes above the river. To feel the enemy out, Jubal ordered Andrews to open fire on the two bridgeheads. The fire was feebly returned—and then came a surprise: the men and guns that had crossed into the downstream bridgehead pulled back from Early's front and went to ground under the riverbank, where they were invisible. Early ordered skirmishers forward to maintain contact. And, if the enemy remained inert, he contemplated detaching two brigades to join Lee.[16]

Curiosity piqued by the Federals' passivity, Early rode to Lee's Hill, one of the higher points on the front (named for the fact that Lee had established his headquarters there during the December battle). There he joined Pendleton and Barksdale, who drew his attention to masses of Union troops moving upstream on the opposite bank. The three generals speculated on the meaning of the movement: were the Federals leaving the Fredericksburg front? Or was this another feint?[17]

By 11:00 A.M., the Confederate commanders had reached no conclusion. Then the situation shifted abruptly. Riding up to the group came Col. Robert H. Chilton, General Lee's chief of staff, with fresh orders. Chilton said that Lee wanted Early to move his entire command, with the guns under Andrews, over to Chancellorsville, except for one brigade and eight or ten guns under Pendleton to be left guarding Fredericksburg. Pendleton was to send all his other artillery to the rear.[18]

This message from Chilton (who happened to be yet another West Point classmate of Jubal Early) was a bombshell. Early and Pendleton were astonished. Sitting on the ground so they could talk quietly, Early, Chilton, and Pendleton carefully went over the orders point by point. To begin with, Early reminded Chilton that since the troops were in the open it would be impossible to move them during the day without alerting the Federals, who could observe the Confederates from Stafford

< 146 >

Heights and from balloons. When the enemy saw that the defense had dwindled to brigade size, they could easily occupy Fredericksburg and seize the hills above the town.[19]

Chilton acknowledged this, but said he assumed that General Lee was also aware of it. The colonel stated that he presumed the commanding general had concluded that having Early's troops with him at Chancellorsville was more valuable than the possession of Fredericksburg and environs, which could easily be retaken once the enemy was defeated on the main battlefield. Besides, Chilton argued, look at all those Federals moving upstream: they could only be marching to reinforce Hooker against Lee.

Early still found it very difficult to accept a change in the straightforward instructions he had gotten from Lee two days earlier. Though a lot of Union troops seemed to be marching away, Early pointed out that there were a great many left, including at least a division on the Confederate side of the river near Deep Run, and another division in the bridgehead farther downstream. Looking at the situation another way, Early was certain he was pinning down a total Union force on both banks that was surely far greater than his relatively puny force could defeat in a head-to-head fight at Chancellorsville. Could Chilton by any chance have misunderstood the verbal orders of his chief? The colonel said he was absolutely sure he had understood Lee's words correctly.

Still skeptical, Early asked why the artillery was to be split up. Chilton explained that Lee needed little artillery in the Wilderness terrain of Chancellorsville, where dense woods made guns hard to use. Sending most of Pendleton's guns to the rear would ensure their safety.[20]

Pendleton wanted to know how long he was supposed to defend the heights against the crushing weight of numbers that would be thrown against him. His guide, Chilton replied, should be the amount of time needed to get the reserve artillery safely off to the rear.[21]

Chilton had spent his whole career in the regular army, mostly in the cavalry; at Buena Vista, in the Mexican War, he had earned a brevet major's rank by rescuing the wounded Jefferson Davis. But he had served the last seven years before the Civil War as a paymaster. And, unlike Jubal and a fair number of others around his age, Chilton's West

Point background (added, in his case, to unbroken military service) had not brought him general officer's rank—even by 1863. Knowing all that, and possibly remembering Chilton as a dim taper from West Point days, Major General Early (one may assume) bore down very hard on the colonel to get him to back away from the orders he purported to bring from Lee.[22]

Colonel Chilton, feeling the heat, must have been heartily glad when a messenger arrived to report that the Union troops occupying the downstream bridgehead had abandoned it. The news appeared to confirm the colonel's assertion that the Federals at Fredericksburg were packing up to join Hooker. Why would they do that? Chilton may have filled the generals in on what was going on out there in the Wilderness. The Federals should be in deep trouble by now—with Jackson marching boldly across Hooker's front to take his right flank by surprise while Lee, with a couple of divisions, pinned him in a defensive position near United States Ford.[23]

Early had no way of judging whether that operation was succeeding; the sounds of gunfire from the west, though heavy, told nothing one way or the other. But with Chilton insisting on the literal accuracy of the orders, which left Early no discretion, he now had to accept the force of General Lee's apparent wishes, despite their seeming illogic and the difficulties involved in carrying them out. Trusting that Lee knew more about the overall operation than he did, Jubal swallowed his doubts and set about doing what the commanding general apparently wanted him to do.[24]

‹‹ HAYS'S BRIGADE was left to man the heights above Fredericksburg, detaching one of its regiments to keep an eye on the Union division in the bridgehead near Deep Run. One of Barksdale's Mississippi regiments remained occupying the town and watching the river bank in that vicinity. These forces had 15 artillery pieces between them. As Pendleton began withdrawing guns, Early set about extricating his infantrymen from their position on the ridge. As this delicate maneuver was concluding, one of Professor Lowe's balloons rose into the brilliant skies over Fredericksburg, and Jubal was sure that the Federals could see every move his men made. It was 2:00 P.M. before he had the division ready to march westward.[25]

As the afternoon waned, the last of Early's regiments was en route to the Plank Road, headed for Chancellorsville. (If the Federals had observed the movement, they had done nothing—so far—to thwart it or take advantage of it.) Now came a shocking new development: not Chilton, but another of Lee's staff, galloping up to transmit Lee's thoughts—this time in writing—following Chilton's return and his report of what he had told Early to do. Those instructions, Lee wrote, were the result of a misinterpretation by Colonel Chilton of the commanding general's actual wishes. Lee had never wanted Early to withdraw from Fredericksburg unless he could do so without undue risk. The element of discretion that had underlain the original orders issued to Early on April 30 remained in full force. Finally, as Early remembered it, the commanding general's new dispatch suggested that if he could hold a substantial enemy force near Fredericksburg by staying there, he would be doing the army as much or more good than by marching to join Lee.[26]

« THE SCENE is vivid in the mind's eye: the lengthening shadows and the slight chill of the late afternoon, the grave faces of Jubal's officers, the lowered gaze of the hapless courier from Lee's staff as Early calls on God Almighty to consign Chilton and all his descendants direct and collateral to the eternal torments of Hell.

Cursing offered great relief. But it solved no problems. What should be done now? It was reasonable to assume that by this time the Federals had seen Early's departure and taken possession of the heights. To return now would mean a fight on most unfavorable terms that could wreck—or at least handcuff—his division and deny its services to Lee on any positive basis. By marching on he would possibly be able to add some muscle to whatever effort Lee was making near Chancellorsville. Lee's note certainly carried the implication that such support would not be unwelcome. Jubal gave what he believed to be the only logical order: "Forward, march!"

Perhaps 20 minutes later another messenger rode up—this time from

Barksdale, whose men were at the rear of the column. The news, dispatched from Pendleton to Barksdale, clarified the situation for Early, though it was hardly reassuring: a large enemy force was crossing the river and preparing to advance on the heights against Hays; the likelihood was that unless he and Pendleton were supported, all the artillery remaining with them would be captured. These developments, the courier said, had led to an immediate decision by Barksdale to turn back toward Fredericksburg.[27]

Though he now knew a bit more about what was happening, Jubal was in as much of a quandary as ever. His decision to keep marching west had rested on the assumption that the Federals had already taken possession of the heights. If, as now seemed possible, they had not yet done so, might there be a chance of fending the enemy off—and fulfilling the crucial mission of protecting Lee's rear? As this thought was forming in Early's mind, Col. John Gordon appeared and volunteered to take his Georgians back to help Barksdale. Would that make sense? It was a brave suggestion, but would Gordon, unsupported, supply that much help in holding the Rappahannock heights? For that matter, would Early's division, less the brigades of Hays, Barksdale, and Gordon, do Lee any good near Chancellorsville?

Here, with a vengeance, was the dispersal of force so sternly prohibited by the military textbooks; in this case, as usual, the prohibition was sound. Fragmenting the division would, at best, neutralize it. Concentrating it in the most useful, timely way meant supporting Barksdale and Hays.[28]

Toward nightfall on May 2—around the time Confederate soldiers shot Stonewall Jackson by tragic mistake in the Wilderness just as he was completing his triumph—the puzzled soldiers of Early's division faced about and started back where they had come from. Their general sent a rider off to tell Barksdale that his decision to return to Fredericksburg was fully approved. A second courier rode to Lee to inform him of Early's decision.

As the troops discovered on arrival in their old positions, the Federals had apparently suspended their advance on the heights. Early learned that the Federals in the Deep Run bridgehead were, at nightfall, no closer to his line than the Richmond Road, which ran beside the river from Fredericksburg.

In the dark, Early deployed his men along the whole front they had originally occupied.[29] The night passed quietly and uneventfully—as far as Jubal could tell. Actually, Sedgwick was very active, employing the hours of darkness to move many of his troops, who had been extended all along Early's front, and concentrate them closer to Fredericksburg. The 6th Corps, some 24,000 strong, was now Sedgwick's principal force, along with a division under John Gibbon detached from the 2d Corps; Hooker had called away the 1st Corps of Maj. Gen. John F. Reynolds, whose men Chilton had seen swarming upstream on May 2.[30]

Sedgwick had sent three divisions across the river—not just the two (or possibly only one) that Early thought might be on the western bank. One of these divisions faced Early's men in the upper bridgehead; one was between Deep Run and Hazel Run. While it was still dark, the third of Sedgwick's divisions entered Fredericksburg from the south, driving out Barksdale's men. Immediately, Federal pontoniers prepared to lay a bridge across the stream near the town.[31]

Thus, on May 3, Barksdale became aware of mounting danger before Early did. The worried Mississippian had slept but little; at one point, when an officer asked if he was asleep, Barksdale fairly shouted, "No, sir! Who could sleep with a million of armed Yankees around him?"

Before dawn, he sought out Early and woke him up with news of the Union activity in and around Fredericksburg, and lodged a complaint about the weakness of his position on Marye's Heights above the town. There, where Barksdale told Early he expected the main attack, the Confederates held a three-mile front with only 1,500 infantrymen. Early told Barksdale he could have Hays's brigade, to be posted in whatever way he thought best. One of Hays's regiments went to reinforce Barksdale's right. Four regiments of the Louisianians were placed on Barksdale's far left, where they linked up with the Alabama Brigade of Brig. Gen. Cadmus M. Wilcox, which had been detached from Anderson's division and ordered on May 1 by Lee to guard Banks Ford.[32]

Jubal, who still thought the main Union attack would fall on his right, did not believe he could spare more than a brigade to reinforce Barksdale, whose men held the strongest section of the line, anchored in the sunken road on Marye's Heights; here Burnside had wasted his army in December. To a logical mind like Jubal's, it would have seemed farcically unlikely that the Federals would make that horrible mistake again. Accordingly, he placed his strength where he sensed the likeliest danger. The brigades of Smith, Gordon, and Hoke (in that order from right to left), aggregating about 6,100 men, occupied the right end of the line on a front of about two miles—about one man per yard. For lack of manpower, there was a gap between the left of Hoke's brigade and Barksdale's right, covered by guns sited to lay a cross fire. (Early had by now recalled all the artillery withdrawn on May 2, and could deploy 48 pieces.)[33]

Unexpectedly, the first Federal attack, launched around 4:00 A.M. on May 3, aimed a brigade straight up Marye's Heights toward the sunken road and the stone wall, where it met with a jolting and costly repulse. This failed attempt (by the Third Brigade of Maj. Gen. John Newton's 3d Division) might have puzzled Early and his men: was it the main assault, or just a heavy demonstration? But its outcome cheered them, as did news from Chancellorsville of a great Confederate success there. Jackson, it seemed, had executed his flanking maneuver and surprised Hooker. With his three divisions, Jackson had scattered one of Hooker's corps and was sweeping rapidly ahead. Nightfall stopped his advance on Hooker's headquarters at Chancellorsville and contributed to the accidental shooting that was to end Stonewall's life.[34]

As the morning brightened, Early peered anxiously across the river from his position on the right, expecting to see blueclad hosts in busy martial motion. He was startled to see instead that Stafford Heights was "bare of troops." This picture, so different from the crowded scenes of previous days and from what he had expected, persuaded Early that the great majority of the Federals in the Fredericksburg neighborhood were on his side of the river, getting ready to attack him, probably on the right. The largest Union force he could see was a contingent, supported by many guns, in the vicinity of Deep Run. These troops attracted

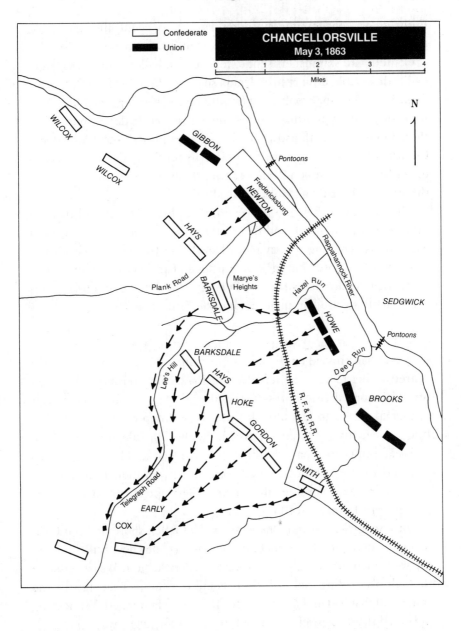

Early's most concentrated attention, since they could, by penetrating the gap between Barksdale and Hoke, split his command in two.

Confederate skirmishers sent to feel out the Federals on the far right had little trouble driving back Union soldiers of the 1st Division under Brig. Gen. William Brooks. But Southerners advancing near Deep Run were stopped, supporting Early's conviction that Federal troops were there in great strength and would be the spearhead of the main attack. Confirmation came when the Deep Run force, the Federal 2d Division under Brig. Gen. Albion P. Howe, started pushing up the ravine cut by the stream, threatening Hoke's brigade.[35]

The threat was thwarted by the terrain as Howe discovered that the movement he intended, and that Early feared, could not be executed without also crossing the ravine of Hazel Run (the other creek tributary), which exposed his flank to musket and artillery fire from Hoke's men. Meanwhile, Barksdale and Pendleton reported at frequent intervals that all was well on their sector of the line.

« BUT ALL was far from quiet. Around 10:00 A.M., a Federal column that had crossed on the newly laid pontoon bridges near the town started trying to turn the left flank of Barksdale's position. This column, Gibbon's division, was frustrated by having to cross two branches of a canal whose 30 feet of width and six-foot depth were spanned by bridges recently rendered impassable by the Confederates. The Federals' attempts to repair the bridges came just as Hays's regiments assigned to the Confederate left were filing into their trenches. No sooner were they in position than their artillery opened fire on the repair parties, which were forced to retire.[36]

Both Sedgwick's turning movements had fallen short, and the Confederate center and left seemed to be holding. But now Early noticed the movement of Howe's men toward Fredericksburg. Was it possible that, all else failing, Sedgwick was going to beat his head against the stone wall that had undone Burnside? It seemed farfetched. Yet nothing indicated that Sedgwick was about to break off and go away.

It was as hard as ever to figure out what the Federals were up to. For all the bustling movement of Union troops and the continual banging of artillery on both sides, there was a strange, menacing inconclusiveness that hung over events and bothered Early mightily. He sent an aide, Lt. William G. Callaway, spurring off to Lee's Hill to find out what was happening on Barksdale's front, which had never been far from Jubal's thoughts all day despite the seeming unlikeliness of a Federal attack there.[37]

Time trickled by. Checking his watch—how long had that infernal Callaway been gone?—Early noticed that it was nearly 11:00 A.M. Impatient for news and worried about Callaway's protracted absence, he hastened to Lee's Hill to see for himself what was happening. From behind, as he rode, he could hear the hurrying hoofbeats of a horse, which soon overtook his. The rider gasped out terrible news: the Union colors were flying from atop Willis's Hill, between Marye's Heights and Lee's Hill! Had the rider seen the flag with his own eyes? No, he had heard about it from someone else, who had seen the colors.

This was undiluted hearsay, impossible to believe without direct, independent corroboration. The general urged his mount forward. But now Early encountered another rider, a courier from Pendleton, whose information seemed to cast doubt on the secondhand account of Union triumph: Lee's artillery chief wrote that the Federals had been driven back, that the line was holding.

The comfort Early got from learning this lasted only a moment. Callaway, finally returning, galloped up to relate that he had left Barksdale and Pendleton on Lee's Hill convinced that they could hold on to their position; but as he had made his way down the hill to rejoin the general, he had seen the enemy ascending Marye's Heights, in the act of capturing the position.

Here, in this unforeseen Union success against terrible odds, was the nightmare specter of a defeat for Early. Many commanders might have quailed—thinking only (or primarily) of simply getting out, of avoiding annihilation. But Jubal was aroused. He was determined to make as much of a fight as he could, and there would be no panic. Callaway was ordered away to tell Gordon to bring three regiments northward along the ridge. The general himself galloped southward on the Telegraph Road to stop anyone fleeing in that direction. (Maj. Andrew Pitzer,

Early's aide, had watched the unfolding Confederate crisis from Lee's Hill; on his own, he turned his horse and rode furiously off to the west, to warn General Lee of what had happened.)[38]

‹‹ AHEAD OF Early on Telegraph Road, clouds of dust, the clatter of hooves, and the rumble of caisson and gun-carriage wheels revealed whole batteries of Pendleton's artillery in full retreat. Above the din, the startled gunners heard Jubal's terrible treble voice damning them and ordering them to halt. With no time to gauge the effect of his order, the general galloped on—finally encountering Barksdale a mile or so to the rear of Lee's Hill. Though his Mississippians were somewhat scattered, Barksdale's force could rally around the 6th Louisiana, the regiment from Hays's brigade, still more or less intact, that had been placed on Barksdale's right flank.[39]

It was from him that Early now probably got a coherent idea of what had happened on that supposedly impregnable sector of the line above the town. After their initial early morning failure against the stone wall on Marye's Heights and the lower slopes of Willis's Hill, the Federals had asked for a flag of truce to recover wounded; the request had been granted by an inattentive Mississippi regimental commander without informing Barksdale. During the cease-fire, the Union soldiers got a glimpse of Confederate weakness as members of the skeleton force (total strength: 900 muskets) showed themselves.

The next Union rush, made both frontally and on the flank by 15 regiments, carried the stone wall position, though at terrible cost. (In both attacks, Sedgwick lost seven percent of his corps, around 1,500 men.) Sweeping on to the summits of Marye's Heights and Willis's Hill, the Federals captured many prisoners and numerous guns, notably some pieces belonging to the proud Washington Artillery of New Orleans. Once the key to the position was in their hands, the Federals quickly moved on to overrun Lee's Hill.[40]

Rallying on the Louisianians and rounding up the Mississippians, Early and Barksdale eventually established a line on good defensive ground at Cox's farm, some two miles behind their original ridge-line position. Smith and Hoke had held on in the old trenches on the right when the left and center collapsed; but since their line could be enfiladed from Lee's Hill, Early pulled them back to Cox's. Gordon, changing direction after starting out to join the general at Lee's Hill, instead rendezvoused at Cox's with the rest of the division, which was reforming in good order by 2:30 P.M. as Hays also reported with the remainder of his brigade.[41]

≪ THUS JUBAL EARLY had scraped through. Under the circumstances, his command was as well off as he had any right to expect. But there were two major blemishes on any optimistic outlook he might have adopted (had he been so disposed). One was the fact that Sedgwick now stood between him and Lee, negating a principal purpose of Early's mission. The other was his essential vulnerability. Jubal did not know Sedgwick's precise numerical advantage, but a guess of more than two to one would have been accurate: Sedgwick had more than 20,000 men to face Early's 10,000 or so.

Tactically, Sedgwick had Early in the bag. The New Englander could have defeated, neutralized, or dispersed the Confederates in his front and made a shambles of Lee's supplies and communications. That done, Sedgwick could then have marched on Lee's rear and executed his end of Hooker's master plan in relative security.[42]

Over the next few hours, two circumstances, both hidden at the time from Jubal Early, intervened to cancel these Union advantages. Perhaps the most important was the relentless pressure that Hooker, through his chief of staff Maj. Gen. Daniel Butterfield, was putting on Sedgwick. Repeated messages, each more urgent than the last, commanded Sedgwick to march to Chancellorsville and smash Lee's rear. Under this pressure, Sedgwick was forced to ignore the hallowed military principle that the leader of a successful attack should finish off— or at least paralyze—the force he has just broken through. In midafternoon, following a brief rest but not waiting to assemble all his divisions, Sedgwick dutifully set off up the Plank Road to the west with just one division—Newton's. Howe and Brooks were ordered to follow; Gibbon was left to occupy Fredericksburg.[43]

Here entered the other saving factor: Confederate Brig. Gen. Cadmus Marcellus Wilcox. His assignment was to guard Banks Ford. But early on May 3, he had personally observed the Federal troops guarding the ford on their side of the river getting ready to move out. According to Lee's orders, as long as Wilcox left a picket to keep an eye on the ford, the Union withdrawal would free him to maneuver elsewhere.

Though his brigade was not under Early's command, Wilcox was in touch with Hays's regiments posted on Barksdale's extreme left. Under mounting pressure, Barksdale had asked Wilcox as well as Hays to send regiments to reinforce the heights. Both commanders had done so, but by the time the regiments had gotten well under way, Barksdale's position had been overrun. Wilcox, riding with the 10th Alabama Regiment, chosen for the reinforcement mission, had received another request from Barksdale after the collapse: join him and Hays and fall back down the Telegraph Road to concentrate on Early.

Outranking Barksdale, and under Lee's direct orders rather than Early's, Wilcox politely declined. From where he was sitting his horse when he got Barksdale's request around noon, Wilcox could see Sedgwick's men advancing from Fredericksburg toward him—and Chancellorsville. Wilcox elected to fall back slowly to the west up the Plank Road, delaying the enemy as much as possible. Sedgwick, initially marching with only the one division, which had spent a hard morning fighting, advanced with caution.

Wilcox's decision was thus absolutely correct. "I felt confident if forced to retire along the Plank Road," he later reported, "that I could do so without precipitancy, and that ample time could be given for reenforcements to reach us from Chancellorsville; and moreover, I believed that, should the enemy pursue, he could be attacked in rear by General Early, reenforced by Generals Hays and Barksdale."

Wilcox, therefore, took over Early's mission of protecting Lee's rear. Meanwhile, Sedgwick—in responding to Hooker's pressure—acted hastily, dispersed his own force (rather than Early's), and ultimately lost his chance either of neutralizing Early or of hitting Lee's rear.[44]

Lee recognized the grave threat that Sedgwick, if left alone, still posed. Alerted by Major Pitzer, the Confederate commander detached four brigades from his effort to finish off Hooker and sent them east under McLaws to oppose Sedgwick on the Plank Road. Meeting Wilcox in his latest defensive position on a low ridge near Salem Church, these

< 158 >

formations awaited a Union attack by Sedgwick, who now deployed two divisions; this assault went in around 5:15 P.M., and was soundly repulsed. A Confederate counterattack then drove Sedgwick's men back more than a mile. By 6:30, the fighting was over. When darkness fell, the quiet of exhaustion settled over the front.[45]

Lee, correctly gauging that Hooker was immobilized on the Chancellorsville front, now decided that he might do more than simply guard his rear; there was a chance, he felt, to destroy Sedgwick. Leaving Stuart with three divisions to keep an eye on Hooker, he ordered Anderson's division to join McLaws at Salem Church. To Early, he sent a dispatch (arriving around 10:00 P.M.) regretting the loss of Fredericksburg and sounding a call for a joint attack by Early with McLaws against Sedgwick. If Anderson were to add his strength to that of the other divisions, the total would be about 23,000 against Sedgwick's 19,000—fair odds for a decisive undoing of the 6th Corps. "I think," wrote Lee, "that you should be more than a match for the enemy."[46] The attack on Sedgwick that finally took shape on May 4 was largely Early's work, partly Anderson's. McLaws had little to do with it; Lee, deciding he was out of his depth, assigned him a supporting role.

Early's division began the operation at dawn by recapturing the heights above Fredericksburg, which were lightly defended. Jubal next contemplated an advance into the broken, hilly terrain north and west of the town, where Sedgwick had withdrawn his force and formed a horseshoe perimeter covering Banks's and Scott's fords. But Early had to wait through most of the day before launching this move so that it could be coordinated with an advance by Anderson, whose division consumed many hours getting into position. When the assault resumed, scant minutes of daylight remained; though the twilight combat was fierce, all action ceased shortly after dark.

During the night, Sedgwick pulled his corps back across the river over pontoon bridges he had ordered laid at Scott's Ford. Gibbon withdrew his division from the town across the bridges there. By Wednesday, May 6, in a dismal rain, the last of Hooker's force was recrossing the Rappahannock—beaten, but largely intact.

<< ROBERT E. LEE's situation as the Chancellorsville campaign began had not been advantageous. He faced a Union army numbering 133,000 men, more than twice his strength of about 60,000. Because of this, the Federals had the initiative. The Confederate supply situation verged on the desperate.[47]

Lee was naturally ignorant of the most threatening element of his predicament: Hooker's plan of offensive, which was excellent. His scheme was to keep Lee guessing by demonstrating on the Fredericksburg front with three corps under Sedgwick. With all or part of his remaining four corps, the Union commander would cross the Rappahannock and approach Lee's rear. If Lee turned to deal with the main body, according to the plan, Sedgwick would attack at Fredericksburg and strike Lee's rear. Hooker actually hoped that Sedgwick would keep Lee so busy and preoccupied that he would not even notice Hooker bearing down on him from the west.

Whichever arm of the pincers drew blood first, Hooker avowed that he would either make Lee "ingloriously fly or come out from behind his defenses and give us battle on our own ground where certain destruction awaits him." If Lee should retreat, Hooker's cavalry, which he had detached to make a grand raid in the Confederate rear, would tie up the retiring Southerners long enough for the Federals to break through Lee's rear guard and force a surrender. Hooker was anticipating Appomattox.[48]

But he was no Grant. Hooker never delivered on his plan. After crossing the Rappahannock, instead of advancing out of the Wilderness into relatively open country and attacking Lee, he halted at the great thicket's edge, waiting for Lee to attack him. And instead of unleashing Sedgwick with 60,000 men (against what turned out to be no more than 11,000 under Early), Hooker siphoned troops away from Sedgwick's front. And he waited to order Sedgwick forward until he himself, tied in knots, was reeling under the attack that Lee, having seized the initiative, duly made.

Lee, perhaps with some advice from Jubal, had read Hooker aright and acted accordingly. After Hooker stalled in the Wilderness, Lee intimidated him and came close to defeating him despite the Federals'

< 160 >

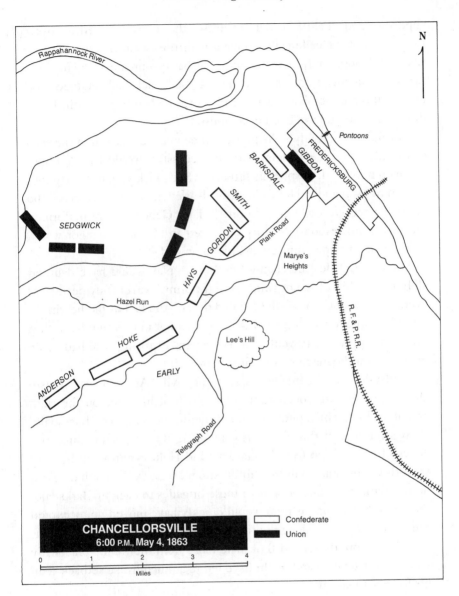

N

Rappahannock River

Pontoons

FREDERICKSBURG

GIBBON

BARKSDALE

SMITH

SEDGWICK

GORDON

Plank Road

Marye's
Heights

HAYS

Hazel Run

R. F. & P. R.R.

HOKE

Lee's Hill

ANDERSON

EARLY

Telegraph Road

CHANCELLORSVILLE
6:00 P.M., May 4, 1863

Confederate
Union

0   1   2   3   4
Miles

superior force. That Lee did not do so, that he was forced to divert troops from Chancellorsville to cope with the threat Sedgwick eventually did pose, only demonstrates the basic soundness of Hooker's plan—as distinct from its execution. If Sedgwick had retained control of all three—or even two—of the corps he had begun with, Lee's difficulties would have been bottomless.[49]

So would Jubal Early's. As things turned out, he was spared the serious trouble that the Federal plan, if successful, would have brought down on him. And, despite his setback at Sedgwick's hands, Early conducted himself and led his troops as well as ever. He truly deserved the praise he received in Lee's report: "Major General Early performed the important responsible duty entrusted to him in a manner which reflected credit upon himself and his command."[50]

The critical role Lee counted on him to play would have daunted all but a handful of senior generals in the army. Never truly perturbed even at the worst times—the garbled orders, the loss of the heights— Jubal had to cope with a situation that was not only intimidating but highly complicated. It would not have been surprising if he had made mistakes; but he made no significant error.

Hindsight would generate its share of cavils. An obvious criticism charged Early with concentrating too much of his force on the right end of his line, which put an excessive defensive burden on Barksdale. Early's rebuttal of this charge is convincing. On the right, three brigades of his division (Smith, Gordon, and Hoke) confronted units of the 6th Corps that he judged to be stronger. Early contended that if he had withdrawn one or more of these brigades to back up Barksdale, the Union troops on his right would quickly have moved up, occupied the vacated position along the ridge and then hit him in the rear. This would have pried him and Barksdale loose from their line "practically without a struggle," and might have led to a much worse setback than his force actually suffered.

As it was, Sedgwick tried his best to avoid the frontal attack—heretofore suicidal—on Marye's Heights, by moving, without success, to outflank that position. It was only as a last resort that Sedgwick violated logic and good sense by imitating Burnside.[51]

Because Lee's rear and its protection were of such prime importance

< 162 >

to Early's mission, Jubal was frustrated when, after losing the heights, he lost his capacity to perform that service. But this circumstance, which was only temporary, was allowed for in Lee's plans. Critics such as James Longstreet were to accuse Early of dereliction in retiring southward down the Telegraph Road, claiming that this was why Lee had to "take Anderson and McLaws from his battle at Chancellorsville to drive back the force threatening his rear." This comment, with its implication of confusion and panic in Early's pullback, was unfounded. Lee's orders to Early were clear: if driven off the heights, he was specifically instructed to withdraw southward and cover the supplies and the railroad. That is just what Jubal did, until he was able to reorganize his command and advance once more to recover the lost ground.[52]

<< LEE'S PROGRAM for May 5 called for a reconcentration of his army and a renewed assault on Hooker. But Fighting Joe had had enough. Lee's scouts, probing north of Chancellorsville early on May 6, found no trace of Federals on the west side of the Rappahannock. Jubal, eventually returning to his old position near Fredericksburg, totted up his losses: in his division, 125 killed, 721 wounded, 500 captured or missing—16 percent of his command. Barksdale counted 45 dead, 181 wounded, and more than 300 prisoners and stragglers, most captured in the Union assault on Marye's Heights.

Lee had not destroyed the Army of the Potomac. But, though Lee's overall losses (12,229) constituted a far greater proportion of his army than Hooker's (15,818, including 5,919 prisoners), the Army of Northern Virginia had won a great victory. No one could doubt it. Yet the Confederates' pride and elation were tempered by the realization that they had paid a fateful price for their triumph. The worst truly did lie ahead, as Early had always felt. The future might now seem distilled in the fall, through mischance, of Lee's most formidable general. "[O]ur rejoicings," Jubal wrote, "over the brilliant and important victory that had been gained were soon dampened by the sad news of the death of General Jackson."[53]

< 163 >

CHAPTER ELEVEN

Watch Charm Victory

*I*N MID-JULY 1863, Early's division formed part of the spearhead
leading Lee's invasion of the North—a movement from Fredericksburg down the Shenandoah Valley that was to unfold as the Gettysburg
campaign. With this initiative, Lee counted on one strategic result and
hoped for three others. He was certain that Virginia could no longer
feed his men and horses; there was no question that Pennsylvania could
fill those needs, at least for the time necessary to get the 1863 crops
established south of the Potomac. More problematical was the goal of
defending Richmond by drawing the Federals away from it and forcing
them to defend their own capital. Lee and others fostered a notion that
bringing war into the North might nourish an apparently burgeoning
antiwar sentiment; this goal seemed almost visionary, but it was worth
the attempt. Finally, it was possible that a successful outcome of the
campaign would induce such powers as Britain and France to recognize
the Confederacy and lend support.[1]

These rather bleak strategic considerations signified far less to General Early than his own immediate military prospects. On July 14, riding
through a grassy field near Winchester, in the Valley of Virginia, he was
already savoring the expectation of a tactical tour de force. That day
he led his men across country west of the town, which was in Federal
hands. The cross-lots route he was taking was essential to a scheme
aimed at surprising a Union fort, key to Winchester's defenses; but the
unmarked approach entailed the risk of getting the column badly lost.
The general rode along the line of march to his favorite regiment, the
13th Virginia, and asked its commander, Col. James B. Terrill, for a

scouting party of an officer and 20 men. The colonel recommended Company H, under Capt. Samuel Buck, whose members were from Winchester, and knew the country.

Captain Buck fell in beside the general's horse at the head of the column, marching along and chatting. As they walked, the captain's orderly sergeant, James Haymaker, called out to the general, reminding him that all Company H's men lived nearby, "and would do the work up clean if he would let us go and see our girls." Buck recounted that "the general laughed, and said he would see about it."

Careful on this occasion to the point of fussiness, Early augmented the expertise of Buck and his men with the guidance of a civilian gentleman from the vicinity named James Baker, who withdrew when the column reached its destination, a low wooded ridge west of the town. Ordering the troops to get some rest following their ten-mile march in blistering heat, Early took Captain Buck and his company off on a reconnaissance. Buck was told, as he remembered, "to deploy the company as skirmishers and find out, without bringing on a battle, the position of the enemy."

To avoid a fight, Buck himself carefully moved forward 50 yards in front of the company line, from the woods into an orchard. Soon, he looked down on three earthen enemy forts: one was near the town, the second in front of and closer to the ridge he was on, the third over to the left on the other side of a road leading from Winchester to Pughtown. In the nearest fort, the Federals were still strengthening the earthworks.

Buck drew some fire, and started back to report what he had seen to Jubal. The general was anxious to see for himself, and Buck guided him to the point in the orchard where he had made his observations. Eager to see more, Early ordered Buck to pull the top rails off a fence at the edge of the orchard. The captain warned Jubal of the danger, but did as he was told.

Trying, under Jubal's enthusiastic spur, to jump the lowered fence from a halt, his horse half refused, landing with front legs on one side and hind quarters on the other. Buck remembered that in

this "healthy" position, the enemy saw us and the way the bullets whizzed about us is still indelibly impressed in my mind, and the

way the General lifted his horse back from the fence convinced
me that he was satisfied and we both retreated to the edge of
the woods, he cursing the Yankees at every step. Turning to me
sharply, he said, "Buck, you stay here with your men and watch
this point, reporting any move of the enemy and I will relieve you."
As he rode off he again turned and began to curse the Yankees,
saying, "I will attend to them. You wait until you hear my signal
gun and you will see some fun from this point."

In the excitement of the next few hours, Jubal forgot to relieve Buck
and his men. But he did deliver the "fun" he had promised—as well
giving the 13th Virginia a reward for its service on this day, June 14,
1863: assignment as the garrison of Winchester after its capture from
the Federals in what was to be the opening phase of the invasion of
Pennsylvania and the Gettysburg campaign. The 13th Virginia Regiment would be spared that trial.[2]

« AT WHAT many would see as the high point of Confederate fortunes,
Jubal Early could scarcely lose for winning. And in conception, execution, and results, his role in the Second Battle of Winchester would
represent one of the most satisfying episodes of Early's entire military
career. It is true that the combat of June 14 was comparatively small in
scale, and that Early acted not alone but in coordination with others.
(He was serving under a familiar and congenial commander, Richard
Ewell, who had campaigned over the same Valley terrain with Stonewall Jackson the year before and knew the layout intimately.) Besides,
the Federals proved inept and comparatively feeble. Yet the action,
particularly from Jubal's point of view, was a jewel of an operation.
Its glitter reflected the noonday morale of his men (following Chancellorsville) no less than the radiance of his own professional and martial
qualities and those of his officers.

For Ewell, the fight and its outcome were of great significance. In
his handling of the 2d Corps in its first action since Jackson's death,
he found his achievements compared favorably with those of the great
Stonewall himself.[3]

« THE DEATH of Thomas Jackson had faced Robert E. Lee with an intractable problem: how to replace him. In the general reorganization of the Army of Northern Virginia following Hooker's defeat on the Rappahannock, Lee sifted the available personnel. Among several candidates for Stonewall's mantle, he decided on Richard Ewell, recovered from his Groveton wound and amputation well enough, it appeared, to ride his horse and stump around adequately on a wooden leg, sometimes with the aid of crutches and sometimes not. Ewell would take over Jackson's old corps, newly designated the 2d in a realigned three-corps army. (In the new table of organization, James Longstreet became commander of the 1st Corps, and A. P. Hill of the 3d.)

Ewell, a wiry fellow, may have recovered from the physical effects of his wound, but its effects on his mind were harder to gauge. A rival of Jubal Early in his eccentricities of appearance and speech (he had a lisp), Old Bald Head also challenged Early as a master of profanity until, in the spring of 1863, he ended a lifelong bachelorhood by marrying the forceful widow Lizinka Brown, an old friend. Under her influence, he gave up swearing (which spawned jokes about Ewell's subservience to commanders other than Robert E. Lee). He also renounced his intolerance, long shared with Early, of spouses traveling with their officer husbands on campaign. As a newly married man, Ewell showed his respect for his helpmeet—as well as a certain absentmindedness—in his manner of introducing her: "My wife, Mrs. Brown, sir." [4]

As ill tempered as Early on occasion, Ewell was also truly kind of heart, more openly generous than Jubal; his men worshiped him notwithstanding his relentless marching and strictness about baggage. "We can get along," he said, "without everything but food and ammunition."

As a soldier, his best qualities were reliability and pugnacity. Nor did anyone dispute Ewell's scrappiness, intelligence, and charisma. But there were questions about his qualities of leadership: unlike Jubal, who had been given independence in greater and greater measure, Ewell, serving under the occasionally baffling but invariably exacting supervision of Stonewall, had comparatively little experience with self-directed operations. He was not accustomed to acting without explicit orders. Would he now show that he had the initiative required to manage a corps—a formation that was larger in the Confederate army than in the Union?[5]

From Jubal Early's point of view, Ewell's appointment as successor to Jackson was a piece of very good fortune. From Malvern Hill through Second Manassas, Ewell seems to have marked Early as an able and combative soldier, a man after his own heart; Ewell had supported Early as his successor in command of the division Jubal had led during Ewell's long medical leave.[6]

<< THE ROUTE of Richard Ewell's corps down the Valley was blocked by a 9,000-man Federal division under Maj. Gen. Robert H. Milroy. As Early probably knew, Milroy was hated by the local citizenry (who referred to him as "the Dog of the Virginia Valley") for his aggressive and highhanded treatment of civilians. Milroy dealt with the Valley inhabitants as he thought they deserved; he suspected them of supporting if not actively engaging in guerrilla warfare against his force.[7]

Besides Early's division, Ewell's corps consisted of two other divisions, led by Maj. Gen. Robert E. Rodes (promoted for services under Jackson at Chancellorsville) and Maj. Gen. Edward Johnson, an unknown quantity as far as Ewell was concerned; both were able if somewhat colorless. The corps also marched with the cavalry brigade of Brig. Gen. A. G. Jenkins, and with a battalion of artillery under Lt. Col. H. P. Jones.[8]

Nearing Winchester on June 13, Ewell knew the ground well enough to make shrewd decisions as to the positioning and assignment of his divisions. Armed with intelligence that Milroy had placed a detachment in Berryville, east of Winchester (presumably to guard against an approach from that direction) Ewell dispatched Rodes, with Jenkins's cavalry, to seize that town. Johnson was ordered to follow the main road from Front Royal straight on to Winchester. For Early, the script was far more interesting. Knowing that the fortifications of Winchester were dominated by high ground to the west of town, Ewell sent his old division in that direction.[9]

All day on the 13th, Early maneuvered the division closer to his objective. "The troops"—and presumably Early too, though he does not say so—"then lay down on their arms and spent the night in a drench-

< 168 >

ing rain." First thing in the morning, Early ordered Hays and Gordon forward to seize a height called Bower's Hill, from which he had a view of Winchester and the terrain to its north and west. The weather had cleared; visibility was good. As Jubal was sweeping the landscape with his field glasses, Ewell joined him. The two discovered immediately that the high ground Ewell had ordered Early to take as a way of overcoming the defenses of Winchester had itself been fortified. These breastworks, known as the West Fort, thus covered and supported the town's main defenses, called the Flag Fort (its pole sported a large United States garrison flag); in its turn, the Flag Fort was supported by a strong redoubt, called the Star Fort, to the north. Capturing the West Fort from Early's present axis of advance would involve an attack under flanking fire from the Flag Fort. Fortunately, Early knew of yet another patch of ground even higher, and even farther to the west, which dominated the new fortifications and all the other Federal works. From this height, Early told Ewell, the West Fort might be taken—possibly by surprise.[10]

Early received orders to leave a brigade and some guns on Bower's Hill "to amuse" the enemy from there; with his other three brigades— those of Smith, Hays, and Hoke (the latter under the command of Col. Isaac E. Avery)—Jubal was to make his way by a roundabout route to the high ground he had picked out, from which he could theoretically open the defenses of Winchester like a can of sardines. If this move were successful, Johnson would then hurry to cut off Milroy's retreat. When it was all over, the 2d Corps would have swept the Valley clear of organized Federal force.

Gordon, with two batteries of guns and a contingent of Maryland troops (who had been ordered to join Early on his approach march),[11] remained on Bower's Hill. The balance of the division, with several batteries under Colonel Jones himself, moved leftward, some of the way on the road, much of it off, guided by Mr. Baker and Captain Buck's Company H. No sign of the Federals was seen along the route.[12]

To protect his rear, Early detached the 54th North Carolina Regiment. He posted it where the field his division had been crossing abutted the intersection of the Romney Turnpike with a farm track leading north. This rough route gave onto the high ground from which the attack would be launched.[13] Arriving there, Early found a wooded position that would be excellent for concealing men and guns until they were ready for attack, and well within artillery range of the objective.[14]

The woods ran down to the base of the hill surmounted by the West Fort. An orchard at one end of Early's position and a cornfield at the other offered excellent sites for the Confederate batteries, which could be deployed to lay a converging fire on the fort.

In Jubal's reconnaissance, as recounted by him, he saw no pickets facing in his direction, nor even any lookouts watching his ridge. (This contradicts, or at least departs from, Buck's account, which speaks of flying Yankee bullets. Buck's reminiscences, written long after the fact, may have incorporated some embroidery on actual events, though Buck seems a reliable witness overall. Early, for his part, always played down his personal reaction to enemy fire; in this instance, he may have decided it was unworthy of mention.)[15] He did note that the Federals' attention seemed riveted on Gordon's position on Bower's Hill, which they were slowly approaching with skirmishers and a body of infantry.[16]

As Jubal was reconnoitering, Colonel Jones was placing his guns at the edge of the woods, where they could be pushed into the open by hand at the proper moment. After a brief rest, the men of Hays's brigade were moved down to the edge of the woods at the bottom of the West Fort hill, within 1,000 yards of the objective.[17] Hays was ordered to keep everyone hidden and quiet until the artillery opened fire, then move to the attack when he felt that the defenders were sufficiently softened up by shot and shell.

All this took time—until late afternoon. When all was ready, around 5:30 P.M., Jones ordered the gunners to run his 20 pieces into firing position; almost instantly, they all opened fire on the West Fort. Forty-five minutes of concentrated gunnery—answered by generally inaccurate counterfire—pounded the defenders before Hays led his brigade out of the woods, across a small field, and up the West Fort hill. Emitting their "terrible, long shrill [rebel] yells" as they ascended, the Louisianians had to negotiate an abatis, but they reached the top in good order, entered the fort and seized it, capturing some of the defenders and six guns.[18]

Two of the captured artillery pieces were turned on Union troops ad-

< 170 >

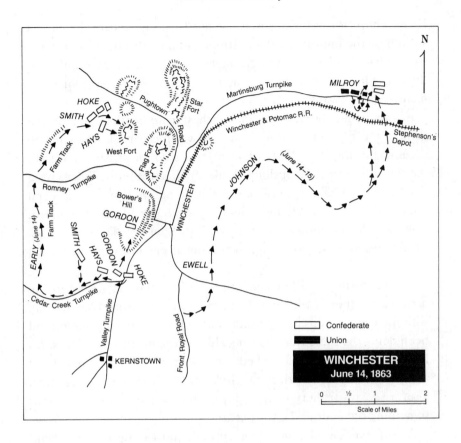

N

HOKE
SMITH
Pughtown
Star Fort
Martinsburg Turnpike
MILROY
HAYS
Farm Track
Winchester & Potomac R.R.
West Fort
Flag Fort
Stephenson's Depot
Romney Turnpike
WINCHESTER
JOHNSON
(June 14-15)
Bower's Hill
GORDON
EARLY (June 14)
Farm Track
SMITH
GORDON
HAYS
HOKE
EWELL
Cedar Creek Turnpike
Valley Turnpike
Front Royal Road
KERNSTOWN

☐ Confederate
■ Union

WINCHESTER
June 14, 1863

0   ½   1   2
Scale of Miles

vancing from the Flag Fort to support the victims of Hays's onslaught. The gunfire drove these reinforcements back.

Most of the Federals in the West Fort withdrew under Hays's attack. As the Louisianians entered the fort, Early sent Smith's brigade forward in support. He told Jones to move some of his pieces into the West Fort, and rode over to take a look at the captured hill himself. The general could see that the Federal troops who had been advancing toward Gordon on Bower's Hill had abandoned that enterprise and taken to their heels.[19]

From his position with Johnson, Ewell tried to keep track of what was happening over at the West Fort. Eyes bleary from constant peering through his field glasses, he fancied he saw Jubal standing on the parapet. "Hurrah for the Louisiana boys!" Ewell shouted. "There's

Early! I hope the old fellow won't be hurt!" At that instant, Ewell was shaken by the impact of a bullet striking him in the chest—but it was a spent ball that left only a black and blue mark. Dr. Hunter McGuire, the corps medical director, aiming to make Ewell stay still for a few moments, took away the general's crutches.[20]

At this point, the defenses of Winchester were still intact. All the guns in the Flag and Star forts were now turned on the Confederate occupiers of the West Fort—though Jones's dozen pieces, fired from the fort's commanding position, made an effective reply. There were also "masses of infantry" visible in and near the two remaining Federal forts. If these forces held their ground, Jubal believed that their defeat would call for a coordinated attack by all three of Ewell's divisions. As Jubal pursued these thoughts, darkness put an end to the day's action.[21]

<< WHILE EARLY had been maneuvering and then attacking in the northwest corner of the field, Johnson had been skirmishing actively with the Union troops in the eastern edge of the town, and Gordon had been doing the same from Bower's Hill. These diversionary measures had apparently distracted the Federals' attention "from the point of real attack," as Early summarized the situation, "which enabled us to effect a surprise with artillery in open day upon a fortified position." It was something right out of the textbooks.

As the evening of June 14 progressed, Jubal came to the conclusion that Milroy was done for. On receiving the news that Johnson was hurrying to cut off the Federal retreat, and that Rodes was en route to seize the Union supply dump 22 miles to the north in Martinsburg, Early perceived that the situation of the Union troops remaining in and around Winchester was untenable. He guessed they would probably try to escape during the night. So did Ewell. (Most of the Federals in Berryville had already gotten away from Rodes and Jenkins.)[22]

At daybreak, it was clear that Milroy's men had pulled out. Early ordered his brigades forward in pursuit along the road to Harpers Ferry. When they reached Stephenson's Depot, some six miles north and east of Winchester, they learned that Johnson had arrived there ahead of the Federals and captured a large fraction of Milroy's command. Mil-

< 172 >

roy himself, with a few men, had escaped, riding through the night to Harpers Ferry on the backs of mules and horses unhitched from guns and wagons. Jubal ordered the pursuit abandoned.[23] Johnson kept it up for a time; though he was dumped into Opequon Creek when his horse stepped in a hole, he later claimed that he had captured 30 men "with his opera glass." [24]

« EARLY'S ACCOUNT of this affair, written in his matter-of-fact prose, scarcely conceals the glee he must have felt at the time and forever after. He was not alone. Normally taciturn, Maj. Jed Hotchkiss, Ewell's (formerly Jackson's) indispensable topographical engineer and map-maker, expressed the universal elation when he wrote his wife on June 15: "This has been one of the most complete successes of the war; our men behaved splendidly." [25]

In their own honor, the men fashioned a Confederate flag out of a number of captured Stars and Stripes, then ran it up the flagpole of the main fort. Early and Ewell, celebrating together in Winchester on the 16th, frolicked with the town's ladies, who waved their handkerchiefs in delight at the deliverance of their town. Asked to say a few words, the ex-bachelor Ewell lisped, "I can't make a speech to ladies. I never made a speech to but one lady in my life. My friend General Early can speak. He will address you ladies." Jubal, the persistent bachelor, had his rejoinder on the tip of his tongue: "I have never been able to make a speech to one lady," he declared, "much less to so many." [26]

As the two generals bantered, the reason for their good humor was manifesting itself in tangible and highly satisfying forms. An escort was marching 3,358 prisoners off to Richmond. Jones and his artillery officers were pondering what to do with the 23 guns, including two 24-pounder howitzers, that had fallen into their hands. The cost of these prizes was a toll of Confederate casualties totaling 269—Early's division having lost 30 killed and 144 wounded.[27]

Ewell departed for Pennsylvania on June 16. He left Early behind to command in Winchester for two days and to organize the mountains of captured matériel in the town. Jubal did his best in this line, depre-cating the value of the effort: "as usual . . . the contents of the wagons and the stores in town were considerably plundered by stragglers and followers of our trains . . . and . . . there was great waste, and perhaps misappropriation . . . as always seemed unavoidable on such occasions."

Since—as Jubal saw it—little would avail against the eternal greed and dishonesty of persons connected with supplies, it must have been much more gratifying for Early to reflect on the beautiful watch charm of a victory just won. Capt. William Seymour of the 6th Louisiana had talked to a captured Yankee colonel who was full of admiration for the flanking maneuver Early had used to take West Fort. Describing this conversation to Jubal, Seymour had "tickled" him by recounting how "the 'Fed' declared that the Johnny Rebs had lied in reporting that Stonewall Jackson was dead—that there was no officer in either army that could have executed that maneuver but 'Old Jack.' " [28]

Maybe so. But had it really settled anything or made any significant difference? It certainly felt decisive enough. Ewell, outnumbering Milroy almost two to one, had expelled the Federals from the Valley. The Northern high command seems to have regarded the outcome as decisive. As the historian Edwin Coddington puts it, Milroy's defeat at Winchester struck the Federals as "a humiliating fiasco which seemed to furnish further proof to the world of the irresistible power of the Army of Northern Virginia."

To Lee, however, the power of his army lay for now largely in its aggressive maneuvering. He valued speed of advance well above Milroy's destruction. Lee had even ordered Ewell not to lay siege to Winchester if it meant delaying his advance northward. If necessary, Ewell was to bypass the town's garrison. (Indeed, Milroy himself seems for a time to have thought that was what would happen.) [29]

Jubal was almost certainly aware of all this. Still, it had been such a great satisfaction to whip the odious Milroy, and do it in such an exemplary fashion. If Jubal hugged the triumph to his bosom, he deserved the pleasure it surely gave him. Certainly he should have savored this victory. Though more significant achievements lay in the future, the June 14 fight at Winchester was to be the ultimate in his unbroken string of clear-cut military successes.

General Jubal A. Early. *Library of Congress*

Jubal's father, Joab Early.
Aleice Pinkerton

Jubal's mother, Ruth H. Early.
Aleice Pinkerton

John D. Imboden (left), a rabid secessionist in 1861, later served under Jubal in the Valley. *Library of Congress* J. E. B. Stuart (right): an acceptable cavalryman in Early's view. *Cook Collection, Valentine Museum, Richmond, Va.*

James Longstreet (left), Lee's "war horse," was Jubal's principal postbellum antagonist. *Cook Collection, Valentine Museum, Richmond, Va.* D. H. Hill (right) was successively Jubal's superior, subordinate, and friend. *Meserve Collection*

Commanding the pugnacious Louisianians, Harry T. Hays (left) was a valued brigade commander. *Cook Collection, Valentine Museum, Richmond, Va.* P. G. T. Beauregard (right), Jubal's first battlefield commander, in peacetime became a friend in need. *Library of Congress*

William Barksdale (left) of the Mississippi Brigade was Jubal's staunch support at Chancellorsville. *Library of Congress* Richard S. Ewell (right), who succeeded Stonewall Jackson, was Early's friend until Jubal succeeded him. *Library of Congress*

Thomas J. Jackson (left) acknowledged Early's contribution to Stonewall's narrow victory at Cedar Mountain in August 1862. *Library of Congress* "Extra Billy" Smith (right), former and future governor, could hardly have enjoyed his service under Early. *Library of Congress*

In September 1862, Confederate troops pause on their march through Frederick, Maryland. *Frederick Historical Society*

Early's West Point classmate, John Sedgwick (left) of Connecticut was a stubborn and perspicacious battlefield antagonist. *Cornwall Historical Society* Cadmus Marcellus Wilcox (right), a little-known Confederate hero at Chancellorsville, helped both Early and Lee emerge triumphant in that battle. *Library of Congress*

"Fighting Joe" Hooker was widely respected—but not by Jubal, who had known him at the Military Academy. *Library of Congress*

A non-West Pointer who ended the war commanding the 2d Corps, John Brown
Gordon (left) was most capable, but underrated by Early. *Library of Congress*
Robert E. Rodes (right) was surprisingly colorless in view of his ability. *Library of
Congress*

Federal Maj. Gen. Robert H. Milroy
became known to inhabitants of
Winchester as "the Dog of the Virginia
Valley." *Library of Congress*

An erratic but resourceful Union cavalryman, William W. Averell (seated), was an occasional Early nemesis. *U.S. Army Military History Institute*

John McCausland (left) was an audacious horseman who followed Jubal's orders and got the job done—up to a point. *West Virginia State Archives* The Texan Thomas L. Rosser (right), a West Point friend of George A. Custer, referred to himself as "Savior of the Valley" in the fall of 1864. *Library of Congress*

"Black Dave" Hunter (left) was fortunate not to have been captured by Early. *Library of Congress* Thomas H. Carter (right) was one of the few subordinates Early never reproached. *Collections of the Virginia Historical Society*

Stephen Dodson Ramseur (left), according to Early, sacrificed his life to save the Valley Army at Cedar Creek in October 1864. *North Carolina Division of Archives and History* George Crook (right) was judged by Early to be one of his most capable wartime adversaries. *Library of Congress*

If not delayed by Lew Wallace (left) and his scratch defense force at Monocacy Junction, Early's Valley Army might have penetrated the defenses of Washington in July 1864. *Library of Congress* Commanding the Union 6th Corps, Horatio G. Wright (right) was unable to prevent Early's army from regaining the Valley after the Washington raid. *Library of Congress*

Jubal's men, withdrawing virtually unmolested after menacing Washington, transport their booty across the Potomac into Virginia. *Library of Congress*

The Maryland home of Francis Blair, an important man in Northern political affairs, was Jubal Early's field headquarters during his foray against Washington. *Library of Congress*

Philip H. Sheridan made numerous mistakes but ended as the author of Jubal's undoing. *Library of Congress*

In August 1864, men of Kershaw's division, covered by artillery in the foreground, march to join Early in the Valley. Smoke marks fires set by orders of the Union command to destroy the region's usefulness as a granary. *Frank and Marie T. Wood Print Collections, Alexandria, Va.*

Fitzhugh Lee (left), who would become governor of Virginia, earned Jubal's respect as a cavalry leader, and the two became good friends. *Library of Congress* John Pegram (right) succeeded to the command of Early's old division after the death of Rodes at Winchester in September 1864. *Library of Congress*

James L. Kemper (left), Early's friend from Mexican War days, was important in postbellum Virginia politics, serving as governor from 1874 to 1877. William Mahone (right), long at odds with Early over politics and Gilded Age business ethics, backed away from a possible duel after he dared attack the lieutenant general's conduct in the Civil War. *Library of Congress*

Robert E. Lee mounted Traveller for this postwar portrait by Michael Miley. *Collections of the Virginia Historical Society*

Jubal Early in old age. *Library of Congress*

PART THREE

CHAPTER TWELVE

Essay in Retribution

CROSSING THE Potomac on June 22, 1863, heading into the enemy's country via Boteler's Ford below Shepherdstown, Jubal Early's division brought up the rear of Ewell's corps, which was still the spearhead of Lee's bold invasion of the North. Just before crossing the river, Jubal calculated his division strength at 5,611 officers and men; he had detached two regiments (besides the 13th Virginia, occupying Winchester) to escort prisoners to Richmond. Supporting his infantry, Early was once again assigned Jones's battalion of artillery, along with the 17th Virginia Cavalry under Col. William H. French. Up ahead, moving through the luxuriant Pennsylvania countryside toward Chambersburg, were the divisions of Edward Johnson and Robert Rodes. To the rear, in columns that stretched all the way back up the Valley to the vicinity of Winchester, the two corps of James Longstreet and A. P. Hill marched toward the Potomac.

The men in ranks—and their officers—were in high spirits that owed much to a sense of vindication. They felt invincible. And they relished treading the sod of a foe whose legions (under the likes of Pope and Milroy) had trampled so harshly on Southern soil. The air they breathed smelled sensuously of vengeance.

With the men in this mood, and since one of the principal purposes of the invasion was the opportunity it offered the Army of Northern Virginia of living off the fat Pennsylvanian land, Robert E. Lee saw that wholesale pillage, and worse, was a great danger. To Lee, the risk lay not only in the moral reprehensibility of marauding and stealing private property (not to mention bodily injury to civilians), though these concerns were important. Even more threatening was the prospect of a complete breakdown of army discipline. Besides, the commanding general hoped that a well-behaved Confederate army that treated civilians decently would help feed antiwar sentiment in the North.

On June 21, three days after Ewell's leading regiments crossed the Potomac, Lee issued strict orders regulating the procurement of supplies while the army was in the North. Under General Orders No. 72, Lee established elaborate procedures for requisitioning and paying for supplies according to local market values. Only certain Confederate officers (e.g., chiefs of ordnance and medical departments) were authorized to requisition property. Civilians who resisted the requisitions risked having their assets seized without cash payment, but even so they were to be given an itemized, priced receipt.[1]

In their thinking about these matters, Lee and many other Civil War generals had recourse to relatively humane rules of war formulated in Europe during the eighteenth century. Under those guidelines, the levying of "contributions" on cities by invading armies was a recognized form of military blackmail. Lee therefore probably had little trouble reconciling his conscience with this approach to procurement, which would be employed repeatedly during the campaign.[2]

In any case, the restrictions of General Orders No. 72 were aimed primarily at maintaining discipline among the soldiers of Lee's army, not at cosseting the citizens of Pennsylvania. The orders explicitly set forth the dangers to the Confederate cause of imitating "the barbarous outrages upon the unarmed and defenseless and the wanton destruction of private property, that have marked the course of the enemy in our own country." The commanding general concluded by exhorting "the troops to abstain with most scrupulous care from unnecessary or wanton injury to private property, and he enjoins upon all officers to arrest and bring to summary punishment all who shall in any way offend against the orders on this subject." Wise, high-minded, and generally effective throughout the army, this directive would not be obeyed with uniform zeal.[3]

‹‹ BY THE 24TH, marching without sight or sign of the enemy, Early's division was camped near the western slope of South Mountain in the hamlet of Greenwood, Pennsylvania, on the road between Chambersburg and Gettysburg. Early soon discovered that Greenwood was the site of the Caledonia Iron Works—a furnace, forges, and a rolling mill, with a storehouse and a sawmill, belonging to Thaddeus Stevens, the Radical Republican congressman. The general and many others in his command knew that Stevens regarded them and all other Confederates as criminal renegades. Perhaps acting on this perception, and probably with at least tacit permission from Early, his men helped themselves to provisions, horses, and other property belonging to Stevens, with little or no effort to comply with General Orders No. 72.[4]

Next day, at Ewell's request, Jubal rode to Chambersburg, where the corps commander, accompanying Rodes's and Johnson's divisions, had his headquarters. There, along with the reinforcement of the 35th Virginia Battalion of cavalry under Col. Elijah V. White, Early received orders based on Lee's instructions to Ewell. Jubal was to take his division over South Mountain and proceed, via Gettysburg, to York. His assignment was to cut the Northern Central Railroad between Baltimore and Harrisburg, and wreck the railroad bridge at Wrightsville, where a branch line crossed the broad Susquehanna on its way from York to Philadelphia. After completing these tasks, the division was to rejoin the rest of the corps in the neighborhood of Carlisle.

For this expedition, the instructions were to travel as light as possible. Early reduced his trains drastically. Only the divisional ambulances and 15 empty wagons were to carry requisitioned supplies; each regiment was permitted but three wagons: one for medical supplies, one for ammunition, and one with cooking equipment. Everything else was to be sent back to Chambersburg. Baggage was reduced to what men and officers could carry on their backs or their saddles.[5]

When it came to impedimenta, this was always the state of affairs most agreeable to Jubal, and his account of the severe requirements (aboard the wagons, "no baggage whatever was allowed for officers") reveals his profound satisfaction with Ewell's orders. All would march and fight as unencumbered as human nature would allow, and would do so for the remainder of the campaign. There is no mistaking the professional satisfaction in Early's tone when he recounts that "we saw no more of our trains until we crossed the Potomac three weeks later."[6]

The division wasted no time breaking camp on the morning of the 26th. But before setting out on the march across South Mountain to Gettysburg and York, Early took time to attend to a chore that must have given him a satisfaction well beyond the professional. He gave his pioneer party—in Early's command a kind of permanent fatigue detail organized to do the division's dirty jobs ("burying dead Yankees and horses")—a pointed order: burn Thaddeus Stevens's iron works.

Early admitted that this was an act of retribution. As such, it was of course a direct violation of Lee's General Orders No. 72. Early never acknowledged that. Moreover, no one ever challenged his flagrant insubordination, though it unequivocally demonstrated that as a senior general he was capable of disobeying orders, even those of Robert E. Lee, if he saw fit.

In his *Autobiographical Sketch*, Early justified the burning as an act of war:

> The enemy had destroyed a number of similar works, as well as manufacturing establishments of different kinds, in those parts of the Southern States to which he had been able to penetrate, upon the plea that they furnished us with the means of carrying on the war, besides burning many private houses and destroying a vast deal of private property which could be employed in no way in supporting the war on our part; and finding in my way these works of Mr. Stevens, who—as a member of the Federal congress—has been advocating the most vindictive measures of confiscation and devastation, I determined to destroy them.

Early asserted his own independent responsibility in burning the factory ("neither General Lee nor General Ewell knew I would encounter these works"). General Early drew a distinction between Stevens's property, which he considered a lawful target, and that of his unoffending employees; their homes, Early said, "were not molested." [7]

That was not strictly true. Then and later, in the course of the campaign, Early's men and other Southerners broke the windows of the workers' houses. But the injury to the employees went far beyond random vandalism, a symptom of indiscipline that Early would hardly have countenanced. Though the bellicose Stevens suffered severely, his was a one-time loss worth perhaps $65,000 (admittedly a lot of money in 1863). But the peaceable workers, some 200 of them, permanently lost their means of earning a living.

General Lee, following Early along the Chambersburg-Gettysburg route, discovered the destruction, and was upset. He told Sweeney that workers and their families who were in need could draw on the army's quartermaster for supplies. But to Early he uttered not one recorded word of rebuke for disobeying his direct orders.

Nor did Richard Ewell ever admonish Early, at least in public. This is somewhat surprising in view of Ewell's own very strict interpretation of General Orders No. 72. One witness to this disciplinary zeal was a member of Jubal's own family—his 15-year-old nephew, John Cabell Early. John, who had been sent by his father Samuel to serve on General Ewell's staff, later recalled seeing four Confederate soldiers of Rodes's division who had been caught stealing vegetables in Carlisle. The culprits were "tied together and marched about the streets with a sign . . . on their backs which read, 'These men have disgraced themselves by pillaging women's gardens.'"[8]

It was raining when the division reached the other side of South Mountain and approached Cashtown. Early had heard that a small enemy force occupied Gettysburg. He determined to bag this garrison. But the Federals, untrained lumps of cannon fodder, ran away at the first approach of hostile troops. Jubal was amused by the sheer rapidity of their withdrawal. "It was as well," Early later reported, "that the regiment took to its heels so quickly, or some of its members might have been hurt, and all would have been captured." Of 750 men in the regiment, all but 175 (claimed as prisoners by Jubal) escaped.[9]

‹‹ UNDEFENDED, Gettysburg was stingy with the bounty the Confederates had expected to find there. The only item in even reasonably adequate supply was a stock of horseshoes and nails, which Early requisitioned in its entirety.

A few of the men, conducting their own search operation, broke into some houses and made off with property whose owners had fled to

Philadelphia. A little way from the railroad station, Early discovered food rations in a train of a dozen cars, issued them to Gordon's brigade, and then set fire to the train and a bridge on the tracks outside the town. Liquor from taverns and storehouses was divided among the men. Some of them, notably the Louisianians, got very drunk.

On June 27, under continuing rain on muddy roads, the worst hangover cases straggled badly on the way to York, 27 miles from Gettysburg. A halt was called a few miles outside York, the strength of whose defenses was unknown.

Not even a company of militia garrisoned York, it turned out; the town was surrendered by a delegation of elders who traveled out to the Confederate camp to offer their submission. Sending his cavalry off to destroy road and rail bridges across the Susquehanna between Hanover Junction and York, Early entered the town, ordering Gordon to keep marching to Wrightsville; there he was to seize the railroad bridge, establish a bridgehead, and wait for the rest of the division to join him.

By Jubal's apparent reckoning, York was ten times as wealthy and important as Gettysburg; on arrival, he demanded payment of $100,000 in addition to massive quantities of hats, shoes, and socks, along with enough food to supply the division for three days. A body of citizens was appointed to work on these demands, which were largely satisfied, though the committee came up short on the money and the shoes. But Early and his quartermaster could rub their hands at their acquisition, among other items, of 3,500 pounds of sugar, 3,000 gallons of molasses, and many tons of fresh beef, bacon, and salt pork. Fifteen hundred pairs of shoes were forthcoming, and bundles of greenbacks worth $28,000—a satisfactory haul under the circumstances.[10]

<< IMPRESSED BY the ease of his movement through the Pennsylvania countryside in the face of an "utterly inefficient" militia, Early conceived an intrepid plan. Though he had been ordered to destroy the railroad bridge at Wrightsville, Jubal now determined to secure it, move his division across the Susquehanna, cut the Pennsylvania Railroad, and take Lancaster. After exacting whatever he could from the citizens there, he would assault Harrisburg from the rear—presumably in co-

< 182 >

operation with Ewell's other two divisions. In the attack, or in retreat if that seemed indicated, Early planned to achieve a kind of horse-marines' mobility by mounting his entire division on horses and mules to be requisitioned from farmers who had moved their animals across the river for safekeeping in the face of Lee's army. Then, destroying bridges, railroads, and canals as they went, Early's men would withdraw across the Susquehanna west of Harrisburg, bearing large quantities of booty. In the absence of the Army of the Potomac, which was now beginning to move into Pennsylvania, parts of this audacious scheme might have worked. But luck was against it from the first.

Arriving in Wrightsville, Gordon discovered the railroad bridge in flames. The fire had been set by Pennsylvania militiamen, members of a detachment of about 1,000 manning trenches west of Wrightsville. Gordon's Georgians brushed this defense aside, though not in time to save the bridge. But as firefighters joining a bucket brigade of towns-men the Confederates were effective in putting out flames that had leapt from the bridge to neighboring houses, and they deserved the credit they got from the citizens for helping to save the town.[11]

But Early's dream of a flying column died with the embers of the ruined Wrightsville span. The cavalrymen under French and White had been diligent in their destruction of all the other feasible bridges to the west; Jubal had to be content with the literal carrying-out of his orders.

Retracing its steps to rejoin Ewell, Early's division marched back into York. Perhaps he was warned by the unruly Wrightsville blaze that had burned some houses and threatened the rest; perhaps his conscience was uneasy over the human consequences of his own incineration of the Caledonia Works. Whatever his reasons, Early avoided damage to civilian property in York. He even refrained from burning railroad cars, shops, and other facilities there, though they were legitimate military targets. Still, he would not openly admit that the possible "mischief" to noncombatants of such an act was not justified by "the barbarous policy . . . pursued by the enemy in numerous similar cases."

Early explained this position in a proclamation issued before his departure. The statement was intended to impress the people of York with his generosity in letting them off so easily, and to persuade them that they owed their problems more to a despotic Federal government than to "the spirit of humanity which has ever characterized my government and its military authorities." The general proclaimed:

> Had I applied the torch without regard to consequences, I would have pursued a course that would have been fully vindicated as an act of just retaliation for the many authorized acts of barbarity perpetrated by your own army upon our soil. But we do not war upon women and children, and I trust the treatment you have met with at the hands of my soldiers will open your eyes to the monstrous iniquity of the war waged by your government upon the people of the Confederate States, and that you will make an effort to shake off the revolting tyranny under which it is apparent to all you are yourselves groaning.[12]

<< EARLY WOULD later heap praise on the Confederate army, including his own command, for its relative lenience in the invasion of Pennsylvania. He was encouraged in this by the fact that Lee himself did. In General Orders No. 73, read out on June 27, the commanding general lauded his men on their good conduct and exhorted them to keep it up. In their public statements, both generals were guilty of pomposity, if not outright hypocrisy. Early was certainly exaggerating outrageously when he asserted that "the invasion of Pennsylvania . . . for the forbearance shown to the invaded country, is without a parallel in the history of war in any age."

All the same, Lee's attempt to control the behavior of his army and limit its destructive effect on civilians was impressive. Certainly Early was partly right when he said that the inhabitants were spared "indignities," though the definition of the term depends on its user's point of view. Women and children were not maltreated, though they surely suffered when the Confederates took all their food. There were no recorded rapes. But it is hard to see how uncompensated loss of goods and the means of livelihood do not qualify as "indignities."

Early was dead wrong when he claimed that "no houses had been burned or pillaged" (though few private dwellings were purposely set afire). And he achieved absurdity when he claimed that, on his route

< 184 >

at least, "not even a rail had been taken from the fences for firewood." The larcenous stragglers of both armies only began their depredations by stealing fence rails, going on to pinch anything else they could find. Soldiers in ranks were little better; camping on successive nights on one Franklin County farmer's land, they consumed 12,550 fence rails for firewood, tent poles, and the like.[13]

As for Jubal Early's burning of the Caledonia Works, it was one of the very few such acts deliberately carried out against private property other than railroad facilities during the entire Gettysburg campaign. Though the works was technically a producer of war matériel, it is worth wondering whether it would have been destroyed if it had not belonged to Stevens. As old as war, the justification for its destruction, barely veiled behind a convention of civilized, professional eighteenth-century-style soldier's rhetoric, was cold-blooded retribution.

< 185 >

CHAPTER THIRTEEN

Change of Heart

ATE ON JUNE 29, 1863, a courier from General Ewell arrived with orders: Early was to march his division west and join the rest of the corps. The courier also delivered information from Lee: the enemy was moving north; it was time to concentrate the army.[1]

At dawn on the 30th, the division was on the march toward Heidlersburg. There it was to rendezvous with Ewell, who had moved from Carlisle with Rodes's division; Johnson's division, under orders issued previously, had been sent from Carlisle to Chambersburg to guard Ewell's trains and reserve artillery.[2] At Heidlersburg, Ewell told Early that Lee planned to concentrate near Cashtown, and ordered him to march his division there next day, by way of Hunterstown and Mummasburg. A look at the map—an excellent one that made it unnecessary to rely on local guides—showed Jubal that the road to Hunterstown was circuitous; he determined to take the Gettysburg road from Heidlersburg, then turn off when that route intersected with the road to Mummasburg.

A galloper from Ewell caught up with Early not long after he started south from Heidlersburg on July 1. Head straight for Gettysburg, Jubal was told; A. P. Hill's corps was there confronting an enemy force that had pushed westward out of Gettysburg toward Cashtown. Early was informed that Rodes was also being ordered to Gettysburg.[3]

The day before, June 30, marching on the town from the west, two of Hill's divisions had bumped into Brig. Gen. John Buford's division of Union cavalry. Buford, a tough, capable professional, had dismounted his men; they had held on against the increasing pressure of infantry attacks until reinforced, on July 1, by the Union 1st and 11th Corps under Maj. Gen. John Reynolds and Maj. Gen. Oliver O. Howard. The Army of the Potomac, now commanded by Maj. Gen. George Gordon Meade (replacing Hooker), was also starting to concentrate.[4]

Riding with his lead regiment, Early came in sight of Gettysburg about 2:30 P.M. He could see that Hill's divisions fighting the Federals about a mile west of the town had now been joined by Rodes's men, who had approached via the Mummasburg Road. Jubal noted that Federal troops opposing Rodes overlapped his left flank and seemed to be pushing him back on that side. Visible about a mile behind the town was a hill on which Early observed Union artillery sited to fire on all the approaches to Gettysburg from the north. It was hard to tell, from his position below the hill crest and some distance from it, whether the guns were supported by infantry.[5]

Early's brigades formed up for battle with Gordon's on the right of the road; Hays's Louisianians straddled the road in the center, with Avery's men on the left. Smith's brigade was in reserve, with some men pulled back to face east and defend against any Federals who might approach Early's exposed left flank. At this point Early had no real idea how badly Rodes, who was hard-pressed not only on his left but all along his line, needed help. But Jubal's intervention was most timely— and though unplanned by Lee, Ewell, or anyone else, devastatingly effective.[6]

Jubal, the old gunner, saw a perfect site for his artillery, which he posted off the Heidlersburg Road pointing west into the flank of the Union lines punishing Rodes. Opening suddenly, the fire of Jones's guns stopped the Federals where they were, just as Gordon's brigade began a headlong charge over a narrow stream called Rock Creek and up a low hill anchoring the Union right flank. Seizing the heights after a short, bloody fight, Gordon's men turned west to enfilade the bluecoats, who tried to change front; but Gordon attacked as they were executing this difficult maneuver, and the Federals turned and ran for the town. Many were shot down in their flight; Gordon's Georgians, chasing the fugitives, captured many more.

Early's other three brigades also advanced. The contingents of Hays and Avery were followed by Smith's Virginians along with the artillery. The first two units were wading through Rock Creek about the time that Gordon's brigade, pursuing what turned out to be members of Howard's 11th Corps, ran into a stubbornly defended second line just outside the town. Early, riding over to discuss the situation with Gordon, saw that Hays and Avery were in a better position than the Georgians for an attack on this line. Gordon was ordered to hold fast; the other brigades, pushing forward under heavy shellfire mixed with canister, shattered the defense that had stopped Gordon and pursued the Federals into and through the town—seizing many prisoners and two guns. Hays encountered house-to-house resistance inside Gettysburg, but subdued it and pushed on. Avery steered to the left of the town, confronting the northeastern approaches to the high ground—Cemetery Hill, as it was called—that rose about 80 feet above the center of Gettysburg.[7]

Almost irresistible up to this point, the forward momentum of Early's division slowed markedly, partly because of the enormous crowd of Federal prisoners milling around in the streets of Gettysburg. But though he was momentarily stuck, Jubal became aware that Rodes was advancing successfully to the right of the town. If Smith's brigade moved up quickly to support Avery and Hays, Early believed that he and Rodes could nail down what was turning into a dramatic victory—of the sort the Confederates were getting so used to.[8]

<< AROUND 3:00 P.M., the successful result of the battle for the town began to become evident. Early rode in search of Ewell or Lee, hoping to report his situation and communicate his opinion that the attack should be pressed—though he now apparently felt that he and Rodes would need support from the troops of A. P. Hill. Jubal found neither of his superiors, but he did encounter an aide on the staff of Maj. Gen. Dorsey Pender, one of Hill's division commanders; the officer was advised to ride straight to Hill and tell him that one of his divisions, if sent eastward, could help ensure the capture of Cemetery Hill.[9]

As the July 1 fighting began to die down, the most urgent question on the minds of the Confederate commanders was *what next?* The immediate tasks were to secure the town and organize the thousands

< 188 >

of prisoners and the captured equipment. Looking further ahead, the answer was more complex.

Lee, whose army was by no means concentrated on July 1, had neither wanted nor expected a battle on that day. His basic instructions to Hill and Ewell—not to bring on a general engagement—had been diluted by events, but they remained in force. Of the troops available near Gettysburg, Lee was only aware of the condition of Hill's men, whom he had accompanied from Cashtown; by late afternoon, many of them had already fought very hard and suffered severely.[10]

Of Ewell's situation Lee knew little. He could see Cemetery Hill from his position on Seminary Ridge, a low elevation to the west of Gettysburg, and he understood that capturing the heights south of the town would be an excellent thing. Ewell's men, the commanding general felt, were closest to that objective; whatever their condition, they were the only troops for the job. Lee duly wrote an order to Ewell to take Cemetery Hill. But not knowing what shape his 2d Corps was in, Lee made the order discretionary—to be carried out only if Ewell thought the operation was "possible," and if, by attacking, he would not bring on a general engagement. He also promised to ride over and talk to Ewell soon. The order was given to a young staff officer, who mounted and rode off in search of Ewell.[11]

The condition of Ewell's corps was equivocal. Like Lee, Ewell lacked a key formation of his command: Johnson's division, which was still on the road, marching eastward from Cashtown. Rodes's division was badly depleted by casualties from the afternoon's combat. Practically speaking, Ewell was down to one division—Early's, which had lost relatively few men.[12]

Early was sent for. Ewell might have already known that Jubal, tracked down previously by a staff officer, was trying to cope with a problem raised by General Smith. Extra Billy had informed Early of word he had received that an enemy column was advancing westward along the York Road. Early doubted the report; but to be safe, he sent Gordon back, with his brigade, to support—and supervise—Smith.[13]

When Early, obeying Ewell's summons, appeared at his field headquarters, the corps commander sought his views. Ewell learned that

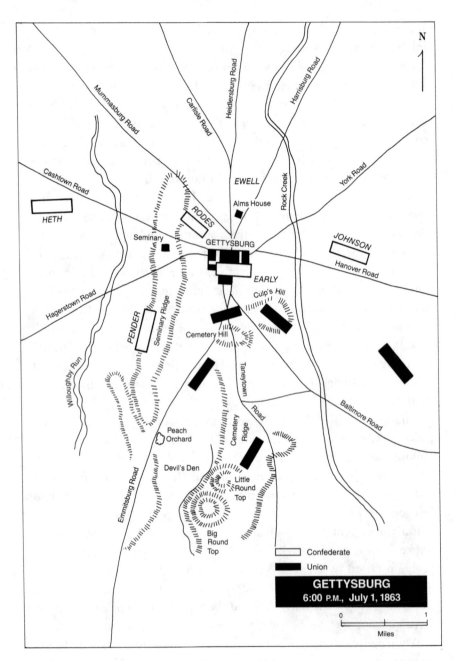

N

HETH

Mummasburg Road

Cashtown Road

Carlisle Road

Heidlersburg Road

Harrisburg Road

EWELL

RODES

Alms House

Rock Creek

York Road

Seminary

GETTYSBURG

JOHNSON

Hanover Road

Hagerstown Road

PENDER

Seminary Ridge

EARLY

Culp's Hill

Cemetery Hill

Willoughby Run

Taneytown Road

Baltimore Road

Peach Orchard

Cemetery Ridge

Emmitsburg Road

Devil's Den

Little Round Top

Big Round Top

Confederate

Union

GETTYSBURG
6:00 P.M., July 1, 1863

0   1

Miles

Jubal believed an attack on Cemetery Hill would be successful. But he felt success required support by additional troops supplied from A. P. Hill's corps. Asked where Johnson ought to be placed when he arrived, Early indicated a position on the left of the corps line, opposite Culp's Hill, a wooded, rocky elevation east of Cemetery Hill that dominated that height, and seemed unoccupied. If he arrived in time, Johnson could attack Culp's Hill in coordination with Early's Cemetery Hill thrust.[14]

Ewell accepted both pieces of advice—sending the appropriate orders to Johnson, and to Lee a declaration of his intent to assault Cemetery Hill with a contingent request for support from A. P. Hill. This dispatch was on its way to the commanding general when the attack order from Lee to Ewell arrived. Acknowledging Early's suggestion to Hill (sent via Pender's aide), Lee regretted that no support would be forthcoming from the 3d Corps; he urged Ewell to go ahead and seize the heights if he saw fit. The staff major who brought this note told Ewell that Lee appeared to think it would not take much to drive the Federals off the hill.[15]

Ewell evidently felt differently. Especially in Johnson's absence, and without help from Hill, the corps commander believed he needed Early's division intact, with both Smith's and Gordon's brigades in the line, if he were to have a chance of bringing the assault off. The difficulties were formidable. Avery, for example, faced the enemy across a mile of rugged ground that rose to the Union guns on the crest of Cemetery Hill; advancing up the slope, his men would have to scramble over numerous stone and wooden fences. Hays, inside Gettysburg, had to proceed along narrow streets enfiladed by artillery from the crest of the hill as well as sharpshooters on the slope and in houses at the edge of town. Then he confronted the slope itself, hundreds of yards of broken terrain defended by artillery and infantry in unknown but possibly substantial strength. The defenders presumably included the thousands of Federals who had escaped capture in Gettysburg and had reached safety behind the crest.[16]

To see some of this for himself, Ewell rode toward the hill, accompanied by Early. Union sharpshooters took these targets, two of the oddest-looking generals in either army, under fire. Ewell was undismayed by the sniping; he had earlier taken a minié ball smack in his peg leg. Asked by John Gordon if he was all right, Ewell had expounded on the awful consequences if the bullet had instead hit a limb of flesh and blood. "No, no," Ewell had insisted, "I'm not hurt. But suppose that ball had struck you; we would have had the trouble of carrying you off the field, sir. You see how much better fixed for a fight I am than you are. It don't hurt a bit to be shot in a wooden leg."

For all his apparent sangfroid, Ewell was disturbed by the artillery he could see on the hill crest. Also visible there was what his staff aide and son-in-law Maj. Campbell Brown called "quite a long line of infantry."[17]

Ewell weighed the risks in the balance with the discretion Lee had given him. The defenses were probably strong. The available striking force was down to two brigades. There would be no help from the rest of the army. Almost 4,000 prisoners remained in the Gettysburg neighborhood, a burden and a potential menace. To the east, whatever Early might say, Union troops could be advancing toward the corps' dangling left flank.

Ewell insisted on riding out and looking in person for the supposed enemy off to the left; he even thought he saw Union skirmishers. Not possible, Early replied; Gordon was well within musket range of hostile skirmishers, but no one was firing. What Ewell saw turned out, finally, to be Confederates (Smith's men, at that). All the same, the corps commander wanted to make absolutely sure, and ordered a staff officer off to check; on his way back, he was to reconnoiter up Culp's Hill. Early detailed one of his aides to go along too, then returned to the town to make sure that the brigades of Hays and Avery were securely positioned for the night.[18]

In the end, the discretion Lee had given Ewell prevailed. Ewell decided not to launch any aggressive moves, at least until Johnson showed up. When he did, Ewell could always send his relatively fresh men up the putatively defenseless slopes of Culp's Hill. From its summit they could presumably dominate and neutralize Cemetery Hill. There would be no need for the costly attack there that Lee had—so uninsistently—called for.[19]

< 192 >

« IT WAS ALMOST dark when General Lee, true to his promise, dismounted outside Ewell's headquarters in the home of the superintendent of Gettysburg's almshouse. The two generals sat outdoors to take advantage of a cool evening breeze and chatted—they had not spoken face to face since June 9—while they waited for Early, whom Ewell had summoned on Lee's arrival. Rodes sat with them.

Jubal rode up in the company of his nephew John, who was returning to headquarters with some corn he had found in a shed up the road. His uncle told him to give the corn to the staff's horses, and John followed Jubal to a porch not far from where the horses were hitched. There he saw Lee and his companions, whom Early now joined.[20]

The boy heard the officers try to come to grips with the "what next" question that bedeviled the Confederates at Gettysburg. There seemed to be tacit agreement that it was too late to organize an assault on Cemetery Hill that day; the subject never arose. Ewell brought his commander up to date on casualties (as many as 2,500 from Rodes's division), prisoners (thousands) and his plans for Johnson (sending him to occupy Culp's Hill).

Lee ignored this information. His reply was a terse query: "Can't you, with your corps, attack on this flank at daylight tomorrow?"[21]

It was a natural question coming from an aggressive general like Lee. It was the more understandable—though Lee's listeners did not know it—in light of a conference he had had earlier with Longstreet, the man he trusted most in the absence of Jackson. To Lee, the only real option was to attack; but Longstreet had urged a complex flanking maneuver instead. Longstreet's idea was to put the Army of Northern Virginia between Meade and Washington and bring on a defensive battle on ground well chosen by him and Lee.[22]

If Longstreet, a known advocate of the strategic defensive, was against attacking Meade at Gettysburg, Lee probably expected—at any rate, hoped—that the combative Ewell, the gallant Rodes, and the aggressive Early would be heartily in favor. In that case, his faith in them was to be crushed.

Early, as Ewell's articulate spokesman, uttered a resounding "no" to Lee's question about a 2d Corps attack. It was in character for Jubal to speak up, in spite of his subordinate status, but he evidently felt that he knew more about the terrain than the other men did—having ridden around a lot of it during the day, and having been in the neighborhood a few days before.

Jubal specifically rejected the idea of an attack on Cemetery Hill on July 2. He pointed to the problems of approach: the rugged ground, the fences, the distance to the crest. The Federals were undoubtedly reinforcing the position already, and by morning they would be very strong.

As Jubal reported the conversation later, he suggested that a better focus for an attack would be on the right, against the heights known locally as Little and Big Round Top that dominated the entire Gettysburg landscape. Confederate possession of these hills, in Early's view, would render the Federal position untenable.

Ewell agreed with this analysis, and so did Rodes. In Early's account, Lee accepted his assessment without comment. Then the commanding general asked if it might not be prudent to pull the 2d Corps around to the right, in line with Hill on Seminary Ridge; if Ewell's corps stayed where it was, it seemed to Lee that his line, stretched too thin, would be vulnerable to attack in Ewell's sector. "Then perhaps," Lee said, "I had better draw you around towards my right, as the line will be very long and thin if you remain here and the enemy may come down and break through it."

Once again it was Early who spoke. Lee need not worry, he said; the terrain favored the defense. "On that part of the front it was more difficult for the enemy to come down from the heights to attack us than for us to ascend and attack him, difficult as the latter would have been." Jubal added that withdrawal from a position won at considerable cost would demoralize the men, and would force him to leave his badly wounded in the hands of the enemy.[23]

Again, Ewell concurred. Rodes was also in accord. Lee must now have been seriously worried. Generals from whom he had probably expected unquestioning support for his offensive scheme were holding back—unanimously declaring they could not do what they must have known he urgently wanted them to do. Moreover, their dissent was not confined to the overarching question of whether or not to attack; it extended to practical questions of position. He wanted them to move; they found manifold reasons to remain where they were. Lee's command style was collegial, both because he was courteous by nature and because he had become accustomed to giving Longstreet and Jackson the maximum discretion. He scarcely knew how to issue peremptory orders to these generals to do what he wanted. Their demurral was thus a factor, and an important one, in his own decision-making.

But it must have come as a shock to find Ewell and his commanders so inert. In just a few hours, something had apparently happened to their states of mind—especially those of Ewell and Early; Rodes was merely following their lead. Since taking over the 2d Corps, Ewell had seemed forceful. But on July 1, a new caution had been manifest— at any rate, since the capture of the town. To Lee, it spelled irresolution. Early, always notoriously assertive, had urged aggressiveness as late as sundown. Now even he was eloquent in erecting obstacles to Lee's will.[24]

What had happened to change Early's attitude is a mystery, at least in part. Some explanations seem clear enough. With his memories of Malvern Hill and Williamsburg, he could logically have been expected to shy away from attacking artillery supported by infantry in a stout position that was surely being made stronger with every minute that passed. But simply stating such an objection was obviously insufficient; Jubal could presumably read Lee's mood well enough to realize that it would not do to recommend the whole army's disengagement and retreat as an alternative to attack by the 2d Corps. In that light, his suggestion of an attack on the right makes sense.

What does not make sense is Early's resistance to the change of position Lee wanted. Lee clearly believed the 2d Corps was capable of attacking on July 2. Thus, in Edwin Coddington's thoughtful view, the intent of Lee's question about moving the corps (as reported by Early) sounds wrong. If attack on the left was not feasible, it would have been only logical for Lee to want the 2d Corps moved over to cooperate with an attack on the right.

But, according to Early, that is not the form Lee's question took: Lee's choice of words emphasized the 2d Corps's vulnerability; in suggesting the move, Lee seemed concerned that the 2d Corps might not

< 195 >

be able to defend itself if it stayed in place. None of the other witnesses ever challenged this version of the conversation. Still, the problem remains. Why, given his yearning for an offensive, would Lee have suddenly started fussing about the 2d Corps's *defensive* capabilities?

The mystery of Jubal's balkiness is crucial because he was so important an actor in the meeting. His role was that of an advocate, skilled in discourse. He did the talking, speaking for Ewell as if he could read the pale cast of his commander's mind, and all of it came right off the top of his head. (It is hard to see how or when Early, Ewell, and Rodes could have conferred before Lee's arrival; yet it almost seems as if they did, so perfect was their unanimity.)

In the course of the meeting, Lee must have been disagreeably struck by the demeaning role Ewell cast himself in by backing away from his obligation to explain his own position, and by permitting Early to run the corps commander's end of the meeting as spokesman. As to why Ewell did this, Lee apparently thought Ewell was demonstrating paralysis in the face of his new responsibilities. For that matter, Ewell's passive reliance on Jubal may indeed have grown out of a dismaying sense of his own inadequacy. If so, Old Bald Head, knowing and trusting Early's grasp of a difficult situation and his ability to outline it clearly, simply let him take over.[25]

General Lee evidently felt he had no choice but to accept Early's counsel: attack on the right, using the 1st and 3d Corps. But Hill's corps was badly mauled, and Longstreet's was not yet all present; the division of Maj. Gen. George Pickett had been left in Chambersburg as rear guard pending the arrival of John Imboden's cavalry to assume that task. Longstreet's other divisions, under Hood and McLaws, were the only available troops fresh enough for a major offensive on the Confederate right.

Years later, Early recounted Lee's out-loud thinking at this critical point in the conference. As if talking to himself, the senior general presumably said, "Well, if I attack from my right, Longstreet will have to make the attack. Longstreet is a very good fighter when he gets in position and gets everything ready, but he is so slow." Whether or not Lee ever uttered these words (he almost certainly did not), they

< 196 >

would detonate with terrible effect in the explosive controversy waged between Early and Longstreet in times to come.[26]

Before Lee left, it was agreed that an attack would be launched on the right as soon as possible on the morning of July 2. On the left, Ewell would make a show of attacking, and would be prepared to push a real assault home if he saw a chance of assisting the main operation or of exploiting its success.

<< SOMETIME AFTER the generals' conference ended, the two staff officers sent earlier to investigate the enigma of the Federals on the York Road returned to headquarters. On their way back, they had ridden up Culp's Hill and discovered it unoccupied. Elements of Johnson's division that were entering their assigned position could apparently now take the hill without opposition. Early and Rodes were sitting with Ewell in a fence corner when the young lieutenants rode up. They indicated that possession of the hill would, like seizure of the Round Tops, render the whole Union position indefensible.

Ewell asked Rodes whether he thought Johnson should occupy the hill now—tonight. Rodes replied that the men were probably dead beat after their march from Chambersburg; whatever their condition, he felt that taking the hill would make no difference one way or the other. Ewell put the same query to Early, who answered: "If you do not go up there tonight, it will cost you 10,000 lives to get up there tomorrow."[27]

Ewell would order Johnson up the hill, but "Allegheny Ed" would not capture it that night—or ever. Somewhat earlier, Johnson, not waiting for further instructions, had set up his attack and sent a party up the hill in advance. This group had bumped into a substantial contingent of Union troops on the heights, and had been driven off. A little later, Johnson was handed a dispatch taken from a captured Federal runner: it indicated that Ewell might now be facing the Union 5th and 12th Corps as well as the 1st and 11th; the 12th could well be on or near Culp's Hill, with the 5th a scant four miles away to the east. In a note to Ewell, Johnson said he would hold off attacking Culp's Hill until he heard from his corps commander.

Upsetting though it may have been, Johnson's news created no new

< 197 >

command problems for Ewell. He had already heard from Lee: no attack was to be launched from the Confederate left until Longstreet's offensive, announced by his guns, was under way.[28]

<< ON JULY 2, Jubal Early was ready to go on the attack from earliest light. But it was a long, frustrating wait. Darkness had actually fallen when Ewell's men, in a ragged, uncoordinated attempt to support Longstreet, surged forward against the heights on the 2d Corps's sector of the line.

During the night of July 1–2, in order to get a jump on the enemy in any attack on July 2, Jubal had stealthily pushed the brigades of Hays and Avery forward until they were under cover from artillery fire behind a low ridge near the base of the hill, half a mile closer to its summit than they had been. Hays was given command of both brigades. When word finally came that the main show on the right would begin around 4:00 P.M., Early made other changes. Though he left Smith's men on the York Road to guard the flank, Early moved Gordon's brigade back in toward town and positioned it behind Avery as a reserve. At some point, Early and Rodes made a pact to stay in touch and attack together, with Rodes supporting Jubal from the right. To support Rodes, Ewell asked Brig. Gen. James Lane, replacing the wounded Dorsey Pender in command of Hill's nearest division on the right, to coordinate with the 2d Corps attack. Lane was noncommittal; feeling pressed by time, Ewell never pursued the plan by getting in touch with Hill.[29]

At 6:30, Ewell decided to send his whole corps forward—though he had no more reason to expect success then than he had had at any time from dawn on. (A particularly disturbing sign of Union strength in Ewell's sector was the total suppression by Federal counterbattery fire of Confederate artillery supporting Ewell's advance.) Johnson ran into heavy resistance on Culp's Hill and never achieved more than a partial success, though he eventually seized and held some trenches partway up the slope on the far Confederate left. Early did much better, but he was unable to hold onto his gains.[30]

Partly protected from artillery fire by the steep slope of Cemetery Hill, some of Early's 3,500 men reached the crest. Masked by the failing light and smoke of battle, and abetted by the weakness of op-

< 198 >

posing troops cut up and demoralized in the previous day's fighting, a few of Hays's Tigers and Avery's Tar Heels got as far as the Federal guns on the hill and were trying to take them as darkness fell. In the murk, the antagonists fought with bullets, handspikes, bayonets, clubbed muskets, and rocks.

A moment came, as the struggle died down, when it seemed as if the two Confederate brigades, which had captured four Union colors, had brought the operation off. But there was no support to help them hold against the inevitable Union counterthrust, whose imminence was announced by the bumping, clanking, and muffled voices of men closing in on the Confederates from behind the crest.

Gordon, Early's closest reserve, was not up there because he and Early had seen or heard no signs that Rodes, per agreement, was moving forward, and Early would not reinforce the setback that he foresaw in Rodes's absence. When the Federal counterattack hit, it drove Early's assault brigades back down the hill. Fortunately, the darkness enabled the Southerners to retire without much further loss.[31]

Over on the Confederate right, Longstreet had also come close to success in a costly attempt to seize the lower end of Cemetery Ridge. Commentators, analyzing the desperate struggle of Hood and McLaws in the Peach Orchard and the Devil's Den, would speculate on the outcome if Early and Rodes had prevailed in their attempt on Cemetery Hill. At the time, quite a number of witnesses thought that the momentary breakthrough by Hays and Avery, if properly backed up, might have generated the great victory so sorely needed by Confederate arms at Gettysburg. Certainly the Tigers, who lost nearly half their strength in the Gettysburg campaign, were loud in blame of Rodes and even Hays, accusing their officers of indifference, and railing that others had let them down after they had grasped triumph.[32]

Why did Rodes fail to advance according to his arrangement with Early? Among several possible reasons, perhaps the most important was Rodes's acceptance of a warning from two of his brigade commanders: Brig. Gen. Stephen Dodson Ramseur—later to serve under Jubal—and Brig. Gen. George Doles, officers with reputations for both sagacity and bravery. They told Rodes that Federal defenses on their sector of Cemetery Hill were too strong to be attacked without prohibitive loss.

Rodes believed them; and when he heard that Early's assault brigades were pulling back, he canceled his own attack.[33]

‹‹ ON JULY 3, the day made famous by George Pickett and his catastrophic charge, Early, along with most of Ewell's corps, remained in roughly the positions they had occupied two days before. Johnson, though reinforced by Smith's brigade, was driven in heavy fighting from the trenches he had taken on July 2 on Culp's Hill. Outside of a few skirmishers and pickets, no other 2d Corps troops so much as fired a shot.

On July 4, Independence Day, the day Vicksburg, Mississippi, surrendered to Ulysses S. Grant, the armies faced each other under cloudy skies that later poured down rain. Next day, Lee opened the last act of the Gettysburg campaign as he began the withdrawal of his army, weakened by the loss of more than 20,000 killed, wounded, and missing, to Virginia.[34]

‹‹ "IT'S ALL my fault," said General Lee after the battle, which few could then deny was a Confederate defeat. Broadly speaking, he was right; so was Freeman, his chronicler, in saying that next to Malvern Hill, Gettysburg was Lee's worst-fought battle. But his was not the only fault. Ewell was as frank as Lee in acknowledging his own shortcomings. In a conversation with a fellow general months after the battle, Ewell said it took "a dozen blunders to lose Gettysburg and he had committed a good many of them."

If Ewell made mistakes, was Early responsible, as a trusted subordinate and adviser, for any of them? The chief accusation against Ewell is indecisiveness on July 1 when, it is alleged, a resolute continuation of the successful attack on Gettysburg would have carried Cemetery Hill and guaranteed a Confederate victory. Some—many of them former subordinates of Jackson—went to their graves asserting that Stonewall would have captured the heights. Though anyone would have found Thomas Jackson a hard act to follow, it is not difficult to find arguments in defense of Ewell (Early himself later entered a quite sweeping defense). It certainly seems reasonable to ask how Ewell was expected to assault a position of unknown strength with two unsupported brigades of troops already exhausted by a very hot July day spent in hard marching and fighting.[35]

But if Ewell was wrong on July 1 in not launching an onslaught on Cemetery Hill, Early cannot be named as an accomplice. He repeatedly urged the attack on Ewell, even though he recognized that its success depended on support from the army's 3d Corps.

Ewell was certainly wrong in letting Jubal be his mouthpiece in the conference with Lee. Nevertheless, a charge of presumption against Early—for taking over the meeting from Ewell—seems just, though Ewell could have shut him up at any point. Jubal felt qualified to speak up by virtue of his familiarity with the local terrain, but it was very much in character at any time for him to assume as much control of a situation like the Lee conference as he could, acting as if he, rather than Ewell, should have been commanding the corps.

On the other hand, the substance of Early's comments in the meeting was probably sound enough. In assessing the chances of a July 2 assault on the Confederate left, the Early-Ewell-Rodes consensus was astute, though passivity was not what Lee wanted, and though none of the generals then had the slightest idea of the defensive strength they faced. (In fact, they confronted elements of four Union corps.) As it turned out, Early's abortive success in seizing the heights late in the day indicates that a well-coordinated corps assault along its whole front from Culp's Hill to Cemetery Hill might have had a chance.

In opposing the change of position that Lee wanted the 2d Corps to make, Early and Ewell were surely wrong. Aligning the corps with those of Hill and Longstreet on Seminary Ridge would have enabled Lee to concentrate all his force against Meade's main position, which stretched along Cemetery Ridge. Leaving the 2d Corps in place, in a position dictated primarily by the direction and circumstances of its approach to the town on July 1, in effect forced Lee to divide his army. Even so, there might have been some merit in a synchronized "one-two" combination of attacks on both the right and the left on July 2. But with Hill so weak, Early's and Ewell's reluctance to endorse such a course threw Lee back on his 1st Corps, which was expected to attack alone with only serendipitous support, if any, from the 2d and 3d.[36]

When the 2d Corps did join the action toward sunset, its moves were so badly coordinated that it fell far short of a decisive performance. Though Lee should have done more to coordinate action on both his wings, the lack of coherence on the left was Ewell's fault; Rodes, Johnson, and especially Early played their parts as best they could.

<< THE MYSTERY of Jubal's change of heart, one moment a passionate advocate of the attack, the next a voice of prudence, urging the status quo, is essentially insoluble. The answer is certainly not a sudden loss of nerve. Overweening arrogance—a feeling that he should have been and therefore somehow actually was in charge of the 2d Corps—might explain his taking a dominant role in the conference, but it fails to account for his choice of a cautious, passive, static course of action.

A less direct answer may emerge from a nature imbued with skepticism and pessimism. Jubal's aggressiveness was of the alert mind and the fighter's gut, not of the chivalric high heart valued by Lee. That soaring spirit, oblivious of all risk, was what Lee was calling to on the evening of July 1. But Early was listening to a darker summons sounded from the gloom and uncertainty he sensed in the mood of Richard Ewell. For the first time, perhaps, Early truly felt—though unconscious of his feeling—that the Southern cause might be a forlorn hope.

< 202 >

<< CHAPTER FOURTEEN >>

"A Great Mind to Curse"

ESTLESS IN CAMP, Jubal was fiddling around one evening in November 1863, trying to fix a makeshift table whose rickety legs denied it a level surface. The table resisted the general's efforts, and he appealed to a staff officer, Maj. John W. Daniel (a staunch friend who would become a United States senator).

"John," said Early, "I have a great mind to curse. Do you think it would do any good?"

"No, sir," said Daniel thoughtfully. "I do not curse myself and do not like to hear anyone else do so." [1]

The major was tactfully evading his commander's sardonic question, but the fact remained that cursing would have done nothing to help fix the table—or to mitigate the great misfortune, still uppermost in everyone's mind, that had befallen Early and the Army of Northern Virginia just a few days before at Rappahannock Station.

<< THE DEFEAT was full of portent for the Army of Northern Virginia, and the culmination of a cycle of frustrations for Lee. Ever since Gettysburg and a period of rest and refitting that lasted through early September, Lee had been hoping to maneuver Meade into a battle in Virginia. His resources were limited. Besides Stuart's cavalry, Lee commanded only two corps: Hill's and Ewell's. Longstreet had been detached to serve under Braxton Bragg in the west. Other units had been sent to reinforce Charleston, South Carolina.

In early October, the opportunity to strike the Army of the Potomac seemed at hand: Meade was near Culpeper; Lee was on the Rapi-

< 203 >

dan near Orange Court House. Outnumbered eight to five, he was nevertheless determined to threaten Meade's right flank, force him to withdraw, and then hit him while he was moving.

On October 9, the Army of Northern Virginia started marching, with Hill's corps swinging wide around Meade's flank via Sperryville and Ewell's aiming more directly at the enemy, though on inferior roads that slowed his corps' advance. By the 14th, it was clear that Meade was pulling back, presumably into the Washington defenses.

That day, Hill's corps caught up with Union troops fording Broad Run near Bristoe Station on the Orange & Alexandria Railroad. Hill had surprised the Federals on the move; his men cheered an order to attack, even though Hill had but two brigades to send in, the bulk of his corps not yet having joined him. Unfortunately for his troops, Hill was unaware of a 3,000-man corps of Federal infantry concealed behind the railroad embankment. Hill's two assault brigades, taking the fire of this hidden force, were badly cut up, losing 1,378 killed and wounded.[2]

Following this one-sided clash, the Federals pulled out. Early's division, leading Ewell's corps, nipped at the backsides of the withdrawing enemy, but to no effect. Largely owing to Hill's impetuosity, Meade was able to complete a successful withdrawal to the neighborhood of Centreville, where he began digging in.[3]

Lee, eager to sustain the momentum of his offensive, considered following up. But Meade had withdrawn his men rapidly, marching them 40 miles to avoid the Confederate flanking movement. Also, supplies for the Southern army were uncertain in the devastated northernmost region of Virginia. To shorten his communications and ensure provisions of some sort for the coming winter, Lee pulled the army back to the Rappahannock, occupying a defensive line south of the river as November began.[4]

Lee posted Hill's corps along the Rappahannock west of the Orange & Alexandria Railroad; Ewell occupied the river line east from the railroad—at the wrecked Rappahannock Bridge—to Kelly's Ford. Here was the most insecure sector of the line. Because Federal guns could dominate the ford from high bluffs on the north bank, Lee abandoned the idea of defending the crossing at the river itself; he set up his defense farther south, out of range of artillery on the bluffs.

To threaten the flank of any Union assault on Kelly's Ford—and tempt the enemy to divide his force—Lee resurrected a complex of fortifications, originally built in 1862 by the Confederates, on the north side of the river near the defunct railroad bridge. A pontoon bridge there was now the only means of crossing; a dam downstream made the Rappahannock unfordable in the vicinity of the railroad.[5]

Ewell was ordered to man these defenses in shifts, with a brigade from Early's division alternating with one from Edward Johnson's. Lee and Ewell thought the earthworks reasonably strong because the defenders could anchor both flanks on the river. Early disagreed. To his eye, the entrenchments were vulnerable in a number of ways. The defenses on the right of the position could be approached within 100 feet by an enemy using the railroad embankment as cover. In front, there were no obstructions such as ditches or abatis, and higher ground to the north offered the Federals a dominant position for artillery. On the left, the line of earthworks followed the river as it bent southward, forming a salient at right angles to the trenches on the right. Finally, Confederate artillery, posted so as to defend the crossing, could not command the north bank of the river.[6]

On November 7, Hays's Louisiana Brigade manned the entrenchments, with four guns of the Louisiana Guard Artillery. Hays himself was on court-martial duty, and the brigade was under the temporary command of Col. Davidson Penn, a 27-year-old Virginia Military Institute graduate and friend of Jubal's. Around 11:00 A.M., Penn became aware that very heavy Federal forces were slowly moving toward his position; he sent word to Early, who was at his headquarters some distance to the rear of the river line. Penn sent another dispatch around 1:00 P.M., reporting a Union column heading toward Kelly's Ford and stating that the enemy was still advancing on his position. By two o'clock, it was apparent to Penn that he was dealing with two Union corps (as it turned out, the 5th and 6th, combined under John Sedgwick).[7]

When Early received Penn's first message, he sent word to Ewell

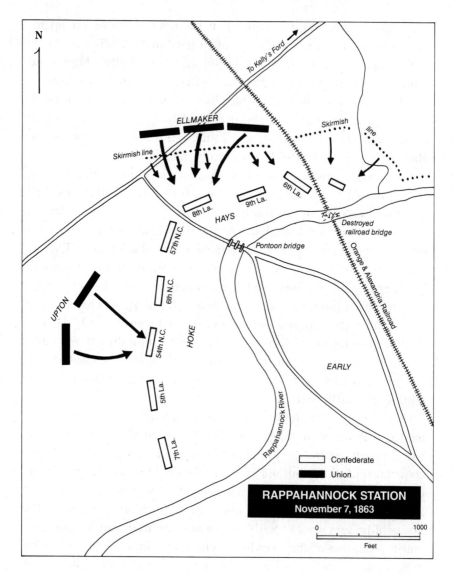

N

ELLMAKER

Skirmish line

Skirmish line

8th La.

9th La.

6th La.

HAYS

To Kelly's Ford

Destroyed
railroad bridge

57th N.C.

Pontoon bridge

Orange & Alexandria Railroad

6th N.C.

UPTON

54th N.C.

HOKE

EARLY

5th La.

Rappahannock River

7th La.

Confederate

Union

RAPPAHANNOCK STATION
November 7, 1863

0   1000

Feet

and Lee. Ordering his other brigades forward to the river line from
their camps, he rode hastily to see for himself what was going on. On
the way, he encountered Lee, who had not received his note. At the
river, Jubal crossed the pontoon bridge and trotted out ahead of his
skirmish line. Penn's information was accurate: massive Federal forces

were moving very slowly and cautiously toward the earthworks so as to surround it.[8]

After discovering a large gap at the point of the salient between two of the Louisiana regiments, Early clattered back across the pontoon bridge and fired off orders to bring up Hoke's brigade (under Col. Archibald Godwin in the absence of Hoke, off on detached duty) to reinforce Hays's men. Then Jubal rode to join Lee on a rise behind the river, where they had a fairly good view of the situation on the north bank, though they were under artillery fire. Lt. Peter Hairston, one of Jubal's aides, had a horse killed under him by a shell he was convinced was fired at the command party: Lee, Early, and Brig. Gen. John Pegram, in charge of the former brigade of Extra Billy Smith, who had left the army to become governor of Virginia. Ewell was absent—preoccupied, by his own account, with a separate Union attack on Kelly's Ford. (Ewell also reported that he had never received Early's dispatch, and had heard "no report of artillery or other indications of an attack" at the bridgehead.)[9]

Around 4:00 P.M., Hays rode up and crossed to assume command of his brigade, which had been forced to pull in its skirmishers and was taking punishment from Federal guns posted on the high ground to the front. Confederate artillery on the south bank lacked the range to reach the Union guns, leaving it to the four Louisiana pieces on the north bank to reply as best they could to the heavier and more effective Federal fire.[10]

Hays arrived about the same time as Godwin, with part of Hoke's brigade, which plugged the gap between the Louisiana regiments in the salient. They were in time to stop the first concerted Federal attack. But they were much too late to prevent disaster as the November twilight gave way to darkness that was the more obscure on account of dense smoke. Under this cover, the Union attackers advanced aggressively, moving against the left and right ends of the Confederate line.

The defenders fired a couple of volleys before the advancing Federals simply overpowered them following a brief, savage surge of hand-to-hand fighting. The action was one of the few during the war in which bayonets were actually used. "Here," wrote a Union participant, "the unusual sight of death by bayonet wounds was witnessed, a dozen or more Confederate soldiers showing bayonet wounds, as well as some Union dead."

There were actually few dead or wounded; most of the losses, some 1,600, were Confederate prisoners. (Sedgwick reported capture of more than 1,200, including at least four colonels and three lieutenant colonels.) Of the two Southern brigades in the bridgehead—about 2,000 men—only about 450 escaped. Some Louisiana units virtually ceased to exist: in the 5th Louisiana, which had mustered 122 men before dark on November 7, only one officer remained to answer roll call the next morning.[11]

Of these developments Lee and Early remained in almost total ignorance. They could see muzzle flashes through the deepening dusk but a southerly wind, blowing from behind their backs as they peered into the murk, silenced the sounds of firing. Lee, interpreting the flashes as the fire of skirmishers, declared the Federal activity a mere reconnaissance in force; it was now too late, he believed, for the enemy (who had never made a night attack against the Army of Northern Virginia) to attempt anything significant until morning. With that, the commanding general announced his retirement for the night.[12]

Early was not so sure, though Lee's confidence that the Federals would make no night attack calmed his fears somewhat. On the assumption that all was well in the bridgehead, he ordered his aide Maj. Sam Hale across the bridge to tell Hays and Godwin to send parties back to draw rations for their men. On his return, Hale reported that the situation had seemed under control on his arrival; but as he was recrossing the river he ran into a couple of Hays's men who told him that the enemy had broken into the fortifications. Hale denounced the report as false. But Jubal, not reassured, now ordered Pegram's brigade up to defend the bridge, and sent Daniel over the span to investigate matters on the other side.

The major never even got across the bridge; he encountered Hays himself on a frantic, lathered horse. In panic when a Federal musket was fired near its head, the animal had bolted; steering his mount at the bridge, the general had managed an escape from the debacle unfolding on the opposite bank. Hays told Daniel that most of his brigade had been captured, and that Godwin's men were cut off from the bridge.

Peter Hairston, returning from the rear with a fresh horse, heard all this and also learned that all four artillery pieces had been taken.[13]

Early became a helpless and horrified witness of the brief fight God-win's survivors put up across the water. "I had the mortification of seeing the flashes of their rifles, and hearing their capture without being able to render them the slightest assistance." The only thing he could do was strengthen the defenses of the bridge in case the enemy tried to follow the few fugitives using it to escape. Many of these were shot into the water; those trying to swim did so in defiance of the already lethal cold of November. Few made it. When he thought he had allowed enough time for the last man capable of getting away to cross the bridge, General Early ordered it destroyed.[14]

<< THE RAPPAHANNOCK Station action, in Freeman's words, was "a disaster unlike any experienced by the troops in all their marching and fighting. Every rank and grade from headquarters to guardhouse was humiliated." Lee was taken by surprise, along with Early and Ewell, who was absent throughout the entire episode. Sixteen hundred and seventy-four of the army's best men were gone. The Richmond *Whig*, editorializing after the fight, lamented the loss of the Tigers; though decimated at Gettysburg, "the nine hundred remaining Louisianians were worth their weight in gold. . . . If they are now lost to Lee's army, we know not where the material will be found to replace them." [15]

Jubal's reaction to the affair, "the first serious disaster that had be-fallen any of my immediate commands . . . since the commencement of the war," was bitter regret. But he did not consider himself respon-sible for the reverse, asserting that he had voiced objections to the position ahead of time. Dining a few days after Rappahannock Station with Robert Chilton (bearer of the jumbled order at Chancellorsville and now a brigadier general), Early must have had to bite his tongue when Lee's aide blamed the design of the bridgehead position on Jubal: "You, General Early, thought it a strong one; those works were yours."

"No, sir," Jubal replied, calmly enough. "I objected to the engineer-ing and pointed out where I thought it was bad." [16]

Early may not have felt responsible, but he recognized that others might find fault. With characteristic touchiness, he reminded Lee of his offsetting accomplishments during the Gettysburg campaign—particularly the capture of 27 guns and over double the number of prisoners taken from him at Rappahannock Station. Of the four Louisiana Guard pieces the Federals had seized there, Early wrote, two had been captured from them at Winchester and one at Antietam.[17]

Early gave Sedgwick and his commanders little credit for bravery and martial skill, attributing their success in the fighting to the weight of numbers—as if all 30,000 members of the Union 5th and 6th Corps had assaulted the 2,000 men of his brigades at once. Actually, as Lee recognized, the front of the position was far too narrow for anything like such numbers to have attacked the earthworks simultaneously; the bridgehead fell to two adroitly and aggressively handled Union brigades—about 2,100 men in all.[18]

His line on the Rappahannock compromised, Lee now had to fall back behind the Rapidan. His mood must have been grim. Following the fiasco at the Station, he faced the fact that since opening the Bristoe campaign scarcely a month before, he had suffered more than 4,000 casualties. Meade had lost barely 1,000 men in the same period, though Lee did not know this. Nor did Lee know that he would never again be able to bring his whole army as far north as the line of the upper Rappahannock.[19]

‹‹ THE LOSS OF his brigades on November 7 depressed Jubal. For a couple of days after the defeat, according to Peter Hairston, the general also felt physically unwell. Hairston respected and liked his commander, describing him in a letter home as "decidedly a character—a fine officer, very active and energetic in the discharge of his duties with some peculiarities which render him very amusing."

In his letters and a diary, Hairston reported and commented on these idiosyncracies. He found much to admire in Jubal's skill as a tinkerer who repaired furniture and other articles. "General Early busy mending his spurs and his trunk lock," Hairston's diary noted on November 21; "he has quite a mechanical genius." The general was also adept at fabricating useful objects: in an 1864 letter, Hairston described helping him make a bedstead. "We cut some pine poles and made the legs . . . then nailed them together with some planks and then in Robinson

Crusoe fashion we cut some cedar poles and made a spring bottom to it. He calls it his patent night cottage bedstead." [20]

Less benign are images of Early's command style. His faithful aide, Andrew Pitzer, returned from a furlough just after Rappahannock Station, leaving a sick child at home, and torn between his duty to the army and his responsibility to the child. His greeting from Jubal:

"Well, Major Pitzer, you have played Hell."

"How so, general?"

"Why, you went away and let us get into a difficulty."

When Pitzer, reasonably enough, replied that he did not see how he could have prevented the "difficulty" if he had been present, Early had a last, if rather lame word: "You might have given us information." [21]

Lt. Col. Alexander ("Sandie") Pendleton, seeking leave to cope with the loss of his fiancée to a rival, received the benefit of Jubal's world-weary advice on the subject of women. The general admitted that the first time a woman discarded him he thought the world was coming to an end. The last time, he avowed, he did not mind. The general declared that he "left the room laughing and went to the faro bank and won $200." The camp, he advised Pendleton, was no place for a woman; in any case, it would be better to wait for the war to end before thinking of marriage. [22]

<< PENDLETON WAS Richard Ewell's chief of staff, inherited by Early when he took over temporary command of the 2d Corps on November 12 after Ewell, his wound acting up, departed on sick leave. Jubal would be in command of the corps during Lee's final campaign with the Army of Northern Virginia in 1863—the confused and inconclusive "skirmishing at Mine Run," as Early called it. [23]

Curiously inert following his victory at Rappahannock Station, Meade acknowledged pressure from Washington and stirred himself as November waned. His plan, to turn Lee's right flank and force the Rapidan line, was sound enough, but it fell afoul of Lee's superior intelligence, which revealed his adversary's intent in time to launch countermoves. Early was stationed on the right of the Confederate line in the broken Wilderness country south of the Rapidan, laced with minor roads and innumerable runs, or small watercourses. He was ordered, on the frigid night of November 26, to take his corps to meet Union forces reported by cavalry to be advancing across the lower Rapidan fords.[24]

Early's own division, under Hays, led the march, followed by Rodes and Johnson. Rodes's men, moving northeast, encountered Federals advancing onto high ground near Locust Grove on the morning of November 27. Hays soon joined forces with Rodes, but Lee hesitated to attack the Union position, which was very strong, until Johnson arrived. Traveling by a route longer than the roads used by the other two divisions, Johnson's contingent was delayed in its arrival until about noon.

Just as his division came up on Rodes's left flank, Johnson got word that his ambulances and wagons, traveling in the middle of his column, had been attacked by skirmishers. The capable Johnson, obeying a good rule of thumb for commanders in doubt, rode rapidly to the rear to make sure. When he reached the scene of action, he found his rearmost brigade hotly engaged with very substantial Union forces. Quickly forming a line of battle, Johnson ordered his men to attack.[25]

Johnson's division was up against the Union 3d Corps, which had crossed the Rapidan at Jacob's Ford, and was potentially in a position to attack Early's flank and rear. That this did not happen owes much to the confusing nature of the terrain, which prevented coordination of the Federal units (and hampered the Confederates as well). The ineptitude of the Federal corps commander, Maj. Gen. William H. French, also played a key part, as did the ferocious self-confidence of the gray-clad infantry. By nightfall, following a disjointed seesaw fight, Johnson had succeeded in checking the Union 3d Corps, which blocked the forward movement of the 6th Corps on the roads to the 3d Corps's rear. Johnson's combat at Payne's farm was costly to both sides, though Johnson came out ahead; he inflicted 952 casualties on the Federals, while losing 545. With Rodes and Hays holding at Locust Grove, the Army of the Potomac was stalled.[26]

But Lee did not feel strong enough for a major offensive move of his own—at least not yet. High ground to the west of Mine Run offered safe defensive positions from which the Confederates could stand off any assault by Meade; after dark, Lee pulled all his people back to the new position. There they dug in, working hard to fortify their line and keep warm through the gelid night. (Confederate Col. John Haskell called Mine Run "the coldest place we ever undertook to campaign in.")[27]

Early's corps now manned the left of the Confederate line, with Hill on the right. They could see the Federals entrenched on their own ridge east of Mine Run; but the expected Union attack did not come—on the 28th, the 29th, or the 30th. Finally, on December 1, Lee decided to push forward once again. The enemy, he found, had departed.

Lee could have kicked himself for letting Meade escape. "I am too old to command this army," was his bitter self-reproach. "We never should have permitted those people to get away."[28] Jubal had no grounds on which to reproach himself, having filled in for Ewell with aplomb. Critics, notably Freeman, have wondered whether he should not have sent Hays or Rodes to support Johnson on November 27. The question is readily answered: first, no one knew how strong the Federals at Locust Grove were, or what they intended. Second, in the tangled Wilderness countryside, it would have been difficult to intervene in the fight that Johnson had gotten into against French without risking great confusion in the dense woods. (This encounter was, in fact, a graphic preview of the Wilderness battle to come.) It would obviously have been a good thing if Early had been able to reinforce Johnson, but as Freeman essentially acknowledges, it was just not practicable.[29]

Freeman may be closer to the mark in implying a third possible reason for Early not to have sent Johnson support: he had no real idea where the fighting was taking place, and admitted in his report that he "could not see any portion of the troops engaged." It would have been logical for Early himself, as corps commander, to join Johnson and at least see what was happening; the fact that he never did suggests that he did not know where Johnson was. This may indicate, as Freeman thinks, that Early's sense of direction was underdeveloped. More likely, the possibility of getting lost in the chaotic landscape— and being captured—made him cautious about galloping indiscriminately off toward the sound of the guns. All he could really do was stay put, well aware that Johnson was capable of taking care of himself.[30]

« MOVING INTO the territory vacated by the Federals, Confederate troops discovered devastation: farms ruined, with stock killed, crops and barns burned, houses vandalized and stripped of valuables. Jubal cited, as a particularly horrible example, "a little tanyard" visible from Meade's headquarters near Locust Grove. The Federals, he said, had burned the tannery and the owner's house, and destroyed the leather and the hides.[31] "Such wanton barbarity," wrote Early in his report, "could have been perpetrated only by a cowardly foe, stung with mortification at the ridiculous termination of so pretentious an expedition."[32]

In such thunderous denunciations, Early's mind was beginning to forge an unbreakable connection between what he saw as the Yankees' uncivilized behavior and their craven ineptitude. Rage blinded him to his own illogic. At Mine Run, he was partly right, but as time passed, he would be increasingly mistaken. In the future, the Union army's "barbarity" would be more and more a part of a deliberate, rationalized military policy. However outrageous from a Southern viewpoint, this program would be untainted by "cowardice" in the accepted, chivalric sense; on the contrary, it would depend for its effectiveness on a bold departure from conventional views on the ethics of war.

CHAPTER FIFTEEN

The Trouble with the Cavalry

I N WINTER Jubal carried his idiosyncratic style of dress to an extreme. Whether it was an affection or a concession to the pain of arthritis aggravated by the cold—probably some of both—the effect was pronounced. As described by the correspondent of a Georgia newspaper, Early's head was "encased in a net striped woolen skull cap drawn about his ears"; his body was "contained within the embraces of a Virginia cloth overcoat, striking his heels"; and his lower limbs were "covered with leggings of the same material wrapped from the feet upwards as high as the knee with white tape." [1]

Swaddled against the chill in mid-December 1863, the general was in winter quarters near Orange Court House. Richard Ewell, declared fit, had returned to take charge of the 2d Corps and Early had resumed command of his division. As he anticipated the cold months' tedium, it must have been a relief when orders came on the 15th from Lee: Jubal was to undertake another independent command—a temporary but urgent assignment.

The emergency was a large cavalry raid launched by the Union command in western Virginia. Brig. Gen. William W. Averell, riding at the head of 2,500 horsemen, had thrust southward from New Creek to cut the Virginia & Tennessee Railroad at Salem, in Roanoke County. Brig. Gen. John Imboden, guarding the Valley with only a brigade of Confederate cavalry and some local volunteers, had appealed to Lee for reinforcements, as had the Western Virginia Departmental commander, Maj. Gen. Samuel Jones. [2]

Jubal's assignment was the capture or destruction of Averell and his

< 215 >

party. In this task he would fail, and he would later blame the outcome on a lack of disciplined, reliable cavalry. The fault-finding was somewhat unfair, since Averell's escape owed much to his own skill and determination; also working against the Confederates were bad luck, terrible weather, and faulty information. Still, there was enough ineptitude to justify some of Early's anger, at least for the moment; later in the winter, he would discern further instances of incompetence and poor discipline on the part of his cavalry. Unfortunately, in the long run these incidents taught Jubal little about discriminating among different units of cavalry. They merely fed a deepening prejudice against all cavalry. This bias, rooted in Early's revulsion against the behavioral lapses of some horsemen, would distort his military judgment and rob him of many of the advantages offered by judicious use of the mounted arm.[3]

<< FROM ORANGE, Early took the train to Staunton, in the Valley. He was followed by two infantry brigades that had been detached from A. P. Hill's corps and assigned to the Valley, commanded by Brig. Gen. Edward Thomas and Brig. Gen. Henry Harrison Walker. Jubal arrived on the 16th, the same day—as he read in a dispatch from Lee— that Averell appeared in Salem, which was undefended. The Federals promptly set about wrecking railroad property and destroying large quantities of supplies intended for Longstreet in Tennessee.[4]

Early's mission was apparently simple. The Federal raiding party would have to return whence it had come; the Confederates were between their enemy and his base. There were, to be sure, a considerable number of routes available to Averell as he finished his work of destruction and prepared to withdraw. But Early had the advantage of numbers, at least on paper. Besides the infantry brigades borrowed from Hill, Early was assigned two cavalry brigades under Brig. Gen. Fitzhugh Lee, detached from Stuart's command, to add to the brigade of John Imboden.

Also available from the Western Virginia Department commanded by Jones was a brigade of infantry under Brig. Gen. John Echols, based in Lynchburg, and cavalry, including a contingent under Col. William L. Jackson. For lack of forage, Jackson's troopers were largely dismounted; they were stationed at Jackson's River Depot on the Vir-

< 216 >

ginia Central Railroad. There they were in a good position to block Averell, especially if he returned the same way he had come—via Callaghan's Station and New Castle, or on nearby parallel roads. Altogether, these Southern units may have comprised as many as 6,000 men, outnumbering the Federals nearly three to one.[5]

Jones hoped to block Averell on the Callaghan's Station–Covington line or force him to swing wide. The Federal raiders, Jones thought, would then have to head north either through rugged country to the west, or push to the east—closer to Echols—via Covington or Clifton Forge on the Jackson River, where bridge crossings offered good defensive positions. In this stretch, the river was deemed unfordable.

Jones sent Early a dispatch describing his plans and dispositions and suggesting that Jubal send his infantry down to Morris Hill, outposting the Jackson River line and Callaghan's. The same dispatch announced that Jones had left a small cavalry force to watch Clifton Forge and Covington and to inform Early immediately if it appeared that Averell was headed that way.

Early never received this message, which fell into the hands of Averell. The Union officer, reading his adversary's mail, drew the natural inference that Clifton Forge and Covington were presently guarded by skeleton forces; he therefore resolved to take that route, believing that he could beat Early to the river crossings.[6]

Averell's thinking was sound. But he had not outsmarted Early. On December 16, Jubal ordered Imboden to take his brigade from his camp west of Staunton to Covington, to guard the bridges there and be ready to slide westward to cover Callaghan's if Averell should choose that line of escape. Imboden's most direct route to Covington required a number of crossings over the Little Calf Pasture, Big Calf Pasture, and Cow Pasture rivers; these were rendered impassible the night of the 16th by torrential rains ("such a rain as I have seldom seen," Early wrote). Imboden was forced to take a more circuitous easterly route. Meanwhile, Fitz Lee, newly arrived, was ordered to join Imboden at Covington with one of his brigades as soon as possible. (The other brigade, under Col. Thomas Lafayette Rosser, was assigned to guard Early's rear and disrupt enemy communications in the neighborhood of Front Royal.)

Early's planning now seemed certain to bring success. According to

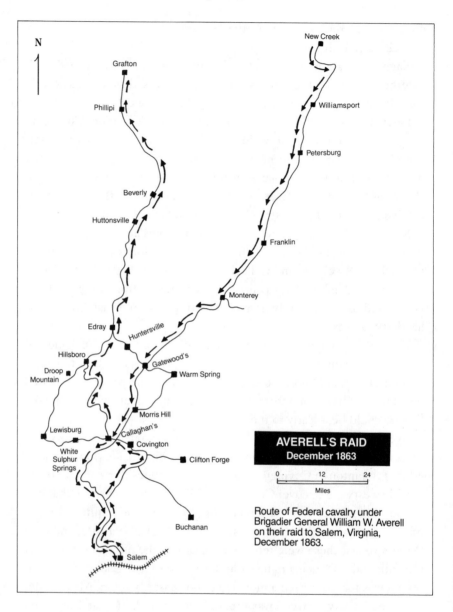

AVERELL'S RAID
December 1863

0 — 12 — 24
Miles

Route of Federal cavalry under
Brigadier General William W. Averell
on their raid to Salem, Virginia,
December 1863.

a telegram from Confederate sources in Lynchburg, the weather had immobilized Averell; he was indeed retracing his steps northward, but his retreat had been halted, according to the telegram, by high water on Craig Creek north of Salem.[7]

This information was basically inaccurate. Craig Creek was in flood as reported. But Averell was undeterred. He pushed on, crossing Craig Creek not once but seven times as his column, some four miles long, struggled north on the primitive river road. The route zigzagged back and forth over the swollen, turbulent stream, which was full of broken ice, slush, and fallen timber.[8]

The next telegram to Early from Lynchburg was as misleading as the first, but its consequences had a more direct impact on the Confederate plan of action. According to the second message, Averell had turned back to Salem. Having no reason to doubt this, Early promptly informed Fitz Lee, who had hooked up with Imboden as planned. Given discretion by Early, the two men on the scene concluded that Averell would now try to escape to the east—via Buchanan. They turned their steps in that direction. By the time the mistake was corrected, Averell had flown; on December 19 he crossed the Jackson River at Covington and gained two days' march on the Southern cavalry column that had come so close to tracking him down.[9]

Averell's passage across the Jackson River was opposed by the largely dismounted troopers of William Jackson's command, reinforced by a few home guards. These men, about 500 strong, were outnumbered three to one by Averell's force, which surprised them, pushed them aside, and captured both bridges. Jackson had prepared the bridges for burning, but his order to set the fires went astray and the crossings fell. Still, Jackson's men recovered from their initial shock and put up a good fight: attacking Averell from the rear, they managed to capture more than 100 Federals and a substantial number of horses. Averell felt desperate enough to burn the bridges himself on the 20th after the bulk of his command had crossed. This destruction marooned a regiment of Federal cavalry and most of the Union wagons and ambulances on the south bank, where the vehicles fell into Confederate hands. Nevertheless, the stranded Federal troopers managed to get away, crossing the river over a ford that Jackson knew nothing about.[10]

Jackson, a kinsman of Stonewall's who would come to be nicknamed "Mudwall," had failed. Not yet knowing all the facts, Early cast no blame, but he certainly withheld praise. In his official report, dated December 24, Early mentioned Jackson's claim to have captured 200 prisoners and most of Averell's wagons—though Jubal was skeptical about that degree of success. He could find no fault with Fitz Lee or Imboden, whose inability to catch Averell he sourly credited to the "erroneous information" transmitted from Lynchburg.

But for all this evenhandedness, Jubal seemed unable to refrain from lashing out, his target being the one cavalry commander not directly involved with the hunt for Averell: at the very end of the report, he appended a blast at Rosser, operating well to the north. Rosser's horses, Early stated, were "broken down" (whose were not?) and "his men a good deal scattered, he having accomplished nothing toward interrupting the enemy's communications." If the volatile Rosser heard about this criticism (as he might have), it could hardly have generated warm feelings toward General Early.[11]

Meanwhile, facts about the Jackson River fight not immediately known to Early were becoming available to others. Another report was filed two days later than Early's, written by Maj. Edward McMahon of Jones's staff. The document, sent from Covington, was a scathing indictment of Jackson and his troops. Among McMahon's numerous charges: Jackson divided his force; he made no preparations for meeting the enemy or blocking their movement, other than a fence he had his men build across the road; he sent no scouts farther than four miles from his camp before one of the provost guards ran into camp to announce that the Federals were approaching; Jackson made no battle plan; as local commander, he was not to be found during the crisis.

McMahon also stated that the trapped Union cavalry regiment that escaped finally did so after making three attempts—all unsuccessful—to surrender. At the time, according to the major, most of Jackson's men were "running about plundering and gathering up property abandoned by the enemy." That was bad enough. But the men who were not busy taking possession of Union matériel, McMahon reported, were committing crimes against local civilians ranging "from burglary down to rape."[12]

Neither Jackson's conduct nor the alleged misdeeds of his men were ever investigated. But though unproved, McMahon's catalog of military errors and lapses of discipline—including the perpetration of crimes—was just what Jubal was teaching himself to expect of cavalry unless commanded by the swashbuckling likes of Fitz Lee, a fellow West Pointer and a nephew of the commanding general.

« IN PARTICULAR, Early found ample grounds for criticizing Imboden. In January 1864, Imboden was absent from the Valley, his place taken temporarily by Col. George H. Smith. Imboden was a political figure of considerable importance in the neighborhood of Staunton; along with Henry A. Wise, he had been one of the hotheads bent on making war even before Virginia seceded. This reputation enabled him to wield a more effective influence over his men than Smith could exert.

During Imboden's absence, infractions of discipline, more or less petty, came frequently to Jubal's attention; these lapses he attributed to the unreliable character of the troopers and the laxity of their officers. It would not have been hard, for example, to find men in Imboden's brigade who got away with refusing to serve anywhere but near their homes in the Valley. Many troopers, Jubal asserted, were deserters from other parts of the army. Whoever they were, their military utility seemed, to Jubal, almost nil. With Imboden away, he found it difficult even to arrange for routine scouting: the troopers' conduct seemed at best to generate disorder—at worst outright evil. In early 1864, the murder of a sergeant in Imboden's brigade by a lieutenant epitomized the unit's depravity for Early. He wrote to Robert E. Lee in bitter protest.[13]

But he did not confine his expressions of disdain for Imboden's command to the written word. Everyone within the sound of Early's penetrating voice became familiar with his views—and soon enough, so did Imboden. His outraged reaction was to be expected. On his return from leave, he challenged Early in a complaint written to General Lee, demanding a chance to defend himself in a court of inquiry. He protested against "sneers unofficially and publicly made which are calculated if true to bring me and my command into disrepute and contempt," and accused Early of doing him and his men "gross injustice by yielding

< 221 >

to the promptings of prejudice rather than reason." Imboden's protest was aptly expressed. By this period of the war, Early's criticisms of fellow officers were growing increasingly harsh and intemperate, whether justified or not.

Imboden's complaint, proceeding through channels, received Early's official endorsement. He approved the idea of a court of inquiry, saying he believed it would result in an improvement of Imboden's brigade. Jubal noted the unit's "very bad state of discipline" and its consequent gross inefficiency: he would not like, he said, "to have to rely on it in any emergency." Lee's reaction to Imboden's letter was disapproval of the court of inquiry as not "advantageous"; the harm it would do in the public release of anger would offset any possible good.[14]

<< It was all too true that Imboden and Jackson represented the least reliable among the formations of Confederate cavalry, which differed in quality to a degree it would have paid General Early to study more systematically than he did.

Though a critical shortage of horses was a major source of trouble, the cavalry's principal weakness was lack of discipline. Furnishing his own horse, many a cavalryman regarded himself as his own commander. Officers might take it on themselves to decide which orders from above they would deign to obey, which they would ignore or defy. An arrogant complacency often fed these attitudes. The conspicuous bravery and proficiency with horses that often made the Southern cavalryman such a formidable fighting man often went with membership in the more affluent classes. Many of these patricians believed with all their being that "high-born freemen and gentlemen [did] not require the rigid discipline of regulars to make them soldiers." [15]

As to that, the Confederate horseman's definition of what it meant to be a soldier could be fairly loose. Under Confederate law, joining the service usually meant an enlistment for the duration of the war. But to many of the mostly young men who signed on, the act of enlistment in a cavalry regiment carried no unalterable obligations to government or army—no ties, for example, to a specific unit, or even a commitment to serve outside the home state. One Louisiana regiment accepted "independents ('peacocks,' the boys called them), that is, they were willing

< 222 >

to fight with us and do guard duty, but would not be sworn in; they wanted to reserve the right to leave when they were so disposed." [16]

Such indifference to accepted forms of regulation was far from universal. But the example of the "peacocks," cited by the historian Stephen Z. Starr, helps explain why many men who actually were sworn in nevertheless contributed to what Starr calls the "greatest failing of the Confederate cavalry, namely absence from the ranks."

A man without a horse could not, of course, take his place in ranks. The loss of a horse might not simply dismount its rider, but remove him completely from the field—at least for a time. If a mount died or was disabled in battle or on the march, the trooper who failed to capture a remount from the Yankees was allowed 30 days to find another horse, which he often went home to do. Horses grew scarcer as the war went on; the search for a suitable mount might be long and difficult, the charms of life at home correspondingly alluring. In many cases, of course, absence without leave eventually shaded into outright desertion. In other situations, it did not, except perhaps technically; the absentee would eventually drift back to his regiment, or join up with some other outfit. [17]

Confederate cavalry units most prone to such breaches tended to be those commanded by men like Imboden and Jackson. The troopers were recruited locally, their training and capability limited by the relatively shallow military grounding of their leaders, who had both been educated as civilians and trained as lawyers. Not surprisingly, the most efficient mounted formations were more likely to be led by professionally trained officers such as Fitz Lee, and Thomas Rosser (both West Point graduates), though Wade Hampton, a prewar planter, was a brilliant exception. Off to one side, regarded askance by many officers of all arms, were the so-called Partisan Ranger units, authorized by the Confederate government to make raids into enemy territory and perform other irregular services. Of these, the most celebrated—and effective—were the Rangers commanded by the dapper and elusive Col. John S. Mosby. Jubal Early regarded them all as freebooters pure and simple. [18]

<< COLONEL ROSSER, whose brigade augmented and later replaced Fitz Lee's cavalry in early January 1864, despised irregulars as much as Early. Rosser, a West Point classmate and bosom friend of George A. Custer, was a large, impetuous 29-year-old Virginia native who had grown up in Texas. As a cavalryman, he would never enjoy Jubal's entire trust. But on one subject presently uppermost in Early's mind, Rosser's views were unexceptionable. After ten days or so in the Valley, he unburdened himself, in a dispatch to Robert E. Lee, of a broad attack against the troops "known as partisans." Rosser called the irregulars a "nuisance and an evil to the service." His chief complaint, among many, was the fact that the irregular troopers often lived in or near their fields of operation, sleeping at home and exempted from normal military chores such as scouting, guard duty, and picket duty. This, along with other privileges enjoyed by the irregulars, such as being allowed to keep all their loot for themselves, generated discontent in the regular ranks.[19]

The message got through. The commanding general, forwarding Rosser's missive to the War Department, recommended that the "law authorizing these partisan corps be abolished." The Confederate Congress quickly passed legislation doing away with Partisan Rangers—though authorizing the War Department to make sweeping exceptions (Mosby's contingent being a notable example).[20]

<< ROSSER'S OWN capabilities were put to the test not long after he dispatched his condemnation of partisan troops to General Lee. On January 28, Early set off on a raid from the neighborhood of New Market in the Valley with Rosser's brigade, two units of mounted scouts, a brigade of infantry, and a battery of four guns. Imboden, under a cloud, was left behind with the other infantry brigade to guard the Valley.

Crossing North Mountain, the raiding force reached Moorefield, West Virginia, described by Early as "a most beautiful and fertile valley surrounded by high mountains" on the South Fork of the South Branch of the Potomac. There the general received word that a Union wagon train was moving south from New Creek to Petersburg, and would be within striking distance—just over Patterson Mountain from Moorefield—on the following day. Rosser took his troopers and the artillery across the mountain early in the morning and captured 50 wagons.[21]

Rosser then rode off, under orders from Early, to get north of Petersburg and block the retreat of that town's garrison, which Jubal proposed to attack with his infantry—expected to be on hand by nightfall. The foot soldiers, the same Georgians serving under Thomas who had bolstered Early's right at Cedar Mountain 18 months before, marched northward along the ridge of Branch Mountain. The weather had turned milder, but up on the ridge it was brisk, "with nothing," as Early wrote, "but wild inaccessible mountaintops and deep ravines on each side as far as the eye could reach."

In this moment, Early revealed a lighter side—and a familiarity with literature—seldom seen in public. Someone evidently told the general that the men wondered, as soldiers will, what they could be doing in this wilderness in the dead of winter. Writing later, Jubal obviously enjoyed telling the end of the short tale: when the men came in sudden "view of the beautiful valley of Moorefield and saw spread out before them what Johnson might have taken as the original of his ideas of the 'Happy Valley' in Rasselas, they burst into wild enthusiasm at the unexpected scene, so beautiful and inviting even in the midst of winter and with the tread of an invading enemy upon it."

The Georgians' doubts vanished, Early reported. And when the column reached Moorefield later in the day, even Dr. Johnson would have had trouble improving on what happened next: ". . . a large number of beautiful girls rushing out to see and welcome 'our' infantry, a sight that had not met the eyes of those warm-hearted beings" since Confederate forces had retreated through the town in 1861. The incident obviously cheered everyone up, from the citizens of Moorefield to the Georgian veterans and General Early himself.

His comments reveal not only a rare gentleness of humor, but a happy appreciation of nature. Here, also, was an optimistic and complimentary recognition of civilian acceptance of the war. In Moorefield and elsewhere, occasions for expressing such sentiments would henceforth be in very short supply, along with the sentiments themselves.[22]

<< EARLY'S PLAN to defeat the Union defenders of Petersburg was foiled by the retreat of the garrison at his approach. But Rosser continued his part of the mission, destroying B. & O. bridges and rounding up some 800 head of cattle. Jubal, most satisfied with Rosser's conduct on this expedition, not only recommended him for promotion to brigadier general, but forgave him—in some measure, at least—for a breach of discipline committed just before the raid. This transgression had offended two powerful Early crotchets: his prejudice about cavalrymen, and his abhorrence of wives in or anywhere near camp.[23]

Rosser was a newlywed, whose wife, Betsey, was so precious to him that he installed her in Staunton shortly after joining Early in the Valley. Just before leaving on his expedition to Moorefield, Rosser rode into Staunton to see her—without permission; Early found out and undoubtedly gave Rosser a tongue-lashing. He also reported the incident to Lee. Rosser, an ambitious man who had by now formed a dislike for his commanding officer, was indignant. In a letter to his bride, he described himself sitting "in his cold tent, wishing he was with Betsey," and calling Early "a miserable old rascal" for reporting him to Lee. Still, he promised Betsey, who was probably begging him to restrain himself, "to be a good boy and stay in camp." [24]

After the raid, Rosser asked Jubal for a furlough, which Early promised to consider when the Valley became more quiet. Meanwhile, Early wrote to Lee praising Rosser: "I have conceived a very high opinion of him as a cavalry officer, notwithstanding the affair I mentioned to you of his coming [to Staunton] after his wife."

In the same letter, Early applied to Lee on his own behalf for leave to go home to Franklin to take care of personal business; he also saw an opportunity, while in Rocky Mount, to "rectify" some "discontent with the war and some lukewarmness in the cause." The leave was granted, and in mid-February Jubal headed home for a couple of weeks.[25]

If and when he thought of Rosser while at home—and later—Early was undoubtedly glad of the younger man's success, which reflected well on Jubal. But Early was ambivalent about Rosser, wanting to think well of him, yet mistrustful. He may have been right in his doubts. On the eve of the Moorefield raid, Rosser was hatching larcenous plans

< 226 >

to procure "many nice things" for Betsey in response to a "memorandum" she had sent her husband. The source of these gifts for Betsey was to be a "strong scouting party" Rosser had sent down the Valley, its military mission to locate Union troops at points from which they might threaten the flank of the planned Moorefield expedition.

What was on Betsey's list is a mystery, and so is the means of procurement. But it is difficult to imagine that she was ordering up darning needles and cotton thread, or that the members of the scouting party, operating mostly behind enemy lines, were expected to buy the things she wanted in local stores. It seems obvious that the troopers were to obtain the "nice things" in any way that came to hand.

The scouting party's mission was a success. On his return from the Moorefield raid, Rosser informed his wife that his presents for her were in his possession and that he would bring them with him when he came to her on furlough.

Had Early known even the bare outlines of this, of course, he would have had everyone connected with it arrested and court-martialed. Rosser's career might have suffered badly, and Early's ambivalence toward him, which survived the war and eventually yielded to friendship (though not lifelong), would soon have hardened permanently—and not unjustifiably—into angry and suspicious disapproval.[26]

CHAPTER SIXTEEN

On a Darkling Plain

*I*N SPRING Jubal put on a new uniform and was resplendent—even comely. That, at any rate, was how General Lee saw him following Jubal's return from leave. In late March 1864, writing to a young cousin, Margaret Stuart, Lee described Early as "handsomer than ever. He looks bright in his new garments and the black plume in his beaver gives him the look of a gay cavalier." [1]

There is gentle irony in this remark; Lee might have been sharing a small joke at Jubal's expense with his "fair kinswoman." (Lee, not without affection, called Early "my bad old man," hardly the image of the perfect gentle "cavalier.") But it was not in Lee to distort or invent the basic facts about the new uniform—which bear out Jubal's contention that, given time and opportunity, he could take as much trouble with his appearance as the next man. Perhaps he had been inspired by a reunion with Julia during his leave in Rocky Mount. Certainly, on his return to camp, his spruce appearance showed that his spirits were high and that he looked forward to a resumption of campaigning as the season warmed. [2]

He probably had questions about his role in the campaign to come—whether he would continue at the head of his division or become corps commander. Dick Ewell, who had suffered a bad fall from his horse in January, seemed increasingly unfit to carry on in charge of the 2d Corps. Ewell's illness at the time of the Mine Run campaign had not disabled him more than a short time, but Lee felt great concern about his subordinate's ability to withstand hard field conditions. Ewell's artificial leg was of crude design; though he could ride his scruffy horse, Rifle, surprisingly well, walking was difficult and painful.

In this setting, Early's relations with Ewell were doubtless heavily influenced in the spring of 1864 by anticipation of taking over for the ailing senior general. Military and domestic circumstances encouraged Early in this presumption. The corps was in winter quarters near Orange Court House; Ewell was living with his new wife and her daughter in a private house some distance away. This arrangement absented Ewell from camp to a certain extent and put Early in a position to act for him as if in command of the corps. At the July 1 Gettysburg conference with Lee, Jubal appears to have behaved, even in Ewell's presence, as corps commander in fact if not in name. This would have been much easier with the lieutenant general actually out of the picture, even momentarily; Ewell himself admitted he was based too far from the army to see much of it. As for Jubal, his feelings about wives in wartime may have inflamed his attitude toward Mrs. Ewell, who had taken control of Ewell's entire life. One observer said that she "manages everything from the General's affairs down to the courier's who carries his dispatches. All say they are under petticoat government." It is likely Early deplored the demoralizing effect of such a dominating woman on her husband, who was absolutely besotted with love for her.[3]

Here was cause for a quarrel. A man in love is seldom inclined to tolerate criticism of his beloved. Jubal was not so reckless as to criticize Lizinka to Ewell's face. But as outspoken as Early was, any verbal strictures may well have reached the new husband's sensitive ears.

And Ewell may have had other grievances against Early. Greatly as Ewell respected him, Jubal was a subordinate, and that was what he would remain until officially promoted and assigned to higher command. This was a development that Ewell may well have foreseen, but the senior general, who stubbornly resisted acknowledging his own physical decline, would naturally have resented any usurpation of his position. Likely as not, Early, in his highhanded way, assumed authority he did not possess in some important matter and gave his superior grave offense. He may have done it more than once. Finally, on April 27, Early must have gone much too far: Ewell put him under arrest for "conduct subversive of good order and military discipline."

That has the sound of insubordination, an offense of which Jubal was demonstrably capable.

The details of this incident are lost—repressed by higher authority for the sake of morale and army solidarity. Lee rescinded the arrest order, while declaring that Early was to blame and calling his conduct "inexcusable." The army commander asserted the urgent military necessity of concord among his generals. But even from its obscurity, the episode throws a harsh light on Early's ambition and its baleful effect on a long relationship with a superior to whom he owed much of the advancement he had already secured. Given Early's willful nature, it is not really surprising that he pushed Ewell too far and too hard, though the incident was not repeated; nor did it result in a public feud.[4]

The surprise is the fact that Ewell did not really follow through in discouraging Early's attitude, even allowing him to resume the ascendancy that had generated the tensions leading to the arrest incident. In fact, the two men were to reenact the July 1 Gettysburg scene at the first major eastern battle of 1864—Early asserting his judgment in a situation where Ewell was unassertive. The result was a blunder, as at Gettysburg—and, in this case, the loss of a glittering chance to defeat the Army of the Potomac.

« IN VIRGINIA, the opening clash of the war's final phase pitted Lee against a new opponent, Ulysses S. Grant. Promoted to lieutenant general and given authority over all the Union armies, Grant devised a master plan for the 1864 campaign that envisaged an advance against the Confederates on several fronts: in the south and west, the principal drive would be Maj. Gen. William T. Sherman's lunge from Chattanooga to the vital rail and supply center of Atlanta; in the east, Maj. Gen. Benjamin Butler, stationed south of Richmond in the Bermuda Hundred, was to advance with 30,000 men on Petersburg and the Confederate capital; in addition, a Union force under Maj. Gen. Franz Sigel was assigned to march southwest up the Shenandoah Valley, severing Confederate communications with the west and seizing the vital granary between the Blue Ridge and the Alleghenies. (Largely because of the Federal generals' incompetence, Butler's and Sigel's ventures would fail.)[5]

Lee's major concern was the Army of the Potomac, with which Grant had chosen to pitch his headquarters tent. That army was still commanded by George Meade. Under Grant's constant eye, he was given the mission of fighting and defeating Lee.[6]

Grant's pugnacity and persistence as a commander in the West had recommended him to Abraham Lincoln, who knew that his political fortunes in November 1864 depended on victory—or some appearance of its prospect—well before election day. Unspoken was the assumption that Grant was to gain this victory in any way he could.

<< LEE FACED his opponent with about 60,000 combat troops, against roughly 100,000 in the Army of the Potomac. As Grant began pushing columns of infantry across the lower fords of the Rapidan into the battle-scarred rectangle of the Wilderness on May 4, the Confederate ranks did not yet include the 10,000 men of Longstreet's corps, which had been sent back to Lee from the west but were still on the march to join him. Yet Lee, for all his weakness, determined to strike Grant while he was in motion and before he could attack the Army of Northern Virginia. Shifting his two available corps eastward from Orange, Lee sent Ewell's men up the Orange-Fredericksburg Turnpike in the direction of a ramshackle stage station known as the Old Wilderness Tavern. The divisions of Rodes and Johnson led the march, with Early bringing up the rear. The 3d Corps under A. P. Hill moved on the parallel Plank Road toward Parker's Store and the Wilderness Church.[7]

With new leaf growth deepening the opacity of the scrubby Wilderness tangle in spite of a late spring, an early glimpse of the enemy was a vast advantage. This edge seems to have gone to the Federals advancing down the Pike toward Ewell's leading brigades. Suddenly attacked on May 5, these units fell back, to be relieved by Early's division. Gordon's brigade of Georgians led a successful counterattack and stabilized the Confederate position; by nightfall, the 2d Corps, constituting Lee's extreme left, was dug in on a line astride the pike about a mile from the Wilderness Tavern, where Grant had established his headquarters.

Lee assumed the fighting would resume next day, and was bent on seizing the initiative. Late on May 5, the army leader sent two successive written orders to Ewell, telling him that he was to attack on the 6th or at least arrange his forces so as to support attacks that Lee planned to launch on the Confederate right.[8]

Next day, the Federals opened their own offensive. They chose Hill's corps as their principal target, driving the Southerners back to a small clearing where Lee had set up his headquarters. The attackers threatened to split Lee's army and capture him. As if on cue, Longstreet and the 1st Corps arrived in time to reverse the dire momentum of the battle; then, seeing a chance to turn the Federals' left flank, "Old Pete" executed a counterstroke that began to create the impetus of a decisive Confederate victory.

The wounding of Longstreet by his own men—an eerie reprise of Jackson's fall only a few rods away the year before—drained the promise from this chance of triumph. Though Longstreet would recover, his loss, now and for months to come, was a dreadful setback for the Confederates.[9]

<< AT CHANCELLORSVILLE, Jackson's bid had been perhaps Lee's only chance of victory. In the Wilderness, Longstreet's attempt, aborted by his wounding, was but one of two solid opportunities offered to Lee by Grant.

The second opening arose from a tactical circumstance that bore a bizarre resemblance to the situation exploited by Jackson in May 1863. As at Chancellorsville, the Union right flank was in the air, although this was not immediately apparent to the Confederates.

The Federal weakness was discovered by Gordon on the morning of May 6. Though the Federals concentrated their offensive that day on Hill's sector, they did not ignore Ewell's corps, striking the center of Early's division front heavily and repeatedly around 5:00 A.M. The line held—at considerable cost. Meanwhile, on the far left of Early's line, occupied by Gordon's brigade, the situation was relatively quiet.[10]

<< JOHN BROWN GORDON was a 32-year-old Atlanta lawyer and entrepreneur who had raised his own company of north Georgia miners (known as the Raccoon Roughs) at the outset of the war and had risen quickly. Gordon had distinguished himself at Antietam, where he was

badly wounded. He was an attractive figure, a tall, erect man who rode superbly and fought with ferocious tenacity. He was an inspiring leader. "Gordon always had something pleasant to say to his men," one observer noted, "and I will bear testimony that he was the most gallant man I ever saw on a battlefield." [11]

When night fell on May 5, Gordon sent out skirmishers to reconnoiter his front. On their return some hours later, these scouts reported that they had found the enemy flank in the woods a short distance ahead. Gordon's line, the scouts added, overlapped the Federal position by a considerable margin.

To Gordon, whose "mind throbbed with the tremendous possibilities to which such a situation invited us," there seemed a chance of turning the Union flank. But that appearance might be a trap. Gordon moved with caution, sending other scouts out to check the findings of the first reconnaissance, with additional instructions to see whether supporting troops were backing up the dangling Union position. The second party confirmed the earlier report: the Federals were in a position to be devastated by an attack from the flank. Moreover, it appeared there were no supporting units within at least two miles.

Still unwilling to credit the scouts' report without making his own investigation, Gordon called for his horse and set out to the north, accompanied by members of the earlier scouting parties. Riding toward the Rapidan, Gordon found an empty landscape. Then, on his return to the Confederate lines, he dismounted and crept, with a scout, through the underbrush. Soon, as he later wrote, he could hear "an unsuppressed and merry clatter of voices." A yard or two more on hands and knees, and Gordon could see "the end of General Grant's temporary breastworks. There was no line guarding this flank. As far as my eye could reach, the Union soldiers were seated on the margin of the rifle-pits, taking their breakfast." [12]

It was about 9:00 A.M. Swiftly, Gordon rode in search of Early and Ewell, ordering a staff officer, Thomas G. Jones, to do the same. The Georgian was eager to impart his news and submit a plan for an attack that would sweep around Grant's flank and roll up his army.

Jones found Ewell, but Early was not with him, possibly busy posting the troops of a brigade under Robert Johnston that Ewell had de-

< 233 >

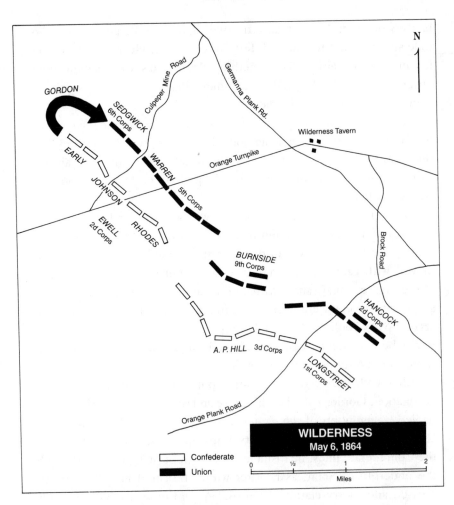

GORDON

SEDGWICK
6th Corps

Culpeper Mine Road

Germanna Plank Rd.

Wilderness Tavern

N

EARLY

WARREN

Orange Turnpike

JOHNSON

5th Corps

EWELL
2d Corps

RHODES

BURNSIDE
9th Corps

Brock Road

HANCOCK
2d Corps

A. P. HILL   3d Corps

LONGSTREET
1st Corps

Orange Plank Road

WILDERNESS
May 6, 1864

Confederate

Union

0   ½   1   2

Miles

tached from Rodes's division to strengthen the 2d Corps's left flank. This flank, Ewell believed, was in danger from Union forces reported by cavalry to be moving east and south from Germanna Ford on the Rapidan; Early's orders were to guard against such a threat.[13]

On Early's return, Jones laid out his brigade commander's plan. Early rejected it instantly, on grounds not only that Federal troops were threatening the army's flank, but that a reserve Union corps under Ambrose Burnside was poised close behind the Union right; this force, Early asserted, was capable not only of thwarting Gordon's plan but of menacing the entire Confederate position. If Gordon's attack failed and Burnside launched a counterthrust, Ewell had no reserve to repulse it.[14]

The argument persuaded Ewell. At this point, Gordon himself rode up and joined the conference. For a quarter of an hour, he urged his plan—in vain. His case, based on the evidence of his own eyes, was dismissed, even when he offered to absorb all responsibility for failure.[15]

Thus nothing was done. The morning and much of the afternoon wore away while Ewell's troops and those opposing them—members of John Sedgwick's 6th Corps—snoozed and smoked in their rifle pits.[16]

Over on the Confederate right, meanwhile, the fighting raged. Following Longstreet's wounding, the brigades he had sent into the attack maintained it as best they could. But the Wilderness, which quickly disorganized advancing troops and allowed those in retreat to escape without great damage, frustrated Lee's hope of a decisive stroke. He must have wondered as the day passed what Ewell was doing to comply with the urgent directives of the previous evening.

At this point in the story, according to most narrators, Lee rode over to Ewell's headquarters to find out what was going on. In this version, Lee asked what Ewell could do to relieve pressure on the right, where Federal resistance was stiffening and casualties were mounting. Ewell, Early, and Lee discussed the matter for a while; then Gordon, who was present, broke in and described his plan to Lee. After hearing Gordon, the army commander asked Ewell and Early why they had not executed the plan when first proposed. Whatever the generals had to say, it evidently did not satisfy Lee, who thereupon personally ordered the attack.

Making Lee an active participant in the dispute over the practicability of Gordon's plan makes a good story, especially from Gordon's standpoint. But it has a flaw: Gordon himself is the only source—unsupported by any other, including his own official report, submitted on July 5, 1864. Neither Ewell nor Early mentioned it in official or unofficial writings. The story first appeared in Gordon's *Reminiscences*, published in 1903, after all of the principals except himself were dead. Did the Georgian invent the Lee conference with Ewell, Early, and himself?

In his 1989 biography of Gordon, Ralph Lowell Eckert does not go so far. With respect and some reluctance, Eckert forgives Gordon his "mistake" in recalling (in some detail) a meeting that may never have taken place. Eckert surmises that "the passage of years substantially distorted the general's recollection of the events" and doubts that Gordon "attended such a conference or that Lee directly issued such an order." Though Lee's principal biographers have accepted Gordon's version, Eckert's analysis makes a great deal of sense. Early claimed, in his *Autobiographical Sketch*, that he suggested that Ewell issue the attack order to Gordon; in his official report, Ewell confirms this; Gordon's report says Early gave the order. Postwar correspondence between Lee and Gordon, which Eckert cites, shows that Lee did visit Ewell's sector and talk to Gordon on May 7. But no one who might have been there—except Gordon—said that Lee ever left the right wing of his army on May 6, at any rate in order to visit Ewell.[17]

« AT SOME POINT on the 6th, the senior officers of the 2d Corps were informed of the actual whereabouts of Burnside's corps, which had marched far from the Confederate left and became engaged on the right. But the afternoon was well advanced before Ewell or Early made or ordered a reconnaissance of the terrain originally scouted by Gordon—and realized that he had been right: the Federal flank still dangled, with no supporting Union troops in its rear.

Around sundown, the order for the attack was finally given: Gordon's brigade was to make the assault supported by Johnston's. As Gordon later reported, Ewell and Early now gave Gordon complete support.

The assault was a smashing triumph—at least for a short time. Initially, it succeeded in creating enormous confusion among the Union troops that received the opening shock. Two Union brigades ran away, shedding their weapons as they fled and creating considerable panic.

But John Sedgwick was quick to meet the crisis, rallying troops and erecting breastworks that helped slow the Confederate advance. An even greater impediment was the encroaching darkness, which, along with the dense growth, helped disorganize the attackers. The assault faded as night shut the battlefield down.[18]

Most of these circumstances were simply part of the grim insanity of the Wilderness battle. Still, the attack, if made earlier in the day when Confederate fortunes on the right were ripening in the light of Longstreet's counterstroke, might have had a decisive effect.[19]

Gordon's losses, compared to the overall level of casualties in the Wilderness, were light on May 6. The assaulting brigades lost 60 men while Federal losses were some 400 killed and wounded along with several hundred prisoners, including two brigadier generals. General Early lost the services of Major Daniel, one of his most valued staff officers, who was maimed while trying, at Jubal's instigation, to keep the attack from losing cohesion in the gathering dusk.[20]

« THE CONDUCT of Ewell and Early on May 6 resonates with the disturbing overtones of their relationship. Here was the corps commander, under reiterated written orders to carry out some sort of offensive operation on the 6th—orders that gave him less discretion than Lee had hitherto been accustomed to vouchsafe. Here, in Gordon's initiative, was an opportunity to carry out those orders with the promise of a smashing victory. True, the prudent commander must scrutinize such opportunities very carefully, knowing that a shrewd enemy may be employing a ruse. But Gordon, a trustworthy subordinate, had sent out two successive scouting parties and then spent upward of an hour and a half perusing the situation in person.

Ewell could logically have been expected to approve the attack urged by Gordon sometime during the morning—if it had not been for Early. Ewell's disapproval grew directly from Early's attitude, even though Jubal's opposition was illogical, being based on inadequate knowledge. When supplied with more complete information, Early changed his mind.

Why was Ewell, who heard the arguments of both subordinates, unable to make the logical decision—the one, moreover, that Lee had virtually mandated? There is no clear answer to this question. But one explanation may lie in Early's evident assumption of his own infallibility. Where it impinged on Gordon, this attitude apparently led Early to dismiss the brigade commander's potent initiative simply because it came from a subordinate, a man, moreover, untrained at West Point. And, whatever its merits on the evidence, the plan did not fit the conclusions about enemy movements and dispositions that Early, as divisional commander, had reached. Case closed.

Where Ewell is concerned, Jubal's attitude about his own incontrovertibility is harder to define. But Early seems to have somehow convinced Ewell that he, the senior officer, should defer, more or less without question, to the junior general's judgment. Possibly Ewell, baffled and distracted by the chaotic conditions on the Wilderness battlefield, daunted by his responsibilities, tortured by his wound, and ever willing to rely on Early, unwittingly adopted this point of view and the passive role that accompanied it. An eloquent indication of Ewell's passivity is his failure to urge an alternative to Gordon's plan. There is no evidence that he ever called Lee's orders of May 5 to Early's attention, as if to say, "We have orders to do something aggressive, general; if we don't do this, we must do something else. What do you suggest?" In any case, Early, who may have been ignorant of Lee's orders (he never mentioned them), certainly did not act on them.

‹‹ THE WILDERNESS battle was a grim standoff—though Grant, numerically superior, suffered a greater percentage of casualties (about 17,000, or 15 percent) than his opponent (7,500, or 12 percent). Lee had succeeded in neutralizing the power of Grant's mighty army, at least for the time being. In the past, such an outcome might well have persuaded a Federal commander in Grant's situation to back away, pulling his army across the Rapidan to rest and refit.[21]

Instead, the Army of the Potomac, far from withdrawing, slid ponderously off to the southeast. Fighting ceased momentarily while Grant resumed his thrust toward Richmond, and Lee maneuvered to block the way. As Lee was absorbing the harsh message of Grant's relentless style of warfare, the Southern leader also had to cope with immediate problems of command.

Probably because Ewell had ignored Lee's May 5 directives, the commanding general seems to have held him principally responsible for the lost opportunity against the Federal right. Whatever blame Lee may have also attached to Early, it did not prevent him from including Jubal in his initial list of possible candidates to replace Longstreet as head of the 1st Corps. A staff officer agreed that Early was a good choice on grounds of ability—but noted that Jubal's acid tongue had made him too many enemies in the corps. Richard H. Anderson was Lee's eventual choice.[22]

During the furious combat of May 5 and 6, Powell Hill had been almost too ill to function. By the 7th, he was clearly incapacitated. Early was an obvious interim replacement for Hill, and Jubal took over the 3d Corps on May 8. He handed the temporary command of his own division to John Gordon—an acknowledgment of the Georgian's capacity as demonstrated on May 6 and his paramount status among Early's brigadiers.[23]

‹‹ IN SLIPPING to Lee's right, Grant precipitated the exhausted armies into a race for possession of the strategically vital crossroads hamlet of Spotsylvania Court House, about 12 miles south of the Wilderness battlefield. Lee was able to win the race as Anderson's men marched through the night of May 7–8 and Confederate cavalry blocked the routes of Federal forces moving south.

Early, leading the 3d Corps, arrived in the vicinity of Spotsylvania in time to help drive back a Federal attempt to get around the Confederate left flank. Lee then formed a line with Anderson on his left, Ewell in the center, and Early on the right. In the climactic fighting on May 12, when Grant assailed Ewell's front (forming the salient known as the "Bloody Angle"), Jubal's role as a corps commander was initially confined to lending three brigades to reinforce Ewell in the salient. These units helped Gordon, leading Early's own division, contain the Federal assault, which had come close to shattering the center of Lee's line; the Union onslaught had captured more than 4,000 prisoners including Gen. Edward Johnson and Gen. George H. Steuart.

Jubal, operating under the proximate (though unofficial) supervision of Powell Hill, who was offering advice from an ambulance close to the front, also sent two brigades to assail the left flank of the Union attackers. Soaked by intermittent, violent rains, these brigades collided with units of Burnside's 9th Corps forming up to assault the Confederate right. The Union plan was foiled, and Burnside's men were driven off with substantial losses.[24]

Early ordered a resumption of the flanking maneuver at the point where the encounter with Burnside had interrupted it. But 3d Corps troops abandoned the move, with Early's approval, when they ran into terrain broken up by gullies and creased with bristling Federal entrenchments in successive lines.[25]

Following this long day of bloody crisis, the 3d Corps was largely inactive. Knowing that these exhausted regiments were not being endangered by any order of his might have eased Jubal's mind in contemplating his ambiguous role. He was temporary commander of a corps whose officers and men he did not know well and whose regular leader was disconcertingly near at hand. Through the ensuing week, Early was surely conscious of Hill in his ambulance, as close to the lines as he could get and ready at any moment to lend "the aid of his personality to Gen. Early," as a correspondent reported in the Richmond *Enquirer* on May 20.[26]

On that day, no doubt gratefully, Jubal turned the 3d Corps over to Powell Hill once more and returned to the command of his own division, riding south on May 22 to catch up with the 2d Corps. Responding to a resumption by Grant of his southward movement around the Confederate right, Ewell had marched, with his badly depleted force, to the neighborhood of Hanover Junction. As the armies were departing the shambles of the Spotsylvania battlefield, John Gordon was promoted to major general and given the command of the division until recently headed by Edward Johnson, a captive at Spotsylvania. Thus did General Lee recognize Gordon for his share in the problematic victory in the Wilderness, and his aggressive and efficacious conduct in the terrible fighting of May 12 at Spotsylvania. In a general order, Lee also publicly thanked Early for his service as the 3d corps commander "in the late trying emergency."[27]

« FOR RICHARD EWELL, the pace of movement and combat, virtually unrelieved for three weeks, was now unendurable. Ill with diarrhea, he was forced to ask Early to take over—a step made official on May 29 by Lee, who relieved Ewell and made Early temporary commander of the 2d Corps.[28]

Feeling better after a couple of days, Ewell chafed to resume his place at the head of his corps. He reported for duty. Lee, not so sure that Ewell was fit physically or mentally, put him off: the corps, the army commander told Ewell, was in line of battle confronting the enemy, and "I do not think any change at the present time would be beneficial." [29]

Ewell knew that Early was in the neighborhood of Mechanicsville, where on May 30 the corps had attacked Federal forces trying to maneuver around the Confederate right toward the Chickahominy River. He may have known that the attack had failed.

The assault had been ordered by Lee, who saw a chance to halt the Federals' southeastward maneuvering by hitting a portion of the Union force that had crossed Totopotomoy Creek in the neighborhood of the 1862 Seven Days' battles. To bring this about, Early and the 2d Corps, supported by Anderson's 1st Corps, was to advance eastward toward Bethesda Church, near a crossroads about two miles south of the creek.

Rodes's division encountered the Federals first, forcing a Union brigade to withdraw east toward the church. The ensuing action threw a spotlight on Brig. Gen. Stephen Dodson Ramseur. Highly regarded— at least by his superiors—for boldness combined with good sense, the 27-year-old Ramseur had been given command of Early's division on Jubal's elevation to corps command. Ramseur now brought his division forward, with Pegram's brigade leading the column. Pegram, wounded at the Wilderness, had handed temporary command over to Col. Edward Willis (of the 12th Georgia), with whom Early and Ramseur were riding when the division came under fire from a lone artillery piece in a patch of woods to the north.

Though the single gun could not have been doing much damage, Ramseur's impulse, communicated to Early, was to suppress the fire. The corps commander disagreed; but after considerable discussion, Ramseur was authorized to take Pegram's brigade, backed up by one of Rodes's brigades, and reconnoiter. Not long after the probing force moved forward, the crew of the offending artillery piece limbered up and withdrew out of the woods into a line of earthen fortifications on the opposite side of an open field. Marching through the woods and out into the field, the Confederates confronted a concentration of guns in the works. Still, they kept on moving ahead—until, having reached the middle of the field, the two brigades were dropped in their tracks by concentrated fire from the massed artillery. The 49th Virginia, which had seen so much, lost all its field officers; Willis was killed, along with many in Pegram's brigade and others, including Col. James B. Terrill, commanding the 13th Virginia.

This was a costly, inauspicious debut for Ramseur as a division commander, and Early must share some of the blame, particularly for not demanding that Ramseur make a more careful reconnaissance. Early should also have tried harder to take advantage of available support from Anderson's corps, which had been assigned that role. Meanwhile Grant, undeterred by the abortive attack, was able to slide his left farther south and east.[30]

Whatever his views about this outcome, Ewell felt increasingly beleaguered. By June 1, he was pulling bureaucratic strings. He wrote to Col. Walter H. Taylor, Lee's assistant adjutant general, asserting that his doctor, the 2d Corps's medical director Dr. Hunter McGuire, agreed with him that he had not been in better health since the beginning of the campaign.[31]

Taylor doubtless reported the letter to his chief. Lee, by now convinced that Ewell was too frail to serve in the field, took up his own pen and composed an administrative memorandum to Ewell that effectively removed him from the corps command. The Confederate Congress, Lee wrote, had just passed a bill calling for emergency promotions; Early was to be made a lieutenant general and given the 2d Corps— at least until the current Union threat was at an end. Ramseur would become a major general and command Early's division. There were to be other promotions of a similar character. In the meantime, Lee suggested that Ewell accept appointment as head of the Richmond defense forces.[32]

The emergency powers built into the recent legislation gave Lee a way to soften the blow to Ewell, since it allowed him to emphasize the officially temporary nature of Early's appointment; but the one-legged general, probably nursing suspicions of Early suggested by Mrs. Ewell, was not satisfied. Like Powell Hill, he stayed with the troops instead of putting himself to bed; he tried to appeal to President Davis; finally, he confronted Lee, and seems to have suffered the commanding general's displeasure. In the end, he took the Richmond defense job.[33]

The situation gave Early genuine cause for concern. Ewell's vain efforts to get himself reinstated must have been the gossip of the whole army. For many reasons, among which some guilt and embarrassment presumably mingled with considerable affection for his former chief, Early took pains to disarm Ewell's suspicions and assuage his hurt feelings. In a June 5 letter to Ewell, Jubal denied that he had had any involvement in the change of command, and reminded the senior general that it was supposed to be only temporary. Early went further, stating that he would have been "grateful" if Ewell had remained in charge "all the time."

In any case, Lee's views about the dangers of a change in the face of crisis were understandable, Early said; he was quite sure that the army chief's position was not based on "dissatisfaction" with Ewell. Jubal announced clearly that he did not want any misunderstandings to arise between him and Ewell on account of the command change, or for any other reason—such as the arrest incident in the spring. "I further assure you," he finished, "that I retain no unpleasant feeling on account of the little affair at the Rapidan, but hope that the cordial, friendly relations that have always existed between us will continue in future." [34]

This hope may have been empty. Contemplating his new and much reduced status as leader of local defenses—albeit those of the capital— Ewell may have wished he could have been closer to the action at Cold Harbor. There Grant, who was trying to overwhelm his adversary with sheer violence, sacrificed thousands of men on June 3 against the stubborn defense mounted by the Army of Northern Virginia, in which the 2d Corps played its part with Early in charge. After the battle, which temporarily eased Federal pressure on the Army of Northern Virginia, a bitter diversion for Ewell may have been reading communications from his stepson Maj. Campbell Brown. The major was still serving on the 2d Corps staff under Early, who seems to have been shaking things up.

"Everybody is disgusted," Brown reported in one letter. "Old Early did not ask me how you were, but I made my speech so that he will hear it. . . . Two of the best of the Signal Corps (the Wynn brothers) have applied to be relieved. Early set them to minding horses—they being gentlemen will not stand it. He is kicking up a row in everything he comes near." In the same letter, Brown hinted that Jubal might have been wondering what the major was writing home about him. "I intend seeing little of Early," wrote Brown, "and will get along finely. He looks at me like a sheep-stealing dog, out of the corner of his eye, and when I reported myself for duty this evening, was astonished at this peculiarity—very different from his usual manner."[35]

Campbell Brown's tone in writing to his mother's husband indicates that he knew his reader would not take offense at his words. Richard Ewell was no longer Jubal Early's defender. Yet in the circumstances, Ewell was not being altogether fair. Early had deserved his promotion, and he was the most logical officer to succeed the incapacitated Ewell in command of the 2d Corps. Ewell was being stubborn and unrealistic in his efforts to hold on to command of the corps.

If Jubal was aware that all was not well between him and the former corps commander—he never revealed such awareness—it undoubtedly puzzled him. He had, after all, made an effort to reassure and conciliate Ewell in a personal letter. What more could he have done? As he settled into his new assignment, Jubal probably gave little conscious thought to the matter, settling whatever blame there might be on Ewell—and especially on Mrs. Ewell. But there could be no doubt that in gaining the highest command he could hope for in this war he had lost the trust and close affection of one of the most devoted friends he would ever have.

CHAPTER SEVENTEEN

Lynchburg Rescued

O N JUNE 12, 1864, Robert E. Lee summoned Jubal Early to his headquarters for the most momentous conference the two men would ever hold. The subject of the meeting was an assignment of solemn importance: command of a diversionary corps to be detached from the Army of Northern Virginia for operations in the Shenandoah Valley. This force was to have the primary goal of frustrating Grant's destructive plans in that theater; later, if it seemed feasible, the Confederate column was to slice down the Valley, cross the Potomac—and threaten Washington. That maneuver might induce Grant to detach troops from eastern Virginia and relieve the strain on Lee's defense of the capital.[1]

« THIS PLAN was a bold response to Union pressure that had only barely let up since early May. At that point, apart from the threat posed by Meade's Army of the Potomac, the Confederate commander had had to worry about subsidiary menaces presented by Maj. Gen. Benjamin Butler's force in the Bermuda Hundred peninsula and Maj. Gen. Franz Sigel's in the Valley.

An idyllically beautiful green rift set between the Blue Ridge in the east and the Alleghenies in the West, the Valley of Virginia was ideally suited to military operations, as Early and Lee well knew. Under the farmer's ax and plow since the eighteenth century, the terrain was clear and open, a good place to maneuver large bodies of troops. Distances were tidy; the Valley, set roughly on a southwest-northeast axis, was about 20 miles broad at its widest point opposite Strasburg.

The geographic orientation of the Valley and its topographical manageability had already made it important to both sides in the Civil War, notably in the campaign of 1862, which established Stonewall Jackson's reputation. The Valley offered Southern strategists a broad avenue between the Confederacy and the heart of the North, leading to the rich towns of Maryland and Pennsylvania, and to the back door of the Northern capital.

To the Union, the Valley represented less of a strategic opportunity, largely because the rift's southwest-northeast orientation led an invader away from—rather than toward—the Confederacy's vitals. But the rift did offer the North two opportunities. Sheltered behind the Blue Ridge, Federal forces could maneuver up and down the Valley, threatening the western flank of the Confederate capital at Richmond. More important was the fact that the Valley lay athwart two vital rail lines: the Virginia & Tennessee Railroad, carrying matériel from Knoxville to Lynchburg and Richmond; and the Virginia Central, running to Richmond from Staunton through Waynesboro. The Virginia Central was particularly vital in moving troops and supplies between Richmond and the Valley.

The most essential supplies produced in the Valley were crops and livestock to feed the increasingly hungry Army of Northern Virginia, and forage to sustain the thousands of horses on which it depended. Obviously, Federal possession of the Valley, even temporarily, represented a grave danger to the Confederates' ability to prosecute the war.[2]

« As HAD so often happened, Federal clumsiness helped ease some of the strain on Lee. By early June, Butler had allowed himself to be penned up in his river-bound cul-de-sac by numerically inferior Confederate troops (under Gen. P. G. T. Beauregard) defending Bermuda Hundred Neck. Lee could also cease worrying about Sigel. The German-born Union general, leading a 6,500-man column southward, had met defeat on May 15 at New Market and had pulled his force back down the Valley.[3]

The Confederates could rejoice at the significance of Sigel's undoing, which had cost the Federals precious time. The German had seemed on the point of seizing Staunton, not only the most important western station on the Virginia Central Railroad, but also a major hospital center and supply depot. On May 14, Sigel's force had marched into New Market, some 42 miles north of Staunton. There, the next day, it had collided with a force built around two small infantry brigades under Brig. Gen. Gabriel Wharton and Brig. Gen. John Echols; these units were supported by John Imboden's cavalry brigade and reinforced by some local militia and the cadet corps—more than 200 spirited martial acolytes—of the Virginia Military Institute. This improvised contingent, about 5,000 men led by Maj. Gen. John C. Breckinridge, had overcome the Federals in a sharp, bloody fight lasting upward of seven hours.[4]

The Confederates, at the cost of 43 dead and 477 wounded and missing (ten cadets were killed or died of wounds), had won one of the most important secondary battles of the war, which—a matter of much mystical significance to many—had taken place on the first anniversary of Stonewall Jackson's funeral. The victory thwarted an immediate Union occupation of the upper Valley. This grim prospect would have forced Lee to send troops desperately needed at Spotsylvania to defend the Valley. Such a sacrifice of strength in the face of the Army of the Potomac might have cost the Confederates their capital. As it was, following New Market, Lee felt he could transfer Breckinridge and his scratch force from the Department of Western Virginia back to the east to lend support in the Cold Harbor campaign.[5]

Unfortunately for the Confederates, Sigel's reverse did not deflect Grant from his purpose in the Valley. He was at Spotsylvania when he got the news in a telegram from his chief of staff, Maj. Gen. Henry Halleck, who ended his message by naming Maj. Gen. David Hunter as the officer whom the Washington authorities wanted to put in Sigel's place.[6]

Hunter assumed command of the Federal Valley force on May 19, with orders to move toward Staunton and Lynchburg, destroying railroad communications and supplies, and eventually either returning to the lower Valley or joining Grant near Petersburg. On June 5, marching toward Staunton, Hunter encountered a small Confederate force under Brig. Gen. William E. ("Grumble") Jones near Piedmont. Hunter thrashed this contingent badly, wounding or killing about 600 Confederates (Jones was among the dead) and capturing more than a thousand prisoners. The 3,000 Confederate survivors headed for Waynesboro—abandoning Staunton—and ended by withdrawing all the way to Lynchburg.[7]

Entering Staunton unopposed on June 6, Hunter's troops were the first armed Union soldiers to occupy the town since the onset of war. On the 8th, 10,000 reinforcements—infantry under Maj. Gen. George Crook and cavalry led by Brig. Gen. William Averell—more than doubled Hunter's numbers to 18,000. In Washington, this aggregation seemed just large enough to be worthy of the designation "Army of the Shenandoah" soon to be conferred by Edwin M. Stanton, the Union secretary of war. But the two days Hunter spent in Staunton waiting for these reinforcements were to represent very expensive hours when the campaign accounts were settled up.[8]

For the moment, Hunter basked in a glow of pride and self-satisfaction. As he was preparing to leave Staunton, he received a telegram that must have confirmed his sense of well-being. From the secretary of war, the message congratulated Hunter on his victory at Piedmont and his occupation of Staunton, and continued: "These brilliant achievements wipe out the antecedent disasters to our arms in former campaigns in the Shenandoah Valley." [9]

From Staunton, Hunter proceeded to Lexington, brushing aside a weak though persistent resistance offered by Confederate cavalry under the 27-year-old Brig. Gen. John C. McCausland that was part of the West Virginia command. Falling back through Lexington, McCausland enlisted the VMI cadets to help defend their institute. When it became obvious that the Federals would prevail, the cadets were ordered to hurry off to Lynchburg to bolster the garrison.

Hunter's forces entered Lexington on June 11. That day the Union general showed an aspect of his attitude toward war that went well beyond strictly professional behavior.[10]

Hunter ordered the torch put to the buildings of VMI. Though this act could have been justified on military grounds, the burning also included the house of Stonewall Jackson. During the search before Jackson's house was set on fire, his sister-in-law, Mrs. Margaret Junkin Preston, managed to hide his sword from Hunter's men under her voluminous skirts; when she was forced by the flames to leave the house, she hid the sword in the privy.[11]

Washington College, next door to the military institute, could hardly have been considered of military importance. But Hunter ordered it burned, too. Though the Federal soldiers who were given the order balked, other men showed no compunction in incinerating the Lexington home of Governor John Letcher. This destruction was in retaliation for what Hunter called a "violent and inflammatory proclamation" issued during Letcher's recent term as governor and calling, as Hunter alleged, for guerrilla warfare against Union forces.[12]

Hunter's Lexington raid accomplished little of military value. And it cost him invaluable time. Hunter spent three days in Lexington, twice as long as he should have in order to arrive in Lynchburg before the Confederates had a chance to strengthen its defenses. With even 36 hours at Hunter's disposal, Lynchburg would inevitably have fallen to him, and Early would have had great difficulty in recapturing it.

<< IN HIS BEHAVIOR at Lexington, Hunter showed himself one of the more bizarre characters of the Civil War. Virginia-born, the general was a West Point graduate who had served in the Mexican War; Jubal Early had met him in Mexico and liked him. Few Confederates had reason to like Hunter now. A fanatic abolitionist despite his origins, Hunter, known in the old army as "Black Dave," was a broad-shouldered, swarthy man whose troops declared that he dyed his raven hair and sickle-shaped "Hungarian-style" mustaches. Prone to fierce attacks of anger, the general, a deeply religious teetotaler who neither smoked nor cursed, yielded to no man in matters of principle. Still, he seemed irrational at times. One of Hunter's subordinates noted that the general's judgment was flawed by prejudices and antipathies "so intense and violent as render him at times quite incapable of taking a fair and unbiased view of many military and political situations."[13]

One example was notorious. In command at Fort Pulaski, Georgia, in April 1862, Hunter had freed all the slaves in Florida, Georgia, and South Carolina. The general also raised the U.S. Army's first regiment of black volunteers. Hunter did all this on his own authority, and

President Lincoln, not yet ready to manumit the slaves or enlist black troops, had to annul both actions. The horrified Confederate response was to declare Hunter an outlaw. Military units had orders to deny him, if captured, treatment as a prisoner of war and hold him "in close confinement for execution as a felon."[14]

For a soldier of his day, Hunter's fanaticism was extreme; it would significantly influence the campaign to come. Professional though he was, his treatment of noncombatants ran against the grain of the times. In an era when tradition and the laws of war still drew a sort of line to protect noncombatants from the warrior's drawn blade, Hunter made war on civilians with a certain gusto; many were the dwellings he ordered put to the torch.

Burning out civilians and destroying their provisions was justified by Hunter as reprisal for aggression against his force by Valley-based partisans and guerrillas, particularly those led by Colonel Mosby. Even to Union officers like Col. Henry A. Du Pont, Hunter's artillery chief, this pretext was "untenable." Though some of the guerrillas were indubitably local residents, they were the minority, and very few of Mosby's men lived in the Valley; most were residents of Loudoun County, to the east. Within days of assuming command in place of Sigel, Hunter responded to an attack by mounted partisans on a Federal supply train near Newtown by sending cavalrymen to set fire to a house from which shots had been fired at the train. Any repetition of the incident, Hunter warned, would be punished by the burning of "every rebel house within five miles of the place at which the firing occurs." (On May 30, another attack on a wagon train produced an order from Hunter for the burning of the entire town of Newtown; but the officer in charge of the detail refused to obey the order.)

The pretext for destruction did not have to be so specific as the interception of a supply column. In his journal, Col. David Hunter Strother, Hunter's kinsman and chief of staff, noted that on May 27 "the General asked me to go into Woodstock to ascertain who the parties were that attempted to confuse our scouts yesterday as he wished to burn a few houses."[15]

Retaliation against civilians for the acts of guerrillas is a common military reaction. But Hunter's fundamental motivation was vindictiveness, demonstrated by the fact that not even his relatives were exempt from his depredations. In Charles Town, in the lower Valley, for example, Hunter burned the house of his cousin Alexander Hunter, allowing the family to save nothing from the flames. Some of the general's own staff found his conduct repugnant. In the sarcastic words of Colonel Du Pont, "it was often ludicrously though painfully amusing to hear the . . . general himself inquiring anxiously after the health of 'Cousin Kitty,' 'Aunt Sallie,' 'Cousin Joe,' or 'Uncle Bob,' from some nice old Virginia lady in smoothed apron, silver spectacles and in tears, or some pretty young rebel beauty in homespun, without hoops and in a towering passion—our soldiers meanwhile cleaning out the smokehouses and the granaries by wholesale . . . with horses, cattle, sheep, bacon, pigs, poultry and so forth, only to be recalled in ecstatic dreams." [16]

« A MORE CONGENIAL opponent for Jubal Early can scarcely be imagined. Hunter appeared not only as a barbaric destroyer like Pope and Milroy but an outlaw zealot whom it might be Early's fully sanctioned privilege to hang from a tall tree.

To that potential pleasure was added the allure of independent command. For Lee, the choice of Early as his instrument to derange Grant's plans and sustain the momentum of Confederate arms was not only obvious but fortunate—at least relatively. It was true that there was really no one else: among the few possible alternatives, Longstreet was disabled, Ewell and Hill weakened by ill health and no longer to be relied on for work as challenging as the Valley mission; Anderson was too inexperienced in independent command. Lee knew that Jubal, with all his faults, was familiar with the Valley, and had the necessary daring tempered by generally good judgment (though the Wilderness episode weighed somewhat against that claim). Lee knew that Early was, in fact, unmatched for boldness and intensity by anyone in the army since Stonewall Jackson. Jackson's Valley veterans who were with Early scarcely loved him, but they and the others in the corps would follow him almost anywhere. [17]

« THE MARCH commenced at three o'clock on the morning of June 13. An assistant surgeon wrote home next day to say that his unit traveled "the road to who knows where," but he felt calm in the knowledge that "Early would carry the war to Africa to beat the Yankees" if necessary.[18]

The secrecy mentioned by the doctor was almost complete, since Lee had persuaded Jefferson Davis to keep knowledge of the movement from the newspapers—something the Confederate government had hitherto been reluctant to do. Neither Grant nor Hunter had any inkling that Jackson's old Valley army was heading west. But Early and Lee were equally ignorant of Hunter's whereabouts, though Breckinridge had been sent hurrying back to the Valley with his two attenuated infantry brigades (barely 2,100 men) following Hunter's Piedmont victory.

After maneuvering for nearly a week to find Hunter, Breckinridge learned that his adversary was en route to Lynchburg. The Kentuckian arrived in that vital center of communications, manufacturing, and military medicine on June 16. There his infantry, with a few horse artillery pieces and Imboden's cavalry (described as "wild" by an officer on Breckinridge's staff), was able to reinforce the skeletal garrison, mainly composed of convalescent wounded and sick men.[19]

Meanwhile, Early hustled the 2d Corps westward toward the rail center of Charlottesville. There the troops could take trains on the Orange & Alexandria Railroad to Lynchburg; alternatively, they could take the cars of the Virginia Central to Staunton, in the event that Hunter was still that far north. The 2d Corps reached Charlottesville on June 17, having marched 80 miles in four days. Tireless, Early himself rode ahead, arriving on the morning of the 16th.[20]

The price paid by the Confederate column for this Jacksonian celerity was high: pulling the corps's guns had become too much for some artillery horses, and the men, according to one brigade commander, were weakened by their march to the point of being unfit to fight. But as Early knew, speed of movement was now especially vital. On arrival in Charlottesville, Early was handed a wire from Breckinridge: Hunter was only 20 miles to the west of Lynchburg and coming on rapidly.[21]

For the exhausted infantry of the 2d Corps, there was to be no rest from the necessity of getting to Lynchburg as fast as possible. But merely putting the troops aboard trains was no guarantee of speed. Still

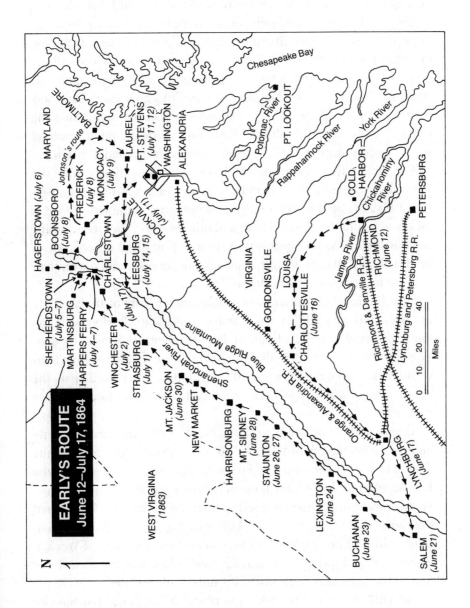

EARLY'S ROUTE
June 12–July 17, 1864

N

Chesapeake Bay

PT. LOOKOUT

Potomac River

Rappahannock River

York River

BALTIMORE

MARYLAND

HAGERSTOWN (July 6)

Johnson's route

BOONSBORO (July 8)

FREDERICK (July 8)

MONOCACY (July 9)

LAUREL

FT. STEVENS (July 11, 12)

WASHINGTON

ALEXANDRIA

SHEPHERDSTOWN (July 5–7)

MARTINSBURG

HARPERS FERRY (July 4–7)

CHARLESTOWN

LEESBURG (July 14, 15)

ROCKVILLE (July 11)

COLD HARBOR

Chickahominy River

RICHMOND (June 12)

PETERSBURG

WINCHESTER (July 2)

STRASBURG (July 1)

Shenandoah River

Blue Ridge Mountains

VIRGINIA

GORDONSVILLE

LOUISA

CHARLOTTESVILLE (June 16)

James River

Richmond & Danville R.R.

Lynchburg and Petersburg R.R.

MT. JACKSON (June 30)

NEW MARKET

HARRISONBURG

MT. SIDNEY (June 28)

STAUNTON (June 26, 27)

Orange & Alexandria R.R.

LYNCHBURG (June 17)

WEST VIRGINIA (1863)

LEXINGTON (June 24)

BUCHANAN (June 23)

SALEM (June 21)

0 10 20 40
Miles

vivid after three years, bitter memories of unreliability among civilian managers of the Orange & Alexandria Railroad aroused Jubal's deepest suspicions. Late on the morning of the 16th, he telegraphed Breckinridge to "send off at once all engines and cars . . . to this place, including everything at [the railroad's] disposal. I will send troops as soon as I get cars. . . . See that there is no lack of energy in railroad management, and give me information from time to time." An hour later, Early was even more worried about his rail transport. "Let me know what the railroad agents can and will do," Early told Breckinridge in a second wire. "Everything depends upon promptness, energy and dispatch."

The same telegram documented Early's stern intentions toward the railroad managers if they should fail him: "Take the most summary measures and impress everything that is necessary in the way of men or means to insure the object. I have authority to direct your movements, and I will take the responsibility of what you may find it necessary to do. I will hold all railroad agents and employees responsible with their lives for hearty cooperation with us." [22]

Even this level of pressure was insufficient. In spite of all that Early and Breckinridge could do or say, trains available in Charlottesville on the 17th could only board half of Early's infantry—Ramseur's division and one brigade of Gordon's. The rest were ordered to drag their weary bones down the track toward Lynchburg, to be picked up on the trains' return. Artillery and wagon trains departed, via local roads, at daybreak. [23]

After a journey of five hours over the 60-mile rail distance, Early entered Lynchburg with Ramseur's division around 1:00 P.M. on the 17th. He was disconcerted on arrival to find that Breckinridge, who had been injured when his horse was killed and fell on him at Cold Harbor, was temporarily confined to bed; the Kentuckian had turned over command to General D. H. Hill, who happened to be in Lynchburg. (Hill had been relieved of his command in the Army of Western Tennessee, and was awaiting reassignment.) This was awkward; Early had not been on easy terms with Hill since Williamsburg.

But Hill, a superior in 1862, was now a subordinate, and military protocol could govern the relationship between the two men. Much more troublesome for the prospects of defending the city was the dilapidation of the trains creaking down the line from Charlottesville. Early would doubtless later hear how the rear car of one train derailed on a bridge near Lynchburg. The train was going so slowly that it was possible to catch the engineer's attention and get him to slow down even more so that the derailed car could be pushed from the span. But some of the men, fearing that the disabled car would drag the whole train off the bridge, jumped. A couple were killed under the wheels; others were caught in the bridge timbers and badly hurt before the train, steaming clear of the derailed car, could proceed to the Lynchburg depot.[24]

Jubal knew that even when the cars brought the rest of his infantry, he would probably still be vulnerable. As of the 17th, he certainly was. Besides Gordon's and Ramseur's men, Lynchburg's defense that day included Breckinridge's two brigades, the survivors of the Piedmont defeat, and the cadets, along with a few home guards and convalescents; none of the 2d Corps artillery had arrived. Imboden's brigade—unreliable as it had long seemed to Early and now appeared to Breckinridge, who felt it had not been effective enough in locating Hunter—constituted the only cavalry. In all, Early could only expect to have about 8,000 men to oppose Hunter's 18,000 on the 17th.[25]

A glance at the map revealed that Lynchburg lay open to assault from the north, west, and south, with the James River at the Confederates' backs. Those circumstances could not be changed. But Early's first look at the city's defenses, as laid out by Hill, showed that the existing entrenchments were too close to the city's center, needlessly exposing the town and its inhabitants to artillery fire. Jubal determined to move the main defense line farther out into the countryside west of the city, the direction from which Hunter was approaching.[26]

‹‹ IT IS HARD to estimate what Hunter knew or guessed of Early's situation. But he evidently failed to realize that he had only to increase his pace to grasp a stunning success. By nightfall on June 15, he and his men, having crossed the Blue Ridge over the Peaks of Otter, were in Liberty, 24 miles from Lynchburg. McCausland's 1,400 cavalrymen had harassed the Union column, using one well-mounted squadron to block the easy route down the road, and posting dismounted men on the flanks. McCausland himself supervised the burning of the bridge

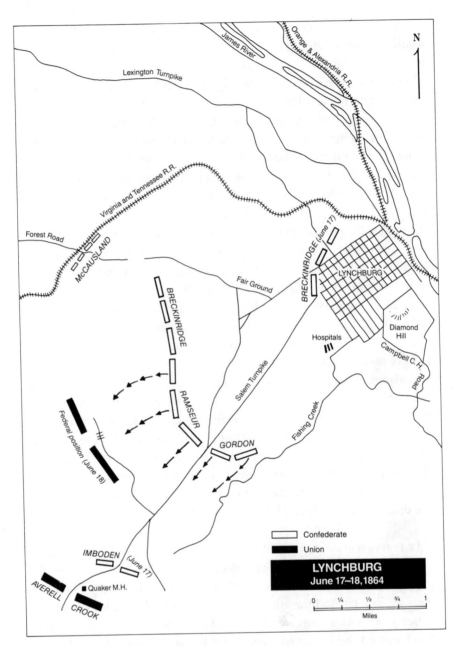

N

Lexington Turnpike

James River

Orange & Alexandria R.R.

Virginia and Tennessee R.R.

Forest Road

McCAUSLAND

BRECKINRIDGE (June 17)

LYNCHBURG

Fair Ground

BRECKINRIDGE

Hospitals

Diamond Hill

Campbell C. H. Road

RAMSEUR

Salem Turnpike

Federal position (June 18)

GORDON

Fishing Creek

IMBODEN

(June 17)

Quaker M.H.

AVERELL

CROOK

Confederate

Union

LYNCHBURG
June 17–18, 1864

0   ¼   ½   ¾   1
Miles

across the James at Buchanan, escaping at the last minute under the flaming span in a small boat.[27]

Notwithstanding McCausland's efforts, hard marching would have put the Federals inside the virtually defenseless city by the end of the next day, June 16. But they spent the day destroying the line of the Virginia & Tennessee Railroad, and at dark they were only seven miles closer to their goal.[28]

The Federals leading the march when it resumed on the 17th were Averell's cavalrymen. They were stopped about four miles west of Lynchburg by Imboden's weary men fighting dismounted from behind fence rails near a stone Quaker meeting house. Calling for support, Averell was joined by Crook's infantry, and the combined force—nearly 10,000 men—began preparing for an assault on the puny Confederate defense. This was the situation when Early, riding out with Hill to find sites for his revised defense line, arrived at the meeting house. Seeing immediately that Imboden could never fend off the impending Union attack without assistance, Early sent a galloper back to summon the two leading brigades of Ramseur's division. These were to advance from their position near the town to a redoubt two miles to the west, where a pair of guns was already in place. There the Federals must be held.[29]

When Crook and Averell sent their men forward in line of battle, Imboden's exhausted troopers lost their remaining resolve and pulled out. Galloping back to find Ramseur's brigades, Jubal met them, then turned and rode ahead of their line to confront the Federals. The bugler of the Stonewall Brigade sounded the charge, and Early, standing in his stirrups and leading Ramseur's skirmishers straight ahead, shouted at the enemy as if the bluecoats could hear him over the battlefield din: "No buttermilk rangers after you now, damn you . . ."

The epithet, from a current popular song (about a "desolate soldier"—the "buttermilk ranger"—who wants to go home), was a slap at the hapless troopers of Imboden's command. Though Jubal's blood was up, it was an unfair aspersion: Imboden's men, like McCausland's, had helped delay Hunter, and had held Averell's more numerous and better-armed troopers until frayed nerves and exhausted bodies could hold on no more.[30]

It was long enough. The timing and verve of the Confederate infantry charge that Jubal led drove the Federals back. Though the artillery exchanged fire for a time, and Union cavalry challenged McCausland on the road from Liberty, there was no more fighting of any importance on the 17th.[31]

<< DURING THE NIGHT, to conceal their weakness and generate doubt in the minds of Hunter and his men, Early had the Confederates in the town make up-to-date use of an ancient ruse. While the balance of the 2d Corps infantry was still en route from Charlottesville, the men already inside Lynchburg were not asleep. They ran an empty train up and down the tracks, in and out of the depot, punctuating the sounds of locomotives and cars clanging and thundering over the switches with cheers, band music, and sounds of rejoicing.[32]

The stratagem worked. Until around noon on the 18th, Hunter enjoyed a substantial numerical advantage, but he failed to exploit it, even though the Confederates could not defend all the roads approaching the city. Around midday, tired of waiting for Hunter to attack, Early launched a sharp assault of his own that caught Hunter's troops sitting on their heels. Hunter managed to contain the Confederate threat with a counterblow that drove the attackers back to their lines; but when the fight died down, the Union commander decided he had had enough.

To justify his unaccountable loss of heart, Hunter, convinced his army was short of ammunition, conceived the idea that he had withstood a major offensive by Early's whole force, which the Union commander believed outnumbered his troops by a two-to-one margin. (The Lynchburg defenders would only number about 12,000 when all Early's troops were assembled late on June 18.) Beginning on the night of the 18th, Hunter's chastened Army of the Shenandoah gathered itself and withdrew westward.[33]

Poised to attack Hunter on the 19th, Early realized during the night that his quarry was retreating. Frustrated, he contemplated a night attack—but decided to wait in case Hunter might not be withdrawing but moving to attack Lynchburg from the south, or to cross the James and march east to join Grant. Dawn was breaking before he could be sure which direction Hunter had taken; the price of Early's prudence was a night's head start for the Army of the Shenandoah.[34]

< 258 >

Once doubts were resolved, pursuit was immediately organized, with infantry following the Federals westward while the cavalry ranged north toward the Peaks of Otter; they were to get ahead of Hunter and block his escape routes so that Early's infantry could overtake and finish him. In a dispatch to Lee written at 9:30 A.M. on the 19th, Early reported that the "enemy is retreating in confusion, and if the cavalry does its duty we will destroy him." Jubal clearly disliked having to rely on his buttermilk rangers; bad luck and undeniable ineptitude—not to mention hunger, thirst, and fatigue—would unhappily confirm his prejudice. Confederate infantry, marching in brutal heat, did catch up with Hunter's rear guard at Liberty, killing numerous troopers of Averell's command and losing a fair number themselves. But the Confederate cavalry took the wrong road and never had a chance of doing "its duty."[35]

Hunter ended by making good his escape over the Blue Ridge to Salem. From there, the Union column embarked on a ten-day march through the dry, inhospitable West Virginia mountains to Charleston.

In choosing this route of withdrawal, Black Dave, evidently fearing that he would be cut off and defeated in a fighting retreat down the Valley, stepped entirely off stage. Though he extricated his force with only 940 casualties, he also subtracted it totally from Grant's order of battle for more than a month. Even more damaging was the fact that he left the route to Washington wide open.[36]

<< ON JUNE 21, Early abandoned Hunter to his own devices and swung north, retracing his adversary's footsteps toward the Potomac, and asserting the dominance of the Valley that Hunter had so unexpectedly handed over to him.

Riding in Hunter's tracks, Jubal observed "heart-rending" scenes. Years later, his wrath was unabated: "Houses had been burned, and women and children left without shelter," he wrote in his *Autobiographical Sketch*. "The country had been stripped of provisions and many families left without a morsel to eat. . . . The time consumed in the perpetration of those deeds was the salvation of Lynchburg, with its stores, foundries and factories, which were so necessary to our army in Richmond."

<< CHAPTER EIGHTEEN >>

"The Most Exciting Time"

*M*OVING NORTH down the Valley as Hunter withdrew westward, General Early's column marched through Lexington on June 23, 1864. One soldier described the veterans filing past Stonewall Jackson's grave—arms reversed, flags dipped—in "a hush as deep as midnight." Jubal said nothing about this moment in his writings, but like his men, he must have been hoping that Stonewall's indomitable ghost would bless their defiant venture.[1]

General Early had let his weary legions, now known as the Army of the Valley, rest on June 22. It was the first time off they had enjoyed for ten days—a period in which some had marched more than 150 miles. The general's headquarters that day were near the Hollins Institute, a female seminary where, the grapevine said, Jubal was paying his respects to one of the teachers who was an old flame.[2]

It is more likely that Early was in his tent pondering his future movements, though the proximity of young females undoubtedly pleased him. He had two options. In sending the 2d Corps off to relieve Lynchburg, Lee had given its commander a choice: after defeating Hunter—or driving him out of the Valley—Early could turn east and rejoin the Army of Northern Virginia; alternatively, he could move aggressively down the Valley toward the Potomac to threaten Washington, throw a scare into the Federal administration, and divert energy and manpower from the Richmond-Petersburg front to the defense of the Union capital. In that case, Grant might even be forced to break off the Petersburg siege to relieve Washington.[3]

To many it seemed hardly credible that Early would—or could—

capture Washington, though if he were to do so even for a short time the consequences could be far-reaching: the possibilities included the sacking of the United States Treasury and its coffers and the destruction of the Union army's main supply depot—its warehouses bulging with food, medical supplies, arms, and ammunition. The government might even be forced to evacuate. Such reverses could slow the Union war effort to a crawl—maybe even bring it to a halt, if only momentarily. Northern war-weariness, profound and growing as 1864 passed its mid-point, might be pushed to extremes of apathy and despair in the chaos attending even a temporary Confederate occupation of Washington.[4]

Still more remote—but dazzling—was the possibility that capture of the Union capital might change the relationship of the Confederacy to such foreign powers as Britain and France, which might recognize Richmond—and lend active support to the Southern cause.[5]

No one who knew Early at all well could have doubted which of his options he would choose, though he was most conscious that the enterprise entailed tremendous risks. Simply by crossing the Potomac and moving on Washington, he would be inviting a crushing defeat; and whatever happened in or around the capital, Early's little army could not remain in Maryland for long. If Union forces were to concentrate in his rear before he could cross the river again, they could cut off his escape route and possibly destroy his entire cohort.[6]

But it was only in Early's mind that a cool professional voice enumerated these dangers. In his heart, whatever the stakes, he was already preparing to teach his enemy a classic lesson in the strategic use of a small, agile force, marching quickly and fighting hard. The performance would be brilliant enough to have impressed Stonewall himself. And the result would represent a kind of high-water mark in the Confederate fortunes of war: as Early unfolded his raid through Maryland toward Washington, he would slice closer to the heart of the Union than any Northern soldier had yet approached the vitals of the South.[7]

<< EARLY SHOWED his resolve in a message to Lee on June 30. "The troops," he wrote, "are in fine condition and spirits, their health greatly improved. . . . If you can continue to threaten Grant, I hope to be able

to do something for your relief and the success of our cause shortly. I shall lose no time." [8]

Yet for all Jubal's brave words, as the Army of the Valley began its rapid move northward, its ability to accomplish even part of its task might have struck an objective observer as questionable. Infantry strength was about 10,000 muskets; cavalry and artillery added up to around 4,000. The artillery, Early's own branch, was his bulwark. The cavalry, through indiscipline, would leave Jubal vulnerable, though he would aggravate the problem by refusing to come to grips with it personally. [9]

Compounding their fatigue, the foot soldiers were chronically hungry ("Bread! Bread! Bread!" men shouted when Early rode near). Worst of all, in terms of their efficiency, was the condition of their feet. Though Early had submitted an official request for shoes before leaving the Chickahominy, many of the men and even some company officers lacked footgear. In a letter to another former Confederate general after the war, Early remarked on the suffering of men he saw on the march with their feet "tied up in rags which were clotted with blood." [10]

As the Valley Army entered Staunton on June 27, the general hoped that he might find shoes there; none were on hand. But he did get word that shoes were on the way by rail, and that they might arrive within a day. Early decided to wait 24 hours—and then, if necessary, move north without the shoes. Staunton contained enough wagons so that the shoes could be sent on after him as he moved down the Valley. Also, after the hectic activity of recent days, the army needed to gather many other kinds of supplies, from rations to ammunition. [11]

‹‹ DURING THE WAIT, the general made changes in organization designed to strengthen his force. First, he had to solve a number of morale problems—most created by attrition.

Two of the army's four infantry divisions were relatively free of such problems. The units led by General Rodes (experienced and reliable) and General Ramseur (only 27, but already a bright star) were depleted but unified; their brigades were solid, integrated ranks of Virginians, Georgians, North Carolinians, and Alabamans, commanded by familiar officers. Their only complaints were the normal gripes of veteran soldiers.

The division commanded by General Gordon was another matter. Though the unit's problems were none of Gordon's making, they were potentially destructive. Troubled and angry, the division was composed of ill-suited fragments of 14 regiments taken from five brigades so shrunken by casualties that they were no longer functional as fighting units. Gordon's command included remnants of Virginia regiments from Jackson's old "foot cavalry" division, survivors of the proud "Louisiana Tigers" brigades and other units. Few regiments contained more than 200 men. In many cases, having lost all their own officers, Gordon's troops had come under the orders of strange superiors, to whom the men they commanded were also strangers. In the combat ranks of the Civil War, these circumstances were demoralizing.

Early attacked the problem in a roundabout way. The solution he devised also took care of another problem—what to do with John Breckinridge, who had marched to Lynchburg with the remnants of the scratch division that had beaten Sigel at New Market. Combining this division with Gordon's, Early created a miniature corps and put it under Breckinridge, whose distinction, Early hoped, would help lead the unhappy troops out of at least some of their troubles; Breckinridge was also named the army's second-in-command.[12]

« THE ONLY SERIOUS problem for the artillery, commanded by Brig. Gen. Armistead L. Long, was a shortage of horses. Long had about 40 pieces in three batteries commanded by able men—Lt. Col. William Nelson, Lt. Col. Carter Braxton, and Maj. William McLaughlin. (There were also three horse artillery batteries, equipped with a total of ten guns.) Finding horses would not be easy. Southern horseflesh was becoming increasingly scarce, and showing signs of wear and tear after three years of war. For Early's cavalry as well as his artillery, horses were a festering problem—added to the others that were either all too real or existed only in the commanding general's capacious portmanteau of prejudices.[13]

Seen as a partial solution to some of these difficulties was a new command structure for the cavalry division of the army. Its four brigades (under Imboden, McCausland, Mudwall Jackson, and Brig. Gen. Bradley Johnson, an energetic native of Frederick, Maryland) now came under the overall command of Maj. Gen. Robert Ransom. A West Point graduate (class of 1850) and old army dragoon, Ransom was an officer noted for his poor health and circumspection who had been commanding infantry until sent in mid-June to assume leadership of the cavalry in Lynchburg. That assignment had been the answer to pleas sent to Richmond from Lynchburg by Breckinridge, who, like Early, distrusted Imboden as a cavalry leader.[14]

In his final preparations for the trans-Potomac expedition, General Early displayed a hitherto unmatched hostility toward excess baggage on the march. Wagon trains were to be cut to the barest minimum: his own headquarters would march with but one six-horse wagon, with a four-horse wagon allotted to each commander of a division or brigade; for every 500 men and officers, Early allowed a wagon to carry cooking utensils. Nothing more was permitted. Orders required that "regimental and company officers must carry for themselves such under-clothing as they need for the present expedition." All else was to be left in Staunton.

Hardly anyone was happy to get this order. But Early would allow no exceptions—least of all himself. To complaints voiced later by Father James Sheeran, a chaplain with the Louisiana Brigade, Jubal described his own predicament, declaring that he had brought with him "but one pair of drawers and had to do without them whilst they were being washed."[15]

<< WHEN JUBAL EARLY marched the Army of the Valley from Staunton toward the Potomac, his enemy had no idea what he was doing. With Hunter out of touch—still retreating over the West Virginia mountains—the Federal authorities had scant knowledge of what had happened at Lynchburg. As late as July 3, Grant himself was unaware that Early had left the eastern Virginia theater with his troops.[16]

By July 4, Early, virtually unopposed in his march from Staunton, was in full control of the Valley. That day, Breckinridge crossed the Potomac at Shepherdstown with his column, and the next day Early followed with the rest of the army. Scant Union force opposed the cross-

< 265 >

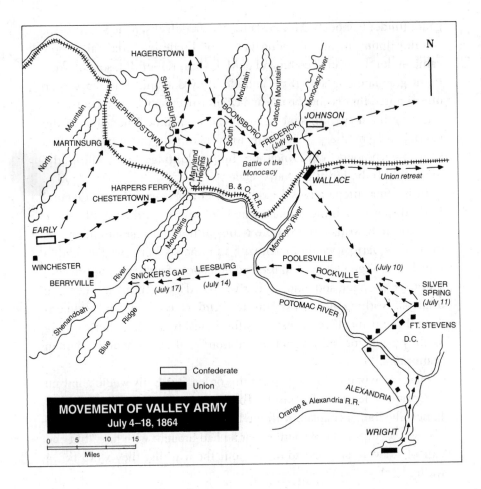

MOVEMENT OF VALLEY ARMY
July 4–18, 1864

ings. The Federals under Sigel who had been guarding the Baltimore
& Ohio Railroad took up a defensive position on Maryland Heights
opposite Harpers Ferry. Crammed with heavy guns, the Union position on the Heights blocked the Confederates' most direct route to
Washington.[17]

Early stayed in the neighborhood for a day following the crossing of
his army. The principal reason for the pause was the desperate need
for shoes, which he had hoped might catch up with him. But the delay
also gave the general a chance to consider the merits of attacking and
destroying the force on the Heights forthwith. If he could do so, he

would not only open the most rapid approach to the Union capital, but also eliminate a threat to his rear while he was thrusting eastward.[18]

As Early's force lingered on the north bank of the Potomac, a rider spurred into camp and dismounted at the general's tent. The horseman was Capt. Robert E. Lee, Jr., carrying a message of great secrecy and importance: a Union prison camp at Point Lookout, on the Maryland shore near the mouth of the Potomac, was to be attacked and the Southern prisoners set free. The main effort would be by sea, but the dispatch from Lee instructed Early to provide support by detaching cavalry to operate near Baltimore as a diversion and even take part in the rescue operation if needed.

The plan must have sounded vague and risky; Captain Lee said even his father knew little more than the bare outlines of the project. But the rewards of success were potentially enormous, measured in the numbers of Confederate prisoners at Point Lookout. Seventeen thousand men held there, if released, would add a whole new corps to Lee's armies—and possibly swell Early's striking force to a strength capable of truly substantial damage to the North.

In his reply to General Lee, handed to the captain as he prepared to mount and ride back to his father, Early outlined his strategic situation (Sigel's blocking the short route to Washington; Early's plan to dislodge him). Now, Jubal declared, he would sidestep the obstacle, which in any case appeared too strong to be attacked without heavy loss; he would march north to the passes through the South and Catoctin mountains used by Lee two years earlier, and head toward Washington via Frederick, detaching cavalry northward from there to lend a hand with the Point Lookout scheme.[19]

« ON JULY 7, wagons arrived with shoes for all who needed them. No sooner were the new laces tied up than Jubal ordered the advance. With his slender force, he was now all by himself in enemy country. From here, movements would have to be swift and sure. A staff officer, Maj. Henry Kyd Douglas, marveled later at Early's daring: "Jackson being dead, it is safe to say no other General in either army would have attempted it against such odds."

Yet Early's response to the danger showed a judicious caution. Unwilling to operate among a population roused to anger against an invader—and perhaps hoping that even at this late date some Marylanders might join the Confederate cause—he emulated Lee in 1863 in issuing strict orders against pillaging. The requisition of supplies would be permitted, but anything taken was to be paid for in Confederate money or certificates to be redeemed later for cash. Violators would be tried and punished by summary court-martial.[20]

To these strictures against waging war on civilians, there was to be a characteristic exception: economic warfare waged by Jubal Early himself. Some of Maryland's more affluent citizens were to be shaken down. To soften his prospective victims up, the general ordered cavalry to ride hard through the countryside, generating an appearance of potency and—it was to be hoped—striking fear into the hearts of armed Union foes and rich native burghers alike.

Whole towns were targeted. McCausland was dispatched to Hagerstown to demand $200,000, the sum that Early calculated the city could raise on short notice. If the money were not paid, the town would be put to the torch. But McCausland, probably groggy with fatigue, slipped up: he dropped a digit from his ultimatum and only exacted $20,000. This was a sum raised with relatively little difficulty by the citizens of Hagerstown, though they also had to furnish McCausland's troopers with 1,500 suits, a like number of shoes or boots, with socks and shirts to match, and 1,900 pairs of drawers—plenty of spares.[21]

<< THE EFFECT of this extortion was dramatic. Panicky word of rebel horsemen riding loose and demanding money all over Maryland and even in Pennsylvania began circulating freely; the rumors hit Baltimore and Washington with the impact of grapeshot.[22]

Concern reached the highest level. President Lincoln intervened personally, as he seldom did now that Grant was in command of the Union's armies. The president directly ordered Halleck to summon Hunter, who had reached Charleston on June 30, back to the Valley immediately. Lincoln also asked the governors of Massachusetts, New York, and Pennsylvania to send drafts of 100-day recruits to reinforce the defenses of Washington.[23]

Grant, unpersuaded until now that Lee would detach any sizable

< 268 >

force from the defense of Richmond, began to take notice. Catching up with the unfolding reality, Union intelligence generated unmistakable evidence that Early and a significant array of Confederates were operating in ever closer proximity to Washington. Grant urgently wanted to obliterate the invading forces while ensuring the safety of the capital; he offered to send Halleck a corps from the Army of the Potomac. Thus, without having made any contact with hostile troops in Maryland, Jubal Early achieved a major objective of his expedition: diversion of Federal resources from the siege of Petersburg.

In his perverse way, Halleck diverged from Grant's and Lincoln's reactions to Early. Washington's defenses might indeed need reinforcements—Grant having siphoned off most of Washington's garrison to replace his casualties in the campaign from the Wilderness to the James—but surely, Halleck stated, an entire corps would be superfluous. Halleck noted that Grant's muster rolls included some 2,500 dismounted cavalry, many of them convalescents. Halleck thought these men, easily spared from the Petersburg front, would supply sufficient stiffening for the capital's defenses. Grant compromised, sending the dismounted cavalry and one division of the 6th Corps from the Petersburg lines, to be followed by the rest of the corps "if necessary." [24]

<< WHILE THESE high-level negotiations over troops for Washington's defense were going on, no Union force actually stood between Early's invading column and its goal. But one man had already started acting on the threat: Maj. Gen. Lew Wallace, later to become famous as the author of *Ben Hur*. At age 37, Wallace, an Indiana lawyer-politician who had served as a lieutenant in the Mexican War, found his career in abeyance. He was manning a desk as commander of the U.S. Army's Middle Department, with headquarters in Baltimore.

Wallace was close to the corridor between Harpers Ferry and the capital. He resolved to see what could be done to deflect the invaders or at least slow them down enough to allow reinforcements to reach Washington. Despite his gaunt, melancholy looks, Wallace was an optimist; but he was also astute and level-headed. He saw a promising defensive position at Monocacy Junction, two miles east of Frederick. [25]

On the Monocacy River, a tributary of the Potomac, the Junction not only joined spurs of the B. & O. running from Harpers Ferry and Frederick to Baltimore, but also lay between the Washington and Baltimore pikes leading east from Frederick. To defend the Junction, Wallace could call on very few troops—some 3,000 men, including Maryland Home Guards under Brig. Gen. Erastus Tyler, and a few 100-day militia. Though he was able to round up a small contingent of mounted militiamen, Wallace lacked reliable cavalry until July 6, when 230 men from the 8th Illinois trotted into the Junction in search of the invaders; Wallace promptly attached them to his defense force. He was lucky; the 8th Illinois had a reputation as one of the best cavalry regiments in the volunteer service.[26]

Wallace was in luck again on July 7, when a train came chuttering down the line from Baltimore, transporting elements of the 6th Corps under Maj. Gen. James Ricketts. Dispatched at Grant's order and traveling by water from the vicinity of Richmond, the division, 3,350 men strong, had disembarked at Baltimore and was en route to Harpers Ferry. When Ricketts—dark, bluff-spoken, and stout—heard Wallace's news of Early's likely presence to the west, he promptly agreed to serve under Wallace's orders.[27]

<< As he pushed eastward through the gaps in the Catoctins on July 8, Jubal Early unwittingly possessed an advantage never again to be his: he outnumbered the Federals, mustering about 14,000 to Wallace's 5,800. Approaching Frederick,[28] Confederate skirmishers pushed the defenders out of the town early on the 9th. Master of the town, Early took personal charge of his economic warfare campaign. He summoned the city's leading citizens and demanded a $200,000 contribution. The town fathers protested: the population was only 8,000, their assets but $2,200,000 in all. Pay, replied Jubal, or suffer the consequences. The citizens asked for time to find the money, and Early relented.

In the meantime, he had sent Bradley Johnson's brigade off to carry out Lee's orders to provide a diversion for the Point Lookout rescue attempt. To McCausland, he had given orders to ride out to the southwest and make sure all telegraph wires and rail connections between Maryland Heights and Washington were cut. Then he was to secure a bridgehead across the Monocacy. The rest of the Army of the Valley would follow.[29]

<< GENERAL EARLY'S conference with the leading inhabitants of Frederick lasted well into a splendid, balmy summer morning; he joined his command after it had started to deploy, to the accompaniment of gunfire from both sides, for the assault on Wallace's position. Sitting his horse, Early saw that the stream was less than 20 yards wide, running from northeast to southwest. The flat, open ground on the western side was scored by the Washington and Baltimore pikes, which converged at Frederick; both roads crossed the Monocacy roughly at right angles, forming a large letter A with the river as crossbar.

The Baltimore Pike spanned the river on a stone bridge almost two miles to Early's left; a little right of center, a covered wooden bridge carried the Washington Pike across the stream. The general knew nothing yet of a ford about three-quarters of a mile downstream from the Washington Pike, off to the right. On the east bank, he could see a ridge that dominated the river, the Washington Pike and the Junction.

The branches of the B. & O. running to Baltimore from Frederick and Harpers Ferry joined near the river on the west bank and then crossed on an iron trestle. Close to the railroad bridge on the near bank of the river, the general could see a blockhouse, not far from which a howitzer belched an occasional shell. Fire from both left and right ends of the Union position disclosed additional artillery.

Early lacked firm knowledge of Federal strength—he estimated the defenders had 7,000–8,000 men—but a quick sweep of his eye was enough to reveal many bluecoats in line of battle. Seeing that the Federals had covered all three crossings, Early was certain that the bridges would be too well guarded to be attacked frontally without unwarrantable loss of men and time. He hoped he could push across the river well downstream from the bridges and outflank the Union defense line on his right, aiming to get behind the bridges and gain the Washington Pike.

Early's plan was uncomplicated. Rodes's division, deployed to the left, was to demonstrate and skirmish with the defenders of the stone

< 271 >

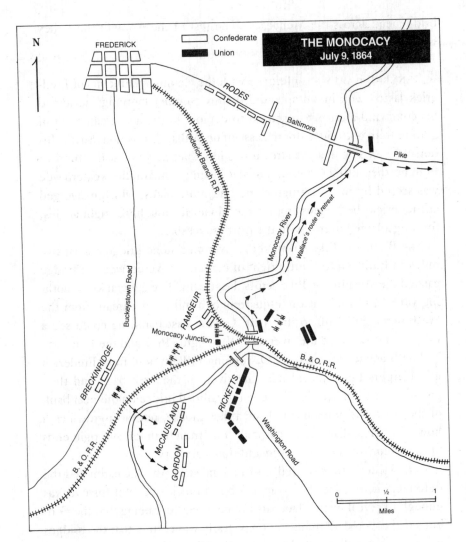

against Union soldiers guarding the covered wooden bridge and the blockhouse. Probably calculating that he was only opposed by militia, Early would assign just one of Breckinridge's divisions to the task of pushing the defenders out of his way.[30]

‹‹ ACCOMPANYING BRECKINRIDGE on the right, Jubal rode up and down, looking for a place to cross the stream. By 11:00 A.M., as the morning ripened, Early was still searching. The sun broiled the ground, pushing the temperature to 90 degrees, where it would remain most of the day. The gathering heat reminded the general that time, along with his chances of reaching Washington before Grant sent reinforcements, was slipping away.

At this critical moment, McCausland's cavalry brigade, returning from its telegraph- and rail-cutting mission, trotted into view near the river—then crossed. They had found the ford that had eluded Early and his staff. The grayclad troopers dismounted and launched an impulsive attack on the rising ground in front of them, which was thickly sown with bluecoats.

Early could more than likely see that the effort was doomed, though he later acknowledged the movement as "brilliantly executed." The troopers did manage to drive the Federals back a short distance. Up to this point, the Southerners had no notion that their adversaries were veterans of the 6th Corps, placed there at the order of Wallace, who had guessed that Early would avoid hitting the bridges head on, and try a flanking movement across the ford.[31]

Identification of the Federals as battle-hardened killers came quickly. As the cavalrymen moved, they were winnowed by a terrible fire from infantrymen who lay low until the Southerners came close, then stood to shoot. The troopers, badly hurt by this gale of lead, fell back. But they reorganized and went forward in a second attack, trying to capture a farm held by two Federal brigades. But though momentarily successful, this effort was also a failure as the defenders rallied and tumbled the played-out troopers back down toward the river.

Despite their rough handling, McCausland's men, who now withdrew, had shown Early how to cross the Monocacy with a body of infantry strong enough to smash through to the Washington Pike. Turning to Breckinridge, Early ordered him to dispatch Gordon's division to deliver a full-scale attack.

Gordon led his division over the stream and formed a line of battle, planning to place the main emphasis on his right and try to outflank the

Union left. The initial onslaught, led by the brigade of Clement Evans, encountered intense volleys of musketry that slowed the Confederate advance once again. Then, to thwart the Southerners' turning movement, Ricketts ordered his men to change front in order to deny the attackers an open flank on the Union left. Pivoting on its right, which was anchored on a rise near the Monocacy, the Federal line halted roughly parallel with the Washington Pike.

Against the new Union formation, a fresh attack was mounted—without success—by the brigade of Brig. Gen. Zebulon York, a 44-year-old Maine native who had made a fortune planting cotton in Louisiana. Gordon, convinced that he no longer had any chance of turning the Federal left flank, decided that his men would have to attack straight along the Monocacy's east bank and blast the Federals off the rise anchoring their right flank.

Around 4:00 P.M., Gordon ordered Brig. Gen. William Terry to get his brigade of Virginians ready. Gordon himself led as the assault column moved out.[32]

As Terry's men approached their task, it was as if they sensed that this was the most critical moment in the battle. To Pvt. John Worsham of the 21st Virginia (a veteran of "Jackson's foot cavalry"), the next few minutes were the "most exciting time I witnessed during the war."

Enthusiasm overwhelmed the Virginians with a "martial delirium," as Gordon called it, that called forth shouts of "At them, boys!" and "Charge them! Charge them!" Their ardor propelled the attackers over a fence, up the hill, and down on top of the Federals, who fled across a small stream. In its waters, Gordon remarked, "the dead and wounded of both sides mingled their blood . . . ; and when the struggle was ended a crimsoned current ran toward the river."[33]

Supporting Terry, Gordon's other brigades pushed forward along the whole line. The Union position gave way under the mounting Confederate pressure. Ricketts's men, ordered to retreat, began a ragged movement toward the Baltimore Pike. They were not closely pursued by Gordon, whose division was exhausted and weakened by casualties.

With the withdrawal of Ricketts's division, the battle was over. Most of the Federals on the west bank escaped across the railroad trestle. Tyler's men guarding the stone bridge on the Baltimore Pike were able to fulfill their mission of covering the retreat, though not all accomplished their own escape. Overwhelmed by the pursuit of Rodes and Ramseur, they lost about 200 prisoners.[34]

That loss accounted for a little less than half the total of 586 men missing from the Federal rolls after the battle, along with 123 killed and 603 wounded—a total of 1,294. Southern losses, most of them in Gordon's division, included at least 250 killed and 650 wounded; of the wounded, 420 or more had to be left behind in Frederick.[35]

« DRIVEN FROM THE Monocacy and out of Early's way, Wallace was defeated. But his worsting in the field belied his true strategic achievement.

Wallace had, in a real sense, worsted Early. The Union commander had accomplished his purpose: to slow the invaders down. The battle ended too late on the 9th for Early to resume the march on Washington before nightfall. The encounter on the Monocacy, having used up a whole day, altered the Confederate timetable. It was a setback for Early that prompted an acknowledgment by Grant, writing his memoirs, of Wallace's achievement: "General Wallace contributed on this occasion, by the defeat of the troops under him, a greater benefit to the cause than often falls to the lot of a commander to render . . . by means of a victory." [36]

If no Wallace had appeared, or if Early had been able to beat Wallace in less than a day, it seems clear that the fortunes of the Confederate expedition would have shone far brighter than they did.

« THE NOMINAL VICTOR, setting up camp near the railroad bridge that night, got two pieces of news, one good, the other unsettling, though far from completely bad. The cheerful intelligence was from Frederick, where Early's aides had collected the $200,000 he had demanded; Frederick's elders, learning of the Confederate victory at Monocacy Junction, had decided to pay up.

The other item of news was confirmation that the main Federal strength on the Monocacy had been men of the Third Division, 6th Corps, Army of the Potomac. This conclusion was drawn from the stiff Union resistance during the day, from the uniforms and blue Greek cross badges of dead and wounded Federals, and from questioning of prisoners.[37]

In one highly important sense, identification of the 6th Corps was good; it meant that Jubal's odds-on gamble had already paid off in drawing Federal strength away from the Richmond-Petersburg front. On the other hand, if more than a division were involved—if the whole 6th Corps lay between Early and his goal—the Valley Army's outlook was clouded at best. Whatever the case, the stakes in a venture never less than extremely hazardous were mounting by the moment.

« CHAPTER NINETEEN »

"More Formidable Than Ever"

*I*N MARYLAND and northern Virginia, the weekend of July 9–10, 1864, was American summer at its most malevolent, setting records of heat and drought. Forty-seven days had passed without rain. No one who has suffered through the Potomac region's terrible July weather can doubt the weary discomfort of all the participants in Jubal Early's raid on Washington, raiders and defenders alike.[1]

But for Early, all material considerations shrank to invisibility beside the greatest challenge of his life: to reach Washington before Federal reinforcements could arrive to block a triumphant entry into the city— an event that would crown his career and shape the very destiny of the Confederacy.

The same preoccupation, seen from the opposing point of view, dominated the thoughts of official Washington. Toward midnight on July 9, news of the Monocacy battle came in, relayed from Wallace over the wire to General Halleck and President Lincoln. The unease of the authorities inside the capital, sweating in their wool suits and uniforms, increased sharply.[2]

Suddenly, the fact that Washington had always been a logical major goal for the Confederates was once again uppermost in everyone's mind. This time, the danger had been slow to register. The alarm raised by the two Manassas battles had long since subsided; Lee's invasions of 1862 and '63 had only indirectly menaced the capital. And it had been half a century since the last—the only—actual attack, when the British had put President James Madison to flight and burned the White House and the Capitol, among numerous other buildings. Since May

1864, the Confederate threat had apparently receded; General Grant, maintaining a steady—if costly—initiative, seemed to have placed the Confederates on the strategic defensive, neutralizing Lee's power to harm Washington. This development, along with the need to replace Grant's losses in 1864, had justified drastic reductions in the defenses of the Union capital.[3]

Secretary of War Stanton, knowing how weak these defenses now were, quietly arranged to have his personal hoard of gold ($5,000 of his own and $400 belonging to Mrs. Stanton) removed from his house and hidden in the residence of his clerk. Otherwise, it seemed, not much was happening at the War Department. In *Reveille in Washington*, her matchless history of the capital at war, Margaret Leech summarized the prevailing atmosphere: "Like a secret cult, the War Office was wrapped in impenetrable mystery. It had no information to give anyone about the invasion, and seemed to find the whole subject faintly distasteful."[4]

Absence of solid information led, in time-honored fashion, to the spread of rumor and misstatement. Refugees pouring into the city from the Maryland countryside fed the spate of hearsay. In the aftermath of the Monocacy fight, one Union soldier wrote, "pale-faced, anxious men solemnly asserted that certain information had been received at the War Department that at least 50,000 veteran soldiers were marching with Early." Late on the night of the battle, by the same account, a man in the bar at Willard's Hotel told the assembled drinkers that Wallace had been "disastrously defeated, and that our disordered troops were in full retreat." In the small hours, the story grew even more dire: Wallace's army had been annihilated, and government clerks were packing money, records and books in boxes for evacuation to New York.[5]

Skeptical voices decried such concerns as exaggerated, claiming that the Confederate incursion, if there was one, involved "a light party"— no more, perhaps, than a few cavalry. But others heeded the reports of grayclad hosts; the correspondent of the New York *World* opined that there were nearly 40,000 invaders in Maryland, with another 60,000 just across the Potomac in close support. Hearing such talk, worriers in Washington shuddered when, like Stanton, they contemplated the actual state of the capital's defenses.[6]

‹‹ ON PAPER—even on the ground—they were formidable. Girdling the District of Columbia on both sides of the Potomac on a peripheral line 37 miles long, engineers had constructed a system of more than 60 enclosed earthen field forts, built on prominent features about 1,000 yards apart. Between the forts throughout most of the line were networks of trenches and rifle pits. Behind the line, connecting roads made it easy to move troops and supplies from one strong point to another according to need. The whole complex was supported by 643 guns and 75 mortars.[7]

For all its unassailable aspect, the system had a major flaw: the scarcity of men to guard the fortifications and serve the guns. According to one 1862 report, adequate defense of the capital required 37,000 men: 25,000 infantry, 9,000 artillerymen, and 3,000 cavalry for outpost duty. But virtually every able-bodied man assigned to the Washington garrison had been sent to the Army of the Potomac during the months since the Wilderness to replace the job lots of casualties there and at Spotsylvania, Cold Harbor, and all the desperate lesser fights of the war's grisliest campaign.[8]

The consequences were lamentable. In July 1864, the garrison replacements for the infantry at Washington included members of the so-called Veterans Reserve Corps, a stouthearted but enfeebled aggregation of invalids and convalescents, accoutered in uniforms of a sickly light blue. Alongside these sad fellows, whom their Southern adversaries characterized as the "condemned Yankees," were untrained 100-day militiamen from various states. Some of these men, assigned to serve the guns, scarcely knew one end of a cannon from the other. To outpost the 37-mile perimeter of forts and trenches, and to scout the approaching enemy, Halleck, the senior officer in Washington, had only about 100 cavalrymen scattered on both sides of the river. In all—notwithstanding a paper strength of 31,000 men in the Washington garrison—Halleck could man the capital's ramparts with only 9,600 soldiers, a term that was at best a doubtful characterization of the available ragtag and bobtail.[9]

« GENERAL EARLY was probably largely ignorant of these circumstances. But despite the evidence of Federal strength at the Monocacy, he sensed great opportunity. Anxious to seize the moment, he had his army stirring in time for a sunrise departure from the Junction on Sunday, July 10. Out front as he apparently wished to be, McCausland trotted into the rising sun with his troopers, followed by Breckinridge in charge of Gordon's division and his own, now under the direct command of John Echols. Rodes marched in second place. Ramseur was left at the Junction to cover men detailed to dismantle the iron railroad bridge; they were to bring up the rear when the work was done. (The bridge defied all efforts to wreck it.)[10]

On the march, along roads turned to suffocating corridors of dust by the drought and the passage of thousands, the ordeal of marching and fighting with little food and rest seriously thinned the ranks. Heat prostration felled hundreds of men and horses. Straggling among Union prisoners as well as Confederates softened and pulled the column of men, animals, and wagons like a strand of taffy. Progress was further slowed by Federal cavalry—including regulars hastily assembled in Virginia and sent out on the Washington-Rockville Road—sniping and slashing at the flanks and rear of the march. But officers enforcing Early's orders to close up and keep moving and the strength of veterans whom nothing seemed to faze pushed the head of the column into Rockville, 20 miles from the Monocacy, by nightfall. Most of the army stopped at Gaithersburg, six miles farther west. By this time, Early's expedition was more of a stumbling procession than a coherent force prepared to capture a capital.[11]

Still, property owners along the line of march fared badly at the hands of Early's army. Though occasionally "secesh" sympathizers greeted his men, the Confederates' behavior alienated many more Marylanders than it attracted. Indeed, Jubal worried about the very small numbers of Southern adherents greeting his advance. Almost none had ventured out from Washington, which indicated that the inhabitants felt that his entrance into the city would be vigorously opposed. If so, perhaps they felt that way because heavy reinforcements had already arrived.[12]

« AT DAWN ON MONDAY, July 11, the Confederate raiders were about a day's march from the outskirts of the capital. The night had been so hot that those in the invading columns who had tried to sleep had only been able to doze. Lurching to their feet as reveille sounded, they set off into another oven of a day.

Early's plan was to arrive at the ramparts before nightfall, march into the city, and stay until Bradley Johnson arrived with his cavalry and—perhaps—the liberated prisoners from Point Lookout. However fantastic that scheme might have looked, the day's pressures left Jubal no time to brood about it. Before daylight, he was mounted, riding after McCausland, who was still out ahead. Rodes led the infantry this day, with Ramseur behind him and Breckinridge in the rear. In Rockville, a conference with McCausland and other commanders refined the plan; McCausland would take the Georgetown Pike to Tennallytown, just inside the District. The infantry (with Imboden's and Mudwall Jackson's cavalry out ahead) would swing east, aiming for the vital entrance to the capital via the Seventh Street Road. General Long, the artillery commander, was to push guns close up behind the leading infantry regiments.[13]

« AS THE VALLEY ARMY approached Washington, the Federals' best information indicated that the invaders were moving toward the capital's northwest perimeter from the direction of Frederick. Grant may have been confident of at least local advantage against the raiders; with reinforcements, the Union forces manning the line opposite Early's axis of advance might even outnumber the Confederates.[14]

Halleck, not so sure, had importuned Grant on July 10 to send the remainder of the 6th Corps. In addition, Halleck requested the Union 19th Corps, newly arrived in Virginia from Louisiana, where it had been lightly employed in the ill-fated Red River campaign. Grant duly dispatched the rest of the 6th Corps and part of the 19th Corps forthwith. As Halleck sweated out Sunday's blistering afternoon and evening at the War Department, he had to be content with reinforcements, mostly veterans, of about 11,000 men.[15]

But until they arrived—sometime on Monday, at the earliest—the forts standing in the invaders' path could only be manned by two regiments of raw militia; no men could be spared to occupy the rifle pits between the forts. Of the dismounted cavalry, which had arrived along with Ricketts's division and had been shipped to Washington via Baltimore, 2,000 were too sick to serve; only 500 were fit. (These were the men that Halleck had so recently felt would be all the reinforcements he would ever need.) The bottom of the manpower barrel was in sight: hastily organized companies of government clerks, useless stragglers and malingerers rounded up by the provost marshal, and paunchy Republican political operatives from the Union Leagues.[16]

<< "I PUSHED ON as rapidly as possible," Early later wrote, "hoping to get into the fortifications around Washington before they could be manned." It must have been frustrating to witness the evaporation of this expectation in the heat; the mercury touched 94 degrees before the sun had long been up. "We pulled on as best we could," recalled a Georgian soldier named G. W. Nichols, who also noted the collapse of his comrades from exhaustion and sunstroke. But though officers, including Early himself, rode up and down the columns trying to inspire the marchers with visions of capturing Old Abe in his own White House, the best that even the strongest could do was to put one aching foot slowly in front of the other and just keep going.[17]

It is likely that Early, despite the hostility of the weather, and though generally ignorant of the enemy's plans and moves, clung to his hopes. His opinion of Union competence and tenacity, never high, had not risen much following the Monocacy fight. Perhaps the fools had blundered again. Jubal pushed his horse into a gallop and overtook his cavalry, skirmishing with Federal troopers, shoving them back down the Seventh Street Road. Finally, the Union horsemen took refuge in a fort. Spying out the works with his binoculars from a distance of about half a mile, Jubal then dismounted and checked a map supplied by Maj. Jed Hotchkiss.

The general learned that he was looking at Fort Stevens, a major bastion of the District's defenses. And as he looked, his heart leapt; he could see that "the works were but feebly manned." The defenders looked like militia—some of them wearing linen dusters instead of the blue coats of Grant's fighting troops.[18]

Had Jubal won the footrace? For the moment, it appeared that he had; and if, as seems likely, he followed the reasoning suggested by the situation, a weakly defended approach of this importance could mean that Washington itself was "but feebly manned." If Fort Stevens could be taken, Jubal's "foot cavalry" might march into Washington and seize what the historian Frank E. Vandiver called "the greatest prize ever offered to an American soldier." The prize was within reach; Jubal could see the Capitol dome looming through the haze to the south.

But the dome might just as well have been a mirage. The Valley Army's racing speed was certainly an illusion. It had not really won the race, a fact that was all too plain in its present lack of concentration. Of the 12,000–15,000 Southerners who had departed from the Monocacy, perhaps 3,000 were in any condition to fight; just another 7,000, in various states of debilitation, were nominally available but not much use. In any case, few of those fit for combat were on hand. Indeed, as Jubal could clearly see, the army presently threatening Fort Stevens consisted of himself, a few staff officers, and a handful of cavalry. These troopers, now dismounted, were deployed as skirmishers, probing the Federal defenses. But they were patently too few, particularly without artillery support, to storm the fort.

The nearest infantry, with guns, was Rodes's division, moving down the Seventh Street Road from Silver Spring. But straggling had diluted the division's available strength. It was easy enough for Early to order Rodes to attack Fort Stevens; but the division commander, unable to array enough men in line of battle, could only throw skirmishers out into the terrain in the fort's front—farmland with houses and barns and an occasional patch of woods.[19]

Priceless minutes crept by in the fierce heat as Jubal awaited the arrival of Rodes's laggard rear brigades. Glasses at his eyes, he watched the fort intently, as if its image, brought close by optical magnification, could bring success closer. Then the image changed. Around 1:30 P.M., Early spied clouds of dust—and not long after, a substantial contingent of Federal infantry entering the fort. Dust veiled but did not conceal the deep blue of their uniforms.[20]

< 283 >

So Grant, it seemed likely, had reinforced the capital with his veterans. But maybe he had only sent enough men to stiffen the defenses at this one point; or perhaps these bluecoats were only well-outfitted militia. Either way, other approaches might still be as vulnerable as Fort Stevens had been just short minutes ago. To find out, Early cantered down the line to his right in search of McCausland, who had been sent to probe the Tennallytown defenses on the Georgetown Pike. But the young cavalry general's news was bad; he reported far too much manpower in the line guarding the pike to be attacked with success, certainly by his few way-worn regiments of troopers.[21]

Early rode back to the Fort Stevens front to see how Rodes was doing. Once again the field glasses came out as he and Rodes reexamined the defenses. By now, it was plain to the generals that even fresh troops would have great difficulty in an assault. As Early recalled it later, the fort's upper regions offered a platform for numerous very heavy guns of the type Jubal could well remember from Fredericksburg; "a tier of lower works" also contained "an immense number of guns." Considering other aspects of the defenses, ranging from "curtains and ditches in front" to "palisades and abbatis [sic]," Early added them all up and deemed them to be of an "impregnable character." [22]

<< IT WAS A POSER. Here was the Valley Army, which Lee had risked losing Richmond to detach for this foray, in front of the enemy's capital. Considering Lee's gamble, the hundreds of miles marched, and the casualties at the Monocacy, was the army now, like Hunter at Lynchburg (odious thought!) to slink away in the night without even trying to grasp the prize? Jubal's wrathful soul rejected the very idea. On the other hand, in his cooler soldier's thoughts he had to ask himself how the thing was to be done. Lee would scarcely thank him for losing his army by reckless action. Early knew the defenses were strong, but he knew far too little of the strength manning them.[23]

With night approaching, it was time to reorganize, to see where matters stood. Early left Rodes's division to fight "the battle of Fort Stevens"—an affair of marksmen, skirmishers, and long-distance artillery fire—and made his way back toward Silver Spring. There, a couple of miles from the fort, stood the house of Francis Preston Blair, a man

< 284 >

powerful in the affairs of Maryland and the Union. Oddly, in this time of uncertainty and peril Blair had gone fishing in Pennsylvania, leaving his house empty. The mansion had been requisitioned for Valley Army headquarters. Not far away was the house, also unoccupied, of Montgomery Blair, Francis's son and Lincoln's postmaster general, who had accompanied the elder Blair on the fishing trip. The Southerners made no use of this mansion, though a guard was posted to protect it.[24]

Realizing that the chance for doing anything significant before nightfall was fast evaporating, Early called his senior officers together for a council of war. Breckinridge, Gordon, Rodes, and Ramseur assembled in the evening, in the Blair dining room; wines from the Blair cellar were opened and sampled as the commanders discussed their situation. It must have been a wry moment for Breckinridge, who, as vice president, had often sipped Francis Blair's wine in that house. It was there that he had made his decision to throw in his lot with the Confederacy. Now, there were jocund toasts hailing the imminent capture of Washington and the triumphant return of John Breckinridge to the vice president's chair in the Capitol.[25]

General Early, while savoring his glass, brought the gathering back to business as he put the harsh dilemma to his lieutenants. Despite the lack of intelligence about Federal strength inside Washington, the army had to do something forthwith. The danger of simply remaining in place was compounded by reliable knowledge—a report in a Northern newspaper—that Hunter was back in the Potomac region, and could be expected to arrive in Harpers Ferry shortly. It would not be long before the passes through South Mountain and the fords across the Potomac would be sealed up in the Valley Army's rear.

Nevertheless, Early asserted that failure to try an assault on the capital would be a terrible waste. All the generals spoke—though not all may have agreed with their commander's resolve. The commanding general announced that the army would attack in the absence of information received overnight that might indicate a different course.[26]

In the small hours came a courier bearing that information. Sent by Bradley Johnson, whose men were busy up near Baltimore creating panic, cutting telegraph wires, and wrecking rail connections between Washington and the North, the galloper brought word, gathered through intelligence sources in Baltimore, that two Union corps were en route to Washington. Hard information from the Monocacy identified the 6th Corps. But what—and where—could the other corps be? Bradley's message identified it as the 19th Corps. This tended to confirm the military rumor mill, which had been generating reports that the 19th Corps, transferred from Louisiana, had reached Virginia and was under orders to proceed to Washington.[27]

Wispy though the evidence might be, Early could not ignore it. Hitting the Washington defenses head on would be hard enough if they contained but one veteran corps; the presence of two corps would make the assault prohibitive. More information—reliable information—was badly needed. Until he had it, Early decided to cancel the attack, pending a last look at sunup on Tuesday, July 12.

« "As soon as it was light enough to see, I rode to the front and saw the parapet lined with troops," Jubal was to remember. It was no illusion. At about the time, on the previous day, that Early had been riding forward to join Mudwall Jackson on the Seventh Street Road, Maj. Gen. Horatio G. Wright had been supervising the disembarkation of parts of the First and Second Divisions of the Union 6th Corps (the Third Division, Ricketts's, was in Baltimore with Wallace). Many of these men would be in or near the lines by midafternoon on July 11, to be joined shortly by two regiments of the 19th Corps. By dawn on July 12, the bulk of the Federal reinforcements were in position in rear of the ramparts at Fort Stevens and other strong points facing the Confederates.

It seemed hopeless. Even if the Valley Army should break into the city through the defenses facing it, how might it fare then? Given unknown reserves that might outnumber the raiders two to one or better, advancing against house-to-house defenses would be costly. The whole Confederate force might be trapped inside the city and annihilated. In that case, Johnson, trying to rejoin from upper Maryland—Early had learned that the Point Lookout expedition had been canceled—would be cut off and destroyed as well. It was like that awful time at Warrenton Springs in 1862; now, the stakes were immeasurably higher and the responsibility was solely in Early's hands. But so was the discretion.[28]

General Early made his final decision. He would remain in place during the day on July 12, then withdraw toward the Potomac fords under cover of darkness. He would abandon his greatest chance for glory, after having "arrived in sight of the dome of the Capitol and given the Federal authorities a terrible fright." [29]

Planning the withdrawal, Early now sent orders to recall Bradley Johnson from upper Maryland. Scarcely dismounting since they had left the Valley Army on Saturday, Johnson's troopers had performed the classic mounted raiders' function of destroying communications; they had generated consternation in the countryside as far north as Wilmington, Delaware. In a mood to avenge Hunter's burning of Governor Letcher's house, Johnson's men had also burned—at Johnson's behest—the country house of Maryland's unionist governor A. W. Bradford. [30]

From Johnson's viewpoint, it was just as well that the Point Lookout project had been called off; as of July 12, he estimated he was a day's march from the rendezvous at the prison camp, 12 hours behind schedule. With the best will in the world, it is hard to see how he could ever have made a success of his end of the scheme. Heat and hard marching had worn down his men and horses; that had understandably slowed the expedition's progress. But, astonishingly, Johnson and Maj. Harry Gilmor, another Marylander and a principal subordinate, had also wasted much precious time visiting relatives and friends in upper Maryland. Of one such visit, Johnson later spoke of "the charming society, the lovely girls, the balmy July air and luxuriant verdure of 'Mayfields,'" as his host's place was called. Had he known of it, Jubal would have found this sort of summertime soldiering grounds for arrest and court-martial, and he would have been right. (Nevertheless, Johnson would be a close associate of Jubal's in years to come.) [31]

<< As JOHNSON turned his steps southwestward to rejoin Early, most of the Confederate troops outside Washington were able to stay quiet, resting in the shade. But Southern sharpshooters and skirmishers maintained their aggressiveness as the day wore on and this finally provoked a Federal reaction. To drive the skirmishers back and flush the marksmen out of houses they were using as cover, the Union command called

< 287 >

for a sortie by a brigade of the 6th Corps under Col. Daniel G. Bidwell. The brigade started forward around 6:00 P.M., braving fire from
the Confederate skirmishers and sharpshooters. Then it encountered
artillery and musket fire from Rodes's division. Calling for support,
Bidwell pressed on, pushing the Confederates back. The affair looked,
for a time, like a ripening battle—one that might not be easy for Early
to break off. Then, as darkness swept over the field, the firing died
down. For the Valley Army, it was just as well. Jubal knew how close
his men were to the limit of their resources: a determined night assault
on the Southerners by a force of fresh veterans might have had serious
consequences. But for some reason, the action was being broken off.
In Jubal's mind, likely as not, the explanation was the enemy's innate
stupidity. But darkness and heavy casualties in Bidwell's command—
25 percent or more killed and wounded, every regimental commander
hit—seem the more substantial reasons.

In any case, the end came none too soon for the Confederates, even
though their combat losses during the two days in front of Washington
were fewer than 100 men. It is hard to imagine Early sighing with relief; but he might have turned his head and fired a particularly vigorous
gobbet of spit from the plug in his jaw as he shifted his mind from the
day's peril to the night's movement.[32]

« STILL PRESIDING over Francis Blair's house (where dirty dishes and
empty bottles were left on the table to be discovered later by the Federals), Early summoned Gordon and Breckinridge. They would lead the
withdrawal, to be followed by Rodes and Ramseur. The route would be
the Seventh Street Road back to Rockville, and from there via Pooles-
ville to White's Ford. A select rear guard of 200 officers and men would
remain behind during the night to picket the Seventh Street Road until
the cavalry of Jackson and McCausland and—at some point—Johnson
could relieve them.[33]

Maj. Henry Kyd Douglas's mouth must have gone a bit dry when
General Early chose him to command the rear guard. The general,
Douglas remembered, was "in a droll humor, perhaps one of relief, for
he said to me in his falsetto drawl: 'Major, we haven't taken Washington, but we've scared Abe Lincoln like hell!' "

The major, unafraid of Early (who liked him for it) but perhaps not greatly pleased to be chosen for his post of danger, shot back: "Yes, general, but this afternoon when that Yankee line moved out against us, I think some other people were scared blue as hell's brimstone!"

Breckinridge (how scared had he been? His fate as a captive might have been most uncertain) found this exchange vastly amusing. Laughing, he asked, "How about that, general?"

"That's true," replied Jubal, "but it won't appear in history!" Douglas, of course, took care that it should appear. But the reason many narratives repeat the exchange is that Jubal had the aplomb not only to admit he was scared but to assert his control by making a joke of it. Early's final word was a cue, if ever there was one, for all present to laugh at the commanding general's witticism.[34]

<< THE RETREAT to the Potomac went smoothly, free of pursuit or even effective harassment by any major Federal force. Bradley Johnson's men, arriving after midnight, helped Jackson break up a Union cavalry thrust against the Valley Army's rear. Grant and Lincoln had been most anxious that Early not escape across the Potomac; but a muddled command structure and hesitancy at the highest military levels in the capital conspired to put a whole day's march between the raiders and Washington before any significant pursuit would be organized.[35]

The withdrawal was hampered by the hundreds of prisoners and a parade of captured horses and cattle. But the Valley Army was across the Potomac with its spoils on July 14, and went into bivouac between White's Ford and Leesburg.

General Early was irked when word reached him that, somehow or other, Montgomery Blair's house had caught fire and burned to the ground. The cause of the blaze may have been a Union shell; guns at Fort Stevens undoubtedly fired at the house, and a guard at the mansion, a company officer of the 53d North Carolina Infantry, claimed to have put out three fires set by Union shells before he withdrew.[36]

Early, of course, had no idea how the blaze started. He denied later charges that he had ordered the house burned, though he believed that "retaliation was fully justified by the previous acts of the enemy."[37]

« "IT WOULD have been a queer finale of the campaign in Virginia," wrote Confederate War Department bureaucrat Robert Kean in a July 16 diary entry, "if while Grant is besieging Petersburg, Early was to capture Washington." [38]

Kean's sense of irony was dead accurate. Still, Southerners enduring the grind of the Petersburg campaign badly needed Early's raid to be a dramatic success. Hopes ran high, as even Kean reflected in his declaration that "Early, Breckinridge, Rodes, Gordon and Ramseur are men to dare and do almost anything." John E. Claiborne, an officer serving at Petersburg, shared the general expectation. Life in the beleaguered city was depressing, he complained in a letter to his wife in North Carolina. Union shells had driven many of the inhabitants into the countryside, where they suffered privations. "What they live on," Claiborne wrote, "their Heavenly Father only knows. He who feeds the birds I trust will remember his suffering ones." In the same letter, Claiborne, with almost desperate optimism, cited Early's expedition as a counterweight to these woes: "I hope Early's advance into Pennsylvania [sic] will act as a deviation from our coasts & that the war may soon be carried to their doors again." [39]

Southern newspapers had been sounding the same inspiriting theme, a paean to the genius of Bobby Lee in sending his most daring lieutenant back over the border to taunt and terrorize the behemoth of the North. Swelled by this publicity, Early's reputation and even his popularity rose to their wartime peak. Expectations of a dramatic victory ran so high that perhaps the least that might have satisfied it was a quick smash-and-grab operation in the District, with a flag from the Treasury or even the Old Soldier's Home (Lincoln's summer White House was on the grounds) as a trophy. Seizure of Baltimore would have been an acceptable substitute prize.

When the actual outcome was revealed, the letdown was severe. Some papers denounced what they trumpeted as Early's failure, which seemed the more abject because it was such a close call, like the gap of millimeters that separates the home run from the foul ball. The drinking at Francis Blair's house was mentioned, in dark tones, as a possible reason for the fiasco. Other journals, while bemoaning the near miss, thanked Early for what he had accomplished—particularly in bringing back herds of horses and cattle from Maryland and ensuring the harvest of crops in the Shenandoah Valley.[40]

If this had been all that Early's expedition had gained, it would, for a Confederacy facing mounting hunger, have been substantial, though not enough to soothe the pangs of frustration. Were there other accomplishments that, along with these, would have been adequate to offset the lack of an unequivocal triumph? Perhaps not in the fickle public mind. But General Lee, whose opinion was the only one Early even considered, thought the operation had been a success. Lee's summary of his reasons for coming to this conclusion is vague and matter-of-fact. Much more succinctly, the same reasons, with details added (along with an undeniably partisan flourish), were given by Jubal's old friend John Warwick Daniel in a speech following Early's death in 1894. In 30 days, Daniel pointed out, Early had:

1. Driven the 18,000-man army of Hunter out of the Valley and rendered it ineffective for many weeks.

2. Immobilized Franz Sigel's 6,000 men at Harpers Ferry.

3. Defeated Wallace at the Monocacy and sent him "whirling into Baltimore" with his 6,000 men.

4. Diverted parts of two corps from Grant's principal theater of operations around Petersburg.

In a fifth point, Daniel credited Early with transferring "the seat of war from Central and Piedmont Virginia, where it menaced the rear of Lee, to the borderline of Northern Virginia on the Potomac." If Daniel was referring to the ouster of Hunter from the Valley, this is partly correct, though the main "seat of war" always remained near Petersburg. It might be more accurate to credit Early with creating an entirely new theater of war in the Valley; just to contain the Valley Army following its successful withdrawal from Washington, Grant would be forced to establish a special Federal army of 36,000 men and mount a time-consuming, costly contingent campaign. By compelling this diversion of strength from the principal Union effort in Virginia, Early would prolong the war many months.

Those accomplishments lay ahead. To date, as Daniel later summarized the campaign, Early had already established some noteworthy statistics. "The march of Early," Daniel stated, "from Cold Harbor by Charlottesville, Lynchburg, Salem, Staunton, and Winchester across the Potomac and the Monocacy . . . to Washington and back to Virginia between the 13th of June and the 14th of July, a distance of 510 miles, an average of sixteen miles a day, is, for length and rapidity, without a parallel in our own or any modern war."[41]

Acknowledging that the statement was made by a worshipful friend noted for his oratorical flair, and allowing for some rail travel and for minor inaccuracies in the figures, one must accept the general validity of Daniel's claim. Under the circumstances, comparison with Stonewall Jackson is irresistible: during 48 days in spring 1862, Jackson marched his men 676 miles, an average of 14 miles a day. That rate would have left Stonewall 90 miles short of Early's mark at the end of 30 days.

It is true that Jackson's men lacked the experience of Early's; but numerically, Stonewall operated on relatively even terms against the Federals, who rarely deployed more than 20,000 against Jackson's 17,000—most of them in far better condition than the exhausted scarecrows in Early's ranks, and all of them volunteers. Early's Valley Army almost never mustered more than 14,000, pitted against almost three times as many during the course of the 1864 campaign. Also, in 1864, the Valley Army had to battle record temperatures and drought, while Jackson's force campaigned in the comparatively temperate Valley spring.[42]

What Jackson never did (though of course he might even have captured Washington, had he lived) was lay siege to the Northern capital. In doing that—at least in some sense—for two days, Early, just as he said, had shaken the nerves of Abe Lincoln and everyone else in authority in Washington, and brought the conscious fear of war to the people of Washington and the North more vividly than anyone ever had or would again. When the New York *Tribune* published an article describing the bafflement of the Union military command as Early approached Northern territory, gold prices shot up to $285 an ounce. Many Northerners were profoundly dejected. "I see no bright spot anywhere," a New Yorker wrote in his diary, "only humiliation and disaster." Others in the North, notably Lincoln's political opponents, were heartened; as one Democratic paper, looking ahead to the 1864 elections, editorialized, "Lincoln is deader than dead."[43]

For the Confederates, political damage to the North's commander in chief was a welcome bonus. Considering the broader canvas of world affairs, one of Lee's remoter hopes for Jubal's raid had been diplomatic recognition for the Confederate States by foreign powers. He was to be disappointed. But Early unquestionably made the world take notice. Contemplating the events of July 9–14, the *Times* of London seemed to discount Grant's tightening hammerlock on Petersburg and the movement of Maj. Gen. William T. Sherman's host into Georgia as signs that the days of the Southern cause might be numbered. On the contrary, the *Times* boomed, "the Confederacy is more formidable as an enemy than ever." Whoever believed that was, as Frank Vandiver points out, the victim of a ruse; but an effective ruse, in war, is often as good as a battlefield triumph. In bringing this one off, Jubal Early was, himself, more formidable than ever.[44]

PART FOUR

« CHAPTER TWENTY »

"The Altar of Revenge"

I N LATE JULY 1864, circumstances unfolded in ways that deepened Jubal Early's furious hatred of the Northern enemy. Events also exacerbated his contempt for the military acumen of his foe. Directly or indirectly, these two perceptions were to influence Early's conduct more profoundly than virtually any others for the rest of the campaign— and for the balance of his life.

« AS THE Valley Army rested on the south bank of the Potomac, its potency was gratifyingly apparent to some of its members. Sgt. Maj. Joseph McMurran of the 4th Virginia Infantry felt triumphant. The result of the raid, McMurran believed, would be final. "Now the prospect of peace encourages all and even the people of Maryland say that Lincoln will now have to make a proposition for an 'armistice'— . . . It's the boldest and most successful move of the war." [1]

Morale among the veterans of the raid, contemplating their booty, was undoubtedly high. But many, like Caleb Linker, were frustrated by the near-miss aspect of the expedition: in a letter home Linker complained that having beheld the Union capitol, the raiders had not actually "accomplished anything." [2]

At the time, Early himself was playing down his army's accomplishments in a report to Lee from the Leesburg encampment. Since Lee was one of the few men in authority—another, perhaps, was Jefferson Davis—whom Early truly respected, this note of caution was genuine; whether or not Jubal knew of the *Times* of London's pronouncement on the "formidable" prowess of the Confederacy, he acknowledged that he felt he had disappointed the commanding general. But characteristically, the report was far from a *mea culpa*. On the contrary, it emphasized the essential fact (well known to Lee) that the raid had all along been a forlorn hope. Chances of success had not been increased, Early complained, by the performance of his cavalry. This routine indictment was, on the record of the Washington raid, something of a delusion. But Jubal was right on one point. Reciting the principal strategic lesson he had learned, Early declared unequivocally that "Washington can never be taken by our troops unless surprised when without a force to defend it." [3]

For the moment, then, General Early felt that his mission was complete, and proposed returning his corps to the Army of Northern Virginia. General Lee disagreed. Though Early's force was back in the Valley, its diversionary mission need not come to an end. Besides tying down Federal forces assigned to prevent a renewed penetration of Maryland, Early would be in place to protect the vital crops of the Valley region (the wheat crop, it was said, was the largest in years); and finally, if Grant decided to concentrate all available Union forces around the Confederate capital, Early could "then retire into the Valley and hang upon and threaten the enemy's flank should he push on toward Richmond." At this date, neither Lee nor Early had any idea that the mission might be extended in yet another—an unprecedented—direction. [4]

<< EARLY WAS also ignorant of the pressures his presence in the Valley was already exerting on Grant and his subordinates in that theater—pressures that were to have far-reaching effects on the remainder of the 1864 campaign. Grant wanted badly to bring his 6th and 19th Corps troops back to the Petersburg siege. But though most of the 19th was in Washington, ready to be shipped southeast, General Wright (commanding the entire 6th Corps and one division of the 19th) was in contact with Early in Virginia; Grant hesitated to pull Wright's men back as long as there was any chance of successful action by them against the Valley Army.

Meanwhile, Hunter was once more back on the scene, having occupied Harpers Ferry on July 14, the same day Early reached Leesburg.

Grant ordered Hunter to pursue Early, not only with his own forces, but with almost anything animate he could lay his hands on—"veterans, militiamen, men on horseback, everything that can be got to follow."[5]

To deal with Early, Hunter dispatched his most aggressive subordinate, General Crook, with a 9,000-man force of infantry and cavalry to Purcellville, seven miles west of Leesburg. Hunter himself concentrated on a renewal of his incendiary campaign against noncombatants. His initial intention was to burn both the city of Charles Town, which he assumed to be a nest of guerrillas, and all of Clarke County, just west of the Blue Ridge. Clarke's offense, in Hunter's view, was to have cast only two votes against the Ordinance of Secession in 1861.[6]

By mid-July, as Union military authorities later estimated, Crook and Wright were in position to slice into Early's flanks and perhaps even get south of him. But lacking clear overall direction of their efforts, the two Union generals hesitated. On July 17, Early slipped away from them and crossed the Blue Ridge through Snicker's Gap, forded the Shenandoah River and camped on its west bank. Next day, the Valley Army bloodily rebuffed the Federals as they pursued through the gap and tried to attack across the Shenandoah. Still, though some Confederates, holding a strong defensive position, may have thought the Federals easily repulsed, the price was high: casualties in Rodes's division were proportionately as great as those suffered by Gordon's men at the Monocacy.[7]

<< ALSO ON JULY 17, Grant ordered Hunter to scorch the earth. It was an especially significant moment. Grant had decided that the Union armies must not only deny the Confederates use of the Valley but also destroy it. Hunter was told to "make all the Valley south of the B. and O. a desert, as high up as possible. I do not mean that houses should be burned, but every particle of provisions and stock should be removed, and the people notified to move out."

The general in chief added another element to this order—a terrible confirmation that the war, in his mind, had entered a final desperate phase. Hunter's men, Grant decreed, were "to eat out Virginia, clear and clean, as far as they go, so that crows flying over it, for the balance of this season, will have to carry their provender with them."[8]

Hunter proceeded to comply, though he flatly ignored the clause prohibiting the destruction of dwellings. On July 17, the same day he received Grant's order, he burned the house of his first cousin Andrew Hunter, a prominent Charles Town lawyer who had prosecuted John Brown for murder and treason in 1859 on behalf of the United States. Soon after, the general ordered the destruction of other houses, including one belonging to Edmund J. Lee, a distant cousin of Robert E. Lee, where Hunter's own niece, Helen, had been welcomed as a refugee until recently. Three days after the burning, Mrs. Edmund Lee wrote a letter calling anathema down on Hunter's head: "Hyena-like you have torn my heart to pieces . . . ; and demon-like you have done it without a pretext of revenge, for I never saw or harmed you. . . . No prayer can be offered for you! Were it possible for human lips to raise your name heavenward, angels would thrust the foul thing back again." [9]

Early learned about these doings and chewed them over in his mind. It was obvious, as he later wrote, that Hunter "had been again indulging in his favorite mode of warfare. . . . I now came to the conclusion that we had stood the mode of warfare long enough, and that it was now time to open the eyes of the people of the north to its enormity, by an example in the way of retaliation." [10]

While he considered what sort of reprisal to take, General Early pushed his foes clear out of the Valley. In doing so, he presided over two fairly significant engagements in Virginia: the first was a stinging rebuff to the courageous and intelligent Ramseur, one of Early's favorite division commanders; the other was a vindication of Ramseur, who combined with Gordon and Breckinridge to inflict a sharp defeat on George Crook.

On July 18, as Crook and Wright were trying to attack Early across the Shenandoah, Hunter sent more troops to support Crook. The reinforcements did not arrive in time to do any good, but Union infantry commanded by Col. Rutherford B. Hayes, a future president of the United States, and cavalry under William Averell, Jubal's old Valley adversary, represented enough of an additional threat to suggest withdrawal of the Confederate force up the Valley to a position near Strasburg where Early could better protect his deep-laden wagon train. In preparation for this move, Early wanted to block Averell, who was moving forward—Hayes having halted with a portion of the infantry ten miles from Snicker's Ferry. Early detached Ramseur on July 19 and sent him north toward the Union cavalry.[11]

From Confederate cavalry outposting the Valley roads, Ramseur learned that the force marching toward him was inferior to his; he looked forward eagerly to overwhelming it as he formed his line near Stephenson's Depot, north of Winchester. But Averell upset Ramseur's expectations. Emerging from thick woods, his troopers smashed into Ramseur's left, turning the flank, and sent it reeling; two regiments, as Ramseur disgustedly described the outcome, "broke & ran like sheep." The terror was contagious, spreading to the right of the line, which likewise routed and fled "in the most perfect panic I ever saw." Ramseur lost four guns, and one of his brigade commanders, who was captured along with 250 other Confederates; losses in killed and wounded came to 203.[12]

The chance to vindicate Ramseur and further humiliate the Federals soon followed. At Strasburg, Early received word that many of the Union troops that had reinforced the Washington garrison and pursued him into Virginia were leaving the Valley.[13] Early's response was to move his entire force northward once again. On July 24, the Valley Army encountered forces under Crook, in the neighborhood of Kernstown (where Stonewall Jackson had been repulsed in 1862). Early, perceiving that Crook had somehow left his left flank vulnerable, sent Breckinridge with his own division to strike the exposed flank. Meanwhile, Ramseur, Rodes, and Gordon advanced against the Federal center and right, and the entire Union line gave way. Leaving nearly 1,200 casualties on the field, Crook's command retreated all the way through Winchester to Bunker Hill, 12 miles north.

Early believed that a reasonably efficient cavalry would have enabled him to capture or destroy Crook's whole force. As it was, Stonewall's vindication at Kernstown was incomplete; Jubal's foe escaped. Next day, in evident apprehension of renewed invasion, the worsted Federals withdrew across the Potomac and organized a defense of the approaches to Washington.[14]

<< ONCE MORE in control of the entire Valley, Early returned to the matter of reprisals. Vengeance for Hunter's "mode of warfare," Early decided, was to be a raid on Chambersburg, Pennsylvania. The choice of that town grew out of the economic warfare campaign waged against the cities of Hagerstown and Frederick, Maryland, earlier in July; Chambersburg (population 5,256 in 1860) was chosen as a community sufficiently large and well endowed to come up with a substantial sum of money. Also, it was well within reach, just over the Maryland-Pennsylvania border. Finally, since that boundary was the Mason-Dixon Line, there could be no mistaking the identification of Chambersburg with the Northern cause.

The greenbacks taken from Hagerstown and Frederick had been turned over to the Confederate government. This time, Early determined that any funds collected would be tendered directly to the families of those burned out by Hunter's orders.[15]

As the instrument of this scheme, Early chose General McCausland, known to his men as "Tiger John," a VMI graduate who had fought Hunter at Lexington and Lynchburg. The mission obviously called for cavalry, which could swiftly cover the 25-odd miles to Chambersburg from the Potomac crossings near Martinsburg, accomplish the mission, and withdraw rapidly.

McCausland was summoned on July 28 to General Early's headquarters, now in Martinsburg, and given his orders. The young general was to assemble his command and the brigade of Bradley Johnson, along with a horse artillery battery of four guns, a total of about 2,800 men; he was to cross the Potomac at McCoy's Ferry and proceed via Clear Spring, Maryland, and Mercersburg, Pennsylvania, to Chambersburg. There he was to read a proclamation to the citizens, written by General Early and dated July 24, that called on them for the sum of $100,000 in gold or $500,000 in "current Northern funds"; if they did not pay, their town, the proclamation coldly stated, would "be laid in ashes." This would be done, the document specifically set forth, "in retaliation" for the houses burned at Hunter's order.[16]

With the cash in hand or the city in ruins, McCausland was to take 50

< 302 >

hostages from among the leading citizens of the town and then set forth
on the return ride to the Valley. En route, he was to enter Cumberland,
a coal-mining town in western Maryland. There he was to demand a
sum similar to that levied on Chambersburg; failing receipt of payment, he was to burn the town and wreck colliery equipment at the
pits. Finally, after crossing the Potomac, McCausland was to attack the
New Creek station on the B. & O., and destroy track, rolling stock, and
other assets of the railroad before rejoining Early in the Valley. Along
the way, going and coming, McCausland and his men were ordered
to seize and send or bring back all the cattle and horses they could
collect.[17]

The raiders were across the Potomac and into Clear Spring, "thick
as flies" (in the words of a local observer), by 11:00 A.M. on July 29.
In and near the town, besides laying hands on livestock, the Confederates took other things, including money, from businesses and private
houses. McCausland's troopers rode on to Mercersburg, arriving in the
early evening. After a four-hour rest stop (spent by some in burglarizing
stores and holding up civilians), the column pushed on.

Early on July 30, troopers were sent into Chambersburg on foot to reconnoiter. Mounted men soon followed, to occupy the place and block
roads leading out of it. Warned in good time and well organized, the
few bluecoats stationed in Chambersburg had already pulled out; not a
single Federal soldier was to be found in the city, though a few hours
earlier it had been the headquarters of Maj. Gen. Darius N. Couch,
commanding the Union army's Department of the Susquehanna.

Around 6:00 A.M., McCausland, Johnson, Harry Gilmor, and other
officers were tucking in to breakfast at the Franklin Hotel. At the end of
the meal, McCausland sent Gilmor off to round up the 50 leading citizens specified in Early's orders. But before they could be assembled,
a captain on McCausland's staff who had been in Chambersburg in
1863 during the Gettysburg campaign recognized an acquaintance from
the year before, a lawyer named J. W. Douglas. The captain showed
Douglas Early's proclamation, then urged him to speak to influential
people and "see that the money is forth coming [*sic*], for I assure you
that this order will be rigidly enforced."[18]

Unfortunately for Douglas—and Chambersburg—no one believed him. It may have been the warworn aspect of the Confederate troopers, with their ungainly Enfield muskets (few sabers) and their threadbare scraps of uniform. Though some were now riding plump, shiny Pennsylvania-bred horses, what real harm could such tatterdemalions be capable of? Or it might have been Chambersburg's relative immunity from serious depredations in earlier incursions by the Southerners. In 1862, when Jeb Stuart had raided through the town, and in 1863, under the strict orders against pillaging issued by General Lee, the city had suffered little from marauding Confederates.[19]

However that may have been, at least some of the town's citizens were actually provoked to mirth by the ultimatum they were now hearing from the Confederates. Informed of this reaction, a frustrated McCausland ordered the bell rung in the courthouse, calling the citizens to assemble in the town center. Those who appeared at this summons were joined by a group of their more prominent brethren who had been rounded up by Gilmor. Among these people there was no agreement about the ransom demand. Some said the town lacked the resources to pay; others declared proudly that no payment, however small, would ever be made. Time was passing. The citizens' palaver sounded to McCausland as much like bluffing and delaying tactics as anything else. Already aware that Averell was somewhere in the vicinity, McCausland must have been worried about being caught in the city by a relief force.

Nevertheless, to find the money, McCausland gave the town fathers a grace period. How much grace remains one of the most controversial aspects of the whole affair; McCausland claims he allowed six hours. But it seems clear that only two or three hours passed before the city began to burn. Perhaps McCausland, writing well after the fact, gave himself too much credit. Just as likely are two other possibilities: one, he grew increasingly fearful of being trapped and wiped out (and correspondingly doubtful that the citizens would meet the ransom demand); two, he simply lost control of his men.

Even before the order to burn the town was officially given, which might have been around 9:00 or 10:00 A.M., fires began to break out here and there. At the same time, contemporary accounts speak of Confederate soldiers robbing citizens at gunpoint in the street, taking personal property ranging from hats and boots to watches and silverware. Men forced their way into stores and rifled their contents at random—strutting around in women's clothing, stuffing their pockets with candy and cinnamon. Officers were also probably guilty of comparable acts; in his reminiscences, the Maryland cavalryman George Wilson Booth, who was at Chambersburg, wrote that he saw General McCausland himself emerging from a shop with an armful of books. The most single-minded thieves were soldiers who broke into private houses and ransacked them for money and jewelry and silver spoons. Some citizens, like S. M. Royston, bartender at the Montgomery Hotel, lost everything of value they had.[20]

The Montgomery bar was doubtless one of the sources for the liquor that some men quickly found. Intoxication was added to the mounting horror of the scene; local accounts speak of "drunken and infuriated soldiers" in the streets; Johnson reported that troopers "paraded . . . in every possible disguise and paraphernalia, pillaging and plundering and drunk." Johnson summed the situation up when he declared, "Every crime in the catalogue of infamy has been committed, I believe, except murder and rape."[21]

No civilian seems to have died directly at the hands of McCausland's troopers. One newspaper, the Baltimore *American*, alleged rape in an 1869 article, blaming the worst behavior on Virginian (as distinct from Marylander) participants: "It was the Virginia cavalry that burned Chambersburg," the paper alleged. "They have in several cases ravished women on their route."

This was blatant sensationalism. Probably the worst threat to the women—it was certainly bad enough—was a scene described by a local bookseller: "Bundles were fired on women's backs, ladies were forced to carry back into the houses articles they had saved from the flames; drunken wretches danced upon the furniture and articles of value and adornment, women's persons were searched in the most undecent [*sic*] fashion; oaths and foul language abounded . . ."[22]

It was against this background of random destruction that parties of cavalrymen began setting fires in a systematic way. Inhabitants were evacuated from their houses; some—though not all—were allowed to take some belongings with them. In dealing with these civilians, some of the incendiaries found that numerous owners were willing, even anxious, to pay ransom for their property. Johnson mentioned this in his official report, having witnessed a scene in which a "quartermaster, aided and directed by a field officer, exacted ransom of individuals for their houses, holding the torch in terror over the house until it was paid. These ransoms," Johnson went on, "varied from $750 to $150, according to the size of the habitation. Thus, the grand spectacle of a national retaliation was reduced to a miserable huckstering for greenbacks." [23]

Booth and Johnson were among those on the Confederate side who found the whole business shameful, not excepting the retributive order to burn the town. One officer, Col. William Peters, a former University of Virginia professor commanding the 21st Virginia Cavalry, simply refused to obey the order, which he received verbally from McCausland, on grounds that his adversaries in Chambersburg were mainly unprotected women and children. McCausland had Peters arrested—but never pressed charges of insubordination.[24]

Peters was not alone in his refusal; other officers ordered their men to refrain from setting fires, and helped civilians rescue belongings from burning buildings. One officer, a Mason, set a guard on the Masonic Hall to protect it. Most of the Confederates, as suggested by Fielder Slingluff of the 1st Maryland (also Booth's regiment), were neither criminals nor do-gooders; they were just following the orders they had been given, though many of these men also helped civilians rescue their property.[25]

Whoever wreaked it, the destruction was of cataclysmic dimensions for the citizens of Chambersburg. The whole center of the city was devastated, with some 550 buildings burned, including 278 houses and businesses, along with 271 barns, stables, and other auxiliary structures. More than 2,000 inhabitants lost their homes—just under half the population. The only death associated with the fire was that of an old black veteran of the underground railroad, who had settled in Chambersburg years earlier after escaping from bondage in the South. He died the night of the fire from unknown causes—perhaps from inhaling smoke, or overcome by the horror of seeing his home destroyed by men he could only have regarded as defenders of slavery.[26]

« PULLING OUT of Chambersburg about noon, McCausland left an enormous pillar of black smoke rising from the burning city, and a shattered citizenry, stunned and weeping, in the vacant lots and adjacent meadows of Chambersburg.[27]

On arrival in Chambersburg with his 2,600-man division, Averell pressed after the Confederate raiders, finding the trail well marked with burning barns and discarded loot. But the Union column, short of fit horses, did not continue the pursuit after dark, or the Federals might have caught McCausland in McConnellsburg, Pennsylvania, about 16 miles west of Chambersburg. On July 31 and August 1, the Confederate column, pursued by Averell, withdrew toward the Potomac, which they crossed at Old Town. Sharp skirmishes at Cumberland and New Creek—where the raiders were not successful in carrying out their mission—punctuated the southward movement toward Moorefield, "the very spot for rest," as the exhausted Slingluff envisioned it. There, on August 6, the raiders drew rein and unsaddled for the first time in nine days. Johnson's brigade, with the guns, bivouacked on the west bank of the South Branch; McCausland's Virginians crossed the river and settled down on the east bank, McCausland choosing to sojourn at a friend's private house in the village of Moorefield, some three miles from his command. Men and horses enjoyed their repose only a few hours before retribution overtook them.[28]

Late on the 6th, Averell's scouts arrived within hailing distance of the Confederate pickets, who seemed unaware of the Federals' proximity.[29] At dawn on the 7th, Averell's advance units captured the Southern outposts before they could give the alarm. Averell's brigades easily surprised Johnson's sleeping encampment.

"Then the shooting and the sabering commenced," as one Northern witness recalled, "the enemy crying out for quarter." Caught with their loot from the raid, and with the stink of fire in their clothes, the Southern horsemen harbored bad consciences, and many expected to be killed on the spot. Some fought desperately, but most put up little resistance. Those of Johnson's men not killed or captured swarmed across the river, closely followed by the Federal troopers, who routed McCausland's brigade in its turn.[30]

In small groups, mostly on foot—there had been scant time to saddle up and mount—the Southerners fled through the town, yelling "Go on!" as they sought the safety of the mountains. The inhabitants watched aghast. One lady, standing on her porch, shouted, "Shame! Oh, shame! Go back and fight! If we had our South Branch men here they would not run!" A Confederate soldier challenged her right to rebuke him, and summed up the disintegration of discipline among the raiders: "Madam, if your South Branch men had been over in Pennsylvania stealing as much as we have, they would run, too." Everyone had come a long way from Early and Rosser's triumphal entry into Moorefield back in January.[31]

Johnson and McCausland fled along with everyone else. Actually, the two leaders were able to ride, though their joint command had lost some 400 horses, all four guns, and 420 men captured, as well as 150 killed, wounded, and missing. (Averell's losses were nine killed and 32 wounded.)[32]

It was probably just as well that General Early was not on hand at his base camp in Mount Jackson to greet the fugitives as they trailed in from the scene of their undoing. They did so, remarked Early later, "in great disorder, and much weakened. This affair," he rightly concluded, "had a very damaging effect on my cavalry for the balance of the campaign."[33]

« DID THE burning of Chambersburg accomplish anything in military terms? Was the North impressed? And even if so, was the burning morally justified? Under the laws of war, Chambersburg was an open town, unarmed and undefended. To protect the city, Couch had carefully evacuated all military supplies as well as troops. Chambersburg harbored no guerrillas.[34]

Even in mid-1864, as Grant issued draconian burn-and-destroy orders, and as Sherman advanced on Atlanta, the burning out of noncombatants was not yet an accepted—or even a widely acknowledged—military doctrine. As the analyst George E. Pond put it in 1885, "The conflagration of towns in pure retaliation would have devastated the Border states without military gain; and such a bootless sacrifice was the holocaust of Chambersburg on the altar of revenge."

This statement resonates with nineteenth-century high-mindedness. But on the overall strategic effect of the raid, Pond was wrong. He even contradicted himself higher up in the same passage. "In simply sensational effect," Pond wrote, "Early's second incursion had been as remarkable as the first, for he had caused almost as great a stir with two cavalry brigades and four guns as if he had used his entire army." Harrisburg became choked with refugees from the Cumberland Valley of Pennsylvania; orders went out for the building of fortifications as far west as Pittsburgh, where there was much talk of an imminent raid.[35]

With Early seemingly poised—despite the debacle at Moorefield— to go on the rampage once again in Maryland and Pennsylvania, thus threatening Washington, Grant could no longer contemplate bringing the 6th and 19th Corps back to him at Petersburg. Finally, casting the raid's effects in terms that Grant, obsessed as he was with railroads, instantly registered, McCausland's incursion had distracted troops normally assigned to guard the vital B. & O.; this had enabled Early, using his infantry and such other cavalry as the brigades of Imboden and Jackson, to lay violent hands on the railroad more destructively than ever before. Lee must have been aware of all these considerations; and though he never authorized the burning of Chambersburg—and can hardly have explicitly approved of it—the commanding general undoubtedly appreciated its contribution to the Confederate cause. Certainly his ordnance chief, Josiah Gorgas, approved of the burning. "It gives," he wrote, "intense satisfaction."[36]

<< AS TO THE rights and wrongs of the Chambersburg affair, Early never entertained so much as a twinge of doubt—whatever the qualms of his officers. To begin with, he hoped that the incident would deter the Federals and make them forbid predatory behavior by people like Hunter. Otherwise, he simply searched out his own laws of war, "the laws of retaliation," and based his justification on them. These "laws" were not really restrictive. On the contrary, in the words of one com-

mentator, they revived "immemorial liberties of warriors which the progressive and humanitarian 19th century liked to believe had been abandoned as relics of ancient barbarism."[37]

Jubal Early knew all that. Still, as a lawyer, he would presumably have pointed to military legalisms that justify, for example, retaliatory executions of enemy prisoners for the killing of captives in hostile hands. The main difference in this instance, never explicitly acknowledged by Early, was the obliteration of the traditional (eighteenth- and nineteenth-century) distinction between military and civilian interests. At Chambersburg, the interests in question—mainly houses and stores owned by civilians—had no intrinsic military significance.[38]

Thus the operation was brutal confirmation that the war had now moved irreversibly beyond the safe confines of custom—a tableau of men in uniform maneuvering and confronting combatant adversaries on more or less uninhabited fields of battle. The citizens of Chambersburg were the only Northerners to learn this truth directly, though many Southerners, like Jubal Early, already knew it and many more would come to know it: the lives and fortunes of noncombatants, having become counters in the currency of military blow and counterblow, were being inexorably drawn into the system of war. The barriers were down.

Even so, Chambersburg need not have burned. The primary element of retaliation in the demands made on the town, Early wrote in an 1882 letter to the editor Edward Bok, was the money; the threat of burning was just the inducement for the town to come up with the gold or the greenbacks. It was unfortunate that the city fathers had refused to believe the threat. It was a simple swap arrangement: ransom for safety. Nevertheless, Early took the concept much farther than any Confederate officer ever had or would. In his mind, the citizens of Chambersburg had no rights that he was bound to respect. As he wrote to Bok, it would have been proper to burn Chambersburg even if there had been no need for the money to compensate Edmund Lee, Andrew Hunter, and others: "I would have been fully justified, by the laws of retaliation in war, in burning the town *without giving the inhabitants the opportunity of redeeming it*" (emphasis added).[39]

In the same letter, and in his memoirs, Early absolved his subordinates of all blame or responsibility. Serenely, he shouldered the whole burden. "For this act," he wrote, "I alone am responsible, as the officers engaged in it were simply executing my orders and had no discretion left them. Notwithstanding the lapse of time which has occurred and the result of the war, I see no reason to regret my conduct." He never changed his mind.[40]

A Worthy Opponent

*T*HE CONFEDERATE rout at Moorefield undoubtedly raised the spirits of William Averell and his troopers. Their victory gained him a brevet promotion to major general. But he may have been the only significant Union figure on the scene who was anything but grimly concerned in the wake of the Chambersburg raid. What almost everyone worried about was the continuing menace posed by Jubal Early.

Grant became fully aware of the worsening situation along the Potomac on the day Chambersburg burned—which was also the day the crucial mine attack on the Petersburg front failed with terrible loss of life and none of the results the Federals had hoped for. For that matter, Grant's expectations for the entire 1864 campaign—which both he and Lincoln knew must be decisive—had so far been disappointed: Sherman had not captured Atlanta; Grant had not yet taken Richmond or defeated Lee. Compounding the danger represented by Jubal Early and the Valley Army was the political requirement that a renewed Confederate invasion of the North must again draw Federal troops away from the Richmond-Petersburg front for the defense of Washington.[1]

Indeed, the gravest peril in all of this was political. The lack of tangible success on the battlefield, added to the bloody horror of recent Union casualties, nourished the war-weariness of the Northern people. And in his campaign for reelection, Abraham Lincoln faced a Democratic opponent, George B. McClellan, who exploited the voters' yearning for peace. "Little Mac" was an able politician despite his lack of success as a military leader, and he was now in an ideal position to conflate his own failings with the present unsatisfactory progress in the war and blame it all on the Lincoln administration, not least Grant. The shock of the Chambersburg raid, with its fiery images of war on civilians, greatly enhanced McClellan's fortunes. McClellan styled himself a War Democrat. But if he won the election—as Lincoln fully expected he would—the antiwar stance of his party could well bring him to negotiate with the Confederates for an end of the fighting; the result would inevitably be some sort of victory for the Southern cause.[2]

‹‹ ONE ESSENTIAL step in regaining control of this high-stakes game, as Grant saw it, was the appointment of a general operating independently of the War Department and reporting directly to him. This officer would take full charge of a drive to wipe out Early's army. A subordinate assignment, but still crucial, would be the destruction of the Valley as a granary for the Confederacy—even as a place capable of supporting an army. At the core of the mission would be Grant's orders to "get south of the enemy, and follow him to the death."[3]

Working closely with Lincoln, Grant managed to circumvent the War Department bureaucracy and arrange for the appointment of an officer capable of doing what Grant expected. The choice, replacing Hunter (who resigned), was a truly worthy opponent for Jubal Early: Maj. Gen. Philip Henry Sheridan. Thirty-three years old in 1864, Sheridan, commanding the cavalry corps in the Army of the Potomac, was barely five feet five inches tall, with broad shoulders and a robust chest. Everyone noticed Sheridan's head, which had a slightly flattened aspect in profile, with a pronounced bump in back. This conformation made it difficult for Sheridan to wear a hat, which he usually carried in his hand. The ensemble was disproportionate, almost grotesque; the man was described by Lincoln as "one of those long-armed fellows with short legs that can scratch his shins without having to stoop over to do it." An odd-looking runt on foot, Sheridan became almost magnificent when he mounted his great black charger, Rienzi.[4]

When he rode along a line of soldiers on Rienzi, intense, waving his hat, shouting phrases of inspiration, Sheridan could be a source of tremendous enthusiasm, which stirred men to surpass themselves. One cavalry officer likened Sheridan's leadership to "an electric shock. He was the only commander I ever met whose personal appearance in the field was an immediate and positive stimulus to battle." It was a great gift, which he combined with steely aggressiveness generally tempered by cool judgment.[5]

Like Rienzi's coat, black was the color of Sheridan's hair and full beard, a striking contrast—added to his youth and short stature—with Early, who never approached the magnificent, afoot or on horseback. But the two men had brilliant, penetrating dark eyes in common, along with unmusical voices, great energy, and "untiring vigilance," as one witness saw Sheridan.[6]

Despite this aura, Sheridan was not without faults as a commander, notably in his tendency to hog credit in good times and blame subordinates when things went badly; yet he possessed abundant good sense, and showed it in unconventional ways. For instance, violating the venerable tenet that gunners must die defending their pieces, he once praised artillery officers who abandoned their guns after firing them until the last moment—saving themselves and their crews to fight another day.

Sheridan's men mistrusted his appointment at first, holding his youth and short stature against him; but when they got used to him, they came to like him, dubbing him "Little Phil." They generally approved of his unostentatious way of going about his job. His disdain for the trappings of rank—elaborate encampments, swollen retinues, and other manifestations of martial pomp—was most welcome.[7]

With these attributes, Sheridan had risen very swiftly—especially in recent months. A son of Irish immigrants, he had begun life in Albany, New York, but had grown up in Somerset, Ohio, where he attended a local school until the age of 14. At that point he dropped out to earn his living working in various local enterprises—and to acquire a knowledge of accounting that was to be useful later. A beneficiary of the U.S. Military Academy's minimal admissions standards at that time, the young man entered West Point with the class of 1852. At the Academy one of his friends was George Crook, whom he had known earlier and who was to become a trusted colleague and close adviser. Sheridan's graduation came a year late; the delay resulted from his suspension for attempted assault on a cadet sergeant with a bayonet—a display of pugnacity that recalled Jubal Early's West Point days.[8]

As a second lieutenant, Sheridan served eight years on the frontier—most of that time as an infantry officer, though he also commanded a unit of dragoons attached to his infantry regiment. As war commenced in 1861, Sheridan served briefly as a first lieutenant and then as a captain under Col. William T. Sherman in the 13th U.S. Infantry in Missouri. Summoned in September 1861 to serve as a quartermaster at St. Louis, headquarters of Maj. Gen. Henry W. Halleck, the departmental commander, Sheridan put his bookkeeping skills to work. He did so aptly enough, in a series of unexciting staff jobs, to establish a reputation for competence with Halleck, whose influence would grow.[9]

In May 1862, Sheridan got a choice combat appointment—command of the 2d Michigan Cavalry—and a colonel's eagles. In this new role, he exploited victory in a minor clash at Booneville, Mississippi, in July 1862, and had the pleasure of hearing himself described by superiors as "worth his weight in gold." The tangible result was promotion to brigadier general and the command of the 11th Infantry Division—little more than a month after advancing from captain to colonel. As a division commander at Stone's River (December 31, 1862–January 2, 1863), he got credit for rescuing Maj. Gen. William S. Rosecrans's army by repelling three attacks and then staging a slow, stubborn withdrawal. As a major general—as of March 1863, to date from December 1862—he served with distinction commanding a corps at Chickamauga and Missionary Ridge; there, he appeared in a glorious light, under Grant's eye, helping to sweep Bragg's army off the summit.[10]

Sheridan's appointment to command the cavalry under Meade and Grant in the Army of the Potomac followed Grant's promotion to lieutenant general and assignment to the leadership of all the Union armies. Sheridan proved to be an energetic and effective cavalry leader despite his lack of experience in command of mounted troops. He overcame personnel problems—two out of his first three division commanders had less experience with cavalry than he did—shortages of fit and suitable horses, and hostility from General Meade, who was convinced that Sheridan was too young and inexperienced for his new post. With Grant's backing, Sheridan succeeded, scant weeks before the Wilderness campaign was to open, in freeing his troopers from onerous picketing duties—imposed by Meade's order—that were wearing down both their horses and their own health and morale. Later, he managed to take the cavalry corps on a raid around Lee's whole army, fighting a battle at Yellow Tavern on May 11 that culminated in the death of the legendary Confederate leader Jeb Stuart.[11]

<< GENERAL SHERIDAN assumed his new post as head of the Army of the Shenandoah, as his command was designated, on August 7. When he took over, the army, of decidedly uneven quality, was hardly more than a loose aggregation. Still, with 35,000 infantry and 8,000 cavalry, it was the largest Union force ever to serve in the Valley—a telling acknowledgment of the region's importance to the North. At the army's heart was the 6th Corps, commanded by Horatio Wright, a solid, reliable if uninspired leader. Two of the division commanders, Maj. Gen. George Getty and Maj. Gen. David Russell (the latter a friend of Sheridan), were regular officers capable of commanding the corps. The third divisional commander, Maj. Gen. James B. Ricketts (Early's principal antagonist at the Monocacy), had begun the war leading a regular battery at First Manassas, and had commanded his division for two years.

The 6th Corps's brigade commanders were men of experience and ability; some like Emory Upton, were potentially gifted. The corps, with three divisions and some 12,000 men, included the proud Vermont and New Jersey Brigades. But everyone was worn out with the recent futile marching in pursuit of Early. Too many weary months in the Army of the Potomac had exposed the corps to too many defeats and too many casualties.[12]

Next in value to Sheridan came the 19th Corps, which differed from the 6th in having enjoyed unbroken success. But the meager sum of its experience, in the Red River campaign in Louisiana, could hardly compare with the accumulated battle wisdom of the 6th Corps. Commanded by Maj. Gen. William H. Emory, a capable 52-year-old West Pointer known to the troops as "Old Brick Top" for his reddish sandy hair, the 12,000-man 19th Corps was perhaps less favored than the 6th in its divisional leaders, Brig. Gen. William Dwight and Brig. Gen. Cuvier Grover. A regular, Grover was handicapped in having to shuffle eastern and western troops together in his large and unwieldy division. Dwight, a volunteer officer, was reliable in a fight, but he had trouble

< 316 >

understanding Emory's by-the-book orders, a limitation that created problems in the day-to-day running of Dwight's division. As Sheridan assumed command of the Army of the Shenandoah, Grover's division of the 19th Corps had yet to join.

The Army of West Virginia (soon to be redesignated as the 8th Corps), served under George Crook, a talented officer with a flair for tactics who enjoyed the full confidence of his men. The corps, some 8,000 strong,, furnished the balance of Sheridan's infantry. Largely made up of hard-bitten West Virginia mountain men, Crook's ranks were known for their marching ability and their pugnacity. But they had been marched off their feet by Hunter and thoroughly beaten by Early; their morale was at full ebb. The two division commanders, Col. Joseph Thoburn and Col. Isaac H. Duval, were judged capable by Regular Army Capt. Henry A. Du Pont (Crook's artillery chief), though neither had attended the Military Academy.[13]

Du Pont's command included three of the army's 12 batteries of guns, with 16 pieces. The artillery of the 19th Corps comprised three batteries with a total of 12 guns, and the 6th, with half the army's batteries, had 24 pieces. Most of these guns were Napoleons, with a few Parrotts and three-inch rifles.[14]

In accord with Sheridan's views about cavalry employment and his sense that the Valley was an ideal place for cavalry to operate, the Army of the Shenandoah was filled out with a substantial body of horsemen, arguably the best in the Union armies. Grant detached two divisions from the Army of the Potomac under Brig. Gen. Alfred Thomas Archimedes Torbert, a 31-year-old graduate of the Military Academy, and sent them to be added to other contingents already in or near the Valley: these were William Averell's division; an outfit led by Brig. Gen. Alfred Duffié; and a brigade under Col. Charles R. Lowell, Jr. Sheridan appointed Torbert chief of this (unofficial) cavalry corps, which numbered about 8,000 men. Under him, Brig. Gen. Wesley Merritt and Brig. Gen. James H. Wilson would head the two divisions detached from Meade (Wilson's would not yet be on hand when Sheridan took over the army).

More than Early, Sheridan understood and cared about his mounted arm. Moreover, in most respects the cavalry of his army merited the commanding general's approval. Improvements in ways of procuring good mounts and taking proper care of them had enhanced the troopers' mobility. Their fighting ability had been enormously increased by the issuance to more and more men of breech-loading, repeating Spencer and Sharps carbines. Brig. Gen. George Armstrong Custer, one of Torbert's brigade commanders, endorsed the weapons as "the most effective the cavalry could adopt." Wilson flatly declared that it made all the difference: "Green regiments that you couldn't have driven into a fight with the [muzzle-loading] old arms, became invincible." Trooper W. F. Scott of the 4th Iowa Cavalry reported that from the time his regiment received the weapons, it "expected to win, and even acquired a sort of habit of looking upon every approaching fight as a 'sure thing.'" Few Confederate troopers could have felt so optimistic at this stage of the war.[15]

Finally, Sheridan must have believed that his own ideas—though few of them were original—about how to use the mounted arm in congenial terrain had fitted his hand with a superb weapon against Early's tough, mobile infantry and whatever cavalry he might have. A down-to-earth soldier, Sheridan thought of cavalry primarily as mounted infantry—a role in which the Spencer was notably deadly. But he did not ignore the value of the mounted charge where it could exploit the shock of a solid mass of horsemen against defenders on foot in the open.

The Confederates, oppressed by the superiority of numbers in the Union cavalry regiments—compared to their own cavalry and even to their strength in infantry and artillery—naturally saw the same things from the opposite viewpoint. As Capt. Samuel Buck of the 13th Virginia put it, Early's men began to develop a "morbid fear of the hard-charging Union horsemen."[16]

Under the circumstances, it was not surprising that the Confederate high command decided to replace Robert Ransom, noted for his bad temper and for weeks too ill to serve on horseback, as chief of Early's cavalry. The replacement was Lunsford Lomax, a 29-year-old native Rhode Islander, a West Pointer, and an experienced cavalryman; as a regimental commander he had helped chase William Averell in the Valley in 1863. Lomax was promoted to major general and sent to take over Early's five slim cavalry brigades (by Ransom's estimate, about 4,000 men) under John Vaughn, John Imboden, Bradley Johnson, William Jackson, and John McCausland. In his diary entry for August 20, J. Kelly Bennette, the 8th Virginia Cavalry's medical orderly, registered a favorable reaction to Lomax's succession: "I don't know anything of General L. except what he shows in his face but it cannot be a change for the worse for I take it that there are few meaner men unhung than this Robert Ransom." [17]

<< AT HIS headquarters at Bunker Hill, Lieutenant General Early could have read about Sheridan's appointment in the Washington *Chronicle* of August 8. But it was one of Early's least favored horsemen, John Imboden, who put the Valley Army commander wise with respect to Sheridan's command—the three Union infantry corps, along with a lot of cavalry, that were assembling in the neighborhood of Harpers Ferry. With a numerical advantage of three to one, Sheridan's force, when concentrated, would pit about 43,000 fighting men against roughly 13,000 effectives on Early's side (4,000 cavalry along with 9,000 infantry and artillery).

At this point, Sheridan had no inkling of his numerical superiority; but even if he had guessed it, he would still have done well to tread warily in the face of the Army of the Valley, which, despite its weakness in cavalry, was one of the most formidable fighting organizations in American history. Early's infantry division commanders—Breckinridge, Gordon, Wharton, Rodes, and Ramseur—were as capable as any other half-dozen Confederate combat leaders. The men commanding brigades—notably Cullen Battle, Bryan Grimes, and William Terry— were more than equal to their responsibilities. The fighters in the regimental ranks were among the "heroes," like those who had endured to reach the Antietam two years earlier, of Lee's 1864 army. They looked the part, according to a Union officer who had observed some of them in the spring of 1864, remarking that "a more sinewy, tawny, formidable-looking set of men could not be. . . . Their great characteristic is their stoical manliness."

The Confederates were conscious of their potency: Lt. Col. J. Floyd King, one of the Valley Army's three proficient artillery battalion commanders, wrote in a letter home of the "splendid army" in which he served under Early, a "good general." With King, the other artillery commanders—Lt. Col. Carter Braxton and Lt. Col. William Nelson—deployed their superb batteries under the army's chief of artillery, Col. Thomas H. Carter, the replacement for Long, who had been disabled.[18]

If he knew any of this, Sheridan was not daunted. He gave orders for a forward movement that was to lift the curtain on a nerve-racking struggle of jabbing and probing, marching and countermarching as the new antagonists felt each other out.[19] Early was on his guard, knowing himself to be the weaker numerically, and therefore unable to out-maneuver Sheridan by crossing the Potomac and feinting at Washington again; there was too much risk that Sheridan might cut him off from the south and destroy him (just as Grant and Lincoln hoped). Sheridan, with a marked respect for Early's infantry, also held back. Much of his hesitancy flowed from poor intelligence: he believed that Early commanded between 20,000 and 30,000 men. He was also under restraint by Grant, who—though still eager to finish Early off—was keenly aware of the high political price to be paid for any reverse.[20]

<< ON AUGUST 10, Sheridan advanced south from Halltown, outside Harpers Ferry, to Berryville. This movement opened the elaborate martial gavotte that was to occupy the next five weeks. Almost as delib-erate as an eighteenth-century European campaign, the armies' evolu-tions took place in a quadrilateral of the lower Valley. This rectangle was approximately defined by lines drawn between Halltown in the northeast, Berryville in the southeast, Winchester in the southwest, and Shepherdstown in the northwest. The field of action was roughly bounded on the east by the Shenandoah, which joins the Potomac at Harpers Ferry. The Valley Pike, a metaled road well suited to rapid marching (it was called "the race course of armies"), formed the west-ern boundary. Opequon Creek, which bisects the quadrilateral from north to south, was one of its most important features, as the historian Jeffrey Wert has remarked. The network of minor roads connecting the numerous small towns in the region crossed the Opequon at numer-ous points that became important to the armies as each sought to gain a positional advantage on the flank or in the rear of the other. In the

< 320 >

meantime, as long as Sheridan occupied Berryville—actually, his army commanded a line between Berryville and Charles Town, 14 miles to the north—he was in a position to threaten Winchester, about ten miles west of Berryville across the Opequon.[21]

Early's response to Sheridan's step to the front, which would put pressure on the Confederates' right flank if they remained at Bunker Hill, was a corresponding step back—to cover Winchester. Sheridan led the next movement, sliding westward on August 11 toward Winchester to cut the Opequon fords and block Early's retreat up the Valley. Once again, Early stepped back in timely fashion. His men withdrew out of the arena of maneuver, to the neighborhood of Strasburg, occupying the precipitous ridge of Fisher's Hill. An excellent defensive position, Fisher's Hill lies athwart the Valley between North Mountain, an arm of the Alleghenies, and the Massanutten, a massif 45 miles long running from Strasburg to Harrisonburg and dividing the Valley; east of the Massanutten, it is known as the Luray Valley. The Massanutten was cut by only one east-west road, carried over the ridge on a pass known as the New Market Gap, about 20 miles south of Strasburg. The Massanutten ridge terminated at its northern end in a peak known as Three Tops, where the Confederates maintained an observation post and signal station that the Federals tried repeatedly and unavailingly to capture.

Sheridan brought the introductory figure of the martial ballet to a close on August 12 by occupying the north bank of Cedar Creek. At this point, Sheridan had achieved some success: he had maneuvered Early out of the lower Valley, away from the B. & O. and the short route to Washington, access to both of which was an important element of Early's mission.[22]

Over the next couple of days, the armies held their positions. But Early was far from idle—then or ever. To mislead the enemy as to Confederate numbers, he ran his men ragged in the brutally hot weather—marching them silently to the rear at night, then back to the front at daylight, with bands tootling and flags waving. The troops lost sleep and scarcely had time to eat; one soldier wrote in his diary that the effect on him and his fellows was "the worst ever saw [*sic*]" as they marched bleary-eyed around the clock, snatching green apples from trees along

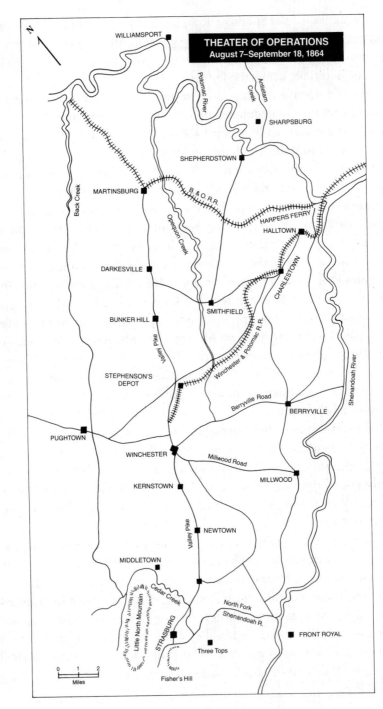

THEATER OF OPERATIONS
August 7–September 18, 1864

the road as they passed. Bryan Grimes, a North Carolina brigade commander, felt admiration for Jubal's wiliness: "Old Early outgenerals us all," he wrote to his wife, "for no one can guess when he is going to move . . . and the Yankees begin to think him ubiquitous." 23

« JUST AS Grant and Sheridan courted victory in the Valley but were anxious not to suffer defeat, Lee and Early were aware of the corresponding pressures on them. All four men were reacting to the intimate relationship between events in the Valley and elsewhere, particularly in Washington and on the Richmond-Petersburg front. To help Early gain an advantage that would allow him to take the initiative, his commanding general subtracted forces from the defense of the Confederate capital and sent them to the Valley. Maj. Gen. Richard H. Anderson, in temporary charge of Longstreet's 1st Corps, headed west with the 3,500-man division of Maj. Gen. Joseph B. Kershaw and a battalion of artillery under Col. Wilfred E. Cutshaw. To support these troops, the high command also dispatched the cavalry division led by Fitz Lee. 24

Before Anderson and Early could concentrate in the Valley, Sheridan had a fleeting opportunity to assail Anderson and deal with him separately before turning on Early. But Sheridan thought the entire Confederate 1st Corps had arrived with Anderson—an impression Lee may have sought to create in sending the corps commander to accompany only one of the corps's three divisions. Sheridan's wariness drew sustenance from Grant, who thought the Confederate reinforcements would bring Early's strength to 40,000, too much for Sheridan to attack. 25

« LITTLE PHIL now inaugurated the second major phase of the elephantine dance of maneuver; he pulled his main body back from Cedar Creek. Sheridan was glad to leave the place, condemning it as a poor defensive position, along with almost all the others he had found south of the Potomac. "The position [at Cedar Creek]," Sheridan complained to Grant, "is a very bad one as I cannot cover the numerous rivers that lead in on both of my flanks to the rear." Two months later, this hardheaded assessment would doubtless come back to haunt him. 26

The Army of the Shenandoah, pulling back through Winchester and pausing in Charles Town, eventually withdrew all the way to Halltown, where it could occupy high ground and secure both flanks firmly on the Shenandoah River. Reinforced in its own turn by the remainder of the 19th Corps (Grover's division), the Federals dug in.[27]

<< FOR THE Union cavalry, the process of withdrawal down the Valley included the execution of Grant's orders to lay the land waste. The fires were already alight by dawn of the 17th, consuming "barns . . . and, it is probable, dwellings, mills and factories . . . on the Front Royal and Winchester roads," according to Marcus Buck, a local resident. "One of the first was Mr. Thos. McKay's barn. This continued till about noon. God save the poor sufferers and enable them to bear this terrible calamity, and may He also make the Yankees sensible of their great wickedness." As they burned standing hay and wheat as well as barns and houses, the blueclad cavalrymen rounded up cattle, horses, and sheep in herds that increased as they were driven northward through the thickening pall of smoke.[28]

Sheridan's retreat was observed from the signal station on Three Tops, along with the signs of destruction. As he mounted a pursuit, Early's thoughts would certainly have echoed Marcus Buck's—though if he had ever believed in the deterrent effect of the Chambersburg raid, he must have been wondering about it now. Certainly the flames stoked the inferno of his hatred toward the Union destroyers, from the roving mounted patrols doing the burning on up to Sheridan himself. All that might have been lacking to bring his fury to perfect intensity was to have heard or read Grant's orders respecting the Valley and Sheridan's interpretation of those orders, which echoed Grant's own thinking and adumbrated the policy of Union terror that would soon take its best-known shape in Sherman's march from Atlanta to the sea.

Sheridan set forth his own views about this policy in his memoirs. These ideas must already have been firmly planted in his mind in 1864. They would have derived in part from Grant's unmistakable attitude; but they also would have been the product of Sheridan's own evolving personal philosophy of total war, one that almost surpassed, in its clear-eyed ferocity, the seminal thinking of his chief.

"I endorsed Grant's programme," Sheridan wrote,

for I do not hold war to mean simply that lines of men shall engage each other in battle, and material interests be ignored. This is but a duel, in which one combatant seeks the other's life; war means much more, and is far worse than this. Those who rest at home in peace and plenty see little of the horrors attending such a duel, and even grow indifferent to them as the struggle goes on, contenting themselves with urging those who are able-bodied to enlist in the cause, to fill up the shattered ranks as death thins them. It is another matter, however, when deprivation and suffering are brought to their own doors. Then the case appears much graver, for the loss of property weighs heavily with the most of mankind; heavier, often, than the sacrifices made on the field of battle. Death is popularly considered the maximum of punishment in war, but it is not; reduction to poverty brings prayers for peace more surely and more quickly than does the destruction of human life, as the selfishness of man has demonstrated in more than one great conflict.[29]

« To MANY of the skeptical and the disillusioned in the North, Philip Sheridan's withdrawal to secure lines in Halltown smelled of ignominy and defeat; it was too much like the retreats of such former luminaries as Hooker and Burnside. A shower of brickbats descended on Sheridan as critics demanded his relief and prophesied a renewed invasion of Maryland and Pennsylvania. Sheridan staunchly informed Grant that there was "no occasion for alarm," and reported that one of his goals in pulling back was to tempt Early to try an invasion so that the Army of the Shenandoah could trap and annihilate him. But Lincoln and Grant, who had chosen Sheridan, must, at least inwardly, have winced at the all too familiar public clamor.[30]

On Jubal Early, Sheridan's withdrawal had much the same effect as on the Northern public: it incubated doubts of Sheridan's abilities. These uncertainties were soon to hatch as a full-fledged, permanent contempt for his adversary that would prove to be most unhealthy. Jubal, in fact, was falling into the trap of overconfidence, which he based on a scornful underestimation of his opponent. "The events of the last month," Early later wrote, "had satisfied me that the commander opposed to me was without enterprise, and possessed an excessive caution which amounted to timidity. If it was his policy to produce the impression that his force was too weak to fight me, he did not succeed, but if it was to convince me that he was not an energetic commander, his strategy was a complete success." [31]

If Sheridan really hoped to lure his adversary into a trap, he was to be disappointed. Instead, on the 21st, in weather suddenly turned cool and rainy, Early attacked—but with Rodes's and Ramseur's divisions only. The fight lasted all day, Rodes suffering the most Confederate losses—160 men to the Federals' 250—but was inconclusive. The armies stood pat for the next few days, staying in close contact and skirmishing frequently. [32]

Increasingly convinced of his adversary's diffidence, Jubal tried to provoke Sheridan on August 25 by moving all but one of his divisions northwestward up the Potomac toward Shepherdstown; Anderson's men were left at Halltown with a handful of cavalry to "amuse" the Federals, as Early put it. His maneuver showed recklessness; if Sheridan had used his whole force to attack Anderson, outnumbered ten to one, Lee would have lost a third of his 1st Corps. Early's rashness, which would grow more evident, may have been intended to draw Sheridan out of his safe Halltown lines.

But Early was actually stymied: first, he was too feeble to make a successful frontal assault on Sheridan at Halltown, and unable to turn either of the Federals' river-anchored flanks. Second, though he feinted at it, he dared not actually cross the Potomac. [33]

Accordingly, Jubal decided to return once more to his former position at Bunker Hill. In response, Sheridan (easier in his mind after being momentarily flustered by Early's demonstration near the Potomac) moved again to the line of the Opequon between Charles Town and Berryville. In this line, which would shortly be heavily fortified between Berryville and Summit Point, Sheridan could hold off almost any attack by the Confederates. For his part, Early, at Bunker Hill, once more within reach of the B. & O. and the Potomac, was in a position to fulfill his mission.

As the last week of August commenced, the curtain descended on the first act of the encounter between Early and Sheridan, with the armies in roughly the same positions they had been in as the curtain had risen. The major changes were in Early's unshakably negative appraisal of his adversary, and in the conversion of the eastern portion of the lower Valley from a sort of oasis—compared, say, to the fought-over countryside farther to the southeast—to the kind of wasteland uniquely created by war.

For now, despite the odds against him, Jubal knew his value: he was holding three infantry corps and three cavalry divisions clear of Lee's lines at Petersburg. Outnumbered, he had been able to keep the Federals off balance, and prevent their uninterrupted use of a key railroad. He had held onto territory in the western lower Valley that was capable of sustaining his army, while keeping the enemy away from the ripening crops in the upper Valley.

As for Sheridan, he was—as Early saw him—but one more incompetent scoundrel whose time would come. That Sheridan, on the contrary, was already in the process of neutralizing the Valley Army, or that it was Early's time that could be coming, never entered the Confederate commander's head.[34]

Fateful Lapse

A SOAKING RAIN sluiced down, blown horizontal now and then by a wind that swirled leaves and twigs into a man's face. The weather aggravated the bad temper of a lone Confederate picket of the Valley Army on the night Early ordered it back to Bunker Hill. The soldier's ire grew as hour after hour passed without relief; finally it occurred to him that the army had "departed without warning," leaving him behind.

As he trudged after it, "wet, forlorn and very angry," the picket recalled later, he tripped over a low stone wall in the dark. Goaded to fury by his fall, the man was "accosted by a lonely horseman who came plodding along through the mud, his nag's hoofs splashing it over me as he rode by. He wanted to know who I was and what I was doing there, and in the same breath cursed me for a straggler and fired at me a volley of abuse.

"With the first word," continued the picket, "I knew it was old Jube. That shrill voice and that style of interrogative scolding could not be counterfeited." Emboldened by rage, the soldier realized he "had the call on the old man." In the dark, the general's stars and his face were invisible. No one would expect the private to know the commander's voice or even "recognize him as an officer when outside his own lines and unattended."

The picket cocked his weapon with a click and ordered the horseman to halt. "He knew the sound and slowed up his tongue a little until I could ask him who he was. He replied that he was General Early. He could easily tell from my speech that I was not a Federal.

I told him he lied; that I believed he was a Yankee spy." The picket declared his intention to arrest the horseman and take him to camp. "Then the old fellow started his swearing again, and as I had a good deal of grist on hand, I started an opposition that fairly took his breath away." When the soldier tested the general by asking him the whereabouts of Gordon's command, Early refused to say. "I told him," the soldier recalled, "that satisfied me he was not General Early, but a spy, and that he had to go with me to camp. He saw he was in a bad box, and screeched at me to go through Winchester and I would find General Gordon camped out on the Front Royal pike about four miles from town. With this he hurled a final shot or two at me, and putting spurs to his horse, went flapping and flopping off into the deeper darkness like an ill-omened old raven with an impediment in his croak. What upon earth he was doing out there by himself I could never understand." [1]

Jubal's solitary ride could have had a number of explanations: he might have been looking for stragglers, as he claimed, or checking on the pickets. Whatever he was doing, the fact that he was alone could have been an expression of a feeling he seems sometimes to have nursed: that all would be well if only he could fight the war by himself, relying on no one and nothing but Jubal Early.

‹‹ AT THE START of September 1864, the entire ambience of the war was shifting. On September 2, Maj. Gen. William T. Sherman reported that he had captured Atlanta. This news came hard upon the victory of Adm. David Farragut in Mobile Bay; Sherman's accomplishment, trumpeted in the North the day after the Democrats had nominated George McClellan for president and embraced a peace platform, reversed the decline in Lincoln's fortunes. Virtually overnight, the sagging spirits of the Northern people commenced a revival. It began to seem, to some at least, as if the ghastly losses might not have been in vain. [2]

These facts would have direct consequences in the Valley. The same was true farther east, where the armies at Petersburg contended for Richmond. The intimate relationship between events on the Petersburg front and those in the Valley now became even more painfully clear to Lee and Early. As Sherman was swooping down on Atlanta, efforts by Grant to tighten the siege of Petersburg were also successful. Pushing its right flank north of the James, the Army of the Potomac forced Lee to extend his line to cover Richmond. Federal forces also denied the Confederates the use of the Petersburg & Weldon Railroad, a vital supply line. Feeling the added pressure, the Southern commanding general asked Early for the return of Anderson and Kershaw's infantry, with Cutshaw's battalion of artillery.[3]

Lee's request sounded reasonable. Sheridan, to Early's eye, seemed inert. Lee's need for the troops was acute. Under the circumstances, Anderson and Early probably agreed on the logic of sending the 1st Corps division back to Petersburg, even though it represented almost 20 percent of the Valley Army's infantry force. Kershaw's troops left the Valley on September 14.[4]

<< EVENTS NOW began to move with dramatic speed. As soon as he learned (from a spy) that Anderson and Kershaw had left, Sheridan formed a plan to occupy Newtown on the Valley Pike. This would throw his force across Early's communications—"get south of him," in Grant's phrase. Sheridan would then bring the Valley Army to battle on his own terms and destroy it.[5]

As Sheridan was pondering this project, Grant began to exchange his long-standing endorsement of Sheridan's circumspection for a mounting sense that it was high time for a winning stroke on the Shenandoah: the crops in the upper Valley must not be allowed to ripen for the harvest; the B. & O. Railroad could not continue to be exposed to Early's depredations, which threatened Washington's coal supply for the coming winter. The Federal commander drew up a plan of attack for the Army of the Shenandoah.[6]

On September 16, Grant, with his plan in his pocket, traveled to Charles Town and summoned Sheridan to meet him there. At the conference, held under a large oak tree, the younger man spoke of his own aggressive plans and declared that he could "whip" the enemy. When Grant asked when he could be ready, Sheridan promised to attack by Monday, September 19. Satisfied, Grant simply said: "Go in."[7]

< 330 >

« GENERAL EARLY, unaware that Kershaw's departure might make a serious difference to him, acted as if it were of no consequence whatsoever. In August, before succumbing to his delusions about Sheridan's pusillanimity, he had been prudent enough to withdraw up the Valley to Fisher's Hill the minute he learned that Sheridan, occupying the same Charles Town–Berryville line he now held, was in a position to attack him. This had been judicious recognition that his little army, numbering 12,500, was dangerously outmanned by Sheridan's big one, 38,000 strong.[8]

Now, with Kershaw departed, the relative strengths were about the same once again. But instead of placing his troops to make a defensive move as he had in August, Early divided his forces. His reasons for doing this were largely rooted in his contempt for Sheridan. They also grew out of his more rational conviction that his mission required him at all feasible times to threaten Maryland (and Washington) and keep the B. & O. Railroad in a perpetual state of ruin.

On the 17th, General Early heard that repair crews were working on the rail line near Martinsburg, 22 miles north of Winchester. To thwart the repairs, he rode off, leading the divisions of Rodes and Gordon, along with Braxton's battalion of artillery and a brigade of cavalry under Lomax. Breckinridge, with Wharton, was left at Stephenson's Depot, about six miles north of Winchester, with King's artillery battalion. Their assignment was the protection of the army's flank. Ramseur's division, with Nelson's artillery, guarded the Berryville Pike leading west from the Opequon to Winchester.[9]

Henry Kyd Douglas was among those on the staff who mistrusted Early's move. Their sense of danger was suggested by Douglas later, when he wrote that on the day that Early rode north, "the air seemed to have a sulphurous smell." Another observer used the image of a fragile necklace to describe the situation: in "the presence of a largely superior force and an untried commander, Early had his troops stretched out and separated, like a string of beads with a knot between each one."[10]

The Martinsburg expedition turned out to be an exercise in pointlessness. The repair crews whose work was to be disrupted were nowhere in sight. The cavalry wrecked a railroad bridge, and supply officers bought coal for the army's forges with their Union currency. The commanding general accompanied a party that broke into the telegraph office. There he found copies of telegrams that revealed Grant's visit to Sheridan two days before. This news must have shaken Jubal. It certainly upset a Georgian in the ranks named G. W. Nichols when he heard about Grant's talk with Sheridan: "This made us private soldiers feel very bad," Nichols acknowledged, "for we knew if it were true, we would soon have trouble."

Rodes's men led the posthaste march back up the Valley, arriving breathless at Stephenson's Depot at dark. Gordon, reaching Bunker Hill the night of September 18, got orders to move to Stephenson's at dawn next day. The knots on the string were loosened, and the beads were closer together. But Ramseur, on the Berryville Pike, and Gordon, at Bunker Hill, were still 14 miles apart late on the 18th. Early's hopes of timely concentration seemed to rest most heavily on Rodes, about six miles from Ramseur.[11]

<< SHERIDAN'S COMBAT intelligence was not solely dependent on spies. He had established a special corps of mounted scouts, some of them (known as the "Jessie Scouts") outfitted in Confederate uniform, who were becoming more efficient all the time. By noon on the 18th, three hours after Early's arrival in Martinsburg, Little Phil was aware that his adversary had split his force. The Union general's response was rapid. He changed his original plan; now he would attack directly westward toward Winchester up the Berryville Pike and obliterate Ramseur. He would then be "south of the enemy," in position to cut off the rest of Early's army and destroy it.[12]

Sheridan's plan was simple. James Wilson's cavalry division would cross the north-flowing Opequon before dawn on the 19th. The troopers would ride westward up the pike, which ran through a ravine known as the Berryville Canyon, to sweep aside Ramseur's pickets. That accomplished, Wilson's horsemen would hold the pike at the point, two miles west of Opequon Creek, where the road ran up a hill and emerged from the canyon.[13]

This natural cut, narrow and wooded, ended in relatively open country about 500 yards east of the position manned by Ramseur's infantry.

< 332 >

Ramseur's defensive position straddled the pike two miles east of Winchester; the line anchored its flanks on two tributaries of Opequon Creek—Red Bud Run to the north and Abraham Creek to the south.[14]

As Sheridan planned it, most of his infantry, the 20,000 men of the 6th and 19th Corps, would march through the defile and deploy in flat terrain; the 6th would lead. Then, supported by their artillery, the Federal infantry would attack the 2,000 defenders under Ramseur. The 10,000-man 8th Corps would be in reserve on the east bank of the creek. Finally, at a signal from Sheridan, it would march southwest around Ramseur's right flank and block the Valley Pike above Winchester. Meanwhile, Averell's and Merritt's cavalry would cross the Opequon farther downstream. They would then sweep west and feel out the remainder of Early's force, with the aim of enveloping it from the north and pushing it into the arms of the Federal infantry.[15]

« AS THE SUN rose on the Third Battle of Winchester, or Opequon Creek, as the Federals styled it, Sheridan's plan worked well for a time. Wilson's troopers, leading Sheridan's advance, had to withstand the severe fire laid down by the dismounted men of Jackson's cavalry brigade, supporting Ramseur with the help of a battery of horse artillery. They halted the Union progress for a time. But the much stronger Federal cavalry soon secured the exit from the canyon. Quickly, the leading infantry brigades of the 6th Corps deployed on the plateau and attacked Ramseur's position. The initial assault was so effective that some Southern units broke and ran—a horrifying echo of Ramseur's humiliation in July at Stephenson's Depot. As the panic spread, the young general rode at the runaways, shouting vainly at them to halt. Then, seizing a musket, he grabbed it by the muzzle and brained one of the leading fugitives. After he had done this a number of times, the running ceased.[16]

All the same, Ramseur was forced to withdraw his division a few hundred yards to the west and post it on more favorable ground. There, in a final redemption of July's fiasco, it was able to dam the Federal surge. Douglas, a witness to the conduct of these troops through three campaigns, particularly admired this performance: "Never," he wrote, "did that division or any other do better work."[17]

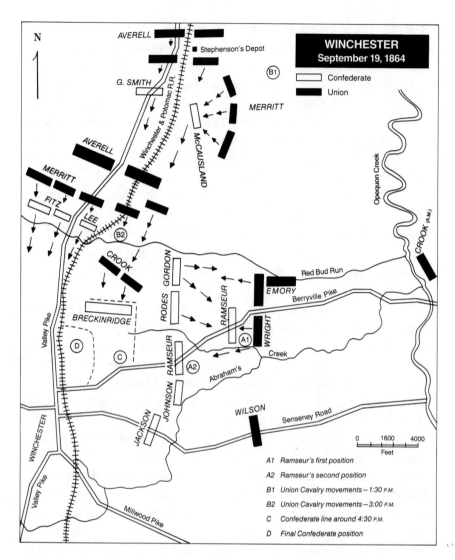

N

AVERELL

Stephenson's Depot

WINCHESTER
September 19, 1864

B1

☐ Confederate
■ Union

G. SMITH

MERRITT

AVERELL

Winchester & Potomac R.R.

McCAUSLAND

Opequon Creek

MERRITT

FITZ

LEE

B2

CROOK (A.M.)

CROOK

RODES GORDON

RAMSEUR

Red Bud Run

EMORY

Berryville Pike

RODES

BRECKINRIDGE

Valley Pike

D

C

RAMSEUR

JOHNSON RAMSEUR

A1

WRIGHT

A2

Creek

Abraham's

JACKSON

WILSON

Senseney Road

WINCHESTER

Valley Pike

Millwood Pike

0   1600   4000
Feet

A1   Ramseur's first position
A2   Ramseur's second position
B1   Union Cavalry movements — 1:30 P.M.
B2   Union Cavalry movements — 3:00 P.M.
C   Confederate line around 4:30 P.M.
D   Final Confederate position

Word of the attack reached Jubal at Stephenson's Depot, where he had pitched his tent in Rodes's bivouac. Alerting Rodes, Early mounted and rode hastily to Ramseur's side, arriving as the young general was frustrating the opening Union attacks. At that point, Early's dominant feeling should have been deep gratitude to Ramseur for what appeared to be his purchase of enough time to enable the Valley Army to concentrate.[18]

It turned out be sufficient. Rodes was the first to bring his command into line, around 9:00 A.M. He posted his division to Ramseur's left. Gordon's division, arriving soon afterward, took position to Rodes's left, with its left flank on Red Bud Run. Gordon's arrival presented the Federals with a defensive line some four times stronger than it had been since dawn.

Gordon's promptness in getting his division to the battlefield was remarkable. He had marched his men 14 miles through most of the night. Finally, trying to save precious minutes, he abandoned the Valley Pike altogether to cut cross-lots to the scene of combat. General Early should have been grateful to Gordon as well as to Ramseur.[19]

And to Sheridan. It is easy to imagine the gleeful cackle of Jubal's laughter had he known of the ghastly mix-up in which Sheridan had tangled his army. Despite orders to leave all but essential wagons behind, Horatio Wright, the 6th Corps commander, had pushed his entire supply train into the narrow confines of the Berryville Canyon along with his artillery and his 10,000 men. Wright thus generated a massive bottleneck that delayed the deployment of two of his own three divisions and blocked access of the 19th Corps to the battlefield. In the canyon, a bedlam of cursing teamsters, stalled vehicles and guns, furious generals and immobilized infantry divisions destroyed Sheridan's schedule and, for a time, canceled his numerical superiority.[20]

Thanks to Sheridan's poor judgment, the Valley Army's concentration was substantially complete at least one hour before Wright could deploy his whole corps. More time went by while the divisions of the 19th Corps filed out of the canyon and went into line to the right of the 6th Corps.

It was about 11:00 A.M. The cavalrymen of Bradley Johnson and Mudwall Jackson covered the Confederate right flank south of Abraham's Creek. From there the Valley Army's line now ran from Ramseur's position just north of that stream across the largely wooded plateau to Gordon's post just south of Red Bud Run. North of the run, cavalrymen of Fitz Lee's division, supported by a battery of horse artillery, watched the left flank.[21]

<< THE MAIN Union attack went in at 11:40 A.M. At that hour, Col. Thomas Carter and General Early were sitting their horses near Braxton's battalion of artillery. Seven guns were positioned on a ridge behind Gordon's men, who were occupying a patch of woods across a large open field in front of the artillery. The Federal attack, by elements of the 19th Corps, began in a blaze of success; some of Gordon's men were driven out of the woods toward the line of cannon.

"To open fire upon the enemy," as Carter recalled the situation, "would kill our own troops, as they filled the space between us and the enemy, and both were in canister range." Braxton proposed that the guns be doubled-shotted with canister; Carter agreed. If the grayclad infantry could only get out of the way, he reasoned, and "if time and space enough remained to play double-shotted canister with full effect upon the advancing lines," the Federals could be stopped cold.

"The situation was as critical and stirring as could be conceived," Carter remembered. "General Early, without infantry support, considered our capture certain, and properly enough, galloped off to save himself. With a steadiness and courage that knew no faltering, the men stood to their posts. The lieutenants sat on their horses like equestrian statues, save that they drew their pistols for close quarter contest."

The pistols were not needed. At a range of 60 yards, the "guns fired as one, when the front line of the enemy was almost close enough to feel the flame of the powder. For a moment, the smoke hid all from view. When it cleared away, we had the joy to see . . . a field of flying, disorganized men, scudding for the woods." The guns had shattered the attack; as Nathan Dye of the 24th Iowa wrote to friends, "There is one great mystery and that is how . . . so many of us got off alive." [22]

<< SUCH SKILLFUL and intrepid use of artillery helped create a glittering Confederate opportunity. Gordon observed the Federals' flight from the guns on his own front. He also saw Union columns farther to the right veering south to follow the route of the Berryville Pike, as Sheridan had ordered them to do. That order had been a grave mistake. In its effect, Gordon perceived the day's great chance for the Valley Army: a gap opening between the two parts of the Federal force (the

19th and 6th Corps). Conferring quickly with Rodes, Gordon hatched a plan on the spot for an immediate counterattack by their two divisions into the gap.[23]

At this moment Rodes, struck behind the ear by a shell fragment, dropped stone dead from his horse. Stifling his horror, Gordon took command of both divisions and urged the men to the assault.

General Early, who no doubt actively participated in this aggressive plan, was once more present on the field. Capt. Robert Park of the 12th Alabama passed him while running forward: "I lifted my hat to the old hero . . . and noticed how proudly he witnessed our impetuous advance."[24]

Surging forward, the two Confederate divisions succeeded in wrecking Grover's and Dwight's divisions of the 19th Corps, and fought Sheridan's prize infantry, the vaunted 6th Corps, to a standstill. Charging or retreating back and forth in the open countryside, men stood and fired volleys at each other from ranges so close their cartridge papers hit the opposing ranks in the face.

By about 1:30 P.M., following a bold Union counterattack, the contending infantry forces were standing their ground. Both had apparently had enough: Early feared overextension of his slender strength, which had already suffered severely; Sheridan was handcuffed, his two principal infantry battering rams disabled or immobilized.[25]

To Early, the Confederate counterattack had not originally signified an attempt to shatter Sheridan's force so much as a means of staving off the destruction of Ramseur. In this aim he and Gordon were signally successful. The Valley Army had thrown a force twice its size onto the defensive and covered a half square mile of ground with 1,500 casualties, most of them in blue uniform. If Early had disposed of an infantry reserve on the field, he might have defeated Sheridan then and there.[26]

As it was, despite his weakness, Early actually thought he *had* won— and assumed that Sheridan, like Pope or Burnside, would soon break off and retreat. Sheridan would not have agreed. Of the troops so far not engaged, the Northern commander could claim a preponderant strength: the 10,000-man 8th Corps under Crook versus Breckinridge's 1,800-man division under Wharton; Union cavalry under Torbert and Averell, 9,000 strong, opposed to perhaps half that number under Fitz Lee (including the brigades of McCausland and Imboden). Yet, for several hours at least, this numerical disparity had had little significant effect on the fighting, which was now shifting to the arena north of Winchester.

Not much had happened there during the morning. Warned in good time of the Federals' approach across the northern Opequon crossings, Breckinridge had moved his force eastward to within a mile of the creek.[27]

As Sheridan's main infantry attack began around 11:40 A.M. east of Winchester, Breckinridge got orders from Early to withdraw his command farther toward Winchester and align it astride the Valley Pike north of the town. The shift made basic sense: Wharton's shriveled division was Jubal's last infantry reserve. Early was well aware that Sheridan had not yet committed the two divisions of Crook's 8th Corps.[28]

As the fighting died down east of the town, it was beginning in earnest to the north. About 1:30, 15 regiments of Wesley Merritt's cavalry division fell upon the five attenuated regiments of McCausland's brigade and sent them skittering "over the cleared fields like so many sheep," as one Union horseman described their flight. Col. George Smith, commanding Imboden's brigade, tried to check the Union onslaught; but under simultaneous pressure from front and flank, the Southern formation broke up as its troopers galloped off in the wake of McCausland's routed brigade. The retreat halted in a patch of pine woods a mile to the rear. There the burly Fitz Lee succeeded in rallying the humbled fragments of the two Valley brigades around the "regular" brigade commanded by Brig. Gen. William H. Payne.[29]

They were not nearly strong enough. Averell, riding up the Valley Pike, had now joined Merritt, adding his two brigades to the brilliant youngster's three (Merritt was only 30). The two Union divisions, sabers drawn, bands playing, flags and banners unfurled, moved southward astride the Valley Pike. In the officially submitted words of George Custer, a military image-maker *par excellence*, the spectacle "furnished one of the most inspiring as well as imposing scenes of martial grandeur ever witnessed upon a battle-field. No encouragement was required to inspirit either man or horse."[30]

Fitz Lee's response to this imposing sight was to attack—before the Federals could hit his men and throw them off balance. In the fight that ensued, the blue horsemen prevailed, stout numbers and plump, sound horseflesh against skeletal regiments and starved, leg-weary nags. Trying to prevent yet another flight by his Confederates, Lee suffered a serious bullet wound in the thigh and had to join the now universal retreat of Southern cavalry on Early's left flank.[31]

« THE UNION momentum in the battle accelerated further around 2:00 P.M. as Sheridan launched his remaining infantry—Crook's 8th Corps—against the Confederates facing east, falling on Gordon's and Wharton's divisions. Fighting built in intensity as the Federals struggled forward across the boggy ground near Red Bud Run and drove the Confederates back some distance. To meet the attack, Gordon had refused his line, and Wharton's men extended it to the west; the effect was to bend the Confederate position into the shape of an inverted L.[32]

Southern resistance seemed to be stopping the 8th Corps's advance. Crook, seeking support, got little from the battered 19th Corps; but the 6th Corps pushed forward against Ramseur once more. Sheridan now put his numerical superiority to work. He ordered the 6th and 19th Corps to wheel northward toward Crook and the cavalry. And, spurring Rienzi up and down the blazing line of infantry combat, he invoked his own dazzling image, shouting "We've got 'em bagged, by God!" and stirring his men to heroic effort against the stubborn Confederate opposition.[33]

Exhorting General Getty of the 6th Corps, Sheridan said, "Press them, General, and they'll run." But he was also telling Getty and others that he had given orders to Torbert to attack with his cavalry corps. By this time, Merritt and Averell had advanced to a point just outside Winchester. Arrayed in line across the pike, the Union horsemen hurled themselves forward in one of the few great cavalry charges ever delivered on American soil.[34]

The shock of this onset, launched across open country, blew the divisions of Gordon and Wharton to shreds. Here and there, men and officers tried to rally their troops; Colonel Carter was wounded by a shell fragment while urging fugitives to hold on. (He managed to avoid being captured, Nelson taking his place in command of the Valley Army's guns.)[35]

In this desperate moment, the gunners fought as fiercely as any Southerners at Winchester, and—in contrast to their fellows in other arms—few ran away when the battle went badly wrong. Guns were inevitably captured as the Northern horsemen sabered gunners and overran their positions, but most of Early's artillery was limbered up and driven out of danger by the intrepid crews. (Early reported the loss of three pieces.) Some crews elected to keep firing as long as they possibly could. As gunners prepared to fire yet one more round from one cannon, a shell got stuck in the barrel; men running to the rear past the gun warned the crew it was about to explode.

Early himself came on this nerve-racking scene, and yelled, "Stop that, you damned fools! You'll kill yourself [*sic*] and anybody about you." Not recognizing the army commander, one gunner thought he was some local farmer, and shot back: "Go to hell, you damned old clodhopper!" The gun was somehow safely extricated.[36]

But the Confederate defenses in the base of the inverted L were by now shattered. As they gave way, the flank and rear of Ramseur's and Rodes's divisions (the latter now commanded by Bryan Grimes) lay uncovered in the L's vertical before the advancing Federal cavalry and the infantry of Crook's corps. Ordered by Early to refuse his left flank, Grimes strove to obey amid a wild scene of confusion he described in a letter home: "horses dashing over the field, cannon being run to the rear at the top of the horses' speed, men leaving their command, and scattering . . ."[37]

Early tried to organize the retreat, fast becoming a rout, as best he could. He sent Wickham's brigade of cavalry to check the push of Torbert's divisions. Ramseur's division, which retained its cohesion, formed a line across the pike south of the town. There it was to protect the supply trains, which made a successful withdrawal, and to act as rear guard. The troops of Gordon and Grimes, scattered, disorganized, some in panic, filtered through this line and commenced a long night of retreat. For the first time in the history of Stonewall Jackson's 2d Corps, they had been driven by a Union assault from a field they had held.[38]

« BY NIGHTFALL on September 20, Early had pulled his force together. He aligned it in the excellent position athwart the Valley at Fisher's Hill that he ought to have been in the day before. Early determined to make a stand there, "in the hopes that the enemy would be deterred from attacking me in this position, as had been the case in August." [39]

But the case was different in September. Early's Winchester losses (1,707 killed and wounded) had reduced his effective force to fewer than 10,000 men. Against this, Sheridan could muster 33,000; his casualties (5,018, including missing) had hurt him, but not, proportionately, as badly as Early's had damaged him. The result was that while Sheridan still had all the strength he needed to do his job, Early was now too feeble to do his. [40]

The Confederate general stationed his troops in a line along the crest, placing Lomax's cavalrymen, dismounted, on the far left next to North Mountain. (Payne's and Wickham's brigades, under the overall command of the latter, were detached and sent into the Luray Valley to block the approaches to the New Market Gap.) To Lomax's right, Early positioned the men of Rodes's division, now under the command of Ramseur. Next came Ramseur's old division, which had been handed over to a 32-year-old graduate of West Point, Brig. Gen. John Pegram. To his right, occupying earthworks next to the Valley Pike where it ran over Fisher's Hill, was Gordon's division. Gabriel Wharton's small division completed the alignment on the far right. Of all these contingents, the least reliable—certainly in Jubal's mind—were those covering his left flank, which was the more vulnerable. [41]

John Breckinridge, possibly, might have counseled better dispositions. But Breckinridge was no longer available. Under orders from Richmond, he had left on September 20 to resume his duties in command of the Department of Southwest Virginia—an assignment he had never officially left. He was needed there, according to the Richmond authorities, to cope with a "bad state of affairs in West Virginia and East Tennessee." Jubal, who had also lost the services of Rodes and Fitz Lee in the same 72-hour period, missed the Kentuckian keenly. "He had ably cooperated with me," Early later wrote, "and our personal relations were of the most pleasant character." [42]

<< THE VALLEY ARMY was fortunate that Sheridan gave it a day or so of respite before resuming the offensive. When the Army of the Shenandoah rolled up to the foot of Fisher's Hill on September 20, Sheridan pondered his options while he positioned his infantry. He and his corps commanders agreed in rejecting a head-on assault. Nor did anyone like the idea of a flanking movement around the Confederate right, which would have to be made in full view of the signal station on Three Tops. The plan finally adopted was to send Crook's corps to outflank the Confederate left by approaching it under the forest cover on the steep slopes of North Mountain. To distract the Southerners and reinforce Crook's flank assault, the 6th Corps, supported on its right by Averell's division of cavalry, would move up to a position within half a mile of the fortified Fisher's Hill ridge. The 19th Corps was to skirmish and demonstrate on the left. Sheridan ordered the bulk of his cavalry, under Torbert, into the Luray Valley to seize the New Market Gap and cut the Confederates off.

By the morning of September 22, all was prepared. Crook began his march over North Mountain as soon as he could, hoping to emerge from the woods with enough daylight left to accomplish his aim.

Early, watching what he could see of Sheridan's preparations for the assault, now concluded that he would not be able to withstand it. Jubal had not changed his mind about Sheridan, but he was nonetheless capable of acting prudently. As he recalled the decision in his memoirs, "I knew my force was not strong enough to resist a determined assault." He gave orders to pull back off the ridge at nightfall. Most unfortunately for him, however, it was well before dark when Crook brought his hard-bitten columns out of the woods and attacked Early's dismounted cavalry.[43]

<< THE FIGHTING began about 4:00 P.M. Surprise was not complete— Crook's movements had been spotted an hour earlier, though nothing effective had been done with the intelligence—but the effect of the assault on the demoralized troopers of Johnson's, Jackson's, and Smith's brigades was devastating. Rout was in the air from the very outset. "Our cavalry rolled down like the swine with an overdose of devils," as

< 342 >

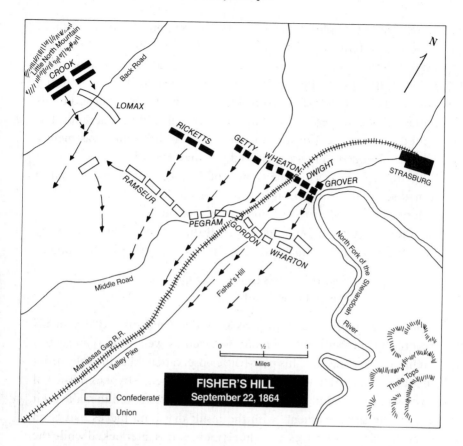

FISHER'S HILL
September 22, 1864

☐ Confederate
■ Union

a Southern infantryman remembered it. While the dismounted cavalry-men bolted to the rear, Ramseur threw his nearest brigades across the Federal line of advance—with some effect. But one Southern brigade went astray in the precipitous terrain, allowing Crook's attackers to get ever farther into the Confederate rear and flank. Ramseur's men now started to run—a flight that gained momentum as the three divisions of the Union 6th Corps moved forward onto the heights and got into the Confederate works. At the same time, the 19th Corps began advancing to join the battle.[44]

With its line unhinged on the left and two corps attacking it in front, the Valley Army essentially disintegrated—men, horses, and guns clawing their way off the ridge and whirling south up the Valley Pike as fast as they could go. General Early, riding around in the atmosphere of unfolding disaster, tried at one point to stem the flight of North Carolinians belonging to Bryan Grimes's brigade. The nearest organized troops were men of the 13th Virginia, Jubal's favored old bulwark, now part of Pegram's division; Early yelled at them, ordering them to shoot down the fugitives. Jubal must have been shocked to his toenails when his pet regiment not only refused to obey that order, but pelted off after the North Carolinians. The 13th Virginia was merely the first of Pegram's regiments to take to their heels.[45]

South of Fisher's Hill, the coming of darkness finally put an end to a mad scene in which disorganized groups of Federals captured Confederates too tired or too stubborn to run anymore. One demoralized Southerner sat down, built himself a little fire and commenced singing. His refrain, to some who heard him, was a wry summary of their plight:

> Old Imboden's gone up the spout,
> And Old Jube Early's about played out.[46]

Fourteen guns were lost. Early duly defended his artillery in his report, but perhaps not everyone behaved as well as at Winchester. Henry Du Pont recalled his post-battle observation "that the sole outlet of a large enclosed field work was completely blocked by the collision of two pieces of Confederate artillery which had attempted to make their exit at the same moment, with the result that both pieces had been overturned with carriages and wheels more or less interlocked while the 12 horses were pinned to the ground by their traces and intermingled in all sort of fantastic attitudes—an incident which effectively prevented the withdrawal from the redoubt of the remaining pieces, which were all captured."[47]

Most of the Valley Army, still intact despite its second severe drubbing in almost as many days, halted after its night's retreat at Woodstock, 25 miles south of Fisher's Hill.

Casualties in killed and wounded (30 and 210, respectively) were not as bad as they might have been, though Early estimated that half of his 995 missing men were prisoners. Among the dead was Sandie Pendleton, victim of a firefight in the dark. Pendleton had married in spite of Jubal's advice, and his wife was carrying his unborn child at his death.[48]

Ironically, Torbert's mission to get into the Valley Army's rear via the Luray Valley was a dismal failure; with but two brigades of cavalry, Wickham's force used a stout position behind Overall's Run at Milford to stop Torbert's superior force and encourage its eventual withdrawal northward. Sheridan was furiously upset by this. Nor was Little Phil happy about the failure of the mercurial Averell to mount an organized pursuit of the Valley Army down the pike in the aftermath of the Fisher's Hill battle. Averell would lose his command.

<< THOUGH WICKHAM'S men had essentially saved his army, and though Torbert and Averell had demonstrated the imperfections of Northern cavalry, Early was too shaken to take an objective view. A tendency to lash out, exaggerated by present circumstances, got squarely in the way of that. He blamed his twin defeats on the weakness of his own horsemen and the insuperable strength of his adversary's. In a breathless letter to Robert E. Lee dated September 25, Early asserted that at Winchester he would have defeated Sheridan's infantry, "but his cavalry broke mine on the left flank, the latter making no stand, and I had to take a division to stop the progress of the former and save my trains, and during the fighting in the rear the enemy again advanced and my troops fell back, thinking they were flanked. The enemy's immense superiority in cavalry and the inefficiency of the greater part of mine has been the cause of all my disasters. In the affair at Fisher's Hill the cavalry gave way, but it was flanked." This would have been tolerable, Early stated, if the troops had not panicked—something he was perfectly aware troops tended to do when even suspecting they were flanked. "[W]ithout being defeated they broke, some of them fleeing shamefully." [49]

Was it carelessness or a sort of fatalism that had counseled Jubal to place these scorned soldiers on his more vulnerable flank? Early never completely abandoned his good judgment. But in times of trouble, he seems to have ignored the dictates of his own native wariness, and to have done so almost petulantly, as if his egoism furiously denied the necessity of adjustment. His decision on placing the cavalry may thus be evidence of a self-destructive streak brought out by failure, of which there would be future instances. In any case, Jubal accepted none of

< 345 >

the onus for his failures. Nor did he give his opponent or the fighting prowess of the Federal rank and file the slightest credit for their successes.

On the contrary, Early attributed the fact that his army still existed—with trains intact and most of its artillery—to Sheridan's lack of skill and energy. Sheridan, he wrote, should "have crushed Ramseur" at Winchester "before any assistance could have reached him, and thus ensured the destruction of my whole force." Later in the day, using the "immense superiority in cavalry which Sheridan had, and the advantage of open country," the Union general should, by Early's lights, "have destroyed my whole force and captured everything I had." There is truth in both statements. But there is none in Early's assertion, published in 1867, that Sheridan "should have been cashiered for this battle [of Winchester]." Nor was Early justified (in 1867 and later) in attributing "my escape from utter annihilation to the incapacity of my opponent." Sheridan's promotion to permanent rank of brigadier general was not an empty gesture. Neither was the 100-gun salute that Grant ordered fired throughout the Federal armies to honor Sheridan following *each* of the September battles. Lincoln's reelection was now assured.

Condemning Sheridan, Early was of course unwittingly damning himself. As Pond points out, Ramseur's exposure to potential destruction at Winchester was a direct result of Early's decision to divide his force. As for the Union cavalry, Early was just as wise to its superiority before the battle as after; this knowledge, in Pond's view, "should have dissuaded him from risking engagement in that open country." [50]

In his communications with Lee, Early had suggested, very sensibly, that Kershaw should be immediately returned to him. (How clear it must have been now that Kershaw, if present at Winchester, might have been the key to a Confederate victory!) In his letter to Lee of the 25th, Early promised "to do the best I can" on Kershaw's arrival, but expressed "apprehension at the result" since the enemy's "superiority in cavalry gives him immense advantage." Early's troops, he said, were "very much shattered, the men very much exhausted, and many of them without shoes."

Lee's reply, sent September 27, was calm and encouraging. True, the defeats were regrettable, but the situation was not beyond remedy.

Kershaw would of course be sent back to the Valley. Offering mild criticism, Lee said he had the impression that Early had "operated more with divisions than with your whole strength. . . . [S]uch a course is to be avoided if possible."

As to the prospect of more help, that was out. "I have given you all I can; you must use the resources you have so as to gain success. The enemy must be defeated, and I rely on you to do it." Shortages of arms, shoes, and ammunition would be made up if possible. Even the deficiencies of the cavalry were correctable, Lee asserted. He urged Early to reorganize it: give one brigade to Payne, another to Wickham. Lomax could certainly "bring out" the rest.

In his desire to buck Early up, Lee waxed almost delusional at the end of his letter, both about the cavalry and about the general situation in the Valley. "The men"—meaning the cavalry troopers—"are all good and only require instructions and discipline. The enemy's force cannot be so greatly superior to yours. His effective infantry, I do not think, exceeds 12,000 men. We are obliged to fight against great odds. A kind Providence will yet overrule everything for our benefit." [51]

‹‹ READING THIS, no one not made of stone could fail to have taken comfort—despite the gross error in Lee's estimate of Sheridan's strength, one of the meticulous Lee's worst mistakes throughout the war. But Lee, Dutch uncle–fashion, also managed to convey his annoyance—at Early's breathlessness, his wild swing at the cavalry, his unwillingness to shoulder blame. Lee's comment about operating by single divisions must have stung; it certainly became the virtually unassailable justification for similar criticism by others.

But, except for his initial separation of force before Winchester, Early had handled his army, once concentrated, with as much coordination as could have been expected. And, abetted by Sheridan's mistakes, Early's vigorous efforts had approached success. The main difficulty at Winchester was simply this: Early never should have risked battle there in the first place. In the fight at Fisher's Hill, there was little chance for coordination after Sheridan had outmaneuvered Early and rolled up his line. Lee did not comment on Early's unwise disposition of his troops in a line too lengthy for his resources.

If Jubal felt the weight of Lee's displeasure—subtle though its expression was—the feeling would have reflected a deeper emotion he could never have acknowledged. All the posturing, the arrogance, even the imperturbability under pressure may have been compensation for a profound vulnerability that was always clearly visible in his touchiness. Early respected Lee as a soldier and looked up to him as a man. But after Winchester and Fisher's Hill there was far more to it than that. He sensed Lee as a true friend in adversity—an adversity scarcely glimpsed until now. Even Lee's reproofs came wrapped in a warm mantle of support and encouragement. In gratitude and affection, Early must have felt bound to Lee by a bond as strong as any between two men. He would be striking no pose when he went to work, after the war, to beatify Lee's memory before the world.

"The Stars Had Fallen"

"AND THEN THAT NIGHT," wrote a Southern witness named N. M. Burkholder, "from one fine point of observation . . . for miles glowing spots of still burning buildings [were] visible—tongues of flame still licking about heavy beams and sills—flames sometimes of many colors from burning grain and forage. . . . [W]ith the numerous camp fires lying nearer, bright-spotting the black face of night, it seemed to us the firmament had descended—the stars had fallen. It looked just that way. Think of it, we said: Looking downward to see the stars! The sight was unique, wonderful, awe-inspiring. Until this day no such desolation had been witnessed since the war began. What were we coming to? What would all this end in?" [1]

« As SEPTEMBER ENDED, Sheridan withdrew down the Valley. He had pursued Early as far south as Port Republic. But though Torbert's cavalry raided through Staunton and Waynesboro, tearing up railroad property, the Federals had failed—in the face of the Confederates' courage and skill—to catch the Valley Army and bring on a final battle. Now Little Phil, operating 80 miles south of Martinsburg and worried about supplies, grew leery of attacks on his lengthened communications. [2]

As he had in his August withdrawal, Sheridan used his cavalry as a rear guard and as incendiaries to carry out his mission of havoc. This time the devastation was even greater. Between September 29 and October 8, the troopers of Wesley Merritt's division (just one of the three Union cavalry divisions in the Valley) burned barns, mills, and crops—and drove off livestock—worth more than three million 1864 dollars. The effect on the population, with winter coming on, is chillingly apparent in the fact that the total expropriation and destruction in that period encompassed 20,397 tons of hay, 435,802 bushels of wheat, 77,176 bushels of corn, 10,918 beef cattle, 12,000 sheep, and 15,000 hogs.[3]

As the Army of the Shenandoah fell back, it left "a smoky trail of desolation," as Frank Myers of the 35th Virginia Cavalry put it, "to mark the footsteps of the devil's inspector-general, and show, in a fiery record that will last as long as the war is remembered, that the United States, under the government of Satan and Lincoln, sent Phil Sheridan to campaign in the Valley of Virginia."[4]

Southern cavalry, ordered to track the retreating Federals and harry the barn burners, seethed with fury—or deserted to be with their kinfolk. Many were Valley residents witnessing the destruction of homesteads belonging to their own families or friends. The scenes they encountered were grim: smoldering ruins; horses shot in the fighting, now decomposing along with slain farm animals; buzzards (infested with lice) and flies feeding on the putrescent carcasses. Mixed in with this wreckage were the squalid traces of Federal campsites, littered with half-eaten pieces of poultry and other animals, broken jars of preserves and pickles sampled and left to rot, and the ever-present festoons of civilian clothing and bedding.[5]

<< QUITE APART from the inescapable evidence of devastation, October was a time of growing troubles for Early. This was true even though the picture brightened considerably in some ways. The arrival of Kershaw's 3,100 men, who joined the Valley Army in Port Republic on September 26, more than made good Confederate losses in the two September battles, although casualties among the officers were crippling: in Ramseur's division, Cox's brigade of five regiments lacked any officers above the rank of captain; Battle's five regiments counted three field officers; Cook and Grimes each had two.

About October 5, Thomas Rosser arrived with his brigade to reinforce Fitz Lee's cavalry division, of which Rosser took command, Wickham having resigned to serve in the Confederate Congress. The

< 350 >

return of Cutshaw's artillery battalion—three batteries of four guns each—raised the number of the Valley Army's guns to 35.[6]

Notwithstanding these augmentations, the morale of the Valley Army was poor; many of the officers and men had lost faith in their general. In early October, Bryan Grimes, once bursting with optimism and faith, was expressing a newly somber viewpoint in writing to his wife. On the night of September 22, he had told her, he had felt for the first time that "we would not establish the Confederacy."[7]

In Grimes's view, the men in ranks had picked up a mood of hesitancy from Early, who followed Sheridan's army as it withdrew down the Valley, but did so with considerable circumspection. Whatever their mood, the soldiers still knew how to act their part. In the days following Fisher's Hill, they had behaved well, once recovered from their sour, shamefaced reaction to the rout there. The very next day, Floyd King reported in a letter home, Early had had to "accomplish the hardest move on the military board, to retire under fire before an enemy numerically his superior across open fields. For 12 miles, this movement was carried out with great deliberation and steadiness."[8]

But the ordeal of the troops generated a failure of spirit that vitiated their remarkable fighting ability. One of the men recognized this, stating that in the future Early's force "would not repel an attack with the same composure and courage as formerly . . . hence the almost universal opinion among the soldiers that we were liable to break the first time we were vigorously attacked."[9]

Moreover, the impact of defeat in two major engagements inside of a week had loosed a flood of criticism and hostility in Richmond. Loud were the outcries among the journalists and politicians, never scarce or inarticulate, who counted themselves Early's foes.

There was much worse to come. As October unfolded, Jubal's fortunes and those of the Confederacy were to suffer two telling setbacks: a sorry rout in a cavalry fight that did nothing to temper Early's mistrust of his mounted arm; and utter catastrophe in a climactic battle in which a Southern victory seemed, at one point, all but certain.

< 351 >

« IT WAS EARLY's misfortune that his principal critic in Richmond was Virginia's energetic governor, Extra Billy Smith, with whom Jubal had never been on very friendly terms. Smith's military proficiency, despite his loudly proclaimed lack of West Point credentials, no doubt irked Jubal. Smith, who had already served a term as governor (Early's Mexican War commission bore Smith's signature), was a man accustomed to high office; his career as Early's subordinate must have been fairly disagreeable.

In October 1864, Smith retaliated. In a private meeting with Robert E. Lee and in a subsequent exchange of letters with the commanding general, Smith denounced Early's conduct in the Valley campaign and called for his relief. In one letter to Lee, Smith declared that it was his duty as governor to pass along evidence of Early's failings that Extra Billy had recently received from an officer—whom Smith did not name—serving in the Valley.

Smith's informant wrote of a lack of faith in the commander among the rank and file. He also criticized the general's coldness toward his men, and condemned poor communication between him and them— no salutes, "no pleasure, much less enthusiasm and cheers" when he rode along the line of march.

The next comment is truly telling: "The army once believed him a safe commander, and felt that they could trust to his caution, but unfortunately this has been proven a delusion and they cannot, do not, and will not give him their confidence." Smith recommended that John Breckinridge relieve Early, and ended his letter by invoking his own lofty status as "Chief Magistrate of Virginia" and imploring "prompt and immediate action."

In his response, General Lee was characteristically tactful but firm. Acknowledging the gravity of Smith's charges against Early, Lee made it clear that he did not accept them. "As far as I have been able to judge at this distance, [Early] has conducted the military operations in the Valley well. Of the care that he takes of his men and the estimation in which he is held by them, I have no means of judging, except from what I witnessed when he was serving with me." Lee finished by telling the governor that he could take no action on the charges without the name of Smith's informant. "Justice to General Early requires that I should inform him of the accusations made against him and of the name of his accuser. The matter can then be officially investigated."

Many others besides Smith wanted an end to Jubal's leadership of the Valley Army. Early's performance, in the popular view, was all the more deplorable because it had foreclosed the aura of invincibility inaugurated by Jackson and long attached to Confederate arms in the Valley. This sentiment was reflected in the Richmond *Enquirer*, which printed a hostile editorial on September 27. The paper demanded Jubal's removal from his post, and put forward the name of James Longstreet as his successor, though Longstreet had not yet recovered from his Wilderness wound.

Lee acknowledged the role of public opinion in the matter of Early's conduct. But the commanding general declined to be influenced by popular views. He expressed this attitude in a masterly stroke ending the written exchange with Smith and deflating the governor's basic arguments. These, Lee attested with suave tact, were largely hot air in the absence of personal knowledge on Smith's part or of an identifiable witness. As to public opinion of the conduct of military affairs, Lee noted that it is unreliable; for security reasons, the public cannot be told enough about operational details to acquire "the facts essential to a fair and intelligent opinion."

Results are thus the only measure the public has for judging a commander's performance. "I think you will agree with me," Lee urged, that an opinion based solely on results "is not as safe a guide as a knowledge of all the circumstances surrounding the officer, his resources as compared with those of the enemy, his information as to the movements and designs of the latter, the nature of his command, and the object he has in view."

Whatever the case, the commanding general had, he wrote, no intention of arguing with Smith. As far as Lee was concerned, Early had "conducted his operations with judgment, and until his late reverses rendered very valuable service considering the means at his disposal." General Lee told Smith that he deplored "these disasters as much as yourself," but was not convinced that they should be attributed to "such want of capacity on the part of General Early as to warrant me in recommending his recall." Lee thanked the governor for his interest and "the zealous support you are always ready to render the army," and temporarily staved the crisis off. President Davis and Secretary of War Seddon promptly endorsed this result.[10]

But the crisis went well beyond the governor's influence. The question of competence was broadened to include personal conduct. The Savannah *News* printed a dispatch from its correspondent reporting that, at the Battle of Winchester, General Early drank frequently from a black bottle. In response to this report, Confederate Senator James L. Orr of South Carolina moved a resolution calling on the Senate Military Committee to investigate the September defeats in the Valley, suggesting that they had come about through the alcoholic overindulgence of General Early. During the debate on the motion, Senator Benjamin H. Hill of Georgia even identified the spirits consumed at Winchester as apple brandy.

Jubal's response to Orr's motion was rapid. He wrote a letter to the chairman of the Military Committee. In it he challenged the committee to conduct a full investigation to prove or refute the allegations of Orr and Hill, which must have reflected widespread hostility, suspicion, and doubt among all sorts of influential people in Richmond. It was fortunate for Early that his friend Breckinridge, who happened to arrive in the capital about this time, was able—as an unimpeachable and knowledgeable witness—to attack the reports and gossip about Early's intoxication as totally unfounded. The Senate backed away from Orr's resolution. Thanks to Lee and Breckinridge, Jubal was safe—for a while.

‹‹ AMONG THOSE in the Valley Army who might have had a problem with drink, Thomas Rosser was as logical a candidate as Early. Although swearing off liquor was commonplace among nineteenth-century American males, Rosser—at least once and in writing—promised his beloved Betsey to refrain forever from the consumption of spirits. Whatever Rosser's drinking habits, Early was doubtless glad to have him join the Valley Army. The 600 troopers of Rosser's so-called Laurel Brigade brought the strength of Lee's and Lomax's attenuated cavalry divisions to a total of as many as 5,000 men.[11]

Symbolic of victory, the laurel in the brigade's nickname—and on its flags and uniform badges—reflected its record of success from its beginnings under the celebrated Turner Ashby. Rosser's own view of his potential contribution to the Confederate effort west of the Blue Ridge led him to call himself, or permit others to dub him, "the Savior of the Valley." [12]

Early ordered Rosser to pursue Sheridan and "harass the enemy as much as possible." Rosser was to keep track of Sheridan's movements, which might, Early thought, take the Union forces east of the Blue Ridge; alternatively, Sheridan might detach some of his men to Washington for shipment to Grant. Until he knew Sheridan's intentions, Early proposed to keep his infantry at New Market. From there, he could either move rapidly across the Blue Ridge or down the Valley. In the meantime, if Rosser saw a chance "to strike a blow," he was to do so without waiting for orders. [13]

Pushing ahead, Rosser was immediately successful in attacks on the rear guards thrown out by Custer and Merritt. On October 7, Rosser reported, the Southern troopers killed and wounded a "considerable number," and captured "about fifty prisoners," along with some wagons and ambulances, a number of horses, and "nine forges with their teams." Next day, Rosser's command continued to beat up the Federal rear guard by sustaining their performance of the 7th. [14]

At any rate, Sheridan was "mad clear through" at what was happening. On the 8th, he summoned Torbert and directed him "either to give Rosser a drubbing or get whipped himself." [15]

On the morning of October 9, Rosser's headquarters were with three brigades of his force (3,000–3,500 men) occupying a ridge line astride the Back Road, west of the Valley Pike and just south of Tom's Brook, a tributary of the Shenandoah. Rosser's position, supported by six guns and buttressed by stone walls and fence rail breastworks, was ideal for dismounted fighting. Lomax, with three smaller brigades numbering about 1,500 men, defended a similar line on the pike.

About 7:00 A.M., Rosser's line began to take heavy artillery fire. The Confederates next faced a head-on attack in the center of their line by three regiments, mounted and dismounted, which were unable to advance very far. Custer, in command west of the pike, brought up a brigade in support of the regiments trying to make the frontal assault, and sent two regiments to turn Rosser's left flank. All this skirmishing and maneuvering took almost two hours.

Then, hearing the charge sounded by Federal bugles, the Southerners reeled under a second attack. Their center held, but the men on the left could not prevent the turning movement; as soon as they saw their line flanked, they ran—with the rest of the command close behind. On the pike, Lomax's brigades encountered a similar fate at Merritt's hands; like their fellows, they held the center but gave way on their right flank. They too took flight, in the same state of confusion and disorder as their comrades.[16]

The culmination was a Confederate stampede. Up the pike and the Back Road, the Southerners broke and galloped to the rear, some thundering through the town of Woodstock. Rosser's men fled 20 miles before they drew rein; Lomax's contingent finished under the wing of Early's infantry in New Market, 26 miles from Tom's Brook.

"Woodstock Races," the Federals called it. Counting nine of their men dead, 48 wounded, and none captured or missing, Custer and Merritt collected 350 prisoners, all but one of Rosser's 12 guns, and virtually every wagon, ambulance, and caisson belonging to the Valley Army's cavalry. In addition, the Confederates lost about 50 men killed and wounded. Sheridan was highly pleased, and Secretary of War Stanton sent all hands a warm telegram of felicitations on their "brilliant victory."[17]

It was certainly decisive. As George Custer correctly declared, "Never since the beginning of this war had there been witnessed such a complete . . . overthrow of [Confederate] cavalry." At least one astute Southern witness gave credit to Sheridan and his cavalry, "which is made out of firstclass fighting stuff." The same man, a gunner, bemoaned the "shameful way our cavalry . . . fought, bled and died a-running rearward," and allowed that it "was enough to make its old commander, General J. E. B. Stuart, weep in his grave. Ring down the curtain on that scene, for the cavalry played a regular exeunt act."[18]

« THOUGH HIS state of mind on getting news of Tom's Brook must have been bleak, Jubal's response was one of his corrosive gibes: "The laurel," he said, "is a running vine." But by now, he was resigned to the feebleness of his cavalry. "It would be better," he concluded disconsolately in a letter to Lee, "if they could all be put into the infantry; but if that were tried I am afraid they would all run off." [19]

These notes repeat a familiar theme. Yet, in considering the responsibility of Rosser himself, Early was surprisingly forgiving. Perhaps he did not know that Rosser's own subordinates were not so tolerant, blaming him for recklessness in taking on the masterful cohorts of Custer—Rosser's West Point friend—and the relentless Merritt. Col. Thomas T. Munford, a brigade commander in what had been Fitz Lee's division, proclaimed the loss of confidence in Rosser by all the officers of his brigade: "They knew he could fight and was full of it, but he did not know when to stop, or when to retire." [20]

Early certainly knew how bad it had all been. But he refrained from recrimination. In a letter to Rosser on October 10, Early cited the Federals' advantages in numbers and equipment as the causes of the previous day's "reverse." Still, Jubal urged, "we must not be dispirited but reorganize and try again." It was as if Early were taking a leaf from Lee's book—accepting what could not be undone and encouraging his shaken subordinate to pull himself and his command together and prepare for success. [21]

<< CONTEMPLATING his future moves in the wake of two sharp, successive setbacks, Early considered withdrawal up the Valley. The devastation wrought by Sheridan was already affecting the Confederates' ability to subsist where they were; a move toward their base of supplies around Staunton would have made logistical sense.

Instead, Jubal chose the aggressive option: he would stay where he was and try, if he could, to accomplish a final, triumphant victory over the Federals. Such a success would avenge the Southern defeats, confirm Sheridan's incompetence once and for all, and solve the worst of Early's supply problems, at least for a while. Most important, Sheridan's undoing would reopen the lower Valley and reinstate the circumstances required for Early's pursuit of his original missions. The morale of his army would revive, and the cause of the Confederacy would gain a breathing spell. [22]

Sheridan did not dream of any such outcome. To him Winchester, Fisher's Hill, and Tom's Brook demonstrated beyond doubt that Early was finished. Little Phil believed, with perfect conviction, that the campaign was at an end, and communicated his belief to Grant. Sheridan also proposed that the bulk of his army return to bolster Grant's siege of Petersburg. On October 12, Sheridan actually began this process by ordering the 6th Corps off to Washington for shipment to Grant by water.[23]

Grant saw things quite differently. Specifically, he revived the long-cherished notion of an offensive mission, outside the Valley, for Sheridan's army. Let Little Phil tear up the Virginia Central Railroad around Charlottesville and Gordonsville and destroy the James River Canal; Grant believed that these interruptions of the Confederate supply line would help strangle Lee at Petersburg as effectively as the physical presence of Sheridan's men, horses, and guns with the Army of the Potomac.[24]

<< EARLY, on the lookout for Sheridan, found him on the line of Cedar Creek. The lieutenant general launched a probing attack on October 13 from Hupp's Hill, with guns and a brigade of Kershaw's division against Thoburn's division of the Federal 8th Corps. It was a sharp, fiercely contested fight that lasted through the morning and caused about 180 Southern casualties; the Federals lost about 200.[25]

Next day, a wire from Stanton asked Sheridan to come to the capital to confer: a "consultation on several points is extremely desirable," the secretary's telegram said. With Early on his front doorstep, Sheridan disliked leaving his army; but the Washington conference offered a chance to declare his independence of the bureaucracy and get on with the war. Still, Sheridan did not depart until large scouting parties sent out by Custer and Emory (commanding the 19th Corps) had reported the Confederates' withdrawal southward to Fisher's Hill. From there, Sheridan persuaded himself, "the enemy . . . could not accomplish much."[26]

Sheridan had not ridden far en route to catch a train to Washington when he received a troubling message from Horatio Wright, whom he had left in charge of the army. Federal signalmen, Wright noted, had picked up a message wigwagged from Round Top Mountain and addressed to General Early, on Fisher's Hill. Translated with the aid of a captured Confederate cipher book, the signal said: "Be ready to move as soon as my forces join you and we will crush Sheridan. LONG-STREET."

It seemed a transparent ruse. It therefore bothered Sheridan, who hastily backed away from his previous certainties about the impotence of the Valley Army. What if Longstreet should actually be on his way? The stolid Wright sounded apprehensive in the cover note he sent with the signal: he would "hold on here until the enemy's movements are developed," adding that he only feared "an attack on my right, which I shall make every provision for guarding against and resisting."

Wright's apprehensions were professionally correct. The right flank of a Union army holding a line on Cedar Creek would have to rest on the creek itself, where it turns northward near the Back Road. Confederate cavalry crossing the creek near this flank—the stream was easily forded here and there—could operate in largely open terrain where units of horsemen could charge, wheel, and maneuver to their hearts' content.[27]

Reminded of this, the Union commander could not shake off his worry: Cedar Creek was indeed a miserable position, largely because of that flat, open right flank. The left flank, anchored on the Shenandoah—a wider, deeper stream than Cedar Creek—was less insecure, especially because of the bulk of Massanutten Mountain, which descended almost sheer to the right bank of the river. This topography would hamper the Confederates in bringing up attacking troops, who would then have to cross the river on fords that could be safely covered by pickets and cavalry.

Still, the Union commanding general did not think it necessary to break off his trip and return to his army. He concluded that the "Longstreet" signal was, after all, a trick, which indeed was the case. (Jubal had conceived and written the message himself, in order to keep Sheridan from sending troops off to Petersburg.) In a hasty note to Wright, Sheridan urged him to strengthen his position as best he could. Then Little Phil climbed back on Rienzi and continued his journey to Washington.[28]

<< BENT ON ATTACK, General Early knew he could succeed only by turning a flank of his opponent's position; a frontal attack would have to cross the creek and advance uphill against entrenchments. The plan that evolved from this realization would throw the greatest weight of the Valley Army—the 2d Corps under Gordon—against the relatively weak Union left flank; this force would approach the Shenandoah by a narrow, primitive trail that wound through the terrain south of the river and emerged near Bowman's Ford. Crossing the river there, the 2d Corps would proceed a mile or so inland before opening its attack. Kershaw would make his assault across Cedar Creek at Bowman's Mill. The artillery, with Wharton, would wait for the assault to begin before advancing behind Kershaw across the creek and aiming straight down the pike to Middletown. Rosser, with the bulk of the cavalry, would operate against Union horsemen on the Confederate left, while a brigade under William Payne would cross the Shenandoah with Gordon and dash to Union headquarters in the mansion of Belle Grove, a few hundred yards west of the river—and capture Sheridan.

It would have been better for Early if Sheridan had slept—and perhaps been captured—at Belle Grove the night of October 18–19. Instead, the Union commander stayed in Winchester en route back from his meeting in Washington (where, ironically, he had persuaded Halleck and Stanton that he should send the 6th and 19th Corps back to Grant). Almost all other arrangements made by the Army of the Shenandoah seemed favorable to the Southern scheme's success. Most of the Federal cavalry was over on the right, removed from the infantry fight that Early figured he could win—with the aid of surprise. Sheridan's weakest infantry, the 8th Corps, manned the left end of the Union line, east of the pike, supported by a brigade of cavalry. West of the pike, the 19th Corps's position on Cedar Creek was strong—well dug in on ground elevated above the creek and stiffened with timber breastworks and abatis. Its defenders hardly expected to be attacked; no one in the Federal camp did, though Wright had prudently ordered a reconnaissance in force, first thing on the 19th, by Grover's division of the 19th Corps. Held in reserve and guarding the right flank, nearer Middletown than the creek, the 6th Corps lay east of a ravine cut by Meadow Brook, a tributary of the creek running parallel to the Valley Pike.²⁹

≪ AT 5:30 A.M. on the 19th, Gordon and Kershaw attacked at almost the same moment, charging through dawn twilight obscured by a dense fog. Between them, they picked up the Union 8th Corps, and flung it, in shocked, bloody, and disorganized fragments, several hundred yards to the rear. The Confederates began taking prisoners, some barely dressed, others caught abed in their tents, dazed and "scared to death," as one North Carolina soldier remembered it.

After the initial encounter, Gordon's and Kershaw's men joined forces. Together, they surged across the pike and fell upon the left flank, now exposed, of the 19th Corps. Though alerted by the yelling and firing to the east, these defenders were also cut down and swept away by the sheer momentum and ferocity of the Southern onslaught.

Hand-to-hand fighting, recalled by some as among the most savage of the war, was a feature of this phase of the battle, with the deadliest combat raging around the Union colors. "Men seemed more like demons than human beings," one Federal soldier remembered, "as they struck fiercely at each other with clubbed muskets and bayonets." A veteran captain in the Vermont brigade never forgot the blood: ". . . splashes of blood, and zig-zag trails of blood, and bodies of men and horses. I never on any battlefield saw so much blood as on this of Cedar Creek. The firm limestone soil would not receive it, and there was no pitying summer grass to hide it."

The Federals fought and died—or ran. By the time the battle was 30 minutes old, Gordon later noted, "we had captured nearly all the Union artillery; we had scattered in veriest rout two thirds of the Union army; while less than one third of the Confederate forces had been under fire and that third intact and jubilant. Only the Sixth Corps of Sheridan's entire force held its ground."³⁰

≪ THE FOG, which hung over the battlefield until midmorning, magnified the normal confusion of combat almost beyond comprehension. The persistent murk may explain why the divisions of Ramseur and

Pegram, having dispersed the elements of the Union 8th Corps facing them at the outset, halted on the pike north of Belle Grove. As they came up on the road, Pegram's men were placed between two of Ramseur's brigades, so that the two divisions were mingled. The organization of the 2d Corps was no longer coherent; Gordon, in command of the corps, was absent, having ridden with Evans, now on the left end of the Confederate line.

From the Ramseur-Pegram line, skirmishers crossed the road and probed toward Meadow Brook; a detachment scouted Middletown. Then, some time between 7:00 and 7:30 A.M., the skirmishers fell back, reporting enemy infantry ahead.[31]

The force opposing the 4,000 men under Ramseur and Pegram was, of course, the Union 6th Corps, numbering about 8,000. Those odds would not necessarily have daunted the Southerners if the fog had not concealed the Federals' dispositions. Had Ramseur and Pegram been able to see better, it might have occurred to them that they controlled the battlefield. They held the Valley Pike, which ran along the highest ground on the field. From there, one of their divisions could have hit the 6th Corps in its left flank while the other marched through Middletown to straddle the pike north of the village, enfilade any future Federal defensive position west of the road, and block the enemy's avenue of retreat. Kershaw and Evans, with Wharton and the artillery in support, could then have finished the 6th Corps off.

Such a sequence of thoughts apparently never did occur to either Pegram or Ramseur. They remained idle where they were for the better part of a crucial hour. As Wert points out, a matchless offensive opportunity "slipped unseen past the Confederates."[32]

<< AROUND EIGHT o'clock, Pegram would get orders from Gordon to move across the pike and search out the Federal 6th Corps. This was about the time Kershaw and Evans ran into parts of that corps as they pressed their attack through the disorganized 19th Corps. The fight put up by the 19th and 8th Corps before they were overwhelmed had purchased time for the 6th Corps, under James Ricketts, to get ready for battle; rallied and reorganized, some 8th and 19th Corps units were incorporated into the 6th Corps line. Even so, the onslaught of Kershaw

< 362 >

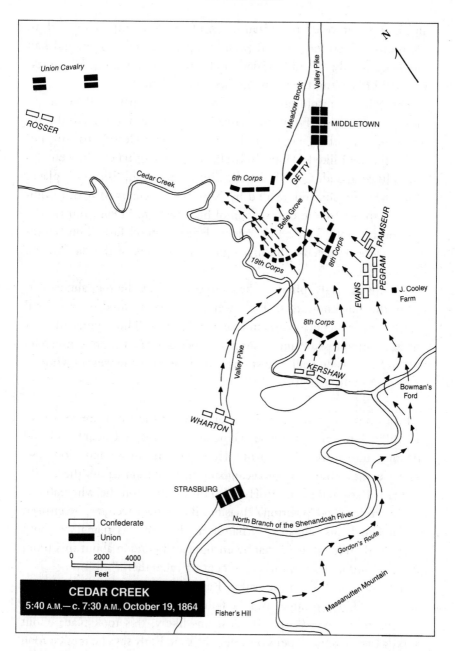

Union Cavalry

ROSSER

Meadow Brook

Valley Pike

MIDDLETOWN

Cedar Creek

6th Corps

GETTY

Belle Grove

RAMSEUR

PEGRAM

19th Corps

8th Corps

EVANS

J. Cooley Farm

8th Corps

KERSHAW

Bowman's Ford

Valley Pike

WHARTON

STRASBURG

☐ Confederate
■ Union

0   2000   4000
Feet

North Branch of the Shenandoah River

Gordon's Route

Massanutten Mountain

Fisher's Hill

CEDAR CREEK
5:40 A.M.—c. 7:30 A.M., October 19, 1864

and Evans unraveled the organization of the 6th Corps's 1st and 3d Divisions, which fell back, the 1st losing a third of its men and half its officers. Only the 2d Division, under Brig. Gen. George W. Getty, remained to defend the honor of Sheridan's infantry.

This was an absolutely critical moment in the battle. Pegram, attacking with one of Ramseur's brigades, and with newly arrived artillery support, put lethal pressure on Getty's men; Getty's 3d Brigade, under the well-liked Daniel Bidwell, nearly broke when Bidwell was mortally wounded. Col. Winsor B. French, who took Bidwell's place, rallied the brigade (dominated by New York regiments) with a command inspired by the desperation of his situation: "Don't run till the Vermonters do!" The 2d (Vermont) Brigade stood fast. The Southerners were repulsed—the first significant setback of the day for the Confederates.[33]

But the Federals, blinded like everyone else by the fog, almost certainly did not know this. They were also able to fend off a second attack, one launched by Bryan Grimes's brigade. Then, persuaded by the Southern pressure and unsupported besides, the Union commander pulled his division back to a stronger position on a rise west of Middletown—the village graveyard.[34]

<< LARGELY BECAUSE Confederate accounts of the battle are so scarce, it is difficult to determine when General Early crossed Cedar Creek and assumed direct overall command. He began the day around 1:00 A.M. with Kershaw, but did not accompany that division across the creek. Instead, Early rode back to Hupp's Hill to check on the whereabouts of the artillery and Wharton's division. By his own account, he crossed Cedar Creek just ahead of Wharton as the sun was rising, at about 6:15. Early remembered that he encountered Gordon about this time, though Gordon never mentioned meeting Jubal then.[35]

In most narratives of the battle, Early's first act in taking over command from Gordon came after the failure of Grimes's attack on Getty's division of the 6th Corps. If, as seems likely, this took place about 8:15, a two-hour gap opens between the time Early says he met Gordon and the point where he assumed direct command.

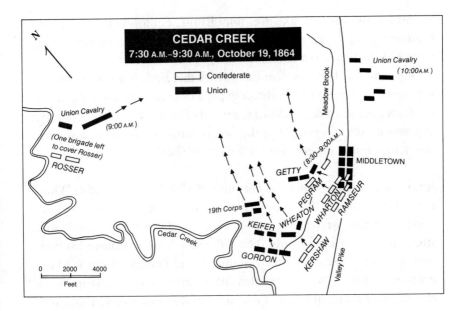

All battles are confusing; in reconstructing them, even a few days or hours after the fighting has ended, men's memories lurch and falter. Because of the fog, which was thickened by battle smoke, Cedar Creek was an unusually confused scene. Yet, even allowing for the chaos, it is enormously difficult to resolve the two-hour anomaly in the chronology of the Cedar Creek battle as it relates to the whereabouts of Jubal Early. It is nearly impossible to reduce the gap to as little as one hour.

Where Early was and what he was doing in that interval is a mystery. Might he have been back with Carter and the artillery, establishing fire from the right bank and organizing the guns' crossing of the creek? This seems unlikely, at best. No account mentions it (Carter later wrote a lot about the battle), and Carter was more than capable of carrying out those assignments without supervision.

It is fairly certain that Early had a conversation with Gordon at some point in which the Georgian reported the successes of the early morning—including 18 guns captured and 1,300 prisoners. It was presumably after that conversation, whenever it took place, that Gordon handed control of the general engagement over to Early, and rode off to find his division and take over from Evans. Following the confused, headlong action of the morning, Gordon's division had ended up on the far left of the Confederate infantry line.

One comes, at last, to a disturbing sense that Early was not in control. Whatever he was up to, whatever explains the chronological hiatus, it suggests a certain mental lethargy, a mood of hesitancy and uncertainty, that was clearly discernible in the first order he issued after assuming command, and in his conduct for the rest of the day.[36]

<< EARLY WAS riding down the pike toward Middletown ahead of Wharton's division when he encountered Ramseur and Pegram, who reported that they were facing the 6th Corps, and that they needed more strength on their right. Early then ordered Wharton to move his division up, "and directed Generals Ramseur and Pegram to put it where it was required." The thrust of this order, vague and ambivalent, was a clue to Jubal's state of mind. It may have made sense to give the generals discretion in the placing of Wharton's men—they were on the spot, they knew what they were up against—but giving them joint discretion diluted everyone's authority and increased the chances that Wharton's division would be misemployed.[37]

As it was. Who gave the next order is unclear, but the result was unfortunate. In view of the fact that all three Confederate generals seem to have believed that they were opposed by the entire 6th Corps, Early should have ensured that in any subsequent attack, Wharton's force would have been added to the combined strength of the other Confederate divisions, at least those of Ramseur and Pegram.

But the commander made no such provision. Instead, he accepted the arguments of his subordinates. In their report to the army commander, those officers undoubtedly mentioned hunger, fatigue, and heavy casualties (absences, at any rate) in their ranks. By contrast, Wharton's men were comparatively fresh. So, in the end, Wharton's understrength formation, about 1,400 men, supported by only one battery of guns, went up all by itself against the stubborn fighters of Getty's division. Like the brigades of the Confederate 2d Corps that had preceded them, they were repulsed. "At the critical moment," as one Northern chronicler described it, "just as the charging line, strain-

< 366 >

ing up the hill, gained the summit, the steady veterans countered upon it with a terrific threefold blow, a sudden deadly volley, a fierce charge and a mighty shout, and dashed it in pieces down the ridge."[38]

This use of the only reserve division Early had was indeed misguided. Even more mistaken was his failure to grasp the elemental tactical importance of the pike. Instead of committing Wharton in what turned out to be a fruitless attack, Early would have done better to send the division down the pike through Middletown. That way, he could have turned the Federals' left and gained their rear, with a grip on Sheridan's line of communications. That was the key to the battle.

<< EARLY TOTALLY missed seeing this, just as Pegram and Ramseur had. Even in the fog, a personal reconnaissance might have acquainted him—or them—with the one thing they needed to know. But Early was soon able to see more of what was happening right in front of him. Just as the survivors of Wharton's attack were recoiling "in some confusion," as Early recalled it, the sun burned the remaining fog off and revealed the Federal position, "and it was discovered to be a strong one." Early's next order was sound: he told Carter to direct the concentrated fire of every available piece at the Union position.[39]

As Carter was seeing to the laying of the guns that had crossed the creek, Early got his first disturbing intelligence of eastward movement by units of Federal cavalry. "In the meantime," the general later wrote, "a force of cavalry was advancing along the Pike, and through the fields to the right of Middletown, thus placing our right and rear in great danger." This was a fact; the Confederate line was now an inverted horseshoe, with its right facing west along the pike, and with nothing between that flank and the Union horsemen but the street grid of Middletown. Early assigned Wharton, with Payne's cavalry, to get ready to "hold the enemy's cavalry in check."[40] On the other flank, however, the Federals on the cemetery hill now packed up and withdrew to the north, occupying part of a line in some woods below Middletown with the rest of the 6th Corps; this new line was also made up of 8th and 19th Corps troops.[41]

Early ordered Kershaw to march east to replace Pegram, whose division the commanding general sent up through Middletown to help cope

< 367 >

with the cavalry in that neighborhood. Apart from that concern, Jubal seemed to feel now that all was going marvelously well. Around ten o'clock, he rode toward Middletown, obviously reveling in a sense of victory. Capt. S. V. Southall, a staff officer, wrote that Early's face "became radiant with joy, and in his gladness, he exclaimed, 'the sun of Middletown, the sun of Middletown!'"

This paraphrase of Napoleon's legendary exclamation at Austerlitz was one of Jubal's ironic private jokes; Bonaparte, too, had been outnumbered, 85,000 to 70,000. But Jubal's unusual *joie de vivre* was a true indication of his sense of vindication. This, he must have felt, was the triumph that would reverse the tide of evil fortune that had been rising against him and the Confederacy. Here was his moment of revenge against Sheridan. "I wonder," Jubal said, "what they will make of this brigadier general in the regular army, now?"—referring to his adversary's promotion to that permanent rank following Winchester.[42]

The feeling of triumph was, of course, seriously misplaced. It was true that much had been accomplished. Two Federal corps had been torn to pieces, losing most of their artillery. But they had been able to reorganize to some extent. And, thanks to the 6th Corps's 2d Division, which had done heroic work against major portions of the Valley Army, Wright had been able to reconstitute the Federal infantry line around the nucleus of the 6th Corps—"as hard a crowd as could be found," in the words of an admiring Union artilleryman. Meanwhile, as of 9:00 A.M., Wright had finally ordered Torbert's cavalry to move over toward Middletown to block any Confederate advance, and now the troopers of Custer's and Merritt's divisions were arriving.[43]

In fact, far from asserting triumph, Early's offensive, which he had built entirely around his infantry and artillery, was in irons. Union infantry had slowed him down, and Union cavalry was tying him up.[44]

Though never forgetting the threat of the Union cavalry, the general had been deceived by the withdrawal of Getty's division, which, it seems almost certain, Jubal thought to be the entire 6th Corps. Though orderly, the pullout reinforced the Confederate commander's sense that he had the bluecoats on the run.

Consolidating his position, Jubal moved Kershaw and Ramseur up to occupy the cemetery hill crest the Federals had abandoned. At about the time he was doing this, John Gordon joined him, and the two had one of the most famous conversations in the history of the Civil War.[45]

« GORDON's *Reminiscences* record the dialogue as he remembered it. "Well, Gordon," Early exclaimed, "this is glory enough for one day. This is the 19th. Precisely one month ago to-day we were going in the opposite direction."

"It is very well so far, general," replied the Georgian, "but we have one more blow to strike, and then there will not be left an organized company of infantry in Sheridan's army." Gordon indicated what he, like Early, saw as the whole Federal 6th Corps, which must have been still making its way back to the wooded line north of Middletown, and said he had ordered "every Confederate command then subject to my orders to assail it in front and in both flanks" and finish it off. He had also directed Carter to "gallop along the broad highway with all his batteries and with every piece of captured artillery available, and to pour an incessant stream of shot and shell upon this solitary remaining corps . . ."

"No use in that," Jubal countered; "they will all go directly."

"That is the Sixth Corps, general. It will not go unless we drive it from the field."

"Yes," Early declared, "it will go too, directly."

Gordon recorded no reply, but described his sense of shock at Early's attitude. "My heart went into my boots," he wrote, and reminded his readers of "the fatal halt on the first day at Gettysburg," and the lost chance to strike "Grant's exposed flank on the 6th of May in the Wilderness." This was the same sort of ghastly error, Gordon believed. "And so it came to pass that the fatal halting, the hesitation, the spasmodic firing, and the isolated movements in the face of the sullen, slow and orderly retreat of this superb Federal corps, lost us the great opportunity, and converted the brilliant victory of the morning into disastrous defeat in the evening."

This colloquy became the principal count in an indictment of Early for the debacle at Cedar Creek: that he threw away, by hesitating at this precise moment, a heaven-sent occasion for the destruction of Sheridan's army.[46]

« GORDON WAS quite right in saying that the 6th Corps would not depart without being driven. And Gordon's indictment is fair, in the sense that by halting, Early failed to *win* the battle. This is true even though some sort of halt was almost inevitable; the army was blocked by Union cavalry in front and on the right, and it badly needed a breathing space to reorganize itself after the frantic morning.

But Gordon never leveled a much more serious charge: that Early *lost* the battle by persisting in his underestimation of Sheridan, by ignoring timely warnings of danger, and through a curious numbness of mind and spirit that Gordon may have sensed at this meeting and perhaps at other times during the day.

Another reality that Gordon had difficulty facing—at least in his later writings—was the pillage, by his men and those of other formations, of the Union camps. In his memoirs, Gordon quoted officers of lofty and lowly rank to support his assertion that the reports of plundering had been exaggerated. But John G. Williams, a Virginia lawyer who rode as a courier for Gordon at Cedar Creek, knew better. He recalled that the morning attack had badly disorganized Gordon's division, "and the men commenced immediately to plunder the camps of the enemy who had left everything behind." Another witness, Capt. Samuel Buck of the 13th Virginia, asserted that half of Early's men left their ranks to search the Union camps for loot—and for necessities. By 8:00 A.M., many soldiers had been without food for at least 12 hours.[47]

At the time, Gordon may have been aware of what was happening with his men. Early had witnessed the straggling personally, and he could see the exhaustion of the men who remained in ranks. "It was now apparent," as he reported to Lee on October 21, "that it would not do to push my troops further. They had been up all night and were much jaded." He noted that "many of our men had stopped in the camp to plunder (in which I am sorry to say that our officers participated)." Their dereliction, if they were guilty as charged, exacerbated an already acute shortage of officers.

Early decided "to content myself with trying to hold the advantages I had gained until all my troops had come up and the captured property was secured." The general gave orders for sending the prisoners and the seized artillery and supplies to the rear.[48]

‹‹ GORDON MAY have been unfair in accusing Early of wasting a golden opportunity to sweep his opponent from the field. But after a pause of an hour or so Early should have advanced in pursuit of whatever opportunity there might have been. His chances of success were growing dimmer by the hour, and in not aggressively attempting to secure victory, he erred more grievously than he ever had before. It was a moment demanding the high heart of a Lee—or a Gordon. Early could not answer that call.

Thus did he revert to the cautious side of his nature. His pugnacity yielded to what he saw as clear evidence that he could do little more, at least for the time being, with his army—exhausted, scattered, and disorganized as it was. As for the future, it appears that he intended, certainly at some point, to press ahead once more against the enemy. But his judgment about how and when to do so became clouded: his wishful conviction that he had won the battle was at odds with his more practical worries about the Union cavalry and his knowledge that Federal infantry was still in the field and still potent. Resolution of this inward conflict may have come from Early's contempt for Sheridan; Jubal could have simply assumed that the Yankee general would "go, too, directly." Holding that view, all Jubal would have felt he had to do was wait, and Sheridan would take his army away.

‹‹ A MAJOR FLAW in this assumption was Sheridan himself, who was only just arriving on the field. Little Phil, who had spent the night of the 18th–19th in Winchester, had been awakened by pickets alarmed at the heavy firing to the south in the early morning hours. Sheridan hurried to the sound of the guns—horrified, as he traveled, by the sight of an army apparently stricken by panic and "thoroughly demoralized." An aide sent to find out what was happening soon returned with news that the Army of the Shenandoah had been beaten; Sheridan's headquarters was in enemy hands.

Unpersuaded, the general began approaching men and urging them to return to the fight—vowing that he himself would sleep in his camp that night "or in hell." Some were inspired to cheer and start walking south. More and more joined them as Sheridan, dropping Rienzi into a ground-eating canter, rode on, waving his cap and urging the men back to the fray. His eyes, a staff officer noted, had "the same dull red glint I had seen . . . when, on other occasions, the battle was going against us."

Near Newtown, the general saw the first groups of organized troops. Soon he was riding by the embattled survivors of Getty's division and the rest of the 6th Corps, who gave him a wild cheer, and a minute later he was among a group of his ranking subordinates, including Wright, Emory, Crook, and Torbert. Sheridan's legendary ride was at an end. It was about 10:30.[49]

From Wright and others, Sheridan learned that appearances in his army's rear were somewhat misleading. Since the morning, Wright, Emory, and Crook had worked hard in their commander's absence to patch things together; the situation facing him, Sheridan decided, was basically manageable.[50]

First, expecting a renewed Confederate assault at any moment, the general decided he wanted to pull his infantry into a more cohesive line anchored on the 6th Corps, with the 19th Corps on the right and Crook's corps in reserve. Custer's cavalry division was ordered back to the Federal right. Overall, the position offered a good defense; many of the troops were now concealed in woods, and cavalry guarded the flanks. But defense was not Sheridan's purpose. When all was in readiness, he decided, the army would move forward and fall upon the left flank of the Confederates.

To inspire the troops for this counterblow, Sheridan's chief of staff, Maj. George Forsyth, suggested that the general ride along the entire line of soldiers, two miles long, so that everyone could see him and respond to his aura. He did so, mounted on his gray charger Breckinridge (the horse was booty from Winchester), waving his cap and shouting. "We'll get a twist on these people yet," he bellowed. "We'll raise them out of their boots before the day is over!" The men cheered, seemingly "from throats of brass," in one witness's phrase, "and caps were thrown to the tops of the scattering oaks."[51]

It was an extraordinary performance, one that very few other generals could have matched. On this day, Sheridan possessed the one thing he needed to turn a beaten rabble into a conquering host: a gift for battlefield leadership second to none.

But he wanted to wait before giving the attack order—even though he knew his aura was not imperishable. Rumors had reached him that Longstreet was actually on his way to the battlefield. Not until he was sure that neither Longstreet nor anyone else was approaching with reinforcements for Early would he give the signal for the assault.

<< GENERAL EARLY consolidated his line about the time Sheridan was issuing orders for the composition of his—around 11:30 A.M. The Confederate line was three miles long. Not chosen for its suitability for defense, the Valley Army's position was simply the most northerly it had reached before being stopped by fatigue, attrition, and the Federal cavalry.

Based on no particular physical feature, the position was isolated and almost untenable for a force under attack, especially by superior numbers; its flanks were highly vulnerable. At the right end of the Southern line, Payne's slim brigade covered the flank, with Wharton to his left. Across the pike, Pegram connected his right with Wharton's left, extending his own left to Meadow Brook. West of the stream, from right to left, were the divisions of Ramseur, Kershaw, and Gordon.[52]

A hush settled over the battlefield as each side waited: Sheridan holding on for word of Longstreet; Early for Sheridan to depart, as had Banks, Pope, Burnside, and Hooker when they had lost a battle. If Jubal had heard the cheering for Sheridan, he had apparently drawn no particular conclusions from it. Anyway, had not Sigel's men—or whoever they were—cheered before withdrawing that night at Warrenton Springs?

Men on both sides slept, weary with the length of their terrifying day. Meanwhile, signs of threats to the Southern position began to accumulate, particularly on the weak left flank. Gordon, apparently aware that this flank was in the air unless he tried to link up with Rosser, extended the line westward to his left. Unfortunately, this opened a quarter-mile gap between two of the brigades in his own division. Attempts to find

Rosser were unavailing; in one of the cavalry skirmishes, Custer had jumped on Rosser and driven him back to Minebank Ford. The three companies of Georgians sent to find the Confederate cavalry ended by establishing a tenuous line with one man every 30 paces.

Gordon sent to Early for reinforcements. When successive staff officers returned with nothing constructive to report, Gordon rode off in person to Early's headquarters in the neighborhood of Middletown. As Gordon remembered this conference, he told Early that it was urgent that he "reinforce the left and fill the gap, which would prove a veritable deathtrap if left open many minutes longer." But Early had no reserve troops available as reinforcements. Stretch out your line, Early told the Georgian, and take a battery of guns with you when you return.

Swallowing this, Gordon "rode back at a furious gallop to execute these most unpromising movements. It was too late. The last chance passed of saving the army." At the very least, Early should have listened to some of Gordon's advice. At any rate, Jubal should have ridden back with Gordon to see just how bad the situation on his left was. It was as if Jubal's irrational views of Gordon, of Sheridan, and of his own claims to success thus far had paralyzed his mind and chilled his heart. The result was a strange passivity in the face of terrible danger.[53]

‹‹ THE THREAT was fulfilled about four o'clock. Reliable intelligence that Longstreet was nowhere around had reached Sheridan at roughly 3:30. Half an hour later, bugles sounded the advance. Bluecoats of the 19th Corps found the gap in Gordon's line and penetrated it, isolating Evans and flanking the main line farther east, "rolling it up like a scroll," as Gordon remembered it. Notwithstanding their growing disarray, the beleaguered Southerners put up a stubborn fight on the left for about 30 minutes. Then, as Custer's cavalry appeared in awful array on the Confederate flank, the line gave way. "Regiment after regiment, brigade after brigade, in rapid succession was crushed," Gordon remembered, "and like hard clods of clay under a pelting rain, the superb commands crumbled to pieces."[54]

The resulting pressure on Kershaw's left unhinged the position of his division, which fled; the men were convinced by the panicky shouts of their comrades that they were surrounded by cavalry. "Like a monster wave struck by the headland," one of Kershaw's officers recalled, the division streamed back, "carrying everything before it by its own force and power, or drawing all within its wake."[55]

Over on the Confederate right, Merritt's cavalry succeeded, after two unfruitful attempts, in overwhelming a battery that had been punishing the Union troopers all day, and then in pushing Payne and Wharton out of the way; Devin's brigade now galloped on and seized the turnpike bridge over the creek.[56]

Ramseur's division, in the Confederate center, withstood the on-set of Sheridan's 6th Corps for a considerable time—90 minutes, by Early's calculation. A nucleus of some 600 fighters, supported by six guns, held on even though men frightened by knowledge of Union cavalry in their rear were steadily leaving the ranks. The musket fire was so intense that Ramseur had two horses killed under him in quick succession. He grabbed the reins of a third horse and was preparing to mount when a bullet ripped through his chest, wounding him mortally. As his men carried him to the rear, his division broke, and all, like their comrades to their left, showed the Federals their heels. Ordered to withdraw by Early, who was nearby, Wharton's and Pegram's forma-tions were unable to maintain cohesion for long; within minutes, they scattered and fled. In the ensuing chaos, the wounded Ramseur was captured; he was to die in Federal hands, visited, as he sank, by West Point friends including Custer and Merritt.[57]

As daylight was fading, those officers and their mounted commands had completed the process begun by the Federal infantry. Now their ranks galloped down on the fugitive masses of the Valley Army. "As the sullen roar from the horses' hooves beating the soft turf of the plain told of the approach of the cavalry," Gordon recalled, "all effort at orderly retreat was abandoned." Still, resisting the mass fear of the routed majority, islands of men gathered here and there around a gun or two, and attempted—at least for a while—to fight. As Major Forsyth of Sheridan's staff saw it, these "Confederates fought splendidly—des-perately even. They tried to take advantage of every stone fence, house or piece of woods on which to rally their men and retard our advance. Their batteries were served gallantly and handled brilliantly, and took up position after position."[58]

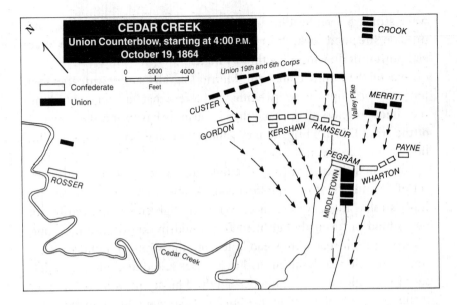

At this point, skill and bravery were no longer enough. Gordon himself was forced to make a precipitate escape from Federals about to surround him and a small group of men he had rallied on the pike south of Cedar Creek. He jumped his horse off a cliff beside the road in the darkness, crashing down with his mount to the bottom in a fall that knocked both horse and rider unconscious. Coming to unhurt after the action had swept southward, Gordon remounted his shaken but uninjured steed and rode through open fields dotted with clumps of Confederates in full retreat.[59]

Later, General Early remembered trying to rally troops after crossing Cedar Creek, and again at Hupp's Hill, without avail. Maj. Marcellus N. Moorman, an artilleryman whose guns had been captured, encountered the general "some 300 or 400 yards west of the creek. Desperate, for his men would listen to nothing, he bawled out, 'Run, run, G—— d—— you, they will get you!' "[60]

The soldiers' panic seemed inexplicable to Jubal. To his eye, at least in hindsight, the Union pursuit was "very feeble"—and thus, "could 500 men have been rallied . . . who would have stood by me, I am satisfied that all my artillery and wagons could have been saved." Compounding the disaster was a traffic snarl on a bridge across a little stream between Strasburg and Fisher's Hill, which some panicky teamster had blocked with a disabled and abandoned wagon. The wreck had created a pileup of artillery, wagons, and ambulances; Jubal recounted that "as there was no force to defend them, they were lost."

After a pause on Fisher's Hill, the scattered fragments of the Valley Army, bereft of its guns and all the captured equipment, along with most of its own wagon train, streamed through the remainder of the night toward New Market, 32 miles from the scene of battle. An officer in Kershaw's division remembered the scene:

> Up the valley this routed, disorganized rabble (it could not be called an army) marched, every man as he saw fit, here a General at the head of a few squads called regiments, or a Colonel or Captain with a few men at his heels, some with colors and some without; here a colonel without a man, there a score or two of men without a commissioned officer . . .
>
> At one place we passed General Early, sitting on his horse by the roadside, viewing the motley crowd as it passed by. He looked sour and haggard. You could see by the expression of his face the great weight upon his mind, the deep disappointment, his unspoken disappointment.[61]

Last Stand

"THE YANKEES got whipped; we got scared." This terse analysis, reported by both Hotchkiss and Douglas, was Jubal Early's immediate comment on the Battle of Cedar Creek. Like most aphorisms, it simultaneously exaggerates and oversimplifies. Yet in seven insightful words it summarizes a battle that, in its turn, encapsulates the entire campaign.[1]

Had the Yankees been whipped at Cedar Creek? Well, hardly. Sheridan had ended the day in undisputed possession of the field, along with 24 Confederate guns, hundreds of the enemy's wagons (besides his own recaptured wagons, guns, and camps), 14 battle flags, and 1,200 prisoners. Later approximations of Southern losses would be substantial: one summary counted 1,860 dead and wounded in addition to the men captured, for a total of 3,100, or 18 percent of the Confederate force.[2]

Informed of Sheridan's accomplishment, Grant ordered a 100-gun salute fired by the Army of the Potomac, and wired Secretary Stanton calling Sheridan "one of the ablest of generals." President Lincoln, whose reelection Little Phil's triumph had virtually assured, sent him "the thanks of the nation, and my own personal admiration and gratitude."[3]

Yet in a sense it was true that the Federals had been worsted. Compared to the Confederates, their casualties were only a slightly more significant proportion of their army: 5,764 had fallen—569 killed, 3,425 wounded, a 20 percent rate of loss. But they had lost almost twice as many men in absolute terms. Moreover, these casualties weakened their infantry corps to the point where, having arrived back in their camps as Sheridan had promised, they stayed put, leaving the pursuit to the cavalry—which did not follow up effectively. Once again, the coup de grace never fell on the defeated Southerners; what was left of their army remained strategically intact.[4]

Above all, the Confederate tactical accomplishment, though nullified, was stunning, as Sheridan himself admitted. With only about five-eighths the strength of its adversary, the Valley Army had executed an unprecedented night march and flank attack, achieving almost total surprise and routing the greater part of the Federal force while driving the remainder back upward of two miles. Early's failures and errors of generalship, added to circumstances beyond his control—particularly, the debilitated physical condition of his men—conspired to cancel the rewards of Confederate success.[5]

What about the second half of Early's comment on the battle? Had "we got scared"? Well, yes. The Federals had certainly taken a beating, but in the end, the Valley Army had run away. And by the use of the first person plural, Jubal included himself in a kind of general indictment. To be sure, his personal conduct was nothing if not exemplary. He never left the most hotly contested part of the field after the Federal onslaught began at 4:00 P.M., and when the rout commenced, tried desperately to rally resistance. But in the phrase "we got scared" he seems to have acknowledged that as commander he suffered, from midmorning on, a failure of nerve—a loss of confidence in himself, his army, and his cause.

This lapse was rooted in the shadowed recesses of his bitter and pessimistic soul. Yet, if even the ebullient Grimes could feel doubts about the future of the Confederate cause, why not the much more saturnine Early? It seems evident that he, too, had been affected by the defeats at Winchester and Fisher's Hill—and that he knew it.

That is, at moments he knew it. Sending Hotchkiss to Richmond on October 22 with dispatches for General Lee, Early directed his engineer (as Hotchkiss recorded in his diary) not to tell the commanding general that "we ought to have advanced in the morning beyond Middletown, for, said [Early], we should have done so." Hotchkiss agreed wholeheartedly with this assessment, but—ever loyal to Early—he probably did not mention it to General Lee.[6]

Early's conscious acceptance of his own responsibility for—and culpability in—the Cedar Creek disaster was eloquently expressed in his written report to Lee, dated at New Market, October 21. Toward the end of this lengthy official account of the recent battle, Early wrote:

It is mortifying to me, general, to have to make these explanations of my reverses. They are due to no want of effort on my part, though it may be that I have not the capacity or the judgment to prevent them. I have labored faithfully to gain success, and I have not failed to expose my person and set an example to my men. I know that I shall have to endure censure from those who do not understand my position and difficulties, but I am still willing to make renewed efforts. If you think, however, that the interests of the service would be promoted by a change of commanders, I beg you will have no hesitation in making the change. The interests of the service are far beyond any mere personal considerations, and if they require it I am willing to surrender my command into other hands.[7]

<< UNFORTUNATELY, the moments of self-knowledge were obscured by self-deception. Most notably, Early made a concerted effort to lay the blame for the defeat on the officers and men of the Valley Army. Immediately after the battle, the general wrote a stiff message of "censure and reprimand" to his troops, which he ordered to be distributed to the lean regiments that had reassembled at New Market. This "sharp lecture," as Early described it, declared the men solely responsible for losing the battle (when victory was in their grasp) through misconduct. Early accused many, including officers, of "yielding to a disgraceful propensity for plunder," of succumbing to "an insane dread of being flanked and a panic-stricken terror of the enemy's cavalry."[8]

Though the famous "foot cavalry" were to be goats, Early particularly exempted the artillery from his general condemnation. Carter's guns, "throughout, from first to last, in this as well as in all the actions I have had, behaved nobly, both officers and men." An official letter to Colonel Carter expressed the army commander's "high appreciation" of the "good conduct and gallantry" of the gunners. "The strictures"

< 380 >

aimed at other troops were, Early stated, "not applicable to your command." In his report, Early attributed this "good conduct to the vast superiority of the officers. Colonel Carter and all his battalion commanders richly deserve promotion." 9

As to the plundering, the guilt of the men was a stain; that officers had looted was abominable. But Early took the indictment yet one more step: he conceived the astonishing suspicion that Gordon himself was guilty of pillage. In his diatribe assailing the conduct of the troops, Early made dark reference to "the officer who pauses in the career of victory to place a guard over a sutler's wagon, for his private use." 10

In hatching this notion about Gordon, General Early evidently picked up a garbled—and widely current—account of an actual incident: during the morning attack Gordon had stopped a wagon, apparently carrying ammunition, that was going to the rear, and ordered it to turn around and follow the advancing Confederate troops. Told by the driver that it was some officer's headquarters wagon, Gordon had released the vehicle.

Gordon confronted Early about the sutler's wagon—and, it seems likely, an alleged accusation by Early that had gotten back to Gordon to the effect that the Georgian had been late in attacking. The two generals, according to Jones of Gordon's staff, had some "very fierce interviews." Gordon spoke of asking for a court of inquiry, and threatened to request a transfer, but was deterred from both gestures by the harm that would come from publicizing the generals' breach.

But the collision was essentially an outgrowth of Early's effort to divert blame. In Gordon's case, it did not work. Gordon and Early patched things up after a while; Early seems to have found reasons to stop believing the sutler's wagon story. But though the two resumed ostensibly normal relations, the conflict would live on.11

« ONCE MORE, in Richmond, voices rose, loudly laying blame on Jubal and calling for his dismissal. And again, enemies in the Senate accused him of drunkenness. The sources of these outcries were refreshed by hostile feelings among the public: Jefferson Davis received a letter from a J. C. McComb, of Augusta County, Virginia, asserting that "there will never be anything but defeat and disaster until Gen'l Early has been relieved of the command . . . men and senior commanders have lost all confidence in their leader." McComb went on to cite local views to the effect that the Valley Army's troubles arose from "too free use of ardent spirits both by officers high and low." [12]

The clamor of accusations against Jubal reached such a pitch that he finally felt the need to write once more to the Senate Military Committee. In his letter he defended his overall performance in the campaign since June, citing his deliverance of Lynchburg, his raid on Washington after a march of 500 miles, and his diversion of two corps from Grant. He demanded "further inquiry into the causes of the recent reverses in the Valley of Virginia." This inquiry, Early wrote, should probe the truth of allegations about the Valley Army commander's drinking and investigate charges that subordinate officers had been deterred from complaining to superiors by fear of vengeance.

It is true that in this letter Jubal was wise enough to acknowledge his own errors. But he spoiled the gesture by not making it wholeheartedly. "I see now," he wrote, "where I might have done things that were not done and avoided others which were done, *provided I had had the same knowledge of facts then which I now have*" (emphasis added).

Jubal tackled the matter of drink head on. "I utterly deny," he wrote, all charges of drunkenness, and he challenged his detractors to produce "any responsible man who will state that he has ever seen me under the influence of intoxicants in the camp, on the march, or in battle." [13]

<< No such man could be found; the accusation was baseless, as Thomas Jones testified years later in a letter to Early's friend John Daniel. "I was very close to him [at Middletown]," Jones wrote, "and shared with him the joy he must feel at the victory, and recall having some curiosity to see just what he would say when he came up and how he would take it. The statement about his being intoxicated . . . was the vilest sort of slander."

This testimony was echoed by Capt. (later Maj.) Samuel J. C. Moore, Sandie Pendleton's replacement as Early's chief of staff. In an 1889 article, Moore wrote, "I was in daily contact with Gen. Early both officially and personally at all hours of the day and night, on the march and in camp, and I never saw him give evidence by word, manner or act, of having taken too much liquor." Moore acknowledged that on "Oct. 19th [Early] was excited, it may be elated," but never, in Moore's view, at the sacrifice of his ability to function. Capt. W. W. Old, an aide-de-camp with Early from May to August 1864, slept in Early's tent and rode everywhere with him during that period. Old told John Daniel (admittedly one of Early's most devoted supporters) that he never knew the general to be "under the influence of liquor." Old allowed that Early "occasionally but most carefully and abstemiously took a little whisky. I never saw him take what might be called a good drink." Old added that the general was often "weak & feeble" from much riding, day and night, "looking into every detail and keeping everybody up to the mark."[14]

Was Jubal Early's capacity to carry out his military duties impaired by overindulgence in alcohol? That he liked to drink, on occasion, and that his rough, tobacco-chewing, profane ways consorted with prevailing Nice Nelly ideas about drunkenness, is incontrovertible. So is the fact that many other officers fell—though perhaps not so vividly—into the same category. But it is also true that many such men, unlike Early, did some of their tippling with politicians and political generals who were in a position to help them if they got into trouble. Early, too prickly and too vulnerable, in his way, to make an easy matter of such politicking, chose to refrain entirely. When his enemies reached for sticks to beat him with, the drinking charge offered a handy cudgel.

Unfortunately, the story about Jubal's condition at the banquet for the Maryland regiments in late 1861 invites belief. But that took place during a lull in the pressures of war, when there was hardly any fighting or marching to challenge the keen military intellect of General Early. He tended to be restless and bad-tempered at such times; his churlish behavior over the toast to the heroes of Bull Run may have been no more than a particularly nasty outburst of choler. Whatever the truth of Jubal's condition that night, there is no evidence whatsoever that he ever took more than an insignificant amount of alcohol when challenged by any military situation involving movement or combat. Those who knew him best accepted this as a fact.

<< BUT THINGS reached the point, finally, where so much damage had been done that facts were irrelevant. Lee would not yield in any obvious or precipitate way to the clamor for Jubal's relief. But the uproar was too loud to be ignored altogether; it certainly would not have been wise to recall Early to the Army of Northern Virginia at Petersburg as commander of the 2d Corps. Lee would simply leave his controversial subordinate in place, transferring troops east from the Valley as needed. On November 15, Kershaw's division broke camp and marched away. Well before Christmas, General Early witnessed the departure of the 2d Corps under Gordon, who would command it until the war's end. As the year waned, the lieutenant general would be left in command of Wharton's little infantry division, made up of what remained of the artillery and the cavalry under Rosser and Lomax.

It might have been some consolation that until the 2d Corps left, the mere presence of Early's Army of the Valley persuaded Sheridan to retain the Union 6th Corps, along with the 19th Corps and two divisions of cavalry, even though Grant badly wanted them all at Petersburg. Sheridan was conscious that he had not annihilated his adversary—far from it. He told Grant in late November that cavalry scouts had ascertained that Early "still retained four divisions of infantry and one of cavalry." Sheridan must have believed that the Valley Army was no less capable of going on the attack than it had been following Fisher's Hill, especially if reinforced. Only when the Confederate 2d Corps left the Valley did Sheridan send Grant his 6th Corps.[15]

<< THOUGH EARLY was not contemplating an immediate resumption of the offensive, his thoughts ran in an assertive direction. The general attended church one Sunday with his staff, and listened to a sermon on the Resurrection.

"What would be your feelings on that day?" the preacher asked his congregation. "What would be your feelings at seeing all the dear ones who have gone before rising on that dread occasion? What would be your feelings at seeing those gallant ones who have given up their lives for their beloved country, rising in their thousands and marching in solemn procession?" The preacher and his listeners were thunderstruck

< 384 >

when Jubal loudly answered the question: "I would conscript every damned one of them!" [16]

Early was undoubtedly present at the service less in a spirit of worship than to set a morale-building example. Believing strongly in the value of religion in keeping his soldiers' spirits up, he issued orders for a stricter observance of the Sabbath. And word of the orders for a more pious Sunday observance seems to have appeared in print. Bryan Grimes, writing to his wife, noted that "the papers state that there is a very perceptible improvement in the religious feelings of this army and if so I have been unable to discover it, for I fear we are all an ungodly lot." [17]

Some might have perceived them as an unpatriotic lot as well. The Richmond authorities, trying to bolster troop morale at this disheartening stage of the war, sent emissaries out to orate on the glories of secession and inspire the ranks with *amor patriae*. Early's reaction to this was unequivocal; he not only refused to go to the rallies organized by the tub-thumpers, but heckled them from the entrance to his tent. The men, immensely bucked up by his show of defiance, soon swelled a chorus of heckling. [18]

Judging by this incident, the mood of the men and their commander would seem to have been good, their spirits high. Opinions on this point differed. Not surprisingly, the morale of the Valley Army's remnants at this time was the subject of considerable comment—some favorable and optimistic, some the opposite. One observer, a cavalry trooper with a brigade of Kentuckians sent briefly to the Valley as reinforcements, felt morale was good; as evidence, he mentioned veterans of the Stonewall Brigade bantering with the cavalry. Former governor John Letcher wrote a friend in Richmond about this time, reporting that the Valley force was much improved since "the Cedar Creek disaster, and I have no doubt that they would make a better fight now than they have ever done since they came to the Valley. Notwithstanding all that has been said and written, I consider General Early a good officer and I feel persuaded that he will yet put his revilers to shame, before his Valley campaign closes." [19]

« WINTER IN the Valley can be bitter. In 1864–65, cold and quiet reigned. Conditions were so hard on men and horses as to hamper all but the most necessary and minimal movement. Restless as usual in such circumstances, Early brooded about his scaled-back responsibilities. In the new year, he journeyed to Richmond to see Lee and discuss "the difficulties of my position in the Valley." The senior general, as usual, smoothed the rough places. Early was told that Lee had "left me there with the small command which still remained in order to produce the impression that the force was much larger than it really was, and he instructed me to do the best I could." [20]

It could have been worse. As the winter deepened, Early's command actually expanded—on paper, anyway. On February 20, President Davis appointed John Breckinridge secretary of war, replacing James Seddon, who had resigned in a dispute over war policy with the Confederate Congress. To fill Breckinridge's place as commander of the Department of Southwestern Virginia and Eastern Tennessee, Lee ordered Early to assume responsibility for that district as well as the Valley. [21]

Also on the 20th, Sheridan received orders from Grant to proceed southward toward Lynchburg with his cavalry to get on with the job of destroying rail and canal facilities in and near the city, which he was to capture if he could. Early's sources of intelligence—mainly the observers and signalers still on Three Tops—informed him of Sheridan's preparations for this move; he in turn alerted Rosser and Lomax, who were able to reassemble parts of their scattered commands. [22]

As Sheridan started up the Valley once more, now at the head of two divisions of cavalry led by Custer and Merritt, his 10,000-man force was stronger than Early's by a factor of seven or eight. Rested and refitted, men and horses appeared formidable. Emma Reily, watching the column march through Winchester on February 27, "witnessed one of the greatest spectacles that can be imagined . . . 10,000 cavalry passing the house four abreast, thoroughly equipped in every detail. Their horses, having been in winter quarters so long, had been fed high and curried and rubbed until their coats shone like satin. Each man had a new saddle, bridle and red blanket, and all their accouterments such as swords, belts, etc., shone like gold. It was a grand sight, requiring hours in passing."

Rosser, with barely 100 troopers whose mounts and gear can hardly have compared with Sheridan's, attempted to block the Federal advance near Mount Crawford on March 1, but (Early noted) "was unable to do so." [23]

Early ordered Wharton, with perhaps 1,000 infantrymen, and Nelson, with six guns and fewer than 100 men, to break winter camp and march at first light on the 2d to Waynesboro. There, around midmorning, Early positioned the infantry along a low ridge just west of the town. Their backs were to the South River, which was spanned by but two bridges: one on the road east of town leading to Rockfish Gap, the other a railroad bridge equipped with planks to allow passage on foot and horseback. The line stretched three-quarters of a mile—too long to be covered adequately by the 1,200 soldiers (including Rosser's men) making up Early's command. [24]

All six guns were in the line. Neither flank was anchored on the river or much of anything else. The right end of the line terminated near an orchard and a huddle of cabins not far from the tracks of the Virginia Central; the left entered a stand of trees about 1,500 feet north of the river, but did not exit from these woods where they yielded to open fields about 660 feet from the river. No attempt was made to dig earthworks. A thin, freezing rain, the sodden late-winter condition of the ground, and a lack of time restricted field fortifications to a breastwork of fence rails piled up along part of the line. [25]

Sheridan ordered Custer's division to make the first move against the Confederate line outside Waynesboro. Marching on the unpaved road from Staunton toward the town, the Union troopers lost the satin-and-gold luster that Emma Reily had marveled at. Covered head to toe with mud, they arrived around noon. Custer sent a brigade forward to test the strength of the line. Convinced by brisk and steady musket fire that a head-on assault would be too costly, Custer then sent three dismounted regiments, armed with Spencer carbines, to explore the Confederate left flank—and discovered the gross weakness in Early's line: the gap, about an eighth of a mile wide, between woods and river.

General Early saw the advance of this Union force on his left and

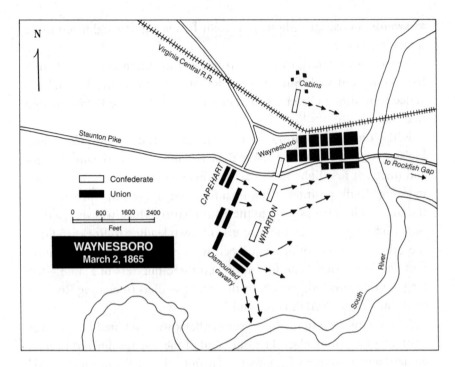

sent a courier to instruct Wharton to deal with it. Before Wharton—
who never received the message—could be found and ordered to the
threatened sector, bugles sounded the Federal attack.

It was about 3:00 P.M. The dismounted Union regiments hit the
Southerners on their left, and a mounted brigade commanded by Col.
Henry Capehart charged through the mud into the center of the Confederate line. The soaked, chilled remnants of the "foot cavalry" were
unequal to their task this day against such an onslaught. One ragged
volley, and they were up and off to the rear, heading for the bridges.[26]

Seeing that "everything was lost," Jubal rode flat-out for the nearest
bridge to forestall the flight of his men and try to stop the oncoming
Federals. The general made it to the bridge ahead of the enemy. But
Capehart's troopers, racing through the town, cut down some Southerners and beat the rest to the river. The Federals crossed, interposing
themselves between the mountain and the line of the river. For most,
retreat was cut off.

It was time to leave. "I rode aside," Early recounted, "into the woods, and in that way escaped capture."

It is difficult to imagine the depths of weariness and chagrin that Jubal Early must have been feeling at this moment. But worse was ahead. He rode to the top of a rise to get his bearings and try to see what was happening. There, he had "the mortification of seeing the greater part of my command carried off as prisoners, and a force of the enemy moving rapidly towards Rockfish Gap," key to the whole position.[27]

The Federals captured nearly every man in the Confederate force—though Rosser and his troopers got away—along with 11 guns (including five left earlier in Waynesboro that Early had hoped to extricate). Sheridan's men also took every wagon, including Early's own headquarters vehicle. Then, with their booty, Sheridan led his force eastward over Rockfish Gap to join Grant in front of Petersburg.[28]

With his staff and perhaps a score of others, including Wharton, General Early struggled over the mountain north of the Gap, through the brush and forest, in the chill rain and oncoming darkness, hoping to reach a supply depot at Greenwood before Custer did—but in vain. Pushing yet farther north to Jarman's Gap, the little party spent a miserable night there, unable to move onward because of darkness and ice on the roads.

<< "THE ONLY solution of this affair which I can give," Early later commented, "is that my men did not fight as I had expected them to do. Had they done so, I am satisfied that the enemy could have been repulsed; and I was and am still of opinion that the attack on Waynesboro was a mere demonstration, to cover a movement south towards Lynchburg. Yet some excuse is to be made for my men, as they knew that they were weak and the enemy very strong."[29]

The last sentence of this statement demonstrates the hold Early still had on reality, though some might call it tenuous. But if the men knew their relative weakness, it was a lesson that Jubal himself seemingly had failed, as a practical matter, to learn; he somehow still expected the troops to fight as they had before the defeat at Winchester. At Waynesboro, so infirm was his grasp of the basic facts of his situation that he could be accused, with some justice, of recklessly hazarding his command—even of compounding its already great danger by placing it in such a grotesquely poor defensive position.

Jubal Early had come a long way since Warrenton Springs and Cedar Mountain, situations in which he had faced danger to his command not only with equanimity but with energetic measures either to avoid peril or to counteract it. At Waynesboro, he was seemingly all delusion and inertia. After everything that had happened, what did he expect his men to do when their exposed flank was turned by Federal cavalry? That the turning movement was carried out by dismounted men— albeit firing repeating weapons—scarcely mattered; the Southerners, at this stage, would probably have run if attacked on that line by infantry.

<< NOT COUNTING a flurry of largely futile activities in which General Early participated over the next four weeks—he was almost captured at least once—the affair at Waynesboro was the end of his war. This is true despite his unflagging willingness to persevere and perform any task he was ordered to undertake—an attitude he presumably showed Lee on a brief visit to the commanding general in Richmond on March 15.

Left without any command save what little remained in the Valley (mainly Lunsford Lomax's cavalry) and in the Department of Southwestern Virginia, Early traveled to departmental headquarters in Abingdon, deep in the commonwealth's western toe, on March 22. It was there, on March 30, that he received a telegram from General Lee bearing official word that Jubal's war was over, once and for all. The wire, promising a letter to follow, ordered Early to relinquish his departmental command to Brig. Gen. John Echols, and turn over his responsibilities in the Valley to Lomax. Rosser had already been ordered to Petersburg with his troopers.[30]

Desperate though he was for capable generals, Lee knew he could not afford the political costs of employing Early in the defense of Petersburg and Richmond—not even in the Department of Southwestern Virginia. After Waynesboro, all the formerly hostile voices were raised, joined now by many new ones. In Charlottesville, for example, a young woman named Laura wrote to her "darling Edith" accusing Early of losing at Waynesboro "through stupidity or drunkenness." The writer stated that the general "just threw away his army." For this opinion,

< 390 >

she cited the authority of General Wharton, as others doubtless were doing: if Early had "fallen back, as everyone expected, to Mountain Top [Rockfish Gap], he could easily have held them back. . . . Now, Gen. Early had so few men that I would not blame him at all if he had not been drunk." [31]

It was time for Jubal to go home. On the way from Abingdon to Rocky Mount, he fell ill, an apparent victim of pneumonia, which prostrated him and made him cough blood. Jubal found refuge for a few days with his sister Elvira McFarland at Marion, in Smythe County. There he rested in bed until he felt well enough to resume his journey, first by rail, later in an ambulance. It was then that word reached him of Lee's surrender at Appomattox.

Lying in the ambulance when he heard the news, Early turned in torment on his litter, groaned, cursed loudly, and cried, "Blow your horn, Gabriel!" [32]

‹‹ THE GENERAL had been in Rocky Mount a few days, staying with a friend, before he got the letter Lee had promised in his telegram of March 30. The letter also bore that date. It was the eve of the day that Grant's final attack commenced—putting such pressure on Lee that he was forced to evacuate Richmond, and to surrender ten days later.

Early printed the entire letter in his memoirs:

My telegram will have informed you that I deem a change of commanders in your department necessary, but it is due to your zealous and patriotic services that I should explain the reasons that prompted my action. The situation of affairs is such that we can neglect no means calculated to develop the resources we possess to the greatest extent and make them as efficient as possible. To this end it is essential that we should have the cheerful and hearty support of the people and the full confidence of the soldiers, without which our efforts would be embarrassed and our means of resistance weakened. I have reluctantly arrived at the conclusion that you cannot command the united and willing co-operation which is essential to success. Your reverses in the Valley, of which the public and the army judge chiefly by the results, have, I fear, impaired your influence, both with the people and the soldiers, and would add greatly to the difficulties which will, under any circumstances, attend our military operations in Southwestern Virginia. While my own confidence in your ability, zeal and devotion to the cause is unimpaired, I have nevertheless felt that I could not oppose what seems to be the current of opinion, without injustice to your reputation and injury to the service. I therefore felt constrained to endeavor to find a commander who would be more likely to develop the strength and resources of the country and inspire the soldiers with confidence; and to accomplish this purpose, I thought it proper to yield my own opinion and to defer to that of those to whom alone we can look for support.

I am sure that you will understand and appreciate my motives, and that no one will be more ready than yourself to acquiesce in any measures which the interests of the country may seem to require, regardless of all personal considerations.

Thanking you for the fidelity and energy with which you have always supported my efforts and for the courage and devotion you have ever manifested in the service of the country, I am, very respectfully and truly, your obedient servant, R. E. Lee, General.[33]

Lee's letter was forthright in laying out the grounds for Early's dismissal. The general in chief also set out his own difficult position, but without whining or making excuses; he retained his high opinion of Early as a soldier, but could no longer act on it without risking the indispensable support of those who did not share it. Lee probably knew Early well enough to assume that he would take it all in the proper spirit.

He did. Jubal was by now much too devoted to Lee to resent anything his commanding general said to him; the letter could only have enhanced his feelings of loyalty and attachment.

« IN A SENSE, everything in Jubal Early's military career before June 1864 was a buildup to his last campaign. In its ending, that campaign seemingly condemns him as a failure. But was the whole effort in the Valley in '64 and '65 a fiasco?

Far from it. Though many believed that Jubal Early's expedition placed a lien on future operations and that it made wasteful use of precious resources, it did yield considerable military benefits for the Confederate cause. Among them (as identified by Terry Moss, a student of Early's career and a professional soldier):

1. The rescue of Lynchburg from Hunter prevented incalculable damage that would have resulted from Federal occupation of that vital transportation and supply center. Hunter's seizure of Lynchburg might have forced Lee's evacuation of Richmond months before it finally took place.

2. The clearing of the Valley in the later part of June removed Hunter completely from the sphere of operations, neutralizing his force and impairing his future usefulness. Not least, the clearing operation made possible the undisturbed harvest of much of the upper Valley's grain.

3. Capture of the Federal depots at Martinsburg and Harpers Ferry as the clearing operation ended helped replenish the increasingly impoverished commissaries of the Confederacy.

4. Destruction of railroads in West Virginia and Maryland seriously hampered Union communications in those regions throughout the summer and into the fall.

5. The advance of the Valley Army upon Washington rattled and immobilized Federal military and civilian authorities. It deepened Northern war-weariness and threatened the reelection of President Lincoln, on which the Union's prosecution of the war depended. Many Northern observers did not fail to notice that in July 1864 Grant had not approached Richmond as closely as Early had come to Washington.

6. Early's raid retarded the momentum of Grant's offensive in eastern Virginia—bringing it to a virtual halt for a time as the Army of the Potomac adjusted to the transfer of troops to the relief of the United States capital.

7. Booty carried back to Virginia by the Valley Army from Maryland—$220,000 in ransom from Frederick and Hagerstown, along with uncounted horses and cattle, with wagons full of food and forage—helped sustain the Confederate war effort.

8. Operations in the Valley from July through the end of 1864 achieved Lee's objective: siphoning troops away from Petersburg. To defeat Early, Sheridan deployed three infantry corps, two and sometimes three cavalry divisions, and as many as 27 batteries of artillery. If available to the Army of the Potomac throughout the summer of 1864, such an array might have shortened the war by many months.

9. Also denied to Grant in his principal struggle with Lee were Sheridan's Valley casualties: 14,500 men killed, wounded, and missing. The equivalent of a Union infantry corps, these losses alone outnumbered Early's total strength at any time during the campaign. His own losses came to less than 10,000.

10. Though weakened by desertion, attrition, and transfer, Early's miniature force was able, in late '64 and early '65, to compel retention in the Valley of substantial Union infantry and cavalry strength. Thus, even in its feeblest condition before the finale at Waynesboro, the Valley Army was exerting a palpable influence on the overall military situation.[34]

Early could take credit for these substantial direct contributions to Confederate fortunes. It was not his fault that the indirect consequences were adverse. To deal with the threat Early posed, Grant found himself forced to straighten out the appalling snarl of the Federal command system, which had consistently helped Lee overcome his material and strategic disadvantages. The threat also impelled Grant toward the solution of another perennial problem: the recurrent use of the Valley by the Confederates as an avenue of aggression into the North; repeated invasions by Confederate columns had affected the morale and the politics of the Union in profound ways. Grant was successful in both these endeavors, which considerably aided Union victory.

The choice of Philip Sheridan to command the force assigned to accomplish these goals was, of course, a crucial decision on Grant's part. Though guilty of many errors, Little Phil met his commander's expectations in using his advantages of strength to persevere against Early—an attitude dramatically demonstrated in his recovery of his army's fortunes at Cedar Creek.[35]

Against Sheridan, Early probably did as well as anyone in the Confederate service could have done, given his circumstances and those of his opponent. (The numerical odds in Sheridan's favor never dropped below two and a half to one, and usually approached three to one.) For that matter, if Early had not underestimated Sheridan so unjustifiably and persistently, he might have done even better. Among Jubal's mistakes, the misreading of his opponent was undoubtedly the greatest. Of his other lapses, his failure to understand and work positively with his cavalry ranked a close second; it certainly put him at a disadvantage against Sheridan, who not only understood his cavalry but knew how to use it in combination with his other arms—a concept to which Early was an almost total stranger.[36]

Other lapses in generalship with which Early has been charged are less easy to demonstrate. After he became a corps commander, Jubal was often accused of employing his divisions piecemeal. Lee thought him guilty of this cardinal transgression (though Lee himself, for example at Gettysburg, was sometimes vulnerable to the charge).

Early's two great Valley defeats do not prove the indictment. It is true that at Cedar Creek, where his behavior in general reflected an unusual lethargy, Early's handling of Ramseur's, Pegram's, and Wharton's divisions was indeed unconcerted and fragmented. At Winchester, on the other hand, though admittedly assisted by Sheridan's own blunders, Early achieved a timely and effective concentration of his infantry and artillery. This concentration was proof against assault in the morning phases of the battle.

Another count in the bill indicting Early's generalship has been his inability to read terrain. Certainly many critics would join Hotchkiss in citing Early's unfortunate choices of position at Cedar Creek and Waynesboro.[37]

In his last two engagements, Early's mind was eerily absent. Illness and mental fatigue, the psychological effects of defeat, pressure generated by the expectations of Lee, an unacknowledged sense that nothing would do any good anyway—some or all of these burdens may have prevented a rational, effective analysis of terrain and other factors in the situations he faced on October 19 and March 2. Thus he may be guilty as charged in these instances, though circumstances are extenuating. Besides, there is a disturbing hint of exhaustion and imminent collapse, of which misjudgment of terrain seems a very small part.

In more normal circumstances, Early may not have had what was called the gift of *coup d'oeil*, the intuitive flair for the analysis of ground possessed by a Marlborough, a Napoleon, or—less incontrovertibly—a Lee. But Jubal did care about it. He retained on his staff perhaps the most gifted and energetic topographical engineer in the Confederate service, Jed Hotchkiss. This officer was available daily to General Early not only as a mapmaker of skill and perception, but as a military engineer trained to appreciate and advise on the role of terrain in tactical situations.

On the positive side, Cedar Mountain demonstrates a good grasp on Jubal's part of terrain and its possibilities. Early quickly saw that the low ridge in the Confederate center that he held was vitally important to the entire position. His perception that the ridge was anchored by the cedar grove and the steps he took to strengthen that anchor were major factors in Jackson's victory. Jackson might also have approved Early's shrewdness in finding and seizing the high ground west of the West Fort at Second Winchester in June 1863.

Early probably felt sure of that, and he certainly knew of Jackson's admiration for his soldierly qualities. Comparisons of Early with Jackson, contemporary and latter-day, are inevitable. Many observers at the time thought that in the absence of Jackson, Early was the only Confederate general capable of bringing off an operation like the Washington raid. In his downfall, Jubal's bitterest critics compared him unfavorably with Stonewall.

The comparisons are tempting, but they are not really apt. Jackson, of course, was never really defeated. And if Early had died at Washington, he might have enjoyed a broad, cordial reputation as one of the greatest military leaders of the South. How, one must ask, would Jackson have done in Early's shoes after mid-June 1864? It is very hard to say. Critics reviling Early for his defeats ignored the contrasts between Jackson's Valley campaign and Jubal's. To begin with, Jackson's cavalry had been better than Early's. Jackson's opponents—Major Generals Nathaniel Banks, John Frémont, and even the reasonably competent James Shields—were nonentities compared to Philip Sheridan. In 1862, the Union generals' problems were vastly compounded by the fragmented command structure in the Valley; two years later, Early faced a much more workable unified command.

<< AGAINST THIS background, a look at some of the external ingredients of Jubal Early's downfall—shared in large measure at that time with all the Confederate armies—provides a useful perspective on his actual degree of success in the Valley. A principal disadvantage was the eternal shortage of supplies, ranging from shoes to food to sound horses, and the flawed Confederate supply system. These shortcomings were not Early's fault. Neither was the inadequate supply and organization of manpower: conscription could not furnish enough men to replace losses; replacements, by and large, had to come from Lee's Army of Northern Virginia (the shuttling of Kershaw's division to and from the Valley is the principal example).

A particular concern was the ghastly attrition among the officers. Setting out for the Valley, Early was lucky to have as good a group of general officers as he did; the battles of the Wilderness and Spotsylvania had cost Lee 37 percent of his generals; both battles had inflicted massive losses on the 2d Corps in the general grades, which had suffered a casualty rate of 62 percent. By June, death, wounds, and capture among field and company grade officers had left many regiments with 50 percent or less of their established complements.

Difficulties with the cavalry partook of both the supply and manpower problems. The horsemen's conduct also dramatized what was perhaps the most disturbing and prevalent problem of all in late 1864 and '65: the Confederate armies' poor morale and deteriorating state of discipline. This was reflected in a desertion rate that had, by March 1865, cut the strength of the eastern Confederate forces by nearly 50 percent, compared to a year earlier.[38]

These deficits of morale were obviously deepened, in the field, by repeated defeats. But to an increasing degree, all citizens of the Confederacy were affected by military failures—regardless of the actual military import of a reverse in this battle or the loss of that piece of territory. The waning of civilian morale, in turn, helped to push the soldiers' spirits into a vicious, downward spiral, which was accelerated by the guilt many fighting men felt at the plight of their increasingly beleaguered families.[39]

Not even an extraordinarily inspiring leader like Robert E. Lee could do much in the face of such powerful material and psychological forces. It was no wonder that Early, more often than not clearheaded in adversity, eventually succumbed, to some degree, to the general hopelessness. And when it came to leadership, if his men could not really love him when things were going well, he gave them scant reason to do so when the war went sour. For his part, Jubal never lost the old ambivalence—born, perhaps, of dealing with volunteers in the Mexican War—toward his troops. In late September, riding past a column of hungry men on the march, he frowned at a chant they set up: "Crackers! Crackers! Give us something to eat!" The general replied, in his grating voice: "Fisher's Hill! Fisher's Hill, damn you!"[40]

PART FIVE

« CHAPTER TWENTY-FIVE »

Reconstruction and Railroad Politics

The South really won the Civil War. Put so baldly, the statement sounds preposterous. And it is certainly very far from the entire truth. Yet some historians have made a convincing case for the proposition that from its very wreckage the old Confederacy succeeded in gaining—or regaining—three crucial goals that had been part of the South's rationale for going to war: white supremacy, states' rights, and the maintenance of honor.[1]

The war had altered the outlines of these concepts, of course. They were nonetheless deeply embedded in Jubal Early's consciousness. He stuck to them ever more firmly as he and his fellow Virginians struggled to absorb the consequences of Southern defeat on the battlefield. Through the difficult period of political transition that the North called Reconstruction, Early would, in his idiosyncratic way, exert a palpable influence on his fellow Virginians and other Southerners.

The tenor of life in postbellum Virginia was complicated; people lived in an environment of bewildering volatility and upheaval. The economic devastation wrought by war generated depression and hardship for most; but for many, including Northern and foreign immigrants, it created a kind of attractive vacuum to be filled by a disturbing new-fangled appetite for wealth (more accurately, economic power). This phenomenon, which drew substance from industrial and technological advances—notably the growth of railroads—was to be summarized in terms of the "New South" and the "Gilded Age."

Early often expressed his detestation of this intrusive, unfamiliar materialism and corruption, visible in the growing influence of Northern financial and business interests in Southern affairs. In Jubal's eyes and others', these developments were balefully associated with the revolutionary change in the political status of newly enfranchised blacks.

In the postwar period, newly freed slaves at first had transcendent hopes: free schools, the vote, and the ownership of land. For blacks, these aspirations would agonizingly fade, until, in the 1880s and '90s, they shrank—and eventually, by the turn of the century, virtually disappeared. Though the defeat of the Confederacy meant that slavery was dead, the whites of Virginia worked hard and effectively to reassert control over the black population, closely regulating the terms of their labor and—notwithstanding concessions such as limited suffrage—restricting their civil rights in every way possible. Despite prohibitions in the Federal constitution, amendments to the state constitution passed as early as 1876 required payment of a poll tax as a condition of voting, and disfranchised anyone convicted of petty larceny. These amendments hit black Virginians, poorer than anyone else, very hard; in 1877, one-fourth of the blacks liable for the tax did not pay, a proportion twice as high as that of the nonpaying liable whites.[2]

‹‹ THESE DEVELOPMENTS were the product of a decade or more following Appomattox. In the immediate aftermath of surrender, Early reacted with characteristic vehemence; he took himself off into voluntary exile—initially, as a soldier sworn to continue fighting. He considered the terms given the Confederates at Appomattox and elsewhere inapplicable to him; he had been present at none of the surrender ceremonies. On May 21, 1865, Early rode southwest from Franklin County with young kinsmen as companions, hoping to join Maj. Gen. Edmund Kirby Smith in the Department of the Trans-Mississippi, where he was, according to report, still prosecuting the war.[3]

Toward the end of June, when Jubal was traversing Alabama, he heard that Kirby Smith had surrendered in his turn. This news did not soften Early's bitter resolve; on the contrary, it only reinforced his desire to "get out from the rule of the infernal Yankees." As he later wrote to Tom Rosser, "I was determined not to give a parole or take the oath either, and rode all the way in arms as if I had been in the enemy's country." Further reinforcement of this attitude likely followed his indictment for treason handed up in June by a Federal grand jury in Norfolk, Virginia; the bill, which also named Robert E. Lee, Richard Ewell, and many others, denounced its subjects as having been "moved and seduced by the devil." [4]

Early reached Texas in August. From there, he intended to travel to Mexico, a purpose he revealed in a letter to Dr. Hunter McGuire. In the same letter, he asked the doctor for casualty figures for the 1864 Valley campaign, beginning with the 2d Corps's march west from Gaines' Mill and ending with the Battle of Cedar Creek. Adding requests for figures on Sheridan's losses and for Little Phil's official reports, Jubal displayed his growing urge to set forth his version of his climactic campaign; this account would be designed not only to rebut the claims, present and future, of the hated enemy, but would also steer Southern critics on the correct course.[5]

The war's history was also much on General Lee's mind. Writing to Early about this time, he asked for a "recapitulation" of Jubal's reports. Because all his own records were lost, Lee wanted to use Early's in a history of the Virginia campaigns. Early might well have welcomed this idea, but he can hardly have been comfortable with a passage in Lee's letter that called on loyal Southerners to stick close to home. "The South," Lee wrote, "requires the presence of all her sons now more than at any period of her history and I determined at the outset to share the fate of my people." [6]

Lee felt he was setting an example. But for some, his apparent submission to Yankee authority was disturbing. Early was probably aware that Lee had applied in June to Andrew Johnson, president of the United States, for a pardon; this act affronted many Confederates because it seemed to acknowledge that the South was guilty of wrongdoing in fighting the war. But, like others, Early completely missed the point of Lee's action: to lead the South out of the valley of the shadow of death, toward the freedom from suffering that could only come with the peaceful rebuilding of the Union.

Leery of the dangers attending land travel to Mexico ("the route over the Rio Grande had become impracticable on account of robbers and guerrillas"), Early took months to find a safe, affordable berth in a ship. It was not until December 27 that he arrived in Veracruz, having trav-

eled via Nassau, Bimini, and Cuba. In Nassau, ragged after his long
journey, he had bought a gray suit that sported Confederate army buttons; it was the first of many such suits he would wear in the course of
his life—a civilian version of uniform.[7]

Indeed, Early's purpose in Mexico, where he settled in the capital, was warlike. He hoped that French sponsorship of Maximilian, the
Austrian-born emperor then ruling Mexico, would ignite a war with
the United States to which Jubal could add his lance and continue to
kill Yankees. But Maximilian, bereft of support in Mexico and largely
ignored by the French emperor Napoleon III (preoccupied by problems
closer to home) seemed increasingly eager to placate the Americans.

Waiting for an outbreak of hostilities that seemed less and less likely,
Jubal worked hard on an account of his last campaign. This work was
of course without remuneration, and Mexico offered almost nothing
by way of gainful employment. After three months, disgusted with
Mexico and Maximilian, whose empire he declared to be "an infernal
humbug," Early decided to transfer his exile to Canada. There, if he
settled near Toronto, he would be closer to home—and communication
with old comrades would be easier. Also, printing his campaign history,
Early felt, would be more practicable there than in Mexico.[8]

Again, months were required to make the move—from Mexico to
Canada via Havana. By August 1866, Jubal was finally installed in
Niagara, just over the Canadian-U.S. border. Visible a half-mile away
across the frontier (as Early wrote Hotchkiss) was "the Yankee Fort
Niagara, at which the cursed old flag, which always reminds me of a
barber's pole, untwisted and ironed out, is always flying."

More congenial was Niagara's Confederate exile population, which
included John Breckinridge and his family. Less agreeable was Jubal's
lack of financial resources: Canada offered as little as Mexico by way
of paid employment. Early could not practice law in Canada without
undergoing a five-year period of probation. He was thrown back on the
charity of his family—forced, as he wrote Sam, to ask "what you can
do to help me, but . . . I fear you can but ill afford it." Indeed, Sam
was struggling, like other Southerners, with a devastated economy in
which money was harder to come by every day. One estimate made a
dozen years after the war put its direct economic damage to Virginia, in-

cluding the uncompensated value of emancipated slaves, at almost half a billion dollars—a nearly unimaginable sum in those days. The few banks still open were charging 1¼ percent per month on paper running longer than 60 days, and no loans on shorter terms were available.[9]

In the fall, Early moved to Toronto, where he published his campaign history in pamphlet form; he paid for the printing (cost: $211) with a draft from brother Bob.

<< THEREAFTER, eking out a threadbare existence with sporadic checks from his brothers and—occasionally—from friends, Early endured through three years the most wintry period of his life. In deepening poverty and worsening health, feeling guilt over his absence from home and his financial dependence, he began work on his complete memoirs in 1867 and corresponded constantly with friends at home in letters that concentrated heavily on the politics of postbellum Virginia and the South. From them he learned early that year of newspaper speculation about his possible nomination as governor of Virginia. Far from persuading Jubal that he had a role to play at home, this notion was denounced by him as "preposterous." Writing to John Daniel, he acknowledged his unfitness, stemming from his volatile temperament, for high public office: "If I were made governor I would have the whole state in another war in less than a week. So it is idle to talk about it, even if there were any prospect of my election." Besides, it was "simply impossible for me to accept a pardon," a prerequisite to holding office.[10]

If asking the hateful Johnson for a pardon was the price of going home, Jubal vowed he would never return. His aversion to Johnson had sprung from the president's approach to Reconstruction, which had begun to unfold while Early was still en route from Mexico to Canada.

Johnson's policy was to appoint provisional governors in the former Confederate states, which were to be brought back into the Union. To accomplish this, conventions called by the governors were to amend the states' antebellum constitutions so as to enfranchise most of the same white men who had been voters before 1861—as long as they swore an oath of loyalty to the United States. Among those disfranchised were former Confederate leaders like Early and men worth $20,000 or more. Like Lee, such notables had to apply personally to President Johnson for their pardons. Early utterly rejected these terms. For him, there was only shame for the South in its states' forced repudiation of everything their governments had done since the outbreak of the war.[11]

The response of Virginia to Johnson's "Presidential Reconstruction" initiative was shaped by the state's first postwar government. This administration was led by Francis H. Pierpont, a hardline antislavery Unionist from the northwestern part of the state who had emerged as the leader of a "Restored Government of Virginia" proclaimed in Wheeling in 1861. The state of West Virginia, which Early condemned as illegal and unconstitutional, would coalesce around this "Restored Government." But as the war ended, it was established under Pierpont in Alexandria, where it functioned as the civilian government in Union-controlled territories of Virginia.[12]

Pierpont moved his regime to Richmond in June 1865—a step taken upon preliminary recognition by Johnson of the "restored" state of Virginia. In October, a new General Assembly, supplanting the wartime legislature that had sat in Alexandria, was chosen in the first postwar election. In the House, 96 of 97 members were old-time Whigs like Jubal; most, like him, had opposed secession in 1861. The Senate lined up in similar fashion.[13]

The lawmakers' identification with antebellum Unionists did not signify sympathy with Pierpont, whose moderate program rested on equal rights for blacks, public works, and free schools. The legislators ignored the governor as they enacted their own highly independent—and markedly traditional—programs.[14]

They began by repealing the "restored" legislature's assent to the establishment of West Virginia. They appealed to President Johnson to free Jefferson Davis, imprisoned at Fort Monroe, and suggested to the president that Robert E. Lee would make a better governor than Pierpont. Though the legislators went along with Pierpont in guaranteeing full payment of Virginia's debt (with interest accrued during the war), they made no provision for public schools—or for enfranchising people of color.

The Assembly did repeal the laws governing slavery, and also mandated equal penalties for offenses committed by whites and blacks. But it restricted the validity of blacks' legal testimony to cases in which they were the sole parties. Maj. Gen. Alfred H. Terry, commanding Federal troops in Virginia, rejected the legislature's stiff new vagrancy law, calling the measure "slavery in all but name."[15]

Though Jubal Early undoubtedly approved this traditionalist legislative course, it was criticized even in some Virginia newspapers. It certainly attracted the disapproving attention of the Radical Republicans who dominated the U.S. Congress after the 1866 elections. These men looked with even greater disfavor on the reluctance of the Virginia legislature to ratify the 14th Amendment to the Constitution, passed by Congress in 1866, which certified the voting rights of former slaves and penalized states withholding such rights with proportional loss of representation in Congress; the amendment also denied federal or state office to anyone who had ever sworn to support the Constitution and then engaged in rebellion. Finally, the congressional Republicans wanted no more of Johnson's "Presidential Reconstruction," which they felt made it too easy for ex-Confederates to hold office. The congressional Republicans were afraid that unreconstructed Confederates and Northern Democrats would band together to rob them of their majority.[16]

Denouncing these Republican doings from Canada, Jubal envisioned a bizarre and apocalyptic resolution of the South's plight that lay with the Radicals themselves. The general declared that he hoped their views would prevail, since he believed that the result would be a resumption of civil war. The shooting would follow formation of a minority government of Northern Republicans allied with Southern blacks, coercively ruling a majority composed of Southern whites and Northern Democrats. This new war would, Early believed, offer the South another chance to achieve its independence.[17]

Though no shooting broke out, Jubal was not completely wrong in his prediction. The Radicals' views did prevail. Passing the Reconstruction Acts in 1867, they abolished the South's state governments, replacing them with military governors appointed in five districts. Maj. Gen. John M. Schofield became governor of Military District Number One, with headquarters in Richmond. His orders were to enroll voters, including every black male and any white men who had not fought against the United States during the war. These voters would elect members of a constitutional convention, its work subject to approval by Congress.

Only with such consent, and after acceptance by the state legislature of the 14th Amendment (and its ratification by enough other states to become the law of the land), would Virginia be readmitted to the Union.[18]

« OF ALL these events, Early was a fascinated—often horrified—spectator. Peering critically at the United States flag across the Canadian border, he endured his exile as best he could—weathering the awful winters, fretting about money, chatting with old Confederates like Breckinridge, working on his memoirs. He still yearned for a fight, and he longed to get home. There, oddly enough—judging by his conscientious voting record when he finally did get home—he probably would have voted, if allowed, though many who shared his views did not. Among like-minded men who could have voted in Virginia in 1867, one in four abstained, allowing the Radicals, led by the federal judge John C. Underwood and Governor Henry Wells, to dominate the constitutional convention elected that year (with seven-eighths of the registered blacks voting). Convention seats went to 73 Republicans and 32 conservatives (largely former Whigs and Democrats). Of the Republicans, 24 were black; 33 were native Northerners or foreigners.[19]

In thunderous tones, General Early condemned the so-called "Underwood constitution" that the convention produced in April 1868. Among other provisions, this instrument called for the ratification of the 14th and 15th Amendments, making blacks citizens with full civil rights. The document enfranchised all adult males, established free public schools, and called for increased taxes on landed property. It also replaced the traditional county government system with a much more democratic township structure. Among its most objectionable provisions, to Early and most white Southerners, was a clause restricting service on juries and in public office—now constitutionally open to blacks—to men who could swear they had never voluntarily gone in arms against the United States. All former federal or state officials who had enlisted in the Confederate cause were disfranchised.[20]

Early was prescient in thinking that the new constitution would be the instrument of Virginia's reconstruction, though he mistook the nature of the transition that would actually take place. He also overestimated the long-term influence of the Radicals, to whom he attributed diabolical powers. While he was right in predicting the part that corruption would play in Virginia's politics, he was wrong in blaming it all on the Radicals and their black clients. The changes he dreaded would, Early thought, be brought about "by some fraud or other, for I believe that the Radicals are capable of perpetrating any iniquity which the wit of man can conceive or the arch-fiend himself can suggest." [21]

Seeking strength in purposeful organization, the minority at the convention forthwith formed the Conservative party and immediately urged voters to turn out and reject the Underwood constitution. But another of the new party's strengths was its response to a broad-based yearning for social stability and breathing space to rebuild and repair the war's ravages—goals that required reinstatement of Virginia in the Union.

This longing was also apparent to Northern financiers and businessmen, including some powerful Republicans. Railroad interests seemed particularly eager to invest in Virginia's future. To some Conservatives, this group, largely composed of outlanders, was abhorrent; others, including a number who saw a chance to make some hay for themselves, regarded the Yankee entrepreneurs with friendlier eyes. The magnanimous aura of Ulysses S. Grant, newly elected president, helped encourage these conciliatory feelings. Knowing that some of the outlanders were offended by raucous denunciations of black voting rights—and particularly by any violent repression in the style of the Ku Klux Klan—the more perceptive Virginia Conservatives modified their positions: though reserving government for whites, these "new movement" men (as some called them) acknowledged the end of slavery and asserted constitutional rights for all Virginians, implying support for blacks' rights to vote and even hold office. [22]

In the fall of 1868, a group of Virginia businessmen formed a Committee of Nine to lobby Congress for readmission of their state to the Union on the basis of universal suffrage and universal amnesty; they appealed to the Senate Judiciary Committee for amendment of the objectionable clauses in the new state constitution. They interviewed President-elect Grant, getting his agreement, in principle, that the test oath and disfranchisement clauses would damage the state's economy by unduly limiting the number and kind of people qualified for political office. The committee also persuaded Grant that if a separate vote were permitted on these clauses the Underwood constitution could be approved, thus furnishing a basis for readmission of the state.[23]

Jubal Early's response to the "new movement" was a metaphor, comparing the Committee of Nine to a whist player in the nine hole, counting on tricks to get out because he had no honors. In other words, the nine were abasing themselves in a shameful way, kissing "the rod that smites them."

But the committee and other groups like it had real support. Once launched, the impetus toward a political arrangement that would hold off the local Radicals while offering Congress a basis for readmitting the state to the Union waxed too powerful to be resisted. Even moderate Republicans were feeling the pressure. When some of them began talking to Conservatives, the result was a split in the Republican party.

In March 1869, just before Early's return to Virginia, the schism became dramatically manifest. A Republican state convention renominated Wells for governor along with a black running mate, Dr. J. D. Harris. (Disaffected Republicans attending the convention pushed Harris's candidacy, knowing it would undermine Wells's chances of reelection.)

Rival nominations, made by men who called themselves "True Republicans," emerged immediately after the Wells-Harris ticket was named. For governor, the schismatics picked Gilbert C. Walker, a New Yorker by birth, now a successful Norfolk financier and manufacturer. His running mate was John F. Lewis, a wealthy Rockingham County farmer who had been a member of the Secession Convention and never signed the ordinance or countenanced the Confederate regime.[24]

A major force behind the scenes in the forging of the Walker-Lewis ticket was William Mahone, a former major general who had served briefly under Early when the latter was in temporary command of A. P. Hill's corps at Spotsylvania. Son of a less than successful merchant, a graduate of VMI, "Little Billy" was a tiny man (weighing less than 100 pounds) of fierce energies and large ambitions.

In the war, Mahone had built a reputation as a capable commander who had attracted the trust and good opinion of General Lee. But he made many enemies—not least Jubal Early. Mahone aroused Early's deepest antagonism as a rival for Lee's favor, as a social inferior (tradesman's son, railroad promoter, money grubber), but mainly as an unsound person who actively sought to make political arrangements with Republicans. Their mutual enmity would furnish Virginia politicians and other gossips with rich conversational fodder for years to come.

Now, as president of both the Southside and the Norfolk & Petersburg Railroads, Mahone was trying to consolidate those lines with the Virginia & Tennessee; the merger would allow him to control rail traffic in southern Virginia and do business directly with western railroads. Mahone had rivals—notably John S. Barbour, owner of the Orange & Alexandria Railroad, controlled by the B. &. O., and the Pennsylvania Railroad, which was seeking to dominate north-south rail business. But Mahone was a powerful leader among the growing corps of businessmen and industrialists who were taking over the Old Dominion's politics and who believed that their enterprises would prosper only through a tranquil process of readmission to the Union. They also felt that such an outcome was more likely under the leadership of Gilbert Walker and John Lewis than that of Wells or anyone else (Mahone had a hand in the nomination of Dr. Harris at the Republican convention).[25]

« THE CONSERVATIVES had already generated their own ticket. At its head was Col. Robert T. Withers, wounded veteran, publisher of the Lynchburg *News*—a man the traditionalists regarded as safely opposed to Republicans and their ilk. Running with Withers was John L. Marye of Fredericksburg (lieutenant governor) and Brig. Gen. James A. Walker (attorney general) of Pulaski County, both kindred souls; Walker had commanded Jubal Early's favorite regiment, the 13th Virginia.[26]

These Conservative candidates found themselves under mounting pressure to withdraw and support the True Republican slate. Expediency argued that Congress was more likely to recognize a candidate like Gilbert Walker than a "red-handed Confederate colonel" like Withers.

The colonel also got word from one of the Committee of Nine that Grant would approve a separate vote on the repugnant clauses only if the Conservative candidates bowed out. They did so.[27]

« ON DECEMBER 25, 1868, Andrew Johnson, the lame-duck president, issued an unconditional amnesty that technically excluded high-ranking officers like General Early, but was clearly intended to pardon all combatants against the United States in the late war. All indictments were dismissed.[28]

"Pardon" was not a word that General Early recognized in his reaction to the amnesty, set forth in a letter to Sam: "Looking upon this proclamation as a final acknowledgement by the government of its inability to hold us responsible under the laws and Constitution as they stood for our resistance to their usurpations and encroachments, I accept it in that light and not as a pardon for any offense committed. I think I can now return without any compromise of principle, and it is certainly a great deal better for me to do so than to remain a burden in the hands of friends who have to submit to the ills of Yankee rule in order to be able to furnish the means on which I live." [29]

Before the liberating news of the proclamation arrived, Jubal had moved to new and more affordable quarters in Drummondville. There, he had to endure some grim December days as winter tightened its grip and the exile contemplated his shrinking hoard of cash. In this period there are signs of another painful issue: a mysterious crisis involving Julia, with whom the general had evidently had a climactic falling out. Replying to a letter from Edmund Irvine, an old Rocky Mount colleague and friend who seems to have been privy to Jubal's most personal affairs, his tone was that of a man wronged and deeply offended. Had Julia, tired of his long absence during and after the war, already become involved with Charles Pugh, the man she would marry in 1871?

Early's letter to Irvine, written in an emotional state that spoiled his usually legible handwriting, suggests that possibility. "As to the person you alluded to," he wrote, "I wish never to hear of her again. That matter did me a great deal of injury at the time, but I tried to do the best I could. I have felt deeply concerned about the children, but the conduct of their mother has been such as to leave me in no doubt about which might and which might not be [illegible]. The whole thing is the source of the deepest regret to me but I certainly [illegible] to do any good, and [illegible] must take their course." [30]

On January 21, 1869, Jubal wrote his niece Ruth, announcing his intention to travel to Missouri on February 2, with the aim of being back in Virginia in the spring—perhaps in April. "I shall be very much delighted to see you all, though I expect the condition of things which I shall witness in Virginia will be very annoying to my feelings." [31]

‹‹ JUBAL WAS back in Virginia in May—settling, in July 1869, in Lynchburg, where he rented quarters over E. Crump's store on Main Street. In the city he could count on the company of Sam and his family; there also, work might be easier to find and more remunerative than in the even more impoverished environs of Rocky Mount and Franklin County.

Physically, Lynchburg was a comparatively compact community. Despite its hilly terrain, its distances were short and easy to walk. In good weather, the journey to Sam's house could have been little more than a stroll, as was more or less true of the distance to the homes of Jubal's friends. [32]

One of the firmest of these, of course, was a devoted comrade and protégé from the war, which had crippled him: John Daniel, now a 27-year-old lawyer living with his young family in Lynchburg. With Daniel, who had political aspirations of his own, Jubal must have spent many evenings talking about Virginia's transition from premier Confederate state to occupied territory—or, perhaps, to something with more of a future.

The immediate focus of their attention was the election of July 6, 1869, which was a clear victory for the True Republican ticket. Voters also ratified the constitution, deleting the restrictive clauses by large majorities. In January 1870, Congress seated members from Virginia for the first time since 1861. Though the price of readmission and home rule had been the acceptance of what Early called a "negro constitution," Virginia had escaped Military Reconstruction—with its accompaniment of Radical-black rule—as it would affect other Southern states for six more years.[33]

‹‹ To GOVERNOR WALKER, the era of his administration was an "age of gigantic material development," typified by such phenomena as the Atlantic cable and the transcontinental railroad. Walker, wanting Virginia to ride this surge of growth, felt that potential investors would be deterred by Virginia's burdensome debt; he aimed to uphold "Virginia's honor" by urging legislation to fund the entire prewar debt, with interest included for the war years. The legislature, ignoring the still-desperate state of the economy, passed the funding bill. The share owed by West Virginia, roughly a third of the total, was withheld; it would not be collected until after the First World War. In the meantime, its share was to be financed by interest-bearing certificates. By 1871, payment of interest alone, some $45 million, absorbed the state's entire income—except for small amounts set aside for public schools. There was no money even to run the state government, which then cost about $1 million annually.[34]

This was the situation inherited by Walker's successor as governor: Early's old friend James L. Kemper. As a veteran wounded in Pickett's charge, Kemper disdained, in traditionalist fashion, to "run" for the post, and was fond of voicing his unhappiness with the passing of "the last of the old Virginia." But he was a true "new movement man." Since the war, he had plunged into business ventures, including railroads, and helped attract enterprising immigrants to Virginia. Early ended by supporting him for old times' sake, though he suspected Kemper of trafficking with Mahone (who would, Early warned, envelop Kemper "like the Devil fish" if he could). Early was right: Kemper courted Mahone's support; their common ground was opposition to the efforts of the Pennsylvania Railroad to take over parts of Mahone's holdings.[35]

But on the question of funding the debt, Kemper's position presumably earned Jubal's unqualified praise. Although Kemper gave lip service to the support of public education, the governor declared that it could not claim an obligation senior to any other government undertaking, including payments on the state's debt. Moreover, since commerce and high finance demanded it, any price was worth paying to guarantee "Virginia's honor"—even the demise of the public schools. Like many other old-line Virginians, Early had never seen any point in educating the masses.

Probably for the same reasons (though hardly with much conviction), Mahone had once championed funding the debt. Now, he was campaigning vigorously for readjustment of the debt, on grounds that the reduction of interest payments would release funds for schools. Having, by the mid-1870s, lost his railroad battles, Mahone now focused his ambitions on politics. As a representative of the new middle class in Virginia, he realized that people presently or potentially of that class might vote for someone who supported free education for their children; in any case, the less affluent (almost everyone) resented having their tax dollars, collected in scarce currency, shipped out of state to bond holders.[36]

In early 1879, Mahone led in the establishment of a Readjuster party. Dominating legislative elections that year, the party passed a readjustment bill, but the governor, a Confederate veteran named Frederick W. M. Holliday, vetoed it. Also in 1879, Mahone won election to the U.S. Senate (where he voted with the Republicans); holding the office made it easier for him to set up the gubernatorial elections of 1881. This time the Readjuster candidate, William E. Cameron, won the state house; in December, another Readjuster, Harrison H. Riddleburger, was elected to the other Senate seat. With their hands on all the important levers, the Readjusters passed their bill, and Governor Cameron signed it. The act underwrote a public school system, state hospitals, and asylums; it repealed the poll tax and outlawed dueling. Above all, it ended the sanctioned definition of "Virginia's honor" as a catchword pretext for ignoring the educational (and other) needs of Virginia's people in changing times.[37]

This remained true even though Mahone wrecked the Readjuster party during the 1880s by overt displays of power hunger and abuses such as demanding salary kickbacks from his appointees. Most of these transgressions were merely unusually blatant instances of the vote-buying, ballot box–stuffing, and general corruption now familiarly associated with money-driven "new movement" politics. This time, however, it created a backlash that drew many Virginians closer to Early in his reverence for antebellum values.

Absorbing Readjusters who repudiated Mahone, the Conservatives renamed themselves Democrats and moved swiftly to seize control of the state's electoral politics. Early joined the Democrats, embedding himself comfortably in the one-party South that was one consequence of the compromise allowing for the election of Rutherford B. Hayes in 1876. The arrangement ended Military Reconstruction, curtailed Republican power, and permitted the South to move more speedily toward its goal of states' rights. While pledging support for public schools, the Democrats vowed to deliver Virginia from the evils of venality, Mahoneism, Republicanism, and black rule. That last charge was a stick with which to beat Mahone, who had used, manipulated, and paid off black voters, as well as poor whites, exploiting their inexperience; they had little real clout.

Mahone clung to an increasingly threadbare fabric of power for a few more years; by 1885, he found himself displaced. That was the year Fitzhugh Lee became governor and John Daniel went to the Senate; both, though thoroughly attuned to the critical new role of business (notably railroads) in Virginia's affairs, were close friends of Early. They were also old Confederates whose political emergence marked a renewed tide of nostalgic veneration for antebellum values, for what the novelist James Branch Cabell ironically called "the paradise in which they had lived for a time, and in which there had been no imperfection," and for "the thin line of heroes who had warred for righteousness' sake in vain." [38]

For Lee, Daniel, and Early, as for many others, these values from an illusory past offered a kind of model for the present and future. At its core was Virginia's honor, now defined in terms increasingly resonant with antebellum emotion; the state debt and public education were no longer real issues.

« FOR EARLY, honor resided intact in the defeated cause of Southern independence. It was now distilled, for him, in the issue of states' rights and white supremacy. An impassioned opponent of secession in 1861, he had defended it vigorously thereafter, and justified his defense by setting the rationale for secession beside the arguments validating the American Revolution. While asserting the same right of the Southern states to withdraw that the colonies had claimed, Early was dismissive of the colonies' standing compared to that of the seceding states. The former, he declared, were mere offshoots of the British Crown; the states were sovereign entities that had actually framed "the government of which they complained."[39]

This was substantially the old Whig version of states' rights promoted by John C. Calhoun and Henry Clay—given an emphatic postbellum twist by old Whig Jubal. Calhoun's position underlay the antebellum stance of the states that seceded, and dovetailed with their rationale for secession. In the war's wake, the emphasis changed. Most Southerners—most Virginians, anyway—acknowledged that slavery was no longer at the core of the states' rights doctrine. Not slavery but Southern independence, a great many asserted, was the principal Confederate war aim. Nevertheless, for most Virginian whites the emotional dynamics of race were essentially the same after the war as they had been before it.

It was true that with slavery dead, the political dynamics of race relations were different. Still, though they admitted blacks as party members, sought black votes, and even nominated black candidates, the Conservatives became known as "the white man's party," and ran for office on the color line. A candidate showing respect for the maintenance of white supremacy drew more votes than an opponent who did not. This fact embodied a concept absolutely vital to the men in power: state control of the relations between whites and blacks in favor of the former.[40]

« THOUGH MAINTAINING silence on slavery—it could not be respectably defended during his later years—Early never changed his views of the institution, which he did defend in a tract entitled *The Heritage of the South*, published posthumously in 1915. Though he never was "an investor in slaves," in the words of his niece (and editor) Ruth, he "possessed" black servants. His attitude toward slavery, Ruth noted, was determined by "familiarity with the institution as it existed in the homes of those to whom it had become a natural condition of life."

These were probably the ideal conditions for absorbing the racism that the institution bred and on which it depended for its continuing existence.[41]

Jubal ended his *Heritage* with a justification of slavery as an uplifting influence: "If . . . slavery has so tutored the negro that immediately his bonds are loosened, he is qualified for the privileges of the ballot box, what a civilizing tendency that institution must have had." But, in the author's view, there could be no question of blacks' being anything but barbaric in their native land. He also felt that blacks could escape that barbarism outside Africa, but only by becoming slaves.[42]

In Virginia, the presence of freed blacks induced dread and loathing in Early. His feelings toward people of color became particularly virulent when they were involved with anything connected to the war or the Confederacy. The intensity of these feelings reached a peak in 1875 over blacks' participation in a public ceremony celebrating the memory of Stonewall Jackson. In March the General Assembly appointed Jubal a member of a board to supervise erection of a bronze statue of Jackson in Richmond. A plan approved by Governor Kemper included volunteer black militia in the unveiling ceremony. Early wrote to Kemper declaring that he would refuse to march in the procession if the blacks were a part of it. Genuinely horrified, Kemper replied, defending the militia's participation as "a pleasing and appropriate honor to Jackson's memory" that also would refute "Radical lies" about white Virginians' exclusion and mistreatment of blacks. Not only that, but Kemper had been told that Mrs. Jackson, the general's widow, was willing to have the black militia march; so were the other Confederate leaders taking part.

Early wrote back, snarling a denunciation of the entire proceeding. He declared his belief that the black marchers would carry pictures of Lincoln and banners promoting the 15th Amendment and would "flaunt" them in the faces of white people. Kemper, fearing that if Early attended the ceremony there would be a race riot, wrote him, "for the sake of the public peace and harmony, I beg, beseech and implore you, for God's sake stay at home." For reasons that are unclear, the militia did not march, though blacks who had been servants in the

Stonewall Brigade stepped out in the parade with the white veterans. Early did not show up.[43]

« AFTER 1885, former Conservatives among the increasingly entrenched Democrats could remember having accepted black suffrage and even having run black candidates (for offices outside the realm of policy). But older attitudes gained growing encouragement from the demands of finance and business for order and stability, and strengthened with time and the ever greater involvement of Virginians with the rewards of commerce. Men who regarded blacks' voting and holding office as a source of chaos and corruption threatening the economic renaissance of Virginia saw to the passage of the state's 1902 constitution. This document repealed the "Underwood constitution" of 1868 that had guaranteed black suffrage. Although the new charter fell well short of canceling voting rights, it hedged them about, conditionally, with a poll tax (paid up for three years), a quiz on the state constitution, a literacy test, and similar obstacles to blacks' registration.[44]

Had he lived to see it, Jubal would have rejoiced. By 1902 it was clear that grotesque and irrational though Early's views may have been, he had expressed, albeit with exaggerated volume and vehemence, the views of many, many Southerners (and not a few Northerners).

In a way, the old Confederates were vindicated. Richard E. Beringer, Herman Hattaway, and their colleagues, in their persuasive book *Why the South Lost the Civil War*, acknowledge that "it may seem to require amazing mental agility to conclude the Confederacy had won victory." But, they argue, if one examines the 100 years between 1865 and 1965, it is clear that the "South had indeed preserved its view of the Constitution, white supremacy, and honor. . . . If the war was lost over slavery and independence, the peace was waged—and won—for states' rights, white supremacy, and honor. In this way, the South could claim 'a moral, if not a military, victory,' conspiring with historians to prove that 'no one—no white man at least—had really lost the Civil War.' "[45] That claim—though he paradoxically saw as pure evil the attendant changes wrought by money men like Mahone—was certainly the one Jubal Early would have made.

CHAPTER TWENTY-SIX

A *Matter of Money*

*F*ROM 1877 UNTIL 1893, at intervals of as little as one month, General Early climbed aboard a train in Lynchburg and arrived, 16 mind-numbing hours later, in New Orleans. It was not that he enjoyed traveling—he came to like it less and less as he got older—or that he felt any particular affection for New Orleans. It was a need for money that persuaded Jubal to make the weary journey so often and so uncomplainingly.[1]

Despising the new emphasis on material values, Early was a man of slender wants and simple tastes, with few obligations to anyone but himself. His expenses must have been modest. Still, the harrowing experience of impoverishment in exile, with its nauseating taste of humiliation and physical deprivation, must have stayed with him. It had been an ordeal that must on no account be repeated.

Jubal's high rank and celebrity as a war leader may have attracted some legal clients, and friends in local government seem to have thrown work in his direction. But even Lynchburg, though important enough to be a focus of such Southern commerce as there was in the 1860s and '70s, seems to have been without much gainful employment for lawyers. At any rate, Jubal tried to supplement his fees, whatever they might have amounted to. In January 1870, he wrote to Jefferson Davis, who had been named president of the Carolina Life Insurance Company, inquiring about the possibility of opening an office as the company's Virginia agent. Davis's reply was encouraging, offering to guarantee all expenses of establishing an agency. But Early can never have been enthusiastic about the insurance business. In April, Davis prodded him, asking for a reply by telegram about whether or not he would take the job. He never did.[2]

Somehow or other, legal work—possibly augmented by assistance from friends and family—kept Jubal going through most of the depressed '70s. Then came an opportunity that was to furnish financial independence for the rest of his life. He would never be a rich man. But he would be able to provide comfortably for himself and remain free from vulgar worries about poverty—and from the need to perform lawyer's work that was growing less and less interesting compared to the continuing and developing struggle for the Confederate cause.[3]

‹‹ THE SOURCE of this pecuniary boon was Jubal's commander at the First Battle of Manassas, P. G. T. Beauregard. In New Orleans, where he had returned after the war, General Beauregard had been approached by the Louisiana State Lottery Company, a large, highly profitable gambling enterprise, chartered as a monopoly by the state, that was being buffeted by charges of venality and fraud. Seeking to imbue its image with a respectability that would be proof against these accusations, the company asked Beauregard to serve as one of two lottery "supervisors"; the choice of the other was up to him. Beauregard initially got in touch with the Confederate cavalry leader Wade Hampton, who was running for governor of South Carolina; Hampton said he would accept if he lost the election. When he won, Beauregard turned, in December 1876, to Early. Would he agree to serve, attending two drawings a year, for a base salary of $5,000?[4]

Jubal hesitated. Beauregard's offer bristled with problems—not least the company itself. Founded by an act of the legislature in 1868, the "La. S. Lot. Co," as Beauregard abbreviated it in a letter to a friend, owed its beginnings—and its lucrative continuance—to large-scale bribery. Its president, a tough, resourceful Gilded Age operator (and self-described Confederate veteran) named Charles T. Howard, had reportedly dispensed $300,000 to Louisiana lawmakers for their assent to the company's establishment. Under the charter, the enterprise was to enjoy a 25-year tax-exempt franchise to run a lottery with no competition permitted in Louisiana. Lottery patrons could play in two semi-annual drawings with large prizes, or in monthly and daily drawings with lesser kitties. The company's only obligation to the state was to provide $40,000 toward the expenses of Charity Hospital in New Orleans.[5]

As a matter of shrewd public relations, the lottery contributed to many other charitable and benevolent causes ranging from flood relief and education to support for the opera. It had little trouble making such altruistic disbursements; gross annual revenues averaged as much as $28,800,000; profits ranged between $8,500,000 and $13,000,000. The value of company stock mushroomed from $35 to $1,200, reliably paying 100 percent dividends. With branch offices in Northern cities such as Chicago, Kansas City, and New York, the lottery attracted 90 percent of its cash receipts from out of state as Americans of all classes and degrees of affluence bought tickets. Ticket prices ranged from 20 cents to $40; the company often split tickets selling, say, for $20 into fractions of $1 each. Some of the cheaper tickets seemed to promise a gratuitous advantage by allowing the player to choose his own numbers.[6]

The handsome prizes awarded to lucky numbers were the attraction. A $1 ticket could return $15,000, a $20 outlay was worth up to $300,000—enormous sums at the time. The dazzling vision of such rewards filled Louisiana's newspaper columns (otherwise stuffed with lottery advertising), but all the puffery hid the price paid by players, many of whom could ill afford it, plunking down their money over the years and never winning anything. Not every paper was cowed or suborned by the lottery. The New Orleans *Democrat* observed that Methuselah, buying a daily ticket throughout his notoriously long life, would have paid a quarter of a million dollars in the hope of winning a bit more than two and a half million.[7]

Advertisements fed the folklore generated by the lottery. The appearance of certain signs was a help: sighting of a stray dog counseled playing number six; a female corpse with gray hair signified 49; the sight of an unclothed woman's leg (if not attached to the player's wife or mistress) was a clear signal to play 11.[8]

Some did win. But it was invariably the lottery company that came out ahead. To begin with, it simply kept most of the receipts; of every $100 that came in, the company paid out only $48 in prizes. Moreover, the company arranged matters—for example, by withholding ticket fractions from sale—so that it could win its own prizes.[9]

With all that wealth, the lottery was the most powerful entity in Louisiana for 20 years. Besides controlling many of the principal organs of the press, the company manipulated the banks and other financial institutions and dominated the legislatures of two decades. One observer reported that the company managers were "the absolute masters of every ward boss and every professional politician in the State of Louisiana, whether he be judge, sheriff, constable, treasurer, member of the [Democratic] State Committee, member of the parish committee." Stuffing money in legislators' pockets, the lottery fought off repeated attempts to stifle it or at least cancel its monopoly. Still, bad publicity persisted; the editor of the unruly *Democrat* was slapped with suits amounting to $90,000 for references to "Howard and his brother thieves," and for predicting that they would shortly be "treated to a short shift and a long rope." That was the ugly talk that Early and Beauregard were supposed to silence.[10]

To Early, the company's difficulties were obvious enough. But there were also vexatious political problems: not only had the legislature been bribed to set the company up, but the entire government, established under Radical reconstruction with an inadmissible "negro constitution," was—at any rate, it recently had been—riddled with Republicans, including freedmen and carpetbaggers. Could Beauregard guarantee, Jubal asked, that the lottery company harbored no carpetbaggers? He could and did, Beauregard replied; otherwise, he would never have had anything to do with it. Besides, Howard was a Confederate veteran and a pillar of New Orleans society. True, John A. Morris, one of the lottery's owners, was a Northerner; but he was also a Democrat and a relative of Confederate Gen. John B. Hood.[11]

‹‹ GENERAL EARLY seems to have considered the lottery enterprise in the spirit of a lawyer deciding whether or not to defend a wealthy client with dubious claims to innocence. He elected to join the company, hammering out an agreement with Howard and Beauregard stipulating that he could withdraw if he smelled trouble, and that he could publicly explain why he had done so.[12]

To earn their stipends—which may have risen to as much as $20,000 a year for Beauregard (a full general) and $15,000 for Early (only a lieutenant general)—the old Confederates had two basic duties to perform: being present in New Orleans at a minimum of two drawings a year; and lending their prestige (and in Early's case, skill in argument) to the lottery company to defend it and to lobby in its behalf in Baton Rouge and Washington. (Apparently Jubal never had to perform lobbying chores, which would have been hateful to him.)[13]

At the drawings they attended in the company's public hall downtown, Beauregard and Early were impressive presences, powerful images in the company's effort to prove that the lottery was honest. Early, standing on a stage by a drum containing tickets, wore his habitual Confederate gray suit; near a drum holding prizes, the white-maned Beauregard, regal in black, put one witness in mind of a French generalissimo in the manner of Napoleon, reviewing his battalions on some Gallic plain. Early removed each ticket from the drum and read the number out, showing the ticket so the audience could read the numerals. Thereupon Beauregard extracted and announced the prize.[14]

Tedious hours would crawl by before all the hundreds of prizes were awarded. A written record of each drawing was kept in a ledger, and at the end, a certificate was drawn up and signed by the generals, who called themselves subscribers or commissioners: "The Subscribers having supervised the single number drawing Class A, Louisiana State Lottery, hereby certify that the above are the numbers which were this day drawn from the 100,000 placed in the wheel, with the prizes corresponding to them. Witness our hands at New Orleans, La., this Tuesday, December 18, 1883." The top prize at this drawing was $150,000.[15]

<< THE ALLURE of the lottery was far from universal. Sentiment ran heavily against the enterprise. Despite the company's control of the legislature, bills for repeal of the charter were occasionally introduced in Baton Rouge, and one actually passed in 1879 and was signed by the governor. Wriggling out from under, the company obtained a federal court injunction against enforcement of the law. In Washington, com-

pany lobbyists (including Beauregard) beat back unremitting efforts by Congress to pass antilottery legislation; no fewer than 11 such bills were introduced just in the first session of the 49th Congress (1885). In 1879, the postmaster general declared all lottery companies engines of fraud and ordered all mail from them or to them to be returned or confiscated by the dead letter department. In Lynchburg, at least, the order was carried out—or so Early alleged in a letter to the company management.[16]

Symbols of rectitude, the generals were dutiful in carrying out their obligations as defenders of the lottery. The task challenged Jubal's powers of advocacy. One persistent charge against the enterprise was cheating. Another was its awarding of prizes to itself. A third was its status as a monopoly. In a tone of conviction—but with arguments that bear little scrutiny—Early answered these accusations in an open letter to the newspapers in June 1878.

There were only three ways, he pointed out, that a lottery swindle could be perpetrated: one, "by a delusive and dishonest drawing"; two, by presenting a drawing different from the actual drawing; three, by "refusal or failure to pay the prizes drawn." Early was not aware, he wrote, that any of these charges had been brought against the lottery; furthermore, if any such accusations were brought, they could not be proved. Early and his colleague had, he asserted, taken more special pains to ensure honesty than had the supervisors of any other lottery; but the fact was that even the drawings they did not supervise were as honest as those they attended.

Jubal did not deny that the company had won some of its own larger prizes. But that was simply because less than half the available tickets had been sold; because the company owned the unsold tickets, it stood to reason that they would win once in a while. (This was a particularly shaky argument, since it did not even attempt to explain why there was no rule against mixing unsold company-owned tickets in the wheel with those purchased by the public.)

On the question of monopoly, Early depended on an even more diaphanous thesis. It was better, he wrote, for an enterprise like a lottery to be a monopoly; there was less chance for fraud and dishonesty if only one person or a few were involved. Otherwise, the field would be open to any grifter who happened to have the wherewithal to pay a license tax.

The clincher was the fact that neither Early nor Beauregard had resigned. Before either general had gotten involved, Jubal pointed out, each had reserved the right to withdraw at any time and publicize his reasons for doing so. The fact that both were still on duty was a clear demonstration that the lottery operation was dead honest.

Apart from the question of probity in running the lottery was the basic issue of the rights and wrongs of gambling, which bothered many Americans. The commissioners did not want, Jubal stated, to get into the matter of the lottery's morality. But he did wish to point to the fact that none other than President James Madison had approved of lotteries, and had authorized them during his administration to finance public works in the District of Columbia. Most of the states had authorized lotteries at one time or another; that most did not have them now, Early argued (harking deftly back to his reasoning on the monopoly question), was because the privilege of operating lotteries had been "improvidently and indiscriminately granted." In the end, the reality of human nature just had to be faced: lotteries, legal or illegal, honest or dishonest, were inevitable, given "the innate propensity of men to take chances and risks." [17]

<< FOR 14 YEARS, such arguments, backed up by the generals' presence at the drawings and combined with astute management, kept the lottery company out of serious trouble. As of 1882, Early and Beauregard were expected to be on hand every month. Meanwhile, the enterprise grew and prospered to an astonishing degree. In 1887, the stock dividend was said to have been 110 percent; a year later it was 120 percent, and reached 170 percent in 1889, dropping to 125 percent in 1890. Another reflection of company fortunes was the level of the top cash prize, which eventually reached $600,000 (though no one ever drew it). [18]

Whether or not Beauregard and Early owned shares in the company is uncertain. They probably did not; but if they did, they would have been imprudent to admit it. Since the enterprise was an in-

< 426 >

tensely private affair, there were probably few shares outstanding in any case. Careful with his money, Early never mentioned his salary or travel expenses in his correspondence. Beauregard, less finicky, complained volubly about his treatment by the company, which—despite its wealth—seems to have been aggressively parsimonious in its policies with respect to compensation and expenses. In August 1883, Beauregard blamed Jubal for a recent cancellation of expense allowances. "I suppose," Beauregard wrote, "that this is the sequel to your yielding so quietly to the reduction of 33% for your traveling expenses. If the co. wishes to economize let it not be at our expense. I have always thought that we accepted the charge of these monthly drawings at too low a rate & when they increased the capital prize to $75,000 we ought to have asked for $700 per mo. We may yet have to do it." [19]

« IT MUST BE doubted whether the company paid the slightest attention to this complaint and numerous others that flowed from Beauregard's pen. Early, knowing a good thing when he saw it, seems never to have bothered to complain about anything.

It is nevertheless possible that Jubal agreed with Beauregard in believing that the lottery company would probably not outlive its charter. Feeling against the lottery in the nation and even in Louisiana, where opposition had never been very strong, was on the rise. As the charter's expiration date approached, the company declared that if the state would renew the charter, it could expect an annual payment of $500,000. When a critic said that was not enough, the lottery management grandly raised the bid to $1,250,000.

Despite this show of generosity, antilottery forces persuaded a majority of legislators to sign a pledge forswearing enactment of a new lottery charter. Overcoming this obstacle, the company engineered passage of a constitutional amendment authorizing another 20 years of life for the lottery. But its power did not reach into the office of the governor, whose veto of the bill was sustained by the legislature. Taking the matter to court, the company managed to get the issue revived as a question on the ballot in the 1892 state election.

But the lottery's ultimate nemesis turned out to be in Washington. Before Louisiana voters went to the polls (where they defeated the charter), Congress acted to forbid the sending of tickets through the mail and outlawed the mailing of newspapers carrying lottery advertisements. An attempt to substitute express services for the post office failed when the express companies refused to do business with the lottery.

It was the end. In 1894, the Louisiana State Lottery Company, arguably the largest American gambling enterprise up to that time, packed up and moved without fanfare to Honduras. Beauregard and Early resigned. Though the commissioners appointed as replacements were close connections of Beauregard's (one was his brother-in-law), the scale of operations was vastly reduced: the new president, Paul Conrad, did not even bother to resign his post as chief executive officer of the Gulf Coast Ice and Manufacturing Company of Bay St. Louis, Mississippi.[20]

Seeking the Lost Cause

T HE NEED FOR money that had led General Early to embrace the Louisiana lottery was different from General Beauregard's need, which was more like an appetite. Beauregard thought in large terms; money was, in his mind, primarily a source of status, as well as a bulwark against the misfortunes of old age. Though Jubal, the returned exile, also regarded money as a shield against a shameful adversity, it was for him essentially a means to an end, freeing him to pursue his perpetual struggle to overturn the verdict of the war's end.[1]

It was all very well to believe—as Early came to do—in the South's gradual recovery, following Reconstruction, of at least some of its war aims, principally white social and political dominance. But it was always very difficult for him and many fellow Southerners to cope with the South's loss of its trial at arms. Nor did his consciousness of that loss diminish with the end of Reconstruction. As late as 1887, Jubal was writing of the ordeal faced by the "true and brave soldier who suffers defeat, while fighting for a just cause, at the hands of a vindictive enemy" and who "suffers the agonies of a thousand deaths. Indeed a real death to many would be preferable."[2]

Not to Jubal. It may be seriously doubted whether the general would ever have sought refuge from defeat's dilemma in death—or that he ever even contemplated suicide. But the rest of the passage quoted is applicable. In Jubal's conscious mind, the justice of the cause was beyond challenge. Moreover, he denied that the correctness of the South's course had any connection with the war's outcome. Might had simply overcome right.

Concepts like the unconscious did not really exist for Jubal Early and most of his contemporaries. But beneath the surface of consciousness, where Southern men and women often knew despair that flickered or raged according to circumstances and temperament, the "agonies of a thousand deaths" arose from far more than bruised *amour propre* and humbled pride. Men like Robert and Fitzhugh Lee, James Kemper, and others, could divert some of the pain by acknowledging the reality—that Northern victory had altered the landscape of their lives—and then try to live according to the new topography.

But there was another issue that was less amenable to such a decisive display of sanity. What, many asked themselves in their heart of hearts, if the cause had *not* been just? A large number of these questioners, acknowledging that the war could not have been righteous if waged to preserve slavery, evaded guilt by loudly denying that the Confederacy had ever fought for that institution; the cause, they said, had been Southern independence, which they had sought in the same spirit as that of the Revolutionary War for American independence. What better proof of that, they asked, than that the Confederate government had contemplated abolishing slavery on its own and recruiting the freedmen as black soldiers in a last-ditch effort to win the war and preserve independence?[3]

But even for these repudiators of slavery, the underlying quandary remained. It was a tangled problem that arose from two closely related sources. First, and perhaps most important, was an evangelical religion prevalent in the South (and much of the North) that bonded the worshiper to God and the devil in a mystical union founded on the conviction that righteousness would ever have its reward and sin would be punished. For believers, the punishment inflicted by defeat could all too logically be traced to their own wrongdoing. Guilt and feelings of alienation troubled their minds; they felt estranged from God. Even for the nonobservant, like Early, religion's influence was pervasive enough throughout their lives to affect their feelings in much the same way it impinged on the emotions of the devout. Jubal's faith in God and Christ appears only dimly in his life; but he certainly believed in the "arch-fiend."[4]

The second source of distress was the fact that Southerners were

Americans, steeped in the unique American legend of success and victory. Until 1865, no white Americans had ever had to come to grips with total collective failure. History, to paraphrase Arnold Toynbee, had always been "something unpleasant that happens to other people."

Suddenly Southerners were America's "other people." As the decades passed, some shed the illusions of fulfillment and innocence once shared with their Northern brethren. Some did not. But all faced the same unpleasantness. As C. Vann Woodward has pointed out, the South "learned to accommodate itself to conditions that it swore it would never accept, and it learned the taste left in the mouth by the swallowing of one's own words." These experiences are not considered part of the American dream.[5]

« AS OF JUBAL EARLY's return from exile, this harsh lesson, which he would never accept, had been clearly set out. For those like him who held back from learning the lesson, resistance to history's chastisement could obviously not extend to the resumption of armed hostilities; the struggle that was waged perforce evolved into a largely unsuccessful attempt to handle the psychological trauma of defeat. This evolution worked itself out in the effort to resolve the dilemmas of sin and failure flowing from the prevailing religion and the current version of the American dream. Distilled in what some observers have seen as a sort of civil religion, the effort became known as the Lost Cause.

Logically enough—given his vehement and articulate irreconcilability—Jubal Early was to become a principal figure in this struggle. He joined with a band of supporters, mostly Virginians and old soldiers, who fought a campaign to rationalize and vindicate the fate of the Confederacy. Their efforts were to have a profound and long-lasting influence on opinion and feeling in the North as well as the South— and in England—about what had happened to the South before, during, and after the Civil War. In wielding that influence, Early and his adherents had the satisfaction of achieving a recognition they had never known during the Civil War.[6]

Their campaign would unfold on three closely related fronts. The first involved the creation of an organization, the Southern Historical Society, to compile and disseminate what Early and his followers regarded as the true story of the war. The core of their doctrine was a declaration that the Confederate soldier was a better fighter—and a better man—than his Union adversary; the Northern enemy was often a foreigner, a member of a mongrel race—seen by one Southern writer as a breed mingling "Yankees, negroes, Germans and Irish."[7]

This notion that the Union soldier was a grosser being than his Confederate adversary had its origin, not surprisingly, during the war. Writing to his wife in May 1864 of the men killed in the Wilderness battle, Bryan Grimes noted the "strange fact" that "the Yankees always turn black and decay rapidly becoming offensive but our soldiers retain for days their natural appearance."[8]

Manning its armies with such material, the North (the argument ran) could only win with the crushing advantage of superior numbers based on its population, which was so much larger than that of the South. The Union hordes were backed up, in this view, by overwhelming industrial and technological might that the South, with its more civilized agrarian tradition, could not match.

Where, it was asked, was the disgrace in losing to such an enemy? Indeed, in a fair fight, the better men would inevitably have won—and thus, in a way, they had won. Certainly, their martial prowess, heroically demonstrated again and again through four years of resistance to the Northern juggernaut, was proof of a moral victory.[9]

The shining symbol of this triumph—and the basis of the campaign's second front—was Robert E. Lee. Early and his supporters, in their writings, speeches, and discourse with other Southerners and the world, worked indefatigably to elevate Lee to the status of a demigod. Lee died on October 12, 1870, not long after Early's return from Canada. The dead general, whose memory Early and others competed to consecrate in monuments and speeches, was canonized. Seen as a Christlike figure, Lee acquired an image of moral purity and martial perfection that raised him—and by association, all male white Southerners—above the level of ordinary men. Such an image was an eloquent denial of defeat: Lee could be trodden down by barbarians, but was ultimately invincible. A society that could produce such a man, it was strongly implied, could do no wrong.[10]

Yet even Lee could be betrayed—undone by the ineptitude and

insubordination of people he trusted. The chief wrongdoer in this category—the third front on which the campaign was prosecuted—was to be James Longstreet. According to Early and his supporters, who wrangled bitterly with Longstreet during the '70s and '80s, Old Pete had committed three unforgivable sins: first, at Gettysburg, he had disobeyed Lee's orders to attack early on July 2, thus forfeiting the victory that would have assured Confederate independence; second, in defending himself against these charges, Longstreet had criticized Lee; third, Longstreet had turned Republican during Reconstruction, an act of betrayal deemed just as heinous as the other two—if not more so.[11]

‹‹ DABNEY H. MAURY, a Virginian living in New Orleans, first conceived the idea of a Southern Historical Society in 1868. Maury (West Point, class of 1846), was a capable wartime cavalry general who served mainly in the West and Deep South. He talked the notion over with such prominent Confederates in New Orleans as Braxton Bragg, Harry Hays, and Beauregard; this group and others organized the society in May 1869. Benjamin Morgan Palmer, a clergyman ardent in the Southern cause, was president; secretary-treasurer was Dr. Joseph Jones, a physician and son of a Georgia preacher and slave owner named Charles Colcock Jones. At its founding, the society asserted its claim to represent authentic Southern views: "No Southern man who has read . . . the unjust and unreasonable history of the late war as compiled by Northern writers for the deception of the world and its posterity, can be satisfied."

Jubal Early would express the society's raison d'être more specifically in a letter to Henry B. Dawson, a magazine editor: "By the reports of the Congressional committee on the Conduct [of the war] contained in eight octavo volumes, the very voluminous reports of the Secretary of War during the war, the messages of the President of the United States during the same time, various other publications by the Government . . . it has been sought to make our cause and our conduct in the struggle for it, odious, and to present a one-sided view of the history of events preceding, attending and following the war."[12]

Though the society, in this early phase, never generated much support outside New Orleans, efforts were made to expand its influence through the appointment of well-known vice presidents in the Confederate states: General Lee, for instance, represented the Society in Virginia; Wade Hampton, head of the Confederate Survivors' Association of South Carolina, was vice president for that state; D. H. Hill was the SHS officer for North Carolina.[13]

Hearing of General Early's return to Virginia, Dr. Joseph Jones wrote to him in August 1869, asking him to give a public address on behalf of the society later in the year or early in 1870. Jubal could not—or did not want to—comply with this request. But Dabney Maury, whose connection with the SHS would continue, wrote to Early regretting his absence, and declaring that the society had been counting on the success of Jubal's lecture to raise funds for its first publishing venture. Not that Maury meant to scold; in another letter he lauded Early's stature among Southerners who had not "apostasized."[14]

On Lee's death in 1870, Early succeeded him as vice president of the SHS in Virginia. Meanwhile, the society struggled to overcome diminishing public interest, its leaders blaming their worsening fortunes on their location in New Orleans. There, they felt, they were on the fringes of the South; the chaos and upheaval of Louisiana's encounter with Reconstruction and the city's preoccupation with business were serious distractions. There was talk of moving the headquarters of the SHS to Richmond. Meanwhile, in hopes of attracting new members and revivifying their organization, the society's elders decided to hold their 1873 meeting at Montgomery White Sulphur Springs in Virginia, watering place of choice for the Southern quality in the years before the war.[15]

Early was informed of this plan and urged to attend the meeting; he was asked to bring from two to five delegates with him. Plainly sensing an opportunity to seize a platform, Jubal interpreted this suggestion very broadly, arranging for the nomination of what turned out to be 22 delegates, including himself. This amounted to nearly half of those attending the August meeting—54 delegates from 12 states, including Kentucky, Tennessee, Maryland, and Missouri. They listened to a speech by Jefferson Davis. They also reorganized the Southern Historical Society, electing Jubal Early as president. Appropriately, the new chief of the SHS was on the agenda as principal speaker.[16]

« THE ADDRESS, given on August 14, 1873, was one of the most important of the dozens Early made over the years. It was eloquent in setting out the ideas and principles of Early's plans for the SHS in its approach to the historiography of the war. The speaker's opening remarks duly welcomed the delegates to the convention and to Virginia, "a State which, however illustrious she may have been in her past record and history, has in our day been rendered still more illustrious by the deeds performed on her soil by soldiers from all parts of the late Confederate States, in defense of the grandest human cause for which man has ever fought." [17]

A central point in the speech was the issue of success or failure in the outcome of the war. Memories of the struggle, Early asserted, would not fade "because we were not successful. The enlightened world does not accept as an infallible maxim that success is the only criterion of merit." Was it not Sir Walter Scott who had said, "Brave blood is ne'er shed in vain"? By "the discerning good and true of all ages and climes," the general went on, "—those who believe that justice, right and truth are as eternal as the throne of Him who is 'from everlasting to everlasting'—it has been, and will continue to be, thought better to deserve success than to achieve it; and by such, the deeds of the virtuous and truly great will always be valued according to their real merit, though success may not have crowned them." [18]

The superiority of deserts to achievement was definite. But even those who doubted it, Early implied, could be sure of one other thing: a harsh punishment awaited the ostensibly successful party in the late conflict for crimes committed in prevailing over the Confederacy. This, he stated, was a universal principle. "Some one has said, 'Nations cannot commit great crimes with impunity, any more than can individuals'; and all history, sacred and profane, vindicates the truth of the remark." (Jubal cannot really have believed this; but he knew it would catch hold of the wishfulness in his listeners' feelings. Certainly he, like they, felt that it *should* be true.)

A principal punishment for such crimes, Early declared, was a civil rot that would spread and bring down in ruins the remains of such republican government as still lingered in the country, North and South.

Meanwhile the question of Southern guilt or innocence in the face of charges of treason remained to be answered. In a telling image, Early placed Southerners before the "bar" of history, where they "must appear, either as criminals—rebels and traitors seeking to throw off the authority of a legitimate government founded by our fathers—or as patriots demanding our rights and vindicating the true principles of the government founded by our fathers." The North was trying, Early asserted, to present the South "in the former character," an image promoted in Northern historical and literary writings and in "the whole scope and tendency of their legislation and government policy." Should Southerners permit this indictment to go unanswered?

"No! A thousand times no! The men who by their deeds caused so many of the battle-fields of the South to blaze with a glory unsurpassed in the annals of the world, cannot be so recreant to the principles for which they fought, the traditions of the past, and the memory of their comrades 'dead upon the field of honor,' as to abandon the tribunal to those before whose immense numbers and physical power alone they were finally compelled to yield from mere exhaustion . . ."

Expanding on this central theme of relative numbers, Early's speech stressed points that were almost always part of his frequent utterances on the subject: the Federals' exaggeration of Confederate strength (and underestimation of their own); the slender manpower resources actually available to Southern arms against the real (and overwhelming) numbers in Union ranks. In general, of course—and in many specific instances as well—the forces of the North did outnumber those of the South; so, in spite of the frequent irrelevance of this disparity on the battlefield, Early was essentially on firm historical ground.

His challenge at White Sulphur Springs was to Northern accounts of the war. Jubal cited "the notable fact that the commanders of the Federal armies, their apologists and eulogists, maintain that they were outnumbered in most of the great battles of the war. McClellan maintains that our numbers were nearly double his own in the battles around Richmond; Pope declares that he was overwhelmed by numbers at second Manassas . . . and General [Andrew A.] Humphreys, chief of the United States Engineer Corps, in his eulogy on Meade, asserts that

the latter was outnumbered at Gettysburg. These are but specimens of
such claims; and it is a little singular that some one has not contended
that Grant was outnumbered at Appomattox." [19]

According to Early, Humphreys had stated at Meade's funeral in
late 1872 that the Federals had only 70,000 infantry at Gettysburg,
with 10,000 cavalry and 4,000 artillerymen, a total of 84,000. (Humphreys evidently cited no source for his figures. It is interesting that,
however he arrived at it, his estimate is only about 1,000 men lower
than the total reached by Coddington in a complicated reckoning based
largely on Federal returns for the two days following the battle.) Early
quoted Humphreys's estimate of Confederate strength as 85,000 infantry, 8,000 cavalry and "a due proportion of artillery." Allowing for only
3,000 artillerymen, the total would come to 96,000 Southerners. [20]

Thus Meade's eulogist perpetuated what Early condemned as the
meretricious tendency of Northerners to endow their enemies with an
imaginary advantage, notwithstanding the fact that Meade's own estimate of his strength (cited by Early from U.S. Congressional records)
was about 95,000. As Early bitterly pointed out, captured Confederate documents, held in Washington, were not yet available to Southern
historians. "Federal officers are exceedingly loath to accept the truth in
regard to our strength, and they try to conceal their own. Hence, as I am
informed, all access to the Federal returns, as well as the Confederate
records in the Archive office, is studiously denied to all Confederates."

But, the speaker urged his audience, look at an estimate of Lee's
strength at Gettysburg, explicitly based on those presumably reliable
captured Confederate records, by the Northern writer William Swinton.
Historian of the Army of the Potomac, Swinton had come up with a
total of 68,352 officers and men in Lee's force. That, Early said, was
much closer to the mark, even though Swinton had included not only
troops of the Army of Northern Virginia but all the men serving in the
regional military department. In his reckoning, Early subtracted troops
left in Virginia (for example, in Winchester) and did not include all
of the substantial reinforcements that actually did join the ANV; the
size of the force actually with Lee in Pennsylvania, Early stated, was
less than 60,000. (Coddington's estimate, based on an official U.S.

Army study in 1886 that included all the Confederate reinforcements, is about 75,000, which, as he correctly points out, is "truly a formidable force.")[21]

Early, in his use of the potent propaganda weapon of the numbers, was not crudely cooking the books. The question of the two sides' strengths in the Civil War has always been vexed, particularly with regard to Confederate returns and estimates based on them. Knowing this, and aware that in a broad general sense Union strengths during the war had been greater—whether or not that meant anything in a given situation—Early used the most reliable figures available to him at whatever time he was writing or speaking, and pushed them gently but firmly in the direction he wanted them to go. The skill he employed in marshaling these "facts" was ultimately much more impressive than the numbers themselves.

« GENERAL EARLY was soon to show an equally impressive grasp of organization, consolidating his new dominance of the SHS by filling its executive committee (Dabney H. Maury, chairman) exclusively with fellow Virginians. All but two, George L. Christian and the Reverend J. William Jones, erstwhile chaplain of the 13th Virginia, were also former Confederate officers. Col. Thomas T. Munford, late of Tom Rosser's cavalry brigade, became the society's paid secretary. When Munford resigned in 1876, he was succeeded by Jones, who remained influential in the SHS as its secretary until 1887.[22]

At two meetings of the society held in Virginia in the months following the pivotal White Sulphur Springs convention, an effort was made to generate a broad regional image for the group by featuring speakers like South Carolina's Wade Hampton and Adm. Raphael Semmes of Alabama; but most of the new members recruited among those attending the meetings were, not surprisingly, Virginians.[23]

The Virginian cast of the society was clearly of great importance to Early. Though he worked to garner support from prominent Confederates in other states, he unquestionably felt that Virginia, his home and Robert E. Lee's, had been the flagship state of the Confederacy during the war, and that it should continue to be dominant in the affairs of the South.

This feeling reflected Jubal's wish to dominate those affairs himself as much as possible; somewhat frustrated in the political arena, he found that the SHS gave him an outlet. Jubal was also reassured by the fact that the SHS gave him great influence with the only people he really felt mattered: the old soldiers. Among them, the general's wrath was something to be dreaded over a period of three decades: as Robert Stiles expressed it, "so long as the old hero was alive in his hill city of Virginia, no man ever took up his pen to write a line about the great conflict without the fear of Jubal Early before his eyes." [24]

The society's organ, initially the Baltimore-based *Southern Magazine*, gave way in 1876 to the *Southern Historical Society Papers (SHSP)*, the society's own monthly magazine. Edited until 1887 by J. William Jones, the periodical was devoted exclusively to the history of the war and the Confederacy. The emphasis was on the feats of Lee and the Army of Northern Virginia. In its first year of publication, the *SHSP* contained 29 articles on the ANV; only five pieces were devoted to armies in the west or elsewhere. In 1877, the content was even more lopsided; the magazine ran 44 articles dealing with Virginia, while five were about other theaters. This chauvinism helped glorify Lee, but it was bitterly resented by such non-Virginians as Longstreet's fellow Georgian Lafayette McLaws, who seems always to have hated Early, though he scarcely knew him personally. [25]

Even so, for 40 years, the *SHSP* was to be the single most influential vehicle, North or South, for the views of Early and his cohorts. Though interest in these views—and in the war—rose and fell over the years, sometimes inflicting hard times on the society, the *SHSP*'s influence was palpable. Texas appropriated funds to buy 150 sets of bound volumes for every college library and for the public schools. The *New England Historical Register* informed its readers about the *Papers* and warned that "no library, private or public, which pretends to historic fullness, *Can Afford To Be Without These Volumes.*" Capitals and italics also appeared in comments on the *SHSP* in the *London Saturday Review*, which declared that the magazine offered "a mass of information relative to the late War, *Without A Careful Study Of Which No Librarian, However Limited His Scope Should Venture to Treat Any Engagement Of That Interesting Story.*" [26]

As the Virginians—and a few others—refought the war's battles in the *SHSP*'s pages, they could feel they had an audience for their cherished themes: the justice of the cause, the irresistible Cyclopean strength of the North, the superiority of the Confederate soldier, and the genius of their great leaders, Jackson and Lee.

« JACKSON'S FAME had almost surpassed Lee's in the years immediately following the war; Stonewall's monument in Richmond, unveiled in 1875, was the first such memorial in the old Confederate capital. (Early, as noted, was one of the commissioners appointed by the government for that monument; he was also president of a citizen's group, the Jackson Memorial Association.) As late as 1881, 12,000 devotees thronged a ceremony at Metairie Cemetery in New Orleans for the dedication of a monument to Jackson; Jefferson Davis, the main speaker, declared that the South "gave its whole heart to Jackson," and that Europe held him up as "the great hero of our war." But it was Lee's star, after his death, that rose in the pantheon of Confederate heroes, ever higher and brighter so as to outshine all others.[27]

Jubal Early was the principal force behind this elevation of Lee to a status that was to transform his image almost out of the human realm—into that of a "marble man," to use the coinage of the historian Thomas L. Connelly. Early was by no means the sole agent of this transformation, but his was the driving, organizing hand.

Little in the way of memorial organization took place before Lee's death. Appointed president of Washington College at Lexington, Virginia, in 1865, Marse Robert's view of his public duty after Appomattox was to help the South put the war behind it. Five years after the war, Bradley Johnson proposed a Confederate veteran's organization, to be headed by Lee, but the general discouraged the effort; he feared disapproval by the Federal authorities that would slow the already sluggish pace of the sectional reunion and economic recovery he favored. As the living leader, Lee had to be deferred to; no one dreamt of stepping in and usurping his place.[28]

Lee's death changed that. Within a month, Generals Johnson and Early had established the Association of the Army of Northern Virginia, which became the most powerful veterans' organization in the South until the formation, in 1889, of the United Confederate Veterans.[29]

Early was galvanized by Lee's death, though he had been unable, on account of pressing legal business, to attend the funeral. William Nelson Pendleton, Lee's old artillery chief and now minister of the general's church in Lexington, received a letter from Early explaining that court cases pending in Franklin County had kept him there to represent old clients whose interests could not be left to proxies. This can be believed; Jubal would undoubtedly have attended the funeral if he could possibly have done so. In his letter to Pendleton, Early recognized that the "loss is a public one, and there are millions of hearts now torn with anguish at the news that has been flashed over the wires to all corners of the civilized world."[30]

A public loss called for a public response. Within two weeks of Lee's passing on October 12, 1870, Early wrote a card to the newspapers calling a meeting in Richmond for November 3, to found an organization dedicated to the perpetuation of Lee's memory. The purpose would be to erect a statue or other memorial to Lee in Richmond, where the leader's body was to be permanently buried; this project was to be the principal monument to the dead general.[31]

That was important. The haste with which the November 3 meeting had been called was in part a response to efforts along the same lines already afoot in Lexington. Some of Lee's friends and associates there, including the Reverend Pendleton, had met the very day of the general's demise to discuss formation of a group dedicated to the erection of a memorial in Lexington, where Lee and his family had lived for the past five years. Looking down the road, if Lee were to be ceremonially entombed with a suitable monument in Lexington, the college, which had hired him largely in order to exploit his name in the raising of scarce funds, could continue to do so with greater chances of success than if he were buried—or even memorialized—somewhere else.

The Lexington group's initial aims were a mausoleum for the general, an appropriately colossal statue on the college grounds, and the assemblage of material for a book to be entitled the "Lee Memorial Volume." The men most active in the organization were Pendleton (its president), Professor William Preston Johnston (son of the famed Confederate Gen. Albert Sidney Johnston, killed at Shiloh), and William Allan, also a professor and once Stonewall Jackson's ordnance chief. These men ran things, but they made careful efforts to adorn their organizational hierarchy with figures like John C. Breckinridge, invited to be honorary president, and the likes of P. G. T Beauregard and Jubal Early, asked to accept posts as state vice presidents.[32]

In this Lexington-based organization and its plans, Early doubtless perceived a competitive thrust that needed to be blunted—but no real threat. In fact, he took some pains to recruit the Lexington people as participants in *his* project.[33]

On November 3, Early and other speakers addressing the assemblage in Richmond's Presbyterian church duly disparaged the Lexington group; but that was far from their whole purpose. The point, as Early asserted, was that "an enduring monument" to Lee ought to be in Richmond, "accessible to all his boys." Early's audience was highly sensitive to that theme; support for a Richmond monument went well beyond a mere response to a challenge from a rival group. As Dabney Maury put it in a letter to Early, the men at the meeting were heeding "the general and strong wish of the people of Virginia—which was so beautifully expressed by one of [Lee's] old soldiers recently, 'that when the grand reveille shall sound, he will be found in the midst of his boys, whom he loved so well.' "[34]

One notable orator, John B. Gordon of Georgia, Jubal's old subordinate and adversary, also urged that Lee's remains be brought to Richmond, because that was the only fit resting place for such a great leader. In defining Lee's greatness, Gordon struck the chord that probably stirred the gathering more than any other. It became an essential theme—the concept of Lee's invincibility: "Lee was never really beaten," Gordon stated. "Lee could not be beaten. Overpowered, foiled in his efforts, he might be, but never defeated."[35]

One obstacle to the new association's aims—one that Early certainly knew about—was the Lee family. William Allan had written to Jubal from Lexington on October 25 that "there is no probability of [Lee's] remains being removed from here." Mrs. Lee did not want that. Allan acknowledged that there might be a possibility of reinterring the body in Richmond at some point in the future, but that in any case "a fit mausoleum should here be made."[36]

Early ignored Allan's letter, though—perhaps because—it contained much praise of the general's steadfastness "against and amidst the trials of the last five years." Allan's tone was too fawning ("Alas, there are not many like yourself who have held out . . ."). His letter offered a further irritant in suggesting that the Richmond monument plans were "merely local steps."

That anything taking place in Richmond, the heart and hub of the Confederacy, could have been categorized as "merely local" doubtless struck Jubal as ludicrous. But as he must have known, Richmond was headquarters for yet another memorial group founded and dominated by the same kinds of patrician women who had guarded the lobby of the Secession Convention at Mechanics Hall in 1861. The Ladies' Lee Monument Association, led by a fierce spinster named Sarah Randolph, wanted Lee's body buried in Hollywood Cemetery, his grave to be adorned with a large bronze sculpture of the general on horseback. The women's group, established the week before Early's Lee Monument Association was organized, competed for contributions with it and the Lexington organization; the ladies held themselves aloof until 1886, refusing to join forces with anyone. Finally, Fitz Lee, then governor, persuaded the women to hand their collections ($15,602.17) over to Early's association, which by that time had been incorporated into the state government and was under Lee's direct control. The women's intransigence had been largely provoked by Early, who "found them a rather hardheaded set," and refused to have anything to do with them— even when they assured him his "soldiers'" organization would get any money they collected.[37]

The women, though few in number, worked hard and effectively, displaying a gift for raising funds that the men might have envied. Quickly establishing a network with similar women's groups throughout the South, they called for a regional canvass on November 27, 1870, soliciting the participation of the South's churches, "Christian or Hebrew," as local fund drive centers. It worked; the canvass pulled in $3,000 just from Savannah, Georgia. Smelling blood, the ladies hired an agent to travel through the region and promote their memorial project, a course of action that raised $16,000.[38]

Early's group retaliated by hiring its own agent (Bradley Johnson even suggested that Jubal himself, with his "gifts of gab," should be the agent). Paid and unpaid, emissaries of the competing memorial groups were soon scouring the South for members and contributions. Though Early himself tried—particularly in a newspaper card dated February 17, 1871—to distance himself publicly from all antagonism between contending memorial groups, he made no bones about his feelings in private. Jubal wanted peace, but only on his terms. Writing to Pendleton, who had turned down an invitation to serve on the Richmond association's executive committee, Early warned him he was making a mistake. It was not, Jubal reminded Pendleton, the memory of Lee as president of Washington College that needed to be preserved, but as "the great, good and glorious commander of the Confederate Armies, and the pure and unselfish patriot."[39]

Despite peace-making efforts on both sides, rivalry between the two organizations broke out in open warfare in the course of 1871, with accusations and other verbal unpleasantness flying like minié balls. Officials at Washington and Lee University (as it was now called) were criticized in the newspapers of eastern Virginia for battening on the memory of Lee. The Richmond monument people charged the Lexington association with callousness in using Mary Lee's grief to extort her agreement to her husband's burial there. The Lexington men fired back, accusing the Lee Monument Association of "malignant and scandalous behavior," particularly in pestering Mrs. Lee about moving the body to Richmond; this had caused her such "pain and annoyance," it was said, that she had requested an end to these importunings. The Richmond forces contended, for their part, that they had offered the widow a plot in Hollywood Cemetery and that she had accepted.[40]

The quarrel eventually subsided into a corrosive stalemate, which Early correctly regarded as a growing obstacle in his own path. This impasse abated late in 1871 when William Preston Johnston sent Early an invitation to speak at Lexington on the occasion of General Lee's birthday. Early accepted the invitation, and in doing so also embraced the compromise that Johnston had offered in November 1870: a memorial tomb for Lee in Lexington, and a commemorative statue in Richmond.[41]

« ON JANUARY 19, 1872, in the chapel of Washington and Lee University, Early delivered another pivotal address. This speech established a virtual Lee cult, and affirmed Early's own leadership of it. The theme of the speech was the portrayal of Lee as "the head and foot, the very life and soul of his army" and of that army as unsurpassed in history. The speech was constructed chronologically, touching on such campaigns as the Peninsula, where numerical odds running heavily against the South had not prevented Lee from defeating the Northern behemoth.[42]

But Early's principal example in making this case was the Wilderness–Spotsylvania–Cold Harbor campaign of 1864, which Jubal credited Lee with having won. Lee, said Early, displayed such "boldness and fertility" in this campaign that, given the ANV's slender numbers, "it appears like a romance," incredible. As to that, Early said, "General Lee, himself, was aware" of the problem of credibility. He had written "a letter to me, during the winter of 1865–6" that said: "It will be difficult to get the world to understand the odds against which we fought."[43]

Through the 1864 campaign, Grant—in Early's view—acted the incompetent role that would have doomed him in the absence of the North's wealth in "numbers, steam-power, railroads, mechanism and all the resources of physical science." After Cold Harbor, Early stated, Grant—though reinforced by troops from Maj. Gen. Benjamin Butler's force—had been "compelled to take refuge on the south side of the James, at a point to which he could have gone by water . . . without loss of a man. His original plan of the campaign was thus completely thwarted."[44]

In this summary, Jubal ignored the fact that Grant was determined to destroy Lee's army, no matter what the cost. But whether or not Lee had "thwarted" Grant's campaign plan, the death of the Confederacy had to be acknowledged. In doing so, Early laid heavy emphasis on Grant's brute strength. The speaker recalled what Lee had said to him as Grant was preparing to cross the James: "We must destroy this army of Grant's before he gets to James River. If he gets there, it will be a siege, and then it will be a mere question of time." That meant, Early explained, that Lee knew that the Federals' crossing of the James would put them beyond the offensive reach of the ANV and enable them, by a process of attrition, to wear down the "gradually diminishing nerve and sinew of the Confederate soldiers." [45]

Thus even the outcome at Appomattox, Early continued, was a demonstration of Lee's "superiority over his antagonist, in all the qualities of a great captain, and of the Confederate soldier over the Northern. . . . General Lee had not been conquered in battle, but surrendered because he had no longer an army with which to give battle." [46]

‹‹ AT GETTYSBURG, it was James Longstreet who had failed, as Early put it to his listeners. In the Lexington speech, this charge, leveled for the first time in public, was made with little of the stridency it would acquire later on. To begin with, Jubal disposed, with suave dispatch, of the problem of Ewell's hesitancy, abetted by Jubal, to attack Cemetery Hill on the morning of July 2. Early recounted the discussion with Lee, Ewell, and Rodes as if it had been obvious from the outset that such an assault by the 2d Corps was scarcely worth considering, at least as the ANV's principal effort. Then he had Lee deciding to make the attack from "our right on the enemy's left," and leaving "us for the purpose of ordering up Longstreet's corps in time to begin the attack at dawn the next morning." [47]

But not until 4:00 P.M. the next day, Early said, was that corps ready to move on the attack. Between daylight and four o'clock in the afternoon, Early noted, Meade had concentrated his whole army. Even so, the objectives of Longstreet's assault had not been occupied by Federals until late afternoon: "Round Top Hill, which commanded the enemy's position, could have been taken in the morning without a struggle." [48]

Longstreet had let Lee down, Early averred, by second-guessing his orders. This "miscarriage" had occurred not only on July 2, Early stated, but also on the 3d, when Pickett's charge had not been "properly" supported "according to the plan and orders of the commanding general. You must recollect," Early lectured his audience, "that a commanding general cannot do the actual marching and fighting of his army. These must necessarily be entrusted to his subordinates, and any hesitation, delay or miscarriage in the execution of his orders, may defeat the best devised schemes." [49]

That was the basic line: success evaded Lee at Gettysburg (though it was far from a defeat); the fault was Longstreet's, who, by not promptly and enthusiastically executing Lee's orders, had betrayed him and the South. Early left the impression, of course, that Lee had actually ordered Longstreet to attack at dawn on the 2d.

Lee gave no such order. But the impression that he did so was reinforced, in a Lee birthday speech in 1873, by William Pendleton, who claimed to have heard of the order from Lee himself. This canard was repudiated by former Lee staff officers like Venable and Charles Marshall who were charter members of the Lee cult and no admirers of Longstreet. Pursued by Northern publishers who sniffed a good story, Pendleton refused their overtures; but he permitted the "dawn order" fabrication to be attributed to him in the *Southern Magazine* in 1874. Once in print, Lee's issuance of such an order came to be widely credited. [50]

Longstreet did not immediately respond. But he would not suffer such calumnies forever in silence. The vendetta between him and his detractors that was to ensue would resound cacophonously down the decades, dwarfing but not obscuring other feuds waged by the Lee cult, led by Early, against men seen to be critics of Lee.

<< THE STRUGGLE to cut down the hero's presumed enemies seems to have required more effort than positive promotion of the hero's image. Nevertheless, this shining perception of Lee became established in the early '70s, and changed little thereafter until the turn of the century, when Lee's status as a hero rose from the regional to the national level.

The imprinting of the cult-sponsored image was boosted by an "authorized" account of Lee's life. Jubal Early had declined, probably on tactical grounds, to contribute to the "Lee Memorial Volume" that represented one of the Lexington Association's three principal goals. The "Memorial Volume," in fact, languished—largely because Charles

Marshall, assigned to write a centerpiece summary of General Lee's military career, never managed to finish it.

In this frustrating situation, J. William Jones, the Lexington Baptist minister who was to become editor of the *Southern Historical Society Papers*, saw an opportunity; he approached the Lee family, and persuaded them to allow him access to family archives and to the unfinished manuscript of the "Memorial Volume." Using these materials, Jones wrote and brought out *Personal Reminiscences, Anecdotes and Letters of General Robert E. Lee* in 1874. Despite its fulsome tone and its unrelieved emphasis on the domestic and military virtues of its hero, this influential biography was to become a major source for later Lee biographers.[51]

Other writers following Jones's lead found that people wanted to read about Lee, for the most part because, as Connelly rightly points out, the general was a genuine paragon. Lee himself would not have agreed; he was afflicted with feelings of failure and personal unworthiness. The world, however, saw him differently. Not only did he have the proper antecedents to appeal to a snobbish, patriotic age. Not only was he capable, unlike most mortals, of getting through West Point without a single demerit. He was also truly wide and deep of character, and—despite a furious temper and a certain hot-blooded relish for battle that led him sometimes to squander lives—a man of large spirit and high mind capable of great kindness, tolerance, and fidelity. He was also a military chief of outstanding ability, whose capacity to lead men was matched by his talent for reading opponents' intentions, taking risks, and seizing an effective initiative. He was, moreover, correctly seen as such by his professional peers, his men, and his adversaries.

Not in need of a publicity campaign to ensure his fame and generate admiration, he got one anyway. Its product was an edifice of myth built on the foundation of truth. In time, the image became an icon. Shaping it and influenced by it, men spoke of Lee as "the noblest type of manhood that this age has produced," "a public officer without vices, a private citizen without wrong." To one old staff officer, the general was "so simple as might become the little children 'of whom is the kingdom of heaven.'"[52]

Thus the religion of the Lost Cause, crystallized in the person of

Lee, enabled many Southerners to absorb the fact that what they saw as a just cause, led by an immaculate hero, had failed. Without Lee, it might not have been possible; he was compared to Christ, who sacrificed himself for his followers, his Gethsemane the decision to fight for Virginia, his Calvary Appomattox. Even so, the outcome—like so much else in the situation—was paradoxical. The true Lee was not, as his biographer Clifford Dowdey remarks, at all mythical. Yet he was an extraordinary man, imbued to an outstanding degree with the virtues most valued in his day. Thus he stood as a beacon, more than life-size. "In living by an ideal under God," Dowdey writes, "his being constituted a wholeness that permitted him to transcend all the hostilities and mutations of his time and circumstances. . . . In his service as a public example, the symbol Lee provided for [the South's] fallen civilization was of an ideal larger and purer than life—literally the 'matchless Lee'—and he related as a god to the mythology that grew around the Lost Cause." [53]

<< THE FIRST FRUITS of the Lee memorial movement were harvested in Lexington, on June 28, 1883. That was the day that witnessed the unveiling of the recumbent statue by the Virginian sculptor Edward V. Valentine that commemorates Lee in the Memorial Chapel at Washington and Lee University. Though Early, after the 1872 Lee birthday speech, had ceded a degree of precedence to the Lexington effort, he got something important in return; it was he who was chosen to preside over the unveiling.

In pursuing success for his own principal concern, the Richmond monument, General Early was untiring. By the end of 1872, the Lee Monument Association had achieved a moderate degree of success, largely by developing a sophisticated organization. Techniques were continually refined, until by 1876, Col. S. Bassett French, the association's longtime secretary, was developing plans "to canvass every house in every town in the Southern States," using carefully compiled lists of prominent citizens and urging mayors to appoint local canvassers in each of the cities' neighborhoods. [54]

The Lexington contingent's efforts did not reach so far. Pendleton undertook a fundraising tour of the South. Another project, considered by many to be in doubtful taste, was a life-size steel engraving of General Lee manufactured by the Cincinnati firm of Bostwick & Winter, offered as a premium to potential donors.[55]

In general, the South's impoverishment made raising funds very difficult. The files of the Lee Monument Association contain bundles of tallies from around Virginia of contributions from schoolchildren, including those attending the newly fledged public schools. These contributions are noted as individual gifts of nickels, dimes, and quarters, and were most welcome. Also welcome was the contribution (not specified) of a Boston lady who said she was sending it to improve intersectional relations.[56]

Early himself worked as hard as anyone, canvassing his own family and friends in Lynchburg, lining up people to do the same for their circles, and contributing his own money. A tally sheet dated Lynchburg, January 19, 1876, lists some 140 names, with Jubal Early and family members heading the list; most of the family gave $5 each, though some could manage only $1. Robert Early, Jubal's brother, even contributed $5 for each of his two sons killed in the war: Robert, who fell at the Wilderness, and Willie, slain at Five Forks (April 1, 1865). Jubal's own contribution was $10, the largest individual donation. The smallest was $1. The total collected was $313.[57]

To raise the necessary thousands for a large equestrian statue, this kind of effort had to be repeated endlessly around the region—and it was. Though Early, crying bad taste, disapproved, Colonel French and others organized subscription balls at Greenbrier White Sulphur Springs to raise money. At least one of these balls involved a beauty contest, in which guests were invited to choose (at ten cents per vote) a "Queen of Love and Beauty" and six "Ladies of Honor." "Vote Early! Vote Often!" the flyer exhorted its readers. "And Repeat Until Your Devotion Be Crowned With Victory!" This sort of thing made Jubal wrinkle his nose, but he did not hesitate to buy Louisiana lottery tickets in the name of the Monument Association; two fractional tickets for one-twentieth of "such prize as may be drawn" on Tuesday, August 13, 1889, are in the files. As of December 1880, the books recorded total receipts of $20,575.27.[58]

« FIFTEEN YEARS yawn between the Lynchburg tally and the lottery drawing date (on which there was obviously no payoff). The slow progress of the fundraising—and of other aspects of the monument project—is largely attributable to divisiveness in general and squabbling between the Ladies' Monument Association and Early's group in particular. Work on a design for the monument was held up from the late '70s to the mid-'80s by the women's jealous sequestration of their collected funds, which came to more than any other group had amassed, and their refusal to approve any of the models submitted by aspirant sculptors.[59]

In the mid-'80s, the Ladies' Monument Association was persuaded to throw in with the Early group, which by that time was essentially managed by the governor, Fitz Lee. But controversy refused to subside altogether. Early now favored the selection of Edward Valentine, the Virginian sculptor who had executed the recumbent Lee statue in Lexington. Under Sarah Randolph's influence, the ladies—as the real financial power—preferred a French artist named Antonin Mercié.

To Jubal, it was blasphemy to choose a foreigner when a Virginian, experienced in Lee portraiture and eager to pay further and greater tribute to the hero, was available. Mercié's model was, in addition, wholly unacceptable to Early, who thought the design mounted Lee on "a 'bob-tail horse' looking like an English jockey." If such a thing were unveiled, he said, he was prepared to mobilize veterans of the 2d Corps and demolish it.[60]

Miss Randolph prevailed. She insisted that "genius is cosmopolitan, and while the Virginia sculptors must have every possible chance for winning the prize they should only expect to do so by superiority of merit and not by the accident of place of birth."[61]

It now appeared that the goal was finally in sight. The statue's cornerstone was laid in 1887. On December 1, 1888, Governor Lee wrote Early that the Mercié contract was signed and sealed, and the money for it set aside. A bid for erecting the pedestal had come in and had been accepted at $41,000, but there was only $31,000 in the bank. Could Early see about raising about $12,000 to cover the balance and take care of incidentals and contingencies? "You have already been very very generous, and I have not 'brass' enough—though credited with a good supply—to ask you for more." Perhaps Early could suggest some names of men who could be leaned on for $100 apiece.[62]

Early raised the money. But one more serious obstacle remained. It shortly came to Jubal's attention that the stone that was to face the pedestal had been quarried in Maine! Somehow, Jubal fussed, that would have to be remedied; putting Yankee stone on the base of a statue of Robert E. Lee would simply desecrate it.

"Hold your horses," wrote the governor, "and keep them under the hill, so that you won't get any of them killed." What had happened was easily explained. James Netherwood, the contractor who won the job, was prevented, through the machinations of disgruntled competitors, from buying locally quarried granite. Undeterred, Netherwood ordered stone from a Maine quarry. In any case, the governor wrote, "the main part, probably nineteen twentieths of the stone used in the pedestal is Virginia granite, and only this facing stone is made from stone from abroad. So be as quiet as you can. To a Virginian, the contract was awarded, and the association saves over ten thousand dollars by it. Send us on another ten thousand, and I won't tell anyone how high you have been rearing."[63]

Early subsided. His fundraising activity even included a peace offering to the ladies in the form of a $200 contribution from him directly to them. They were duly grateful, noting that it was "a great happiness . . . to know what a firm friend the defenders, living and dead, of the 'Lost Cause' have in yourself. To that cause you have given the fullest and most perfect allegiance—the fealty of sword, of pen and purse."[64]

On May 29, Mercié's statue was unveiled in ceremonies attended by a crowd estimated at between 100,000 and 150,000 people. It was the biggest Confederate celebration to date, with perhaps 15 times as large an assemblage as had witnessed the earlier unveilings of Lee monuments in Lexington and even in New Orleans. Fitz Lee stepped off at the head of a parade featuring 15,000 marchers and stretching four miles. At the monument site, where the parade wound up, Jubal Early presided, with Dabney Maury, William Payne, J. William Jones, Charles Colcock Jones, John Gordon, John Daniel, and other stalwarts in attendance. Gen. Joseph E. Johnston gravely unveiled the statue as salutes were fired from cannons and muskets.

It is tempting to wonder how much Early had to say about the choice of the speaker on this occasion. He was Archer Anderson—certainly suspect in Jubal's eyes as an industrialist (treasurer of Richmond's Tredegar Iron Works), and member of the Lee Camp, the Virginia arm of the new, more conciliatory United Confederate Veterans' movement that was supplanting the AANV.

Still, the general could hardly have quarreled with the content of Anderson's address. Outlining Lee's war career, the speech dwelt on his army's constant numerical inferiority, and concluded: "Let this monument, then, teach to generations yet unborn these lessons of life! Let it stand, not as a record of civil strife, but as a perpetual protest against whatever is low and sordid in our public and private objects! . . . Let it stand as a great public act of thanksgiving and praise, for that it pleased Almighty God to bestow upon these Southern States a man so formed to reflect His attributes of power, majesty and goodness!" [65]

< 453 >

"Tom-Tom Warfare"

"*I* DO NOT FEEL," Early said in his January 1872 speech in Lexington, "that it is necessary or just to attempt to build up the reputation of the Army of Northern Virginia, or its Commander, at the expense of our comrades who battled so gloriously and vigorously on other fields for the same just and holy cause."[1]

Yet Early used that same speech to launch the attack on Lee's great lieutenant, James Longstreet, an ANV corps commander who had fought on most of the same fields. In a characteristic reaction, Longstreet ignored this opening volley and others that followed it. But when the Georgian did reply, he plunged himself into an acrid, losing feud with Early and his adherents that was to rob Longstreet of his laurels as an authentic Southern hero—and Lee confidant—and portray him as a virtual traitor to the Confederate cause.

Though it was to be the chief vendetta of this kind, it was not the only one. Longstreet was principally guilty in Early's eyes of political apostasy, having joined the Republicans. William Mahone was similarly blameworthy, as well as being tainted by his money-grubbing business interests; but it was in Jubal's role as guardian of the truth about the war that he eventually humiliated Little Billy, who had the temerity to attack Early as a soldier. Early ended by forcing Mahone to choose between backing down or challenging him to a duel. In these encounters, Early generally displayed himself at his most contentious, self-serving, vindictive, and effective; he was not to be deflected, silenced, or overcome.

‹‹ THE UNFOLDING of the Longstreet imbroglio was a classic drama in which his own qualities of pride, honesty, logic, conceit, and stubbornness contributed to his downfall. Old Pete himself prepared the ground on which he was to be sacrificed.

In the late 1860s, Longstreet was living and working as a cotton factor in New Orleans. He had been evolving a postwar political philosophy that stressed acquiescence in the style of Robert E. Lee, whom he also emulated in seeking a Federal pardon. Longstreet's new attitude included acceptance of the Reconstruction Acts as the quickest and surest way back to some approximation of the status quo antebellum; the logical culmination of his political evolution was membership in the Republican Party, which he joined in 1869. "The war," he wrote, "was made upon Republican issues, and it seems to me fair and just that the settlement should be made accordingly."

One aspect of this view, expressed privately, was Longstreet's belief that black suffrage was inevitable, and that Southerners could control this development more effectively as Republicans than in any other way. Control was important, Longstreet was certain, because too much power in the hands of blacks could threaten whites.[2]

The reaction of many Southerners to Longstreet's new party alignment was loud and angry. Not only were they horrified by his embrace of the enemy's abolitionist political soul, but they were sure that Longstreet had turned coat in order to profit materially. At the same time, because he did not express it publicly, these critics did not grasp his white-supremacist rationale for becoming a Republican. Without that ingredient, his attitude seemed blatantly Radical and pro-black.[3]

Longstreet's political activities and attitudes created an ideal atmosphere for the members of the Lee cult to write personal letters and newspaper cards spreading and refining the damaging material about Longstreet's military career that had been introduced in speeches by Early and William Pendleton. Again, Longstreet helped his enemies, writing an injudicious letter to the press in which he implied that he, Longstreet, had done much of Lee's wartime thinking for him, and therefore deserved much credit for Lee's victories. Among many others, this particularly outraged former members of Lee's staff who, though not fervent Longstreet supporters, had hitherto been willing to refute William Pendleton's fabrication of the "dawn order."[4]

One correspondent, congratulating Early on the anti-Longstreet campaign, remarked, "What little reputation Longstreet had as a Confederate general is gone forever." In this assessment, the writer was a bit premature. But what he went on to say sounded the essential thematic note: "You could not have done less, with a due regard to the truth of history, and above all, with a proper reverence for our great leader."[5]

« THE PACE now quickened, as the Northern press smelled a running intramural Southern controversy in which one party was already becoming well known in the North for his pro-Republican views. In late 1877 and early 1878, Longstreet struck back at Lee's adherents in articles in the Philadelphia *Weekly Times*. He enumerated Lee's mistakes in the 1863 Pennsylvania campaign and at Gettysburg, and criticized Stuart, Ewell, and Early for their roles in that battle. These articles, later reprinted in an anthology entitled *Annals of the War Written by Leading Participants North and South*, gained a wide audience.[6]

Lee's main error at Gettysburg, Longstreet wrote, was in not accepting his advice to outmaneuver Meade—sliding around the Union commander's left flank to get between him and Washington—rather than attacking him. Moreover, Longstreet claimed, Lee had admitted his mistake. When after the battle Lee said, "It's all my fault," he was, according to Longstreet, referring directly to his failure to heed Longstreet's counsel. At the same time, Longstreet loftily excused Lee's errors as the product "of a great mind disturbed by unparalleled conditions."[7]

Longstreet never doubted that he would be believed. He was the senior in rank of the Confederate survivors of Gettysburg, and except for Lee, the officer most closely involved with directing the critical events of the battle's second and third days. In some respects, his presentation was unassailable; judicious quotation from letters received from Lee's staff officers blew the sunrise order myth to shreds. Not surprisingly, the reaction of many, including Gen. Joseph E. Johnston, was positive.[8]

The trouble was, as Longstreet utterly failed to see, that Lee's image had already acquired the lineaments of sainthood. To begin with, it was no longer possible to say that he had made any mistakes whatever. Still, perhaps even Old Pete, draped though he was in the shroud of black Republicanism, would have been forgiven if, in discussing Lee's errors, he had used a more worshipful, adulatory tone.[9]

But Longstreet was angry—partly at the old Confederates who had been carping these ten years past at his politics, partly at Lee himself for the fact that he had been canonized. Finally, in a blasphemous fit of conceit, Longstreet made himself Lee's equal. Longstreet claimed that he had bargained with the commander over strategy: he had only agreed to join the Pennsylvania campaign when Lee went along with Longstreet's grand plan, which was calculated to force Meade to attack the ANV—and not the other way around. Longstreet thereby implied that Lee, in attacking the Army of the Potomac, had broken a contract.[10]

<< THUS DID James Longstreet insert his head into the cannon's mouth. The order to fire only awaited a suitable opportunity. This soon materialized, offered by an alien hand. In 1875 and 1877, Louis-Philippe-Albert d'Orléans, comte de Paris, had issued English translations of the first two volumes in his projected multivolume Civil War history. Early and the Virginians had been unfavorably impressed; the count, who had served on McClellan's staff in 1862, found fault with Lee's handling of the Seven Days' and the 1862 Maryland campaigns. Reacting to Early's blunt criticism, the French historian hastened to seek the advice and assistance of the influential Southern Historical Society. He submitted a sort of outline, with some questions, to J. William Jones, editor of the *SHSP*. Reaction and comments, the count apparently hoped, would elicit material for his next volume, which would deal with the Gettysburg campaign. In this overture from France, Early and Jones quickly saw the means of discharging their anti-Longstreet bombshell.

As a Frenchman, the comte de Paris presumably had no North-South ax to grind. In responding to his outline—which was critical of Lee—Early and company could lay out their version of the Pennsylvania campaign in exquisite detail, but without any appearance of bias. In furnishing the disinterested foreigner with correct information, they could be seen as merely doing their evenhanded duty as historians.

« AFTER DUE consultation with Early, Jones arranged for the writing of several articles—based on the Frenchman's propositions—by leaders of the Lee cult, including Fitz Lee, William Allan, and Walter Taylor. Early led off in the August 1877 issue of the *SHSP*, defending the conduct of Stuart, Ewell, and himself at Gettysburg, and assigning the full blame for failure there to Longstreet. The others backed him up.

At the end of his article, Early showed his consummate skill as a polemicist by dimming the spotlight on his, Ewell's, and Stuart's parts in the battle—all doubtful—in order to throw harsh and unflattering illumination on Longstreet's role.[11]

Early's main article had gone to the printer before the publication of Longstreet's first Philadelphia *Times* piece in the issue of November 3, 1877. In a stop-press supplement to his *SHSP* article, Early counterattacked, sounding a cruel note. He was evidently aware that Longstreet's Wilderness wound made writing difficult and painful, and that this forced him to seek help from literary professionals who could take his rough drafts and put them into publishable shape. The Philadelphia *Times* had supplied such assistance, without which the paper would have had trouble printing Longstreet's articles.

In his reaction to the first of these, Early contrived to make this highly understandable circumstance somehow suspect. "That article," he asserted, "is not from General Longstreet's own pen, as is very apparent to those who are familiar with his style of writing." In support of his assertion, Early also cited "assurance from a quarter that leaves no doubt on the subject." Since Jubal did not mention Longstreet's handicap, many readers could hardly avoid the inference that there was something at least faintly reprehensible—a hint of laziness, perhaps—in Longstreet's resort to literary assistance. Whatever the reason for it, Early went on, the "data and material for the article were . . . furnished by [Longstreet]," which made him responsible for "its statements and utterances." Sloth—or perhaps something more serious?— did not cancel any obligation to tell the truth, Early implied.[12]

Whatever the shortcomings of Longstreet's prose, Early and Jones were not content with merely rebutting its content. They turned his own weapons on Longstreet with a master stroke that fairly gleamed with its appearance of fairness and impartiality: indulging the reader who had not yet seen the Philadelphia *Times*, they reprinted Longstreet's first article, verbatim, in the *SHSP*. Longstreet does not appear to have been consulted about this use of his material, but its appearance in the *Papers* lent further credence to the evenhanded historiographical posture of the Southern Historical Society. "For while we are, of course, under no obligation," wrote editor Jones, "*to copy what is published elsewhere* [italics in original], we are desirous of getting at the whole truth, and wish to give every party a fair hearing." What the *SHSP*'s readers got was the unalloyed Longstreet style, with all its truculence and power to alienate—and its "errors," now so apparent to readers carefully tutored in spotting them. The writer was thus convicted by the words of his own laboriously driven pen.[13]

Condemned Longstreet might be. But he was not finished. Reloading, he discharged another fusillade in the February 24, 1878 issue of the Philadelphia *Times*. Stung by Early's assault on his writing methods, he referred to "the ill-natured and splenetic attacks" of "certain wordy soldiers," and went on to say:

> Without proceeding directly against the essential parts of my narrative, they raise a clamor of objection and denial. One of the chief elements of this tom-tom warfare is found in the fact that, owing to wounds received in the honorable service of my country, which have virtually paralyzed my right arm and made it impossible for me to write, save under great pain and constraint, I have been compelled to accept the services of a professional writer. . . . Upon such trifling casuals as this do my enemies propose to build their histories and amend mine. The attempt is at once pitiful and disgraceful.[14]

Early taunted Longstreet in print for such "unmanly" references to his wound. Meanwhile, in the pages of the *SHSP*, the campaign against the Georgian continued through October 1878. The April issue carried a piece by Fitz Lee embodying a letter to him from Maryland's former governor John Lee Carroll, who quoted General Lee to the effect that Gettysburg would have been won if Longstreet had obeyed the orders given him, and had made the attack early rather than late. (Fitz Lee had kept the letter, with its forever unconfirmed imputation, for two years until, as he wrote Early in 1876, Longstreet should come "out with [his] long-promised account of battle of G.")[15]

A reprint of Longstreet's second Philadelphia *Times* article appeared in June, and was duly torn to pieces in the same issue by Early. Longstreet's supposedly willful insubordination on July 2, 1863, was the subject of a polemic by Cadmus Wilcox in the September number. In October, William C. Oates, an Alabama regimental commander, lodged similar accusations.[16]

After 1878, the feud moved off the pages of the *SHSP*. During the '80s, Longstreet wrote four articles for the *Century* magazine (eventually incorporated in the famous anthology *Battles and Leaders of the Civil War*). Since Old Pete never abandoned his egoistic, critical tone, these articles only helped to complete the destruction of his reputation among the numerous readers by now educated to despise him. Clarence Buel and Robert Johnson, the series editors, solicited a rebuttal from Early, who declined—though he permitted the reprinting of previous writings.[17]

It was not that Jubal was tired of smiting Longstreet; as late as 1890, he was writing to the Richmond *State*, calling the Georgian a "renegade" and a "viper," among other things. But amid his satisfaction in expressing his hatred for a man who had attacked him and criticized Lee, Early must have been aware that it had all been said as effectively as possible in the *SHSP*'s so-called "Gettysburg series" of 1877 and '78.

That campaign to destroy a man's name was one of the most extraordinary and cynical manipulations of history in the annals of American publishing. The hand that fine-tuned the campaign was that of a clever lawyer as well as a master editor and writer. Jubal acted the prosecutor, judge, and jury: his weapons were the number and diversity of witnesses (the *SHSP* articles' authors); the defendant implicating himself on the stand (the use of Longstreet's own writings, albeit unauthorized); the marshaling of evidence (the detailed tracking of events in the Gettysburg battle, meticulously accurate in many important respects, and thus the more credible). The total presentation adds up to a carefully contrived tissue of falsehood all the more devastating for its mimicry of justice and fairness. Abetted by Longstreet's own stubborn refusal to protect himself effectively—for that matter, his apparent willingness to dig his own grave—Jubal's victory was almost a foregone conclusion.

The influence of the series' verdict was profound. In his tome entitled *The Rise and Fall of the Confederate Government*, published in 1881, Jefferson Davis quoted lengthy portions of William Pendleton's "sunrise order" speech of 1873. Davis directed possible questioners of Pendleton's veracity to the *SHSP* series, where the cause of the failure at Gettysburg "has been so fully discussed . . . as to relieve me from the necessity of entering into it." [18]

Writing in the *North American Review* in 1889, the highly regarded British soldier and military commentator Garnett Wolseley put his imprimatur on the Gettysburg series. For Wolseley, the *SHSP* articles were positive confirmation of Longstreet's responsibility for the great defeat. Moreover, the Englishman brought this theme to what William Garrett Piston, Longstreet's biographer, has called its "fullest development": in saying "It's all my fault," laying no blame on Longstreet, Lee did more than demonstrate his resemblance to Christ and his total allegiance to the Confederate cause. The commanding general, wrote Wolseley, feared the negative effect on army and civilian morale if he should criticize his lieutenant; thus his refusal to find fault with Longstreet actually proved the Georgian's guilt. This tortured logic, Piston notes, would have been impossible without both the prosecutorial campaign in the *SHSP* and other periodicals, and Longstreet's own self-destructive utterances. [19]

Longstreet's reputation suffered for decades—up to and beyond the Civil War centennial. At his death in 1904, the United Daughters of the Confederacy in Savannah, Georgia, disapproved the sending of flowers to Longstreet's funeral. Condolences to the general's family were withheld by formal vote of the encampment of United Confederate Veterans in Wilmington, North Carolina. (Less than 5 percent of the UCV's chapters approved resolutions paying tribute to Longstreet.) Monuments to Longstreet, the man Lee once called his "war horse," are conspicuous by their absence in a South that erected thousands of memorials to more obscure men. Fifty years after Longstreet's death, only one Georgia bridge, spanning a little-known river, honored the memory of a man on whom Lee had relied as much as any other in his army.[20]

« JUBAL LIKED to say "that I have always deplored controversies between Confederate officers in regard to . . . the late war, and have sincerely regretted having had to enter into such controversies on two or three occasions when they were forced on me by personal attacks or misrepresentations of my own conduct."[21]

This high-minded protestation belies the unalloyed relish with which Jubal conducted his feud with William Mahone. Little Billy's postwar political and business activities had, as noted, long since attracted Early's unfavorable attention. But Jubal's animus toward Little Billy grew exponentially when he saw, in the June 1870 *Historical Magazine* (published in New York State), a biographical article about Mahone. The author was Gen. J. Watts de Peyster, a Northerner; the subject was the brilliance of Mahone's Civil War career and his superiority, as a soldier, to other Confederates including Jubal Early.[22]

It would seem that de Peyster was anything but a literary or scholarly heavyweight. One informant told Early that, "according to friends," de Peyster was "an eccentric old creature with far more money than brains, who could unquestionably be called crazy if it could be established that he ever had brains enough to make a respectable crazy man. He is a member of the 'Knights of the Golden Fleece,' from which order he derives his title of Genl."[23]

Crazy or not, de Peyster was shrewd enough to insert a disclaimer high up in his article. This statement declared that everything in it had been shown to Mahone and "approved by him, as to matters he alone could decide."[24]

It was this disclaimer that put into Jubal's hands the ax with which he would proceed to chop Mahone into small pieces, although in the end Mahone proved almost supernaturally indestructible. Mahone made himself vulnerable to this dismemberment by statements in the article based on wildly inaccurate or untruthful interpretations of events. To cite one egregious example, Mahone claimed that at Spotsylvania he had captured Meade's headquarters and run the Federal general off the field.[25]

As a lawyer and historical critic, Early had no trouble exploiting this weakness. In a long letter to Mahone dated March 21, 1870, Early used de Peyster's disclaimer to establish Mahone as the article's author of record. As such, Mahone was "responsible," in Early's view, for the "very grave imputations upon other Confederate officers conveyed by the language attributed to you."

Early then drew Mahone's attention to statements "in said memoir, which affect me personally." After a passage describing Mahone's actions at Fredericksburg in December 1862, the article's text said, "We shall see that, from this time forward, it was a happy thing for the North that Mahone had to fight as hard, if not harder, against the inertion [*sic*] and incompetency of his superiors than he did against the North."

Early, having been Mahone's superior for a few days in May 1864, was outraged by this remark, although it did not name him. But Early's name did appear further along in a most negative light. In his chatty way, de Peyster told the reader that his own view of Early had been fairly positive; but in reaching it, he had been forced to rely on the "statements of others; while Mahone knew [Early] intimately, and had served under him."[26]

Plunging ahead, Mahone and de Peyster warmed to their task. "Moreover," continued the text, "Mahone's judgment was justified by the proverb, in regard to Early, at West Point: 'that although his name was Early, he was always late.' Mahone said that 'he did not like to fight under him; that Jubal was always hesitating whether to fight or not; he would ride up and down his lines, from fifteen to twenty minutes, debating whether or not to begin; whereas the battle was to be lost or won, meanwhile.'"

Early's reply bristled with disdain and lawyerly menace. "I have no disposition to complain," he wrote on March 21, "of the puerility of the very stale play upon my name, by whomsoever committed." The assertion that Mahone had known Jubal "intimately," Early went on, must have been de Peyster's, since Mahone well knew that "our acquaintance, prior to the eighth of May, 1864, when I was temporarily assigned to the command of Hill's Corps, was of the most casual and limited character." [27]

Early drew Mahone's attention to other objectionable statements in the de Peyster article. A particular point of contention involved the calamity at Rappahannock Station in November 1863. De Peyster gave Mahone credit for advising "strongly" against the building of the bridgehead, quoting Mahone's view of it as a "man-trap" and stating that it was "Early's idea." Not so, answered Jubal; the works were constructed and manned by order of General Lee. But the quotation attributed to Mahone, putting the matter of blame in his words, made Mahone responsible for it.[28]

Take these misrepresentations, Early wrote, and add them to "the direct statement in regard to my habitual conduct in action, made in language claimed to be your own." The sum total was such a serious reflection "on my conduct and judgment as a military commander, that I am sure you will be ready to acknowledge my right to inquire of you whether it is true, that the Memoir above mentioned was submitted to and approved by you before its publication, and whether the language attributed to you, therein, is yours." Laying his groundwork in this careful manner, Early begged the favor of a prompt answer.[29]

Mahone's reply, dated March 30, was brief; it must have made Jubal laugh out loud. "May I request," Mahone wrote, "the loan of the 'Historical Magazine' for June 1870, to which you refer in your letter . . . dated March 21st inst. I have never seen the Magazine." [30]

Two days later, Early sent Mahone a copy of the periodical containing the article. Two months went by. On May 25, Early received a long, rambling letter from Mahone in which he waffled and prevaricated, essentially backing away from responsibility for the statements in the article. Mahone admitted that he had seen the piece, but only in an earlier version published in the New York *Evening Mail*.

On the most sensitive issue—Early's conduct as a commander and Mahone's disinclination to serve under him—Mahone even tried to amend his words somewhat. He now avoided any reflection on Early's personal courage, describing him as "brave enough and untiring as an

officer." But the revised wording mired Mahone even deeper by calling Early "disputatious" to the point where he would argue even with
himself about the proper course of action; therefore, "delay was the
consequence at times, when the battle might be fought and won." [31]

If Mahone thought that would mollify Early, he was sadly in error. It
seems to have taken Jubal five whole days to write the devastating letter
that Little Billy received on May 31. In this very long communication,
Early gave Mahone the lie direct. He referred almost immediately to
the "very awkward dilemma" in which Mahone had placed himself.
"To escape from this dilemma," Jubal wrote, "you have resorted to the
expedient of all men who embark on a career of deception . . . and
like all such men, you have signally failed in your purpose. Your whole
answer is disingenuous and evasive." [32]

Early's principal interest in this quarrel, of course, was his fury at
Mahone for reflecting on his "uniform conduct in action." This reflection, Early declared, was not mere opinion on Mahone's part, but was
offered as a "direct statement of fact. . . . You have not responded to
the question whether you used the language quoted, but have put in
a sort of special plea, very unskillfully drawn, and which I cannot but
regard as a miserable subterfuge."

In the de Peyster article, Early concluded, Mahone was

palpably guilty of a most unsoldierly and unworthy attempt to
establish for yourself a factitious reputation upon the ruins of those
of your brother officers . . .

In the whole Memoir, I have failed to discover a solitary expression of a kind or liberal word or sentiment in regard to any of your
old comrades, from the Commanding General down, save and except General Jackson, under whom you never served, and along
with praise of him is the impudent pretense that his mantle had
fallen on you.

Great God! Stonewall Jackson and Billy Mahone! Hyperion to
a satyr!

I cannot pursue the subject further, and leave you alone in
your glory." [33]

≪ IN THE YEARS following the Civil War, the South was still the home
of the duel (legal or illegal) in North America. Personal honor remained
a potent ingredient in the relations between men. Early's letter of
May 31 had sliced into the most tender and vulnerable core of Mahone's
"very awkward dilemma" by calling him a liar and other unpleasant
names. Mahone now had a choice: either retract the statements in
the de Peyster article that Early found objectionable, thereby suffering
great loss of face; or challenge Early to a duel.

Early seems to have been supremely confident that Mahone would
not challenge him. He was right. On June 3, Mahone sent Early a note
indicating that "there could of course be but one answer" (a duel) if
Early were in possession of all the facts. But he was not. What he could
not know was that Mahone, who declared that he could not "allow myself to be forced into a quarrel," had authorized a "republication of the
memoir, with such corrections as I supposed would remove any just
ground of complaint on the part of yourself or others."

This statement must have reinforced Early's assessment of Mahone's
lack of enthusiasm for fighting. But friends of Mahone, fearing the consequences of a duel, interceded with friends of Early. Negotiations over
a period of weeks produced a framework for reconciliation: Early would
withdraw his "offensive" letter to Mahone, and Mahone would draft
an answer to Early's first letter, acknowledging Jubal's right to question
the statements in the de Peyster article; the new Mahone letter would
also disavow any intention to injure Early or anyone else. In addition,
Mahone would recognize that "injustice" had been "done yourself and
other Confederate officers, by references made to both as well as the
reflection which these references turned upon me."

This final exchange, along with a corrected version of the original
de Peyster memoir, appeared in the August 1871 issue of the *Historical
Magazine*. For the time being, the quarrel subsided.[34]

≪ NEITHER MAHONE nor Early was a man to let a sleeping dog lie.
Yet, though the hostility between the two men intensified as the years
passed, Early had no reason to revive the 1871 controversy; he had,

after all, won that round far more handily and safely than he ever could have through a duel with Mahone.

It made even less sense for Little Billy to revisit the quarrel; he was well aware that Early held onto the entire correspondence, including the May 31 letter that had been formally withdrawn in the agreement of July 1871. Nevertheless, in 1881, Mahone did choose to disinter the old feud, and even tried to breathe new life into it.

Feelings ran high in the political battles of the late '70s and early '80s, as the Funders (supported by Early) and the Readjusters (Mahone and company) fought over the state debt. During the campaign of 1881, with Mahone running for the U.S. Senate, epithets flew back and forth between Mahone and Early with increasing frequency and effect.[35]

Jubal gave a "denunciatory" speech in Richmond in the course of the campaign that questioned Mahone's devotion to the truth. It goaded Mahone into writing a card—"notable," said Early, "only for its absurdity"—that raised the temperature of the mutual vituperation to the levels of 1871. It was through an article in the *National Republican* that Mahone mentioned the old correspondence, in a context that inflated his own present importance vis-à-vis Early's. Sensing the heat, various Northern publications began referring to the ancient quarrel between the two, and their exchange of letters; some published versions of the story, according to Early, were "very erroneous."[36]

Rumors of a duel began to fly. Still sure that Mahone would not challenge him, and fed up with the direction press coverage of the controversy was taking, Early stopped fooling around. Apparently in October 1881, he published the entire correspondence, including the devastating letter of May 31, 1871.[37]

Nineteen pages long, the printed copies of the correspondence, which were sent to many newspapers, included comments by Early. His justification for publishing the entire collection of letters was, as always, his obligation to the truth. "I will say that the object of my correspondence with him was neither with a view of challenging him nor provoking a challenge from him; but was for a very different purpose, which an intelligent reader cannot fail to perceive."

Whatever the veracity of that statement, Early would have the last word in his characterization of Mahone as a coward as well as a liar. "The idea that it was my purpose in making these remarks to provoke him into a duel with me is wholly unfounded—I knew there was no danger of that." [38]

But though undoubtedly damaged, Little Billy—unlike Longstreet —had the true satisfaction of a last laugh. The Virginia legislature, apparently more impressed by Mahone's stature as a very important figure in Virginia politics than by the printing of the letters, elected him to the Senate.

« CHAPTER TWENTY-NINE »

A *Farewell Kiss*

*M*AJ. GEN. GEORGE CROOK, whom Early came to regard as perhaps more capable than any other Federal commander he had faced, visited Lynchburg in 1890, when Jubal was 73 years old. Crook made mention in his diary of sitting up late with Early over drinks. Still serving actively in the U.S. Army, Crook recorded an astringent view of the older man: "While waiting, we met Gen. Early. . . . He is much stooped and enfeebled, but as bitter and violent as an adder. He has no use for the government or the northern people. Boasts of his being unreconstructed, and that he won't accept a pardon for his rebellious offenses. He . . . is living entirely in the past. He has fought his battles so many times that he has worked himself into the belief that many of the exaggerated and some ridiculous stories he tells are true. We sat up with him until after 12 midnight, taking a hot scotch with him the last thing." [1]

Another Northern visitor about this time was Lt. Lyman W. V. Kennon—then serving on Crook's staff—who was working on a study of the 1864 Shenandoah Valley campaign. Kennon had asked Early for an interview; this was granted, and eventually occupied portions of three days in March 1889. Entries in Kennon's diary paint a sharp portrait of the general. At their first meeting, Kennon was struck by Early's tall white hat, his long white beard, and "bright eye that had something of a twinkle in it, and seemed altogether very pleasant." The lieutenant also noted the general's "habit of spitting thro' his teeth, in which he displayed a great deal of skill." When Kennon remarked on Early's neat gray suit, Jubal shot his cuff to show his shirt-sleeve buttons, on which appeared "a Confederate flag, gold with colors in enamel." [2]

In the course of their conversations, the general received the lieutenant in his bachelor digs, up one flight of stairs in a grimy brick building that reminded Kennon of a New York tenement. Admitted to Early's quarters, Kennon was shocked: "The room was so dirty, so poor that at first I was ashamed to look around. It looked like an old, neglected storeroom. A small, round table stood in the middle of the room; on it was piled old papers and letters until it was as full as it was possible to be, a sort of cone of papers. In the corner to the right was another pile of books, papers, etc. Chests and books were piled against the wall [near] the door, which led to a bedroom. This latter was dark, and I only saw the bed, which was made up, and looked clean, the only clean thing about the place."

Kennon described a bookcase bulging with some 200 volumes, mostly law books and Civil War reports. A coal fire smoldered in a fireplace; the carpet covering the floor near the hearth was "worn through, and evidently burned at some time by a coal falling on it from the fire." There were a couple of austere chairs. The only pictures were a photograph of a horse named "Old Whitey," one of Jubal's Shenandoah Valley mounts, and a portrait of Governor John Letcher, "very dusty." Kennon added: "The walls of the room were otherwise bare and dirty, cobwebs and dust around the siding." [3]

General Early apparently liked the young Yankee officer, who flattered him by asking for a photograph—a request readily granted. That afternoon, Jubal conducted the lieutenant on a tour of the Lynchburg battlefield, driving a hired horse and carriage. It was a cold March day; the general had no gloves, so Kennon took the reins on the return drive, which turned out to be "somewhat unpleasant." On the bumpy road, the carriage jounced and jolted in and out of potholes. Not helping, Jubal still grasped the whip, which he held in such a way that it kept popping the horse in the back, "making him nervous and restless." When the carriage hit a particularly bad bump, Early would "ejaculate, 'God A' Mighty,' which, by the way, was a favorite expression of his." Entering the city on the way back to the livery stable where he had hired the rig, the general "pointed out several houses in one street, saying, 'Here is where the accommodating ladies of the town live. There's one of them now, sitting in the window,' pointing to a young and pretty girl sitting on the sill of a second story window."

Kennon was later to be invited to join a gentleman (a Mr. Lyne) in a "call on the Lynchburg ladies," an offer the lieutenant "was forced to decline." This proposal was made during a liquid evening that eventually involved the general and a group of cronies, including Lyne, who gathered in a back room at the saloon of the Norvelle-Arlington Hotel. According to Kennon, "the 'fun was fast and furious,'" enlivened with much laughter, teasing and mock contention, and "good-natured badinage."

At one point General Early announced that he had had enough to drink. Kennon, perhaps emboldened by what he had consumed, suggested just one more round. The drinks were duly ordered, and all hands picked them up, including the general.

"'God A' Mighty,' said he, and the evening was just begun . . ." Among the *convives* was Col. Lawrence S. Marye, editor of the Lynchburg *Virginian*. The colonel, an ordnance officer during the war, had served temporarily on Early's staff at the Battle of Fredericksburg (his family gave its name to the heights there). Others in the party described by Kennon included Robert Yancey, a young lawyer, and an unidentified major who had served with Early in the Valley.[4]

« AS A CHILD during this period, Douglas Southall Freeman glimpsed General Early from time to time, remembering him "dimly as a glowering old man, fiercely chewing tobacco," and "notorious, our nurses would have us remember, for eating a bad little boy every morning at breakfast." Little boys naturally avoided Jubal, but as Freeman points out, their fathers did not. Not that Early was necessarily nice to them. "When he hobbled down to the Arlington Hotel in the morning," Freeman recalled, "he might snarl and swear. Veterans would listen respectfully, and never would answer back. Had he not saved the city at the time of Hunter's Raid? Was he not the embodiment of the Confederacy, . . . unparoled and unreconstructed, a Lieutenant-General in the Army of Northern Virginia?"

Robert Yancey was not a veteran—he had been too young to join

up. Yancey was to enjoy a highly successful career as a Lynchburg lawyer, winning nomination as commonwealth attorney in election after
election. The fact that he was not a Confederate veteran apparently
did not hurt him. Not only was he personally very popular, according
to Freeman, but times were changing. No longer was a Confederate
war record a major factor in political success.⁵ Still, given Early's preeminence in Lynchburg, it cannot have hurt Yancey that he was the
general's friend and drinking companion. For years the lawyer dined
out on stories about Jubal—stories that waxed ever more fanciful as
time passed and Jubal's legendary aura intensified.

One of Yancey's favorite yarns involved the building where Jubal
lived and worked when he was in Lynchburg. In 1890, during one
of his absences, this structure had suffered damage in a fire. Early's
papers had been damaged and thrown into confusion. Moreover, the
city had condemned the building, and workers had even begun to demolish it. Despite the fact that some papers and other belongings had
been removed, Early wanted to check on the condition of his remaining
things. On his return to town, he went to the building, mounted the
stairs, and sat down at his table to take stock.

All of a sudden the building collapsed. Yancey, who was mayor
of Lynchburg at the time, swiftly organized a rescue effort—though
neither he nor anyone else really thought that Jubal had survived. It
took hours to pull timber, lath, and bricks out of the wreckage, but
finally Jubal was revealed, his white campaign hat (on his head) and
his white beard blancoed to unnatural brilliance by a coating of plaster
dust. He was quite unhurt, sitting in his chair where it had remained
when the floor of his room dropped intact to the street level. Instead
of braining him, timbers had formed a protective framework over his
head and kept most of the heaviest debris off him.

As Yancey told it, when Early looked up and saw his friend in charge
of the rescue efforts, he bellowed, "Hey, Bob! Blast my hat to hell, I
didn't know you were up there, boy! Damn it, you go get me a julep."

Yancey did as he was told, returning with not just one but several
juleps. These were lowered to Jubal in a basket as the rescue workers
toiled away and finally extricated him, with at least some of the juleps
under his belt.⁶

« FOLLOWING THE destruction of his quarters, General Early moved in with his nieces at 510 Main Street, the rambling three-story house where brother Sam (dead of pneumonia in 1874) and his wife Henrian had raised the girls and John. Henrian had died early in 1890.[7]

The routine of life now comprised—besides the evenings at the bar of the Norvelle-Arlington Hotel—the frequent trips to New Orleans and a large correspondence. Jubal could work either at home or at the Lynchburg National Bank, where the management had made the directors' room available to him.[8]

Obviously, one of the most important parts of General Early's day was a trip to the post office to dispatch and pick up his mail. He usually journeyed there in a hired carriage with a driver. Some of the mail traffic, following the last Louisiana lottery drawing in December 1893, was doubtless connected with the conclusion of the company's activities in the United States and Jubal's consequent loss of his steady income. Early may have been worried about that during his visit to the post office on February 15, 1894—too preoccupied to watch where he was putting his feet as he descended from the building on the long flight of granite steps leading to the street.[9]

Half crippled by age, his old wound, and his even older arthritic affliction, he missed a step or stumbled somehow, falling and rolling all the way down to the sidewalk. His driver rushed to help him, and postal officials also hastened to his side. They got him into the building again and sat him down in the postmaster's office. The general fumed at all the to-do; when his regular physician, Dr. A. W. Terrell, arrived with a medical colleague, Jubal would not listen to advice from them. That was to be expected. But it was clear to the doctors that he had suffered a bad shock and seemed mentally as well as physically under the weather.[10]

They did persuade him to ride home in the carriage. But when he arrived, he refused to get out and go into the house, insisting on being taken back downtown. There he remained until late afternoon. Dr. Terrell was able to get a good look at his patient that evening; no bones were broken, and his bruises were not serious. But the general was in great pain throughout his back, and his speech was incoherent.

Though refusing to admit that there was anything seriously the matter, Jubal was incapable of leaving his room for two days and three nights. The third day, a Sunday, he brushed aside objections from the doctor and his relatives and ventured forth, riding the streetcar down to the bank, where he spent most of the day. He also went out the next day, returning only at 9:00 P.M.

General Early never left the house again. Sinking slowly over the next two weeks, eating only intermittently, he resisted death with diminishing vigor. Senator John Daniel came down from Washington to be by his side; other old friends—notably William Payne, Bradley Johnson, Fitz Lee, and Dabney H. Maury—came to see the patient. Telegrams and letters flooded in from all over the nation, asking how he was.

The answer: worse and worse. At 10:30 P.M. on Friday, March 2, 1894, Jubal Early died, his hand—according to the *News* of Lynchburg—clasped in John Daniel's.[11]

<< IN A four-column obituary, the *News* printed the customary summary of the general's Civil War career. The piece made almost no mention of his postwar life, though it stated that he was probably worth between $200,000 and $300,000, having received over $400,000 from the Louisiana lottery. With this money, according to the paper, the general had been generous to the "thousand calls upon him from the widows and orphans of Confederate soldiers throughout the South."[12]

The obituary writer, considering the place and time in which he was working, offered a surprisingly candid appraisal of Early as a soldier. True, the death notice makes obligatory reference to efforts by "envious comrades of General Early and rival commanders to disparage his services," and states—stretching the facts a bit—that Cedar Creek was "the sole instance in the long and illustrious career of Early of a disastrous defeat." But the writer makes no final judgment, leaving it to "come out in luminous letters in the veracious record of the Confederate Army yet to be written by the colorless and dispassionate pen of history."

The obituary's appraisal of Early as a man manages to balance candor with an acceptance that stops well short of sentimentality—which Jubal would have hated, as he would have despised any sort of "puffery." "He was a rough diamond," the obituary concludes. "Beneath an exclusive and repellent exterior, he had a warm, sympathetic heart, even as the eagle that soars with an unwinking eye nearest the sun wears beneath his wing the softest down." [13]

‹‹ JUBAL WOULD probably have liked that all right. Was it true?

Yes, as far as it went. For all its evocative imagery, the statement makes no attempt to explain the sources of Early's "exclusive and repellent" characteristics. These arose from his extreme vulnerability—that is to say, his overdeveloped regard for what other people thought of him. Early's way of dealing with his vulnerability was to deny it, and then act on his denial with every ounce of emotional energy he possessed. Those, like General Lee, who divined Jubal's insecurity (so fiercely concealed from the whole world) could command his entire loyalty.

With his gifts of intelligence and zeal, there is no telling how far Early might have gone during and after the war, if only he had been able to redirect the emotional energy he squandered in smothering every sign of his deep fear of his softer side. This expenditure generated his profound pessimism, his sense that all hope was ultimately forlorn. It produced the barren, cobwebbed ambience of his quarters and robbed his life of any substantial enjoyment other than his love for his family. In this aura he was able to relax and love others and be loved. Otherwise, his ostensibly enjoyable contact with fellow human beings was restricted, at least in his later years, to a vapid, boozy good-fellowship with men whom he could easily dominate.

Emotionally handicapped as he was, Early was nonetheless very far from undistinguished in his accomplishments, though his wartime record was marred by its finale and his postwar goals—largely achieved —had an ultimately and profoundly negative effect. Charles M. Blackford, a writer and Civil War engineer officer criticized Early for not doing "all he might have done" after the war "to cheer and sustain the people in their despondency and gloom." But Blackford gave him full marks as a military leader, making a most important point. Commenting on a speech by John Daniel about Jubal delivered late in 1894,

Blackford wrote that Early "had hard lines laid down for him, and did more within them than perhaps any other man could have done."[14]

One might qualify this statement by amending it to read "any other man available to Lee," but it is essentially true. It must also be remembered that Jefferson Davis and Lee supported Early until, almost on the eve of Appomattox, they could do so no longer without undermining their own political credibility.

It was on Lee's credibility that Early built his own postwar career. In exalting Lee and diminishing Longstreet, in flaunting the Confederate soldier as a better man than his mongrel Northern foe, Early spoke to nearly every white Southerner. A person hearing an Early speech or reading an Early article could contemplate Lee and feel the burden of defeat's shame and despair lift; Lee could not be beaten, could not have lost, and if that were true, neither could the reader or listener. Very much a part of this thought was the other major idea promoted by Early: in a fair fight (even numbers, equal resources), no enemy could have beaten the Southern fighting man. What looked like defeat was only the consequence of the fight's unfairness, and of betrayal by renegade scalawags like James Longstreet. Such ideas, like those fueling all effective propaganda, were simple; they directly addressed the tender emotions of enormous numbers of Southerners, among whom very few did not find at least a tiny region of susceptibility in their hearts. For many Americans who are still susceptible, the ideas live on.

In Early's case, of course, susceptibility was virtually all-encompassing. Like an Old Testament prophet, Jubal supported the message by his own extreme example—his "constancy" and intransigence, his unremitting hatred for Grant (even after Jefferson Davis had forgiven the Illinoisan), his refusal to be pardoned or reconstructed or to regard the North, at least in the abstract, as anything but an evil empire.[15]

Ironically, the adoption after 1900 of Lee by Northerners as a national hero—highminded, noble, an ideal American—would have irked Jubal, since it helped foster growing tendencies toward sectional reconciliation. But adding Northerners to Lee's legion of worshipers did not diminish the number or enthusiasm of Southern adherents.[16]

One result was a wave of affection for Early in the South (and even in the North) that elevated him at the end of his life to a popularity enjoyed by few other living Confederates. Regarding him as the living symbol—and substitute for—the heroes Lee and Jackson, thousands of people thought Jubal Early put the sun up.[17]

« THIS SEEMS quite extraordinary under the circumstances and with regard to his whole life. But there is no question that General Early would have been gratified had he witnessed his funeral, held in Lynchburg on March 5, 1894. Early's obsequies dramatized the loving esteem in which he was held. In Richmond, flags were lowered to half-mast; from 3:00 P.M. to 6:00 P.M., the funeral's hours, howitzer salutes were fired in Capitol Square at intervals of five minutes—a total of 36 guns.[18]

Though Early was not a pompous man, the military pomp of his funeral was impressive. The procession, forming on Church Street, included the entire corps of cadets from Virginia Military Institute with their band. Local militia units such as the Fitz Lee Cavalry Troop (35 men), the Virginia Zouaves (35 men), the Lynchburg Light Artillery Blues, and the Lynchburg Home Guard, the last led by the tattered colors of the old 11th Virginia Infantry, held prominent places in the line of parade. More than 300 Confederate veterans marched on foot and horseback, wearing gray sashes.

Behind the draped catafalque of the hearse, drawn by four splendid black horses, walked a soldier leading the general's mount, with his sword on the saddle and boots reversed in the stirrups.

The procession wound its way through the streets, which were thronged with dense crowds, as the *News* reported, standing "with bowed heads." The procession halted at St. Paul's Episcopal Church. There the prominent pews were filled with members of the general's family and with honorary pallbearers, including Generals William H. Payne of Warrenton, Dabney H. Maury of Richmond, Eppa Hunton of Warrenton, Fitz Lee of Glasgow, and Lunsford Lomax of Fauquier (four of the five were cavalry commanders!). Also close to the casket were surviving members of Early's Civil War staff, notably Maj. John Daniel, Maj. Andrew L. Pitzer, Maj. Jed Hotchkiss, Capt. William W. Old, and Maj. Mann Page.

The service was brief. The Reverend T. M. Carson, a veteran chaplain of the Valley campaign, gave the eulogy. As the *News* reported it, the minister recalled the aftermath of the Battle of Cedar Creek, when "General Early's forces were retiring before the almost countless numbers of the enemy." Carson remembered seeing Early on his horse, his head "bowed almost to the saddle." Carson thought it "one of the most pathetic and at the same time one of the most noble pictures he had seen during the war. Bent under the storm, but unconquered and unconquerable!"

En route to Spring Hill Cemetery, according to the *News*, "great crowds followed the march. All along the way the windows, balconies and sidewalks were lined with people, aggregating many thousands." [19]

The grave site, donated by the trustees of the cemetery, was on a hilltop with a view of the Blue Ridge, not far from his headquarters during the Battle of Lynchburg. John Daniel, referring to the honorary pallbearers and the other veterans, later described the "line of gray and wrinkled men, who followed his hearse" to the graveyard, "carrying a tattered flag that told its own story."

The Lynchburg Light Artillery Blues fired a 17-gun salute, echoed by the VMI cadets. A grizzled bugler sounded "Taps."

The casket lay open to the sky, in the fading light of the sun setting behind the Peaks of Otter. Before the coffin was closed and lowered into the ground, the obsequies were punctuated by an incident, not included in the burial service, that would have shocked the living Jubal into an outburst. What happened might also have soothed his troubled soul on its journey to a hereafter for which, as an unbeliever, he was resolutely unprepared. A mourner, unidentified except by Daniel as one of Jubal's "noblest and bravest followers," walked up to the casket, bent over, and planted a farewell kiss on his cold brow. [20]

« ABBREVIATIONS »

Abbreviated titles of books, dissertations, theses, and articles are used throughout the notes, as are shortened names of authors (usually just the last name). Full names and titles appear in the bibliography, which is divided into the following sections: Manuscript Sources; Books; Dissertations and Theses; and Articles, Newspapers, and Periodicals.

In the list below, the institutional abbreviations refer to manuscript sources. The book titles are given full citations in the bibliography.

CWM   College of William and Mary
Duke   Duke University
FCR   Franklin County Records, Franklin County Court
            House
FWCC   J. Wert, *From Winchester to Cedar Creek*
HSP   Historical Society of Pennsylvania
JAE   Jubal Anderson Early
LC   Library of Congress
LL   D. S. Freeman, *Lee's Lieutenants*
OR   U.S. War Department, *The War of the Rebellion:*
            A Compilation of the Official Records
OR Atlas   U.S. War Department, *Atlas to Accompany the Official*
            Records of the Union and Confederate Armies
SHC   Southern Historical Collection, University of North
            Carolina at Chapel Hill
SHSP   *Southern Historical Society Papers*
USAMHI   United States Army Military History Institute
UVA   University of Virginia
VHS   Virginia Historical Society
VSL   Virginia State Library

« NOTES »

CHAPTER ONE: *Foothills Idyll*

1. Wise, *End of an Era*, 219ff.
2. Ibid.
3. Bushong, *Old Jube*, 187; Rolle, *Confederate Exodus*, 123; Wise, *End of an Era*, 228.
4. Wise, *End of an Era*, 228.
5. Samuel S. Early, *A History of the Family*, 14; Sloane, *Early*, 1.
6. John S. Salmon, "Washington Iron Works," in Franklin County Bicentennial Commission, *Bicentennial Reflections*, 16.
7. Ruth H. Early, *Campbell County Chronicles*, 406; Bushong, *Old Jube*, 2; FCR, Deed Book No. 8.
8. Ruth H. Early, *The Family*, 107–8; "Papers Concerning General Jubal A. Early," Smith Papers, VSL.
9. Ruth H. Early, *The Family*, 107–8.
10. Joab Early to JAE, Aug. 7, 1833, JAE Papers, vol. 1, LC; Anne Carter Lee, "Farming in 18th Century Franklin County," in Franklin County Bicentennial Commission, *Bicentennial Reflections*, 14–15; Talbert et al., *Studies in the Local History of Slavery*, 3; FCR, Deed Book 20, p. 483 reflects the sale of 1,350 acres by Joab to his son Samuel for $5,000 on Oct. 23, 1848.
11. Sloane, *Early*, 2, 4, 5; Ruth H. Early, *The Family*, 121.
12. JAE, *Autobiographical Sketch*, xvii.
13. JAE Records, United States Military Academy; Bushong, *Old Jube*, 3.

CHAPTER TWO: *Soldier Apprentice*

1. Boynton, *History of West Point*, 284; Morrison, "U.S. Military Academy" (Ph.D. diss.), 3ff.
2. Ambrose, *Duty, Honor, Country*, 63.
3. Ibid., 66; Ellis and Moore, *School for Soldiers*, 37.
4. Morrison, "U. S. Military Academy" (Ph.D. diss.), 99–100, 112; Bushong, *Old Jube*, 4.

5. Bushong, *Old Jube*, 5–6; Boynton, *History of West Point*, 254–55; United States Military Academy Regulations, 1832, 28 (Regulation No. 101).

6. Morrison, "U.S. Military Academy" (Ph.D. diss.), 100.

7. Lloyd Lewis, *Sherman*, 53–54; Wingate, *Franklin County*, 112; list of contributors to Episcopal Church building fund, 1848, FCR.

8. JAE, *Autobiographical Sketch*, xxiv–xxv.

9. Morrison, "U. S. Military Academy" (Ph.D. diss.), 101; Lloyd Lewis, *Sherman*, 51–52.

10. Bushong, *Old Jube*, 6; Morrison, "U.S. Military Academy" (Ph.D. diss.), 108–9.

11. Joab Early to JAE, Aug. 7, 1833, JAE Papers, vol. 1, LC.

12. Bushong, *Old Jube*, 6; Ambrose, *Duty, Honor, Country*, 90; United States Military Academy Regulations, 1832, Appendix A; Morrison, "U.S. Military Academy" (Ph.D. diss.), 116.

13. Ambrose, *Duty, Honor, Country*, 90, 93.

14. Ibid., 91; Bushong, *Old Jube*, 7.

15. Bushong, *Old Jube*, 7; Morrison, "U.S. Military Academy" (Ph.D. diss.), 116.

16. Bushong, *Old Jube*, 7.

17. Ibid., 8; Lloyd Lewis, *Sherman*, 56; JAE, *Autobiographical Sketch*, xviii.

18. Bushong, *Old Jube*, 8; Samuel H. Early to JAE, Feb. 1, 1834, JAE Papers, vol. 1, LC.

19. Samuel H. Early to JAE, Mar. 23, 1834, JAE Papers, vol. 1, LC.

20. Samuel H. Early to JAE, June 2, 1834, JAE Papers, vol. 1, LC.

21. Bushong, *Old Jube*, 9; Ambrose, *Duty, Honor, Country*, 94.

22. Bushong, *Old Jube*, 10; "Gen. Lewis Addison Armistead," 502.

23. Ambrose, *Duty, Honor, Country*, 90, 95.

24. JAE to Joab Early, Nov. 8, 1835, JAE Papers, vol. 1, LC.

25. Bushong, *Old Jube*, 12–13.

26. Schmitt, "Interview with General Jubal A. Early," 561; Hebert, *Fighting Joe Hooker*, 20.

27. JAE, *Autobiographical Sketch*, xxiv–xxv.

28. Ibid., 14; John C. Pemberton to Anna Pemberton, Dec. 13, 1836, Pemberton Papers, Box 1, HSP.

29. Ambrose, *Duty, Honor, Country*, 90, 96.

30. Ibid., 97.

31. Ibid., 97–100, 102.

32. Bushong, *Old Jube*, 13.

33. JAE, *Autobiographical Sketch*, xviii.

34. Bratt Diary, July 31, 1837, United States Military Academy Library; United States Army Military History Research Collection, *The Volunteer Army*, viii. The introduction quotes Wellington (from Thomas Henderson, *Hints on the Medical Ex-*

amination of Recruits for the Army [Philadelphia, 1840]): "[I]t cannot be denied that in ninety-nine cases out of a hundred some idle, or irregular, or even vicious habit, is the cause of the enlistment of the volunteer."

35. Motte, *Journey into Wilderness*, 199.

36. Peters, *The Florida Wars*, 32–33, 34–35.

37. Bushong, *Old Jube*, 16.

38. Ibid., 16; Motte, *Journey into Wilderness*, 193.

39. Peters, *The Florida Wars*, 162; JAE, *Autobiographical Sketch*, xix.

40. Sloane, *Early*, 6.

41. E. G. Tapton to JAE, Jan. 22, 1838, JAE Papers, vol. 1, LC.

42. Bushong, *Old Jube*, 17; JAE, *Autobiographical Sketch*, xix–xx.

43. Bushong repeats a flowery version, appropriate to the era, of this tale of love and rejection that seems to have been current during Early's lifetime. This romance appeared in print after his death. As the story was told in the newspaper, young Lt. Early, riding on a black stallion, set forth one day into the countryside near White Sulphur Springs. On the road, he passed a carriage, bearing a young lady, that was heading for a stream crossed by a ford. The watercourse, normally a trickle, was swollen on this occasion with "mad, muddy waters" from heavy rain the night before. The carriage entered the stream, and the force of the torrent swept the horses off their feet. Early observed the unfolding calamity, "and realizing the lady's danger, buried his rowels in his horse's side and dashed into the water."

The lieutenant reached the carriage just as the water flipped it over, and the girl went under. But "a second later, she came up almost beside him. Reaching down he caught her by the skirt, and a half minute later he was holding her motionless body in his arms." With his "almost lifeless" burden, Early galloped back to the hotel. When the girl recovered and the other guests heard the story of the rescue, the young officer was the "hero of the hour, and that evening monopolized the Quaker belle's dancing list." For the remainder of a leisurely sojourn at the hotel from summer into autumn, the pair were together constantly; they parted with a promise to meet again at "the White" the following summer. But just before he was to take leave of absence to meet his sweetheart in Virginia, the mail brought the eager suitor an envelope addressed in a familiar hand. Opening it, he read an enclosed clipping with news of his beloved's marriage to another man, and realized "for the first time that she had been toying with his heart."

Tapton's letter establishes a connection between Lavinia, Early, and White Sulphur Springs. It seems clear that he met her there, and planned to meet her again. If she jilted him—as distinct from merely rejecting him—the experience was undoubtedly painful.

In any case, Early was irritated by the story, and repudiated it in its entirety. Early, *Autobiographical Sketch*, xix–xx; Bushong, *Old Jube*, 19; Lynchburg *News*, Mar. 6, Mar. 18, 1894.

CHAPTER THREE: *Military Governor, Country Lawyer*

1. Quarrels over credit and loans led to the bulk of the litigation, much of it bitterly protracted. On February 24, 1851, Joab Early—no longer even resident in Franklin—filed a deposition in a case being tried over a disputed debt of $28.58¼ allegedly owed to John W. Lumsden since November 29, 1833. Franklin County Determined Papers, VSL; Bushong, *Old Jube*, p. 19; JAE, *Autobiographical Sketch*, xxv.

2. JAE, *Autobiographical Sketch*, xxiv.

3. Bushong, *Old Jube*, 19; Sloane, *Early*, 6.

4. Sloane, *Early*, 19; Howe, *American Whigs*, 5; Simms, *Rise of the Whigs in Virginia*, 164, 165, 189.

5. *Journal of the House of Delegates of Virginia*, 48, 49, 54, 56, 59, 74, 107, 182, 208, 246, 281.

6. Samuel H. Early to JAE, Feb. 22, 1842, JAE Papers, vol. 2, LC; Sloane, *Early*, 6; J. L. Coggins to JAE, Apr. 8, 1842, JAE Papers, vol. 2, LC; JAE, *Autobiographical Sketch*, xx.

7. JAE, *Autobiographical Sketch*, xxi.

8. Franklin County Order Book, Nov. 1851, Mar. 1852, FCR.

9. Wallace, "Virginia Volunteers," 54, 55.

10. Ibid., 55; Elizabeth J. Woods to JAE, Jan. 10, 1847, JAE Papers, vol. 2, LC.

11. Wallace, "Virginia Volunteers," 55, 56; JAE to Col. John F. Hamtramck, Jan. 15, 1847 (copy), United States Army Regimental Letterbook, Virginia Regiment, Mss. 10, no. 145, VHS; Jones, "Mexican War Diary," 417.

12. Wallace, "Virginia Volunteers," 57–58.

13. Ibid., 58–59; Jones, "Mexican War Diary," 421, 423–24.

14. Hoyt, *America's Wars and Military Excursions*, 222.

15. Col. John F. Hamtramck to War Department, reporting his arrival in Mexico and status of regiment (copy), n.d., United States Army Regimental Letterbook, Virginia Regiment, VHS; Wallace, "Virginia Volunteers," 63.

16. JAE, *Autobiographical Sketch*, xxi–xxii; Strode, *Jefferson Davis*, 179.

17. JAE, *Autobiographical Sketch*, xxii; Wallace, "Virginia Volunteers," 63.

18. Schmitt, "Interview with General Jubal A. Early," 561.

19. Letter to the author, Aug. 23, 1987, from Mrs. Everett H. O'Dowd, a descendant of Moses Greer Noble, citing his obituary (Oct. 11, 1912).

20. Wallace, "Virginia Volunteers," 70–71.

21. JAE, *Autobiographical Sketch*, xxii.

22. Wallace, "Virginia Volunteers," 75. After practicing law for a while in Franklin, Sam had moved to Kanawha County (now in West Virginia) about 1844 to seek his fortune in the profitable salt-making business. While in Kanawha, Samuel in-

vented a pump, designed to prevent gas explosions, for use in salt manufacturing and oil wells. Joab, his children grown and mostly married (all but Judith and Jubal living outside Franklin County), left in 1847 to work orchards and farmland he had bought in Putnam County, also in what was to become West Virginia. His son Robert was with him in 1850, and possibly earlier. Robert moved to Lexington, Missouri, before the Civil War; Joab joined him after the war, and died there in 1870. Ruth H. Early, *The Family*, 108; Ambler, *West Virginia*, 222-23; Samuel H. Early to JAE, July 2, 1844, JAE Papers, vol. 2, LC; Franklin County Determined Papers, reel 165, Feb. 5, 1850, VSL.

23. JAE, *Autobiographical Sketch*, xxii.

24. Wallace, "Virginia Volunteers," 77.

25. Ibid.

26. Franklin County, Virginia, Census, 1860 (#653 Roll 1346), 1870 (#593 Roll 1647), FCR; Franklin County Marriage Records, Book 1, 95, 213, FCR. The children were Joseph, born 1850; Florence Annie, 1858; Robert, 1860; and Jubal L., 1864. Julia bore a fifth child, Lilly, in 1867. Lilly's father was Charles Pugh, whom Julia married in 1871. Conversation, Oct. 22, 1990, with Jean Early Dugan, great-granddaughter of Jubal and Julia, granddaughter of Joseph; Jean Early Dugan to author, Nov. 7, 1990.

27. Bushong, *Old Jube*, 24. During the late 1840s and 1850s, Early maintained a steady connection with politics and politicians. Running as a Whig, though the party was in decline across the country, Early lost in an election for delegates from Franklin County to the Virginia Constitutional Convention of 1851, which revised the state charter. In 1852, he ran for his old seat in the legislature and lost.

28. Bushong, *Old Jube*, 24; Talbert et al., *Studies in the Local History of Slavery*, 105; Franklin County Determined Papers, reel 167, VSL.

29. JAE to James Reade Clement, Sept. 8, 1859, Clement Papers (#9479), UVA.

CHAPTER FOUR: *A Shedding of Tears*

1. Atkins, "Henry A. Wise" (Master's thesis), 33, quoting Eppa Hunton, *Autobiography of Eppa Hunton* (Richmond, 1933), 13.

2. Atkins, "Henry A. Wise" (Master's thesis), 32.

3. Reese, *Proceedings* 1:438; Virginia Civil War Commission, *Chronology*, 5; JAE, *The Heritage of the South*, 89.

4. Talbert et al., *Studies in the Local History of Slavery*, 71.

5. Virginia Civil War Commission, *Chronology*, 8-9.

6. Bushong, *Old Jube*, 27; Reese, *Proceedings* 1:6-8. President James Buchanan's attorney general, Jeremiah Black, would not give an opinion asserting the right of the Federal government "to make war against one or more states, and require

the Executive to carry it on by means of force to be drawn from other states." Black recommended dumping the problem in the lap of Congress. Nevins, *Emergence* 2:347.

7. JAE, *Autobiographical Sketch*, 89; Virginia Civil War Commission, *Chronology*, 7, 9.

8. Virginia Civil War Commission, *Chronology*, 8–9.

9. Shanks, *The Secession Movement*, 158.

10. Ibid., 159–60.

11. Jeffrey, "Secessionist Party" (Master's thesis), 55; Bushong, *Old Jube*, 29.

12. Atkins, "Henry A. Wise" (Master's thesis), 33.

13. Ibid., 34; Ernst, "Movement toward Secession" (Master's thesis), 175; Shanks, *The Secession Movement*, 161–62.

14. Reese, *Proceedings* 1:103.

15. Ibid., 152–54.

16. Atkins, "Henry A. Wise" (Master's thesis), 55.

17. Ibid., 55–61; Goode, *Reminiscences*, 51–52; McPherson, *Battle Cry*, 258; Samuel McDowell Moore to James D. Davidson, Apr. 6, 1861, in Greenawalt, "Correspondence of James Dorman Davidson," 95–96.

18. Atkins, "Henry A. Wise" (Master's thesis), 59; McPherson, *Battle Cry*, 243.

19. Nevins, *Emergence* 2:391.

20. Bushong, *Old Jube*, 30; Virginia Civil War Commission, *Chronology*, 11; JAE, *Heritage*, 90; Dowdey, *Lee*, 129; Nevins, *Emergence* 2:459.

21. Reese, *Proceedings* 1:427.

22. Ibid., 428–29.

23. Ibid., 429–33.

24. Ibid., 437–38.

25. Ibid., 486–88.

26. Jeffrey, "Secessionist Party" (Master's thesis), 58–59.

27. Ibid., 62–63; Atkins, "Henry A. Wise" (Master's thesis), 71.

28. Atkins, "Henry A. Wise" (Master's thesis), 71; Jeffrey, "Secessionist Party" (Master's thesis), 63–64, 66.

29. Jeffrey, "Secessionist Party" (Master's thesis), 64, 66.

30. Virginia Civil War Commission, *Chronology*, 12; Shanks, *The Secession Movement*, 178–79, 182–90, 263; Dowdey, *Lee*, 131.

31. Reese, *Proceedings* 3:650–51.

32. Dowdey, *Lee*, 131–32.

33. Reese, *Proceedings*, 3:722–23.

34. Dowdey, *Lee*, 132–33; Reese, *Proceedings* 4:23, 24, 27.

35. Reese, *Proceedings* 3:760–61.

36. J. B. Jones, *A Rebel War Clerk's Diary*, 20; JAE, *Heritage*, 92.

37. The conspiracy encompassed a plan to overthrow the elected Convention unless it enacted a secession ordinance forthwith. If not, a group calling itself the

Spontaneous Southern Rights Assembly ("that other assemblage," as the horrified Waitman T. Willey called it) would get the job done. McGregor, *Disruption*,
172–76; Shanks, *The Secession Movement*, 203.

38. Reese, *Proceedings* 4:24; JAE, *Heritage*, 92.

39. JAE, *Autobiographical Sketch*, vii; Borey, *John Letcher of Virginia*, 112–14.

40. McGregor, *Disruption*, 178.

41. Reese, *Proceedings* 4:362.

42. McPherson, *Battle Cry*, 180.

43. John B. Gordon, *Reminiscences*, 325; Stiles, *Four Years*, 189–90. Encountering a rabid Virginian secessionist earlier in the war than the Breckinridge incident,
Early took joyful advantage of the occasion to hurl the man's views in his teeth. Jeremiah Morton, who had been at the 1861 Convention and was, according to Stiles,
as extremist a secessionist as Early was a Unionist. Morton lived near a battlefield,
where he was almost captured by Federal soldiers. Fleeing on horseback, Morton
encountered Early, who was leading troops to meet the enemy. Seeing Morton in
full flight, Early threw a line of men across the road to head off the fugitive, and
shouted, "Hold on, Morton! Are you going for our rights in the territories?" Goode,
Reminiscences, 60.

CHAPTER FIVE: *"The Fun Has Just Commenced"*

1. Squires, "Autobiography and Reminiscences," SHC; JAE, *Autobiographical Sketch*, xxvi; Haskell, "Reminiscences," 32, SHC.

2. John B. Gordon, *Reminiscences*, 317.

3. *OR* 2:500.

4. *OR* 2:883.

5. Long, *Memoirs of Robert E. Lee*, 105; Freeman, *LL* 1:701; *OR* 2:883. In his
memoirs, Col. S. Bassett French, aide to Generals Lee and Jackson, remarks that
all generals in the Confederate army, regardless of age, were called "old." French,
Centennial Tales, 29.

6. *OR* 2:806.

7. A stand of arms comprised one soldier's complete armament, including his
musket or rifle, bayonet, cartridge box, and belt. Faust, *Encyclopedia of the Civil
War*, 712.

8. *OR* 2:851–53.

9. Ibid., 858, 860; JAE, *Autobiographical Sketch*, 55. Early maintained a profound skepticism about civilian railroad personnel throughout the war.

10. *OR* 2:912.

11. The 4th South Carolina, detached from Beauregard's command and sent to
Leesburg before the 6th Brigade was formed, never joined; the regiment's place
was taken by the 7th Louisiana. JAE, *Autobiographical Sketch*, 3.

12. Squires, "Autobiography," SHC.

13. William C. Davis, *Bull Run*, 114; Squires, "Autobiography," SHC.

14. William C. Davis, *Bull Run*, 127–28.

15. Ibid., 128; JAE, *Autobiographical Sketch*, 8.

16. *OR* 2:461–65; JAE, *Autobiographical Sketch*, 8; Longstreet, *From Manassas*, 39. Early's report of casualties was lost. The plunging fire killed nine and wounded 15 in the 7th Louisiana. Terry L. Jones, *Lee's Tigers*, 50.

17. JAE, *Autobiographical Sketch*, 9–10.

18. T. Harry Williams, *P. G. T. Beauregard*, 71, 77; William C. Davis, *Bull Run*, 144; JAE, *Autobiographical Sketch*, 10–11.

19. William C. Davis, *Bull Run*, 144.

20. JAE, *Autobiographical Sketch*, 16–18.

21. Ibid., 18–19.

22. William C. Davis, *Bull Run*, 199.

23. JAE, *Autobiographical Sketch*, 19; William C. Davis, *Bull Run*, 230.

24. William C. Davis, *Bull Run*, 230.

25. JAE, *Autobiographical Sketch*, 21.

26. Freeman, *LL* 1:71.

27. JAE, *Autobiographical Sketch*, 21–22; William C. Davis, *Bull Run*, 230.

28. Freeman, *LL* 1:72.

29. Ibid., 72; JAE, *Autobiographical Sketch*, 23–25, 28; *OR* 2:555; William C. Davis, *Bull Run*, 231.

30. JAE, *Autobiographical Sketch*, 26–28.

31. Freeman, *LL* 1:86n.

32. JAE, *Autobiographical Sketch*, 37.

33. United States Military Academy, *Register of Graduates*, 232.

34. JAE, *Autobiographical Sketch*, 39–40.

CHAPTER SIX: *The Spur of Ambition*

1. Early, *Autobiographical Sketch*, 49; Faust, *Encyclopedia of the Civil War*, 451.

2. JAE, *Autobiographical Sketch*, 47–55; Freeman, *LL* 1:142.

3. JAE, *Autobiographical Sketch*, 54; JAE to Emma Cameron (typescript), Mar. 7, 1883, Daniel Papers (#158/5383, Box 25), UVA.

4. The Confederacy introduced conscription early in 1862, mainly to retain men who had enlisted for one year following Lincoln's inaugural. Winton, "Antebellum Instruction at West Point" (Ph.D. diss.), 133; JAE to James L. Kemper, Feb. 9, 1862, Kemper Papers (#4083), UVA.

5. Ferguson, "Memoirs," 89–90, Ferguson Papers, Duke.

6. Faust, *Encyclopedia of the Civil War*, 847; Freeman, *LL* 1:148ff.

7. Freeman, *LL* 1:174–75; Faust, *Encyclopedia of the Civil War*, 829; JAE, *Autobiographical Sketch*, 67.

8. Freeman, *LL* 1:176–78.

9. Ibid., 179–80.

10. Ibid., 180; JAE, *Autobiographical Sketch*, 68; Faust, *Encyclopedia of the Civil War*, 829.

11. JAE, *Autobiographical Sketch*, 69; Freeman, *LL* 1:181.

12. Freeman, *LL* 1:182–83; JAE, *Autobiographical Sketch*, 69.

13. Daniel Papers (#158/5383, Box 25), UVA.

14. JAE, *Autobiographical Sketch*, 70–71.

15. Freeman, *LL* 1:183–88; JAE, *Autobiographical Sketch*, 69–72.

16. Tucker, *Hancock the Superb*, 87.

17. Freeman, *LL* 1:188; Clark, *Histories of the Several Regiments and Battalions*, 285; JAE, *Autobiographical Sketch*, 72; *OR* 11, pt. 1:569.

18. JAE, *Autobiographical Sketch*, 73; JAE to D. H. Hill, May 7, 1862, Hill Papers, VSL.

19. Report of JAE, June 9, 1862, JAE Papers, vol. 3, LC; *OR* 11, pt. 1:608.

20. Joseph Gardner to JAE, May 24, 1862, JAE Papers, vol. 3, LC; D. H. Hill to JAE, Aug. 1, Aug. 13, 1862, JAE Papers, vol. 4, LC; Freeman, *LL* 1:190.

21. Freeman, *LL* 1:190–91.

22. *OR* 11, pt. 1:607–8; JAE, *Autobiographical Sketch*, 72; Freeman, *LL* 1:192.

CHAPTER SEVEN: *"Very Able and Very Brave"*

1. Dowdey, *Lee*, 264–65; Freeman, *R. E. Lee* 2:529.

2. Freeman, *LL* 2:xxviii.

3. Johnson and Buel, *Battles and Leaders* 2:409ff.

4. Bushong, *Old Jube*, 60.

5. Ibid., 62; Freeman, *LL* 1:595ff.

6. JAE, *Autobiographical Sketch*, 83, 85.

7. Burke Davis, *They Called Him Stonewall*, 268, 277; JAE, *Autobiographical Sketch*, 92; Douglas, *I Rode with Stonewall*, 127.

8. Pope's orders to units subsisting in enemy country provoked Southern feelings to the extent of inspiring a "reprisal order" that denied treatment as prisoners of war to any of Pope's officers who might fall into Confederate hands. Freeman, *LL* 2:150n.

9. Bushong, *Old Jube*, 68; Terry L. Jones, *Lee's Tigers*, 111–13; Burke Davis, *They Called Him Stonewall*, 268, 277.

10. Bushong, *Old Jube*, 69; *OR* 11, pt. 3:664; JAE to Marcus J. Wright, June 19, 1881, July 9, 1881, Wright Papers, SHC.

11. Freeman, *LL* 2:22–23.

12. JAE, *Autobiographical Sketch*, 93–94; Freeman, *LL* 2:24.

13. Freeman, *LL* 2:26.

14. Krick, *Stonewall Jackson at Cedar Mountain*, 58.
15. JAE, *Autobiographical Sketch*, 95–96; *OR* 12, pt. 2:229 (Early's report); Buck, *With the Old Confeds*, 44.
16. *OR* 12, pt. 2:230.
17. JAE, *Autobiographical Sketch*, 97–98; Freeman, *LL* 2:28–29.
18. Ibid., 33; *OR* 12, pt. 2:230.
19. Freeman, *LL* 2:30.
20. *OR* 12, pt. 2:230.
21. Ibid., 230; Freeman, *LL* 2:35.
22. *OR* 12, pt. 2:231; Freeman, *LL* 2:35.
23. Freeman, *LL* 2:36; *OR* 12, pt. 2:231.
24. *OR* 12, pt. 2:231.
25. Freeman, *LL* 2:38; Buck, *With the Old Confeds*, 44–45.
26. JAE, *Autobiographical Sketch*, 99.
27. *OR* 12, pt. 2:231–32.
28. Ibid., 232.
29. Freeman, *LL* 2:43.
30. Ibid., 41.
31. *OR* 12, pt. 2:227.
32. Hamlin, *Old Bald Head*, 122.

CHAPTER EIGHT: *Pinnacle of Pride*

1. Freeman, *LL* 2:73; JAE, *Autobiographical Sketch*, 106–7.
2. JAE, *Autobiographical Sketch*, 107–8; Freeman, *LL* 2:73–74.
3. Freeman, *LL* 2:108–9.
4. JAE, *Autobiographical Sketch*, 110.
5. Freeman, *LL* 2:76; JAE, *Autobiographical Sketch*, 110; *OR* 12, pt. 2:706–7; George H. Gordon, *History*, 64.
6. Freeman, *LL* 2:77n; George H. Gordon, *History*, 65.
7. *OR* 12, pt. 2:650; Blackford, *Letters*, 124–25.
8. Freeman, *LL* 2:76–78; JAE, *Autobiographical Sketch*, 111–13; *OR* 12, pt. 2:705–7; George H. Gordon, *History*, 55n.; Livermore, *Numbers and Losses in the Civil War in America*, 89.
9. *OR* 12, pt. 2:644.
10. Freeman, *LL* 2:103; JAE, *Autobiographical Sketch*, 120.
11. JAE, *Autobiographical Sketch*, 120; Freeman, *LL* 2:110.
12. Freeman, *LL* 2:111.
13. Ibid., 111–12; Early, *Autobiographical Sketch*, 122.
14. JAE, *Autobiographical Sketch*, 123.
15. Ibid., 124; Freeman, *LL* 2:115.

16. Terry L. Jones, *Lee's Tigers*, 121; undated note in Daniel Papers (#158/ 5383, Box 25), UVA; *OR* 12, pt. 2:712.

17. Freeman, *LL* 2:118; Robertson, *A. P. Hill*, 122.

18. Buck, *With the Old Confeds*, 57; JAE, *Autobiographical Sketch*, 126.

19. JAE, *Autobiographical Sketch*, 126–27.

20. Ibid., 127; Robertson, *A. P. Hill*, 125.

21. Freeman, *LL* 2:130.

22. Ibid., 131.

23. Robertson, *A. P. Hill*, 128.

24. Ibid., 128; JAE, *Autobiographical Sketch*, 129.

25. JAE, *Autobiographical Sketch*, 130.

26. Freeman, *LL* 2:134.

27. Smith's sobriquet originated in his reputation for drawing frequent extra payments from the post office for mileage logged by a mail-coach service he operated between Washington, D.C., and Milledgeville, Georgia, in the years 1827–36. A capable man of strong opinions, he went on to command Jubal's own brigade after Early's promotion and Smith's recovery from wounds suffered at Antietam. Faust, *Encyclopedia of the Civil War*, 698; Freeman, *LL* 2:134.

28. *OR* 12, pt. 2:715–16.

29. Elzey resumed duty, with the rank of major general, in December 1862, assigned to the command of Richmond's defenses. Faust, *Encyclopedia of the Civil War*, 242.

30. "Recollections of Jubal Early, by One Who Followed Him," 311–12.

CHAPTER NINE: *"Here Comes Old Jubal!"*

1. JAE, *Autobiographical Sketch*, 134.

2. Ibid., 135; Freeman, *LL* 2:150–51.

3. Freeman, *LL* 2:150; Sears, "The Bloodiest Day," 7; Henderson, *Stonewall Jackson*, 2:209; Dowdey, *Lee*, 300.

4. JAE, *Autobiographical Sketch*, 135.

5. Sears, "The Bloodiest Day," 4, 7; Dowdey, *Lee*, 302.

6. JAE, *Autobiographical Sketch*, 135; *SHSP* 8:437–39; Johnson and Buel, *Battles and Leaders* 2:618; Douglas, *I Rode with Stonewall*, 152.

7. JAE, *Autobiographical Sketch*, 135–37.

8. *OR*, plate 29:2; Sears, "The Bloodiest Day," 10.

9. Freeman, *LL* 2:204, 205–6.

10. *OR* 19, pt. 1:955–56; JAE, *Autobiographical Sketch*, 140–41; Terry L. Jones, *Lee's Tigers*, 129.

11. Freeman, *LL* 2:149–52, 204; Sears, "The Bloodiest Day," 7, 10; Dowdey, *Lee*, 303.

12. Sears, "The Bloodiest Day," 13.

13. JAE, *Autobiographical Sketch*, 142.

14. Sears, *Landscape*, 242.

15. JAE, *Autobiographical Sketch*, 142; *OR* 19, pt. 1:967–69.

16. JAE, *Autobiographical Sketch*, 143; Terry L. Jones, *Lee's Tigers*, 129; *OR* 19, pt. 1:974, 978–79.

17. JAE, *Autobiographical Sketch*, 144; Sears, "The Bloodiest Day," 25.

18. JAE, *Autobiographical Sketch*, 144.

19. Hale and Phillips, *History of the 49th Virginia Infantry, C.S.A.*, 52.

20. The Confederate reinforcements supporting Early in the crucial counterattack on the Confederate left were the brigade of Brig. Gen. Paul J. Semmes, two regiments from William Barksdale's brigade, detached from Maj. Gen. Lafayette McLaws's division, and the brigade of Brig. Gen. George T. ("Tige") Anderson, of D. H. Hill's division. Identification of the Union troops that moved past the battery on the road into the gap in Early's rear is confused. Early believed they were Brig. Gen. George S. Greene's 2d Division of Maj. Gen. Joseph K. F. Mansfield's 12th Corps. More likely they were only the 125th Pennsylvania of the same corps's 1st Division; it was later—though perhaps only a short time—that Greene's division attacked and seized a position in the woods behind the church, potentially the most threatening Federal move of the day so far. If Greene had enjoyed the support of the Union troops driven off with such loss at the end of the action on the Confederate left, Early's—and Lee's—worst fears might have been realized.

These shattered units belonged to Jubal's West Point classmate, Maj. Gen. John Sedgwick, commanding the 2d Division of Maj. Gen. Edwin V. Sumner's 2d Corps. Sedgwick's division lost 2,300 men, most of them shot down in the first few minutes of the counterattack; losses in the brigades of Early, Semmes, and Barksdale were a total of 804, including the serious wounding of Extra Billy Smith of the 49th Virginia, who was subsequently promoted to brigadier general and given command of Early's brigade. Casualty figures for the commands of Grigsby and Anderson are unknown; for Anderson, since his engagement was so brief, losses were probably insignificant. Early and Sedgwick, who was badly wounded at Antietam, would square off again. JAE, *Autobiographical Sketch*, 144–49; *OR* 19, pt. 1:970–71; Sears, *Landscape*, 230 n. 19, 234.

21. Sears, "The Bloodiest Day," 32–33, 37–45; JAE, *Autobiographical Sketch*, 152.

22. Federal casualties at Antietam were 11,657, 15.5 percent of those engaged. McWhiney and Jamieson, *Attack and Die*, 8, 11; *OR* 19, pt. 1:974.

23. Freeman, *LL* 2:256, 259, 264, 266.

24. Freeman, *LL* 2:325.

25. Bushong, *Old Jube*, 106; Stiles, *Four Years*, 190.

26. Greer Diary, Nov. 27, 1862, USAMHI.

27. Freeman, *LL* 2:347; Robertson, *A. P. Hill*, 160–61; Freeman, *R. L. Lee* 2:446.

28. Robertson, *A. P. Hill*, 344.

29. Freeman, *LL* 2:346; Burke Davis, *They Called Him Stonewall*, 356; JAE, *Autobiographical Sketch*, 171.

30. JAE, *Autobiographical Sketch*, 171; Henderson, *Stonewall Jackson* 2:314.

31. JAE, *Autobiographical Sketch*, 172–73; Bushong, *Old Jube*, 111; Freeman, *LL* 2:356; Robertson, *A. P. Hill*, 166.

32. JAE, *Autobiographical Sketch*, 173–74.

33. Ibid., 175.

34. Ibid., 175–76; Henderson, *Stonewall Jackson* 2:320.

35. Bushong, *Old Jube*, 114.

CHAPTER TEN: *Underwriting the Army*

1. JAE, *Autobiographical Sketch*, 190–91.

2. Early's standing with his superiors was very high at this point. Jackson had been communicating with Lee about the desirability of reestablishing a Shenandoah Valley force, at least over the winter; his choice of commander for such a contingent was General Early. But no permanent Valley detachment was to be set up until Early was sent there with his command in 1864. JAE, *Autobiographical Sketch*, 185; Douglas, *I Rode with Stonewall*, 40–42.

3. Terry L. Jones, *Lee's Tigers*, 142–43.

4. JAE, *Autobiographical Sketch*, 192.

5. JAE, *Autobiographical Sketch*, 191; Cooper, *Chancellorsville*, 6–7.

6. Freeman, *LL* 2:524.

7. JAE, *Autobiographical Sketch*, 193.

8. Ibid., 194.

9. Ibid., 195; Cooper, *Chancellorsville*, 16.

10. JAE, *Autobiographical Sketch*, 196.

11. Ibid., 196–97; Freeman, *LL* 2:527, 603; Cooper, *Chancellorsville*, 12.

12. Cooper, *Chancellorsville*, 12; United States Military Academy, *Register of Graduates*, 231.

13. JAE, *Autobiographical Sketch*, 198.

14. Cooper, *Chancellorsville*, 15.

15. Freeman, *LL* 2:603.

16. Ibid., 606; JAE, *Autobiographical Sketch*, 199–200.

17. JAE, *Autobiographical Sketch*, 200; Freeman, *LL* 2:607.

18. JAE, *Autobiographical Sketch*, 200.

19. United States Military Academy, *Register of Graduates*, 232; Freeman, *LL* 2:607; JAE, *Autobiographical Sketch*, 200–201.

20. JAE, *Autobiographical Sketch*, 201; Freeman, *LL* 2:607.

21. Freeman, *LL* 2:608.

22. Faust, *Encyclopedia of the Civil War*, 139.

23. Freeman, *LL* 2:608; JAE, *Autobiographical Sketch*, 201.

24. Freeman, *LL* 2:609.

25. Ibid.; JAE, *Autobiographical Sketch*, 202.

26. JAE, *Autobiographical Sketch*, 203; Freeman, *LL* 2:609n. Hampered by high winds aloft, Lowe's observations were fragmentary. By 5:30 P.M., he was reporting the withdrawal of "nearly all the enemy's force." Sedgwick knew he faced only a division, but was unaware from his own observations that it was pulling out. Hooker's headquarters bombarded Sedgwick with dispatches insisting on the abandonment by the Confederates of Fredericksburg and its defenses, but "Uncle John" found the intelligence hard to believe.

27. JAE, *Autobiographical Sketch*, 203.

28. Freeman, *LL* 2:611.

29. Ibid., 612.

30. Cooper, *Chancellorsville*, 88.

31. Freeman, *LL* 2:613n.

32. Ibid., 613; JAE, *Autobiographical Sketch*, 204–5; Cooper, *Chancellorsville*, 44–45; Bigelow, *Campaign*, 384–85.

33. JAE, *Autobiographical Sketch*, 204, 206; Freeman, *LL* 2:613, 615; Bigelow, *Campaign*, 384.

34. JAE, *Autobiographical Sketch*, 205; Freeman, *LL* 2:614.

35. Freeman, *LL* 2:616; JAE, *Autobiographical Sketch*, 205.

36. JAE, *Autobiographical Sketch*, 206–7; Bigelow, *Campaign*, 387–88.

37. JAE, *Autobiographical Sketch*, 209.

38. Ibid., 208–9.

39. Ibid., 210; Freeman, *LL* 2:617.

40. Freeman, *LL* 2:617–18; JAE, *Autobiographical Sketch*, 208; Winslow, *Sedgwick*, 75.

41. Freeman, *LL* 2:619; JAE, *Autobiographical Sketch*, 210.

42. Bigelow, *Campaign*, 394.

43. Ibid., 394, 397; Winslow, *Sedgwick*, 76; *OR* 25, pt. 1:558.

44. Freeman, *LL* 2:619–25; *OR* 25, pt. 1:856–57.

45. Cooper, *Chancellorsville*, 46; JAE, *Autobiographical Sketch*, 218; Freeman, *LL* 2:626. Freeman charges Early with failure to acknowledge how much he owed Wilcox "then or later." Though Jubal admitted no direct obligation, he did praise the conduct of Wilcox's brigade as "gallant," and gave him unstinting credit for his role in stopping Sedgwick at Salem Church.

46. Freeman, *LL* 2:626; Cooper, *Chancellorsville*, 47; JAE, *Autobiographical Sketch*, 220.

47. Cooper, *Chancellorsville*, 6; Bigelow, *Campaign*, 415.

48. Bigelow, *Campaign*, 8–13.

49. Ibid., 42.

50. Freeman, *LL* 2:653.

51. JAE, *Autobiographical Sketch*, 219.

52. Longstreet, *From Manassas*, 330.

53. JAE, *Autobiographical Sketch*, 234–35; Luvaas and Nelson, *U.S. Army War College Guide*, 349.

CHAPTER ELEVEN: *Watch Charm Victory*

1. Freeman, *R. E. Lee* 2:8–9; Freeman, *LL* 2:690–91, 695–96.

2. Buck, *With the Old Confeds*, 86–88; JAE, *Autobiographical Sketch*, 246.

3. Douglas, *I Rode with Stonewall*, 234.

4. Gordon, *Reminiscences*, 158.

5. Freeman, *R. E. Lee* 3:8–9; Freeman, *LL* 2:690–91, 695–96.

6. Freeman, *LL* 2:690.

7. In communications with the Confederate government, Brig. Gen. John D. Imboden, a Valley resident whose cavalry command accompanied Lee's army, catalogued some of Milroy's offenses. These were connected with Union charges of local guerrilla activity. Imboden assailed penalties of $300 and $700, levied respectively on Job Parsons, of Tucker, and another man in compensation for "guerrilla" robberies. Imboden enclosed letters written to Parsons threatening him with an unspecified penalty for not obeying a Milroy summons to headquarters; another announced that he would be shot and his property burned if he did not pay a $14.25 assessment. Imboden, closing one of these letters, wrote: "Oh, for a day of retribution!" John D. Imboden, *Message of the President*, printed compilation of official communications, E480.5/CB62, VSL. Milroy's reputation was known to such Confederate soldiers as William B. Bailey, Jr., of the 1st Louisiana Artillery; Bailey Memoir, p. 15, USAMHI.

8. *OR* 27, pt. 2:439; Coddington, *Gettysburg Campaign*, 590, 595.

9. Coddington, *Gettysburg Campaign*, 440.

10. Ibid., 460–61; Freeman, *LL* 3:22, 27.

11. Coddington, *Gettysburg Campaign*, 439, 441.

12. Nye, *Here Come the Rebels*, 97; JAE, *Autobiographical Sketch*, 245.

13. Coddington, *Gettysburg Campaign*, 461; JAE, *Autobiographical Sketch*, 244.

14. Nye, *Here Come the Rebels*, 97.

15. JAE, *Autobiographical Sketch*, 246; Nye, *Here Come the Rebels*, 98–99; *OR* 27, pt. 2:463.

16. JAE, *Autobiographical Sketch*, 246.

17. Nye, *Here Come the Rebels*, 97.

18. *OR* 27, pt. 2:478, 495.

19. Ibid., 160; JAE, *Autobiographical Sketch*, 248.

20. Hamlin, *Old Bald Head*, 139; Nye, *Here Come the Rebels*, 101.

21. JAE, *Autobiographical Sketch*, 248-49.

22. Freeman, *LL* 3:27; JAE, *Autobiographical Sketch*, 249.

23. JAE, *Autobiographical Sketch*, 250.

24. Ibid., 250-51; Freeman, *LL* 3:26.

25. Freeman, *LL* 3:27.

26. Hamlin, *Old Bald Head*, 140; Freeman, *LL* 3:27.

27. Scarcely half of Milroy's command escaped Ewell's trap. Of his total losses of 4,443, 3,856 were recorded as captured or missing. Coddington, *Gettysburg Campaign*, 88-89; JAE, *Autobiographical Sketch*, 251-52; Freeman, *LL* 3:27; *OR* 27, pt. 2:463-64.

28. Seymour Journal, June 15, 1863, USAMHI.

29. Coddington, *Gettysburg Campaign*, 86, 89; Freeman, *R. E. Lee* 3:37.

CHAPTER TWELVE: *Essay in Retribution*

1. Coddington, *Gettysburg Campaign*, 154-55.

2. Duffy, *Military Experience*, 166.

3. Freeman, *R. E. Lee*, 3:56-57.

4. Coddington, *Gettysburg Campaign*, 166; Current, *Old Thad Stevens*, 180, 182; Seymour Journal, June 24-26, 1863, USAMHI.

5. JAE, *Autobiographical Sketch*, 255; *OR* 27, pt. 2:464-65.

6. JAE, *Autobiographical Sketch*, 255.

7. Ibid., 255-56.

8. Ewell, touched by John Early's youth and sincerity, took the boy firmly under his wing, making the young fellow stick close to him and "sleep nearby at night." Jubal told John he was too small to be with the army, but did not try to prevent his service with Ewell. Hamlin, *Old Bald Head*, 141, 143; John Cabell Early, "A Southern Boy," 415-27.

9. JAE, *Autobiographical Sketch*, 257-58.

10. Coddington, *Gettysburg Campaign*, 168-69, 168 n. 45.

11. JAE, *Autobiographical Sketch*, 260-61; John B. Gordon, *Reminiscences*, 148-49; Coddington, *Gettysburg Campaign*, 170; *OR* 27, pt. 2:466-67.

12. JAE, *Autobiographical Sketch*, 262-63.

13. Ibid., 264-65; Coddington, *Gettysburg Campaign*, 176. Coddington quotes Maj. Gen. Dorsey Pender, one of A. P. Hill's division commanders, who was more candid in a letter to his wife: "Until we crossed the Md. line our men behaved as well as troops could but here [in Pennsylvania] it will be hard to restrain them for they have an idea that they are to indulge in unlicensed plunder" (*Gettysburg Campaign*, 177).

CHAPTER THIRTEEN: *Change of Heart*

1. JAE, *Autobiographical Sketch*, 263; *OR* 27, pt. 2:467–68.

2. JAE, *Autobiographical Sketch*, 468; Freeman, *LL* 3:92.

3. JAE, *Autobiographical Sketch*, 263, 264, 266; *OR* 27, pt. 2:468.

4. JAE, *Autobiographical Sketch*, 266; Starr, *Union Cavalry* 1:138; Faust, *Encyclopedia of the Civil War*, 89.

5. JAE, *Autobiographical Sketch*, 267.

6. Coddington, *Gettysburg Campaign*, 291; JAE, *Autobiographical Sketch*, 267.

7. JAE, *Autobiographical Sketch*, 268; Freeman, *LL* 3:90; USGS map, Gettysburg, Pa. SW/4—15′ Quadrangle.

8. Coddington, *Gettysburg Campaign*, 296; *OR* 27, pt. 2:469; JAE, *Autobiographical Sketch*, 269.

9. JAE, *Autobiographical Sketch*, 269–70.

10. Coddington, *Gettysburg Campaign*, 315.

11. Freeman, *LL* 3:97.

12. Freeman, *LL* 3:95, 96; Coddington, *Gettysburg Campaign*, 319.

13. *OR* 27, pt. 2:469.

14. Freeman, *LL* 3:96.

15. Lee's views were based on his own observation from Seminary Ridge. He sent Ewell his orders before receiving a report from Col. A. L. Long of his staff, whom he had sent to take a closer look at Cemetery Hill. Long told him the position was held in strength; trying to capture it would be costly and not necessarily successful. Later, Lee acknowledged that the "weakened and exhausted" divisions of Hill and Ewell were in no condition on July 1 to renew an assault on "the strong position that the enemy had assumed." Hassler, *Crisis*, 134; *OR* 27, pt. 2:318; Freeman, *LL* 3:97; Freeman, *R. E. Lee* 3:75.

16. JAE, *Autobiographical Sketch*, 269–70.

17. Freeman, *R. E. Lee* 3:93; Gordon, *Reminiscences*, 157; Brown Diary, Dec. 27, 1869, USAMHI.

18. Ewell was right to be concerned about the threat to his left flank. As of about 5:00 P.M., elements of two divisions of the Union 12th Corps were 1½ miles east of Gettysburg on the York Road. Hassler, *Crisis*, 138.

19. Freeman, *R. E. Lee* 3:98; Coddington, *Gettysburg Campaign*, 319–20.

20. John Cabell Early, "A Southern Boy," 415–27.

21. Freeman, *LL* 3:101.

22. Ibid., 109–10.

23. Coddington, *Gettysburg Campaign*, 364; Freeman, *LL* 3:101, 103.

24. Coddington, *Gettysburg Campaign*, 365.

25. Coddington, *Gettysburg Campaign*, 365.

26. Such an indiscretion would have been unlike Lee, who in any case was— and remained—on excellent terms with Longstreet. A possible reason for believ-

ing Early's account is Lee's mental state. He was upset not only by Longstreet's and Ewell's reaction to his desire to attack Meade, but by the loss of Jackson, the totally unexplained absence of Jeb Stuart and his cavalry, and Lee's consequent ignorance of Meade's strength, dispositions, and intentions. Coddington, *Gettysburg Campaign*, 361, 365n; Freeman, *R. E. Lee* 3:80.

27. "Gettysburg," typescript statement by Capt. [T. T.] Turner, undated, JAE Papers 3:604, LC.

28. Freeman, *LL* 3:103–4; Coddington, *Gettysburg Campaign*, 367.

29. *OR* 27, pt. 2:447, 470; JAE, *Autobiographical Sketch*, 271; Freeman, *LL* 3:130; Coddington, *Gettysburg Campaign*, 429.

30. Coddington, *Gettysburg Campaign*, 428; *OR* 27, pt. 2:504.

31. Coddington, *Gettysburg Campaign*, 436, 439.

32. Terry L. Jones, *Lee's Tigers*, 175, 176.

33. *OR* 27, pt. 2:556; Gallagher, *Ramseur*, 74; Freeman, *LL* 3:135.

34. Coddington, *Gettysburg Campaign*, 536.

35. Jubal's argument goes so far as to claim that capture of Cemetery Hill on July 1 would have done the Confederates no real good because it would not have yielded a decisive defeat of Meade. According to Early, the Federals would simply have fallen back on the Pipe Creek line Meade had designated as his defensive base. *SHSP* 4:260ff., passim.

36. Coddington, *Gettysburg Campaign*, 386–87.

CHAPTER FOURTEEN: *"A Great Mind to Curse"*

1. Hairston Diary, Nov. 11, 1863, Hairston Papers, SHC.

2. Robertson, *A. P. Hill*, 233, 235–39.

3. Graham and Skoch, *Mine Run*, 2.

4. Freeman, *R. E. Lee* 3:188; JAE, *Autobiographical Sketch*, 315.

5. Freeman, *LL* 3:264; Graham and Skoch, *Mine Run*, 6.

6. Graham and Skoch, *Mine Run*, 7; Freeman, *LL* 3:264; *OR* 29, pt. 1:620.

7. Graham and Skoch, *Mine Run*, 17.

8. JAE, *Autobiographical Sketch*, 309, 310.

9. Freeman, *R. E. Lee* 3:191; Freeman, *LL* 3:265; JAE, *Autobiographical Sketch*, 313; Hairston Diary, Nov. 8, 1863, Hairston Papers, SHC.

10. JAE, *Autobiographical Sketch*, 311.

11. Graham and Skoch, *Mine Run*, 19–23, 26; Terry L. Jones, *Lee's Tigers*, 185; *OR* 29, pt. 1:924–26.

12. JAE, *Autobiographical Sketch*, 313; Graham and Skoch, *Mine Run*, 27.

13. *OR* 29, pt. 1:622; JAE, *Autobiographical Sketch*, 313; Hairston Diary, Nov. 9, 1863, Hairston Papers, SHC.

14. JAE, *Autobiographical Sketch*, 314; Graham and Skoch, *Mine Run*, 26.

15. There is no direct evidence that Early complained before the fight about

the engineering of the bridgehead. But it would have been in character for him to register his opinion either with Ewell or Lee the moment he was given responsibility for defense of the position. Freeman, *LL* 3:264, 267; Terry L. Jones, *Lee's Tigers*, 185.

16. Hairston Diary, Nov. 11, 1863, Hairston Papers, SHC; *OR* 29, pt. 1:620.

17. Freeman, *LL* 3:268; JAE, *Autobiographical Sketch*, 316; *OR* 29, pt. 1:626.

18. *OR* 29, pt. 1:626; Freeman, *R. E. Lee* 3:190.

19. Graham and Skoch, *Mine Run*, 29; Freeman, *R. E. Lee* 3:184.

20. Hairston Diary, Nov. 21, 1863, Hairston Papers, SHC; Hairston to wife, Nov. 3, 1864, Hairston Papers, SHC.

21. Hairston Diary, Nov. 13, 1863, Hairston Papers, SHC.

22. Ibid., Nov. 17, 1863.

23. JAE, *Autobiographical Sketch*, 319.

24. Graham and Skoch, *Mine Run*, 38, 40, 41.

25. Ibid., 54; *OR* 29, pt. 1:832; Freeman, *LL* 3:269–72.

26. Graham and Skoch, *Mine Run*, 55–57.

27. JAE, *Autobiographical Sketch*, 321; Haskell, *Reminiscences*, p. 84, Haskell Papers, SHC.

28. Freeman, *R. E. Lee* 3:202.

29. Freeman, *LL* 3:277.

30. Ibid.; *OR* 29, pt. 1:833.

31. Gallagher, *Ramseur*, 89; JAE, *Autobiographical Sketch*, 324–25.

32. *OR* 29, pt. 1:835.

CHAPTER FIFTEEN: *The Trouble with the Cavalry*

1. Richard Ewell's biographer, referring to widespread shortages of shoes and clothing in the Confederate army, mentions rumors that Early shared the men's hardships, electing to wear a pillowslip instead of a white shirt. Hamlin, *Old Bald Head*, 165; Sloane, *Early*, 8.

2. JAE, *Autobiographical Sketch*, 326; *OR* 51, pt. 2:795–98.

3. Bushong, *Old Jube*, 163ff.; *OR* 29, pt. 1:970.

4. *OR* 51, pt. 2:797; JAE, *Autobiographical Sketch*, 327.

5. Starr, *Union Cavalry*, 2:169–70; JAE, *Autobiographical Sketch*, 326; *OR* 33:1135–36.

6. Starr, *Union Cavalry* 2:169.

7. JAE, *Autobiographical Sketch*, 327–28; *OR* 29, pt. 1:970.

8. Starr, *Union Cavalry* 2:168–69.

9. JAE, *Autobiographical Sketch*, 328–29; *OR* 29, pt. 1:970.

10. *OR* 29, pt. 1:952; Starr, *Union Cavalry* 2:171–72; JAE, *Autobiographical Sketch*, 330.

11. Faust, *Encyclopedia of the Civil War*, 392; *OR* 29, pt. 1:970. Rosser felt that

Early was exaggerating the danger from Federal troops' moving up the Shenandoah, and complained of the constant marching and countermarching his men and horses were subjected to. Thomas L. Rosser to wife, Dec. 24, 1863, Rosser Papers, UVA.

12. *OR* 29, pt. 1:946.

13. Ibid., 1086, 1168.

14. Ibid., 1086, 1167–68.

15. Starr, *Union Cavalry* 1:222, 224; Hopkins, *From Bull Run to Appomattox*, 218.

16. Starr, *Union Cavalry* 1:214–15.

17. Ibid., 228–29.

18. Ibid., 229–30.

19. *OR* 33:1081–82.

20. Ibid., 1082.

21. Ibid., 43; JAE, *Autobiographical Sketch*, 333–35.

22. JAE, *Autobiographical Sketch*, 336.

23. *OR* 33:45–46, 1133–34, 1142; Thomas L. Rosser to wife, Feb. 7, 1864, Gordon and Rosser Family Papers (#1171-c), UVA.

24. *OR* 33:1166; Thomas L. Rosser to wife, Jan. 25, 1864, Gordon and Rosser Family Papers (#1171-c), UVA.

25. *OR* 33:1166.

26. Ibid., 1129; Thomas L. Rosser to wife, Jan. 28, Feb. 7, 1864, Gordon and Rosser Family Papers (#1171-c), UVA.

CHAPTER SIXTEEN: *On a Darkling Plain*

1. Robert E. Lee to Margaret Stuart, Mar. 20, 1864, Daniel Papers (#158/5383, Box 25), UVA.

2. Sloan, *Early*, 7.

3. Freeman, *LL* 3:329–33.

4. Hamlin, *Old Bald Head*, 107–8; Daniel, Diary, Apr. 26, 1864, Mss. 511 D2244, VHS.

5. Catton, *Grant Takes Command*, 168–69.

6. Ibid., 153.

7. Dowdey, *Lee*, 417–18; Catton, *Stillness*, 68.

8. *OR* 36, pt. 1:1070; ibid., pt. 2:952–53; Eckert, *John Brown Gordon*, 63–64; John B. Gordon, *Reminiscences*, 237–42.

9. Freeman, *LL* 3:355–67; Dowdey, *Lee*, 435–40.

10. JAE, *Autobiographical Sketch*, 347; *OR* 36, pt. 1:540; undated note, Daniel Papers (#158/5383), UVA.

11. Faust, *Encyclopedia of the Civil War*, 315; Eckert, *John Brown Gordon*, 7, 84; Worsham, *One of Jackson's Foot Cavalry*, 228.

12. John B. Gordon, *Reminiscences*, 243–44; *OR* 36, pt. 1:1077.

13. *OR* 36, pt. 2:962; JAE, *Autobiographical Sketch*, 348.

14. John B. Gordon, *Reminiscences*, 255–56; Thomas G. Jones to John W. Daniel, July 3, 1904, Daniel Papers, Duke; JAE, *Autobiographical Sketch*, 348.

15. Freeman, *LL* 3:370; John B. Gordon, *Reminiscences*, 255–56.

16. *OR* 36, pt. 1:1071.

17. Dowdey, *Lee*, 441; John B. Gordon, *Reminiscences*, 258; Eckert, *John Brown Gordon*, 67–68; JAE, *Autobiographical Sketch*, 348–49; *OR* 36, pt. 1:1071, 1077.

18. Eckert, *John Brown Gordon*, 67–71; JAE, *Autobiographical Sketch*, 350.

19. Smith, *Lee and Grant*, 197; *OR* 36, pt. 1:1071.

20. *OR* 36, pt. 1:1077–79; JAE, *Autobiographical Sketch*, 349–50.

21. Faust, *Encyclopedia of the Civil War*, 827; *OR* 36, pt. 1:133.

22. Freeman, *LL* 3:374, 447.

23. Ibid., 390–91; JAE, *Autobiographical Sketch*, 351.

24. JAE, *Autobiographical Sketch*, 353–57; Freeman, *R.E. Lee* 3:322–24; Robertson, *A.P. Hill*, 270–71.

25. JAE, *Autobiographical Sketch*, 356–57.

26. Robertson, *A.P. Hill*, 270.

27. JAE, *Autobiographical Sketch*, 359; Eckert, *John Brown Gordon*, 79–80; undated citation of Lee's General Order No. 128, May 21, 1864, Daniel Papers (#158/5383), UVA.

28. *OR* 36, pt. 1:1074.

29. Robert E. Lee to Richard S. Ewell, May 31, 1864, Ewell Papers, SHC.

30. Gallagher, *Ramseur*, 115–16.

31. Richard S. Ewell to Walter H. Taylor, June 1, 1864, Ewell Papers, SHC.

32. Robert E. Lee to Richard S. Ewell, June 1, 1864, Ewell Papers, SHC.

33. Freeman, *LL* 3:510.

34. JAE to Richard S. Ewell, June 5, 1864, Ewell Papers, SHC.

35. Campbell Brown to Richard S. Ewell, June 13, 1864, Ewell Papers, SHC.

CHAPTER SEVENTEEN: *Lynchburg Rescued*

1. Vandiver, *Jubal's Raid*, 19; JAE, *Autobiographical Sketch*, 371.

2. Pond, *Shenandoah Valley*, 3–8.

3. Faust, *Encyclopedia of the Civil War*, 98.

4. Pond, *Shenandoah Valley*, 19–20; Thomas A. Lewis, *Shenandoah in Flames*, 35–39.

5. Thomas A. Lewis, *Shenandoah in Flames*, 37–39; Vandiver, *Jubal's Raid*, 5–6; Freeman, *LL* 3:515.

6. *OR* 37, pt. 1:485.

7. Faust, *Encyclopedia of the Civil War*, 584; *OR* 37, pt. 1:95.

8. Stevenson, "*Boots and Saddles*," 282; Pond, *Shenandoah Valley*, 28; *OR* 37, pt. 1:103.

9. *OR* 37, pt. 1:103.

10. Ibid., 37, 39, 91; Faust, *Encyclopedia of the Civil War*, 455.

11. Ibid., 97; Allan, *Life and Letters of Margaret Junkin Preston*, 196.

12. Pond, *Shenandoah Valley*, 30–31; Douglas, *I Rode with Stonewall*, 277.

13. Burr, *Little Phil and His Troopers*, 175; Thompson, "Summer Campaign" (Ph.D. diss.), 68–69; T. Harry Williams, *Hayes of the 23rd*, 192; Du Pont, *Campaign of 1864*, 37.

14. Du Pont, *Campaign of 1864*, 41.

15. Phillips, *Shenandoah Valley in 1864*, 9; Strother, *A Virginia Yankee in the Civil War*, 237; Du Pont, *Campaign of 1864*, 49, 50.

16. Julia Davis, *The Shenandoah*, 247.

17. JAE, *Autobiographical Sketch*, 371; JAE, *War Memoirs*, ed. Vandiver, xx.

18. Moss, "Jubal Anderson Early" (Master's thesis), 13.

19. Ibid.; JAE to Robert E. Lee, June 16, 1864, Venable Papers, SHC; William C. Davis, *Breckinridge*, 437, 439–40.

20. Sheridan, *Personal Memoirs* 1:425–26; JAE to Robert E. Lee, June 16, 1864, Venable Papers, SHC.

21. Moss, "Jubal Anderson Early" (Master's thesis), 13n; JAE, *Autobiographical Sketch*, 371.

22. *OR* 37, pt. 1:762–63.

23. JAE, *Autobiographical Sketch*, 371.

24. McMurran Diary, June 17, 1864, VSL; Casler, *Four Years in the Stonewall Brigade*, 225.

25. Vandiver, *Jubal's Raid*, 40; Thomas A. Lewis, *Shenandoah in Flames*, 59.

26. JAE, *Autobiographical Sketch*, 374.

27. Blackford, *Campaign and Battle of Lynchburg*, 39; *SHSP* 30:299–300; Achilles James Tynes to wife, June 13, 1864, Tynes Papers, SHC.

28. Vandiver, *Jubal's Raid*, 35.

29. Ibid., 39; JAE, *Autobiographical Sketch*, 374–75.

30. Daniel, *Speeches and Orations of John Warwick Daniel*, 541; Dorie to Charlie, July 30, 1864, Soldier's and Officer's Miscellaneous Letters, Confederate States Army Archives, Duke. The song's words, as copied by Dorie for Charlie in her chatty letter, are as follows (probably sung to the tune of "Rye Whiskey"):

> Go away from me, Lincoln, and let me alone,
> I'm a desolate soldier, a long way from home.
> I eat when I'm hungry and drink when I'm dry,
> If a tree don't fall on me I live till I die.

> Go away from me Lincoln
> And let me alone
> I'm a buttermilk ranger
> A long way from home—

31. Vandiver, *Jubal's Raid*, 40.
32. Morris and Foutz, *Lynchburg*, 46; Crook, *General George Crook*, 118.
33. *OR* 37, pt. 1:100.
34. JAE, *Autobiographical Sketch*, 376.
35. JAE, to Robert E. Lee, June 19, 1864, Venable Papers, SHC; Gallagher, *Ramseur*, 124; Vandiver, *Jubal's Raid*, 55.
36. *OR* 37, pt. 1:160; Crook, *General George Crook*, 121, 121n.
37. JAE, *Autobiographical Sketch*, 380; Gorgas quoted in Thompson, "Summer Campaign" (Ph.D. diss.), 72.

CHAPTER EIGHTEEN: *"The Most Exciting Time"*

1. Gallagher, *Ramseur*, 124; Douglas, *I Rode with Stonewall*, 280.
2. Douglas, *I Rode with Stonewall*, 280; Bushong, *Old Jube*, 193.
3. *OR* 37, pt. 1:766.
4. Vandiver, *Jubal's Raid*, 164; Beringer et al., *Why the South Lost*, 319, 323.
5. Vandiver, *Jubal's Raid*, 164.
6. JAE, *Autobiographical Sketch*, 393–94; *OR* 37, pt. 1:346.
7. Vandiver, *Jubal's Raid*, viii.
8. *OR* 51, pt. 2:1028–29.
9. JAE, *Autobiographical Sketch*, 381; Freeman, *LL* 3:558; Cooling, *Raid on Washington*, 23, 305n. 33.
10. Bushong, *Old Jube*, 247.
11. JAE, *Autobiographical Sketch*, 381–82.
12. Ibid., 381; Freeman, *LL* 3:558; John B. Gordon, *Reminiscences*, 317–18; Vandiver, *Jubal's Raid*, 67–69.
13. Vandiver, *Jubal's Raid*, 68–69.
14. Ibid., 68–70; *OR* 37, pt. 1:768–69; JAE, *Autobiographical Sketch*, 381.
15. *OR* 37, pt. 1:768; Cooling, *Raid on Washington*, 17.
16. Cooling, *Raid on Washington*, 33–35.
17. Vandiver, *Jubal's Raid*, 85; *OR* 37, pt. 1:178.
18. JAE, *Autobiographical Sketch*, 385.
19. Vandiver, *Jubal's Raid*, 93; *OR* 37, pt. 1:769–70; Thomas A. Lewis, *Shenandoah in Flames*, 73.
20. Cooling, *Raid on Washington*, 41.
21. Ibid., 42.
22. Vandiver, *Jubal's Raid*, 91–92; *OR* 37, pt. 1:95.
23. Bushong, *Old Jube*, 198.
24. Ibid.
25. Faust, *Encyclopedia of the Civil War*, 799; Vandiver, *Jubal's Raid*, 98; Cooling, *Raid on Washington*, 53, 55.

26. Cooling, *Raid on Washington*, 57.

27. Wallace, *Lew Wallace*, 734; Pond, *Shenandoah Valley*, 57.

28. Pond, *Shenandoah Valley*, 57; Vandiver, *Jubal's Raid*, 97–98; Faust, *Encyclopedia of the Civil War*, 614.

29. Bushong, *Old Jube*, 197; JAE, *Autobiographical Sketch*, 386; Vandiver, *Jubal's Raid*, 107.

30. Vandiver, *Jubal's Raid*, 107–9.

31. Ibid.; Cooling, *Raid on Washington*, 61.

32. Cooling, *Raid on Washington*, 34; Vandiver, *Jubal's Raid*, 115–16.

33. Worsham, *One of Jackson's Foot Cavalry*, 238–39; John B. Gordon, *Reminiscences*, 312.

34. Cooling, *Raid on Washington*, 76–78.

35. Ibid., 79.

36. Grant, *Personal Memoirs* 2:461.

37. JAE, *Autobiographical Sketch*, 387; Vandiver, *Jubal's Raid*, 119.

CHAPTER NINETEEN: *"More Formidable Than Ever"*

1. Cooling, *Raid on Washington*, 90.

2. Ibid., 84.

3. Green, *Washington: Village and Capital*, 261; Hickey, *The War of 1812*, 199–201; Vandiver, *Jubal's Raid*, 130.

4. Cooling, *Raid on Washington*, 88; Leech, *Reveille*, 331.

5. Bushong, *Old Jube*, 206–7; Cooling, *Raid on Washington*, 91.

6. Cooling, *Raid on Washington*, 90; Moss, "Jubal Anderson Early" (Master's thesis), 32.

7. Bushong, *Old Jube*, 203.

8. Cooling, *Raid on Washington*, 93; Moss, "Jubal Anderson Early" (Master's thesis), 34.

9. *SHSP* 30:254; Leech, *Reveille*, 352; Bushong, *Old Jube*, 203.

10. JAE, *Autobiographical Sketch*, 289; Vandiver, *Jubal's Raid*, 119, 120; Cooling, *Raid on Washington*, 103.

11. Cooling, *Raid on Washington*, 103; Vandiver, *Jubal's Raid*, 121.

12. Vandiver, *Jubal's Raid*, 121; Moss, "Jubal Anderson Early" (Master's thesis), 35; JAE, "The Advance on Washington," 756.

13. Vandiver, *Jubal's Raid*, 149–50; Bushong, *Old Jube*, 202.

14. Leech, *Reveille*, 333; Moss, "Jubal Anderson Early" (Master's thesis), 34.

15. Cooling, *Raid on Washington*, 89, 279.

16. Pond, *Shenandoah Valley*, 64; Leech, *Reveille*, 335, 336; Cooling, *Raid on Washington*, 135.

17. JAE, *Autobiographical Sketch*, 389; Cooling, *Raid on Washington*, 110.

18. JAE, *Autobiographical Sketch*, 389; Vandiver, *Jubal's Raid*, 151–52.

19. Vandiver, *Jubal's Raid*, 152–53; JAE, *Autobiographical Sketch*, 390, 392.

20. JAE, *Autobiographical Sketch*, 390, 392.

21. Vandiver, *Jubal's Raid*, 153.

22. JAE, *Autobiographical Sketch*, 390; *OR* 37, pt. 1:347.

23. JAE, *Autobiographical Sketch*, 391.

24. Vandiver, *Jubal's Raid*, 155; Cooling, *Raid on Washington*, 90, 115–16; Welles, *Diary*, 70.

25. Vandiver, *Jubal's Raid*, 155; Cooling, *Raid on Washington*, 136; William C. Davis, *Breckinridge*, 447.

26. JAE, *Autobiographical Sketch*, 392; Vandiver, *Jubal's Raid*, 155–56.

27. Vandiver, *Jubal's Raid*, 155–56; Cooling, *Raid on Washington*, 164.

28. Vandiver, *Jubal's Raid*, 163–64.

29. JAE, *Autobiographical Sketch*, 392; Cooling, *Raid on Washington*, 121, 278.

30. Vandiver, *Jubal's Raid*, 156; Bennette Diary, July 11, 1864, SHC.

31. Vandiver, *Jubal's Raid*, 164, 172.

32. Cooling, *Raid on Washington*, 147–49.

33. Vandiver, *Jubal's Raid*, 171.

34. Douglas, *I Rode with Stonewall*, 285.

35. Cooling, *Raid on Washington*, 183, 187.

36. Vandiver, *Jubal's Raid*, 172; Cooling, *Raid on Washington*, 120–21; Bushong, *Old Jube*, 210.

37. JAE, *Autobiographical Sketch*, 395n.

38. Kean, *Inside the Confederate Government*, 165, 167.

39. Ibid.; John E. Claiborne to wife, July 11, 1864, Claiborne Papers (#3633), UVA.

40. Cooling, *Raid on Washington*, 190; Andrews, *The South Reports the Civil War*, 407–9; Lee, "Were the Rebs Too Groggy to Carry The Day?"

41. Dowdey and Manarin, *Wartime Papers*, 822–23; Daniel, *Speeches*, 545–46.

42. Burke Davis, *They Called Him Stonewall*, 193; Gallagher, Introduction to Early, *Autobiographical Sketch*, xvi.

43. Noah Brooks, a writer who was on the scene in Washington, derided the notion that Lincoln himself was "greatly disturbed" by the threat of the capital's loss. The president's chief anxiety, according to Brooks, was the danger that the invaders might be allowed to escape. Brooks, *Washington in Lincoln's Time*, 162; Moss, "Jubal Anderson Early" (Master's thesis), 27; McPherson, *Battle Cry*, 757–58.

44. Vandiver, *Jubal's Raid*, 174.

CHAPTER TWENTY: *"The Altar of Revenge"*

1. McMurran Diary, July 14, 1864, VSL.

2. Cooling, *Raid on Washington*, 190.

3. Ibid., 191; *OR* 37, pt. 1:349.

4. *OR* 37, pt. 1:346; Cooling, *Raid on Washington*, 191.

5. Pond, *Shenandoah Valley*, 76–77; *OR* 37, pt. 2:301.

6. Thompson, "Summer Campaign" (Ph.D. diss.), 75; Cooling, *Raid on Washington*, 216; Bushong, *Old Jube*, 221.

7. Pond, *Shenandoah Valley*, 80–82.

8. Catton, *Stillness*, 309–10; *OR* 37, pt. 2:301, 329.

9. Cooling, *Raid on Washington*, 215; Douglas, *I Rode with Stonewall*, 285–86.

10. Thompson, "Summer Campaign" (Ph.D. diss.), 84–85n; JAE, *Memoir of the Last Year*, 71.

11. Pond, *Shenandoah Valley*, 86.

12. Ibid., 86–87; Gallagher, *Ramseur*, 131.

13. JAE, *Autobiographical Sketch*, 398.

14. Ibid., 399; Bushong, *Old Jube*, 213; Pond, *Shenandoah Valley*, 96–97, 98; Thompson, "Summer Campaign" (Ph.D. diss.), 66.

15. Bushong, *Old Jube*, 222.

16. Ibid.; *OR* 37, pt. 1:347; Morris and Foutz, *Lynchburg*, 50; Faust, *Encyclopedia of the Civil War*, 455; JAE, *Autobiographical Sketch*, 401–402; "True Copy," JAE to the Municipal Authorities of Chambersburg, Pennsylvania, July 24, 1864, New York Historical Society.

17. Bushong, *Old Jube*, 223: John H. Dawson, *Wildcat Cavalry*, 54.

18. John H. Dawson, *Wildcat Cavalry*, 117–18.

19. Ibid., 119; *OR* 37, pt. 1:329.

20. Alexander et al., *Revenge*, 122; Booth, *Reminiscences*, 129; *OR* 37, pt. 1:355.

21. *OR* 43, pt. 1:7, 994.

22. Alexander et al., *Revenge*, 120–23.

23. Ibid., 123; *OR* 37, pt. 1:7.

24. Alexander et al., *Revenge*, 123–24; Booth, *Reminiscences*, 129.

25. Alexander et al., *Revenge*, 123, 127.

26. Ibid., 132.

27. Ibid., 127; Pond, *Shenandoah Valley*, 102–3.

28. *SHSP* 37:160; Dawson, *Wildcat Cavalry*, 56; *OR* 43, pt. 1:494–95.

29. *OR* 43, pt. 1:493–95; Thompson, "Summer Campaign" (Ph.D. diss.), 108–9.

30. Thompson, "Summer Campaign" (Ph.D. diss.), 108–9; *SHSP* 37:101; Stevenson, *"Boots and Saddles,"* 297–98; *OR* 43, pt. 1:6.

31. Thompson, "Summer Campaign" (Ph.D. diss.), 115.

32. Ibid.; Alexander et al., *Revenge*, 136; Bushong, *Old Jube*, 226.

33. JAE, *Autobiographical Sketch*, 405.

34. *OR* 37, pt. 1:333.

35. Pond, *Shenandoah Valley*, 109–10; Alexander et al., *Revenge*, 132.

36. Pond, *Shenandoah Valley*, 109; Long, *Memoirs of R. E. Lee*, 367; Thompson, "Summer Campaign" (Ph.D. diss.), 120.

37. Phillips, *Shenandoah Valley in 1864*, 15.

38. Ibid.

39. Bok, *Americanization of Edward Bok*, 208.

40. JAE, *Autobiographical Sketch*, 404n.

CHAPTER TWENTY-ONE: *A Worthy Opponent*

1. Moss, "Jubal Anderson Early" (Master's thesis), 47; Catton, *Stillness*, 303–4.

2. McPherson, *Battle Cry*, 771.

3. *OR* 37, pt. 2:558; Moss, "Jubal Anderson Early" (Master's thesis), 49.

4. Wert, *FWCC*, 17; Sheridan, *Personal Memoirs* 1:156–57; Stackpole, *Sheridan*, 121.

5. Stackpole, *Sheridan*, 125; Thomas A. Lewis, *Shenandoah in Flames*, 103.

6. Taylor, "With Sheridan Up the Shenandoah," Ms., Folder #2, 47, Western Reserve Historical Society.

7. Starr, *Union Cavalry* 2:75; Catton, *Stillness*, 316–17.

8. Sheridan, *Personal Memoirs* 1:1–14; Wert, *FWCC*, 20–21.

9. Stackpole, *Sheridan*, 109–12.

10. Faust, *Encyclopedia of the Civil War*, 679.

11. James H. Wilson, *Under the Old Flag*, 1:328–29; Starr, *Union Cavalry* 1:42–43, 2:78, 80.

12. T. Harry Williams, *Hayes*, 232; Thompson, "Summer Campaign" (Ph.D. diss.), 290–91; Wert, *FWCC*, 22; Catton, *Stillness*, 315.

13. T. Harry Williams, *Hayes*, 232; Wert, *FWCC*, 21; Catton, *Stillness*, 314–15.

14. Wert, *FWCC*, 21.

15. Starr, *Union Cavalry* 1:24–25, 163–65, 167–68.

16. Moss, "Jubal Anderson Early" (Master's thesis), 89.

17. Freeman, *LL* 3:575–76; Faust, *Encyclopedia of the Civil War*, 444; Robert Ransom to JAE, Aug. 22, 1864, JAE Papers, vol. 4, LC; Bennette Diary, Aug. 20, 1864, SHC.

18. Dowdey and Manarin, *Wartime Papers*, 832; Wert, *FWCC*, 22, 26.

19. Wert, *FWCC*, 28.

20. JAE, *Autobiographical Sketch*, 406; Thompson, "Summer Campaign" (Ph.D. diss.), 160.

21. Wert, *FWCC*, 30; *Official Military Atlas*, plate 27:1.

22. *Official Military Atlas*, plate 27:1; Wert, *FWCC*, 31.

23. Bushong, *Old Jube*, 229; Moss, "Jubal Anderson Early" (Master's thesis), 49; Bryan Grimes to wife, Aug. 12, 1864, Grimes Papers, SHC.

24. Wert, *FWCC*, 31.

25. Pond, *Shenandoah Valley*, 129; Sheridan, *Personal Memoirs* 1:483; U. S. Grant to Maj. Gen. Philip Sheridan, Aug. 14, 1864, in U. S. Grant Correspondence,

Aug. 7–Dec. 4, 1864, Huntington Library; Thompson, "Summer Campaign" (Ph.D. diss.), 171.

26. Sheridan, *Personal Memoirs* 1:484; Pond, *Shenandoah Valley*, 128.

27. Sheridan, *Personal Memoirs* 1:483–84.

28. Ibid., 484; Hale, *Four Valiant Years*, 400.

29. Sheridan, *Personal Memoirs* 1:487–88.

30. Ibid., 492.

31. JAE, *Autobiographical Sketch*, 415.

32. Thompson, "Summer Campaign" (Ph.D. diss.), 207.

33. Wert, *FWCC*, 38; JAE, *Autobiographical Sketch*, 409; Pond, *Shenandoah Valley*, 139.

34. Wert, *FWCC*, 45.

CHAPTER TWENTY-TWO: *Fateful Lapse*

1. "Recollections of Jubal Early," 312–13.

2. McPherson, *Battle Cry*, 774–75.

3. Pond, *Shenandoah Valley*, 144.

4. Wert, *FWCC*, 41; Thompson, "Summer Campaign" (Ph.D. diss.), 314–15.

5. Thompson, "Summer Campaign" (Ph.D. diss.), 325–26; Wert, *FWCC*, 43.

6. Wert, *FWCC*, 42–43.

7. Ibid., 43; Sheridan, *Personal Memoirs* 2:9.

8. Pond, *Shenandoah Valley*, 152–54; *OR* 43, pt. 1:1003, 1011; Moss, "Jubal Anderson Early" (Master's thesis), 51.

9. JAE, *Autobiographical Sketch*, 414, 419; Thompson, "Summer Campaign" (Ph.D. diss.), 230.

10. Douglas, *I Rode with Stonewall*, 296; *SHSP* 18:247.

11. Wert, *FWCC*, 45.

12. Ibid., 44; Sheridan, *Personal Memoirs* 2:10.

13. Sheridan, *Personal Memoirs* 2:11–13.

14. Ibid., 16–17; JAE, *Autobiographical Sketch*, 420–21.

15. Sheridan, *Personal Memoirs*, 2:11–13; *OR* 43, pt. 1:1011; Thompson, "Summer Campaign" (Ph.D. diss.), 232.

16. Gallagher, *Ramseur*, 141.

17. Douglas, *I Rode with Stonewall*, 296.

18. JAE, *Autobiographical Sketch*, 420; Gallagher, *Ramseur*, 141; John B. Gordon, *Reminiscences*, 321–22.

19. Wert, *FWCC*, 53.

20. *OR* 43, pt. 1:47; Pond, *Shenandoah Valley*, 158n.

21. Wert, *FWCC*, 53.

22. *OR* 43, pt. 1:280; Thomas H. Carter to John W. Daniel, Nov. 28, 1894,

Daniel Papers, Duke; Nathan G. Dye to friends, Oct. 1, 1864, Dye Papers, Duke; JAE, *Autobiographical Sketch*, 422–23.

23. John B. Gordon, *Reminiscences*, 321–22; JAE, *Autobiographical Sketch*, 422–23; Wert, *FWCC*, 66.

24. Wert, *FWCC*, 66.

25. Ibid., 66, 68; Thompson, "Summer Campaign" (Ph.D. diss.), 383.

26. JAE, *Autobiographical Sketch*, 421–23; Thompson, "Summer Campaign" (Ph.D. diss.), 353–54.

27. Moss, "Jubal Anderson Early" (Master's thesis), 53; Starr, *Union Cavalry* 2:271; *OR* 43, pt. 1:61, 455.

28. Wert, *FWCC*, 77–78.

29. Ibid., 78–79.

30. Ibid., 71, 78; *OR* 43, pt. 1:456.

31. Wert, *FWCC*, 78–79.

32. Crook, *General George Crook*, 126–27; Wert, *FWCC*, 81–84.

33. Crook, *General George Crook*, 128; Wert, *FWCC*, 94; *OR* 43, pt. 1:189.

34. Catton, *Stillness*, 336; Wert, *FWCC*, 94.

35. Thomas H. Carter to John W. Daniel, Oct. 10, 1881, Daniel Papers, Duke.

36. Wert, *FWCC*, 95–96.

37. Ibid., 96.

38. John B. Gordon, *Reminiscences*, 319–20; Wert, *FWCC*, 98; Eckert, *John Brown Gordon*, 90–91.

39. JAE, *Autobiographical Sketch*, 429.

40. Wert, *FWCC*, 103; McWhiney and Jamieson, *Attack and Die*, 19–20.

41. Wert, *FWCC*, 110–11; Freeman, *LL* 3:583–84; *OR* 43, pt. 2:877.

42. Wert, *FWCC*, 119; JAE, *Autobiographical Sketch*, 428–29; *OR* 43, pt. 2:876.

43. Sheridan, *Personal Memoirs* 2:35, 37, 40; Crook, *General George Crook*, 129–30; JAE, *Autobiographical Sketch*, 430.

44. Gallagher, *Ramseur*, 149; Wert, *FWCC*, 121. One Confederate artilleryman recorded an even earlier sighting of the Federal troops on North Mountain. "The Yanks have been moving heavy columns of infantry to their right all day," he wrote in his diary. "We can see them plainly climbing up the side of [the mountain]." Berkeley, *Four Years in the Confederate Artillery*, Sept. 22, 1864.

45. Buck, *With the Old Confeds*, 115.

46. McCarthy, *Soldier Life*, 114; Wert, *FWCC*, 127.

47. Wert, *FWCC*, 128; *OR* 43, pt. 1:556; Du Pont, *Campaign of 1864*, 136–37.

48. *OR Atlas*, plate 74:1; Wert, *FWCC*, 127, 128.

49. *OR* 43, pt. 1:557, 558–59.

50. JAE, *Autobiographical Sketch*, 427; JAE *Memoir of the Last Year*, 97n; Pond, *Shenandoah Valley*, 167, 171–72, 185; McPherson, *Battle Cry*, 777–78.

51. *OR* 43, pt. 1:557–58, 559.

CHAPTER TWENTY-THREE: *"The Stars Had Fallen"*

1. *SHSP* 28:105.
2. Pond, *Shenandoah Valley*, 192; Starr, *Union Cavalry* 2:293–94.
3. *OR* 43, pt. 1:443; Phillips, *Shenandoah Valley in 1864*, 19, 22–23.
4. Myers, *The Comanches*, 335.
5. Pond, *Shenandoah Valley*, 200; Phillips, *Shenandoah Valley in 1864*, 21.
6. Wert, *FWCC*, 135, 139; John B. Gordon, *Reminiscences*, 331.
7. Bryan Grimes to wife, Sept. 30, 1864, Grimes Papers, SHC.
8. Bryan Grimes to wife, Oct. 3, 1864, Grimes Papers, SHC; Floyd King to sisters, Sept. 26, 1864, King Papers, SHC.
9. Bushong, *Old Jube*, 247–48.
10. Wert, *FWCC*, 137; *OR* 43, pt. 2:893–98.
11. Thomas L. Rosser to wife, Dec. 24, 1863, Rosser Papers (#1171 a-b), UVA; Stevens, *Battle of Cedar Creek*, 6; Bushong, *Old Jube*, 249–50.
12. Wert, *FWCC*, 161; Thomas A. Lewis, *The Guns*, 64; Booth, *Personal Reminiscences*, 152.
13. JAE to Thomas L. Rosser, Oct. 7, 1864, Rosser Papers (#1171 a-b), UVA.
14. *OR* 43, pt. 1:553.
15. Ibid., 431; Sheridan, *Personal Memoirs* 2:56.
16. Thomas A. Lewis, *The Guns*, 100–102.
17. Starr, *Union Cavalry* 2:298–300; Pond, *Shenandoah Valley*, 204–5.
18. *OR* 43, pt. 1:521; Starr, *Union Cavalry* 2:301.
19. Douglas, *I Rode with Stonewall*, 300; *OR* 43, pt. 1:559.
20. J. D. Ferguson Diary, Oct. 9, 1864, Munford-Ellis Papers, Duke; *SHSP* 13:134–35.
21. JAE to Thomas L. Rosser, Oct. 10, 1864, Rosser Papers (#1171 a-b), UVA.
22. *OR* 43, pt. 2:892.
23. Sheridan, *Personal Memoirs* 2:55; Thomas A. Lewis, *The Guns*, 57.
24. *OR* 43, pt. 2:363.
25. Ibid., 168–69; *OR* 43, pt. 1:372.
26. Wert, *FWCC*, 169.
27. *OR* 43, pt. 2:389; Sheridan, *Personal Memoirs* 2:63; *OR Atlas*, plate 99:2.
28. Sheridan, *Personal Memoirs* 2:64.
29. Pond, *Shenandoah Valley*, 222–23; Wert, *FWCC*, 170–71.
30. Thomas A. Lewis, *The Guns*, 203–4, 205, 211; Wert, *FWCC*, 190; John B. Gordon, *Reminiscences*, 340.
31. Wert, *FWCC*, 203, 206.
32. Ibid.
33. Thomas A. Lewis, *The Guns*, 226–27.
34. Wert, *FWCC*, 208.
35. JAE, *Autobiographical Sketch*, 443.

36. Ibid., 444; Floyd King to sisters, Oct. 24, 1864, King Papers, SHC; Eckert, *John Brown Gordon*, 97–98.

37. JAE, *Autobiographical Sketch*, 444–45; Wert, *FWCC*, 209; Douglas, *I Rode with Stonewall*, 303.

38. Wert, *FWCC*, 210–11; Thomas A. Lewis, *The Guns*, 226–27; *OR* 43, pt. 2:911.

39. Wert, *FWCC*, 210; JAE, *Autobiographical Sketch*, 445.

40. JAE, *Autobiographical Sketch*, 445.

41. Ibid., 445–46; *OR* 43, pt. 1:210, 562; Thomas A. Lewis, *The Guns*, 324.

42. JAE, *Autobiographical Sketch*, 447; Freeman, *LL* 3:603; Calvert and Young, *A Dictionary of Battles*, 302; Thomas G. Jones to John W. Daniel, July 3, 1904, Daniel Papers, Duke.

43. Buell, *The Cannoneer*, 247.

44. Starr, *Union Cavalry* 2:310–11; *OR* 43, pt. 1:562, 613; Wert, *FWCC*, 215.

45. Wert, *FWCC*, 217; Thomas A. Lewis, *The Guns*, 235.

46. John B. Gordon, *Reminiscences*, 341–42.

47. Ibid., 364–69; John G. Williams, quoted in Cedar Creek folder, Daniel Papers (#158/5383, Box 21), UVA; James Mason, quoted in Cedar Creek folder, Daniel Papers (#158/5383, Box 21), UVA; Buck, *With the Old Confeds*, 126; Wert, *FWCC*, 218.

48. *OR* 43, pt. 1:562; JAE, *Autobiographical Sketch*, 448.

49. Wert, *FWCC*, 223.

50. Thomas A. Lewis, *The Guns*, 250–52.

51. Ibid., 255.

52. Wert, *FWCC*, 225.

53. Ibid., 228; John B. Gordon, *Reminiscences*, 347–48.

54. Wert, *FWCC*, 230; Thomas A. Lewis, *The Guns*, 262; John B. Gordon, *Reminiscences*, 348.

55. Thomas A. Lewis, *The Guns*, 278.

56. *OR* 43, pt. 1:450–51, 479.

57. JAE, *Autobiographical Sketch*, 449; Gallagher, *Ramseur*, 162.

58. Thomas A. Lewis, *The Guns*, 280; John B. Gordon, *Reminiscences*, 349.

59. John B. Gordon, *Reminiscences*, 350.

60. Marcellus N. Moorman, "Recollections of Cedar Creek and Fisher's Hill, October 19, 1864," BR Box 306(42), Huntington Library.

61. Thomas A. Lewis, *The Guns*, 291.

CHAPTER TWENTY-FOUR: *Last Stand*

1. Douglas, *I Rode with Stonewall*, 305; *OR* 43, pt. 1:580.

2. Pond, *Shenandoah Valley*, 239.

3. Ibid., 241.

4. Ibid., 240.

5. Sheridan, *Personal Memoirs* 2:95; Wert, *FWCC*, 240, 246.

6. *OR* 43, pt. 1:582.

7. Ibid., 563-64.

8. Copy of address, published in the Richmond *Enquirer*, Oct. 27, 1864, in Daniel Papers (#158/5383), UVA; JAE, *Autobiographical Sketch*, 451.

9. *OR* 43, pt. 1:563; JAE to Thomas H. Carter, Oct. 29, 1864 (MC3 M640), Museum of the Confederacy.

10. Clipping, Richmond *Enquirer*, Oct. 27, 1864, in Daniel Papers (#158/5383), UVA; Eckert, *John B. Gordon*, 102.

11. *OR* 43, pt. 1:583; Eckert, *John B. Gordon*, 102-3; Thomas G. Jones to John W. Daniel, July 3, Dec. 25, 1904, Daniel Papers, Duke.

12. J. C. McComb to Jefferson Davis, Oct. 24, 1864, Letters Received by the Secretary of War (RG 109, M437, Roll 136, M-544), National Archives.

13. JAE to Hon. Mr. Sparrow, Chairman, Committee on Military Affairs, Nov. 28, 1864 (printed by order of the Senate), Confederate States Senate Records, VSL.

14. Thomas G. Jones to John W. Daniel, July 3, 1904, Daniel Papers, Duke; Samuel J. C. Moore, "Account of the Battle of Cedar Creek, 1864" (June 1889), p. 8, JAE Papers, CWM; W. W. Old, biographical notes, Daniel Papers (#158/5383, Box 25), UVA.

15. Sheridan, *Personal Memoirs* 2:98-99.

16. Dennison, *Soldiering in Canada*, 68; Douglas, *I Rode with Stonewall*, 310.

17. Douglas, *I Rode with Stonewall*, 307; Hale, *Four Valiant Years*, 316-17; Bryan Grimes to wife, Nov. 17, 1864, Grimes Papers, SHC.

18. Maddex, *Virginia Conservatives*, 30.

19. "Letters of John Letcher to J. Hierholzer," 138; Mosgrove, *Kentucky Cavaliers in Dixie*, 221.

20. JAE, *Autobiographical Sketch*, 459.

21. Ibid., 461; Freeman, *LL* 3:634.

22. Pond, *Shenandoah Valley*, 251; JAE, *Autobiographical Sketch*, 461.

23. Pond, *Shenandoah Valley*, 252; Hale, *Four Valiant Years*, 499; JAE, *Autobiographical Sketch*, 462.

24. JAE, *Autobiographical Sketch*, 462.

25. Golladay, "Jubal Early's Last Stand," 30.

26. Ibid., 31.

27. Ibid., 32; JAE, *Autobiographical Sketch*, 463.

28. Sheridan, *Personal Memoirs* 2:116, 119; JAE, *Autobiographical Sketch*, 463-64.

29. JAE, *Autobiographical Sketch*, 463-64.

30. Jed. Hotchkiss Diary, Mar. 16, 17, 21, 22, 30, 1865, Hotchkiss Papers, LC; JAE, *Autobiographical Sketch*, 466.

< 512 >

31. Laura to Edith, Mar. 1865, "Charlottesville in the Civil War," Miscellaneous Collection, UVA.
32. JAE, *Autobiographical Sketch*, 466–67; Bushong, *Old Jube*, 280.
33. JAE, *Autobiographical Sketch*, 468–69.
34. Moss, "Jubal Anderson Early" (Master's thesis), 75–76; Wert, *FWCC*, 248.
35. Moss, "Jubal Anderson Early" (Master's thesis), 76.
36. Ibid., 90.
37. Ibid., 91; Freeman, *LL* 3:277.
38. Freeman, *LL* 3:513–14; Beringer et al., *Why the South Lost*, 435.
39. Moss, "Jubal Anderson Early" (Master's thesis), 85–86, 88.
40. Note, n.d., Daniel Papers (#158/5383, Waynesboro folder, Box 25), UVA.

CHAPTER TWENTY-FIVE: *Reconstruction and Railroad Politics*

1. Beringer et al., *Why the South Lost*, 398–417, passim.
2. Foner, *Reconstruction*, 588–92; Maddex, *Virginia Conservatives*, 198, 78n.
3. JAE, *Autobiographical Sketch*, 468.
4. JAE to John Goode, June 6, 1866, JAE Papers, Duke; JAE to Thomas L. Rosser, May 10, 1866, Rosser Papers (#1171 a-b), UVA; Associated Press clipping, n.d., Allen Papers, SHC.
5. JAE to Hunter H. McGuire, Oct. 30, 1865, McGuire Papers (#9320), UVA.
6. Robert E. Lee to JAE, Nov. 22, 1865, JAE Papers, vol. 4., LC.
7. JAE to John Goode, June 8, 1866, JAE Papers, Duke.
8. Rolle, *Confederate Exodus*, 124.
9. JAE to Jed. Hotchkiss, June 8, 1866, Hotchkiss Papers, LC; JAE to Samuel H. Early, June 13, Aug. 8, 1866, JAE Papers, vol. 4, LC; Faust, *Encyclopedia of the Civil War*, 479; Maddex, *Virginia Conservatives*, 36; Smith, "Virginia during Reconstruction," (Ph.D. diss.), 185–86.
10. JAE to John W. Daniel, Feb. 17, 1867, Daniel Papers, Duke; JAE to Samuel H. Early, Mar. 6, 1867, JAE Papers, vol. 4, LC.
11. Foner, *Reconstruction*, 183; JAE to John Goode, June 8, 1866, JAE Papers, vol. 4, LC; JAE to Samuel H. Early, May 15, May 30, Aug. 21, 1866, JAE Papers, vol. 4, LC; JAE to Thomas L. Rosser, Rosser Papers (#1171 a-b), UVA.
12. JAE to John Goode, June 8, 1866, JAE Papers, Duke; Maddex, *Virginia Conservatives*, 26–28.
13. Maddex, *Virginia Conservatives*, 37–39; Rubin, *Virginia*, 138.
14. Maddex, *Virginia Conservatives*, 40–41.
15. Ibid., 39–40; Smith, "Virginia during Reconstruction" (Ph.D. diss.), 17.
16. Maddex, *Virginia Conservatives*, 40; Rubin, *Virginia*, 138.
17. JAE to John Goode, June 8, 1866, JAE Papers, vol. 4, LC.
18. Rubin, *Virginia*, 139.

< 513 >

19. Bushong, *Old Jube*, 294; Maddex, *Virginia Conservatives*, 55–56; Smith, "Virginia during Reconstruction" (Ph.D. diss.), 110.

20. Maddex, *Virginia Conservatives*, 58; Smith, "Virginia during Reconstruction" (Ph.D. diss.), 110; Rubin, *Virginia*, 140.

21. JAE to Samuel H. Early, June 30, 1868, JAE Papers, vol. 5, LC.

22. Rubin, *Virginia*, 140; Maddex, *Virginia Conservatives*, 55–56.

23. Rubin, *Virginia*, 141; Maddex, *Virginia Conservatives*, 70–71.

24. Maddex, *Virginia Conservatives*, 73–75.

25. Ibid., 74; Foner, *Reconstruction*, 412; Faust, *Encyclopedia of the Civil War*, 469; Pearson, *The Readjuster Movement in Virginia*, 69; Freeman, *LL* 3:552, 553.

26. Maddex, *Virginia Conservatives*, 61.

27. Ibid., 76, 78–79.

28. Freeman, *R. E. Lee* 4:381.

29. Bushong, *Old Jube*, 291.

30. JAE to Edmund Irvine, Dec. 7, 1868, JAE Papers, Duke.

31. JAE to Ruth H. Early, Jan. 21, 1869, JAE Papers, vol. 5, LC.

32. John W. Daniel to JAE, July 10, 1870, JAE Papers, vol. 5, LC; Coleman, "The Lion of Virginia," pt. 4, 20.

33. Maddex, *Virginia Conservatives*, 82; Smith, "Virginia during Reconstruction" (Ph.D. diss.), 161–63.

34. Maddex, *Virginia Conservatives*, 91; Rubin, *Virginia*, 144.

35. Maddex, *Virginia Conservatives*, 100–107; Jones, "Conservative Virginian" (Ph.D. diss.), 213; James L. Kemper to JAE, July 26, 1873, JAE Papers, vol. 7, LC.

36. Rubin, *Virginia*, 144–45; Maddex, *Virginia Conservatives*, 250, 257–58.

37. Rubin, *Virginia*, 146.

38. Ibid., 147, 157.

39. Ibid., 158; Early, *Heritage*, 94.

40. Beringer et al., *Why the South Lost*, 400.

41. Early, *Heritage*, 8.

42. Ibid., 113–15.

43. Jones, "Conservative Virginian" (Ph.D. diss.), 299–300; James L. Kemper to JAE, Oct. 22, 23, 1875, JAE Papers, vol. 7, LC.

44. Rubin, *Virginia*, 151–52.

45. Beringer et al., *Why the South Lost*, 417. The quoted statements within the quotation are from John Shy.

CHAPTER TWENTY-SIX: *A Matter of Money*

1. B. W. Wrenn to JAE, Nov. 18, 1886, JAE Papers, vol. 13, LC; Early to Darwin C. Pavey, Mar. 12, 1886, EG Box 16, Huntington Library.

2. Bushong, *Old Jube*, 293; Jefferson Davis to JAE, Apr. 16, 1870, JAE Papers, vol. 5, LC.

3. Bushong, *Old Jube*, 293.
4. T. Harry Williams, *Beauregard*, 298.
5. Ibid., 292; Ezell, *Fortune's Merry Wheel*, 244.
6. T. Harry Williams, *Beauregard*, 292, 293, 294–95.
7. Ibid., 295; Ezell, *Fortune's Merry Wheel*, 246.
8. T. Harry Williams, *Beauregard*, 295.
9. Ibid., 294; Ezell, *Fortune's Merry Wheel*, 247.
10. T. Harry Williams, *Beauregard*, 292; Ezell, *Fortune's Merry Wheel*, 247, 249.
11. T. Harry Williams, *Beauregard*, 298.
12. Ibid., John B. Hood to JAE, Dec. 11, 1876, JAE Papers, vol. 8, LC. Hood appears to have been a possible third candidate for Beauregard's partner as lottery supervisor. But the value of this letter lies in Early's notes, scribbled on the back, outlining his version of an employment agreement with the company.
13. T. Harry Williams, *Beauregard*, 298–99.
14. Ibid., 300.
15. JAE, memorandum, n.d., JAE Papers, vol. 12 (2451), LC.
16. Ezell, *Fortune's Merry Wheel*, 248, 251; P. G. T. Beauregard to JAE, Nov. 17, 1879, JAE Papers, vol. 10, LC.
17. JAE, open letter, June 12, 1878, JAE Papers, vol. 10, LC.
18. Beauregard to M. A. Dauphin, Aug. 23, 1883, JAE Papers, vol. 12, LC; Ezell, *Fortune's Merry Wheel*, 249–50.
19. Beauregard to Early, Aug. 23, 1883, JAE Papers, vol. 12, LC.
20. T. Harry Williams, *Beauregard*, 302–3; Ezell, *Fortune's Merry Wheel*, 247.

CHAPTER TWENTY-SEVEN: *Seeking the Lost Cause*

1. T. Harry Williams, *Beauregard*, 301.
2. JAE to E. L. Cohn, Jan. 22, 1887, EG Box 16, Huntington Library.
3. Beringer et al., *Why the South Lost*, 392–93.
4. Connelly and Bellows, *God and General Longstreet*, 12–19, passim; Charles Reagan Wilson, *Baptized in Blood*, 67–69.
5. Woodward, *Burden of Southern History*, 168–69.
6. Connelly, *Marble Man*, 48.
7. Connelly and Bellows, *God and General Longstreet*, 22, 28.
8. Bryan Grimes to wife, May 18, 1864, Grimes Papers, SHC.
9. Foster, *Ghosts*, 57–58.
10. Connelly, *Marble Man*, 91–98, passim, 100–110, passim.
11. Connelly and Bellows, *God and General Longstreet*, 30–38; Piston, *Lee's Tarnished Lieutenant*, 125.
12. JAE to Henry B. Dawson, Oct. 25, 1873, Smith Papers, VSL.
13. Foster, *Ghosts*, 50.

14. Joseph Jones to JAE, Aug. 12, 1869, JAE Papers, vol. 5, LC; Dabney H. Maury to JAE, Jan. 14, 1870, JAE Papers, vol. 5, LC.

15. Foster, *Ghosts*, 53-54.

16. Ibid., 54; *Proceedings of the Southern Historical Convention*, 5, 12, 18.

17. *Proceedings of the Southern Historical Convention*, 18.

18. Ibid., 22.

19. Ibid., 28.

20. Ibid., 29; Coddington, *Gettysburg Campaign*, 250.

21. *Proceedings of the Southern Historical Convention*, 29-30; Swinton, *Campaigns of the Army of the Potomac*, 310; Coddington, *Gettysburg Campaign*, 249.

22. Foster, *Ghosts*, 54.

23. Ibid.

24. Connelly, *Marble Man*, 51; Stiles, *Four Years*, 188-89.

25. Foster, *Ghosts*, 54; Connelly, *Marble Man*, 73-74; L. McLaws to James Longstreet, Nov. 22, 1887, Tucker Family Papers, SHC.

26. Connelly, *Marble Man*, 72.

27. Connelly, *Marble Man*, 25; Executive Committee, Jackson Memorial Association to JAE, Apr. 19, 1875, JAE Papers, vol. 7, LC.

28. Connelly, *Marble Man*, 46; Foster, *Ghosts*, 51.

29. Connelly, *Marble Man*, 46.

30. JAE to William N. Pendleton, Oct. 13, 1870, Pendleton Papers, SHC.

31. Connelly, *Marble Man*, 43.

32. Ibid., 33; Foster, *Ghosts*, 52.

33. JAE to William N. Pendleton, Oct. 24, 1870, Pendleton Papers, SHC.

34. Connelly, *Marble Man*, 43; Dabney H. Maury to JAE, Oct. 26, 1870, JAE Papers, vol. 5, LC.

35. Connelly, *Marble Man*, 43, 61.

36. William Allan to JAE, Oct. 25, 1870, JAE Papers, vol. 5, LC.

37. Bundle of papers covered by a letter from Jubal A. Early to Governor F. W. W. Holliday, Mar. 11, 1878, Treasurer's Office Inventory, Lee Monument Association Correspondence, VSL; Connelly, *Marble Man*, 45.

38. The relationship between this sum and the funds finally turned over to Governor Lee by the women is interesting; it seems clear, given their energy and talent, that they should have ended up contributing considerably more. In fact, a substantial portion of their collected funds leaked away. In April 1873, the Ladies' Association authorized the loan, at 8 percent, of $7,000 to Thomas Jefferson Randolph, Sarah's father. Security was his 1,200-acre estate, Edge Hill, appraised at $30 an acre. Apart from the potential conflicts of interest involved, the loan was a mistake because the estate carried prior liens (up to $15,000). When Randolph père died, his executor sold the land at the best price he could obtain—$18 an acre—to the nearest buyers, Sarah Randolph's sisters; she took no part because of the involvement of her Memorial Association. As of March 1878, the sisters were

prepared to pay off the loan if the interest were reduced to 6 percent. Early, writing to Virginia's Governor Holliday about the matter, guessed that the money, with the original interest, would amount to two-thirds of the total collected to that point by the women. What they had done with the rest of the money, he sniffed, he had "no idea, and it was a mere accident that I heard of this 'investment.'" JAE to Governor F. W. W. Holliday, Mar. 11, 1878, bundle of papers, &c., Lee Monument Association Correspondence, VSL.

39. JAE to William N. Pendleton, Dec. 8, 1870, Pendleton Papers, SHC; JAE to Southern newspapers, Feb. 17, 1871, Pendleton Papers, SHC.

40. Connelly, *Marble Man*, 44; JAE to William N. Pendleton, Feb. 20, 1871, Pendleton Papers, SHC.

41. Foster, *Ghosts*, 53.

42. JAE, *Campaigns of Gen. Robert E. Lee*, 35.

43. Ibid., 35–37.

44. Ibid., 40.

45. Ibid., 37.

46. Ibid., 40.

47. Ibid., 29–30.

48. Ibid., 30–31.

49. Ibid., 31–32.

50. Connelly, *Marble Man*, 84–85; Piston, *Lee's Tarnished Lieutenant*, 121–22.

51. Connelly, *Marble Man*, 39–40; William Allan to JAE, Dec. 16, 1870, JAE Papers, vol. 5, LC.

52. Ibid.; Connelly and Bellows, *God and General Longstreet*, 28.

53. Connelly and Bellows, *God and General Longstreet*, 29; Dowdey, *Lee*, 630.

54. Connelly, *Marble Man*, 46.

55. Ibid., 37–38; printed broadside advertising the portrait, endorsed by Jefferson Davis, John B. Hood, John C. Breckinridge and others, Pendleton Papers, SHC.

56. Treasurer's Office Inventory, Lee Monument Association Correspondence, VSL.

57. Ibid.

58. JAE to J. William Jones, Aug. 3, 1879, JAE Papers, Duke; flyer for Aug. 18, 1878, Lee Monument Ball at Greenbrier White Sulphur Springs, Lee Monument Association Correspondence, VSL; collection figures in final report of R. M. T. Hunter, Treasurer, Dec. 31, 1880, Lee Monument Association Correspondence, VSL.

59. Foster, *Ghosts*, 98.

60. Ibid.; memorandum, May 1886, Lee Monument Association Correspondence, VSL.

61. Foster, *Ghosts*, 100.

62. Fitz. Lee to JAE, Dec. 1, 1888, JAE Papers, vol. 14, LC.

63. Fitz. Lee to JAE, Jan. 15, 1889, JAE Papers, vol. 14, LC.

64. Ladies Confederate Memorial Association to JAE, Jan. 9, 1890, JAE Papers, vol. 14, LC.

65. Foster, *Ghosts*, 101.

CHAPTER TWENTY-EIGHT: *"Tom-Tom Warfare"*

1. JAE, *Campaigns of Gen. Robert E. Lee*, 41.

2. Piston, *Lee's Tarnished Lieutenant*, 105–6.

3. Ibid., 107–10.

4. Ibid., 127–28.

5. John H. New to JAE, Mar. 23, 1876, JAE Papers, vol. 8, LC.

6. Connelly *Marble Man*, 85; Piston, *Lee's Tarnished Lieutenant*, 132.

7. *SHSP* 5:72–73.

8. Johnston was a target of the Lee cult for criticizing their icon in memoirs (*Narrative of Military Operations*) published in 1874. For that, and for the hatred of Jefferson Davis that Johnston revealed in his book, the cult transformed Johnston's reputation; popular during the war, his postwar profile became that of a ham-handed incompetent who was on the point of wrecking the Army of Northern Virginia until Lee took over following Johnston's wounding at Seven Pines. Connelly, *Marble Man*, 79–80.

9. Piston, *Lee's Tarnished Lieutenant*, 132.

10. Ibid., 132–33.

11. *SHSP* 4:281.

12. Ibid., 282.

13. *SHSP* 5:54–86; *SHSP* 4:282.

14. Sanger and Hay, *Longstreet*, 425.

15. Tucker, *Lee and Longstreet*, 38; Fitz. Lee to JAE, Apr. 24, 1876, JAE Papers, vol. 8, LC. In conversation with Wade Hampton, Carroll quoted Lee in holding Longstreet responsible for losing Gettysburg. "I don't know," Hampton wrote Early, "whether [Carroll] would make the statement publicly but he made it to me at a dinner in Baltimore." Wade Hampton to JAE, Mar. 27, 1876, JAE Papers, vol. 8, LC.

16. Piston, *Lee's Tarnished Lieutenant*, 134–35.

17. Ibid., 144.

18. Connelly, *Marble Man*, 86; Piston, *Lee's Tarnished Lieutenant*, 135; Jefferson Davis, *Rise and Fall*, 2:371–72.

19. Piston, *Lee's Tarnished Lieutenant*, 149. In his memoirs, *From Manassas to Appomattox* (1896), Longstreet took a measure of vengeance upon Early, who was no longer alive to fight back. Writing of Gettysburg, Longstreet maintained— untruthfully—that Early had deliberately held back the brigades of Gordon and William Smith on July 2, and implied broadly that Jubal was a coward: "There was

a man on the left of the line who did not care to make the battle win. He knew where it was, had viewed it from its earliest formation, had orders for his part in it, but so withheld part of his command from it as to make cooperative concert of action impossible. He had a pruriency for the honors of the field of Mars, was eloquent, before the fires of bivouac and his chief, of the glory of war's gory shield; but when its envied laurels were dipping to the grasp, when the heavy field called for bloody work, he found the placid horizon, far and away beyond the cavalry, more lovely and inviting. He wanted command of the Second Corps, and succeeding to it, held the honored position until General Lee found, at last, that he must dismiss him from field service." Longstreet, *From Manassas*, 375.

20. Piston, *Lee's Tarnished Lieutenant*, 169; Connelly, *Marble Man*, 64.

21. JAE to Thomas T. Munford, Feb. 20, 1886, JAE Papers, vol. 13, LC.

22. *A Correspondence*, JAE Papers, CWM.

23. A. M. Chicester to JAE, Oct. 23, 1881, JAE Papers, vol. 11, LC.

24. *A Correspondence*, p. 2, JAE Papers, CWM.

25. "The Early-Mahone Fight," Baltimore *Sun*, Apr. 22, 1881.

26. *A Correspondence*, pp. 2–3, JAE Papers, CWM.

27. Ibid., 3.

28. Ibid., 4.

29. Ibid., 5.

30. Ibid.

31. Ibid., 6.

32. Ibid., 7.

33. Ibid., 14–15.

34. Bradley Johnson to JAE, Apr. 26, 1881, JAE Papers, vol. 11, LC; *A Correspondence*, pp. 17–18, JAE Papers, CWM.

35. Thomas Smith to JAE, Oct. 16, 1881, JAE Papers, vol. 11, LC; William H. Payne to JAE, Oct. 23, 1881, JAE Papers, vol. 11, LC.

36. *A Correspondence*, p. 1, JAE Papers, CWM.

37. R. W. Wooley to JAE, Oct. 26, 1881, JAE Papers, vol. 11, LC; "The Early-Mahone Fight," Baltimore *Sun*, Apr. 22, 1881. There is no date on the printed correspondence.

38. *A Correspondence*, p. 19, JAE Papers, CWM.

CHAPTER TWENTY-NINE: *A Farewell Kiss*

1. Schmitt, "Interview," 548–49, 551, 558, 562. Early deemed Crook and Averell "gentlemen."

2. Ibid., 550.

3. Ibid., 552.

4. Ibid., 553–56.

5. Rebecca Yancey Williams, *The Vanishing Virginian*, 9–10.

6. Ibid., 81–83.

7. William H. Payne to JAE, Jan. 8, 1890, JAE Papers, vol. 14, LC; Ruth H. Early, *The Family*, 110.

8. Lynchburg *News*, Mar. 3, 1894.

9. Coleman, "The Lion of Virginia," pt. 4, 23; Lynchburg *News*, Mar. 3, 1894.

10. Lynchburg *News*, Mar. 3, 1894.

11. Ibid.

12. Ibid. One of Early's more notable beneficiaries was Mary Anna Jackson, Stonewall's widow. Jubal loaned her $1,000 to pay off a debt on land she had bought near the twin cities in Minnesota, which she hoped would one day be valuable enough to provide independence for her daughters. Without the loan, the creditor would have foreclosed. M. A. Jackson to JAE, Oct. 4, 1889, JAE Papers, vol. 14, LC.

13. Lynchburg *News*, Mar. 3, 1894.

14. Charles M. Blackford to John W. Daniel, Dec. 29, 1894, Daniel Papers, Duke.

15. Jefferson Davis to JAE, Apr. 17, 1885, JAE Papers, vol. 13, LC.

16. Connelly, *Marble Man*, 115–16.

17. C. D. Holmes to JAE, May 12, 1889, JAE Papers, vol. 14, LC. Holmes was a former Union officer. Early must have been gratified by his letter, which said in part: "I cannot say I wish you had won, but I can say very decidedly that you deserved to. If you had been supported as liberally as the absurdly lauded [Stonewall] Jackson, I am of the opinion that you would have shown much greater results."

18. Coleman, "The Lion of Virginia," pt. 4, 24.

19. Lynchburg *News*, Mar. 6, 1894.

20. Daniel, *Speeches*, 579–80.

« BIBLIOGRAPHY »

MANUSCRIPT SOURCES

College of William and Mary. Swem Library. Williamsburg, Va.
>   Jubal A. Early Papers
>   > *A Correspondence between Generals Early and Mahone, in Regard to a Military Memoir of the Latter*
>   > Samuel J. C. Moore, "Account of the Battle of Cedar Creek, 1864" (June 1889)

Duke University. Manuscript Department. William R. Perkins Library. Durham, N.C.
>   John W. Daniel Papers
>   Nathan G. Dye Papers
>   Jubal A. Early Papers
>   Samuel Wragg Ferguson Papers
>   > Samuel Wragg Ferguson, "Memoirs"
>   Edmund Jennings Lee II Papers
>   Munford-Ellis Papers (Thomas T. Munford Division)
>   Soldiers' and Officers' Miscellaneous Letters, Confederate States Army Archives
>   Joachim R. Saussy Papers
>   Mary Eliza Fleming Schooler Papers

Franklin County Records. Franklin County Court House. Rocky Mount, Va.

Historical Society of Pennsylvania. Philadelphia, Pa.
>   John C. Pemberton Papers

Huntington Library. San Marino, Calif.
>   Jubal A. Early Papers
>   U. S. Grant Correspondence, 1864
>   Marcellus N. Moorman, "Recollections of Cedar Creek and Fisher's Hill, October 19, 1864"

Library of Congress. Washington, D.C.
>   Jubal A. Early Papers
>   Jedediah Hotchkiss Papers

Museum of the Confederacy. Eleanor S. Brockenbrough Library. Richmond, Va.
    Miscellaneous Letters
National Archives. Washington, D.C.
    Adjutant General, Letters Received (Records Group 94)
    Secretary of War, Letters Received (Records Group 109)
New York Historical Society. New York, N.Y.
    Naval History Collection
    Ms. "True Copy," Jubal A. Early to the Municipal Authorities of
        Chambersburg, Pennsylvania, July 24, 1864
United States Army Military History Institute. Carlisle, Pa.
    William B. Bailey, Jr., "Memoir"
    Campbell Brown Diary, Tennessee Historical Commission Collection
    George Greer Diary, *Civil War Times Illustrated* Collection
    William Seymour Journal, Harrisburg Civil War Roundtable, Gregory Coco
        Collection
United States Military Academy. West Point, N.Y.
    John Bratt Diary
    Jubal A. Early Records
    United States Military Academy Regulations
University of North Carolina. Southern Historical Collection. Chapel Hill, N.C.
    William Allen Papers
    J. Kelley Bennette, Ms. Diary
    Richard S. Ewell Papers
    Bryan Grimes Papers
    Peter W. Hairston Papers
        Peter W. Hairston, Ms. Diary
    John C. Haskell Papers
        John C. Haskell, "Reminiscences"
    Thomas Butler King Papers
    W. N. Pendleton Papers
    William B. Pettit Papers
    Charles W. Squires, "Autobiography and Reminiscences"
    Glenn Tucker Papers
    Tucker Family Papers
    Achilles James Tynes Papers
    Charles Venable Papers
    Marcus J. Wright Papers
University of Virginia. Alderman Library. Charlottesville, Va.
    Barnes Family Papers
    "Charlottesville in the Civil War," Miscellaneous Collection
    John E. Claiborne Papers

BIBLIOGRAPHY

Maude Carter Clement Papers
John W. Daniel Papers
   John W. Daniel, Ms. Diary
Gordon and Rosser Family Papers
James L. Kemper Papers
Hunter H. McGuire Papers
Thomas L. Rosser Papers
Virginia Historical Society. Richmond, Va.
Confederate States Senate Records
John W. Daniel, Ms. Diary
Jubal A. Early Papers
Gustavus A. Myers Papers
Preston Family Papers
United States Army Regimental Letterbook, Virginia Regiment of Infantry
Virginia State Library. Richmond, Va.
Franklin County Determined Papers
D. H. Hill Papers
Lee Monument Association Correspondence
Joseph McMurran, Ms. Diary
Essie Wade Smith Papers
Western Reserve Historical Society. Cleveland, Ohio.
James E. Taylor, "With Sheridan Up the Shenandoah. Leaves from a
   Special Artist's Sketchbook and Diary"

BOOKS

Alexander, Ted, et al., eds. *Southern Revenge! Civil War History of Chambersburg, Pennsylvania*. Shippensburg, Pa., 1989.
Allan, Elizabeth Preston. *The Life and Letters of Margaret Junkin Preston*. Boston, 1903.
Ambler, Charles H. *West Virginia*. New York, 1940.
Ambrose, Stephen E. *Duty, Honor, Country: A History of West Point*. Baltimore, 1966.
Andrews, J. Cutler. *The South Reports the Civil War*. Princeton, 1970.
Beringer, Richard E., Herman Hattaway, Archer Jones, and William N. Still, Jr. *Why the South Lost the Civil War*. Athens, Ga., 1986.
Berkeley, Henry Robinson. *Four Years in the Confederate Artillery: The Diary of Henry Robinson Berkeley*. Edited by William H. Runge. Chapel Hill, 1961.
Bigelow, John, Jr. *The Campaign of Chancellorsville*. New Haven, 1910.
Blackford, Charles M. *The Campaign and Battle of Lynchburg*. Lynchburg, 1901.
———, and Susan L. Blackford, eds. *Letters from Lee's Army; or, Memoirs of Life in*

and out of the Army in Virginia during the War between the States. New York, 1947.

Bok, Edward. *The Americanization of Edward Bok*. New York, 1920.

Booth, George Wilson. *Personal Reminiscences of a Maryland Soldier in the War between the States, 1861–1865*. 1898. Reprint. Gaithersburg, Md., 1986.

Borey, F. N. *John Letcher of Virginia*. University, Ala., 1961.

Boynton, Edward Carlisle. *History of West Point*. 1863. Reprint. Freeport, N.Y., 1970.

Brooks, Noah. *Washington in Lincoln's Time*. Edited by Herbert Mitgang. New York, 1958.

Buck, Samuel D. *With the Old Confeds: Actual Experiences of a Captain in the Line*. Baltimore, 1925.

Buell, Augustus. *The Cannoneer: Reflections of Service in the Army of the Potomac*. Washington, D.C., 1890.

Burr, Frank A. *Little Phil and His Troopers*. Providence, 1888.

Bushong, Millard K. *Old Jube: A Biography of General Jubal A. Early*. Boyce, Va., 1955.

Calvert, Michael, and Peter Young. *A Dictionary of Battles, 1715–1815*. New York, 1979.

Casler, John O. *Four Years in the Stonewall Brigade*. Guthrie, Okla., 1893.

Catton, Bruce. *Grant Takes Command*. Boston, 1969.

————. *A Stillness at Appomattox*. New York, 1958.

Clark, Walter, ed. *Histories of the Several Regiments and Battalions from North Carolina*. Raleigh, 1901.

Cleator, P. E. *Weapons of War*. London, 1967.

Coddington, Edwin P. *The Gettysburg Campaign*. New York, 1968.

Coffman, Edward M. *The Old Army*. New York, 1986.

Connelly, Thomas L. *The Marble Man: Robert E. Lee and His Image in American Society*. Baton Rouge, La., 1977.

————, and Barbara L. Bellows. *God and General Longstreet*. Baton Rouge, 1982.

Connor, Seymour V., and Odie B. Faulk. *North America Divided*. New York, 1971.

Cooling, Benjamin F. *Jubal Early's Raid on Washington*. Baltimore, 1989.

Cooper, H. John. *Chancellorsville 1863*. New York, 1973.

Crook, George. *General George Crook: His Autobiography*. Edited by Martin F. Schmitt. Norman, Okla. 1946.

Current, Richard N. *Old Thad Stevens*. Madison, Wis., 1942.

Daniel, Edward M., ed. *Speeches and Orations of John Warwick Daniel*. Lynchburg, 1911.

Davis, Burke. *The Long Surrender*. New York, 1985.

————. *They Called Him Stonewall*. 1954. Reprint. New York, 1988.

Davis, Jefferson. *The Rise and Fall of the Confederate Government*. 2 vols. Richmond, 1938.

Davis, Julia. *The Shenandoah*. New York, 1945.

Davis, William C. *Battle at Bull Run*. Baton Rouge, 1977.

———. *Breckinridge: Soldier, Statesman, Symbol*. Baton Rouge, 1974.

Dawson, Francis L. *Reminiscences*. Edited by Bell Wiley. Baton Rouge, 1980.

Dawson, John H. *Wildcat Cavalry: A Synoptic History of the Seventeenth Virginia Cavalry of the Jenkins-McCausland Brigade in the War between the States*. Dayton, Ohio, 1982.

Dennison, George T. *Soldiering in Canada*. Toronto, 1900.

Douglas, Henry Kyd. *I Rode with Stonewall*. 1940. Reprint. St. Simon's Island, Ga., 1983.

Dowdey, Clifford. *Lee*. Boston, 1965.

———, and Louis H. Manarin, eds. *The Wartime Papers of Robert E. Lee*. Boston, 1961.

Duffy, Christopher. *The Military Experience in the Age of Reason*. New York, 1987.

Du Pont, Henry A. *The Campaign of 1864 in the Shenandoah Valley*. New York, 1925.

Early, Jubal Anderson. *Autobiographical Sketch and Narrative of the War between the States*. Philadelphia, 1912.

———. *The Campaigns of Robert E. Lee*. 2d ed. Baltimore, 1872.

———. *The Heritage of the South*. Lynchburg, 1915.

———. *A Memoir of the Last Year of the War for Independence in the Confederate States of America, Containing an Account of the Operation of His Commands in the Years 1864 and 1865*. Lynchburg, 1867.

———. *War Memoirs: Autobiographical Sketch and Narrative of the War between the States*. Edited by Frank E. Vandiver. Bloomington, Ind., 1960.

Early, Ruth H. *Campbell County Chronicles and Family Sketches*. Baltimore, 1978.

———. *The Family of Early*. Lynchburg, 1920.

Early, Samuel S. *A History of the Family of Early*. Albany, N.Y., 1896.

Eckert, Ralph Lowell. *John Brown Gordon: Soldier, Southerner, American*. Baton Rouge, 1989.

Ellis, Joseph, and Robert Moore. *School for Soldiers*. New York, 1974.

Ezell, John T. *Fortune's Merry Wheel: The Lottery in America*. Cambridge, Mass., 1960.

Faust, Patricia L., ed. *Historical Times Illustrated Encyclopedia of the Civil War*. New York, 1986.

Foner, Eric. *Reconstruction: America's Unfinished Revolution, 1863–1877*. New York, 1988.

Foster, Gaines. *Ghosts of the Confederacy: Defeat, the Lost Cause and the Emergence of the New South*. New York, 1987.

Franklin County Bicentennial Commission. *Bicentennial Reflections*. Rocky Mount, Va., 1986.

Freeman, Douglas Southall. *Lee's Lieutenants*. 3 vols. New York, 1942–44.

———. *R. E. Lee: A Biography*. 4 vols. New York, 1934–35.

French, S. Bassett. *Centennial Tales: Memoirs of Colonel "Chester" S. Bassett French, Extra Aide-de-Camp for Generals Lee and Jackson, the Army of Northern Virginia, 1861–1865.* New York, 1962.

Gallagher, Gary W. *Stephen Dodson Ramseur: Lee's Gallant General.* Chapel Hill, N.C., 1985.

———. Introduction to Jubal Anderson Early, *Autobiographical Sketch and Narrative of the War between the States.* 1912. Reprint. Wilmington, N.C., 1989.

Goode, John. *Reminiscences of a Lifetime.* New York, 1906.

Gordon, George H. *History of the Campaign of the Army of Virginia under John Pope, Brigadier General . . . from Cedar Mountain to Alexandria, 1862.* Boston, 1880.

Gordon, John B. *Reminiscences of the Civil War.* New York, 1903.

Graham, Martin F., and George F. Skoch. *Mine Run: A Campaign of Lost Opportunities.* Lynchburg, 1987.

Grant, Ulysses S. *Personal Memoirs of U. S. Grant.* 2 vols. New York, 1885–86.

Green, Constance M. *Washington: Village and Capital, 1800–1878.* Princeton, 1962.

Griffith, Paddy. *Battle Tactics of the Civil War.* New Haven, 1987.

Hale, Laura V. *Four Valiant Years in the Lower Shenandoah Valley, 1861–1865.* 1968. Reprint. Front Royal, Va., 1986.

———, and Stanley S. Phillips. *History of the 49th Virginia Infantry, C.S.A.* Lanham, Md., 1981.

Hamlin, Percy G. *Old Bald Head.* Strasburg, Va., 1940.

Hassler, Warren W., Jr. *Crisis at the Crossroads.* University, Ala., 1970.

Haynes, Edwin M. *History of the Tenth Vermont.* Rutland, Vt., 1894.

Hebert, Walter H. *Fighting Joe Hooker.* New York, 1944.

Henderson, G. F. R. *Stonewall Jackson and the American Civil War.* 2 vols. New York, 1927.

Hickey, Donald. *The War of 1812.* Urbana and Chicago, 1989.

Hogg, O. F. G. *Artillery: Its Origins, Heyday and Decline.* London, 1970.

Hopkins, Luther W. *From Bull Run to Appomattox.* Baltimore, 1911.

Howe, Daniel Walker. *The American Whigs: An Anthology.* New York, 1973.

Hoyt, Edwin P. *America's Wars and Military Excursions.* New York, 1987.

Johnson, Robert Underwood, and Clarence Clough Buel, eds. *Battles and Leaders of the Civil War.* 4 vols. 1884–88. Reprint. Secaucus, N.J., 1982.

Jones, J. B. *A Rebel War Clerk's Diary.* Philadelphia, 1866.

Jones, J. W. *Christ in the Camp; or, Religion in Lee's Army.* Richmond, 1887.

Jones, Terry L. *Lee's Tigers.* Baton Rouge, 1987.

Jones, Virgil C. *Gray Ghosts and Rebel Raiders.* New York, 1956.

Journal of the House of Delegates of Virginia. Richmond, 1842.

Kean, Robert G. H. *Inside the Confederate Government: The Diary of Robert Garlick Hill Kean, Head of the Bureau of War.* Edited by Edward Younger. New York, 1957.

Krick, Robert K. *Stonewall Jackson at Cedar Mountain*. Chapel Hill, 1990.

Leech, Margaret. *Reveille in Washington, 1860–1865*. New York, 1941.

Lewis, Lloyd. *Sherman: Fighting Prophet*. New York, 1932.

Lewis, Thomas A. *The Guns of Cedar Creek*. New York, 1988.

———, and the Editors of Time-Life Books. *The Shenandoah in Flames*. Alexandria, Va., 1987.

Livermore, Thomas L. *Numbers and Losses in the Civil War in America*. Bloomington, Ind., 1957.

Long, A. L. *Memoirs of Robert E. Lee*. 1886. Reprint. Secaucus, N.J., 1983.

Longstreet, James. *From Manassas to Appomattox*. Philadelphia, 1896.

Luvaas, Jay, and Arnold W. Nelson, eds. *U.S. Army War College Guide to the Battles of Chancellorsville and Fredericksburg*. Carlisle, Pa., 1988.

McCarthy, Carlton. *Soldier Life in the Army of Northern Virginia*. Richmond, 1894.

McGregor, J. C. *The Disruption of Virginia*. New York, 1922.

McPherson, James M. *Battle Cry of Freedom*. New York, 1988.

McWhiney, Grady, and Perry D. Jamieson. *Attack and Die: Civil War Tactics and the Southern Heritage*. University, Ala., 1982.

Maddex, Jack P. *The Virginia Conservatives, 1867–1879: A Study in Reconstruction Politics*. Chapel Hill, 1970.

Morris, George, and Susan Foutz. *Lynchburg in the Civil War*. Lynchburg, 1984.

Mosgrove, G. D. *Kentucky Cavaliers in Dixie*. Edited by Bell Irvin Wiley. Jackson, Tenn., 1957.

Motte, Jacob Rhett. *Journey into Wilderness*. Gainesville, Fla., 1953.

Myers, Frank M. *The Comanches: A History of White's Battalion, Virginia Cavalry*. Baltimore, 1871.

Nevins, Allan. *The Emergence of Lincoln*. 2 vols. New York, 1950.

Newcomer, C. Armour. *Cole's Cavalry: Three Years in the Saddle*. Baltimore, 1895.

Nye, Wilbur S. *Here Come the Rebels*. Baton Rouge, 1965.

The Official Military Atlas of the Civil War. 1891. Reprint. New York, 1983.

Pearson, Charles C. *The Readjuster Movement in Virginia*. Gloucester, Mass., 1969.

Peters, Virginia B. *The Florida Wars*. Hamden, Conn., 1979.

Phillips, Edward H. *The Shenandoah Valley in 1864: An Episode in the History of Warfare*. Charleston, 1965.

Piston, William Garrett. *Lee's Tarnished Lieutenant: James Longstreet and His Place in Southern History*. Athens, Ga., 1987.

Pond, George E. *The Shenandoah Valley in 1864*. New York, 1883.

Proceedings of the Southern Historical Convention . . . and the Southern Historical Society as Organized: With the Address of Gen. Jubal A. Early. Baltimore, 1873.

Reese, George H., ed. *Proceedings of the Virginia State Convention of 1861*. 4 vols. Richmond, 1965.

Robertson, James I. *A. P. Hill*. New York, 1987.

Rolle, Andrew F. *The Confederate Exodus to Mexico*. Norman, Okla., 1965.

BIBLIOGRAPHY

Rubin, Louis D., Jr. *Virginia: A History*. New York, 1977.
Sanger, Donald P., and Thomas P. Hay. *Longstreet: Soldier, Politician, Officeholder*. Baton Rouge, 1952.
Sears, Stephen W. *Landscape Turned Red*. New York, 1983.
Shanks, Henry T. *The Secession Movement in Virginia, 1847–1861*. Richmond, 1934.
Sheridan, Philip H. *Personal Memoirs*. 2 vols. New York, 1888.
Simms, Henry H. *The Rise of the Whigs in Virginia, 1824–1847*. Richmond, 1929.
Sloane, Kermit V. *Lieutenant General Jubal Anderson Early, C.S.A.* Rocky Mount, Va., 1975.
Smith, Gene. *Lee and Grant*. New York, 1984.
Stackpole, Edward J. *Sheridan in the Shendandoah: Jubal Early's Nemesis*. Harrisburg, Pa., 1961.
Starr, Stephen Z. *The Union Cavalry in the Civil War*. 2 vols. Baton Rouge, 1981.
Stevens, Hazard. *The Battle of Cedar Creek and the Recaptured Guns*. Papers of the Military Historical Society of Massachusetts, vol. 6. 1907. Reprint. Gaithersburg, Md., 1987.
Stevenson, James H. *"Boots and Saddles": A History of the First Volunteer Cavalry of the War*. Harrisburg, Pa., 1879.
Stiles, Robert M. *Four Years under Marse Robert*. Washington, 1903.
Strode, Hudson. *Jefferson Davis*. New York, 1955.
Strother, David Hunter. *A Virginia Yankee in the Civil War: The Diaries of David Hunter Strother*. Edited by Cecil D. Eby. Chapel Hill, 1961.
Swinton, William. *Campaigns of the Army of the Potomac*. 1866. Reprint. Secaucus, N.J., 1988.
Talbert, Roy, Jr., Gary Lee Cardwell, and Andrew L. Baskin. *Studies in the Local History of Slavery*. Ferrum, Va., 1978.
Tucker, Glenn. *Hancock the Superb*. Dayton, Ohio, 1980.
———. *Lee and Longstreet at Gettysburg*. New York, 1968.
United States Military Academy. *Register of Graduates*. West Point, N.Y., 1980.
United States Army Military History Research Collection. *The Volunteer Army*. Special Bibliographic Series, no. 5. Carlisle, Pa., 1972.
United States War Department. *Atlas to Accompany the Official Records of the Union and Confederate Armies*. Washington, D.C., 1891–95.
———. *The War of the Rebellion: A Compilation of the Official Records of the Union and Confederate Armies*. 128 vols. Washington, D.C., 1880–91.
Vandiver, Frank E. *Jubal's Raid*. New York, 1960.
———. *Rebel Brass: The Confederate Command System*. 1956. Reprint. New York, 1986.
Virginia Civil War Commission. *Virginia Joins the Confederacy: Chronology of Events*. Richmond, 1961–65.
Virginia Commission on Constitutional Government. *The Constitution of the United States*. Richmond, 1967.

Wallace, Lew. *Lew Wallace: An Autobiography.* New York, 1906.

Welles, Gideon. *Diary.* New York, 1911.

Wert, Jeffrey. *From Winchester to Cedar Creek: The Shenandoah Campaign of 1864.* Carlisle, Pa., 1987.

Williams, Rebecca Yancey. *The Vanishing Virginian.* New York, 1940.

Williams, T. Harry. *Hayes of the 23rd.* New York, 1965.

————. *P. G. T. Beauregard: Napoleon in Gray.* Baton Rouge, 1957.

Williamson, James J. *Mosby's Rangers.* New York, 1896.

Wilson, Charles Reagan. *Baptized in Blood: The Religion of the Lost Cause, 1865–1920.* Athens, Ga., 1980.

Wilson, James H. *Under the Old Flag.* Westport, Conn., 1971.

Wingate, Marshall. *Franklin County: A History.* Berryville, Va., 1964.

Winslow, Richard Elliott III. *General John Sedgwick.* Novato, Calif., 1982.

Wise, John S. *The End of an Era.* Boston, 1900.

Woodward, C. Vann. *The Burden of Southern History.* Baton Rouge, 1960.

Worsham, John H. *One of Jackson's Foot Cavalry.* New York, 1912.

Worthington, Glenn H. *Fighting for Time, or, the Battle that Saved Washington and Mayhap the Union.* Frederick, Md., 1932.

DISSERTATIONS AND THESES

Atkins, Paul A. "Henry A. Wise and the Virginia Secession Convention, February 23–April 17, 1861." Master's thesis, University of Virginia, 1950.

Ernst, Denessa Glennon. "Movement toward Secession in the *Richmond Daily Dispatch*, 1856 to 1861." Master's thesis, Illinois State University, 1968.

Jeffrey, Thomas E. "The Secessionist Party at the Virginia Convention of 1861." Master's thesis, Catholic University, 1970.

Jones, Robert Rivers. "Conservative Virginian: The Postwar Career of James Lawson Kemper." Ph.D. diss., University of Virginia, 1964.

Morrison, J. L. "The United States Military Academy, 1833–1866: Years of Progress and Turmoil." Ph.D. diss., Columbia University, 1970.

Moss, Terry, "Jubal Anderson Early, Glory to Ignominy: His Shenandoah Campaign, 1864." Master's thesis, University of North Carolina, 1981.

Smith, James Douglas. "Virginia during Reconstruction, 1865–70." Ph.D. diss., University of Virginia, 1966.

Thompson, Paul S. "The Summer Campaign in the Lower Valley, 1864." Ph.D. diss., University of Virginia, 1966.

Winton, George Peterson, Jr. "Antebellum Instruction at West Point and Its Effect on Confederate Military Organization and Operations." Ph.D. diss., University of South Carolina, 1972.

ARTICLES, NEWSPAPERS, AND PERIODICALS

Coleman, Howard. "The Lion of Virginia: The Story of Jubal Anderson Early." Parts 1–4. *Lynchburg Magazine.* March-October 1981.

Confederate Veteran. 40 vols. Nashville, 1893–1932.

Conway, William B. "Talks with General J. A. Early." *SHSP* 30 (1902): 250–55.

Early, John Cabell. "A Southern Boy at Gettysburg." *Journal of the Military Service Institute* 48–49 (May-June 1911): 415–23.

Early, Jubal A. "The Advance on Washington." *Southern Magazine* 8 (1871): 750–63.

"The Early-Mahone Fight." Baltimore *Sun.* April 22, 1881.

"Gen. Lewis Addison Armistead." *Confederate Veteran* 22 (1914): 502–4.

Golladay, V. Dennis. "Jubal Early's Last Stand." *Virginia Cavalcade* 20, no. 1 (Summer 1970): 28–33.

Greenawalt, Bruce S., ed. "Unionists in Rockbridge County: The Correspondence of James Dorman Davidson Concerning the Secession Convention of 1861." *Virginia Magazine of History and Biography* 73 (January 1965): 78–102.

Jones, Robert R., ed. "The Mexican War Diary of James Lawson Kemper." *Virginia Magazine of History and Biography* 74 (October 1966): 387–428.

Lee, Blair. "Were the Rebs Too Groggy to Carry the Day?" Washington *Post.* July 15, 1990.

"Letters of John Letcher to J. Hierholzer, Esq., 1864–65." *William and Mary College Quarterly Historical Magazine,* 2d ser., 8 (1928): 137–140.

Lynchburg *News.* March 3, 6, and 18, 1894.

New York *Tribune.* October 29, 1899.

"Recollections of Jubal Early, by One Who Followed Him." *Century Magazine* 70 (June 1905): 311–13.

Richmond *Daily Dispatch.* August 8, 1873.

Schmitt, Martin F., ed. "An Interview with General Jubal A. Early in 1889." *Journal of Southern History* 11, no. 4 (November 1945): 547–63.

Sears, Stephen W. "The Bloodiest Day." *Civil War Times Illustrated* 26, no. 2 (April 1987): 2–46.

Southern Historical Society Papers. 39 vols. Richmond, 1876–1919.

Staunton *Spectator.* August 12, 1873.

"Tenth Annual Reunion of the Virginia Division, Army of Northern Virginia Association. Address of Major H. B. McClellan of Lexington, Ky., on the Life, Campaigns and Character of Gen'l J. E. B. Stuart." *SHSP* 8 (1880): 433–56.

Wallace, Lee A. "The First Regiment of Virginia Volunteers, 1846–48." *Virginia Magazine of History and Biography* 77 (January 1969): 46–77.

Abraham Creek, 333
Alabama, secession of, 35
Allan, William, on Lee memorial, 442–43
Anderson, Archer, Lee memorial activities of, 453
Anderson, George T., at Antietam, 492 n.20
Anderson, Richard H.
  in Chancellorsville campaign, 159, 163
  as Longstreet replacement, 239
  at Petersburg, 330
  vs. Sheridan, 323
  at Spotsylvania, 239
  in winter quarters, 142
Andrews, Snowden, in Chancellorsville campaign, 145, 146
Antietam, Battle of, 119–29
  prelude to, 117–19
Appomattox, surrender at
  Early nonacceptance of, 402
  Lee conduct at, 446
Archer, J.J., at Fredericksburg, 133–38
Armistead, Lewis A.
  at Malvern Hill, 88
  at Military Academy, 14
Army of the Shenandoah
  establishment of, 238
  Sheridan assigned to, 316
Army of Virginia (Pope's command), formation of, 88–89

Artillery
  at Cedar Mountain, 94–96
  at Fisher's Hill, 344
  at Fredericksburg, 132
  horse shortage and, 264
  at Malvern Hill, 86
  at Winchester
    Second Battle of, 170–71
    Third Battle of, 340
Ashby, Turner, 355
Ashby's Gap, 63
Association of the Army of Northern Virginia, 440–41
Atkinson, Edmund N., at Fredericksburg, 135, 137
Atlanta, Sherman capture of, 329
Averell, William W., 300–1
  in Chambersburg, 307
  at Fisher's Hill, 345
  joining Hunter, 238
  at Lynchburg, 257, 259
  at Moorefield, 307–8
  promotion to major general, 312
  Salem raid of, 215–20
  at Stephenson's Depot, 301
  at Winchester, Third Battle of, 333, 337, 338, 339
Avery, Isaac E.
  at Gettysburg, 187, 188, 191, 192, 198, 199

Avery, Isaac E. *(continued)*
    at Winchester, Second Battle of, 169

Baggage, transportation of, 73
Baker, James, at Winchester, 165, 169
Baldwin, John, at Virginia Secession
    Convention, 49–50
Balloon surveillance, 72, 148
Baltimore & Ohio Railroad
    Early raids on, 309, 330–31
    at Frederick, 271
Baltimore Pike, at Frederick, 271
Banks, Nathaniel P.
    at Cedar Mountain, 98–99
    at Warrenton Springs, 107
"Barbara Frietchie" (poem), 119
Barbour, John S., as Mahone rival, 411
Barksdale, William
    at Antietam, 492 n.20
    in Chancellorsville campaign, 145,
        148, 150, 151, 154–56, 158, 162, 163
    at Fredericksburg, 134, 144
    at Manassas, 66
Bartlett, William H.C., 14
Bartow, Francis
    at Henry Hill, 65
    toast to, 74
Battle, Cullen, capability of, 319
Battles
    Antietam, 119–29
        prelude to, 117–19
    Averell's cavalry raid to Salem, 215–20
    Bull Run (Manassas)
        First, 63–71
            prelude to, 59–63
        Second, 109–16
    Cedar Creek, 358–77
        comments on, 378–81
    Cedar Mountain, 90–99
    Chancellorsville, 143–63
    Chantilly, 113–16
    Fisher's Hill, 341–47

Fredericksburg, 131–39
    prelude to, 130–31
Gettysburg, 187–202, 437, 446–47
    postwar analysis of, 457–61
    retribution before, 177–85
    Winchester leading to, 164–74
Locust Grove, 212
Lynchburg, 254–60
    prelude to, 245–54
Malvern Hill, 85–88
Manassas (Bull Run)
    First, 63–71
        prelude to, 59–63
    Second, 109–16
Monocacy Junction, 269–75
Ox Hill, 113–16
Rappahannock Station, 205–11
Seven Days', 84–85
    at Malvern Hill, 85–88
Spotsylvania, 239–40
Warrenton Springs, 104–7
    prelude to, 102–4
Waynesboro, 387–90
Wilderness, The, 231–39
Williamsburg, 76–83
    prelude to, 75–76
Winchester
    Second, 164–74
    Third, 333–41
    plans for, 332–33
Baylor, Mr., at Virginia Secession Con-
    vention, 50
Beauregard, P.G.T., 56
    at Bermuda Hundred, 246
    in Lee memorial organization, 442
    as Louisiana State Lottery official,
        421–28
    at Manassas, 59, 60, 62–68, 70
    Southern Historical Society and, 433
Bedford County, Virginia, Jeremiah Early
    in, 5
Bee, Barnard, 56
    at Henry Hill, 65

toast to, 74

Belle Grove mansion, Union headquarters at, 360, 362

Benham, Henry W., 18

Bennette, J. Kelly, 319

Bérard, Claudius, 12

Beringer, Richard E., on results of War, 419

Bermuda Hundred, Butler in, 245, 246

Berryville, 168
Sheridan at, 320–21

Berryville Canyon, 332–33, 335

Bethesda Church, action at, 241–42

Bidwell, Daniel G.
at Cedar Creek, 364
in Washington defense, 288

Big Calf Pasture River, Averell's raid and, 217

Big Round Top, at Gettysburg, 194, 197

Black, Jeremiah, on Federal right to war upon states, 485 n.6

Black Dave. See Hunter, David

Blackburn's Ford clash, 60–63

Blackford, Charles M., on Early, 475–76

Blacks
in Conservative party, 417
enslavement of. See Slavery
status after abolition, 402
in Stonewall Jackson memorial ceremony, 418–19
voting rights of, 402, 409, 419

Blair, Francis Preston, house of, Early headquarters in, 284–85, 288, 290

Blair, Montgomery, house of, 285, 289

Blue Ridge (steamboat), explosion of, 30

Bok, Edward, Early letter to, 310

Booneville, Mississippi, Sheridan at, 315

Booth, George Wilson, on Chambersburg pillage, 305, 306

Borst, Peter B., 40

Bostwick & Winter, Lee engraving by, 450

Bower's Hill, at Winchester, 169–72

Bradford, A.W., house of, burning of, 287

Bragg, Braxton
at Military Academy, 18
Southern Historical Society and, 433

Braxton, Carter, 264
capability of, 320
at Martinsburg, 331–32
at Winchester, Third Battle of, 336

Brazos, in Mexican War, 30

Breckinridge, John C.
assignment to Southwest Virginia, 341
capability of, 319
on Early drinking problem, 354
Early mocking of, 52
exile in Canada, 404, 408
at Kernstown, 301
in Lee memorial organization, 442
at Lynchburg, 252, 254–55
miniature corps command by, 264
at Monocacy Junction, 272, 273
at New Market, 247
as secretary of war, 386
at Shepherdstown, 265
at Stephenson's Depot, 331–32
in Washington threat, 280, 281, 285, 288, 289
at Winchester, Third Battle of, 337, 338

Bristoe Station, 204
Jackson at, 107

Brooks, Noah, on Lincoln during Washington threat, 505 n.43

Brooks, William, in Chancellorsville campaign, 154

Brown, Campbell
on Cold Harbor action, 243–44
at Gettysburg, 192

Brown, Lizinka (Mrs. Richard Ewell), 100, 167, 229, 244

Brown, William F., at Cedar Mountain, 94, 98

Buck, Marcus, on civilian property destruction, 324

Buck, Samuel
  at Cedar Creek, 370
  on Union cavalry, 318
  at Winchester, Second Battle of, 165–
    66, 169, 170
Buel, Clarence, Longstreet-Early feud
    and, 460
Buena Vista, Early at, 27–30
Buford, John, at Gettysburg, 186–87
Buford daughter (Early's great-great-
    grandmother), 5
Bull Run (Manassas)
  First Battle of, 63–71
    prelude to, 59–63
  Second Battle of, 109–16
Bunker Hill
  Early at, 326
  troops at, 332
Burkholder, N.M., on camp fires, 349
Burnside, Ambrose
  at Antietam, 127
  at Fredericksburg, 131–35, 138, 142
  McClellan replaced by, 130
  replaced by Hooker, 142
  at Spotsylvania, 239–40
  in Wilderness campaign, 234–36
"Burnside Bridge" (Rohrbach Bridge),
    over Antietam, 120, 127
Bushong, Millard K.
  as Early biographer, xiii
  on Lavinia relationship, 483 n.43
Butler, Benjamin, 230
  in Bermuda Hundred, 245, 246
Butterfield, Daniel, in Chancellorsville
    campaign, 157

Cabell, James Branch, on antebellum
    values, 416
Caledonia Iron Works, burning of, 179,
    180, 181, 183
Calhoun, John C., on states' rights, 417

Callaghan's Station, Averell's raid
    and, 217
Callaway, James, 5
Callaway, William G., in Chancellorsville
    campaign, 155
Cameron, William E., in Virginia legisla-
    ture, 415
Camp Davis, 57, 59
Campbell County, Virginia, secessionists
    in, 35
Canada, Early exile in, 404–8
Capehart, Henry, at Waynesboro, 388
Carbines, effectiveness of, 318
Carlile, John S., at Virginia Secession
    Convention, 40
Carolina Life Insurance Company, 420–
    21
Carroll, John Lee, on Gettysburg out-
    come, 459–60
Carson, Mr., as Montpelier owner, 131
Carson, R.M. (Rev.), at Early funeral,
    477–78
Carter, Thomas H., xiii, 320
  at Cedar Creek, 367, 380–81
  at Winchester, Third Battle of, 336,
    339–40
Cashtown, Lee at, 186
Cass, Lewis, 7
Cavalry
  arms shortage in, 58
  in Averell's raid to Salem, 215–20
  at Fisher's Hill, 345
  from Franklin County, 24
  organization of, 264–65
  problems with, 222–24, 397–98
  Sheridan's handling of, 317–18
Cedar Creek
  Battle of, 358–77
    comments on, 378–81
  Sheridan at, 321, 323
Cedar Mountain, Battle of, 90–99
Cemetery Hill, at Gettysburg, 188, 189,

191–94, 198–201, 497 n. 15

Centreville, Meade at, 204

Century magazine, Longstreet-Early feud
and, 460

Chamberlayne, Ham, at Fredericksburg, 135

Chambersburg
burning of, 304–10
economic warfare against, 302–4
Pickett in, 196

Chancellorsville campaign, 143–63

Chantilly, Battle of, 113–16

Charles Town, Grant-Sheridan conference at, 330

Charlottesville, Early forces arrival at,
252, 254

Chickahominy River, action at, 241

Chilton, Robert H., 209
in Chancellorsville campaign, 146–49

Chinn's Ridge, at Manassas, 68–70

Choice v. Choice, 32–33

Christian, George L., Southern Historical Society and, 438

Church, Albert E., 12

Claiborne, John E., on Washington
threat, 290

Claiborne, Nathaniel H., 7

Clarke County, Virginia, guerrillas
in, 299

Clay, Henry, 23
on states' rights, 417
on Texas annexation, 25

Clear Spring, Maryland, 303

Clifton Forge, Averell's raid and, 217

Cocke, Philip St. George, 59

Coddington, Edwin
on Gettysburg strategy, 195
on Gettysburg troop strengths, 437–38
on retribution, 496 n. 13
on Winchester, 174

Cold Harbor, action at, 243

College of William and Mary
Early's brigade at, 76

Samuel Early at, 6–7

Committee of Nine, for Virginia readmission to Union, 409–10, 412

Committee on Federal Relations, 38, 39,
42, 44–45

Confederate Army regiments
Florida 2d, at Williamsburg, 76
Georgia 12th
at Antietam, 124
at Cedar Mountain, 91–92, 94,
96–99
at Malvern Hill, 86
Georgia 13th, at Warrenton Springs,
103, 105
Louisiana 5th, at Rappahannock Station, 208
Louisiana 7th, at Manassas, 60–61,
63, 64
Louisiana 9th, at Antietam, 122
Mississippi 2d, at Williamsburg, 76
Mississippi 13th, 66
North Carolina 5th, at Williamsburg,
76–81
North Carolina 23d, at Williamsburg,
76, 77, 80
South Carolina 4th, at Manassas, 59
Virginia 7th, at Manassas, 59, 60,
61, 64
Virginia 11th, at Manassas, 61
Virginia 13th
at Antietam, 122
at Cedar Mountain, 97, 98
at Fisher's Hill, 344
at Fredericksburg, 137
at Malvern Hill, 86
at Manassas, Second Battle of,
108, 110
at Winchester, 164, 165
Virginia 17th, at Manassas, 61
Virginia 24th
at Lynchburg, 59
at Manassas, 59, 61–64, 66
at Williamsburg, 76, 77–81

Confederate Army regiments *(continued)*
  Virginia 25th, at Malvern Hill, 86
  Virginia 27th, at Antietam, 122
  Virginia 31st
    at Antietam, 126
    at Malvern Hill, 86
  Virginia 38th, at Williamsburg, 76–78, 80
  Virginia 44th, at Malvern Hill, 86
  Virginia 49th, at Antietam, 122, 126
  Virginia 52d, at Malvern Hill, 86
  Virginia 58th, at Malvern Hill, 86
Confederate Ordnance Department, 58
Confederate Survivors' Association of South Carolina, 434
Connelly, Thomas L., on Lee canonization, 440
Conrad, Paul, Louisiana State Lottery and, 428
Conscription, Early views on, 74
Couch, Darius N., in Chambersburg, 303, 308
Courtney, A.R., at Cedar Mountain, 94
Covington, Averell's raid and, 217, 219
Cow Pasture River, Averell's raid and, 217
Cox farm, in Chancellorsville campaign, 156
Craig Creek, Averell's raid and, 219
Crampton's Gap, fighting at, 119
Crittenden farm, in Cedar Mountain battle, 92
Crook, George, 317
  at Cedar Creek, 372
  Early action against, 300, 301
  at Fisher's Hill, 342, 343
  joining Hunter, 238
  at Kernstown, 301
  at Lynchburg, 257
  at Military Academy, 314
  pursuit of Early, 299
  visit to Early in old age, 469

  at Winchester, Third Battle of, 337, 339
Culpeper, civilian property destruction in, 89
Culpeper Courthouse, cavalry assembly at, 59
Culpeper Road, in Cedar Mountain battle, 91–94, 98
Culp's Hill, at Gettysburg, 191–93, 197, 199, 200
Cumberland, Maryland, action at, 307
Custer, George Armstrong
  on carbine utility, 318
  at Cedar Creek, 368, 372, 374, 375
  Rosser attack on, 355
  at Tom's Brook, 355–56
  at Waynesboro, 387, 389
  at Winchester, Third Battle of, 338
Cutshaw, Wilfred E., 323, 351
  at Petersburg, 330

Daniel, John Warwick, 203
  on Early accomplishments, 291–92
  at Early deathbed, 474
  on Early drinking, 382–83
  as Early friend, 413
  at Early funeral, 477–78
  Lee memorial activities of, 452
  at Rappahannock Station, 208
  as senator, 416
  in Wilderness campaign, 237
Danville Male Academy, Early education at, 7
Davis, Jefferson, 147
  as Carolina Life Insurance Company president, 420–21
  Early meeting with, in Mexican War, 28
  Early respect for, 297
  on Gettysburg outcome, 461
  at Jackson memorial ceremony, 440

at Manassas, 69
postwar imprisonment of, 406
Southern Historical Society and, 434
at Virginia Secession Convention, 38
Dawson, Henry B., Early letter to, 433
de Peyster, J. Watts, on Mahone, 462–66
Deep Run, in Chancellorsville campaign,
    143, 147, 150, 152, 154
Democrat (New Orleans), on Louisiana
    State Lottery, 422
Devin's brigade, at Cedar Creek, 375
Dillard, Hugh, 35
Doles, George, at Gettysburg, 199
d'Orleans, Louis-Philippe-Albert, as Lee
    critic, 457
Douglas, Henry Kyd, 267
    on Martinsburg raid, 331
    in Washington threat, 288–89
    on Winchester battle, 333
Douglas, J.W., as Chambersburg citizen,
    303–4
Douglass, Marcellus, at Antietam, 120,
    122, 124, 128
Dowdey, Clifford, on Lee, 449
Duffié, Alfred, 317
Dugan, Jean Early, on Early children,
    485 n.26
Dunkard Church, in Antietam Battle,
    120, 122, 124–26
DuPont, Henry A.
    command of, 317
    at Fisher's Hill, 344
    on Hunter's retribution, 250, 251
Duval, Isaac H., 317
Dwight, William
    under Sheridan, 316–17
    at Winchester, Third Battle of, 337
Dye, Nathan, on Third Winchester
    Battle, 336

Early, Abner (cousin), 24
Early, Elizabeth (sister), 26

Early, Florence Annie (daughter), 485
    n.26
Early, Henrian (sister-in-law), 473
Early, Henry (uncle), 6
Early, Jeremiah (great-grandfather), 5
Early, Jeremiah (great-great-grandfather),
    5
Early, Joab (brother), 6
Early, Joab (father), 5–7, 11, 13
    Jubal sick leave with, 30
    in litigation, 484 n.1
    move to West Virginia, 485 n.22
    on Texas Uprising, 15–16
Early, John, 6
Early, John (nephew), 181
    at Gettysburg, 193
Early, Joseph (son), 485 n.26
Early, Jubal (grandfather), 5–6
Early, Jubal (son), 31
Early, Jubal Anderson
    accomplishments of, 291–92, 475–76
        in Alabama, 402
    at Antietam, 119–22, 124–29
        prelude to, 118–19
    appearance of, 4
    arrest for insubordination, 229–30
    arthritis onset in, 29–30
    attire of, 4, 55–56, 215, 228, 404,
        469–70
    Averell's raid and, 216–20
    aversion to President Johnson, 405–6
    on balloon surveillance, 72
    Baltimore & Ohio Railroad depreda-
        tion by, 330–31
    at Bethesda Church, 241–42
    birth of, 6
    in Blackburn's Ford clash, 60–62
    at Buena Vista, 27–30
    in building collapse, 472
    at Bunker Hill, 326
    Caledonia Iron Works burning by, 179,
        180, 181, 183
    in Canadian exile, 404–8

Early, Jubal Anderson *(continued)*
  at Cedar Creek, 360, 364–74, 376–77
    comments on, 378–81
  at Cedar Mountain, 90–99
  challenged by picket, 328–29
  Chambersburg burned by, 304–7
    comments on, 309–11
  in Chancellorsville campaign, 143–63
  at Chantilly, 113–15
  characteristics of, 475
  childhood of, 6–7
  children of, 31
  on civilian property destruction,
    71, 214
  at Cold Harbor, 243–44
  concerns over provisions, 117
  on conscription, 73–74
  coping with defeat, 429–31
  criticism of, 352–54, 381–83, 390–91
  cruelty shown by, 27
  Davis meeting with, in Mexican
    War, 28
  Davis respected by, 297
  death of, 474–75
  as Democrat, 416
  dismissal by Lee, 390–92
  economic warfare by, 268–69, 302–4
  education of
    childhood, 6–7
    Military Academy, 8–18
  escape from Waynesboro, 389
  Ewell praise of, 100
  Ewell relationship with, 229–30,
    242–44
  as Ewell replacement, 240–41
  on excess baggage, 72–73, 265
  fall leading to death, 473
  family history of, 5–6
  at Fisher's Hill, 321, 331, 341–47
  at Fort Taylor, 19
  at Fortress Monroe, 18, 26
  at Frederick, 118–19, 270–71
  at Fredericksburg, 133–39

  funeral of, 477–78
  genealogy of, 5–6
  at Gettysburg, 187–202
    comments on, 458–61
  Goode conflict with, 40, 42–44
  on Gordonsville march, 89–90
  Grant, hatred of, 476
  at Groveton, 108–9
  at Hagerstown, 268
  at Heidlersburg, 186
  horse shortage and, 264
  Hunter meeting with, in Mexican War,
    29, 249
  Imboden conflict with, 221–22
  impetuosity of, 56
  impudence to Jackson, 130
  insurance business considered by,
    420–21
  intoxication ascribed to, 74–75, 354,
    381–83
  Jackson compared with, 292, 396–97
  Jackson praise of, 100, 107, 128
  Julia McNealey relationship, 31–32,
    412–13
  lapses in generalship, 395–97
  Lavinia relationship with, 18–21, 31
  as lawyer, 22–25, 32–33, 421, 441
  Lee contacts with. *See under* Lee,
    Robert E.
  Lee memorial activities of, 440–53,
    517 n. 38
  at Leesburg, 298–99
  in Lexington, 261
  on Lincoln election, 41–42
  literary familiarity of, 225
  at Locust Grove, 212, 214
  Longstreet feud, 454–62
  Lost Cause embraced by, 431
  as Louisiana State Lottery official,
    421–28
  on loyalty to state, 51–52
  at Lynchburg, 56–59
    postwar, 413, 469–74

at Lynchburg Battle, 254–60
prelude to, 252–54
as Mahone enemy, 411, 414–16, 462–
68
at Malvern Hill, 85–88
at Manassas Battles
First, 63–71
Second, 109–16
maneuvering against Sheridan, 320–
21, 323–27
at Martinsburg, 331–32
at Mechanicsville, 241
in Mexican War, 25–31
on Mexican War, comments, 15–16
in Mexico, 403–4
sea voyage to, 27
at Military Academy, 8–18
application to, 7
conduct rating, 13–14, 16, 17
as first classman, 16–18
friends at, 17
as plebe, 10–12
as second classman, 14–16
as third classman, 13–14
as military governor of Monterrey,
28–29
military intellect of, 55
at Mine Run, 212–13
at Monocacy, 271–75
at Montpelier, 131
at Moorefield, 224–27
Morton encounter with, 487 n.43
at New Market, 380
nicknames of, 57
on Northern business interests in
South, 401–2
Northerners hated by, 118, 297
in old age, 469–74
at Orange Court House, 215
Pennsylvania invasion by, 177–85
at Petersburg, 226
on Point Lookout rescue expedition,
267, 270

political activity of, in 1840s and
1850s, 485 n.27
at Port Republic, 349
on presidential pardon, 412
profanity used by, 4
promotion of
to brigadier general, 70
to colonel, 52
to first lieutenant, 21
to lieutenant general, 242
to major, 26
to major general, 141
proposed as governor of Virginia, 405
as prosecutor
Floyd County, 25
Franklin County, 25, 32–33
public speaking ability of, 23
on Radical Republicans, 407–9
at Rappahannock Station, 205–10
on readmission of Virginia to Union,
410
recovering from wound in Rocky
Mount, 4–5
refusal to accept Appomattox terms,
402
religion of, 10–11, 384–85, 430
retribution by, 177–85, 302–11
return to duty after wound, 84
at Rocky Mount. See Rocky Mount
in Seminole War, 18–21
Senate Military Committee letter
by, 382
at Shepherdstown, 265–67, 326
Sheridan compared with, 395
slavery views of, 33, 417–18
Southern Historical Society and, 431,
433–36, 438–40, 448
at Spotsylvania, 239–40
on states rights, 416–17
at Staunton, 263–64
in steamboat explosion, 30
on Sumter bombardment, 47
superiors criticized by, 5

Early, Jubal Anderson *(continued)*
Taliaferro apprenticeship, 22–23
temperament of, 23, 74, 116
in Texas, 403
on theft in Hays unit, 141–42
on tobacco economics, 46
on Tom's Brook outcome, 357
treason indictment of, 402
on Underwood constitution, 408–9
as Unionist delegate to Virginia Secession Convention, 35, 37, 39, 41–44,
 46–48, 50–52
veteran's organization founded by,
 440–41
in Virginia House of Delegates, 23–25
on Virginia Military Institute financing,
 24–25
as Virginia secession opponent, 50
voice quality of, 4, 57, 59–60
at Warrenton Springs, 102–7
Washington threatened by, 261–62,
 268–69, 277–89
 comments on, 297–98
at Waterloo Bridge, 103
at Waynesboro, 387–90
on West Virginia statehood, 406
in Whig party, 23–25
at White Sulphur Springs resort, 18–19
on white supremacy, 416–17
in Wilderness country, 211–12, 233–
 34, 236–39
at Williamsburg, 76–83
 prelude to, 75–76
at Winchester, 321
 Second Battle of, 164–66, 168–74
 Third Battle of, 334–38
at winter quarters (1862–1863), 143
on women on campaigns, 73, 226, 211
wounding at Williamsburg, 78, 81
at Wrightsville, 183
writings of
 campaign history, 405
 The Heritage of the South, 417–18

at York, 182–84
Early, Jubal L. (son), 485 n.26
Early, Judith (sister), 6, 485 n.22
Early, Robert (brother), 485 n.22
 Jubal campaign history publication
  costs paid by, 405
 Jubal sick leave with, 30
 Lee memorial activities of, 450
Early, Robert (nephew), 450
Early, Robert (son), 485 n.26
Early, Ruth (mother), 6–7
Early, Ruth (niece)
 as Jubal editor, 417
 letter to, 413
Early, Samuel (brother)
 business ventures of, 484–5 n.22
 career advice to Jubal, 13–14, 22
 at Cedar Mountain, 92, 94–95
 at Chantilly, 114
 death of, 473
 education of, 6–7
 Jubal sick leave with, 30
 at Manassas, Second Battle of, 114
 postwar struggles of, 404
Early, Willie (nephew), 450
Echols, John
 Averell's raid and, 216
 as Early replacement, 390
 at New Market, 247
 in Washington threat, 280
Eckert, Ralph Lowell, on Gordon, 236
Economic warfare. *See also* under Union
 Army
 on Chambersburg, 302–4
 on Clear Spring, 303
 by Early, 268–69, 302–4
 on Frederick, 270, 271, 275
 on Hagerstown, 268
 on Mercersburg, 303
Elzey, Arnold
 command assumed by Early, 89–90
 at Manassas, 67–69, 70
 promotion to major general, 491 n.29

wounding in Seven Days' campaign, 84
Emory, William H.
  at Cedar Creek, 372
  under Sheridan, 316
Enquirer (Richmond)
  Early criticism in, 353
  on Goode-Early debate, 44
Episcopal Church, at Military Academy,
  10–11
Equipment
  requisitioning of, 178–81
  scarcity of, 56–59
  transportation of, 73
Evans, Clement A.
  at Cedar Creek, 362, 374
  at Fredericksburg, 137
  at Monocacy Junction, 274
  in winter quarters, 140
Ewell, Mrs. Richard (Lizinka Brown),
  100, 167, 229, 244
Ewell, Richard S., 72
  at Cedar Mountain, 90–95, 100
  character of, 167–68
  Early praised by, 100
  Early relationship with, 229–30, 242–
    44
  on Early retribution, 181
  Early substituting for, 240–41
  at Gettysburg, 189, 191–200, 497
    n.15, 498 n.26
  at Groveton, 108–9
  as Jackson replacement, 167
  at Malvern Hill, 86–88
  at Manassas, Second Battle of, 107–9
  in Pennsylvania invasion, 178
  physical problems of, 228–29
  at Rappahannock River, 205
  at Rappahannock Station, 209
  as Richmond defense force head,
    242–43
  at Spotsylvania, 239
  treason indictment of, 403
  at Warrenton Springs, 102, 106

in Wilderness campaign, 232, 233,
  235–38
  at Winchester, 166, 168–69, 171–73
  wounding of, 109
Examiner (Richmond), on secession, 37
Extra Billy. *See* Smith, William

Farragut, David, Mobile Bay victory
  of, 329
Federal Army. *See* Union Army
Ferguson, Samuel, 75
"Fighting Joe" Hooker. *See* Hooker,
  Joseph
Fisher, C.F., toast to, 74
Fisher's Hill
  Battle of, 341–47
  Early at, 321
  Early withdrawal to, 331, 358
Flag Fort, at Winchester, 169, 172
Florida
  2d regiment of, at Williamsburg, 76
  secession of, 35
  Seminole War in, 18–21
Floyd County, Virginia, prosecuting
  attorney for, 25
Forno, Henry
  at Cedar Mountain, 90, 95
  at Groveton, 108
  at Manassas, Second Battle of, 108,
    110
  at Warrenton Springs, 102
Forsyth, George, at Cedar Creek,
  372, 375
Fort Magruder, in Battle of Williams-
  burg, 75–80
Fort Monroe, Davis imprisonment at, 406
Fort Stevens, in Washington defense,
  282–84
Fort Sumter, bombardment of, 47, 48
Fort Taylor, 19
Fortress Monroe, 26, 29, 39
  Early at, 18, 26

Franklin, William, at Fredericksburg, 134
Franklin County, Virginia. *See also* Rocky
    Mount, Virginia
  compared with Military Academy, 8
  description of, 3–4
  Early family life in, 5–7
  Early legal career in, 22–25, 32–33
  Early recuperation at, 81
  Jubal Early (grandfather) settlement
    in, 6
  Military Academy applicants from, 7
  militia company from, 24
  opinion on secession, 43
  prosecuting attorney for, 25, 32
  race tracks of, 7
  Unionist delegates to Virginia Seces-
    sion Convention, 35–52
Fraser's Farm, 84
Frederick, Maryland
  action at, 270
  Early at, 118–19
  economic warfare on, 270, 271, 275
Fredericksburg, Virginia
  Battle of, 131–39
    prelude to, 130–31
  Chancellorsville campaign and, 143–63
  Mahone at, 463
Freeman, Douglas Southall
  on Early in old age, 471
  on Locust Grove action, 213
  on Warrenton Springs troop move-
    ments, 105
  on Williamsburg, 80
French, S. Bassett
  Lee memorial activities of, 449, 450
  on "old" as applied to generals, 487
    n.5
French, William H.
  at Locust Grove, 212
  in Pennsylvania invasion, 177
French, Winsor B., at Cedar Creek, 364

Gaithersburg, Early at, 280
Gardner, Fleming, at Manassas, 66
Garnett, Thomas S., at Cedar Mountain,
    90–91
Georgia
  regiments of. *See* under Confederate
    Army regiments
  secession of, 35, 36
Germanna Ford, in Wilderness cam-
    paign, 234
Getty, George
  at Cedar Creek, 364, 372
  under Sheridan, 316
  at Winchester, Third Battle of, 339
Gettysburg
  Battle of, 187–202, 437
    Early summary of, 446–47
    postwar analysis of, 457–61
    prelude at Winchester, 164–74
    retribution preceding, 177–85
    supplies requisitioned from, 181–82
    Union garrison abandonment of, 181
Gibbon, John
  in Chancellorsville campaign, 151, 154,
    157, 159
  at Fredericksburg, 135, 138
"Gilded Age," 401
Gill's Creek, Jubal Early (grandfather)
    settlement in, 6
Gilmor, Harry, 58, 287
  in Chambersburg, 303, 304
Godfrey, Joseph P., 7
Godwin, Archibald, at Rappahannock
    River, 207–9
Goode, John, conflict with Early, 40,
    42–44
Gordon, John B., 142
  at Bunker Hill, 332
  capability of, 319
  at Cedar Creek, 360–62, 364–66,
    369–71, 373–76
  in Chancellorsville campaign, 150, 152,
    155, 157

at Fisher's Hill, 341
at Gettysburg, 187, 188, 191, 192,
  198, 199
at Kernstown, 301
leaving Early command, 384
Lee memorial activities of, 442, 452
at Lynchburg, 255
at Martinsburg, 331–32
at Monocacy Junction, 273–75
pillage by (alleged), 381
promotion to major general, 240
at Staunton, 264
in Washington threat, 280, 285, 288
in Wilderness campaign, 231–37
at Winchester
  Second Battle of, 169, 170, 172
  Third Battle of, 335–37, 339
at Wrightsville, 183
Gordonsville, Pope threat to, 89–90
Gorgas, Josiah
  on Chambersburg burning, 309
  on civilian property destruction, 260
Grant, Ulysses S.
  on Cedar Creek battle outcome, 378
  characteristics of, 231
  circumventing War Department, 313
  at Cold Harbor, 243
  conference with Sheridan, 330
  Early hatred of, 476
  Early pressure on, 298
  political perils of, 312
  as president, 409
  promotion to lieutenant general, 230
  scorched earth policy of, 299
  at Spotsylvania, 239
  on Valley strategy, 358
  in Washington defense, 278, 281,
    284, 289
  in Wilderness campaign, 231–33, 238
Greene, George S., at Antietam, 492
  n.20
Greenwood, Early encampment at, 179
Greer, George, on Montpelier visit, 131

Gregg, Maxcy
  at Fredericksburg, 133
  at Manassas, Second Battle of, 110, 111
Grigsby, Andrew J., at Antietam,
  122, 126
Grimes, Bryan
  capability of, 319
  at Cedar Creek, 364
  on Cedar Creek outcome, 379
  on Early capability, 323
  at Fisher's Hill, 344
  on morale, 351
  on religious status of troops, 385
  on Union dead, 432
  at Winchester, Third Battle of, 340
Grover, Cuvier
  at Cedar Creek, 360
  under Sheridan, 316–17
  at Winchester, Third Battle of, 337
Groveton, Battle at, 108–9
Guerrillas, in Clarke County, 299
Guiney's Station, in Chancellorsville
  campaign, 145

Hagerstown, civilian requisitions from, 268
Hairston, Peter, 6, 59
  on Early idiosyncracies, 210–11
  at Rappahannock River, 207, 209
Hairston, Samuel (Early children's guardian), 6
Hale, Samuel
  at Antietam, 124, 125
  at Cedar Mountain, 97–98
  at Rappahannock Station, 208
Halleck, Henry W.
  naming Sigel replacement, 247
  Sheridan serving under, 315
  in Washington defense, 269, 279,
    281–82
Halltown, Sheridan at, 323–26
Hamilton's Crossing, in Chancellorsville
  campaign, 145

Hampton, Wade, 139
  as cavalry leader, 223
  as governor of South Carolina, 421
  Southern Historical Society and,
    434, 438
Hamtramck, John F., 26–29
Hancock, Abram Booth, 35
Hancock, Winfield Scott, at Williams-
  burg, 76, 80–81
Harpers Ferry
  arsenal at, 49–51
  capture of, 118–19
  Hunter at, 298
Harris, J.D. (Dr.), as governor's running
  mate, 410
Harvey, Daniel, at Williamsburg, 76
Haskell, John, at Mine Run, 213
Hattaway, Herman, on results of War,
  419
Hauser's Ridge, at Antietam, 121, 124–
  27
Hayes, Rutherford B., 300
  election of, 416
Haymaker, James, at Winchester, 165
Hays, Harry T.
  at Antietam, 120, 122, 124, 128
  in Chancellorsville campaign, 148,
    151, 154, 157, 158
  at Gettysburg, 187, 188, 191, 192,
    198, 199
  at Locust Grove, 212
  at Manassas, 60, 63–65
  at Rappahannock River, 205
  at Rappahannock Station, 208
  Southern Historical Society and, 433
  at Winchester, 169, 170
  in winter quarters, theft problems
    in, 141
Hazel Run, in Chancellorsville campaign, 154
Heidlersburg, Early at, 186
Henry, Patrick, as Virginian, 36

Henry County, Virginia, Hairston family
  in, 6
Henry Hill, at Manassas, Battle of, 65,
  66, 68, 69, 112
Hill, Ambrose Powell
  at Antietam, 127–28
  at Bristoe Station, 204
  at Cedar Mountain, 90, 95, 96, 98
  at Fredericksburg, 133–35, 137
  at Gettysburg, 186, 187, 189, 191,
    196, 198, 201
  at Gordonsville, 89
  at Harpers Ferry, 119
  at Manassas, Second Battle of, 109–12
  at Mine Run, 213
  in Pennsylvania invasion, 177
  at Rappahannock River, 204–5
  at Spotsylvania, 239–40
  in Wilderness campaign, 231, 232, 239
Hill, Benjamin H., on Early drinking, 354
Hill, Daniel Harvey
  at Antietam, 127
  at Fredericksburg, 133
  at Lynchburg, 254–55
  at Malvern Hill, 87–88
  Southern Historical Society and, 434
  at Williamsburg, 76–78, 80, 82
Hill, Harvey, at Fredericksburg, 133, 134
Hillroy, J.T., 112
Hoke, Robert F.
  in Chancellorsville campaign, 152, 156
  at Fredericksburg, 137–38
  at Rappahannock River, 207
  at Winchester, 169
  in winter quarters, 140
Holliday, Frederick W.M., as governor, 415
Hollins Institute, 261
Honor, maintenance of, 401, 416–17
Hood, John Bell
  at Antietam, 124

at Gettysburg, 196, 199
as Louisiana State Lottery supervisor
candidate, 515 n.12
at Manassas, Second Battle of, 110
Hooker, Joseph
at Antietam, 122–23
as Burnside replacement, 142
in Chancellorsville campaign, 144–45,
147, 148, 152, 158–62
at Military Academy, 16, 18
Horses. *See also* Cavalry
shortage of, 264
Hotchkiss, Jed, 379
at Early funeral, 477
as topographer, 396
in Washington threat, 282
on Winchester victory, 173
Houston, Samuel, 15
Howard, Charles T., Louisiana State
Lottery and, 421
Howard, Oliver O., at Gettysburg,
187, 188
Howe, Albion P., in Chancellorsville
campaign, 154
Humphreys, Andrew A., as Meade eulogist, 436–37
Hunter, Alexander, house of, burning
of, 251
Hunter, Andrew, house of, burning
of, 300
Hunter, David
appearance of, 249
characteristics of, 249–50
civilian property destruction by, 250–
51, 299–300
Early meeting with, in Mexican
War, 29
at Harpers Ferry, 298
at Lexington, 248–49
at Lynchburg Battle, 252, 255, 257–59
replacement by Sheridan, 313
as Sigel replacement, 247
at Staunton, 247–48

Hunton, Eppa, at Early funeral, 477
Hupp's Hill, action at, 358, 364, 376

Imboden, John
Averell threat to, 215
Averell's raid and, 216, 217, 219–21
as cavalry leader, 223, 265
conflict with Early, 221–22
at Lynchburg Battle, 255, 257
prelude to, 252
on Milroy civilian offenses, 495 n.7
at New Market, 247
at Virginia Secession Convention,
49–50
at Winchester, Third Battle of, 338
Indiana Choice legal case, 32–33
Indians, Seminole, war with, 18–21
Irvine, Edmund, as Early confidant, 412

Jackson, John S., at Virginia Secession
Convention, 40
Jackson, Thomas J. (Stonewall), 56
at Antietam, 120–24
at Cedar Mountain, 90–100
at Chancellorsville, 150
death of, 163, 167
Early command under, 85
Early compared with, 292, 396–97
Early praised by, 100, 107, 128
at Fredericksburg, 131–35, 138
at Gordonsville, 89–90
grave of, 261
at Groveton, 108–9
at Harpers Ferry, 118–19
at Henry Hill, 65
house of, burning of, 248–49
at Manassas, Second Battle of, 109–16
memorial ceremony for, 418–19
monument to, 440
on Pope's threats, 88
promotion to lieutenant general, 128

Jackson, Thomas J. *(continued)*
  at Sharpsburg, 119
  at Warrenton Springs, 102–7
  at White Oak Swamp, 85
Jackson, William L. (Mudwall)
  Averell's raid and, 216, 219–21
  cavalry under, 265
  at Fisher's Hill, 342
  in Washington threat, 286, 288
  at Winchester, 333, 335
Jackson Memorial Association, 440
Jackson River, Averell's raid and, 217, 219, 220
Jackson's River Depot, 216–17
Jacob's Ford, on Rapidan River, 212
Janney, John, as Virginia Secession Convention president, 37–38
Jenkins, A.G., at Winchester, 168
Jessie Scouts, 332
Jesup, Thomas S., 19
Johnson, Andrew (president), pardon for Confederate leaders, 403, 405–6, 412
Johnson, Bradley
  cavalry under, 265
  in Chambersburg raid, 302–6
  at Early deathbed, 474
  at Fisher's Hill, 342
  at Gettysburg, 189, 191, 192, 197, 199, 200
  at Locust Grove, 213
  at Moorefield, 307–8
  in Pennsylvania invasion, 177
  in Point Lookout rescue attempt, 270
  veteran's organization proposed by, 440
  in Washington threat, 285–87, 289
  in Wilderness campaign, 231
  at Winchester
    Second Battle of, 171, 172
    Third Battle of, 335
Johnson, Edward
  at Rappahannock River, 205
  at Spotsylvania, 239

  at Winchester, 168
Johnson, Robert, Longstreet-Early feud and, 460
Johnson, William Preston, Lee memorial activities of, 442, 444–45
Johnston, Joseph E.
  as Lee critic, 456
  Lee memorial activities of, 453
  at Manassas, 62–63, 65, 71
  at Williamsburg, 62–63, 65, 76, 77, 80
  withdrawal to Richmond, 75
Johnston, Robert, in Wilderness campaign, 233–34, 236
Jones, Charles Colcock
  Lee memorial activities of, 452
  Southern Historical Society and, 433
Jones, D.R., at Manassas, 65
Jones, H.P., at Winchester, 168–72
Jones, J. William
  Lee memorial activities of, 448, 452
  Southern Historical Society and, 433, 434, 438, 439
  as *Southern Historical Society Papers* editor, 457–59
Jones, J.R., at Antietam, 120
Jones, Samuel, 215
  Averell's raid and, 217
Jones, Thomas
  on Early drinking, 382
  in Wilderness campaign, 233, 234
Jones, William E., at Piedmont, 247–48
Jupiter River, Locha-Hatchee Ford, in Seminole War, 20

Kanawha County, West Virginia, Samuel Early residence in, 484–85 n.22
Kean, Robert, on Washington threat, 290
Kearny, Philip, at Chantilly, 114
Kelly's Ford, 204–5, 207
Kemper, James Lawson, 26–27
  on blacks in Jackson memorial parade, 418

coping with defeat, 430
Early letter to, 73–74
as governor, 414
at Manassas, 60, 66
Kennon, Lyman W.V., visit to Early in
old age, 469–71
Kernstown, action at, 301
Kershaw, Joseph B., 323
at Cedar Creek, 358, 360–62, 364,
367, 368, 373–75
leaving Early command, 384
at Petersburg, 330
at Port Republic, 350
reassignment to Early, 346–47
King, J. Floyd
defending Early retreat, 351
on Early, 319–20

Ladies' Lee Monument Association,
443–44, 451
"Landing of the Pilgrims" (painting), 14
Lane, James H.
at Fredericksburg, 133
at Gettysburg, 198
Langhorne, Daniel, 57–58
Laurel Brigade, 354–55
Lavinia, as Early friend, 18–21, 31
Lawton, Alexander R.
at Antietam, 121
at Chantilly, 114
Ewell command assumed by, 109
at Manassas, Second Battle of, 108–
10, 114
at Warrenton Springs, 102–6
Lee, Edmund J., house of, burning
of, 300
Lee, Fitzhugh
Averell's raid and, 216, 217, 219, 220
as cavalry leader, 223
coping with defeat, 430
at Early deathbed, 474
at Early funeral, 477

as governor, 416
Lee memorial activities of, 443,
451, 452
at Winchester, Third Battle of, 335,
338–39
Lee, Mary, 444
Lee, Robert E.
at Antietam, 119–29
application for presidental pardon, 403
at Appomattox, 446
on Caledonia Iron Works destruction, 181
canonization of, 432–33, 440–53,
457, 476
career of, Early summary of, 445–47
at Cashtown, 186
in Chancellorsville campaign, 144–51,
158–63
character of, 448
coping with defeat, 430
criticism of, 456–57
death of, 432
Early contacts with
arrest order rescinded by, 230
comments on Early appearance, 228
defended by Early, 352–54
dismissal, 390–92
on Imboden-Early conflict, 221–22
letters
on Cedar Creek, 380
on Fisher's Hill, 345
meetings
on establishment of Valley force,
245, 251
on scaled-back command, 386
praise of Early, 90
presidential pardon request, 403
respect for Lee, 297, 348, 476
engraving of, 450
Ewell assignment to Richmond defense
force head, 242–43
at Fraser's Farm, 84
at Fredericksburg, 131–33

Lee, Robert E. *(continued)*
 funeral of, 441
 General Orders No. 72 on requisitioning, 178–81
 after Gettysburg, 203–4
 at Gettysburg, 189, 192–97, 199–202,
  497 n.15, 497 n.26
 Jackson replaced by, 167
 at Locust Grove, 212
 on loyalty to state, 51
 on McClellan as Pope replacement, 118
 at Malvern Hill, 85–86
 Maryland campaign orders taken
  from, 121
 memorialization of, 441–53
 at Mine Run, 212–13
 Petersburg siege and, 329–30
 on property destruction, 177–78
 at Rappahannock River, 204–10
 reassigning Early troops, 384
 at Seven Days' battles, 84–85
 Smith meeting with, 352
 Southern Historical Society and, 434
 Southern newspapers praise of, 290
 at Spotsylvania, 239
 statues of, 449, 451–52
 treason indictment of, 403
 as Virginia armed forces head, 51
 war records lost by, 403
 as Washington College president, 440
 on Washington threat, 291
 in Wilderness campaign, 231–32, 235,
  238, 239
 on Winchester Battle outcome, 346–48
Lee, Robert E., Jr., 267
"Lee Memorial Volume," 447–48
Lee Monument Association, 443–44,
 449–50
Leech, Margaret, on atmosphere in
 Washington, 278
Lee's Hill, in Chancellorsville campaign,
 146, 155–57
Letcher, John, 49

 home of, burning of, 249
 on troop morale, 385
Lewis, John F., as governor's running
 mate, 410
Lexington, Virginia. *See also* Virginia
 Military Institute
 Early movement through, 261
Liberty, Hunter at, 255
Lincoln, Abraham
 Antietam influence on, 129–30
 concern over Washington defenses,
  268, 289, 292
 election of, southern reaction to, 35,
  36, 38, 41–42, 44
 enemies of, Washington threat and, 293
 on established slavery, 41–42
 Grant promotion by, 231
 Hunter orders annulled by, 250
 reelection of, 312, 329, 346, 378
 on Sheridan appearance, 313–14
 Virginia Secession Convention interview with, 46–47
 Virginia Secession Convention report
  to, 45
Linker, Caleb, 297
Little Calf Pasture River, Averell's raid
 and, 217
Little Round Top, at Gettysburg,
 194, 197
Locha-Hatchee Ford, in Seminole
 War, 20
Locust Grove, action at, 212–13
Lomax, Lunsford
 at Early funeral, 477
 at Fisher's Hill, 341
 at Martinsburg, 331–32
 as Ransom replacement, 318–19
 at Tom's Brook, 355–56
Long, Armistead L., 264
 at Gettysburg, 497 n.15
 in Washington threat, 281
Longstreet, James, 56
 in Chancellorsville campaign, 163

criticism of Lee, 456–57
death of, 461
feud with Early, 454–62
at Fredericksburg, 132
at Gettysburg, 198, 199, 201, 446–47, 498 n.26
on Gettysburg strategy, 193
at Harpers Ferry, 119
at Manassas
First Battle of, 60–62, 64, 66
Second Battle of, 112
message of, interception of, 358–59
monuments to, 461–62
in Pennsylvania invasion, 177
postwar activities of, 455–62
promotion to lieutenant general, 128
proposed as Early successor, 353
replaced by Anderson, 239
sins committed by, 433
in Wilderness campaign, 232
at Williamsburg, 76–77, 82
in winter quarters, 142
López de Santa Anna, Antonio, 15
Lost Cause, religion of, 431, 448–49
Louisiana
regiments of. See under Confederate Army regiments
secession of, 35, 37
Louisiana State Lottery, 420–28
Lowe, J.H.
at Antietam, 128
at Fredericksburg, 148
Lowe, Thaddeus S.C., balloons of, 72, 148
Lowell, Charles R., Jr. , 317
Lumsden, John W., 484 n.1
Lynchburg
Battle of, 254–60
prelude to, 245–54
Early at
education, 7
postwar, 413, 469–74
recruit organization, 56–59

Sheridan ordered to, 386
Lyne, Mr., as Early crony, 471
Lyon, Elijah (Capt.), 19

McCausland, John
cavalry under, 265
in Chambersburg economic warfare, 302–7
civilian requisitions by, 268
communications destruction by, 270
harassment of Hunter en route to Lynchburg, 255, 257
at Monocacy Junction, 273
at Moorefield, 307–8
in Washington threat, 280, 281, 288
at Winchester, Third Battle of, 338
McClellan, George B.
at Antietam, 119–21, 127
at Malvern Hill, 85–86, 88
march to Richmond, 75
as Pope replacement, 118
as presidential candidate, 312–13, 329
replacement by Burnside, 130
at White Oak Swamp, 85
McComb, J.C., on Early drunkenness, 381–82
McDowell, Irvin
at Manassas, 60, 62, 63, 65, 70–71
at Warrenton Springs, 106
McFarland, Elvira Early (sister), 391
McGuire, Dr. Hunter, 172, 242, 403
McKay, Thomas, barn of, burning of, 324
McLaughlin, William, 264
McLaws, Lafayette
at Antietam, 492 n.20
in Chancellorsville campaign, 145, 158, 159, 163
at Gettysburg, 196, 199
resentment of Early, 439
in winter quarters, 142
McLean House, at Manassas, 62

McLean's Ford, on Bull Run, 63–65

McMahon, Edward, Averell's raid and, 220–21

McMurran, Joseph, 297

McNealey, Julia, Early relationship with, 31–32, 412–13

McRae, D.K., at Williamsburg, 79

Madison, James, 277
as Virginian, 36

Madison County, Virginia
Jackson travel through, 130
Jeremiah Early in, 5

Magruder, John, 75

Mahan, Dennis Hart, 17–18

Mahone, William
feud with Early, 462–68
political manipulations of, 410–11, 414–16

Malvern Hill, Battle of, 85–88

Manassas (Bull Run)
First Battle of, 63–71
prelude to, 59–63
Second Battle of, 109–16

Mansfield, Joseph K.F., at Antietam, 492 n.20

Martinsburg
Early raid on, 331–32
supply dump at, 172

Marye, John L., as governor's running mate, 411

Marye, Lawrence S., at Early party, 471

Marye's Heights
in Chancellorsville campaign, 151, 152, 156, 155, 162, 163
at Fredericksburg, 132–33

Maryland Heights, 266

Massanutten ridge, 321, 359

Maury, Dabney H.
at Early deathbed, 474
at Early funeral, 477
Lee memorial activities of, 442, 452
Southern Historical Society and, 433, 434

Maximilian, in Mexico, 404

Meade, George Gordon
at Bristoe Station, 204
at Centreville, 204
at Fredericksburg, 134, 138
funeral of, 436–37
at Gettysburg, 187, 201
hostility toward Sheridan, 315
at Mine Run, 212–13
after Rappahannock Station action, 211

Meadow Brook, in Cedar Creek battle, 361, 362

Mechanics Hall, Richmond, ladies' lobby group in, 34–35, 38

Mechanicsville
action at, 241
fighting at, 84

Mercersburg, economic warfare on, 303

Mercié, Antonin, Lee statue by, 451–52

Merritt, Wesley, 317
at Cedar Creek, 368, 375
civilian property destruction by, 349–50
Rosser attack on, 355
at Tom's Brook, 356
at Winchester, Third Battle of, 333, 338, 339

Metairie Cemetery, Jackson memorial ceremony in, 440

Mexico
Early exile in, 403–4
Houston rebellion against, 15–16
war with, 25–30

Middletown, in Cedar Creek battle, 360–4, 367–9, 374

Military Academy. See United States Military Academy

Miller Farm, at Antietam, 121

Milroy, Robert H.
civilian treatment by, 168
at Winchester, 168, 169, 172, 174

Mine Run, action at, 212–13

Mineback Ford, 374

Mississippi
2d regiment of, 76
13th regiment of, 66
secession of, 35
Mitchell's Ford, at Manassas, 65–66
Mobile Bay, Farragut victory in, 329
Monocacy Junction
Battle of, 269–75
Early at, 118
Monterrey, Early as military governor,
28–29
Montpelier, Early staff dinner at, 131
Moore, Samuel J.C., on Early drinking,
382–83
Moore, Samuel McDowell, at Virginia
Secession Convention, 40
Moorefield
McCausland at, 307
raid at, 224–27
Moorman, Marcellus N., at Cedar
Creek, 376
Morale, problems with, 398
Morris, John A., Louisiana State Lottery
and, 423
Morris Hill, Averell's raid and, 217
Morton, Jeremiah, 487 n.43
Mosby, John S., as cavalry leader, 223
Moss, Terry, on Early's last campaign,
393–94
Motte, Jacob Rhett, on Seminole War, 19
Mount Crawford, action at, 387
"Mud march," at Fredericksburg, 142
Munford, Thomas T.
Southern Historical Society and, 438
on Tom's Brook outcome, 357
Myers, Frank, on civilian property de-
struction, 350

Nelson, William, 264
capability of, 320
at Winchester, Third Battle of, 340
Netherwood, James, Lee statue contractor, 452

New Creek, action at, 307
New Market
Early at, 380
Sigel defeat at, 246–47
"New South," 401
News (Lynchburg), Early death reported
in, 474–75, 478
News (Savannah), on Early drinking, 354
Newton, John, in Chancellorsville cam-
paign, 152, 157
Newtown
civilian property destruction at, 250
Sheridan at, 330
Nichols, G.W.
on Grant-Sheridan meeting, 332
on Washington threat, 282
Nicodemus Hill, at Antietam, 121
Noble, Moses Greer, 29
Norfolk, arsenal at, 49, 51
Norfolk & Petersburg Railroad, 411
North Carolina
5th regiment of, 76–81
23d regiment of, 76, 77, 80
North Mountain, in Fisher's Hill battle,
341, 342
Northern Central Railroad, 179

Oates, William C., on Longstreet-Early
feud, 460
Old, William W.
on Early drinking, 383
at Early funeral, 477
Old Point Comfort, 26–27
Old Wilderness Tavern, 231
Opequon Creek, 320–21
battle at, 333–41
plans for, 332–33
Sheridan at, 326
Orange & Alexandria Railroad, 254, 411
Bristoe Station, 107, 204
Orange Court House, Early at, 131, 215
Ordnance, scarcity of, 56–59

Orr, James L., on Early drinking, 354
Overall's Run, 345
Ox Hill, battle at, 113–16

Page, Mann, at Early funeral, 477
Palmer, Benjamin Morgan, Southern Historical Society and, 433
Park, Robert, 337
Parker's Store, in Wilderness, 231
Parsons, Job, 495 n.7
Partisan Ranger Units, 223, 224
Pate, Anthony, 6
Patterson, Robert, 62
Payne, William H.
  at Cedar Creek, 360, 367, 373, 375
  at Early deathbed, 474
  at Early funeral, 477
  at Fisher's Hill, 341
  Lee memorial activities of, 452
  at Winchester, Third Battle of, 338
Payne's Farm, 212
Peace Convention
  failure of, 41, 44
  proposed by Virginia Assembly, 36–37, 38
Pegram, John
  at Bethesda Church, 241–42
  at Cedar Creek, 362, 364, 366–67, 373, 375
  at Fisher's Hill, 341, 344
  at Rappahannock River, 207
  at Rappahannock Station, 208
Pemberton, John C., at Military Academy, 17, 18
Pender, Dorsey
  at Gettysburg, 188, 198
  on retribution, 496 n.13
Pendleton, Alexander, 211
  death of, 344
Pendleton, William Nelson
  in Chancellorsville campaign, 145, 146, 148, 150, 154–56
  Early letter to, 441

sunrise order speech of, 461
Penn, Davidson, 141
  at Rappahannock River, 205, 206
Pennsylvania, invasion of, 177–85. See also Chambersburg; Gettysburg
Pennsylvania Railroad, 411
Peters, William, on Chambersburg pillage, 306
Petersburg
  siege of, 329–30
  Union troops diverted from, 269
Petersburg & Weldon Railroad, Union control of, 330
Phillips, John R., at Antietam, 126
Pickens, Francis (Gov.), 48
Pickett, George
  in Chambersburg, 196
  at Gettysburg, 200
Piedmont, action at, 247–48
Pierpont, Francis H., as postwar governor, 406
Piston, William Garrett, as Longstreet biographer, 461
Pitzer, Andrew L.
  at Cedar Mountain, 92
  in Chancellorsville campaign, 155–56, 158
  on Early command style, 211
  at Early funeral, 477
  at Warrenton Springs, 102
Plank Road, in Chancellorsville campaign, 158
Pleasant Valley, Virginia, 113
Point Isabel, 27
Point Lookout, scheme for prisoner rescue from, 267, 270, 286, 287
Polk, James K., 25
Pond, George E., on civilian property destruction, 308–9
Pope, John
  at Cedar Mountain, 91, 98, 99
  Gordonsville area threatened by, 88–89

at Manassas, Second Battle of, 107,
110–13
replacement by McClellan, 118
at Warrenton Springs, 106, 107
Port Republic, Sheridan at, 349
Preston, Margaret Junkin, 248–49
Preston, William Ballard, 46–48
Pugh, Charles M., 31, 412
Pugh, Lilly, 485 n.26
Purcellville, Crook at, 299
Putnam County, West Virginia, Jubal
Early in, 485 n.22

Radical Republicans, postwar, 407, 409
Railroads, postwar politics of, 409, 411,
414–15
Ramseur, Stephen Dodson
at Berryville Pike, 332
at Bethesda Church, 241–42
capability of, 319
at Cedar Creek, 361–62, 364, 366–68,
373, 375
death of, 375
at Fisher's Hill, 341, 343
at Gettysburg, 199
at Kernstown, 301
at Lynchburg, 254–57
at Monocacy Junction, 272, 275
promotion to major general, 242
vs. Sheridan, 326
at Staunton, 263
at Stephenson's Depot, 301
in Washington threat, 280, 281,
285, 288
at Winchester, 332–35, 337, 339–41
Third Battle of, 346
Randolph, Edmund, as Virginian, 36
Randolph, George W., 46–47
Randolph, Sarah, Lee memorial activities
of, 443, 451, 516 n.38
Randolph, Thomas B., 26–28
Randolph, Thomas Jefferson, Lee
memorial activities of, 516 n.38

Ransom, Robert
cavalry under, 265
replacement of, 318–19
Rapidan River
action at, 212
withdrawal to, 100
Rappahannock River
crossing, 101–7
Lee at, 204–5
winter encampment at, 140, 142–43
Rappahannock Station, battle at, 205–11
Readjuster Party, 415–16, 467
Reconstruction, 401–19
Reconstruction Acts (1867), 407
Red Bud Run, 333, 335
Red Valley, Jubal Early (grandfather)
settlement in, 6
Reily, Emma, on Sheridan's army appear-
ance, 386–87
Reno, Jesse, at Warrenton Springs, 107
Republican Party, Longstreet in, 455–56
Reynolds, John F.
in Chancellorsville campaign, 151
at Gettysburg, 187
Richmond
defense of, 164
Early recuperation at, 81
McClellan march to, 75
Mechanics Hall ladies' lobby group in,
34–35, 38
Virginia House of Delegates sessions
in, 23–25
Richmond, Fredericksburg & Potomac
Railroad, 132
in Chancellorsville campaign, 145
loan to, 24
Ricketts, James B.
at Cedar Creek, 362
at Monocacy Junction, 270, 274
under Sheridan, 316
in Washington defense, 282, 286
Riddleburger, Harrison H., in Virginia
legislature, 415

Robertson, Beverly, at Warrenton
Springs, 104
Rock Creek, at Gettysburg, 187, 188
Rockfish Gap, Early at, 387, 389
Rockville, Early at, 280, 281
Rocky Mount, Virginia
description of, 3–4
Early residence in
after dismissal, 391
furlough, 226
legal career, 22–25
as Mexican War veteran, 30–31
recuperation, 4–5
Rodes, Robert E.
at Bethesda Church, 241
capability of, 319
death of, 337
at Gettysburg, 187–89, 193–95, 197–
201
at Kernstown, 301
at Locust Grove, 212
at Martinsburg, 331–32
at Monocacy Junction, 271, 275
in Pennsylvania invasion, 177
vs. Sheridan, 326
at Staunton, 263
at Stephenson's Depot, 332
in Washington threat, 280, 281, 283–
85, 288
in Wilderness campaign, 231
at Winchester
Second Battle of, 168, 172
Third Battle of, 335, 337
Rohrbach Bridge, over Antietam,
120, 127
Romney Turnpike, at Winchester, 169–
70
Ronald, Charles, at Cedar Mountain, 90
Rosecrans, William S., Sheridan rescue
of, 315
Rosser, Betsey, 226–27
Rosser, Thomas Lafayette, 350
Averell's raid and, 217, 220

as cavalry leader, 223
at Cedar Creek, 360, 373–74
Laurel Brigade, 354–55
at Moorefield, 224–27
at Mount Crawford, 387
opinion of irregulars, 224
in pursuit of Sheridan, 355–56
at Tom's Brook, 355–57
at Waynesboro, 387
Round Tops, at Gettysburg, 194, 197
Royston, S.M., as Chambersburg citizen, 305
Russell, David, under Sheridan, 316

Salem, Virginia
Averell's raid to, 215–20
Early children education at, 7
Salem Church, in Chancellorsville cam-
paign, 158–59
Saunders, Fleming, 35
Saunders, Judith (grandmother), 6
Saunders, Peter, 35
Schofield, John M., as military governor,
407–8
Scott, R.F., on carbines, 318
Scott, Winfield
Manassas defect blamed on, 71
in Mexican War, 28
Scott's Ford, in Chancellorsville cam-
paign, 159
Secession
of states, 35
Virginia convention on, 34–51
Seddon, James, as secretary of war, 386
Sedgwick, John
at Antietam, 492 n.20
in Chancellorsville campaign, 145, 151,
154, 156–60, 162
at Military Academy, 18
at Rappahannock River, 205, 208
at Rappahannock Station, 210
in Wilderness campaign, 235, 236

Seminary Ridge, at Gettysburg, 189, 194, 201, 497 n.15
Seminole War, 18–21
Semmes, Paul J., at Antietam, 492 n.20
Semmes, Raphael, Southern Historical Society and, 438
Senate Military Committee, Early letter to, 382
Seven Days' battles, 84–85
  at Malvern Hill, 85–88
Seward, William H., 45
Seymour, William, at Winchester, 174
Sharpsburg, Jackson arrival at, 119
Sheeran, Father James, as chaplain, 265
Shenandoah Valley, force established in, 245–46
Shepherdstown, 265–67, 326
Sheridan, Philip Henry
  vs. Anderson, 323
  appearance of, 313–14
  appointment by Grant, 395
  appointment to Army of the Shenandoah command, 316
  at Berryville, 320–21
  cavalry handling by, 317–18
  at Cedar Creek, 321, 323, 358–61, 364, 367, 369–75, 378–79
  civilian property destruction by, 324–25, 349–50
  conference with Grant, 330
  criticism of, 325
  Early compared with, 395
  early military career of, 314–16
  Early opinion of, 325–27
  at Fisher's Hill, 341–47
  at Halltown, 323–26
  as Hunter replacement, 313
  Jessie Scouts under, 332
  leadership style of, 313–14
  Lynchburg orders, 386
  maneuvering against Early, 320–21, 323–27
  at Military Academy, 314

  at Newtown, 330
  at Port Republic, 349
  promotion to brigadier general, 346
  Rosser pursuit of, 355–56
  Stanton meeting with, 358–59
  at Waynesboro, 387
  at Winchester, 333–41
    plans for, 332–33
  at Woodstock, 356
Sherman, William T., 230
  Atlanta captured by, 329
  movement into Georgia, 293
  Sheridan serving under, 315
Shoes, shortage of, 263, 266
Sigel, Franz, 230
  defeat at New Market, 246–47
  at Maryland Heights, 266
  in Shenandoah Valley, 245
  at Warrenton Springs, 107
Silver Spring, Early at, 284–85
Slaughter's (Cedar) Mountain, Battle of, 90–99
Slavery
  abolition of, blacks status after, 402
  Early views on, 33, 417–18
  Goode speech on, 40
  Hunter views on, 249–50
  importance in Virginia, 36
  legal case on, 32–33
  repeal in Virginia, 406–7
Slingluff, Fielder, on Chambersburg pillage, 306
Smith, Edmund Kirby, surrender of, 402
Smith, Francis, 24–25
Smith, George H.
  as Imboden replacement, 221
  at Winchester, Third Battle of, 338
Smith, William (Extra Billy)
  at Antietam, 122, 126, 492 n.20
  in Chancellorsville campaign, 152, 156
  at Chantilly, 114–15
  as Early critic, 352–54
  at Fisher's Hill, 342

Smith, William *(continued)*
  at Gettysburg, 187–89, 191, 192,
    198–200
  at Manassas, Second Battle of, 112
  at Winchester, 169, 171
  wounding of, 492 n.20
South Carolina
  4th regiment of, 59
  secession of, 35
South Mountain
  Early encampment at, 178–81
  fighting at, 119
Southall, S.V., at Cedar Creek, 368
Southern Historical Society, 431, 433–35,
  438–40, 448
Southern Historical Society Papers, 439–40,
  457–61
Southern Magazine, 439
Southside Railroad, 411
Spotsylvania, action at, 239–40
Squires, Charles, at Manassas, 59–60, 62
Stafford, Leroy A., 142
  at Antietam, 122, 126
Stafford Heights
  in Chancellorsville campaign, 146–
    47, 152
  in Fredericksburg Battle, 132, 137
Stanton, Edwin M., 238
  assets protected by, 278
  meeting with Sheridan, 358–59
  on Tom's Brook outcome, 356
Star Fort, at Winchester, 169, 172
Starke, William E.
  at Chantilly, 113–14
  death of, 122
  at Manassas, Second Battle of, 109,
    113–14
  replacement by Jones, 120
Starr, Stephen Z., on Confederate cavalry, 223
State (Richmond), Longstreet-Early feud
  and, 460

Staunton
  Early at, 263–64
  Hunter at, 247–48
Stephenson's Depot, 331–32
  action at, 301
  Milroy troops captured at, 172–73
Steuart, George H., at Spotsylvania, 239
Stevens, Isaac I., at Chantilly, 113, 114
Stevens, Thaddeus, owner of Caledonia
  Iron Works, 179–81, 183
Stiles, Robert, on Early, 439
Stone's River, Sheridan at, 315
Strong, Henry B., at Chantilly, 114
Strother, David Hunter, on Hunter
  retribution, 250
Stuart, Alexander H.H., 46–48
Stuart, J.E.B.
  at Antietam, 120, 121
  in Chambersburg, 304
  in Chancellorsville campaign, 144
  death of, 316
  at Fredericksburg, 134
  at Manassas, 69
Stuart, Margaret, 228
Sumner, Edwin V., at Antietam, 492
  n.20
Sutler's wagon story, 381
Swinton, William, on Gettysburg troop
  strengths, 437–38

Taliaferro, Norborne F., 22, 25
  as judge, 33
Taliaferro, William B.
  at Cedar Mountain, 90–91, 94–98
  at Fredericksburg, 133, 134
  at Groveton, 108
  wounding of, 109
Tampa Bay, Early arrival at, 19
Tapton, E.G., 20–21
Taylor, Walter H., 242
Taylor, Zachary, 27

Telegraph Road, in Chancellorsville
campaign, 155–56, 158, 163
Terrell, A.W. (Dr.), as Early physician, 473
Terrill, James B.
death of, 242
at Winchester, 164–65
Terry, Alfred H., on vagrancy laws, 407
Terry, William
capability of, 319
at Monocacy Junction, 274
Texas
annexation of, 25
Early in, 403
secession of, 35
war in, 15–16
Thayer, Sylvanus, 9, 10
Thoburn, Joseph, 317
at Cedar Creek, 358
Thomas, Edward L.
Averell's raid and, 216
at Cedar Mountain, 96–99
at Fredericksburg, 137
at Manassas, Second Battle of, 110
Thompson, Mrs., boardinghouse, 17
Three Tops observation post, 321
Tiger John. *See* McCausland, John
Times (Philadelphia), in Early-Longstreet
feud, 458–60
Tobacco, economic aspects of, 46
Tom's Brook, action at, 355–57
Torbert, Alfred Thomas Archimedes, 317
at Cedar Creek, 368, 372
at Winchester, Third Battle of, 337,
339, 340
Totopotomoy Creek, 241
Trimble, Isaac
at Cedar Mountain, 90, 95
at Groveton, 108
at Manassas, Second Battle of, 107–
8, 115
promotion to major general, 129

True Republicans, in Virginia, 410
Tyler, Erastus, at Monocacy Junction,
270, 272, 274

Underwood, John C., constitution prepared by, 408–9, 419
Uniforms, similarity between two armies,
64–65
Union Army
civilian property destruction/requisi-
tion by, 299–300
at Culpeper, 89
at Fredericksburg, 138–39
Hunter, 250–51
at Lexington, 248–49
at Locust Grove, 214
at Lynchburg, 259–60
at Manassas, 71
Milroy, 168
Sheridan, 324–25, 349–50
uniforms of, 64–65
Union Army Corps
6th
assignment to Petersburg, 384
at Cedar Creek, 360–64, 366–70,
372, 375
experience of, 316
at Fisher's Hill, 342–43
at Winchester, 333, 335, 337, 339
8th
at Cedar Creek, 358, 360–62, 367
experience of, 317
at Winchester, 333, 339
19th
at Cedar Creek, 360–62, 367, 372
experience of, 316
at Fisher's Hill, 343
at Winchester, 333, 335, 337, 339
Unionist delegates, to Virginia Secession
Convention, 35–52
United Confederate Veterans, 441, 461

United Daughters of the Confederacy, 461
United States Military Academy
curriculum of, 9, 12, 14, 17–18
Early application to, 7
Early at, 8–18
entrance examination at, 11
living conditions at, 10
maxims of, 10
opportunities offered at, 9
religious services at, 10–11
Sheridan at, 314
summer encampment at, 11
Upton, Emory, under Sheridan, 316

Valentine, Edward V., Lee statue by,
449, 451
Valley Campaign
August 1864, 316–27
Early's contributions to, 392–94
October 1864, 352–83
September 1864, 328–51
winter of 1864–1865, 386–91
Valley Pike, 320
Van Dorn, Earl, 72
Vandiver, Frank E., on Washington
threat, 283, 293
Veterans Reserve Corps, in Washington
defense, 279
Virginia
Committee on Federal Relations, 38,
39, 42, 44–45
contributions to Union's origins, 36
northern ties of, 36
regiments of. See under Confederate
Army regiments
secession of, 50
Virginia & Tennessee Railroad, 246, 257
Virginia Central Railroad, 246, 247
Pope threat to, 89
Virginia Constitutional Convention of
1851, 485 n.27

Virginia General Assembly
arms appropriation, 37
Secession Convention established
by, 36
Virginia House of Delegates, Early
representation in, 23–25
Virginia Military Institute
appropriation for, 24–25
burning of, 248–49
cadets from, at New Market, 247
Virginia Secession Convention, 34–51
delegates to, 37
establishment of, 36
interview with Lincoln, 46–47
ordinance of secession passage, 50
other states commissioners in, 38
reaction to Lincoln inaugural address,
41–42
secret session of, 48–49
Voting rights, of blacks, 402, 409, 419

Walker, Gilbert C.
as governor, 414
as gubernatorial candidate, 410
Walker, Henry Harrison, Averell's raid
and, 216
Walker, James A.
at Antietam, 120, 122–24, 128
at Cedar Mountain, 91, 98
at Fredericksburg, 135, 137
as governor's running mate, 411
at Manassas, Second Battle of, 108,
110
Wallace, Lew, 269–71, 273, 275
Warrenton Springs, river crossing at,
102–7
Washington, D.C.
defenses of, 279, 301
Early threat to, 261–62, 268–69,
277–89
threat to, 298
Washington, George, as Virginian, 36

Washington and Lee University (formerly Washington College)
  burning of, 249
  Lee involvement with
    memorial activities, 441–42, 444–45
    as president, 440
    statue, 449
Washington Artillery, at Manassas, 59, 60
Washington Iron Works, Rocky Mount, 5
Waterloo Bridge, Rappahannock crossing at, 103, 106–7
Waynesboro, Battle of, 387–90
Weekly Times (Philadelphia), Longstreet-Early feud and, 456
Weir, Robert W., 14
Weld, Eugene, 7
Wells, Henry, constitution proposed by, 408–9
Wert, Jeffrey, on Valley geography, 320
West Fort, at Winchester, 169–71, 174
West Point. *See* United States Military Academy
West Virginia, statehood of, 406
Wharton, Gabriel
  capability of, 319
  at Cedar Creek, 360, 366–67, 373, 375
  at Fisher's Hill, 341
  at New Market, 247
  at Stephenson's Depot, 331–32
  at Waynesboro, 388–89
  at Winchester, Third Battle of, 337, 339
Whig (Richmond paper), on Rappahannock Station action, 209
Whig party, 23–25, 485 n.27
White, Elijah V., at Chambersburg, 179
White Sulphur Springs resort
  Early at, 18–21
  Southern Historical Society meeting at, 434–36
White supremacy, Early promotion of, 416–17
Whitehead, Dr. (divisional surgeon), 131

Whittier, John Greenleaf, 119
Whittle, Powhatan B., at Williamsburg, 77
Wickham's brigade
  at Fisher's Hill, 341
  at Overall's Run, 345
  at Winchester, Third Battle of, 340
Wilcox, Cadmus Marcellus
  in Chancellorsville campaign, 151, 157–58
  on Longstreet-Early feud, 460
Wilderness, The, 147–48, 160
  campaign in, 231–39
Wilderness Church, 231
Willey, Waitman T., 49
Williams, John G., at Cedar Creek, 370
Williamsburg, Battle of, 76–83
  Early praised for, 90
  prelude to, 75–76
Willis, Edward, at Bethesda Church, 241–42
Willis's Hill, in Chancellorsville campaign, 155, 156
Wilson, James H., 317
  on carbine utility, 318
  at Winchester, 332, 333
Winchester
  assembly at, after Antietam, 128
  Battle of
    Second, 164–74
    Third, 333–41
      plans for, 332–33
  Early at, 321
Winder, Charles, at Cedar Mountain, 90–92, 94–95, 99
Wise, Henry A., 36, 48–52, 221
Wise, John, on Rocky Mount, 3–4
Withers, Robert T., as gubernatorial candidate, 411
Wolseley, Garnett, on Gettysburg outcome, 461
Women, on campaigns, 73
"Woodstock Races," 356

Woodward, C. Vann, on postwar conditions, 431
Worsham, John, at Monocacy Junction, 274
Wright, Horatio G.
    at Cedar Creek, 360, 368, 372
    Early action against, 300
    on intercepted message, 358–59
    pursuit of Early, 298, 299
    under Sheridan, 316
    in Washington defense, 286

at Winchester, 335
Wrightsville
    Early at, 183
    railroad bridge at, 179

Yancey, Robert, 471–72
York, Pennsylvania, Early at, 182–84
York, Zebulon, at Monocacy Junction, 274

B
EARLY

Osborne, Charles C.

Jubal

79856

$29.95

DATE			